CONTENTS

vi-vii WORLD Countries
viii-ix WORLD Cities
x-xi WORLD Languages
xii-xiii WORLD Economic Groups
xiv-xv WORLD International Organisations
xvi SYMBOLS

1 Arctic Ocean

NORTH AMERICA

2-3 North America
4-5 Canada West
6-7 Canada East
8-9 USA West
10-11 USA East
12 USA Alaska
13 Canada West
14-15 Canada Southeast, USA Northeast
16 USA Washington - New York - Boston
17 USA Southeast
18-19 USA South-Central
20 USA Northwest
21 USA Southwest
22 USA San Francisco & Los Angeles
23 Mexico Central
24-25 Mexico & Central America
26-27 Caribbean

SOUTH AMERICA

28	South America
29	South America South
30	South America Central
31	South America Northeast
32-33	South America North
34	Central Argentina
35	Brazil Southeast

EUROPE

36-37	Europe
38-39	Scandinavia
40-41	British Isles
42-43	England & Wales
44	Scotland North
45	Ireland
46	The Low Countries
47	Switzerland & Italy North
48-49	France
50-51	Spain & Portugal
52-53	Italy
54-55	The Balkans
56-57	Germany & Austria
58-59	Europe East-Central
60-61	European Russia, Ukraine & Baltic States

ASIA

62	Asia North
63	Russian Federation East
64-65	Russian Federation West
66-67	Asia South
68-69	Asia East

70-71	Asia Southeast
72-73	China Central
74	Japan & Korea
75	Japan Central
76-77	Burma, Thailand, Indo-China, Malaysia & Singapore
78	Indonesia Central
79	Philippines
80-81	Middle East
82-83	India & West China
84-85	India Northwest & Pakistan
86	India Northeast & Bangladesh
87	India South & Sri Lanka

AFRICA and THE MIDDLE EAST

88-89	Africa
90-91	Iran and The Gulf
92-93	Turkey, Syria & Iraq
94	Israel & Lebanon
95	Africa Northeast
96-97	Africa West
98-99	Africa Central
100-101	Africa South
102-103	Atlantic Ocean

OCEANIA

104-105	Australasia
106-107	Australia
108-109	Australia Southeast
110-111	New Zealand
112	Antarctica
113-192	Index

WORLD Countries

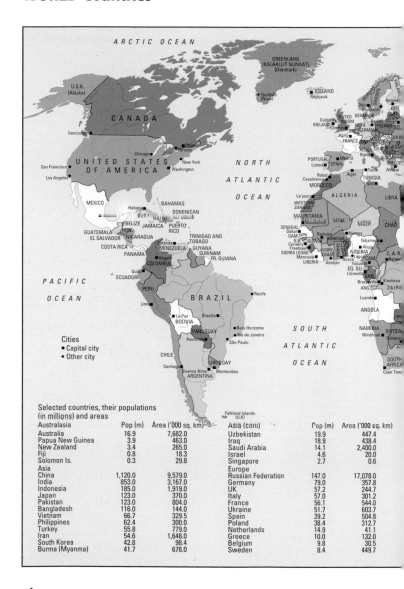

Selected countries, their populations
(in millions) and areas

Australasia	Pop (m)	Area ('000 sq. km)	Asia (cont)	Pop (m)	Area ('000 sq. km)
Australia	16.9	7,682.0	Uzbekistan	19.9	447.4
Papua New Guinea	3.9	463.0	Iraq	18.9	438.4
New Zealand	3.4	265.0	Saudi Arabia	14.1	2,400.0
Fiji	0.8	18.3	Israel	4.6	20.0
Solomon Is.	0.3	29.8	Singapore	2.7	0.6
Asia			Europe		
China	1,120.0	9,579.0	Russian Federation	147.0	17,078.0
India	853.0	3,167.0	Germany	79.0	357.8
Indonesia	185.0	1,919.0	UK	57.2	244.7
Japan	123.0	370.0	Italy	57.0	301.2
Pakistan	123.0	804.0	France	56.1	544.0
Bangladesh	116.0	144.0	Ukraine	51.7	603.7
Vietnam	66.7	329.5	Spain	39.2	504.8
Philippines	62.4	300.0	Poland	38.4	312.7
Turkey	55.8	779.0	Netherlands	14.9	41.1
Iran	54.6	1,648.0	Greece	10.0	132.0
South Korea	42.8	98.4	Belgium	9.8	30.5
Burma (Myanma)	41.7	678.0	Sweden	8.4	449.7

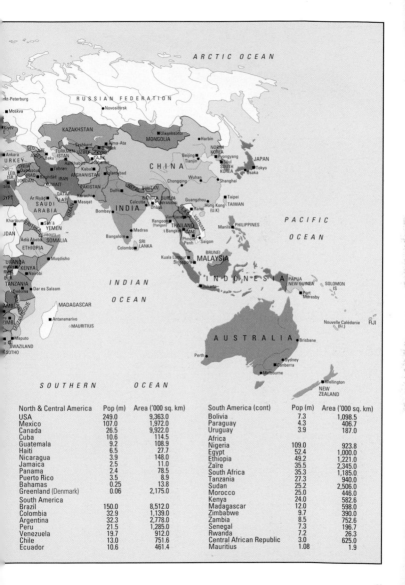

North & Central America	Pop (m)	Area ('000 sq. km)
USA	249.0	9,363.0
Mexico	107.0	1,972.0
Canada	26.5	9,922.0
Cuba	10.6	114.5
Guatemala	9.2	108.9
Haiti	6.5	27.7
Nicaragua	3.9	148.0
Jamaica	2.5	11.0
Panama	2.4	78.5
Puerto Rico	3.5	8.9
Bahamas	0.25	13.8
Greenland (Denmark)	0.06	2,175.0
South America		
Brazil	150.0	8,512.0
Colombia	32.9	1,139.0
Argentina	32.3	2,778.0
Peru	21.5	1,285.0
Venezuela	19.7	912.0
Chile	13.0	751.6
Ecuador	10.6	461.4

South America (cont)	Pop (m)	Area ('000 sq. km)
Bolivia	7.3	1,098.5
Paraguay	4.3	406.7
Uruguay	3.9	187.0
Africa		
Nigeria	109.0	923.8
Egypt	52.4	1,000.0
Ethiopia	49.2	1,221.0
Zaire	35.5	2,345.0
South Africa	35.3	1,185.0
Tanzania	27.3	940.0
Sudan	25.2	2,506.0
Morocco	25.0	446.0
Kenya	24.0	582.6
Madagascar	12.0	598.0
Zimbabwe	9.7	390.0
Zambia	8.5	752.6
Senegal	7.3	196.7
Rwanda	7.2	26.3
Central African Republic	3.0	625.0
Mauritius	1.08	1.9

WORLD Cities

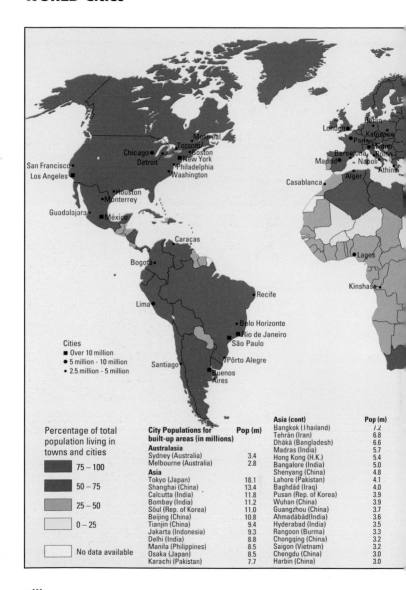

Cities
- ■ Over 10 million
- ● 5 million - 10 million
- • 2.5 million - 5 million

Percentage of total population living in towns and cities

75 – 100	
50 – 75	
25 – 50	
0 – 25	
No data available	

City Populations for built-up areas (in millions)	Pop (m)
Australasia	
Sydney (Australia)	3.4
Melbourne (Australia)	2.8
Asia	
Tokyo (Japan)	18.1
Shanghai (China)	13.4
Calcutta (India)	11.8
Bombay (India)	11.2
Sŏul (Rep. of Korea)	11.0
Beijing (China)	10.8
Tianjin (China)	9.4
Jakarta (Indonesia)	9.3
Delhi (India)	8.8
Manila (Philippines)	8.5
Osaka (Japan)	8.5
Karachi (Pakistan)	7.7

Asia (cont)	Pop (m)
Bangkok (Thailand)	7.2
Tehrān (Iran)	6.8
Dhākā (Bangladesh)	6.6
Madras (India)	5.7
Hong Kong (H.K.)	5.4
Bangalore (India)	5.0
Shenyang (China)	4.8
Lahore (Pakistan)	4.1
Baghdād (Iraq)	4.0
Pusan (Rep. of Korea)	3.9
Guangzhou (China)	3.7
Ahmadābād (India)	3.6
Hyderabad (India)	3.5
Rangoon (Burma)	3.3
Chongqing (China)	3.2
Saigon (Vietnam)	3.2
Chengdu (China)	3.0
Harbin (China)	3.0

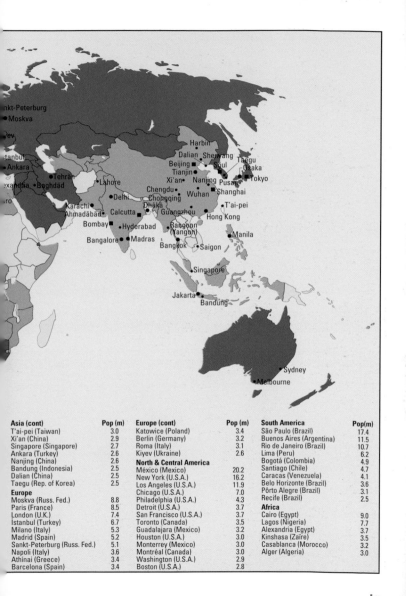

Asia (cont)	Pop (m)	Europe (cont)	Pop (m)	South America	Pop(m)
T'ai-pei (Taiwan)	3.0	Katowice (Poland)	3.4	São Paulo (Brazil)	17.4
Xi'an (China)	2.9	Berlin (Germany)	3.2	Buenos Aires (Argentina)	11.5
Singapore (Singapore)	2.7	Roma (Italy)	3.1	Rio de Janeiro (Brazil)	10.7
Ankara (Turkey)	2.6	Kiyev (Ukraine)	2.6	Lima (Peru)	6.2
Nanjing (China)	2.6	**North & Central America**		Bogotá (Colombia)	4.9
Bandung (Indonesia)	2.5	México (Mexico)	20.2	Santiago (Chile)	4.7
Dalian (China)	2.5	New York (U.S.A.)	16.2	Caracas (Venezuela)	4.1
Taegu (Rep. of Korea)	2.5	Los Angeles (U.S.A.)	11.9	Belo Horizonte (Brazil)	3.6
Europe		Chicago (U.S.A.)	7.0	Pôrto Alegre (Brazil)	3.1
Moskva (Russ. Fed.)	8.8	Philadelphia (U.S.A.)	4.3	Recife (Brazil)	2.5
Paris (France)	8.5	Detroit (U.S.A.)	3.7	**Africa**	
London (U.K.)	7.4	San Francisco (U.S.A.)	3.7	Cairo (Egypt)	9.0
İstanbul (Turkey)	6.7	Toronto (Canada)	3.5	Lagos (Nigeria)	7.7
Milano (Italy)	5.3	Guadalajara (Mexico)	3.2	Alexandria (Egypt)	3.7
Madrid (Spain)	5.2	Houston (U.S.A.)	3.0	Kinshasa (Zaïre)	3.5
Sankt-Peterburg (Russ. Fed.)	5.1	Monterrey (Mexico)	3.0	Casablanca (Morocco)	3.2
Napoli (Italy)	3.6	Montréal (Canada)	3.0	Alger (Algeria)	3.0
Athínai (Greece)	3.4	Washington (U.S.A.)	2.9		
Barcelona (Spain)	3.4	Boston (U.S.A.)	2.8		

WORLD Languages

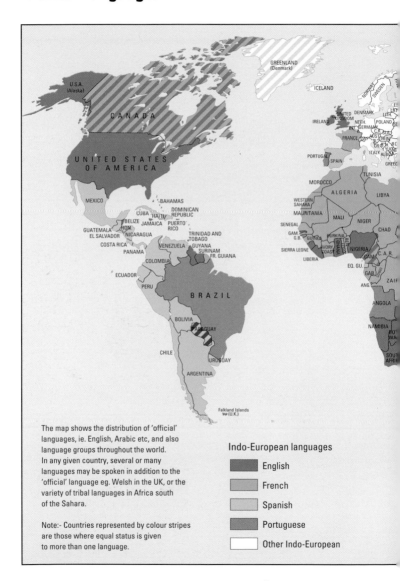

The map shows the distribution of 'official' languages, ie. English, Arabic etc, and also language groups throughout the world. In any given country, several or many languages may be spoken in addition to the 'official' language eg. Welsh in the UK, or the variety of tribal languages in Africa south of the Sahara.

Note:- Countries represented by colour stripes are those where equal status is given to more than one language.

Indo-European languages

- English
- French
- Spanish
- Portuguese
- Other Indo-European

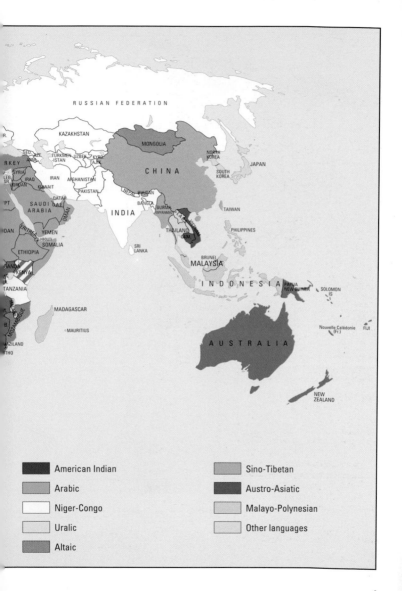

American Indian

Arabic

Niger-Congo

Uralic

Altaic

Sino-Tibetan

Austro-Asiatic

Malayo-Polynesian

Other languages

WORLD Economic Groups

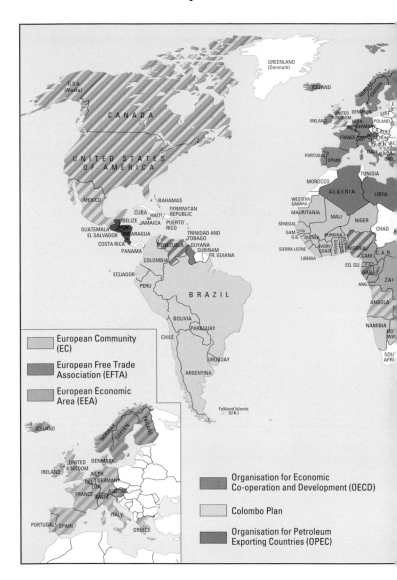

European Community (EC)

European Free Trade Association (EFTA)

European Economic Area (EEA)

Organisation for Economic Co-operation and Development (OECD)

Colombo Plan

Organisation for Petroleum Exporting Countries (OPEC)

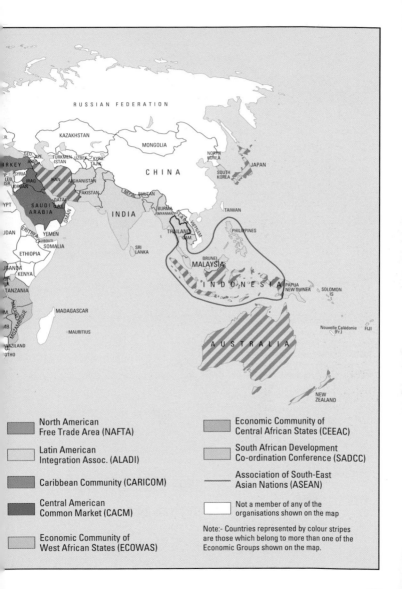

North American
Free Trade Area (NAFTA)

Latin American
Integration Assoc. (ALADI)

Caribbean Community (CARICOM)

Central American
Common Market (CACM)

Economic Community of
West African States (ECOWAS)

Economic Community of
Central African States (CEEAC)

South African Development
Co-ordination Conference (SADCC)

Association of South-East
Asian Nations (ASEAN)

Not a member of any of the
organisations shown on the map

Note:- Countries represented by colour stripes
are those which belong to more than one of the
Economic Groups shown on the map.

WORLD International Organisations

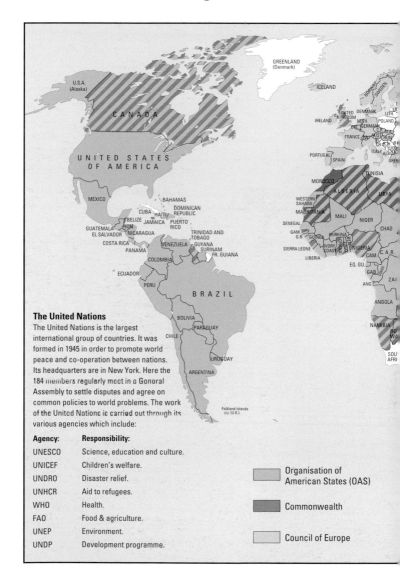

The United Nations

The United Nations is the largest international group of countries. It was formed in 1945 in order to promote world peace and co-operation between nations. Its headquarters are in New York. Here the 184 members regularly meet in a General Assembly to settle disputes and agree on common policies to world problems. The work of the United Nations is carried out through its various agencies which include:

Agency:	Responsibility:
UNESCO	Science, education and culture.
UNICEF	Children's welfare.
UNDRO	Disaster relief.
UNHCR	Aid to refugees.
WHO	Health.
FAO	Food & agriculture.
UNEP	Environment.
UNDP	Development programme.

Organisation of American States (OAS)

Commonwealth

Council of Europe

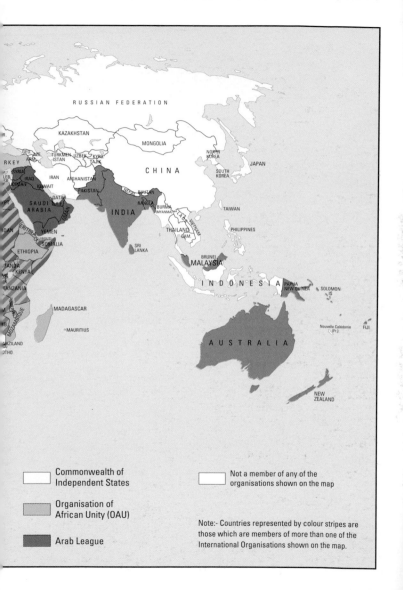

RUSSIAN FEDERATION

KAZAKHSTAN

MONGOLIA

NORTH KOREA

JAPAN

CHINA

SOUTH KOREA

R.
GEO. AZE.
RKEY
TURKMEN-ISTAN
UZBEK.
KYRG.
TAJK.
SYRIA
LEB.
SR.
IRAQ
KUWAIT
IRAN
AFGHANISTAN
PAKISTAN
QATAR
U.A.E.
SAUDI ARABIA
OMAN
NEPAL
BHUTAN
BANGLA.
BURMA
MYANMAR

TAIWAN

INDIA

LAOS
VIETNAM

THAILAND
CAM.

PHILIPPINES

SRI LANKA

BRUNEI
MALAYSIA

I N D O N E S I A

PAPUA NEW GUINEA

SOLOMON IS.

DAN
ERITREA
YEMEN
DJIBOUTI
SOMALIA
ETHIOPIA

GANDA
KENYA
TANZANIA

MADAGASCAR

MAURITIUS

Nouvelle Calédonie (Fr.)

FIJI

MOZAMBIQUE

A U S T R A L I A

AZILAND
OTHO

NEW ZEALAND

| | Commonwealth of Independent States | | | Not a member of any of the organisations shown on the map |

| | Organisation of African Unity (OAU) |

| | Arab League |

Note:- Countries represented by colour stripes are those which are members of more than one of the International Organisations shown on the map.

SYMBOLS

BOUNDARIES

	International
	International under Dispute
	Cease Fire Line
	Autonomous or State
	Administrative
	Maritime (National)

LETTERING STYLES

CANADA	Independent Nation
FLORIDA	State, Province or Autonomous Region
Gibraltar (U.K.)	Sovereignty of Dependent Territory
Lothian	Administrative Area
LANGUEDOC	Historic Region
Lorr **Vosges**	Physical Feature or Physical Region

TOWNS AND CITIES

Square Symbols denote capital cities. Each settlement is given a symbol according to its relative importance, with type size to match.

■	●	**New York**	Major City
■	●	**Montréal**	City
□	○	Ottawa	Small City
■	●	**Québec**	Large Town
□	○	St John's	Town
□	○	Yorkton	Small Town
□	○	Jasper	Village
			Built-up-area

LAKE FEATURES

	Permanent
	Seasonal

OTHER FEATURES

	River
	Seasonal River
=	Pass, Gorge
	Dam, Barrage
	Waterfall, Rapid
	Aqueduct
	Reef
▲4231	Summit, Peak
.217	Spot Height, Depth
⌣	Well
⌂	Oil Field
▲	Gas Field
Gas / Oil	Oil/Natural Gas Pipeline
Gemsbok Nat. Pk.	National Park
..UR	Historic Site
	Main Railway
	Other Railway
- - - - - - -	Under Construction
—•—•—	Rail Tunnel
- - - - - - -	Rail Ferry
	Canal
⊕	International Airport
✦	Other Airport

For pages 102-103, 104-105 only:

xvi

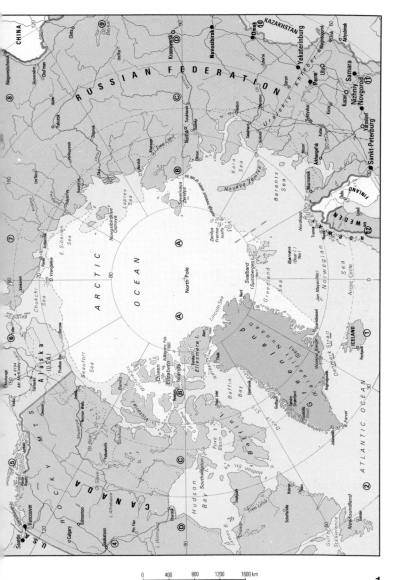

NORTH AMERICA

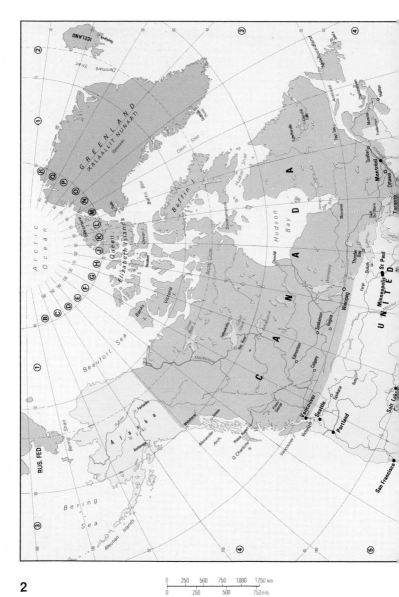

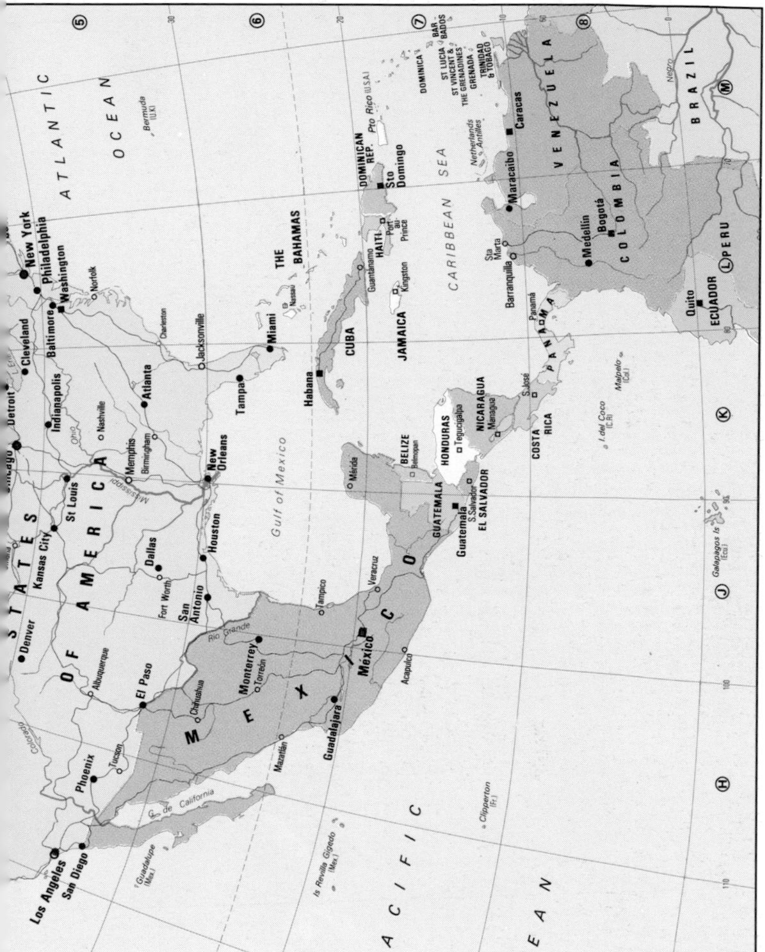

ATLANTIC

OCEAN

Bermuda (U.K.)

UNITED

New York
Philadelphia
Washington
Baltimore
Norfolk
Cleveland
Detroit
Indianapolis
Nashville
Atlanta
Charleston
Jacksonville

STATES

OF AMERICA

Denver
Kansas City
St Louis
Memphis
Birmingham
Dallas
Fort Worth
Houston
San Antonio
New Orleans
Tampa
Miami

El Paso
Chihuahua
Albuquerque
Phoenix
Tucson
Los Angeles
San Diego

Rio Grande

Monterrey
Torreón
México
Tampico
Veracruz
Acapulco
Guadalajara
Mazatlán

M E X I C O

Gulf of Mexico

Mérida

THE BAHAMAS

Habana
CUBA
Guantánamo
Kingston
JAMAICA

DOMINICAN REP.
Sto Domingo
HAITI
Port-au-Prince

Puerto Rico (U.S.A.)

DOMINICA
ST LUCIA
ST VINCENT &
THE GRENADINES
BARBADOS
GRENADA
TRINIDAD & TOBAGO

CARIBBEAN SEA

Netherlands Antilles

Maracaibo
Caracas

VENEZUELA

BELIZE
GUATEMALA
Guatemala
EL SALVADOR
San Salvador
HONDURAS
Tegucigalpa
NICARAGUA
Managua
COSTA RICA
San José
PANAMA
Panamá

Barranquilla
Sta Marta
Medellín
Bogotá
COLOMBIA

BRAZIL

Quito
ECUADOR
PERU

PACIFIC

OCEAN

Clipperton (Fr.)

Is Revilla Gigedo (Mex.)

Guadalupe (Mex.)

G. de California

Tropic of Cancer

Equator

Galápagos Is (Ecu.)

r. del Coco (C.R.)

Malpelo (Col.)

⑤ ⑥ ⑦ ⑧
⑥ ⑦ ⑧
Ⓖ Ⓗ Ⓙ Ⓚ Ⓜ

CANADA WEST

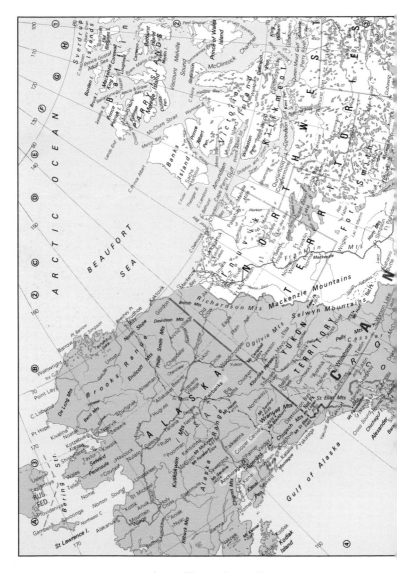

0   200   400   600 km
0   100   200   300 mls

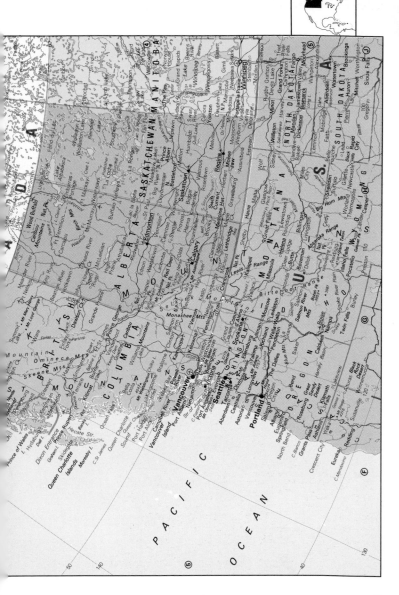

CANADA EAST

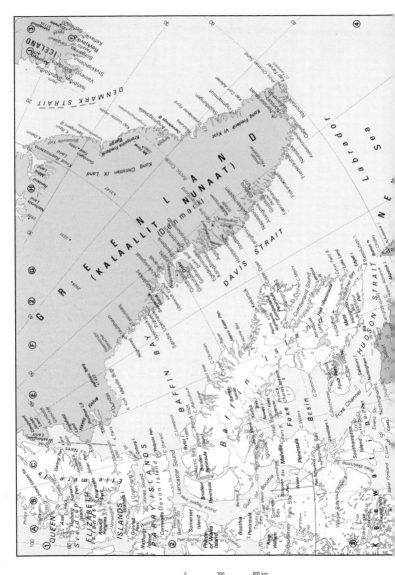

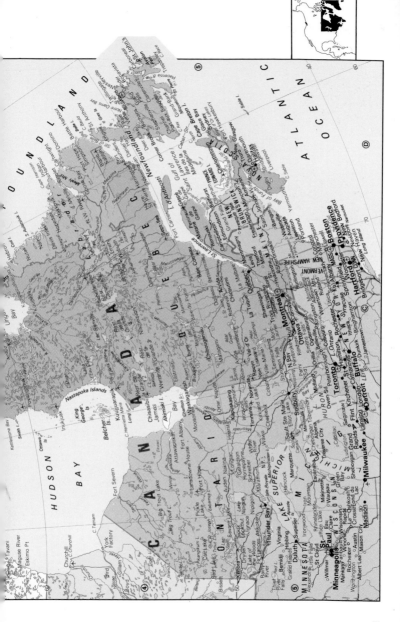

7

USA WEST

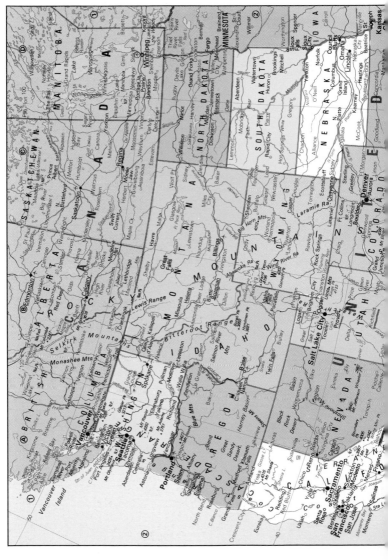

0   100   200   300   400km
0   100   200 mls

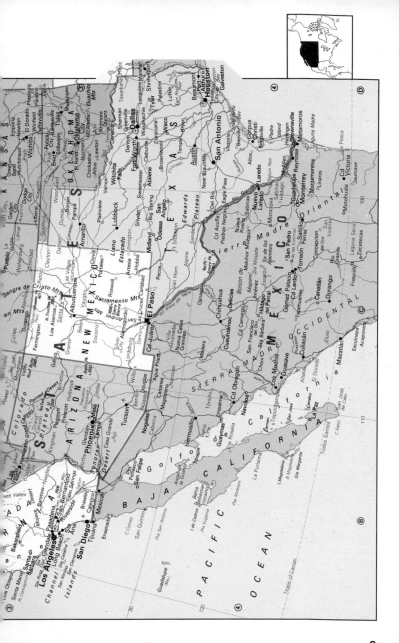

9

USA EAST

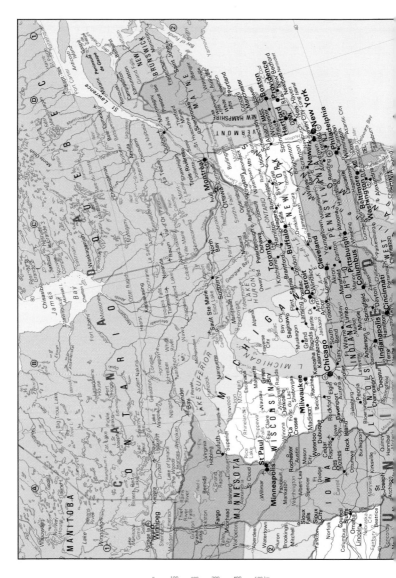

| 0 | 100 | 200 | 300 | 400 | 500 km |
| 0 | | 100 | 200 | | 300 mls |

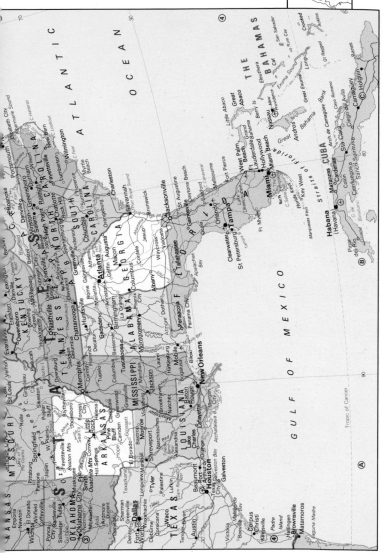

USA ALASKA

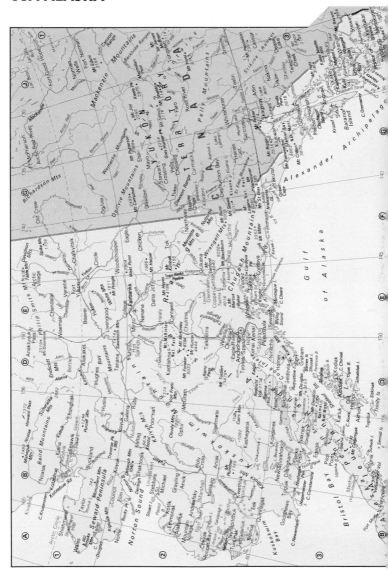

0   100   200 km
0   100 mls

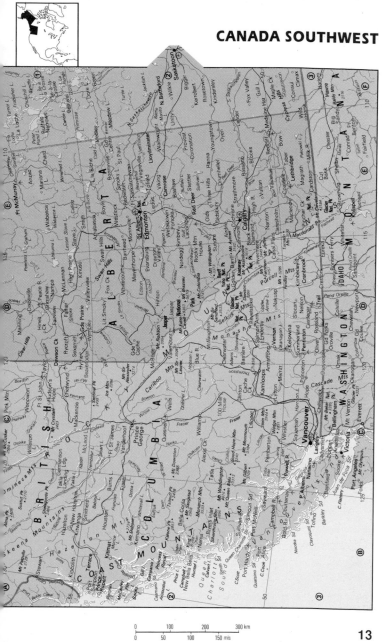

CANADA SOUTHWEST

CANADA SOUTHEAST, USA NORTHEAST

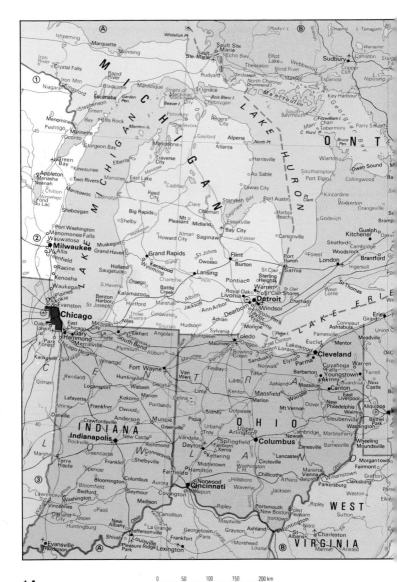

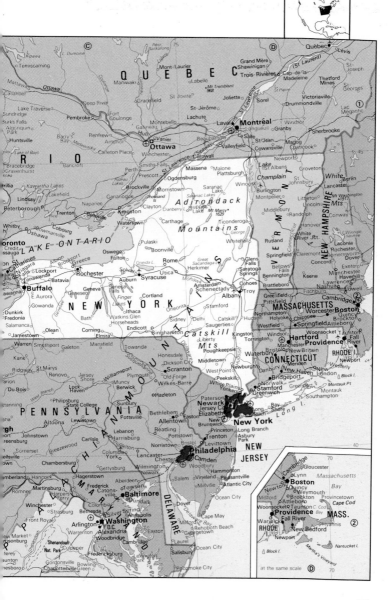

15

USA Washington - New York - Boston

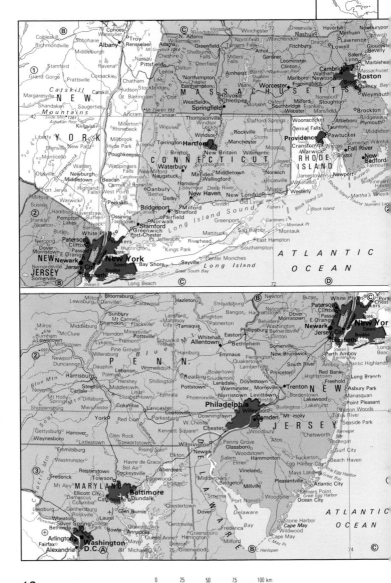

0   25   50   75   100 km

0   25   50 mls

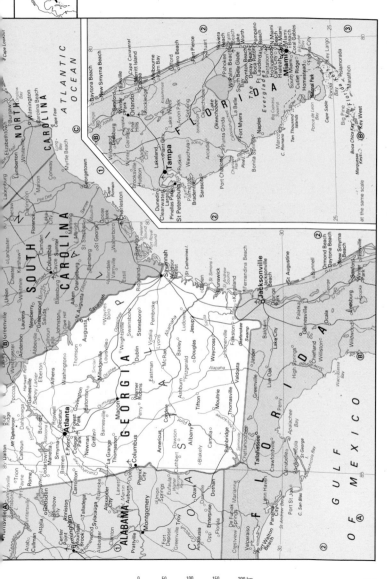

USA SOUTH-CENTRAL

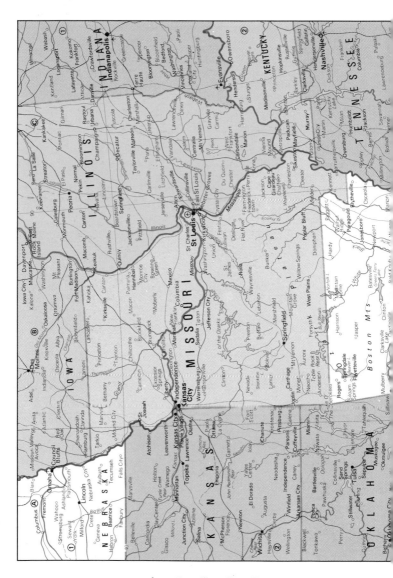

| 0 | 50 | 100 | 150 | 200 km |
| 0 | | 50 | | 100 mls |

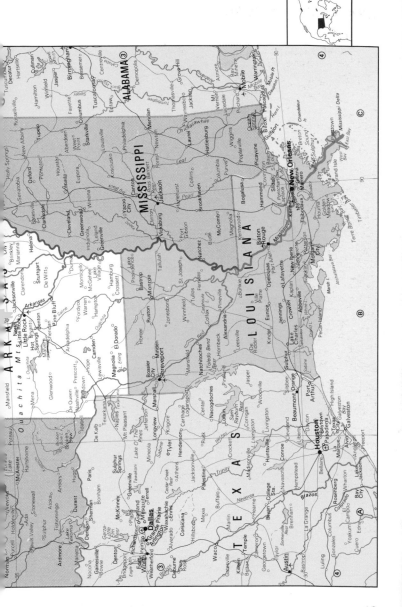

19

USA NORTHWEST

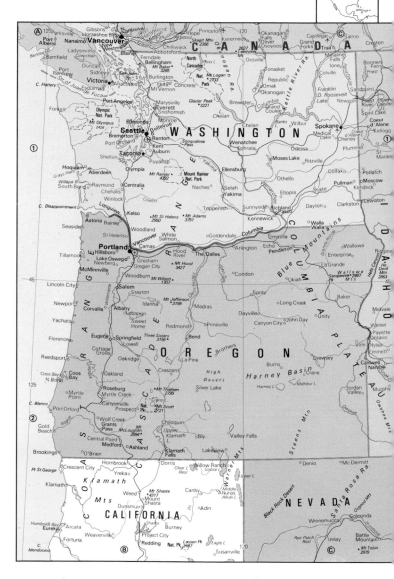

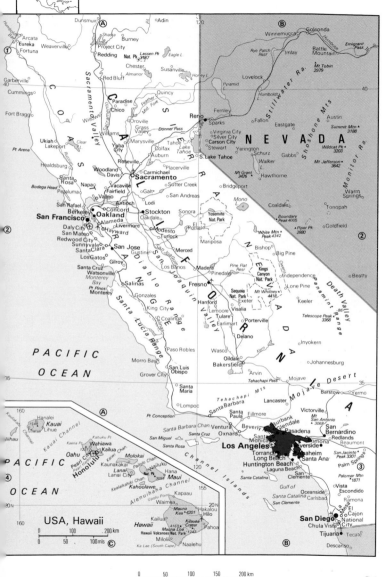

PACIFIC OCEAN

NEVADA

CALIFORNIA

Sacramento

San Francisco
Oakland

San Jose

Los Angeles

San Diego

Death Valley

Mojave Desert

Sierra Nevada

San Joaquin Valley

Santa Lucia Range

Diablo Range

Sacramento Valley

COAST RANGES

USA, Hawaii

Kauai
Oahu
Honolulu
Molokai
Lanai
Maui
Kahoolawe
Hawaii
Mauna Kea 4205
Mauna Loa 4169
Hilo

USA San Francisco & Los Angeles

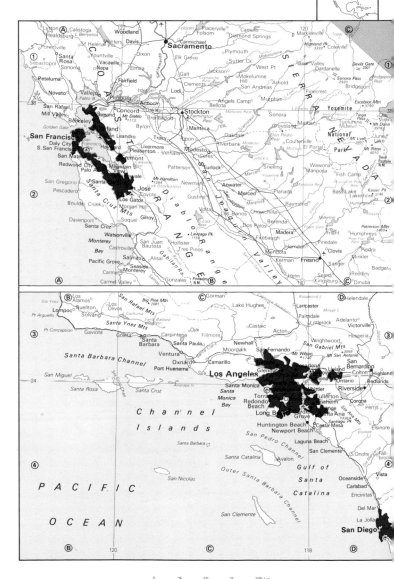

| 0 | 25 | 50 | 75 | 100 km |
| 0 | | 25 | | 50 mls |

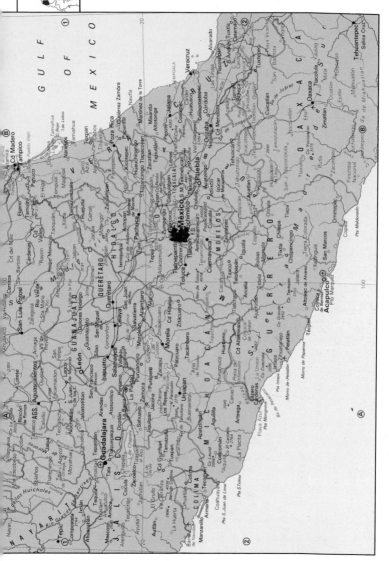

MEXICO & CENTRAL AMERICA

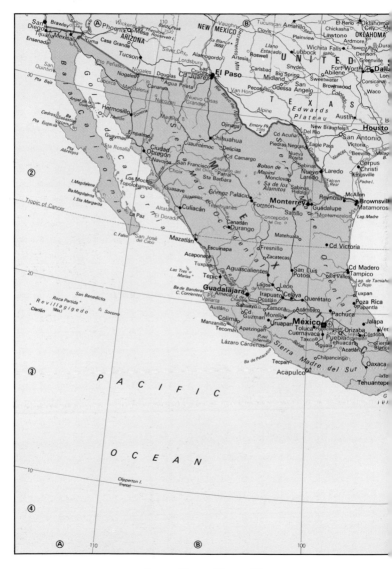

0	200	400	600 km
0	100	200	300 mls

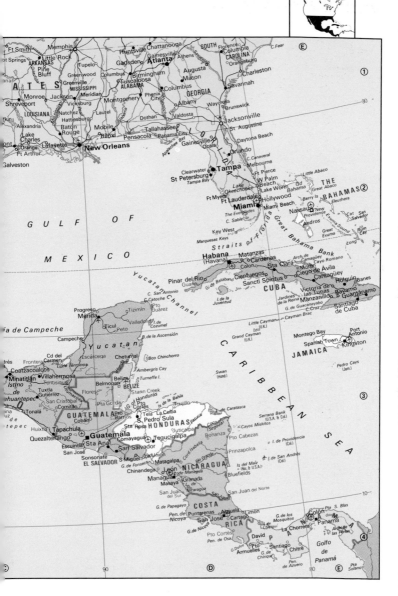

25

CARIBBEAN

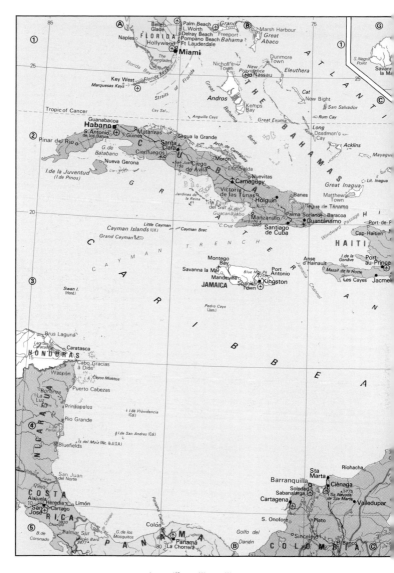

0	100	200	300	400 km
0		100		200 mls

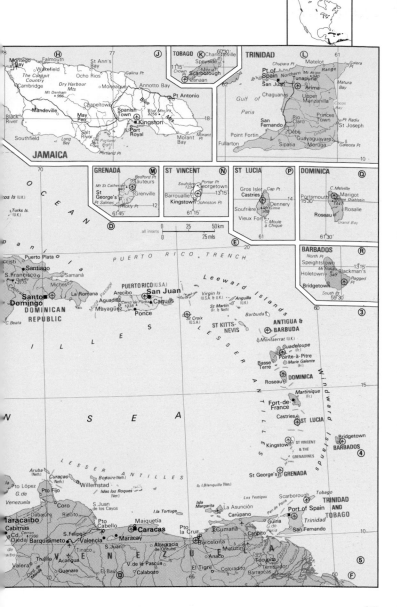

JAMAICA

Montego Bay, Falmouth, St Ann's Bay, Ocho Rios, Galina Pt, **(H)**, **(J)**, **TOBAGO**, **(K)** Charlotteville, Speyside, **TRINIDAD**, **(L)** Matelot, Galera
The Cockpit Country, Wakefield, Moneague, Annotto Bay, 1115', Crown Pt, Morat, Scarborough, Canaan, Chupara Pt, Northern, Mt Aripo, Range, Pt
Cambridge, Mt Denham 986, Chapeltown, Blue Mtn Pk 2256, Pt Antonio, Pt of Spain, Tunapuna, Arima, Matura Bay
Mandeville, Spanish Town, Port Royal, Kingston, 18, San Juan, Chaguanas, Upper Manzanilla
Black River, May Pen, Long Bay, Salt River, Portland Pt, Morant Pt, Morant Bay, Gulf of Paria, San Fernando, Rio Claro, Princes Town, Pt Radix, St Joseph, Cocos Bay
Southfield, **JAMAICA**, Portland Pt, Point Fortin, Débé, Sipatia, Guayaguayare, Moruga, Galeota Pt, Fullarton, 10

70

GRENADA **(M)**
Bedford Pt, Mt St Catherine 840, St Sauteurs, George's, Grenville, St Salines, Hicky Pt, 12
61°45'

ST VINCENT **(N)**
Porter Pt, Soufrière 1234, Georgetown, 13°15', Barrouallie, Kingstown, Johnston Pt
61°15'

ST LUCIA **(P)**
Gros Islet, Cap Pt, Castries, Dennery, 14, Soufrière, Vieux Fort, C. Moule à Chique
61

DOMINICA **(Q)**
Portsmouth, Marigot, 1530', C. Melville, Morne Diablotin 1447, Roseau, Rosalie, Grand Bay
61°30'

all insets 0 25 50 km / 0 25 mls

BARBADOS **(R)**
North Pt, Speightstown, 1315', Mt Hillaby, Holetown, Blackman's, Ragged Pt, Bridgetown, South Pt, 59°30'
(3)

O C E A N

os Is (U.K.), Turks Is. (U.K.)

P U E R T O   R I C O   T R E N C H

Puerto Plata, S. Francisco, Santiago, Samaná, Miches, **Leeward Islands**
cristi, La Romana, **PUERTO RICO** (U.S.A.), **San Juan**, Virgin Is (U.S.A. & U.K.), Anguilla (U.K.)
Santo Domingo, **DOMINICAN REPUBLIC**, Aguadilla, Hato de Ponce 1338, Mayagüez, Ponce, **Caguas**, St Martin (Fr & Neth), Barbuda, St Kitts-Nevis (U.K.)
Duarte 3175, C. Beata, St Croix (U.S.A.), **ANTIGUA & BARBUDA**, Montserrat (U.K.)
L L E S, Guadeloupe (Fr.), Pointe-à-Pitre, Basse Terre, Marie Galante (Fr.), Roseau **DOMINICA**
Martinique (Fr.), Fort-de-France, Castries **ST LUCIA**, 15
S E A, Kingstown **ST VINCENT & THE GRENADINES**, Bridgetown **BARBADOS**, **(4)**
St George's **GRENADA**

L E S S E R   A N T I L L E S

Aruba (Neth.), Curaçao (Neth.), Bonaire (Neth.), Islas los Roques (Ven.), I.Blanquilla (Ven.), Los Testigos, Scarborough, Tobago, **TRINIDAD AND TOBAGO**
la, Pto López, G.de Venezuela, Pto Fijo, Willemstad, Isla Margarita, La Asunción, Pan de Paria, Port of Spain, Trinidad
Coro, S.Juan de los Cayos, I.la Tortuga, Carúpano, Güiria, G de Paria, San Fernando, 10
Maracaibo, Cabimas, Riecito, Maiquetía, Isla, Pto la Cruz, Cumaná, Caripito
Cd. Ojeda, S. Felipe, **Caracas**, Cerro 1990, Barquisimeto, **Valencia**, **Maracay**, Barcelona, Maturín, Tucupita, Temblador
de, Valera, Trujillo, Acarigua, Tinaco, S. Juan, Altagracia de Orituco, Anaco, Colorado, Barrancas
aibo, Guanare, El Baúl, **V E N E Z U E L A**, V. de la Pascua, El Tigre, 60
Cojedes, 66, Calabozo, **(D)**, **(E)**, **(F)**, **(5)**

27

SOUTH AMERICA

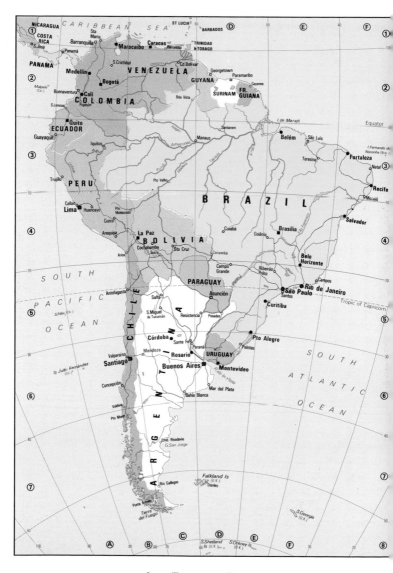

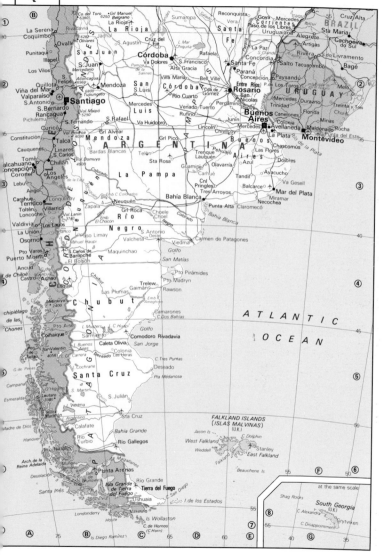

SOUTH AMERICA CENTRAL

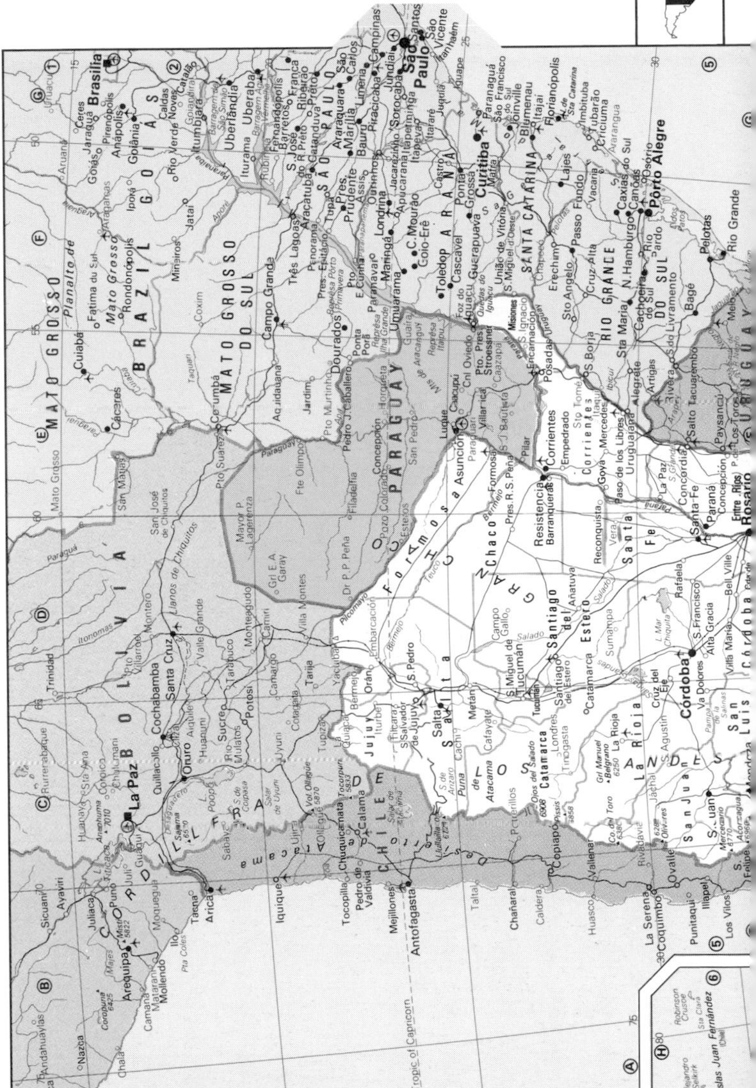

0   200   400   600 km
0   100   200   300 mls

BRAZIL

GOIÁS

Brasília
Brazil
Anápolis
Goiânia
Uberlândia
Uberaba
Ribeirão Prêto
Franca
SÃO PAULO
São Paulo
São Vicente
Santos
Jundiaí
Sorocaba
Campinas
Piracicaba
Araraquara
Pres. Prudente
Marília
Bauru
Londrina
Maringá
C. Mourão
Toledo
Cascavel
Guarapuava
Ponta Grossa
Curitiba
PARANÁ
União da Vitória
Lajes
Joinville
Blumenau
Florianópolis
Itajaí
SANTA CATARINA
Passo Fundo
Caxias do Sul
Canoas
N. Hamburgo
RIO GRANDE DO SUL
Sta Maria
Cruz Alta
Sto Ângelo
Pôrto Alegre
Pelotas
Rio Grande
Bagé
Livramento
Uruguaiana
Alegrete
URUGUAY
Salto
Paysandú

MATO GROSSO
Cuiabá
Cáceres
Planalto de Mato Grosso
MATO GROSSO DO SUL
Campo Grande
Corumbá
Três Lagoas
Dourados
Ponta Porã

BOLIVIA
La Paz
Cochabamba
Santa Cruz
Sucre
Oruro
Potosí
Tarija
Trinidad
CORDILLERA

PARAGUAY
Asunción
Concepción
Villarrica
Pedro J. Caballero
Pilar
Filadelfia
GRAN CHACO
Formosa

CHILE
Arica
Iquique
Antofagasta
Tocopilla
Mejillones
Taltal
Chañaral
Caldera
Copiapó
Vallenar
La Serena
Coquimbo
Ovalle
Desierto de Atacama

ARGENTINA
Córdoba
ANDES
San Juan
San Luis
La Rioja
Catamarca
Santiago del Estero
Tucumán
Salta
Jujuy
Resistencia
Corrientes
Formosa
Posadas
Santa Fe
Paraná
Rosario
Rafaela
Sunchales
Reconquista
Goya
Paso de los Libres
Concordia
Entre Ríos

PERU
Arequipa
Moquegua
Tacna

Tropic of Capricorn

Islas Juan Fernández

Equator

I. de Marajó
C. Maguariho
B. de Marajó
Salinópolis
Bragança
Pará
Capanema
Cametá
Belém
Abaetetuba
Alcântara
Pinheiro
São Luís
Rosário Parnaíba
Monção
Chapadinha
Bacabal
Coroatá
Codó
Caxias
Campo
Teresina
Castelo
Crateus
Imperatriz
Grajaú
Pto Franco

Marabá
Carolina
Balsas
Araguaína

Floriano
Oeiras
Picos
J. do Norte
Crato

Paulistana
S.Raimundo
Nonato

Petrolina
Juazeiro

Camocim Acaraú
Itapipoca Cauaia
Sobral
Sta
Quitéria
Nova
Russas
Morada
Canindé
Aracati
Mombaça
Taúa
Acopiara
Iguatú
Sousa
Patos
Caicó
Cabedelo
João Pessoa
Campina Grande
Talhada Val do
Limoeiro
Caruaru
Olinda
Recife
(Pernambuco)
Garanhuns
Palmares
Barreiros
Palmeira dos Índios
Maceió
Propriá
Arapiraca
Penedo

Rocas
I. Fernando
de Noronha
Pța do Calcanhar

Fortaleza (Ceará)
Quixadá
Mossoró
Natal

PARA
MARANHÃO
CEARÁ
PIAUI
PERNAMBUCO
RIO GRANDE DO NORTE
PARAÍBA
ALAGOAS
SERGIPE
BRAZIL
TOCANTINS
BAHIA
GOIAS
MINAS GERAIS
SÃO PAULO
ESPÍRITO SANTO

Cach. de
P. Afonso
Sen.do Bonfim
Barra
Jacobina
Ibotirama
R.de Jacuípe
Serrinha
Feira de S.
Iaçu
Alagoinhas
Cachoeira
Bom Jesus
da Lapa
Caetité
Valença
Ipiaú
Jequié
Salvador (Bahia)
Vitória da
Conquista
Itabuna
Ilhéus
Januária
Porteirinha
Salinas
Canavieiras
Belmonte
Montes Claros
Itapetinga
Pôrto Seguro
Aracuaí
Sa do Chifre
Itamaraju
Paracatu
Pirapora
Teófilo Otóni
Nanuque
João
Pinheiro
Diamantina
Gov.
Valadares
São Mateus
Corinto
Curvelo
Araguari
Patos
de Minas
Itabira
Cnl
Fabriciano
Linhares
Colatina
Uberlândia
Araxá
Sete Lagoas
Belo
Horizonte
Caratinga
Manhuaçu
Carlácica
Vitória
Vila Velha
Divinópolis
Con.
Lafaiete
Ponte Nova
Cachoeiro de Itapemirim
Franca
João del Rei
Barbacena
Itaperuna
Ribeirão Preto
Lavras
Pocos de Caldas
Juiz
de Fora
Carangola
São João da Barra
Campos
Nova Friburgo
Petrópolis
Volta
Redonda
Barra
Mansa
Magé
Niterói
Rio de Janeiro

ATLANTIC
OCEAN

Tropic of Capricorn

Aruanã
Ceres
Jaraguá
Formosa
Goiás
Pirenópolis
Brasília
Anápolis
São Francisco
Goiânia
Caldas
Novas
Rio Verde
Itumbiara
Barragem de
São Simão
Goiandira
Catalão
Uberaba
Ituiutaba
Barragem Água
Vermelha
Frutal
Fernandópolis
Barretos
Passos
José
do R. Prêto
Barretos
Catanduva
São José
Araçatuba
Araraquara
São Carlos
Marília
Limeira
Bauru
Piracicaba
Prudente
Assis
Jundiaí
Campinas
Jacarezinho
Sorocaba
São Paulo
Londrina
Itapeva
Itapetininga
Santos
Apucarana
São Vicente
Itanhaém
Itararé
Juquiá
Iguape
Castro
Ponta
Grossa
Guarapuava
Curitiba
Mafra
Paranaguá
São Francisco do Sul

0   200   400   600 km
0   100   200   300 mls

SOUTH AMERICA NORTH

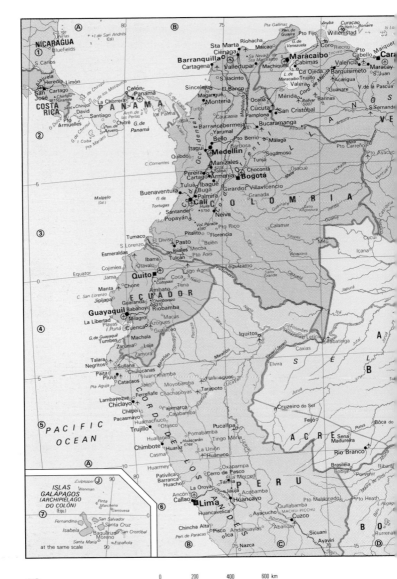

NICARAGUA
Bluefields
S Caribs
Heredia Limón
San José Cartago
COSTA RICA David Santiago
Armuelles
PANAMA
Colón Panamá
La Chorrera
Chitré G. de Panamá

NICARAGUA
Pta Gallinas
Sta Marta
Ciénaga
Barranquilla
Cartagena
Riohacha Maicao
Valledupar Machiques
Aruba Curaçao Bonaire
Pen. de Guajira Pto Fijo Willemstad
G. de Venezuela Coro Riecito Pto Cabello
Cabimas Valencia Maracay
Maracaibo
Cd Ojeda Barquisimeto
Acarigua
Cara
Maiquet
San Juan
L. de Maracaibo Trujillo
Valera
Mérida
Bolívar
Guanare
V. de la Pascua
San Cristóbal
Sincelejo El Banco
Magangué
Montería
Ocaña
Pamplona
Barrancabermeja
Barinas
San Fernando
Turbo Caucasia Yarumal
Barbosa
Málaga
Pto Carreño
Bello
Medellín
Itagüí
Quibdó Manizales
Pereira Chocontá
Cartago Armenia Bogotá
Tuluá Ibagué Girardot Villavicencio
Buga
Buenaventura Palmira Granada
Cali Neiva
Santander
Popayán Pitalito
Pto Rico
Calamar
Mitú
Pasto Belén
Ibales Mocoa
Esmeraldas Tulcán Pto Asís
Ibarra
Otavalo
Quito
Coca
Manta Latacunga
Chone Tena
Ambato
Guayaquil Riobamba
Babahoyo Macas
Milagro
La Libertad Cuenca Gualaceo
Playas Azogues
Machala
Loja
Zaruma
Zamora
Iquitos Leticia Tabatinga
Talara
Negritos Sullana
Paita Chulucanas
Catacaos Moyobamba
Lambayeque Ferreñafe Chachapoyas Tarapoto
Chiclayo Cajamarca
Chepén Celendín
Pacasmayo
Trujillo Huamachuco
Otusco
Huallanca Pucallpa
Chimbote Huaraz Tingo María
Casma La Unión
Huánuco
Huarmey
Oxapampa
Pativilca Cerro de Pasco
Barranca La Merced
Huacho Tarma
La Oroya Jauja
Ancón Acobamba
Callao Lima Huancayo
Huancavelica
Chincha Alta Ayacucho
Pisco Andahuaylas
Ica Abancay
Nazca

COLOMBIA
VE

ECUADOR

PERU

CORDILLERA DE LOS ANDES

PACIFIC OCEAN

Equator

ISLAS GALÁPAGOS (ARCHIPIÉLAGO DO COLÓN)
(Equ.)
Culpepper Wenman
Pinta Marchena
Darwin Genovesa
Fernandina
Isabela Baquerizo Moreno San Cristóbal
Santa Cruz San Salvador
Santa María Española
at the same scale

Cuzco
Machu-Picchu
Sicuani
Ayaviri
BO

0   200   400   600 km
0   100   200   300 mls

32

ATLANTIC

OCEAN

GRENADA
I. de Margarita
St George's
The Grenadines
Tobago
La Asunción *Pen. de Paria*
Carúpano Güiria
Cumaná *G. de Paria* Port of
Cruz Caripito Spain TRINIDAD
Iona Trinidad AND
Anaco Maturín San Fernando TOBAGO
Tigri
El Tigre Tucupita
Barrancas
Cd Bolívar *Orinoco* Cd Guayana Mabaruma
Cd Piar Upata
Charity
Emb. de Suddie
Guri V-en Hoop Georgetown
ZUELA El Dorado New Amsterdam
La Paragua Bartica Linden *Nieuw Amsterdam*
Salto Paramaribo Marienburg
del Angel Nieuw Sinnamary
La Gran *Roraima* Tottness Nickerie Albina *I. du Diable Devil's I.*
Sabana *2180* Apoera Witagron Kourou
Sa Pacaraima *Kaieteur* *Blommestein Meer* Cayenne
Fall *Cabo Orange*
Bonfim SURINAM FRENCH
Sta Elena *Julianatop* Oiapoque
Boa Vista *1280* GUIANA
Sa Parima Lethem
Orinoco Serra Tumucumaque
RORAIMA Amapá
Caracaraí *Ilha de Maracá*
Branco AMAPÁ
puruçuara Sa do Navio
Negro Macapá
Pto Santana *C. Maguarinho*
I. de Marajó
Oriximiná *B. de Marajó* Salinópolis
Óbidos Amazonas Bragança
Manaus Monte Pará Capanema
Tefé Manacapuru Careiro Itacoatiara Santarém Alegre Cametá Belém
Abaeteuba
Coari Aveiro Altamira
AZONAS Itaituba PARÁ Tucuruí
Madeira Pimenta
A *Tapajós*
Z Marabá
Coari I Imperatriz
Juruá L Jacareacanga S. Félix
Lábrea Humaitá Prainha Pto
Serra do Cachimbo Franco
Madeira *Xingu* *Araguaia* Araguaína Carolina
Pôrto Velho Aripuanã
Cachimbo C.do Araguaiá
Abunã *Aripuanã*
Guajará-Mirim *Ji-Paraná* Sa dos Caiabis TOCANTINS
RONDÔNIA Serra dos Parecis São Félix
Guaporé Vilhena *Sa Formosa* *Ilha do Bananal*
VIA MATO GROSSO GOIÁS
Trinidad *Iténez* Pto Artur
Mato Grosso Aruanã Uruaçu

CENTRAL ARGENTINA

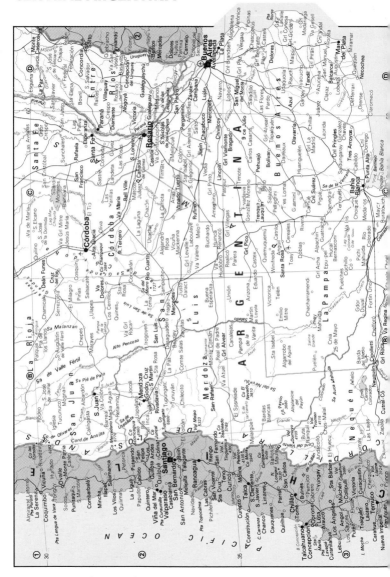

34

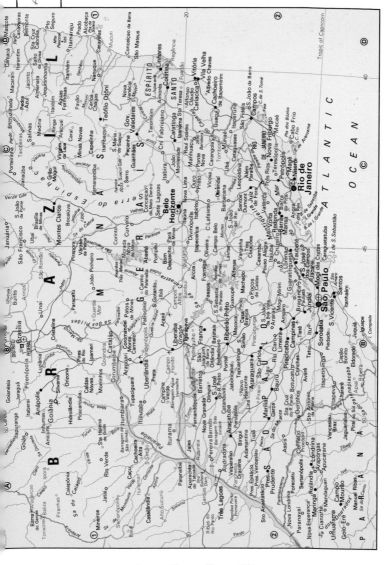

EUROPE

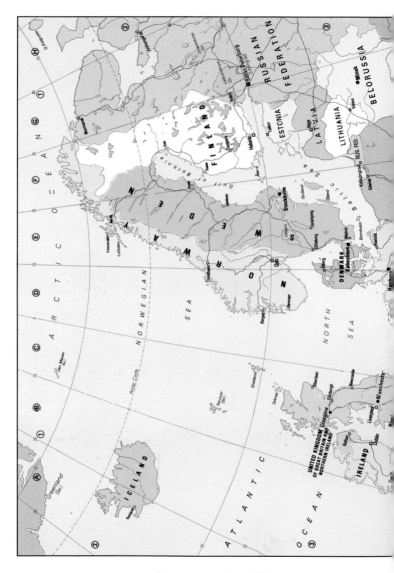

| 0 | 200 | 400 | 600 km |
| 0 | 100 | 200 | 300 mils |

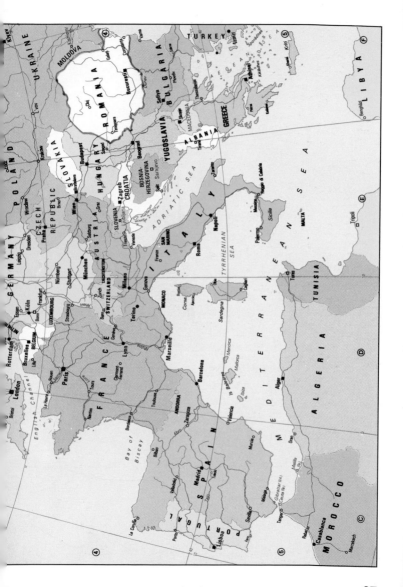

SCANDINAVIA

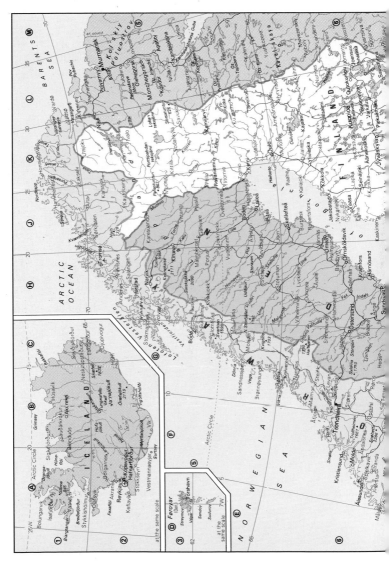

0   100   200   300 km
0   50   100   150 mls

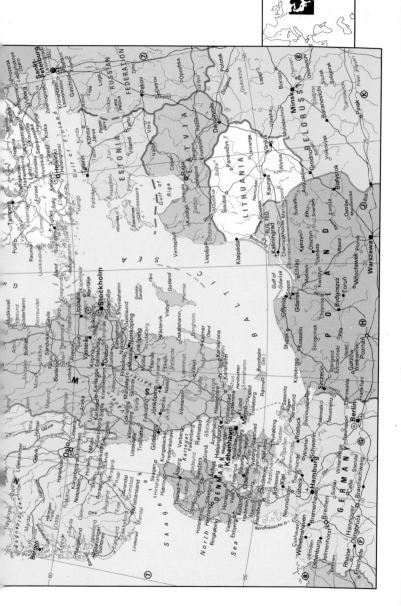

39

BRITISH ISLES

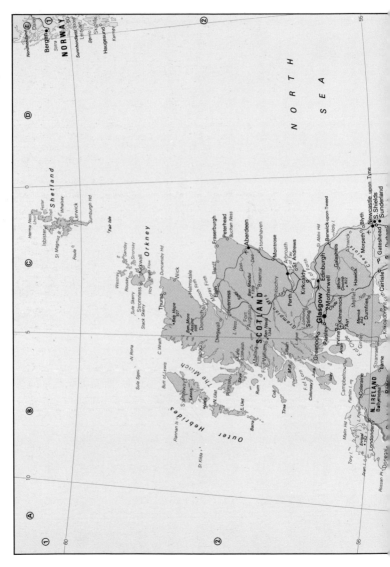

0	50	100	150	200 km
0		50		100 mils

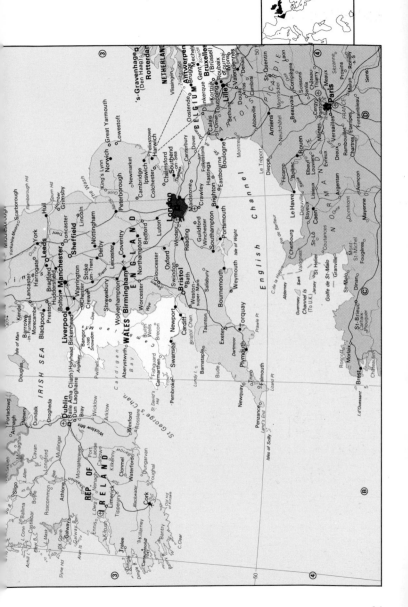

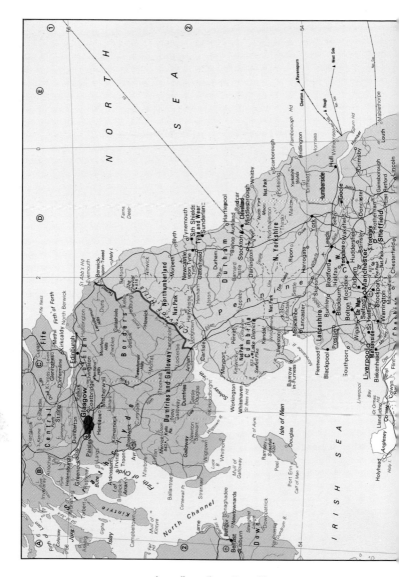

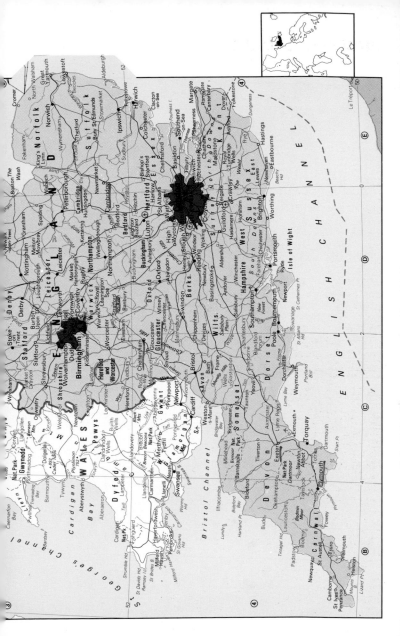

43

Shetland

Unst
Yell
Whalsay
Hillswick
St
Ness
Brae
Bressay
Lerwick
Scalloway
Sumburgh Hd
Fitful Hd
Fair Isle
Foula
Papa Stour
Isbister
The Faither
Herma Ness
Muckle Roe

Orkney

Mainland
Stromness
Hoy
Scapa
Flow
Kirkwall
Westray
Sanday
Stronsay
Eday
Rousay
Birsay
South Ronaldsay
Pentland Firth
Thurso
Dunnet Hd
Duncansby Hd

NORTH SEA

Long Forties
Buchan Deep

Peterhead
Fraserburgh
Buchan Ness
Aberdeen
Girdle Ness
Stonehaven
Montrose
Arbroath
St. Andrews
Dundee
Fife
Firth of Forth
Edinburgh
North Berwick
Dunbar
St Abb's Hd
Eyemouth
Berwick

Grampian
Banff
Keith
Huntly
Dufftown
Ballater
Braemar
Cairngorms
Ben Macdui
Forfar
Perth
Kinross
Dunfermline
Glenrothes
Kirkcaldy
Methil
Cupar

Wick
Lybster
Helmsdale
Brora
Golspie
Dornoch
Tain
Dornoch Firth
Cromarty Firth
Dingwall
Beauly
Inverness
Nairn
Forres
Elgin
Lossiemouth
Moray Firth
Buckie

Thurso
Dunnet Hd
John o'Groats
Duncansby Hd
Hoy
S Ronaldsay
Pentland Firth

C. Wrath
Durness
Eddrachillis Bay
Kinlochbervie
Scourie
Lochinver
Ullapool
Gairloch
Poolewe
Gruinard Bay
Loch Broom
Ben More Assynt
Ben Klibreck
Ben Hope
Tongue
Lairg
Loch Shin
Ben Wyvis
Strathpeffer
Loch Ness
Monadhliath Mts
Kingussie
Aviemore
Grantown-on-Spey
Loch Laggan
Ben Nevis
Fort William
Fort Augustus
Loch Lochy
Invergarry
Kyle of Lochalsh
Isle of Skye
Portree
Raasay
Broadford
Mallaig
Arisaig
Ardnamurchan Pt
Tobermory
Mull
Oban
Loch Awe
Lochgilphead
Inveraray
Loch Fyne
Dunoon
Greenock
Helensburgh
Dumbarton
Glasgow
Paisley
Hamilton
Motherwell
Coatbridge
Airdrie
Falkirk
Stirling
Callander
Loch Lomond
Loch Katrine
Crianlarich
Killin
Loch Tay
Aberfeldy
Pitlochry
Blair Atholl
Loch Rannoch
Loch Ericht
Loch Tummel

Highland
Tayside
Central
Lothian
SCOTLAND
MONTAINS

Western Isles
Lewis
Stornoway
Harris
Tarbert
North Uist
Benbecula
South Uist
Lochboisdale
Barra
Castlebay
Barra Hd
Flannan Is
Butt of Lewis
North Minch
Little Minch
Sea of the Hebrides
Eigg
Rum
Canna
Coll
Tiree
Staffa
Iona
Colonsay
Jura
Islay
Port Askaig
Sound of Jura
Kintyre
Bute
Arran
Firth of Clyde
Morvern
Loch Linnhe
Sound of Mull

Outer Hebrides

0 25 50 75 100 km
0   25   50 mils

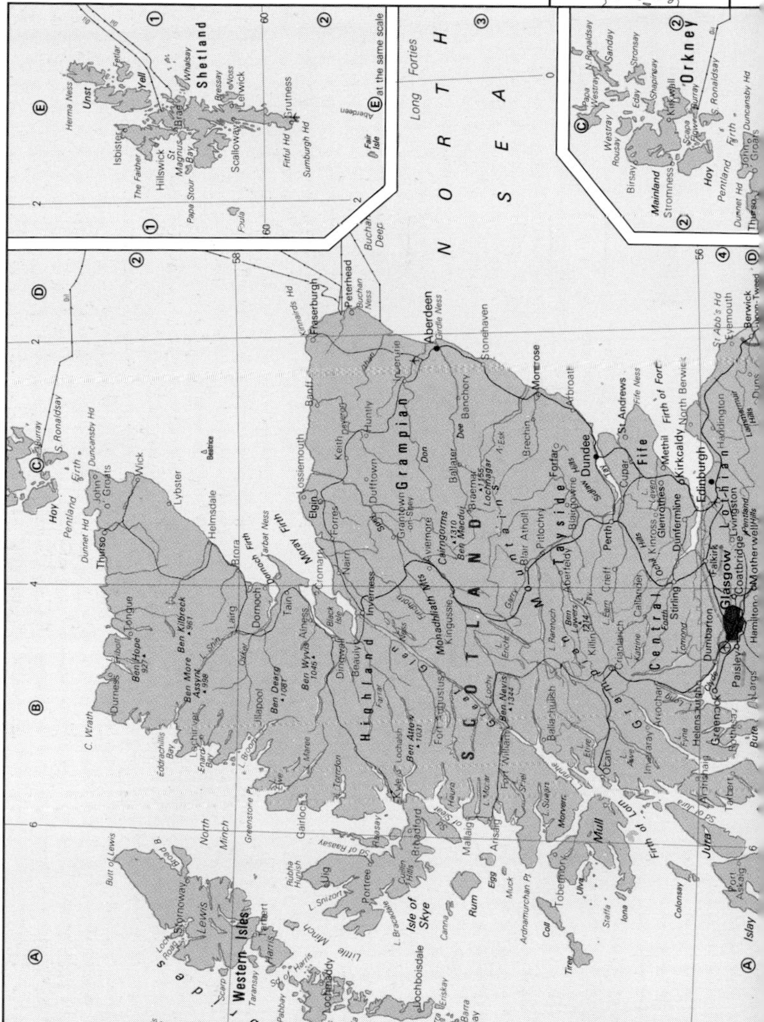

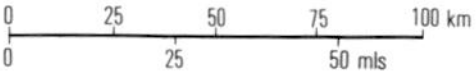

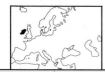

IRELAND

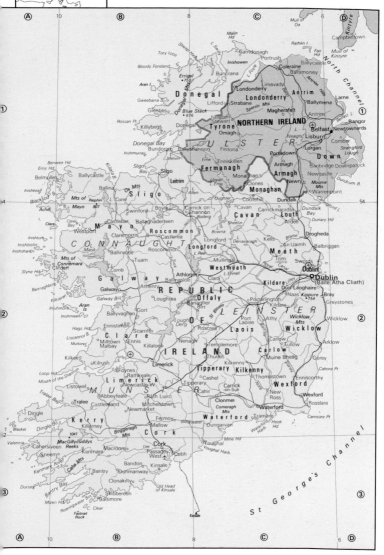

THE LOW COUNTRIES

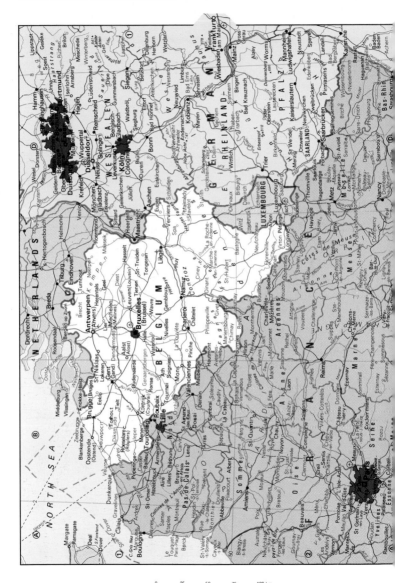

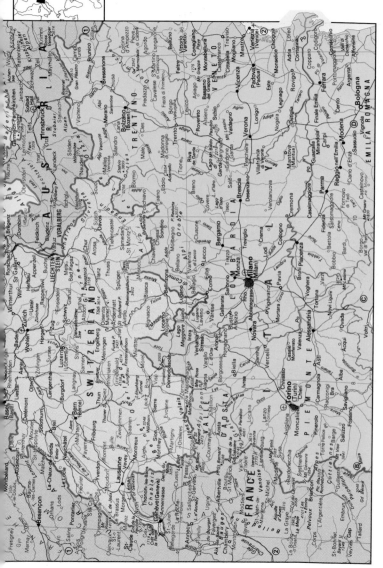

FRANCE

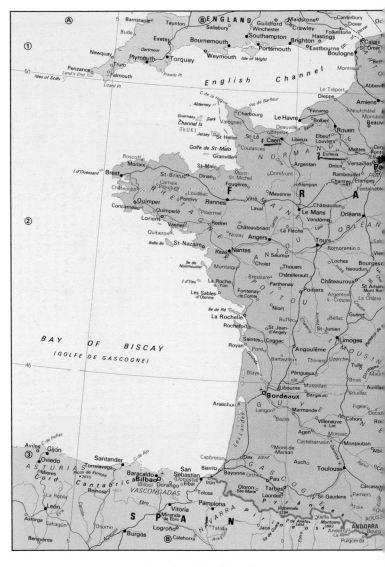

48

| 0 | 50 | 100 | 150 | 200 km |
| 0 | | 50 | | 100 mls |

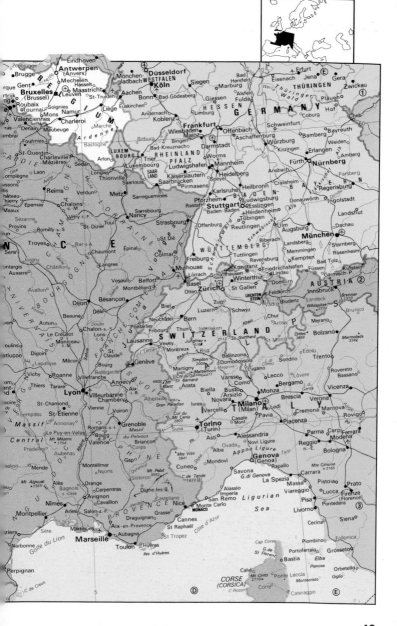

49

SPAIN & PORTUGAL

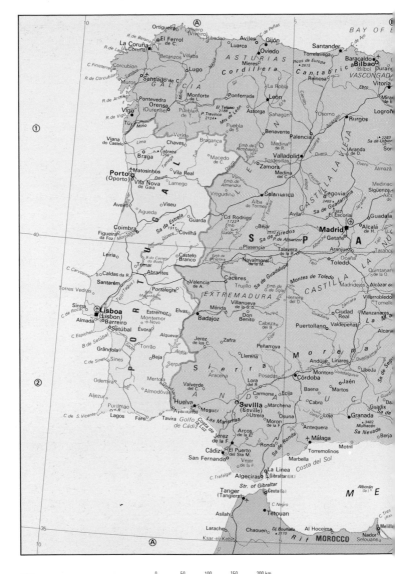

| 0 | 50 | 100 | 150 | 200 km |
| 0 | | 50 | | 100 mls |

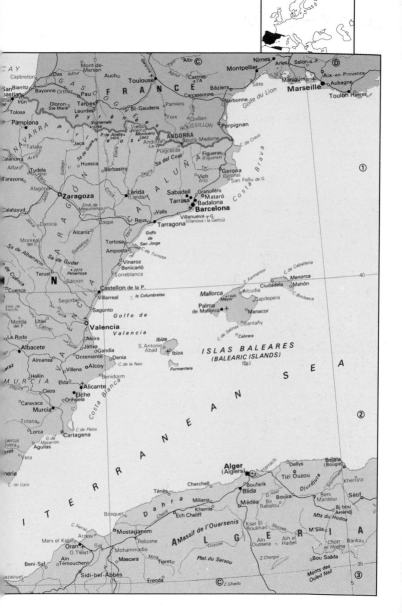

ITALY

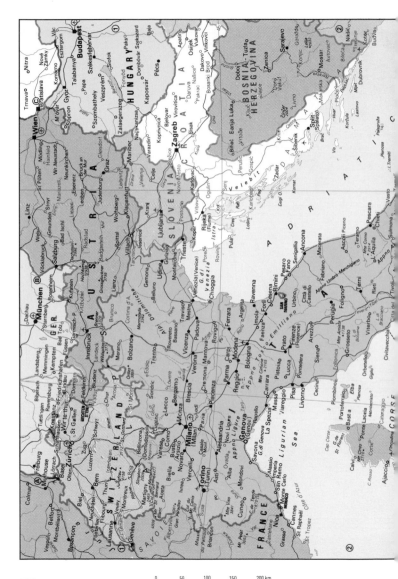

| 0 | 50 | 100 | 150 | 200 km |
| 0 | | 50 | | 100 mls |

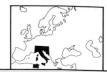
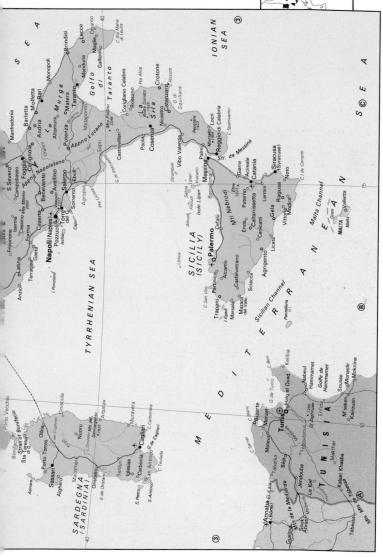

THE BALKANS

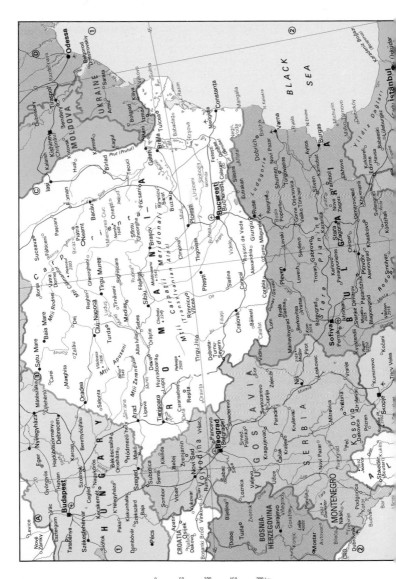

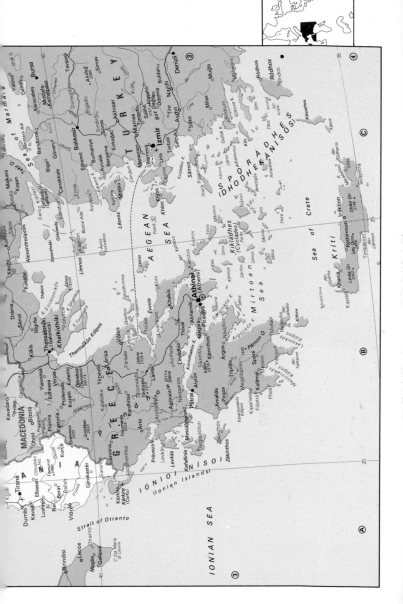

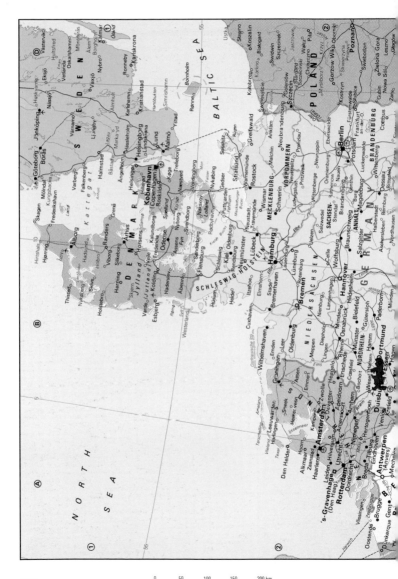

| 0 | 50 | 100 | 150 | 200 km |
| 0 | 50 | | 100 mls | |

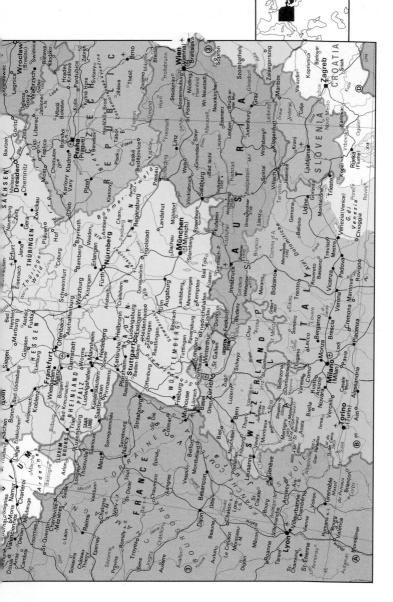

57

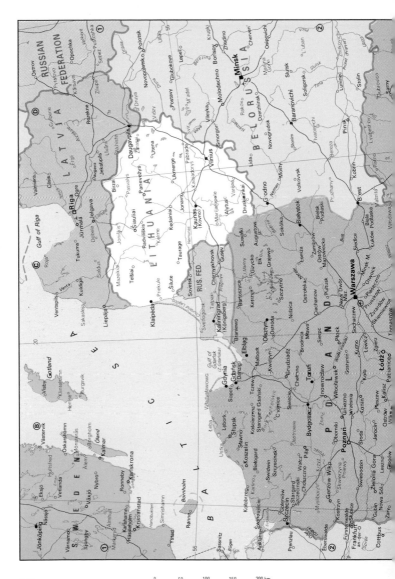

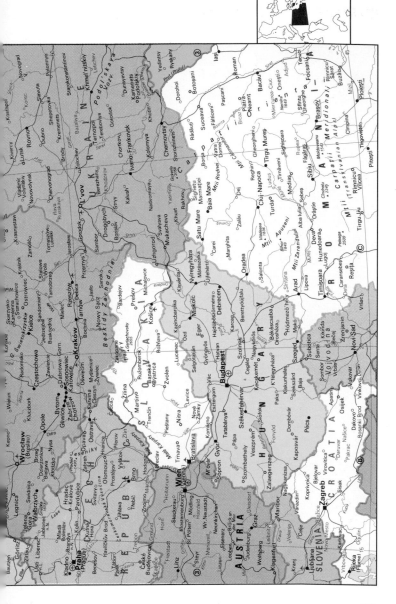

59

EUROPEAN RUSSIA, UKRAINE & BALTIC STATES

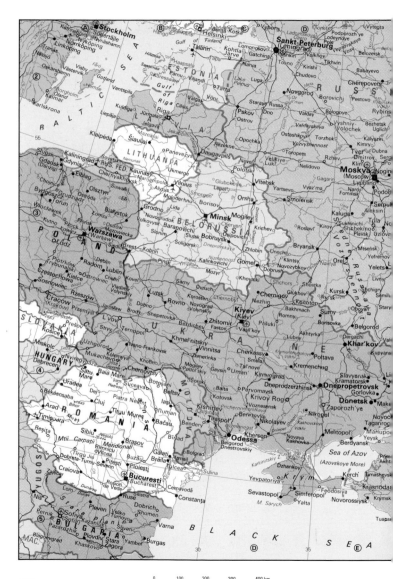

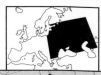

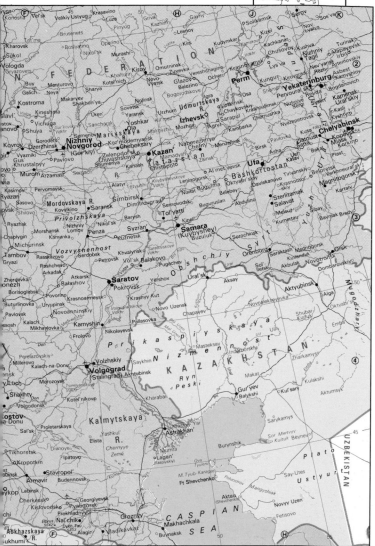

ASIA NORTH

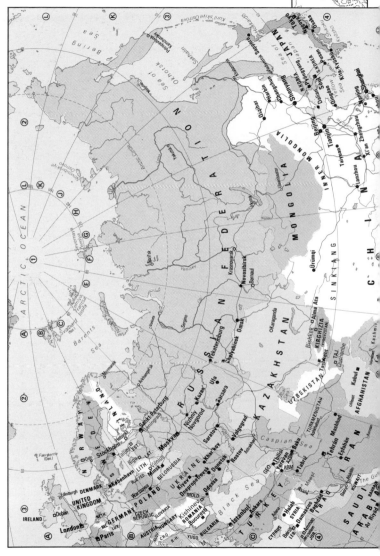

| 0 | 600 | 1200 | 1800 km |
| 0 | 300 | 600 | 900 mils |

SEA OF

JAPAN

Sakhalin

Zaliv Sakhalinskiy

Kuzno-Sakhalinsk

Proliv Nevel'skogo

Tatarskiy Proliv

Komsomol'sk-na-Amure

Amur

Khabarovsk

Sikhote Alin'

Vladivostok

YELLOW SEA

Beijing (Peking)

Tianjin (Tientsin)

Datong

Baotou

Hohhot

Stanovoy Khrebet

Yakutsk

M O N G O L I A

Ulaanbaatar

C H I N A

N E I M O N G O L

Ulan-Ude

Bratsk

Krasnoyarsk

Tomsk

Novokuznetsk

R U S S I A N   F E D E R A T I O N

S i b e r i a

Ürümqi

Turpan

A L T A Y

RUSSIAN FEDERATION WEST

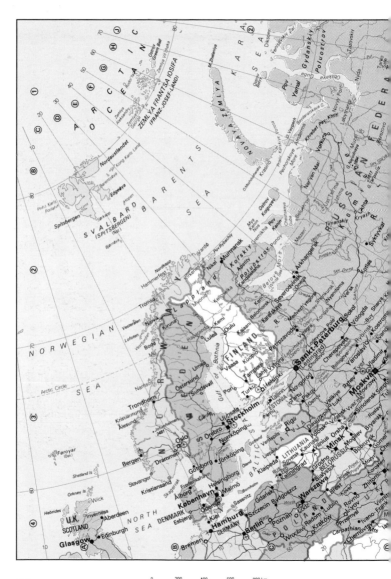

64

| 0 | 200 | 400 | 600 | 800 km |
| 0 | 200 | 400 mls | |

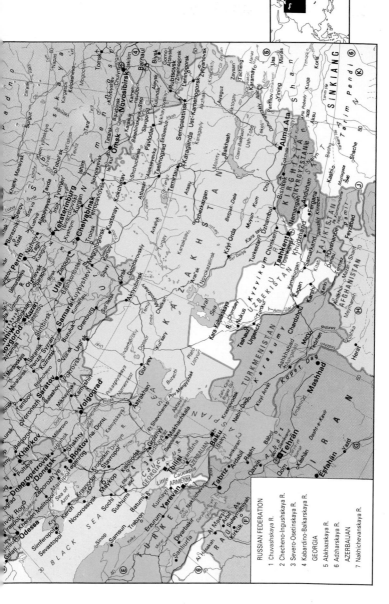

RUSSIAN FEDERATION
1 Chuvashskaya R.
2 Checheno-Ingushskaya R.
3 Severo-Osetinskaya R.
4 Kabardino-Balkarskaya R.

GEORGIA
5 Abkhazskaya R.
6 Adzharskaya R.

AZERBAIJAN
7 Nakhichevanskaya R.

ASIA SOUTH

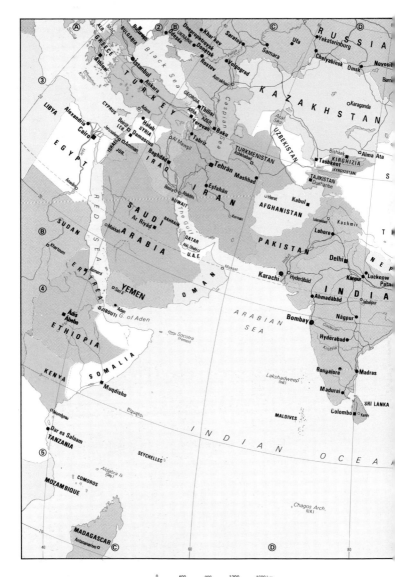

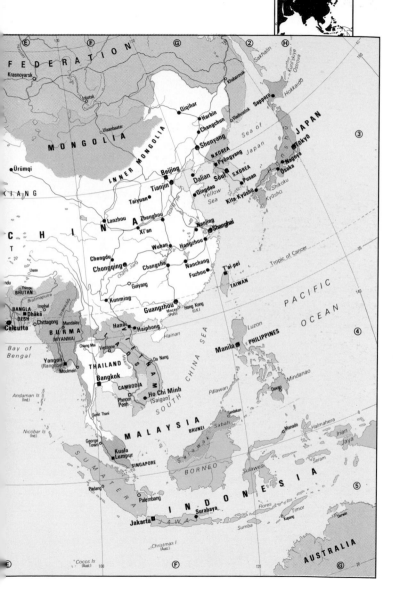

67

ASIA EAST

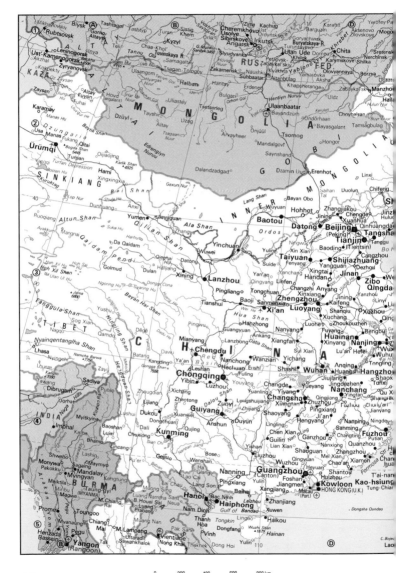

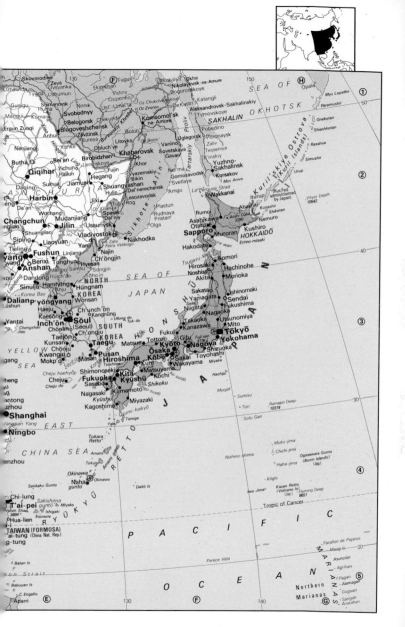

ASIA SOUTHEAST

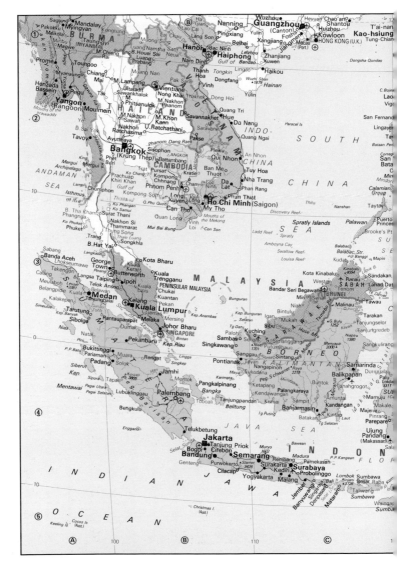

0   200   400   600   800 km
0   200   400 mls

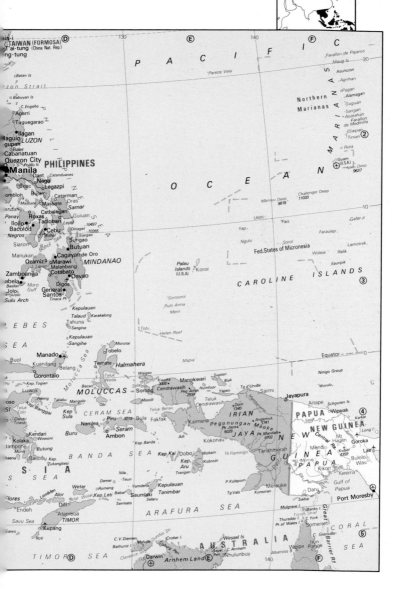

PACIFIC

OCEAN

Farallon de Pajaros
Maug Is.

TAIWAN (FORMOSA) Ⓓ
Ta'i-tung (China Nat. Rep.)
ng-tung

Ⓔ

Ⓕ

Parece Vela

Asuncion
Agrihan
Pagan
Alamagan
Guguan
Sarigan
Anatahan
Farallon
de Medinilla
Saipan
Tinian
Rota

Northern
Marianas

M
A
R
I
A
N
A
S

Batan Is.

zon Strait

C. Engaño
Babuyan Is
Aparri
Tuguegarao
Ilagan
Baguio LUZON
gupan Baler
Cabanatuan
Quezon City
Manila
PHILIPPINES
Boac
Naga
Legazpi
Daet Catanduanes
omblon Bulan
Masbate Catarman
andao Catbalogan
Panay Roxas
Iloilo Tadoban
Bacolod Cebu
Negros Bohol
Siaton
Surigao
Manukan Cagayan de Oro
Ozamiz Marawi
MINDANAO
Zamboanga Malabang
abela Cotabato Davao
Jolo Basilan Digos
Jolo Moro General
Sulu Arch Gulf Santos Tinaca Pt.

Polillo Is.

Samar

Guiuan
Leyte
Dinagat 10265
Siargao

S
E
A

Challenger Deep
11033

Mariana Deep
9818

Guam
(U.S.A.)
9637

Rota

2

Ⓝ

10

Ulithi
Yap
Fais
Faraulep
Gafer Jr.

Ngulu
Sorol
Fed. States of Micronesia

Woleai Ifalik
Lamotrek

Eauripik

3

CAROLINE ISLANDS

Palau
Islands Koror
(U.S.A)

Sonsorol
Pulo Anna
Merir

Tobi
Helen Reef

EBES
SEA

Kepulauan
Talaud Karakelong
Tahuna
Sangihe

Kepulauan
Sangihe Morotai

Tobelo

Mapia

Equator

Ninigo Group

Wuvulu

Manado
Kuandang Belang
Gorontalo
Luyuk Kep. Togian
Talaud
Kep. Banggai
Danau
Towuti
Kolaka Wowoni
tampone Muna
aena Baubau
Butung
Tukangbesi

Ternate Halmahera

Weda

Manokwari
Waigeo
Kwatisore
Numfoor
Bacan
Sorong Cendrawasih
Misool

Supiori
Biak

Tg d'Urville

Sarmi

Aitape Schouten Is.
Jayapura
Wewak

Karkar

4

Moluccas
Peleng Talaibu Mangole
Kep.
Sula
Buru
Namlea
Piru Bula Fakfak
Ambon
Seram

CERAM SEA

Teluk Berau

Kaimana

IRIAN

Dom
1340
Pk. Jaya
5029
Pegunungan Maoke
3741
Pk. Mandala
4702

JAYA

Kokonau

Central Ra.

PAPUA

Sepik

Mt.
Hagen

N
E
W

G
U
I
N
E
A

Goroka
Mendi
Kubor
4359

Lae
Bulolo
Wau

Goroka

BANDA SEA

Kep. Kai
Kep.
Aru
Trangan

Dobo
Wokam
Kobroor

Tk Flamingo

Tanahmerah

PAPUA

Kikori

Kerema

Gulf of
Papua

SIA
SEA

Nila
Damar Teun
Wetar
Romang
Alor Wetar
Endeh Kep. Leti
TIMOR
Atapupu
Dili
Kupang
Roti

Lomblen

Selat Wetar Babar
Sermata

Yamdena
Kepulauan
Tanimbar
Saumlaki Selaru

Kp. Kolepom

Komoran

Tg Vals

Menasah

Saibai
Daru

Port Moresby

ARAFURA SEA

Mulgrave I.
Banks I.
Thursday I. York I.
Pr. of Wales I.

Somerset

Boigu
Torres Strait

C.V. Diemen
Bathurst I.
Melville I.

Dundas Str.
Croker I.

Cape

Gove Arnhem
Pen.

Weipa

5

Great

TIMOR Ⓓ SEA

Savu Sea

Sawu

Clarence Str. Darwin
Arnhem Land Ⓔ
Nhulunbuy

Wessel Is.

AUSTRALIA

140

Albatross Bay

Iron Range

Barrier

CORAL
SEA

Rf.

C. Grenville Ⓕ

120

130

140

Ⓕ

71

CHINA CENTRAL

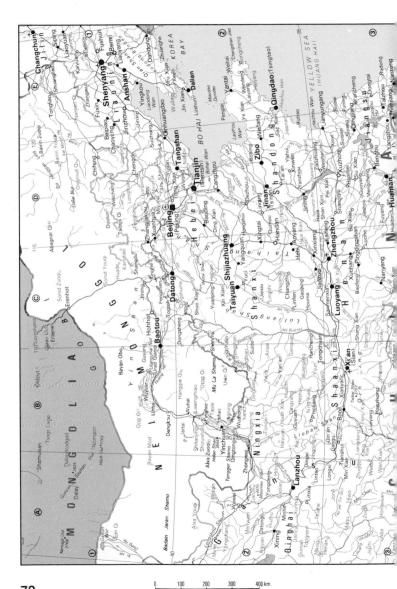

0   100   200   300   400 km
0   100   200 mls

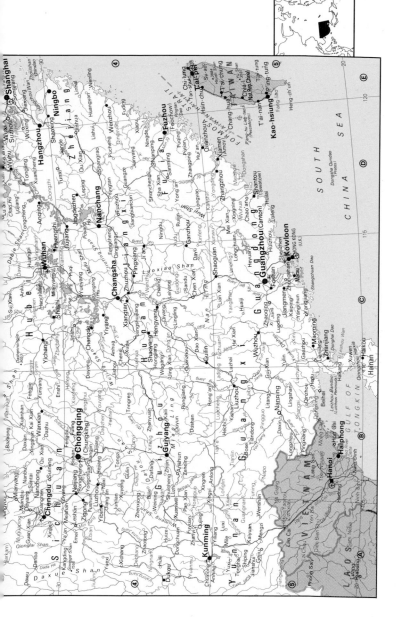

JAPAN & KOREA

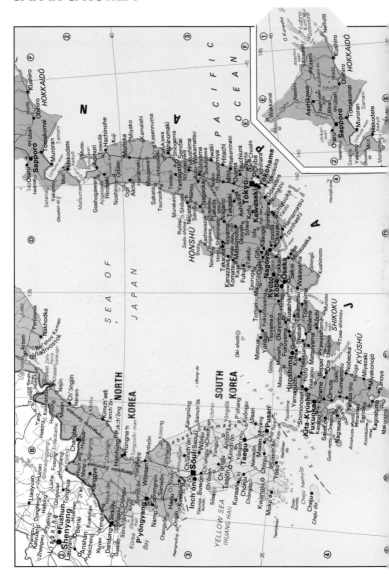

0   100 km
0   50 mls

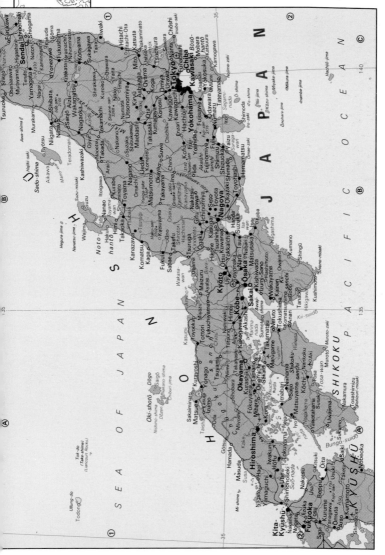

BURMA, THAILAND, INDO-CHINA, MALAYSIA & SINGAPORE

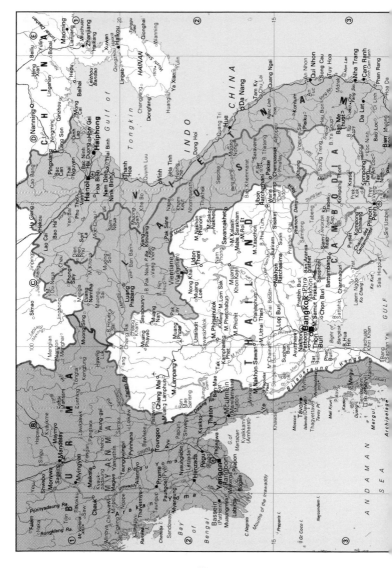

0 100 200 300 400 km
0 100 200 mls

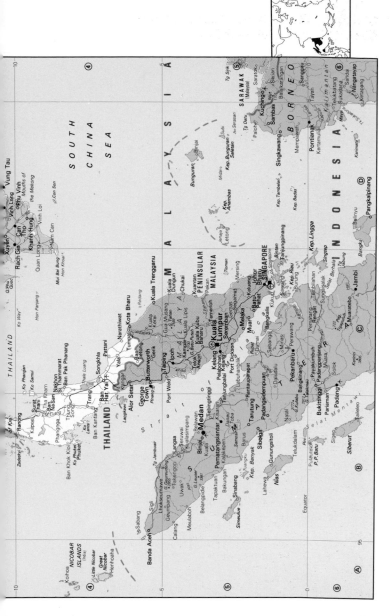

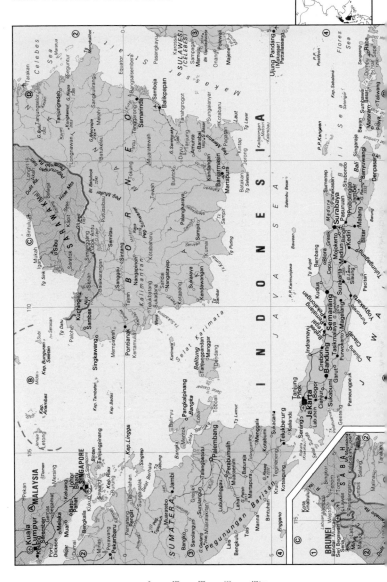

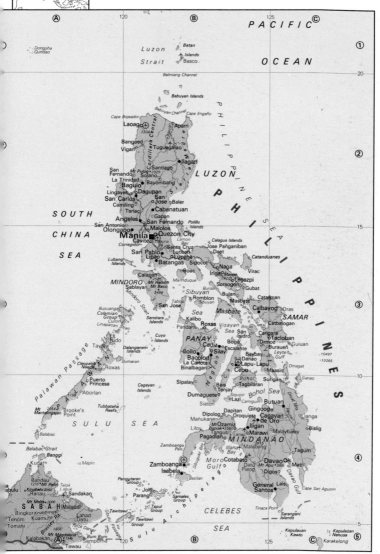

MIDDLE EAST

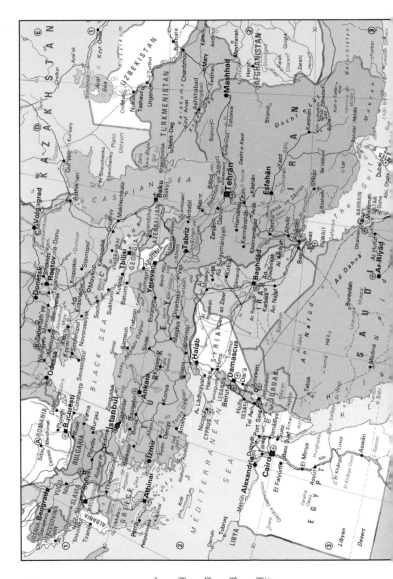

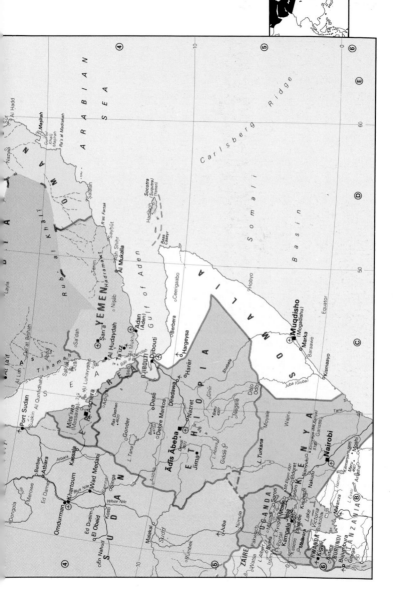

INDIA & WEST CHINA

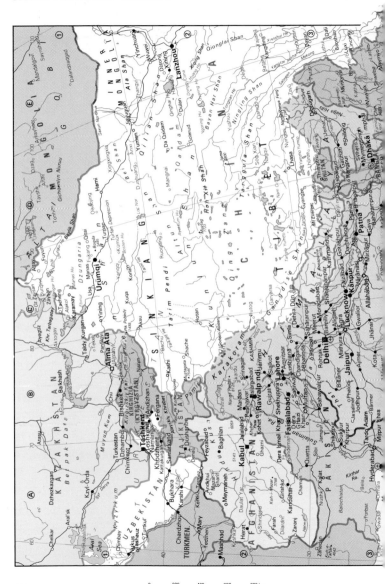

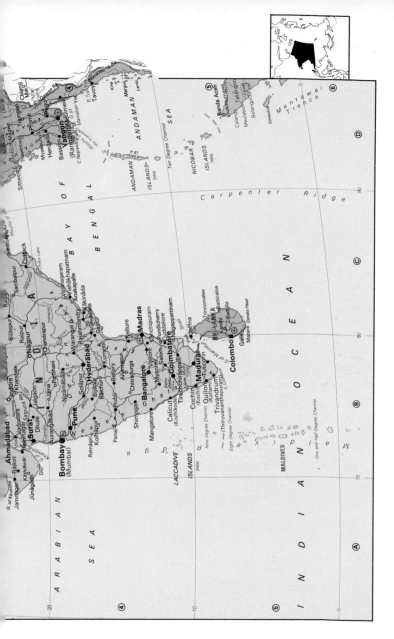

INDIA NORTHWEST & PAKISTAN

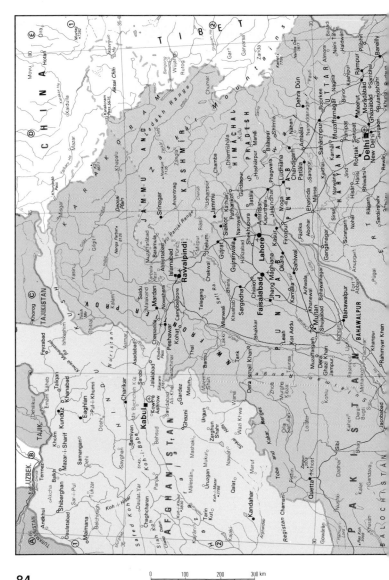

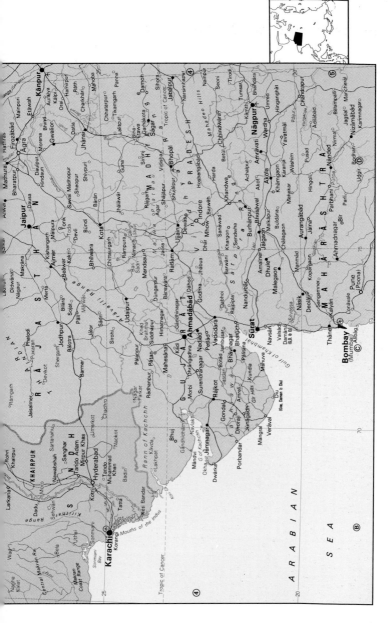

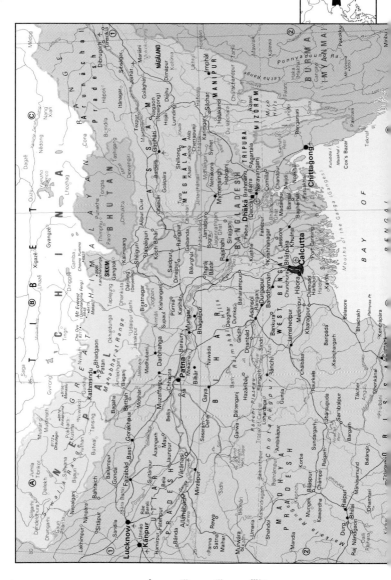

INDIA SOUTH & SRI LANKA

Bombay (A)
Mumbai
Lonavale
Pune MAHARASHTRA
Jilgaon
ibad
rivardhan
Mahad
Wai
Chiplun
Ratnagiri
Satara
Phaltan
Karad
Vite
Sangli
Mirai
Ichalkaranji
Kolhapur
Jamkhandi
Malvan
Vengurla
Belgaum
Panaji
Goa
Daman
Diu
Madgaon
Karwar
Sirsi
Kumta
Dandeli
Bhatkal
Coondapoor
Udupi
Mangalore
Karkal
Kasaragod
Cannanore
Tellicherry Mahe
Badagara
Calicut
(Kozhikode)
Beypore
Ponnani
Androth
Trichur
(Thrissur)
Cochin
(Kochi)
Ernakulam
Kottayam
Alleppey
Kayankulam
Quilon
(Kollam)
Trivandrum
(Thiruvananthapuram)
Kanniyakumari C Comorin
Nagercoil

Ahmadnajar
Parbhani
Purna
Nanded
Bir
Parli
Nirmal
Bodhan
Nizamabad
Jagtial
Mancheral
Belampalli
Sironcha
Jagdalpur
Kotapad
C
Bijapur
Dantewara
Sukma
Daund
Udgir
Barsi
Latur
Solapur
Bidar
Homnabad
Akalkot
Gulbarga
Shahabad
Tandur
Bijapur
Yadgir
Shorapur
Raichur
Bagalkot
Guledagudda
Gajendragarh
Gadag
Koppal
Bellary
Hospet
Guntakal
Gooty
Haveri
Swamihalli
Tadpatri
Ranibennur
Kotturu
Rayadurg
Hirihar
Davangere
Kalyandurg
Dhamavaram
Chitradurga
Kadiri
Bhadravati
Tarikere
Sira
Tumkur
Shimoga
Kadur
Arsikere
Chik Ballapur
Chikmagalur
Dod Ballapur
Hassan
Hole Narsipur
Madikeri
Bangalore
Nanjangud
Mandya
Mysore
Chamrajnagar
Dharmapuri
Krishnagiri
Tiruppattur
Kolar
Gold Fields
Arakkonam
Chittoor
Tirupati
Sri Kalahasti
Vellore
Kanchipuram
Ambur
Javadi
Hills
Tiruvannamalai
Tindivanam
Pondicherry
Salem
Villupuram
Cuddalore
Mettur
Vriddhachalam
Chidambaram
Erode
Coimbatore
Ootacamund
Coonoor
Nilgiri Hills
Tiruppur
Shoranur
Palghat
(Palakkat)
Pollachi
Tiruchchirappalli
Palani
Dindigul
Bodinayakkanur
Kambam
Madurai
Virudunagar
Aruppukkottai
Rajapalaiyam
Paramakkudi
Tenkasi
Tirunelveli
Palayankottai
Tiruchendur
Tuticorin
Gulf of
Mannar

Ahmadnajar
AP

Karimnagar
Warangal
Yellandu
Kottagudem
Khammam
Bhadrachalam
Rajahmundry
Yanam
Kakinada
I
Eluru
Bhimavaram
Vijayawada
Guntur
Tenali
Machilipatnam
Suriapet
Narasaraopet
Chilakalurupet
Chirala
Ongole

ANDHRA
PRADESH

Siddipet
Nalgonda
Macherla
Wanparti
Mahbubnagar
Narayanpet

Hyderabad

Sangareddi
Bhongir
Mahesra

Nandyal
Adoni
Dhone
Giddalur
Kurnool
Kani Giri
Kondukur
Kavali
Nellore
Gudur
Venkatagiri
Proddutur
Cuddapah
Anantapur
Hindupur
Madras
Coromandel Coast

Pulicat L.

KARNATAKA

K

TAMIL NADU

Thanjavur
Kumbakonam
Mannargudi
Karaikal
Nagappattinam
Pt Calimere
Pudukkottai
Kodikkarai

Palk Strait
Pt Pedro
Jaffna
Ramanathapuram
Ramesvaram
Pamban
Bridge
Talaimannar
Mannar
Mullaittivu
Vavuniya
Trincomalee

SRI LANKA
CEYLON
Puttalam
Anuradhapura
Dambulla
Matale
Batticaloa
Chilaw
Kurunegala
Kandy
Nuwara Eliya
Badulla
Negombo
Kegalla
Ratnapura
Colombo
Adam's Pk
7343
Dehiwala-Mt Lavinia
Moratuwa
Opanake
Ambalangoda
Galle
Matara
Dondra Hd
Hambantota

Havankulam
Mannar

MALDIVES

Nine Degree Channel

Minicoy

Eight Degree Channel

Kalpeni

Vembanad
Lake

3

A
75
B
C

0	100	200	300 km
0	50	100	150 mls

AFRICA

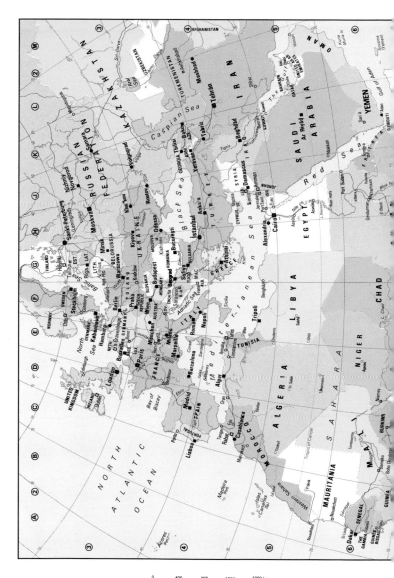

0	400	800	1200	1600 km
0		400		800 mls

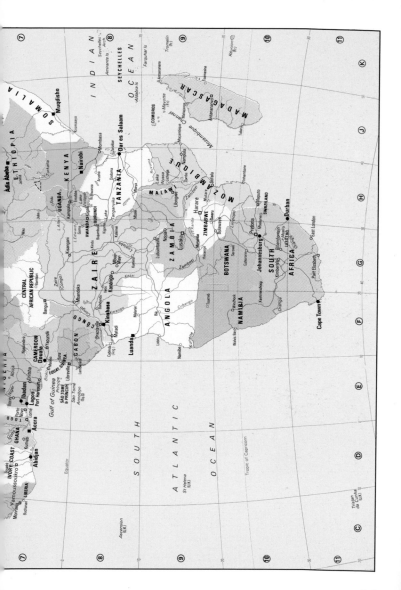

89

IRAN & THE GULF

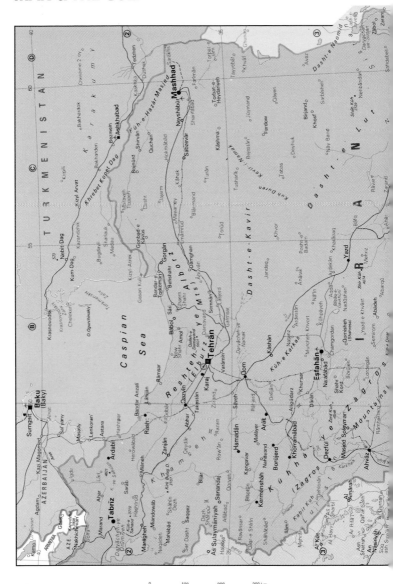

| | 0 | 100 | 200 | 300 km |
| 0 | 50 | 100 | 150 mls | |

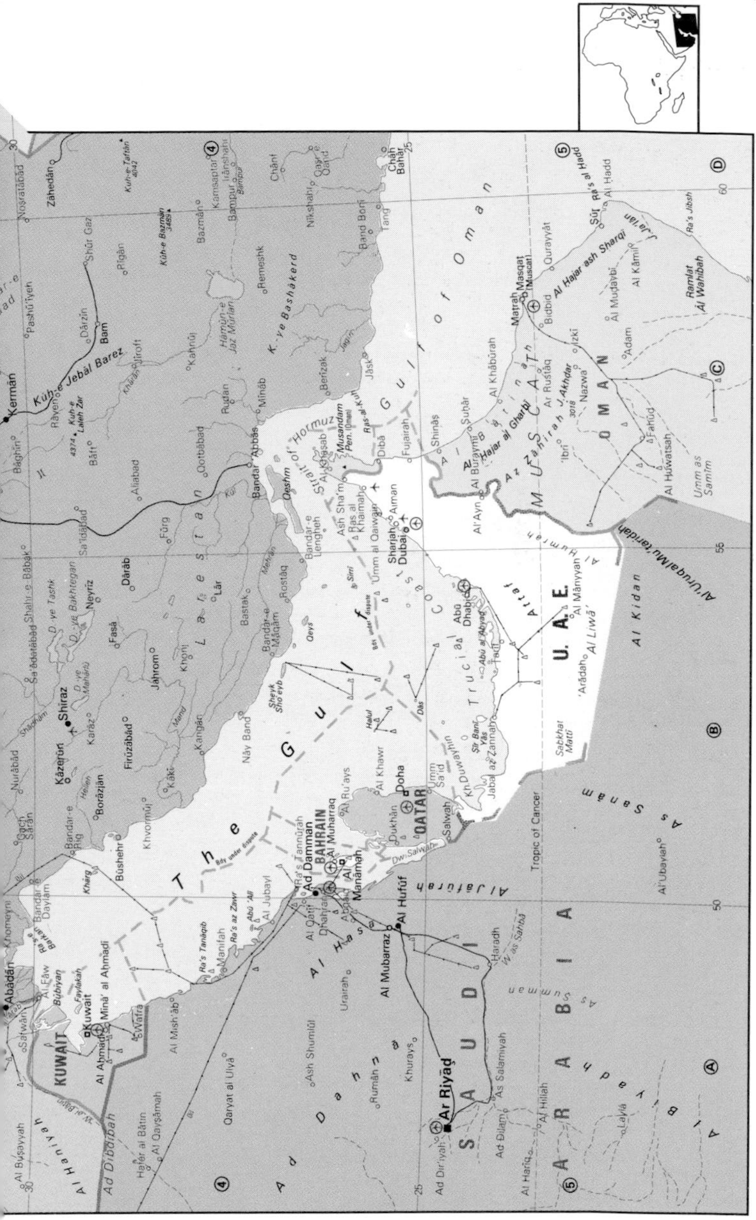

TURKEY, SYRIA & IRAQ

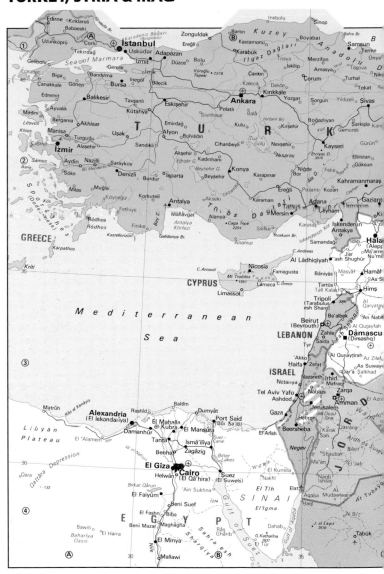

| 0 | 100 | 200 | 300 km |
| 0 | 50 | 100 | 150 mls |

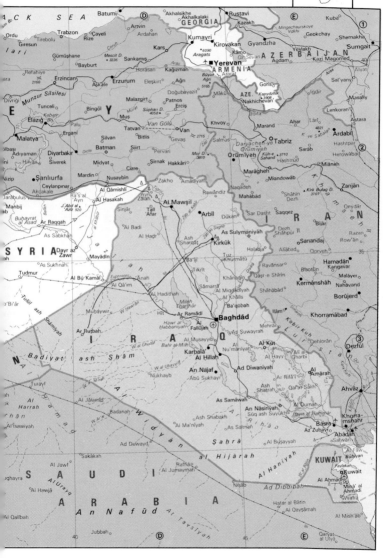

ISRAEL & LEBANON

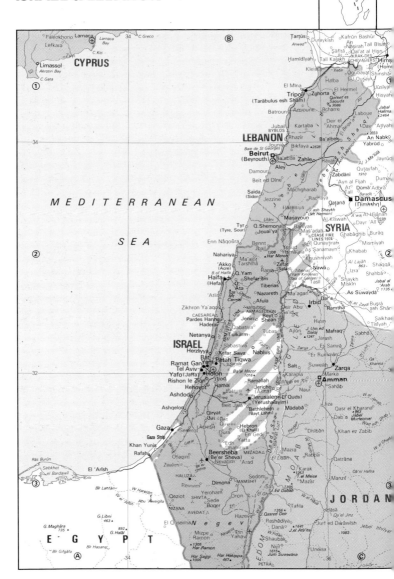

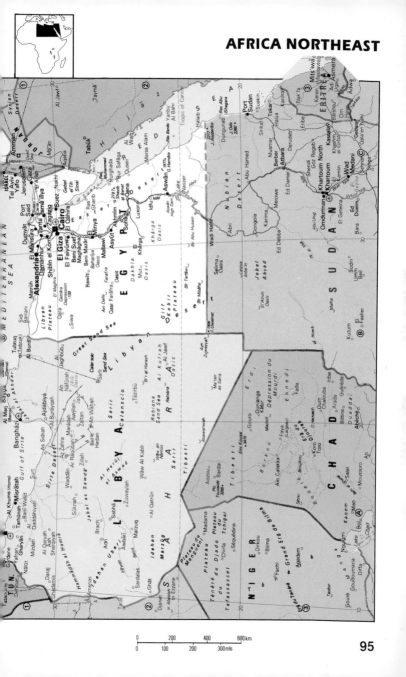

AFRICA WEST

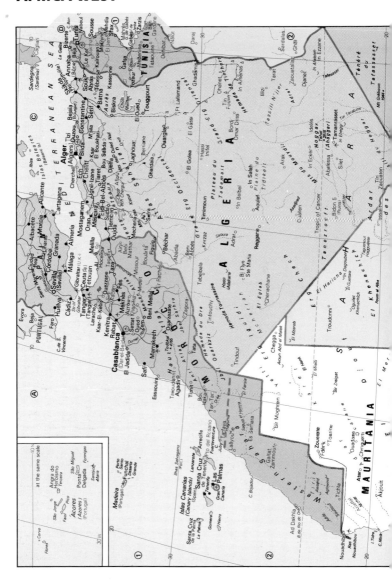

0   200   400   600 km
0   100   200   300 mils

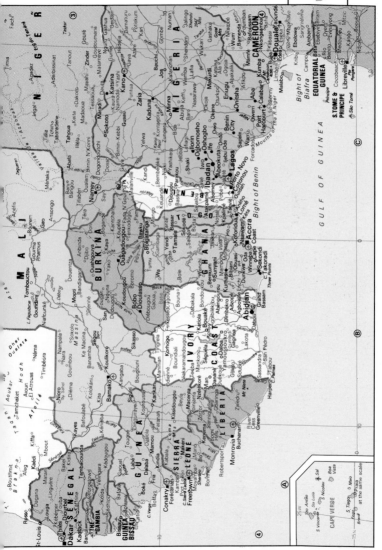

AFRICA CENTRAL

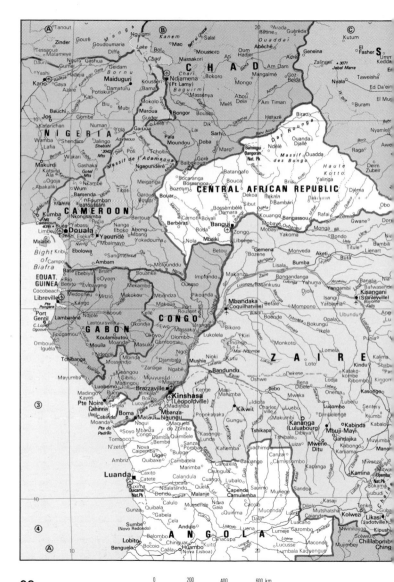

ERITREA

Keren Mits'iwa Massawa
Kassala Barentu Asmera
Khashm Ugai
al Girba
Wad Gedaref Adwa Mersa Fatma
Medani Qala'en Nahl Mek'ele Ed Ta'izz
El Geteina El Senafe
Gezira Ras Dashan Aseb Al Shaykh
Ed Gallabat 4620 Mukha 'Uthman
Dueim El Hawata Dabat Sek'ot'a Adan (Aden)
Senriar Gonder 3657
El Obeid Kosti Simia Obock Gulf of Aden
Bara El Jebelein Dangila Deseé DJIBOUTI
Er Rahad Omm Chob Mts L'Abbé Djibouti
Dilling Ruwaba Renk Burye Zeila Ras Khanzira Karin
Nube Rashad Roseires Debre Bryo Berbera
Mts Belfodiyo Markos Kaboba Guban Burao Ceerigaabo
Kaka Paloich Asosa Nej̄o Fiche Dire Dawa Hargeysa Caynabo 10
Kodok Nek'emte Birhan Harer Laascaanood
Abyei Malakal Abwong Nazir Dendi Awash
Bentiu Fangak Goba Ambo Degeh Bur Warder Aware Ogaden
Meshra Er Reu Ayod Sodo ADIS Asela Golocha Geladi Danan
Sudd Duk Akobo Gore ABEBA Ginir Imi
Faiwil Jima Shashemene Hara Gaalkacyo
Shambe Tor Mizan Yirga Mendebo Fanq
Rumbek Pibor Teferi Alem Mts Danan
Tali Post Maji Abaya 4200 Negeli El Goran Sina Dhaqa
Amadi Kenamuke Bako Arba Minch Gidole Dolo Ceelbuur
Maridi Mongalla Swamp Melka Odo Beled
Juba Guba Mega Moyale Mandera Weyne Xuddur Dirri Meregh
Yambio Torit Lotikipi Luuq Baydhabo Wanle Jowhar
Kinyeti Lokitaung Lake Buur Weyne Buulo Barde
Dungu Laȳo 3187 Turkana Hakaba Uarsciek
Faradje Movo Lodwar Buna Baardheere Afgooye Muqdisho
Watsa Nimule Kitgum Mt Kulal Baraawe (Mugadishu)
Mungbere Aru Gulu 2293 Moroto Marsabit Wajir Jilib Markâ
Arua Soroti Mt Nyiru Kangetet Afmadu Giamame Equator
Dungu Pakwach 2805 Kotido Baardheere
Butia Masindi Mt Elgon Maralal
Mambasa Hoima 4321 Kitale Mado Kismaayo
Kabarole Mubende Bombo Mbale KENYA Gashi
Beni Ruwenzori Kampala Tororo Eldoret Isiolo SOMALIA
Lubero Kasese Jinja Kakamega Nanyuki Garissa Caluula
Edward Entebbe Kisumu Nakuru Nyeri Kirinyaga Raas Qandala Boosaaso
Mt Masaka Kericho Mt Kenya Caseyr Hordiyo
Karisimbe Bukoba Narok Naivasha 5199 Laasqoray Laz
Goma Kigali Ukerewe Embu Ceerigaabo Daua
RWANDA Musoma Ushashi Nairobi Cercar Mts Ras
Cyangugu Bihamulo Mwanza Machakos Qardho Xaafuun
Butare Muyinga Geita Shinyanga Makindu Tsavo Bandarbeyla
Bukavu Nyakabindi Loolmalasin Meru Tsavo Malindi 10
Uvira Kahama Nzega 3648 4565 Moshi Laascaanood
BURUNDI Kigoma Nzega Singida Babati Masai Same Kilifi Evl
Kaliua Kondoa Mbulu Eyasi Steppe Luhoto Mombasa Jiriban Damot
Tabora Sekenke kwale Dabaro
TANZANIA Manyoni Dodoma Tanga Korogwe Gaalkacyo
Uvinza Mpanda Kitunda Mpwapwa Handeni Pemba I.
Kigoma Rungwa Kilosa Morogoro Pangani Hobyo
Kapona Rukwa Mikumi Bagamoyo 50
Mpulungu Nat Pk Sao Kilombero Zanzibar
Sumbawanga Chunya Hill Iringa Dar es Salaam
Kasama Mbeya Rungwe Njombe Mahenge Kisiju Mafia SEYCHELLES
Mansa 2959 Ifakara Kilwa Kivinje Assumption
Isoka Njombe Mohoro Kilwa Kisiwani Aldabra Is
Chinsali Karonga Liwale Lindi
Luwingu Chilumba Masasi Mtwara C. Delgado
Mpika Songea Newala Palma
Mbamba Tunduru Mueda Mocimboa Moroni Grande
Bay Lupilichi Macomia da Praia Comore COMOROS Is Glorieuses
Lundazi Mecula Macaloge Quissanga Mutsamudu Anjouan
Kasungu Metangula Mahéli

at the same scale

AFRICA SOUTH

at the same scale

MAURITIUS

Port Louis
Round I.

St Denis
Réunion
(Fr.)

	0	200	400	600 km
	0	100	200	300 mls

100

SEYCHELLES

Aldabra Is
Assumption
Cosmoledo Is
Providence
Farquhar Is

Is Glorieuses

COMOROS
Moroni Grande Comore
Mutsamudu Anjouan
Mahéli
Mayotte (Fr.) Dzaoudzi

Tj. Babaomby
St Sébastien
Antseranana
Massif
Tsaratanana
Ambilobe Nosy Mitsio Ambre
Nosy Bé
Ambanja
Vohimarina

Is Glorieuses

Analalava
Analalava Antsohihy Befandriana Maroantsetra
B. de Mahajanga
Maromandia
B. de Bombetoka
Mahajanga (Majunga) Marovoay Mampikony Mandritsara C. Masoala
Ambato Boeny Antongila
Tanjona Besalampy Ivongo Soamiandrano Nosy Boraha
Vilanandro Saratanana Ambodifototra
Fenoarivo Atsinana
Tsiroanomandidy Ankazobe Anjozorobe Toamasina (Tamatave)
Nosy Barren Moramanga Vohibinany
Ambatondrazaka
Morafenobe Tsiroanomandidy Antananarivo
Ambatolampy Antsirabe Mahanoro
Miandrivazo Betafo
Manabo Morondava Malaimbandy Atofinandrahana Nosy Varika
Ambohimahasoa Ifanadiana
Manja Fianarantsoa Mananjary
Mangoky Ihosy Ambalavao Manakara
Ankaboao Ivohibe Farafangana
Sakaraha Betroka Vangaindrano
Toliara Midongy
Bekily Isoanala Atsimo
Betioky
Ampenihy Amboasary Tôlañaro
Beloha Tsihombe Ambovombe
Vohimena

MADAGASCAR
(MALAGASY REP.)

Mozambique Channel

Nosy
Juan
de Nova
(Fr.)

Bassas
da India
(Fr.)

Europa
(Fr.)

Canal de Mozambique

Massif de l'Isalo

B de St Augustin

Tropic of Capricorn

Tanjona
Vohimena

ATLANTIC OCEAN

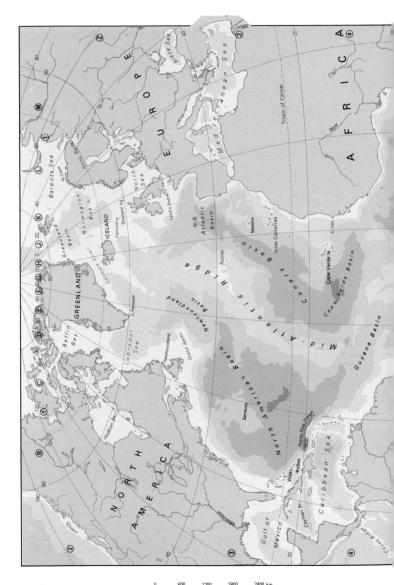

0   600   1200   1800   2400 km
0   600   1200 mls

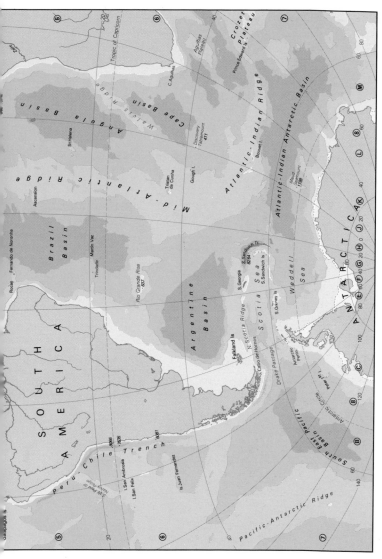

SOUTH AMERICA

ANTARCTICA

Brazil Basin

Argentine Basin

Angola Basin

Cape Basin

Mid-Atlantic Ridge

Walvis Ridge

Atlantic-Indian Ridge

Atlantic-Indian Antarctic Basin

Crozet Plateau

Weddell Sea

Scotia Sea

Peru-Chile Trench

Pacific-Antarctic Ridge

South East Pacific Basin

Tropic of Capricorn

Antarctic Circle

N.Scotia Ridge

S.Scotia Ridge

Drake Passage

Antarctic Pen.

Falkland Is.

S.Georgia

S.Orkney Is.

S.Sandwich Is.

S.Sandwich Tr.
8264

Cabo de Hornos

Rio Grande Rise
637

Trindade

Martin Vaz

Tristan da Cunha

Gough I.

St.Helena

Ascension

Fernando de Noronha

Rocas

C.Agulhas

Agulhas Plateau

Prince Edward Is.

Bouvet I.

Discovery
Tablemount
411

Maud
Seamount
1759

I.San Ambrosio

I.San Felix

Is.Juan Fernández

Peter I Øy

6066
7635
7881

A K H G F E D C B

AUSTRALASIA

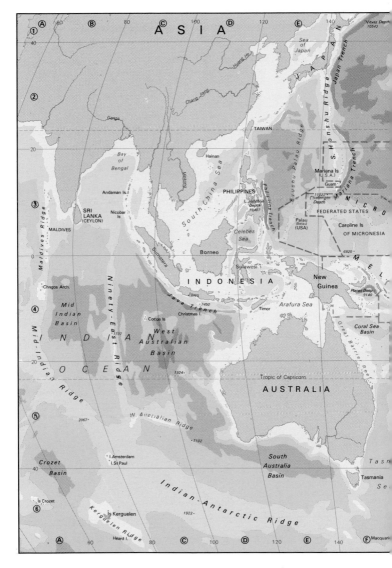

ASIA

Vityaz Depth 10542

Sea of Japan

JAPAN

Japan Trench

S. Honshu Ridge

Chang Jiang

TAIWAN

Ganga

Kyushu-Palau Ridge

Bay of Bengal

Hainan

Mariana Is (U.S.A.)

Mariana Trench

Andaman Is.

MEKONG

PHILIPPINES

Guam

MICRO

SRI LANKA (CEYLON)

Nicobar Is

South China Sea

Mindanao Depth 10497

Challenger Depth

FEDERATED STATES

Maldives Ridge

MALDIVES

Celebes Sea

Palau (Belau) (USA)

Caroline Is

OF MICRONESIA

Chagos Arch.

Borneo

Sulawesi

Sumatera

INDONESIA

New Guinea

6920

MELA

Ninety-East Ridge

Jawa

Java Trench

7450

Timor

Arafura Sea

Planet Deep 9140

Mid Indian Basin

Cocos Is

Christmas I.

West Australian Basin

Coral Sea Basin

1737

Great Barrier Reef

INDIAN

OCEAN

1924

Mid-Indian Ridge

W. Australian Ridge

Tropic of Capricorn

AUSTRALIA

2067

3102

Crozet Basin

I.Amsterdam I.St Paul

South Australia Basin

Tasm

Is Crozet

Tasmania

Se

Indian-Antarctic Ridge

Kerguelen Ridge

Is Kerguelen

1922

Heard I.

Macquari

104

0   600   1200   1800   2400 km
0   600   1200 mls

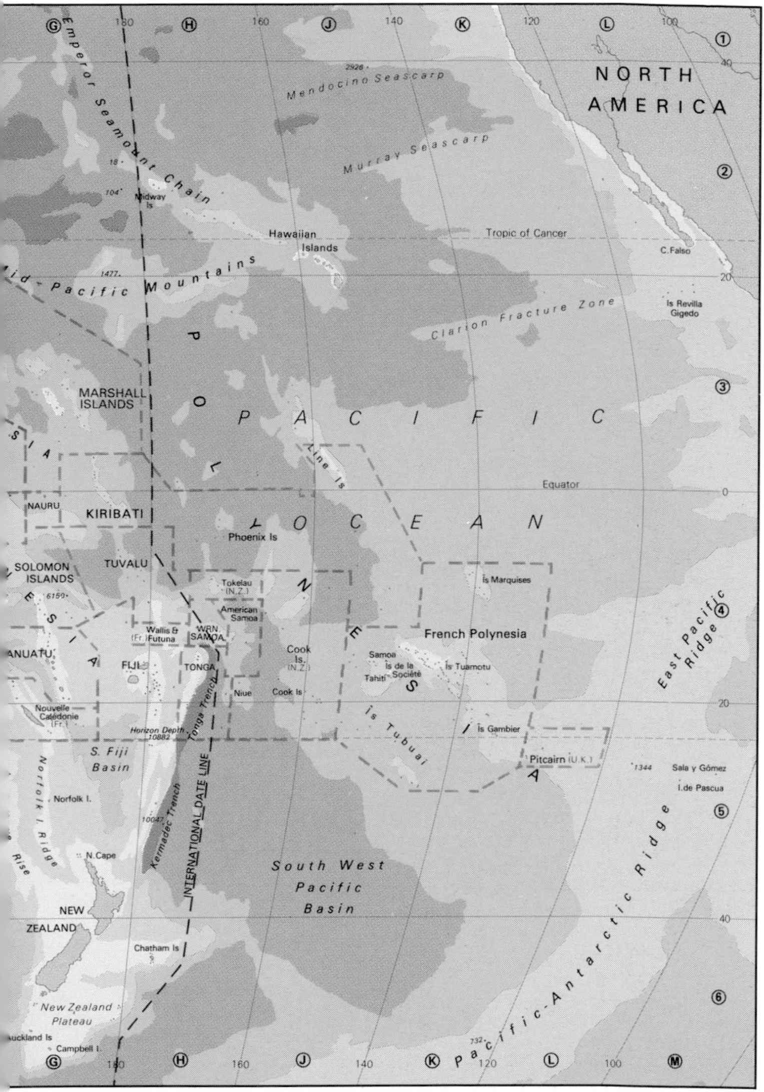
NORTH
AMERICA
Emperor Seamount Chain
Mendocino Seascarp
Murray Seascarp
Midway Is
Hawaiian Islands
Tropic of Cancer
C.Falso
Mid-Pacific Mountains
Clarion Fracture Zone
Is Revilla Gigedo
MARSHALL ISLANDS
PACIFIC
OCEAN
POLYNESIA
Line Is
Equator
NAURU
KIRIBATI
Phoenix Is
SOLOMON ISLANDS
TUVALU
Tokelau (N.Z.)
American Samoa
Is Marquises
Wallis & Futuna (Fr.)
WRN. SAMOA
French Polynesia
VANUATU
FIJI
TONGA
Cook Is. (N.Z.)
Samoa
Is de la Société
Tahiti
Is Tuamotu
East Pacific Ridge
Niue
Cook Is
Nouvelle Calédonie (Fr.)
Is Tubuai
Is Gambier
Horizon Depth 10882
Tonga Trench
S. Fiji Basin
Pitcairn (U.K.)
Sala y Gómez
I.de Pascua
Norfolk I.
Norfolk I. Ridge
Kermadec Trench
INTERNATIONAL DATE LINE
N.Cape
South West Pacific Basin
Pacific-Antarctic Ridge
NEW ZEALAND
Chatham Is
New Zealand Plateau
Auckland Is
Campbell I.

AUSTRALIA

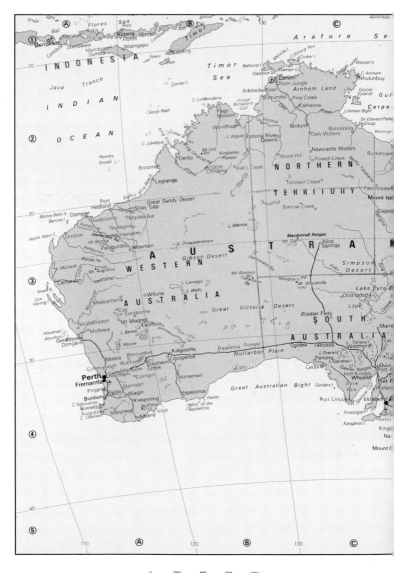

0	200	400	600	800 km
0		200	400 mls	

Gulf of Papua

Daru

PAPUA

Popondetta

Port Moresby

Kokoda

D'Entrecasteaux

Woodlark

NEW GUINEA

Kupiano

Abau

Aus

Samarai

Misima

Louisiade

Arch.

Tagula

Rossel

Kiriwina

Trobriand

Owen Stanley Ra.

Sabai

Torres Strait

C. York

of Wales I.

Somerset

Weipa

Cape

C. Grenville

York

Princess Charlotte B.

Coen

Peninsula

Mitchell River

Laura

Cooktown

Normanton

Mt Bartle Frere

1612

Cairns

Ravenshoe

Innisfail

Croydon

Forsyth

Ingham

Palms

Townsville

Ayr

Charters Towers

Cloncurry

Richmond

Bowen

Hughenden

Proserpine

Collinsville

QUEENSLAND

Selwyn

Winton

Clermont

Sarina

Northumberland

Is

Mackay

Longreach

Barcaldine

Mount Morgan

Emerald

Rockhampton

Blackall

Gladstone

Windorah

Theodore

Charleville

Tarcoom

Bundaberg

Fraser or

Gt. Sandy I.

Quilpie

Miles

Maryborough

St George

Toowoomba

Dalby

Gympie

Cunnamulla

Warwick

Ipswich

Brisbane

Milparinka

Goondiwindi

Lismore

Bourke

Moree

Stanthorpe

Glen

Casino

Innes

Grafton

Wilcannia

Narrabri

Broken Hill

Cobar

Tamworth

Port Macquarie

Menindee

Nyngan

Ivanhoe

Taree

Dubbo

Barrington

1555

NEW SOUTH

Griffith

Bathurst

Maitland

WALES

Orange

Lithgow

Newcastle

Wagga Wagga

Cootamundra

Sydney

Deniliquin

Wollongong

Mildura

Albury

Goulburn

Balranald

Canberra

Swan Hill

A.C.T.

VICTORIA

Shepparton

Mt Kosciusko

2230

Bendigo

Bombala

Horsham

Ararat

Ballarat

Orbost

Hamilton

Melbourne

Bairnsdale

C. Howe

Geelong

Morwell

Sale

Port Fairy

Wonthaggi

Warrnambool

Wilson's Prom.

King I.

Bass Strait

Flinders

Furneaux

Group

C. Grim

C. Barren

Smithton

Burnie

Devonport

Launceston

Queenstown

Mt Ossa

St Mary's

1617

Hobart

TASMANIA

Geeveston

South West C.

South East C.

Coral

Sea

Coral Sea

Island Territories

Willis Group

Coringa Is

Marion Reef

Îles

Chesterfield

(Fr.)

Swain

Reefs

Cato

PACIFIC

OCEAN

Tropic of Capricorn

Norfolk I.

(Aust.)

Lord Howe I.

(Aust.)

TASMAN

SEA

SOLOMON

ISLANDS

New

Georgia

Santa Isabel

Florida Is

Guadalcanal

Honiara

Malaita

Maramasike

San Cristobal

Rennell

Récifs

d'Entrecasteaux

Îles Bélep

Nouvelle

Calédonie

(Fr.)

Île des Pins

Nouméa

Bourail

Muéo

Ouéga

Lifu

NEW

ZEALAND

C. Farewell

Westport

Nelson

South Island

Greymouth

10

20

30

40

150

160

170

AUSTRALIA SOUTHEAST

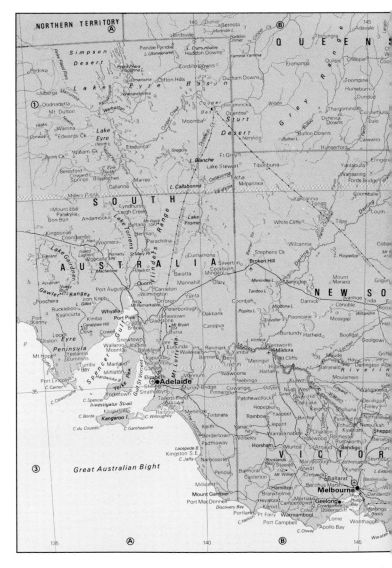

| 0 | 100 | 200 | 300 km |
| 0 | 50 | 100 | 150 mils |

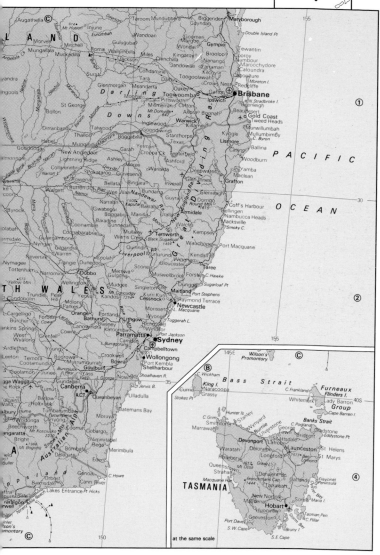

NEW ZEALAND

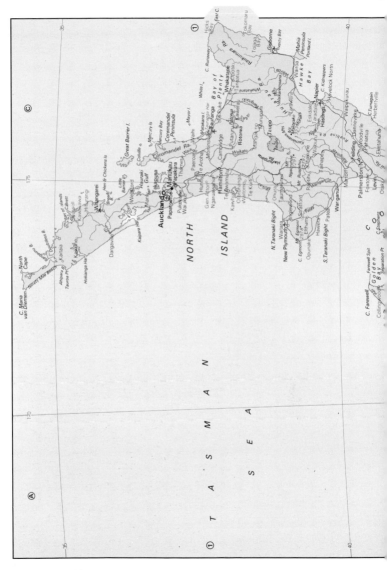

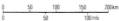

0	50	100	150	200 km
0		50		100 mls

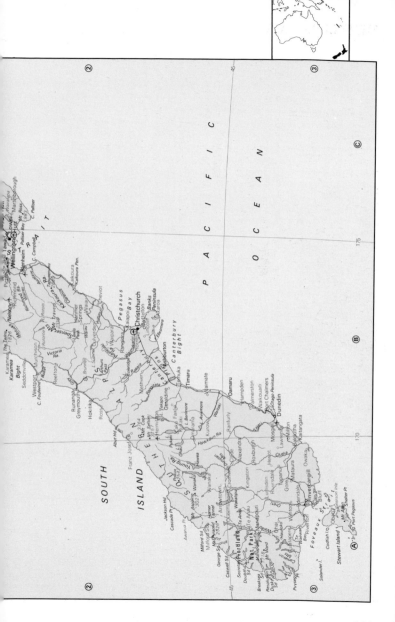

111

ANTARCTICA

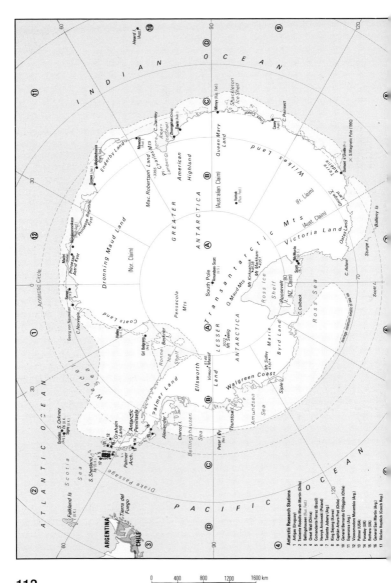

Antarctic Research Stations
1 Artigas (Uruguay)
2 Teniente Rodolfo Marsh Martin (Chile)
3 Bellingshausen (Rus. Fed.)
4 Great Wall (China)
5 Comandante Ferraz (Brazil)
6 Henryk Arctowski (Poland)
7 Teniente Jubany (Arg.)
8 King Sejong (Korea)
9 Capitán Arturo Prat (Chile)
10 General Bernardo O'Higgins (Chile)
11 Esperanza (Arg.)
12 Vicecomodoro Marambio (Arg.)
13 Palmer (USA)
14 Faraday (UK)
15 Rothera (UK)
16 General San Martín (Arg.)
17 Václav Vojtěch (Czech Rep.)

0   400   800   1200   1600 km
0   400   800 mls

112

Index

In the index, the first number refers to the page, and the following letter
and number to the section of the map in which the index entry
can be found. For example, 48C2 **Paris** means that Paris can
be found on page 48 where column C and row 2 meet.

Abbreviations used in the index

Afghan	Afghanistan	Hung	Hungary	Pol	Poland	Arch	Archipelago
Alb	Albania	Ind	Indonesia	Port	Portugal	B	Bay
Alg	Algeria	Irish Rep	Ireland	Rom	Romania	C	Cape
Ant	Antarctica	Leb	Lebanon	Russian Fed	Russian	Chan	Channel
Arg	Argentina	Lib	Liberia		Federation	Gl	Glacier
Aust	Australia	Liech	Liechtenstein	S Arabia	Saudi Arabia	I(s)	Island(s)
Bang	Bangladesh	Lux	Luxembourg	Scot	Scotland	Lg	Lagoon
Belg	Belgium	Madag	Madagascar	Sen	Senegal	L	Lake
Bol	Bolivia	Malay	Malaysia	S Africa	South Africa	Mt(s)	Mountain(s)
Bulg	Bulgaria	Maur	Mauritania	Switz	Switzerland	O	Ocean
Burk	Burkina	Mor	Morocco	Tanz	Tanzania	P	Pass
Camb	Cambodia	Mozam	Mozambique	Thai	Thailand	Pen	Peninsula
Can	Canada	Neth	Netherlands	Turk	Turkey	Plat	Plateau
CAR	Central African Republic	NZ	New Zealand	USA	United States	Pt	Point
Den	Denmark	Nic	Nicaragua		of America	Res	Reservoir
Dom Rep	Dominican Republic	N Ire	Northern Ireland	Urug	Uruguay	R	River
El Sal	El Salvador	Nig	Nigeria	Ven	Venezuela	S	Sea
Eng	England	Nor	Norway	Viet	Vietnam	Sd	Sound
Eq Guinea	Equatorial Guinea	Pak	Pakistan	Yugos	Yugoslavia	Str	Strait
Eth	Ethiopia	PNG	Papua New Guinea	Zim	Zimbabwe	V	Valley
Fin	Finland	Par	Paraguay				
Germ	Germany	Phil	Philippines				

A

57B2 **Aachen** Germany
46C1 **Aalst** Belg
38K6 **Äänekoski** Fin
47C1 **Aarau** Switz
47B1 **Aare** *R* Switz
72A3 **Aba** China
97C4 **Aba** Nig
99D2 **Aba** Zaïre
91A3 **Abādān** Iran
90B3 **Abādeh** Iran
96B1 **Abadla** Alg
35B1 **Abaeté** Brazil
35B1 **Abaeté** *R* Brazil
31B2 **Abaetetuba** Brazil
72D1 **Abagnar Qi** China
97C4 **Abakaliki** Nig
63B2 **Abakan**
    Russian Fed
97C3 **Abala** Niger
96C2 **Abalessa** Alg
32C6 **Abancay** Peru
90B3 **Abarqū** Iran
74E2 **Abashiri** Japan
74E2 **Abashiri-wan** *B*
    Japan
71F4 **Abau** PNG
99D2 **Abaya** *L* Eth
99D1 **Abbai** *R* Eth
99E1 **Abbe** *L* Eth
48C1 **Abbeville** France
19B4 **Abbeville** Louisiana,
    USA
17B1 **Abbeville** S Carolina,
    USA
45B2 **Abbeyfeale** Irish Rep
47C2 **Abbiategrasso** Italy
20B1 **Abbotsford** Can
84C2 **Abbottabad** Pak
61H3 **Abdulino**
    Russian Fed
98C1 **Abéché** Chad
39F7 **Åbenrå** Den
97C4 **Abeokuta** Nig
99D2 **Abera** Eth
43B3 **Aberaeron** Wales

15C3 **Aberdeen** Maryland,
    USA
100B4 **Aberdeen** S Africa
44C3 **Aberdeen** Scot
8D2 **Aberdeen** S Dakota,
    USA
8A2 **Aberdeen**
    Washington, USA
4J3 **Aberdeen** L Can
44C3 **Aberfeldy** Scot
43C4 **Abergavenny** Wales
43B3 **Aberystwyth** Wales
81C4 **Abha** S Arabia
90A2 **Abhar** Iran
97B4 **Abidjan** Ivory Coast
18A2 **Abilene** Kansas, USA
9D3 **Abilene** Texas, USA
43D4 **Abingdon** Eng
7B4 **Abitibi** *R* Can
7C5 **Abitibi,L** Can
61F5 **Abkhazskaya**
    Respublika, Georgia
84C2 **Abohar** India
97C4 **Abomey** Benin
98B2 **Abong Mbang** Cam
79A4 **Aborlan** Phil
98B1 **Abou Deïa** Chad
91A4 **Abqaiq** S Arabia
50A2 **Abrantes** Port
95C2 **Abri** Sudan
106A3 **Abrolhos** *Is* Aust
8B2 **Absaroka Range** *Mts*
    USA
91B5 **Abū al Abyad** *I* UAE
91A4 **Abū 'Alī** *I* S Arabia
91B5 **Abū Dhabi** UAE
95C3 **Abu Hamed** Sudan
97C4 **Abuja** Nig
33D5 **Abunã** Brazil
32D6 **Abunã** *R* Bol
93D3 **Abū Sukhayr** Iraq
111B2 **Abut Head** *C* NZ
95C3 **Abu 'Urug** *Well*
    Sudan
99D1 **Abuye Meda** *Mt* Eth
99C1 **Abu Zabad** Sudan
99D2 **Abwong** Sudan

56B1 **Åby** Den
94B3 **Aby 'Aweigila** *Well*
    Egypt
99C2 **Abyei** Sudan
24B2 **Acambaro** Mexico
24B2 **Acaponeta** Mexico
24B3 **Acapulco** Mexico
31D2 **Acaraú** Brazil
32D2 **Acarigua** Ven
24C3 **Acatlán** Mexico
23B2 **Acatzingo** Mexico
97B4 **Accra** Ghana
85D4 **Achalpur** India
29B4 **Achao** Chile
47D1 **Achensee** *L* Austria
46E2 **Achern** Germany
41A3 **Achill** *I* Irish Rep
63B2 **Achinsk** Russian Fed
53C3 **Acireale** Italy
26C2 **Acklins** *I*
    Caribbean S
32C6 **Acobamba** Peru
29B2 **Aconcagua** *Mt* Chile
31D3 **Acopiara** Brazil
88B4 **Açores** *Is* Atlantic O
    A Coruña = La Coruña
47C2 **Acqui** Italy
108A2 **Acraman,L** Aust
    Acre = 'Akko
32C5 **Acre** State, Brazil
22C3 **Acton** USA
23B1 **Actopan** Mexico
19A3 **Ada** USA
50B1 **Adaja** *R* Spain
91C5 **Adam** Oman
35A2 **Adamantina** Brazil
98B2 **Adamaoua** Region,
    Nig/Cam
47D1 **Adamello** *Mt* Italy
16C1 **Adams** USA
87B3 **Adam's Bridge** India/
    Sri Lanka
13D2 **Adams L** Can
8A2 **Adams,Mt** USA
87C3 **Adam's Peak** *Mt*
    Sri Lanka
81C4 **'Adan** Yemen

92C2 **Adana** Turk
60D5 **Adapazari** Turk
112B7 **Adare,C** Ant
108B1 **Adavale** Aust
47C2 **Adda** *R* Italy
91A4 **Ad Dahna'** Region,
    S Arabia
96A2 **Ad Dakhla** Mor
81C4 **Ad Dalī'** Yemen
91B4 **Ad Damman**
    S Arabia
91A4 **Ad Dibdibah** Region,
    S Arabia
91A5 **Ad Dilam** S Arabia
91A5 **Ad Dir'iyah** S Arabia
93D3 **Ad Diwaniyah** Iraq
93D3 **Ad Duwayd** S Arabia
106C4 **Adelaide** Aust
4J3 **Adelaide Pen** Can
22D3 **Adelanto** USA
    Aden = 'Adan
81C4 **Aden,G of** Yemen/
    Somalia
97C3 **Aderbissinat** Niger
94C2 **Adhra** Syria
71E4 **Adi** *I* Indon
52B1 **Adige** *R* Italy
99D1 **Adigrat** Eth
85D5 **Adilābād** India
20B2 **Adin** USA
15D2 **Adirondack Mts** USA
99D2 **Adis Abeba** Eth
95C3 **Adi Ugai** Eritrea
93C2 **Adiyaman** Turk
54C1 **Adjud** Rom
4E4 **Admiralty I** USA
6B2 **Admiralty Inlet** *B*
    Can
87B1 **Adoni** India
48B3 **Adour** *R* France
96A2 **Adrar** Region, Maur
96C2 **Adrar** *Mts* Alg
96A2 **Adrar Soutouf**
    Region, Mor
98C1 **Adré** Chad
95A2 **Adri** Libya
47E2 **Adria** Italy

14B2 **Adrian** Michigan, USA
52B2 **Adriatic S** S Europe
99D1 **Adwa** Eth
97B4 **Adzopé** Ivory Coast
55B3 **Aegean** S Greece
80E2 **Afghanistan** Republic, Asia
39E2 **Afgooye** Somalia
97C4 **Afikpo** Nig
38G6 **Afjord** Nor
96C1 **Aflou** Alg
99E2 **Afmadu** Somalia
97A3 **Afollé** Region, Maur
94B2 **Afula** Israel
92B2 **Afyon** Turk
95A3 **Agadem** Niger
97C3 **Agadez** Niger
96B1 **Agadir** Mor
85D4 **Agar** India
86C2 **Agartala** India
20B1 **Agassiz** Can
97B4 **Agboville** Ivory Coast
93E1 **Agdam** Azerbaijan
75B1 **Agematsu** Japan
48C3 **Agen** France
90A3 **Agha Jāri** Iran
96A2 **Aghāwīll** *Well* Mor
47D2 **Agno** *R* Italy
47E1 **Agordo** Italy
48C3 **Agout** *R* France
85D3 **Agra** India
93D2 **Agri** Turk
53C2 **Agri** *R* Italy
53B3 **Agrigento** Italy
55B3 **Agrinion** Greece
34A3 **Agrio** *R* Chile
53B2 **Agropoli** Italy
61H2 **Agryz** Russian Fed
6E3 **Agto** Greenland
27D3 **Aguadilla** Puerto Rico
24B1 **Agua Prieta** Mexico
24B2 **Aguascalientes** Mexico
23A1 **Aguascalientes** State, Mexico
35C1 **Aguas Formosas** Brazil
50A1 **Agueda** Port
96C3 **Aguelhok** Mali
50B2 **Aguilas** Spain
23A2 **Aguililla** Mexico
100B4 **Agulhas,C** S Africa
79C4 **Agusan** *R* Phil
93E2 **Ahar** Iran
110B1 **Ahipara B** NZ
85C4 **Ahmadābād** India
87A1 **Ahmadnagar** India
99E2 **Ahmar** *Mts* Eth
46D1 **Ahr** *R* Germany
46D1 **Ahrgebirge** Region, Germany
23A1 **Ahuacatlán** Mexico
23A1 **Ahualulco** Mexico
39G7 **Ähus** Sweden
90B2 **Ahuvān** Iran
90A3 **Ahvāz** Iran
26A4 **Aiajuela** Costa Rica
47B1 **Aigle** Switz
47B2 **Aiguille d'Arves** *Mt* France
47B2 **Aiguille de la Grand Sassière** *Mt* France
75B1 **Aikawa** Japan
17B1 **Aiken** USA
73A5 **Ailao Shan** *Upland* China
35C1 **Aimorés** Brazil
96B1 **Ain Beni Mathar** Mor
95B2 **Ain Dalla** *Well* Egypt
51C2 **Ain el Hadjel** Alg
95A3 **Ain Galakka** Chad
96B1 **Ain Sefra** Alg
92B4 **'Ain Sukhna** Egypt
75A2 **Aioi** Japan
96B2 **Aioun Abd el Malek** *Well* Maur
97B3 **Aioun El Atrous** Maur
30C2 **Aiguile** Bol
97C3 **Aïr** *Desert Region* Niger

13E2 **Airdrie** Can
46B1 **Aire** France
42D3 **Aire** *R* Eng
46C2 **Aire** *R* France
6C3 **Airforce I** Can
47C1 **Airolo** Switz
4E3 **Aishihik** Can
12G2 **Aishihik L** Can
46B2 **Aisne** Department, France
49C2 **Aisne** *R* France
71F4 **Aitape** PNG
58D1 **Aiviekste** *R* Latvia
72B2 **Aixa Zuogi** China
49D3 **Aix-en-Provence** France
47A2 **Aix-les-Bains** France
86B2 **Aiyar Res** India
55B3 **Aíyion** Greece
55R3 **Aíyna** *I* Greece
86C2 **Aizawl** India
100A3 **Aizeb** *R* Namibia
74E3 **Aizu-Wakamatsu** Japan
52A2 **Ajaccio** Corse
23B2 **Ajalpan** Mexico
99B1 **Ajdabiyā** Libya
74E2 **Ajigasawa** Japan
94B2 **Ajlun** Jordan
91C4 **Ajman** UAE
85C3 **Ajmer** India
9B3 **Ajo** USA
23A2 **Ajuchitan** Mexico
55C3 **Ak** *R* Turk
75B1 **Akaishi-sanchi** *Mts* Japan
87B1 **Akalkot** India
111B2 **Akaroa** NZ
75A2 **Akashi** Japan
61J3 **Akbulak** Russian Fed
93C2 **Akçakale** Turk
96A2 **Akchar** *Watercourse* Maur
55C3 **Akdağ** *Mt* Turk
92C2 **Aketi** Zaire
93D1 **Akhalkalaki** Georgia
93D1 **Akhalsikhe** Georgia
55B3 **Akharnaí** Greece
12D3 **Akhiok** USA
92A2 **Akhisar** Turk
58D1 **Akhiste** Latvia
95C2 **Akhmîm** Egypt
61G4 **Akhtubinsk** Russian Fed
60D4 **Akhtyrka** Ukraine
75A2 **Aki** Japan
7B4 **Akimiski I** Can
74E3 **Akita** Japan
96A3 **Akjoujt** Maur
94B2 **'Akko** Israel
4E3 **Aklavik** USA
97B3 **Aklé Aouana** *Desert Region* Maur
99D2 **Akobo** Sudan
99D2 **Akobo** *R* Sudan
84D1 **Akoha** Afghan
85D4 **Akola** India
85D4 **Akot** India
6D3 **Akpatok I** Can
55B3 **Ákra Kafirévs** *C* Greece
55D3 **Ákra Maléa** *C* Greece
38A2 **Akranes** Iceland
55C3 **Ákra Sídheros** *C* Greece
55B3 **Ákra Spátha** *C* Greece
55B3 **Ákra Taínaron** *C* Greece
10B2 **Akron** USA
94A1 **Akrotiri B** Cyprus
84D1 **Aksai Chin** *Mts* China
92B2 **Aksaray** Turk
61H3 **Aksay** Kazakhstan
84D1 **Aksayqin Hu** *L* China
92B2 **Akşehir** Turk
92B2 **Akseki** Turk
63D2 **Aksenovo Zilovskoye** Russian Fed
68D1 **Aksha** Russian Fed
82C1 **Aksu** China

61H5 **Aktau** Kazakhstan
65J5 **Aktogay** Kazakhstan
61J4 **Aktumsyk** Kazakhstan
65G4 **Aktyubinsk** Kazakhstan
38B1 **Akureyri** Iceland
45K5 **Akyab = Sittwe**
65K5 **Akzhal** Kazakhstan
11B3 **Alabama** State, USA
11B3 **Alabama** *R* USA
17A1 **Alabaster** USA
92C2 **Ala Dağlari** *Mts* Turk
61F5 **Alagir** Russian Fed
47B2 **Alagna** Italy
31D3 **Alagoas** State, Brazil
31D4 **Alagoinhas** Brazil
51B1 **Alagón** Spain
93E4 **Al Ahmadi** Kuwait
25D3 **Alajuela** Costa Rica
12B2 **Alakanuk** USA
38L5 **Alakurtti** Russian Fed
93E3 **Al Amārah** Iraq
21A2 **Alameda** USA
23B1 **Alamo** Mexico
9C3 **Alamogordo** USA
9C3 **Alamosa** USA
39H6 **Åland** *I* Fin
92B2 **Alanya** Turk
17B1 **Alapaha** *R* USA
65H4 **Alapayevsk** Russian Fed
92A2 **Alaşehir** Turk
68C3 **Ala Shan** *Mts* China
4C3 **Alaska** State, USA
4D4 **Alaska,G of** USA
12C3 **Alaska Pen** USA
4C3 **Alaska Range** *Mts* USA
52C2 **Alassio** Italy
12D1 **Alatna** *R* USA
61G3 **Alatyr'** Russian Fed
108B2 **Alawoona** Aust
91C5 **Al Ayn** UAE
82B2 **Alayskiy Khrebet** *Mts* Tajikistan
49D3 **Alba** Italy
92C2 **Al Bāb** Syria
51B2 **Albacete** Spain
50A1 **Alba de Tormes** Spain
93D2 **Al Badi** Iraq
54B1 **Alba Iulia** Rom
54A2 **Albania** Republic, Europe
106A4 **Albany** Aust
17B1 **Albany** Georgia, USA
15D2 **Albany** New York, USA
8A2 **Albany** Oregon, USA
7B4 **Albany** *R* Can
34B2 **Albardón** Arg
91C5 **Al Batinah** Region, Oman
71F5 **Albatross B** Aust
95B1 **Al Baydā** Libya
11C3 **Albemarle Sd** USA
50B1 **Alberche** *R* Spain
108A1 **Alberga** Aust
46B1 **Albert** France
5G4 **Alberta** Province, Can
99D2 **Albert,L** Uganda/Zaire
10A2 **Albert Lea** USA
99D2 **Albert Nile** *R* Uganda
49D2 **Albertville** France
48C3 **Albi** France
18B1 **Albia** USA
33G2 **Albina** Suriname
14B2 **Albion** Michigan, USA
15C2 **Albion** New York, USA
92C4 **Al Bi'r** S Arabia
91A5 **Al Biyadh** Region, S Arabia
50B2 **Alborán** *I* Spain
39G7 **Ålborg** Den
93D3 **Al Bū Kamāl** Syria
47C1 **Albula** *R* Switz
9C3 **Albuquerque** USA
91C5 **Al Buraymi** Oman

95A1 **Al Burayqah** Libya
95B1 **Al Burdi** Libya
107D4 **Albury** Aust
93E3 **Al Busayyah** Iraq
50B1 **Alcalá de Henares** Spain
53B3 **Alcamo** Italy
51B1 **Alcaniz** Spain
50B2 **Alcántara** Spain
50B2 **Alcaraz** Spain
50B2 **Alcázar de San Juan** Spain
51B2 **Alcira** Spain
35D1 **Alcobaça** Brazil
50B1 **Alcolea de Pinar** Spain
51B2 **Alcoy** Spain
51C2 **Alcudia** Spain
89J8 **Aldabra Is** Indian O
63E2 **Aldan** Russian Fed
63E2 **Aldanskoye Nagor'ye** *Upland* Russian Fed
43E3 **Aldeburgh** Eng
48B2 **Alderney** *I* UK
43D4 **Aldershot** Eng
97A3 **Aleg** Maur
30E4 **Alegrete** Brazil
34C2 **Alejandro Roca** Arg
30H6 **Alejandro Selkirk** *I* Chile
63G2 **Aleksandrovsk Sakhalinskiy** Russian Fed
65J4 **Alekseyevka** Kazakhstan
60E3 **Aleksin** Russian Fed
58B1 **Ålem** Sweden
35C2 **Além Paraíba** Brazil
49C2 **Alençon** France
21C4 **Alenuihaha Chan** Hawaiian Is
Aleppo = Halab
6D1 **Alert** Can
45E3 **Alès** France
52A2 **Alessandria** Italy
64B3 **Ålesund** Nor
12C3 **Aleutian Range** *Mts* USA
4E4 **Alexander Arch** USA
100A3 **Alexander Bay** S Africa
112C3 **Alexander City** USA
112C3 **Alexander I** Ant
111A3 **Alexandra** NZ
29G8 **Alexandra,C** South Georgia
6C2 **Alexandra Fjord** Can
95B1 **Alexandria** Egypt
11A3 **Alexandria** Louisiana, USA
10A2 **Alexandria** Minnesota, U3A
10C3 **Alexandria** Virginia, USA
55C2 **Alexandroúpolis** Greece
13C2 **Alexis Creek** Can
94P7 **Aley** Leb
65K4 **Aleysk** Russian Fed
93D3 **Al Fallujah** Iraq
51B1 **Alfaro** Spain
54C2 **Alfatar** Bulg
93E3 **Al Fāw** Iraq
35B2 **Alfenas** Brazil
55B3 **Alfiós** *R* Greece
47D2 **Alfonsine** Italy
35C2 **Alfonzo Cláudio** Brazil
35C2 **Alfredo Chaves** Brazil
61J4 **Alga** Kazakhstan
34B3 **Algarrobo del Aguila** Arg
51C2 **Algeciras** Spain
96C1 **Alger** Alg
96B2 **Algeria** Republic, Africa
53A3 **Alghero** Sardegna
96C1 **Algiers = Alger**
15C1 **Algonquin Park** Can
91C5 **Al Hadd** Oman
93D3 **Al Hadīthah** Iraq
92C3 **Al Hadīthah** S Arabia

93D2 Al Haḍr Iraq
91C5 Al Hajar al Gharbī Mts Oman
91C5 Al Hajar ash Sharqi Mts Oman
93C3 Al Hamad Desert Region Jordan/ S Arabia
93E4 Al Haniyah Desert Region Iraq
91A5 Al Hariq S Arabia
93C3 Al Harrah Desert Region S Arabia
95A2 Al Harūj al Aswad Upland Libya
91A4 Al Hasa Region, S Arabia
93D2 Al Hasakah Syria
93C4 Al Hawjā' S Arabia
93E3 Al Hayy Iraq
94C2 Al Hijanah Syria
93D3 Al Hillah Iraq
91A5 Al Hillah S Arabia
96B1 Al Hoceima Mor
91A4 Al Hufūf S Arabia
91B5 Al Humrah Region, UAE
91C5 Al Huwatsah Oman
90A2 Aliābad Iran
91C4 Aliabad Iran
55B2 Aliákmon R Greece
93E3 Ali al Gharbi Iraq
87A1 Alībāg India
51B2 Alicante Spain
9D4 Alice USA
106C3 Alice Springs Aust
53B3 Alicudi I Italy
84D3 Aligarh India
90A3 Aligūdarz Iran
84B2 Ali-Khel Afghan
55C3 Alimniá I Greece
86B1 Alīpur Duār India
14B2 Aliquippa USA
22B2 Alişal USA
93C3 Al' Isawiyah S Arabia
100B4 Aliwal North S Africa
95B2 Al Jaghbūb Libya
93D3 Al Jalamid S Arabia
95B2 Al Jawf Libya
93C4 Al Jawf S Arabia
93D2 Al Jazirah Desert Region Syria/Iraq
50A2 Aljezur Port
91A4 Al Jubayl S Arabia
91C5 Al Kāmil Oman
93D2 Al Khābūr R Syria
91C5 Al Khābūrah Oman
93D3 Al Khālis Iraq
91B4 Al Khasab Oman
91B4 Al Khawr Qatar
95A1 Al Khums Libya
91B5 Al Kidan Region, S Arabia
94C2 Al Kiswah Syria
56A2 Alkmaar Neth
95B2 Al Kufrah Oasis Libya
93E3 Al Küt Iraq
92C2 Al Lādhiqīyah Syria
86A1 Allahābād India
94C2 Al Lajāh Mt Syria
12D1 Allakaket USA
76B2 Allanmyo Burma
95C2 'Allaqi Watercourse Egypt
17B1 Allatoona L USA
15C2 Allegheny R USA
10C3 Allegheny Mts USA
17B1 Allendale USA
111A3 Allen,Mt NZ
15C2 Allentown USA
87B3 Alleppey India
49C2 Aller R France
47D1 Allgäu Mts Germany
8C2 Alliance USA
81C3 Al Liāwi Yemen
91B5 Al Liwā Region, UAE
109D1 Allora Aust
14B2 Alma Michigan, USA
82B1 Alma Ata Kazakhstan
50A2 Almada Port
    Al Madinah = Medina
71F2 Almagan I Pacific O
91B4 Al Manāmah Bahrain
93D3 Al Ma'niyah Iraq

21A1 Almanor,L USA
51B2 Almansa Spain
13B1 Alma Peak Mt Can
91B5 Al Māriyyah UAE
95B1 Al Marj Libya
    Almaty = Alma Ata
93D2 Al Mawsil Iraq
50B1 Almazán Spain
35C1 Almenara Brazil
50B2 Almeria Spain
61H3 Al'met'yevsk Russian Fed
56C1 Almhult Sweden
93E3 Al Miqdadiyah Iraq
112C3 Almirante Brown Base Ant
34A1 Almirante Latorre Chile
55B3 Almirós Greece
91A4 Al Mish'āb S Arabia
50A2 Almodôvar Port
84D3 Almora India
91A4 Al Mubarraz S Arabia
92C4 Al Mudawwara Jordan
91C5 Al Mudaybi Oman
91B4 Al Muharraq Bahrain
81C4 Al Mukallā Yemen
81C4 Al Mukhā Yemen
93D3 Al Musayyib Iraq
44B3 Alness Scot
43C3 Al Nu'māniyah Iraq
42D2 Alnwick Eng
71D4 Alor I Indon
77C4 Alor Setar Malay
    Alost = Aalst
107E2 Alotau PNG
106B3 Aloysius,Mt Aust
34C3 Alpachiri Arg
14B1 Alpena USA
47B2 Alpes du Valais Mts Switz
52B1 Alpi Dolomitiche Mts Italy
47B2 Alpi Graie Mts Italy
9C3 Alpine Texas, USA
47C1 Alpi Orobie Mts Italy
47B2 Alpi Pennine Mts Italy
47C1 Alpi Retiche Mts Switz
47D1 Alpi Venoste Mts Italy
52A1 Alps Mts Europe
95A1 Al Qaddāhiyah Libya
94C1 Al Qadmus Syria
93D3 Al Qā'im Iraq
93C4 Al Qalibah S Arabia
93D2 Al Qāmishli Syria
95A1 Al Qaryah Ash Sharqiyah Libya
92C3 Al Qaryatayn Syria
91A4 Al Qātif S Arabia
95A2 Al Qatrūn Libya
91A4 Al Qaysāmah S Arabia
94C2 Al Quatayfah Syria
50A2 Alqueva R Port
92C3 Al Qunaytirah Syria
81C4 Al Qunfidhah S Arabia
93E3 Al Qurnah Iraq
94C1 Al Qusayr Syria
92C3 Al Qutayfah Syria
56B1 Als I Den
49D2 Alsace Region, France
57B2 Alsfeld Germany
42C2 Alston Eng
38J5 Alta Nor
29D2 Alta Gracia Arg
27D5 Altagracia de Orituco Ven
68A2 Altai Mts Mongolia
17B1 Altamaha R USA
33G4 Altamira Brazil
23B1 Altamira Mexico
53C2 Altamura Italy
68C1 Altanbulag Mongolia
71F4 Altape PNG
24B2 Altata Mexico
63A3 Altay China
63B3 Altay Mongolia
63A2 Altay Mts

    Russian Fed
47C1 Altdorf Switz
46D1 Altenkirchen Germany
34B3 Altiplanicie del Payún Plat Arg
47B1 Altkirch France
101C2 Alto Molócue Mozam
10A3 Alton USA
15C2 Altoona USA
34B2 Alto Pencoso Mts Arg
35A1 Alto Sucuriú Brazil
23B2 Altotonga Mexico
23A2 Altoyac de Alvarez Mexico
82C2 Altun Shan Mts China
20B2 Alturas USA
9D3 Altus USA
91B5 Al'Ubaylah S Arabia
93C4 Al Urayq Desert Region S Arabia
91B5 Al'Uruq al Mu'taridah Region, S Arabia
9D2 Alva USA
23B2 Alvarado Mexico
19A3 Alvarado USA
39G6 Alvdalen Sweden
19A4 Alvin USA
38J5 Alvsbyn Sweden
80B3 Al Wajh S Arabia
85D3 Alwar India
93D3 Al Widyān Desert Region Iraq/S Arabia
72A2 Alxa Yougi China
93E2 Alyat Azerbaijan
39J8 Alytus Lithuania
46E2 Alzey Germany
23B2 Amacuzac R Mexico
99D2 Amadi Sudan
6C3 Amadjuak L Can
74B4 Amakusa-shotō I Japan
39G7 Åmål Sweden
63D2 Amalat R Russian Fed
55B3 Amaliás Greece
85D4 Amalner India
69E4 Amami I Japan
69E4 Amami guntō Arch Japan
100C4 Amanzimtoti S Africa
33G3 Amapá Brazil
33G3 Amapá State, Brazil
9C3 Amarillo USA
60E5 Amasya Turk
23A1 Amatitan Mexico
    Amazonas = Solimões
32D4 Amazonas State, Brazil
28C3 Amazonas R Brazil
84D2 Ambāla India
87C3 Ambalangoda Sri Lanka
101D3 Ambalavao Madag
98B2 Ambam Cam
101D2 Ambanja Madag
1C7 Ambarchik Russian Fed
32B4 Ambato Ecuador
101D2 Ambato-Boeny Madag
101D2 Ambatolampy Madag
101D2 Ambatondrazaka Madag
57C3 Amberg Germany
25D3 Ambergris Cay I Belize
86A2 Ambikāpur India
101D2 Ambilobe Madag
101D3 Amboasary Madag
101D2 Ambodifototra Madag
101D3 Ambohimahasoa Madag
71D4 Ambon Indon
101D3 Ambositra Madag
101D3 Ambovombe Madag
98B3 Ambriz Angola
98C1 Am Dam Chad

64H3 Amderma Russian Fed
24B2 Ameca Mexico
23B2 Amecacameca Mexico
34C2 Ameghino Arg
56B2 Ameland I Neth
16C2 Amenia USA
112B10 American Highland Upland Ant
105H4 American Samoa Is Pacific O
17B1 Americus USA
101G1 Amersfoort S Africa
112C10 Amery Ice Shelf Ant
55B3 Amfilokhia Greece
55B3 Amfissa Greece
63F1 Amga Russian Fed
63F1 Amgal R Russian Fed
69F2 Amgu Russian Fed
69F1 Amgun' R Russian Fed
99D1 Amhara Region Eth
7D5 Amherst Can
16C1 Amherst Massachusetts, USA
    Amherst = Kyaikkami
87B2 Amhūr India
48C2 Amiens France
75B1 Amino Japan
94B1 Amioune Leb
89K8 Amirante Is Indian O
86B1 Amlekhgan Nepal
92C3 Amman Jordan
38K6 Ämmänsaario Fin
56B2 Amersfoort Neth
90B2 Amol Iran
55C3 Amorgós I Greece
7C5 Amos Can
    Amoy = Xiamen
101D3 Ampanihy Madag
35B2 Amparo Brazil
51C1 Amposta Spain
85D4 Amrāvati India
85C4 Amreli India
84C2 Amritsar India
56A2 Amsterdam Neth
101H1 Amsterdam S Africa
15D2 Amsterdam USA
98C1 Am Timan Chad
88L3 Amu Darya R Uzbekistan
6A2 Amund Ringes I Can
4H3 Amundsen G Can
112B4 Amundsen S Ant
80E Amundsen-Scott Base Ant
78D3 Amuntai Indon
63E2 Amur R Russian Fed
33E2 Anaco Ven
20B1 Anacortes USA
55C3 Anáfi I Greece
93D3 'Anah Iraq
21B3 Anaheim USA
87B2 Anaimalai Hills India
83C4 Anakapalle India
12E1 Anaktuvuk P USA
101D2 Analalava Madag
92B2 Anamur Turk
75A2 Anan Japan
87B2 Anantapur India
84D2 Anantnag India
31B5 Anápolis Brazil
90C3 Anār Iran
90B3 Anārak Iran
71F2 Anatahan I Pacific O
30D4 Añatuya Arg
74B3 Anbyŏn N Korea
22C4 Ancapa Is USA
4D3 Anchorage USA
30C2 Ancohuma Mt Bol
32B6 Ancon Peru
52B2 Ancona Italy
16C1 Ancram USA
29B4 Ancud Chile
34A3 Andacollo Arg
108A1 Andado Aust
32C6 Andahuaylas Peru
38F6 Andalsnes Nor
50A2 Andalucia Region, Spain
17A1 Andalusia USA

83D4 **Andaman Is** Burma
83D4 **Andaman S** Burma
108A2 **Andamooka** Aust
38H5 **Andenes** Nor
47C1 **Andermatt** Switz
57B2 **Andernach** Germany
14A2 **Anderson** Indiana, USA
18B2 **Anderson** Missouri, USA
17B1 **Anderson** S Carolina, USA
4F3 **Anderson** *R* Can
87B1 **Andhra Pradesh** State, India
55B3 **Andikithira** *I* Greece
65J5 **Andizhan** Uzbekistan
65H6 **Andkhui** Afghan
74B3 **Andong** S Korea
51C1 **Andorra** Principality, SW Europe
51C1 **Andorra-La-Vella** Andorra
43D4 **Andover** Eng
35A2 **Andradina** Brazil
12B2 **Andreafsky** USA
92B2 **Andreas,C** Cyprus
53C2 **Andria** Italy
11C4 **Andros** *I* The Bahamas
55B3 **Andros** *I* Greece
87A2 **Androth** *I* India
50B2 **Andújar** Spain
100A2 **Andulo** Angola
97C4 **Anécho** Togo
97C3 **Anéfis** Mali
34B3 **Añelo** Arg
63C2 **Angarsk** Russian Fed
38H6 **Ange** Sweden
24A2 **Angel de la Guarda** *I* Mexico
79B2 **Angeles** Phil
39G7 **Angelholm** Sweden
109C1 **Angellala Creek** *R* Aust
22B1 **Angels Camp** USA
71E4 **Angemuk** *Mt* Indon
48B2 **Angers** France
76C3 **Angkor** *Hist Site* Camb
41C3 **Anglesey** *I* Wales
19A4 **Angleton** USA
6G3 **Angmagssalik** Greenland
101D2 **Angoche** Mozam
29B3 **Angol** Chile
14B2 **Angola** Indiana, USA
100A2 **Angola** Republic, Africa
103H6 **Angola Basin** Atlantic O
12H3 **Angoon** USA
48C2 **Angoulême** France
96A1 **Angra do Heroísmo** Açores
35C2 **Angra dos Reis** Brazil
34C3 **Anguil** Arg
27E3 **Anguilla** *I* Caribbean S
26B2 **Anguilla Cays** *Is* Caribbean S
86B2 **Angul** India
99C3 **Angumu** Zaïre
56C1 **Anholt** *I* Den
73C4 **Anhua** China
72D3 **Anhui** Province, China
12C2 **Aniak** USA
35B1 **Anicuns** Brazil
46B2 **Anizy-le-Château** France
4C3 **Anjak** USA
48B2 **Anjou** Region, France
101D2 **Anjouan** *I* Comoros
101D2 **Anjozorobe** Madag
74B3 **Anju** N Korea
72B3 **Ankang** China
92B2 **Ankara** Turk
101D2 **Ankaratra** *Mt* Madag
101D3 **Ankazoabo** Madag
101D2 **Ankazobe** Madag
56C2 **Anklam** Germany
76D3 **An Loc** Viet

73B4 **Anlong** China
73C3 **Anlu** China
18C2 **Anna** USA
96C1 **'Annaba** Alg
92C3 **An Nabk** S Arabia
92C3 **An Nabk** Syria
108A1 **Anna Creek** Aust
80C3 **An Nafūd** *Desert* S Arabia
93D3 **An Najaf** Iraq
42C2 **Annan** Scot
15C3 **Annapolis** USA
86A1 **Annapurna** *Mt* Nepal
14B2 **Ann Arbor** USA
94C1 **An Nāsirah** Syria
93E3 **An Nāsiriyah** Iraq
47B2 **Annecy** France
47B1 **Annemasse** France
76D3 **An Nhon** Viet
73A5 **Anning** China
17A1 **Anniston** USA
89E8 **Annobon** *I* Eq Guinea
49C2 **Annonay** France
27J1 **Annotto Bay** Jamaica
73D3 **Anqing** China
72B2 **Ansai** China
57C3 **Ansbach** Germany
26C3 **Anse d'Hainault** Haiti
72E1 **Anshan** China
73B4 **Anshun** China
97C3 **Ansongo** Mali
14B3 **Ansted** USA
92C2 **Antakya** Turk
101E2 **Antalaha** Madag
92B2 **Antalya** Turk
92B2 **Antalya Körfezi** *B* Turk
101D2 **Antananarivo** Madag
112C1 **Antarctic Circle** Ant
112C3 **Antarctic Pen** Ant
50B2 **Antequera** Spain
96B2 **Anti-Atlas** *Mts* Mor
7D5 **Anticosti, Î. d'** Can
27E3 **Antigua** *I* Caribbean S
Anti Lebanon = Jebel esh Sharqi
21A2 **Antioch** USA
19A3 **Antlers** USA
30B3 **Antofagasta** Chile
45C1 **Antrim** County, N Ire
45C1 **Antrim** N Ire
45C1 **Antrim Hills** N Ire
101D2 **Antseranana** Madag
101D2 **Antsirabe** Madag
101D2 **Antsohihy** Madag
76D1 **An Tuc** Viet
46C1 **Antwerpen** Belg
45C2 **An Uaimh** Irish Rep
84C3 **Anupgarh** India
87C3 **Anuradhapura** Sri Lanka
Anvers = Antwerpen
4B3 **Anvik** USA
6363 **Anxi** China
72A3 **A'nyêmaqên Shan** *Upland* China
47C2 **Anza** *R* Italy
13E1 **Anzac** Can
65K4 **Anzhero-Sudzhensk** Russian Fed
53B2 **Anzio** Italy
74E2 **Aomori** Japan
52A1 **Aosta** Italy
97B3 **Aoukar** *Desert Region* Maur
96C2 **Aoulef** Alg
95A2 **Aozou** Chad
30E3 **Apa** *R* Brazil/Par
11B4 **Apalachee B** USA
17B2 **Apalachicola** USA
17A2 **Apalachicola B** USA
23B2 **Apan** Mexico
64E3 **Apatity** Russian Fed
32C3 **Apaporis** *R* Colombia
35A2 **Aparecida do Taboado** Brazil
79B2 **Aparri** Phil
54A1 **Apatin** Croatia

64E3 **Apatity** Russian Fed
24B3 **Apatzingan** Mexico
56B2 **Apeldoorn** Neth
35B2 **Apiaí** Brazil
33F2 **Apoera** Surinam
108B3 **Apollo Bay** Aust
79C4 **Apo,Mt** *Mt* Phil
17B2 **Apopka,L** USA
30F2 **Aporé** *R* Brazil
10A2 **Apostle Is** USA
10A2 **Apostle L** USA
23A1 **Apozol** Mexico
11B3 **Appalachian Mts** USA
52B2 **Appennino Abruzzese** *Mts* Italy
52A2 **Appennino Ligure** *Mts* Italy
53C2 **Appennino Lucano** *Mts* Italy
53B2 **Appennino Napoletano** *Mts* Italy
52B2 **Appennino Tosco-Emilliano** *Mts* Italy
52B2 **Appennino Umbro-Marchigiano** *Mts* Italy
47C1 **Appenzell** Switz
42C2 **Appleby** Eng
14A2 **Appleton** Wisconsin, USA
30F3 **Apucarana** Brazil
23B1 **Apuico** Mexico
32D2 **Apure** *R* Ven
32C6 **Apurímac** *R* Peru
92C4 **'Aqaba** Jordan
92B4 **'Aqaba,G of** Egypt/ S Arabia
90B3 **'Aqdā** Iran
30E3 **Aquidauana** Brazil
23A2 **Aquila** Mexico
86A1 **Ara** India
17A1 **Arab** USA
81D4 **Arabian S** Asia/ Arabian Pen
31D4 **Aracajú** Brazil
30E3 **Aracanguy, Mts de** Par
31D2 **Aracati** Brazil
30F3 **Araçatuba** Brazil
50A2 **Aracena** Spain
31C5 **Araçuaí** Brazil
94B3 **Arad** Israel
60B4 **Arad** Rom
98C1 **Arada** Chad
91B5 **'Arādah** UAE
106C1 **Arafura S** Indon/Aust
30F2 **Aragarças** Brazil
51B1 **Aragón** *R* Spain
50B1 **Aragón** *R* Spain
33G6 **Araguaia** *R* Brazil
31B3 **Araguaína** Brazil
31B5 **Araguari** Brazil
35B1 **Araguari** *R* Brazil
75B1 **Arai** Japan
96C2 **Arak** Alg
90A3 **Arāk** Iran
76A2 **Arakan Yoma** *Mts* Burma
87B2 **Arakkonam** India
65G5 **Aral Sea** Kazakhstan/ Uzbekistan
80E1 **Aral'sk** Kazakhstan
Aral'skoye More = Aral S
40B2 **Aran** *I* Irish Rep
50B1 **Aranda de Duero** Spain
23A1 **Arandas** Mexico
50B1 **Aranjuez** Spain
75A2 **Arao** Japan
97B3 **Araouane** Mali
29E2 **Arapey** *R* Urug
31D4 **Arapiraca** Brazil
35A2 **Araporgas** Brazil
30G4 **Araranguá** Brazil
31B6 **Araraquara** Brazil
35B2 **Araras** Brazil
107D4 **Ararat** Aust
93D2 **Ararat** Armenia
93E1 **Aras** *R* Azerbaijan
93E2 **Aras** *R* Azerbaijan
75E1 **Arato** Japan
32D2 **Arauca** *R* Ven

34A3 **Arauco** Chile
32C2 **Arauea** Colombia
85C4 **Arāvalli Range** *Mts* India
31B5 **Araxá** Brazil
99D2 **Arba Minch** Eth
53A3 **Arbatax** Sardegna
93D2 **Arbīl** Iraq
47A1 **Arbois** France
39H6 **Arbrā** Sweden
44C3 **Arbroath** Scot
47A1 **Arc** France
47B2 **Arc** *R* France
48B3 **Arcachon** France
17B2 **Arcadia** USA
20B2 **Arcata** USA
23A2 **Arcelia** Mexico
26B2 **Archipiélago de Camaguey** *Arch* Cuba
29B6 **Archipiélago de la Reina Adelaida** *Arch* Chile
29R4 **Archipiélago de las Chones** *Arch* Chile
32B2 **Archipiélago de las Perlas** *Arch* Panama
35B2 **Arcos** Brazil
50A2 **Arcos de la Frontera** Spain
6B2 **Arctic Bay** Can
1C1 **Arctic Circle**
4E3 **Arctic Red** Can
4E3 **Arctic Red** *R* Can
4D3 **Arctic Village** USA
54C2 **Arda** *R* Bulg
65F6 **Ardabīl** Iran
93D1 **Ardahan** Turk
39F6 **Ardal** Nor
96C2 **Ardar des Iforas** *Upland* Alg/Mali
45C2 **Ardee** Irish Rep
90B3 **Ardekān** Iran
46C2 **Ardennes** Department, France
57A2 **Ardennes** Region, Belg
90B3 **Ardestan** Iran
92C3 **Ardh es Suwwan** *Desert Region* Jordan
50A2 **Ardila** *R* Port
109C2 **Ardlethan** Aust
9D3 **Ardmore** USA
44A3 **Ardnamurchan** *Pt* Scot
46A1 **Ardres** France
44B3 **Ardrishaig** Scot
42B2 **Ardrossan** Scot
27D3 **Arecibo** Puerto Rico
31D2 **Areia Branca** Brazil
21A2 **Arena,Pt** USA
39F7 **Arendal** Nor
30B2 **Arenápolis** Brazil
52B2 **Arezzo** Italy
52B2 **Argenta** Italy
49C2 **Argentan** France
46B2 **Argenteuil** France
27F2 **Argentina** Republic, S America
103F7 **Argentine Basin** Atlantic O
48C2 **Argenton-sur-Creuse** France
54C2 **Arges** *R* Rom
84B2 **Arghardab** *R* Afghan
55B3 **Argolikós Kólpos** *G* Greece
55B3 **Árgos** Greece
55B3 **Argostólion** Greece
22B3 **Arguello,Pt** USA
106B2 **Argyle,L** Aust
56C1 **Ärhus** Den
100A3 **Ariamsvlei** Namibia
50B1 **Arian zón** *R* Spain
34C2 **Arias** Arg
97B3 **Aribinda** Burkina
30B2 **Arica** Chile
84C2 **Arifwala** Pak
Arihā = Jericho
27L1 **Arima** Trinidad
35B1 **Arinos** Brazil

33F6 Arinos R Brazil
23A2 Ario de Rosales Mexico
27L1 Aripo,Mt Trinidad
33E6 Aripuana Brazil
33E5 Aripuaná R Brazil
44B3 Arisaig Scot
87B2 Ariskere India
13B2 Aristazabal I Can
34B3 Arizona Arg
9B3 Arizona State, USA
39G7 Arjäng Sweden
61F3 Arkadak Russian Fed
19B3 Arkadelphia USA
65H4 Arkaly Kazakhstan
11A3 Arkansas State, USA
11A3 Arkansas R USA
18A2 Arkansas City USA
64F3 Arkhangel'sk Russian Fed
41B3 Arklow Irish Rep
47D1 Arlberg P Austria
49C3 Arles France
19A3 Arlington Texas, USA
15C3 Arlington Virginia, USA
20B1 Arlington Washington, USA
97C3 Arlit Niger
57B3 Arlon Belg
Armageddon = Megiddo
45C1 Armagh County, N Ire
45C1 Armagh N Ire
61F5 Armavir Russian Fed
23A2 Armenia Mexico
32B3 Armenia Colombia
65F5 Armenia Republic, Europe
107E4 Armidale Aust
13D2 Armstrong Can
7C3 Arnaud R Can
92B2 Arnauti C Cyprus
56B2 Arnhem Neth
106C2 Arnhem,C Aust
106C2 Arnhem Land Aust
22B1 Arnold USA
15C1 Arnprior Can
46E1 Arnsberg Germany
100A3 Aroab Namibia
47C2 Arona Italy
12B2 Aropuk L USA
52A1 Arosa Switz
97A3 Arquipélago dos Bijagós Arch Guinea-Bissau
93D3 Ar Ramādi Iraq
42B2 Arran I Scot
93C2 Ar Raqqah Syria
95A2 Ar Rāqubah Libya
49C1 Arras France
96A2 Arrecife Canary Is
34C2 Arrecifes Arg
23A1 Arriaga Mexico
93E3 Ar Rifā't Iraq
93E3 Ar Rihāb Desert Region Iraq
91A5 Ar Riyād S Arabia
44B3 Arrochar Scot
111A2 Arrowtown NZ
23B1 Arroyo Seco Mexico
91B4 Ar Ru'ays Qatar
91C5 Ar Rustaq Oman
93D3 Ar Rutbah Iraq
47D2 Arsiero Italy
61G2 Arsk Russian Fed
55B3 Árta Greece
23A2 Arteaga Mexico
63B2 Artemovsk Russian Fed
63D2 Artemovskiy Russian Fed
9C3 Artesia USA
111B2 Arthur's P NZ
112C2 Artigas Base Ant
29E2 Artigas Urug
4H3 Artillery L Can
48C1 Artois Region, France
112C2 Arturo Prat Base Ant
93D1 Artvin Turk

99D2 Aru Zaïre
33G6 Aruanã Brazil
27C4 Aruba I Caribbean S
86B1 Arun R Nepal
86C1 Arunáchal Pradesh Union Territory, India
87B3 Aruppukkottai India
99D3 Arusha Tanz
98C2 Aruwimi R Zaïre
68C2 Arvayheer Mongolia
47B2 Arve R France
7C5 Arvida Can
38H5 Arvidsjaur Sweden
39G7 Arvika Sweden
21B2 Arvin USA
94B1 Arwad I Syria
61F2 Arzamas Russian Fed
84C2 Asadabad Afghan
75A2 Asahi R Japan
74E2 Asahi dake Mt Japan
74E2 Asahikawa Japan
86B2 Asansol India
95A2 Asawanwah Well Libya
61K2 Asbest Russian Fed
15D2 Asbury Park USA
103H5 Ascension I Atlantic O
57B3 Aschaffenburg Germany
56C2 Aschersleben Germany
52B2 Ascoli Piceno Italy
47C1 Ascona Switz
99E1 Aseb Eritrea
96C2 Asedjirad Upland Alg
32B3 Asela Eth
38H6 Asele Sweden
54B2 Asenovgrad Bulg
46C2 Asfeld France
61J2 Asha Russian Fed
17B1 Ashburn USA
111B2 Ashburton NZ
106A3 Ashburton R Aust
92B3 Ashdod Israel
19B3 Ashdown USA
11B3 Asheville USA
109D1 Ashford Eng
43E4 Ashford Eng
Ashgabat = Ashkhabad
74D3 Ashikaga Japan
75A2 Ashizuri-misaki Pt Japan
65G6 Ashkhabad Turkmenistan
10B3 Ashland Kentucky, USA
18A1 Ashland Nebraska, USA
14B2 Ashland Ohio, USA
8A2 Ashland Oregon, USA
109C1 Ashley Aust
16B2 Ashokan Res USA
94B3 Ashqelon Israel
93D3 Ash Shabakh Iraq
91C4 Ash Sha'm UAE
93D2 Ash Sharqāt Iraq
93E3 Ash Shatrah Iraq
81C4 Ash Shihr Yemen
91A4 Ash Shumlul S Arabia
14B2 Ashtabula USA
7C3 Ashuanipi L Can
92C3 'Aşi R Syria
47D2 Asiago Italy
53A2 Asinara I Medit S
65K4 Asino Russian Fed
93D2 Aşkale Turk
39G7 Askersund Sweden
84C1 Asmar Afghan
95C3 Asmera Eritrea
75A2 Aso Japan
99D1 Asosa Eth
111A2 Aspiring,Mt NZ
93C2 As Sabkhah Syria
91A5 As Salamiyah S Arabia
92C3 As Salamīyah Syria
93D3 As Salmān Iraq
86C1 Assam State, India

93E3 As Samāwah Iraq
91B5 As Şanām Region, S Arabia
94C2 As Sanamayn Syria
56B2 Assen Neth
56B1 Assens Den
95A1 As Sidrah Libya
5H5 Assiniboia Can
5G4 Assiniboine,Mt Can
30F3 Assis Brazil
93C3 As Sukhnah Syria
93E2 As Sulaymānīyah Iraq
91A5 As Summan Region, S Arabia
99E3 Assumption I Seychelles
92C3 As Suwaydā' Syria
93D3 As Suwayrah Iraq
93E2 Astara Azerbaijan
52A2 Asti Italy
55C3 Astipálaia I Greece
50A1 Astorga Spain
8A2 Astoria USA
61G4 Astrakhan' Russian Fed
50A1 Asturias Region, Spain
30E4 Asunción Par
99D2 Aswa R Uganda
80B3 Aswān Egypt
95C2 Aswān High Dam Egypt
95C2 Asyût Egypt
92C3 As Zilaf Syria
97C4 Atakpamé Togo
71D4 Atambua Indon
6E3 Atangmik Greenland
96A2 Atar Maur
65J5 Atasu Kazakhstan
95C3 Atatisk Baraji Res Turkmenistan
95C3 Atbara Sudan
65H4 Atbasar Kazakhstan
11A4 Atchafalaya B USA
10A3 Atchison USA
16B3 Atco USA
23A1 Atenguillo Mexico
52B2 Atessa Italy
46B1 Ath Belg
13E2 Athabasca Can
5G4 Athabasca R Can
5H4 Athabasca L Can
45B2 Athenry Irish Rep
Athens = Athínai
11B3 Athens Georgia, USA
14B3 Athens Ohio, USA
19A3 Athens Texas, USA
55B3 Athínai Greece
41B3 Athlone Irish Rep
16C1 Athol USA
55B2 Athos Mt Greece
45C2 Athy Irish Rep
98B1 Ati Chad
7A5 Atikoken Can
61F3 Atkarsk Russian Fed
18B2 Atkins USA
23B2 Atlacomulco Mexico
11B3 Atlanta Georgia, USA
14B2 Atlanta Michigan, USA
18A1 Atlantic USA
10C3 Atlantic City USA
16B2 Atlantic Highlands USA
103H8 Atlantic Indian Basin Atlantic O
103H7 Atlantic Indian Ridge Atlantic O
96C1 Atlas Saharien Mts Alg
4E4 Atlin Can
4E4 Atlin L Can
94B2 'Atlit Israel
23B2 Atlixco Mexico
11B3 Atmore USA
101D3 Atofinandrahana Madag
12D3 Atognak I USA
19A3 Atoka USA
23A1 Atotonilco Mexico
23B2 Atoyac R Mexico
32B2 Atrato R Colombia

91B5 Attaf Region, UAE
81C3 At Tā'if S Arabia
94C2 At Tall Syria
17A1 Attalla USA
7B4 Attauapiskat Can
7B4 Attauapiskat R Can
93D3 At Taysiyah Desert Region S Arabia
14A2 Attica Indiana, USA
46C2 Attigny France
15D2 Attleboro Massachusetts, USA
76D3 Attopeu Laos
92C4 At Tubayq Upland S Arabia
34B3 Atuel R Arg
39H7 Atvidaberg Sweden
22B2 Atwater USA
49D3 Aubagne France
46C2 Aube Department, France
49C3 Aubenas France
17A1 Auburn Alabama, USA
21A2 Auburn California, USA
14A2 Auburn Indiana, USA
18A1 Auburn Nebraska, USA
15C2 Auburn New York, USA
20B1 Auburn Washington, USA
48C3 Auch France
110B1 Auckland NZ
105G6 Auckland Is NZ
48C3 Aude R France
7B4 Auden Can
47B1 Audincourt France
109C1 Augathella Aust
57C3 Augsburg Germany
106A4 Augusta Aust
11B3 Augusta Georgia, USA
18A2 Augusta Kansas, USA
10D2 Augusta Maine, USA
12D3 Augustine I USA
58C2 Augustów Pol
106A3 Augustus,Mt Aust
46A2 Aumale France
85D3 Auraiya India
85D5 Aurangābād India
96C1 Aurès Mts Alg
48C3 Aurillac France
8C3 Aurora Colorado, USA
10B2 Aurora Illinois, USA
14B3 Aurora Indiana, USA
18B2 Aurora Mississippi, USA
100A3 Aus Namibia
14B2 Au Sable USA
10A2 Austin Minnesota, USA
21B2 Austin Nevada, USA
9D3 Austin Texas, USA
106C3 Australia Fed. State/ Monarchy
107D4 Australian Alps Mts Aust
37E4 Austria Federal Republic, Europe
46A1 Authie R France
24B3 Autlán Mexico
49C2 Autun France
49C2 Auvergne Region, France
49C2 Auxerre France
46B1 Auxi-le-Châteaux France
49C2 Avallon France
22C4 Avalon USA
7E5 Avalon Pen Can
35B2 Avaré Brazil
90D3 Avaz Iran
94B3 Avedat Hist Site Israel
33F4 Aveiro Brazil
50A1 Aveiro Port
29E2 Avellaneda Arg
53B2 Avellino Italy
46B1 Avesnes-sur-Helpe France

Avesta

39H6 Avesta Sweden
52B2 Avezzano Italy
44C3 Aviemore Scot
111B2 Aviemore,L NZ
47B2 Avigliana Italy
49C3 Avignon France
50B1 Avila Spain
50A1 Aviles Spain
47D1 Avisio R Italy
108B3 Avoca R Aust
43C4 Avon County, Eng
43D4 Avon R Dorset, Eng
43D3 Avon R Warwick, Eng
43C4 Avonmouth Wales
17B2 Avon Park USA
46B2 Avre R France
54A2 Avtovac Bosnia-Herzegovina
94C2 A'waj R Syria
74D4 Awaji-shima B Japan
99E2 Aware Eth
111A2 Awarua Pt NZ
99E2 Awash Eth
99E2 Awash R Eth
75B1 Awa-shima I Japan
111B2 Awatere R NZ
95A2 Awbāri Libya
98C2 Aweil Sudan
99E2 Awjilah Libya
96A2 Awserd Well Mor
6A2 Axel Heiburg I Can
43C4 Axminster Eng
75B1 Ayabe Japan
29E3 Ayacucho Arg
32C6 Ayacucho Peru
65K5 Ayaguz Kazakhstan
82C2 Ayakkum Hu L China
50A2 Ayamonte Spain
63F2 Ayan Russian Fed
32C6 Ayaviri Peru
92A2 Aydin Turk
55C3 Ayios Evstrátios I Greece
43D4 Aylesbury Eng
13D2 Aylmer,Mt Can
94C2 'Ayn al Fijah Syria
93D2 Ayn Zālah Iraq
95B2 Ayn Zuwayyah Well Libya
99D2 Ayod Sudan
107D2 Ayr Aust
42B2 Ayr Scot
42B2 Ayr R Scot
42B2 Ayre,Pt of Eng
54C2 Aytos Bulg
55C3 Ayutla Mexico
76C3 Ayutthaya Thai
23A1 Ayutla Mexico
55C3 Ayvacık Turk
55C3 Ayvalik Turk
86A1 Azamgarh India
97B3 Azaouad Desert Region Mali
97D3 Azare Nig
92C2 A'Zāz Syria
Azbine = Aïr
65F5 Azerbaijan Republic, Russian Fed
32B4 Azogues Ecuador
Azores = Açores
98C1 Azoum R Chad
60E4 Azov, Sea of Russian Fed/Ukraine
Azovskoye More = Azov, Sea of
96B1 Azrou Mor
34D3 Azucena Arg
32A2 Azuero,Pen de Panama
29E3 Azúl Arg
94C2 Az-Zabdani Syria
91C5 Az Zāhirah Mts Oman
95A2 Az Zahra Iraq
96A2 Azzeffal R Maur
93E3 Az Zubayr Iraq

B

94B2 Ba'abda Leb
92C3 Ba'albek Leb
94B3 Ba'al Hazor Mt Israel

99E2 Baardheere Somalia
54C2 Babadag Rom
92A1 Babaeski Turk
32B4 Babahoyo Ecuador
81C4 Bāb al Mandab Str Djibouti/Yemen
71D4 Babar I Indon
99D3 Babati Tanz
60E2 Babayevo Russian Fed
14B2 Baberton USA
13B1 Babine R Can
5F4 Babine L Can
90B2 Bābol Iran
79B2 Babuyan Chan Phil
79B2 Babuyan Is Phil
31C2 Bacabal Brazil
71D4 Bacan I Indon
60C4 Bacău Rom
76D1 Bac Can Viet
108B3 Bacchus Marsh Aust
82B2 Bachu China
4J3 Back R Can
12J2 Backbone Ranges Mts Can
76D1 Bac Ninh Viet
79B3 Bacolod Phil
79B3 Baco,Mt Phil
87B2 Badagara India
72A1 Badain Jaran Shamo Desert China
50A2 Badajoz Spain
51C1 Badalona Spain
93D3 Badanah S Arabia
46D2 Bad Bergzabern Germany
46D1 Bad Ems Germany
47C1 Baden Switz
57B3 Baden-Baden Germany
57B3 Baden-Württemberg State, Germany
57C3 Badgastein Austria
22C2 Badger USA
57B2 Bad-Godesberg Germany
57B2 Bad Hersfeld Germany
46D1 Bad Honnef Germany
85B4 Badin Pak
52B1 Bad Ischl Austria
93C3 Badiyat ash Sham Desert Region Jordan/Iraq
57B3 Bad-Kreuznach Germany
46D1 Bad Nevenahr-Ahrweiler Germany
47C1 Bad Ragaz Switz
57C3 Bad Tolz Germany
87C3 Badulla Sri Lanka
50B2 Baena Spain
97A3 Bafatá Guinea-Bissau
4H2 Baffin Region Can
6C2 Baffin B Greenland/Can
6C2 Baffin I Can
98B2 Bafia Cam
97A3 Bafing R Mali
97A3 Bafoulabé Mali
98B2 Bafoussam Cam
90C3 Bāfq Iran
60E5 Bafra Burun Pt Turk
91C4 Bāft Iran
98C2 Bafwasende Zaïre
86A1 Bagaha India
87B1 Bāgalkot India
99D3 Bagamoyo Tanz
29F2 Bagé Brazil
93D3 Baghdād Iraq
86B2 Bagherhat Bang
91C3 Bāghīn Iran
84B1 Baghlan Afghan
49C3 Bagnols-sur-Cèze France
97B3 Bagoé R Mali
Bagu = Pegu
79B2 Baguio Phil
86B1 Bāhādurābād India
11C4 Bahamas,The Is Caribbean S
86B2 Baharampur India
92A4 Bahariya Oasis Egypt

84C3 Bahawalpur Pak
84C3 Bahawalpur Province, Pak
85C3 Bahawathagar Pak
Bahia = Salvador
31C4 Bahia State, Brazil
29D3 Bahía Blanca Arg
29D3 Bahía Blanca B Arg
34A3 Bahía Concepción B Chile
35C2 Bahia da Ilha Grande B Brazil
24B2 Bahía de Banderas B Mexico
24C2 Bahía de Campeche B Mexico
25D3 Bahia de la Ascension B Mexico
24B3 Bahía de Petacalco B Mexico
96A2 Bahia de Rio de Oro B Mor
35C2 Bahia de Sepetiba B Brazil
29C6 Bahía Grande B Arg
9B4 Bahia Kino Mexico
24A2 Bahia Magdalena B Mexico
24A2 Bahia Sebastia Vizcaino B Mexico
90D3 Bahar Dar Eth
86A1 Bahraich India
80D3 Bahrain Sheikhdom, Arabian Pen
93D3 Bahr al Milh L Iraq
98C2 Bahr Aouk R Chad/CAR
Bahrat Lut = Dead S
98C2 Bahr el Arab Watercourse Sudan
99D2 Bahr el Ghazal R Sudan
98B1 Bahr el Ghazal Watercourse Chad
101H1 Baia de Maputo R Mozam
31B2 Baia de Marajó B Brazil
101D2 Baiá de Pemba B Mozam
32C3 Baia de São Marcos B Brazil
50A2 Baia de Setúbal B Port
31D4 Baia de Todos os Santos B Brazil
100A2 Baia dos Tigres Angola
60B4 Baia Mare Rom
98B2 Baibokoum Chad
69E2 Baicheng China
101E2 Baie Antongila B Madag
7D5 Baie-Comeau Can
101D2 Baie de Bombetoka B Madag
101D2 Baie de Mahajamba B Madag
101D3 Baie de St Augustin B Madag
94B2 Baie de St Georges B Leb
10D2 Baie des Chaleurs B Can
7C4 Baie-du-Poste Can
72B3 Baihe China
72C3 Bai He R China
93D3 Ba'iji Iraq
86A2 Baikunthpur India
Baile Atha Cliath = Dublin
54B2 Băilesti Rom
46B1 Bailleul France
72A3 Baima China
17B1 Bainbridge USA
12B2 Baird Inlet USA
4B3 Baird Mts USA
72D1 Bairin Youqi China
72D1 Bairin Zuoqi China
107D4 Bairnsdale Aust
79B4 Bais Hung
54A1 Baja Hung
9B3 Baja California State, Mexico

24A1 Baja California Pen Mexico
61J2 Bakal Russian Fed
98C2 Bakala CAR
97A3 Bakel Sen
8C2 Baker Montana, USA
8B2 Baker Oregon, USA
6A3 Baker Foreland Pt Can
4J3 Baker L Can
4J3 Baker Lake Can
9B3 Bakersfield USA
90C2 Bakharden Turkmenistan
90C2 Bakhardok Turkmenistan
60D3 Bakhmach Ukraine
38C1 Bakkafloi B Iceland
99D2 Bako Eth
98C2 Bakouma CAR
66A4 Baku Azerbaijan
Baky = Baku
92B2 Balá Turk
79A4 Balabac I Phil
70C3 Balabac Str Malay
78C2 Balaikarangan Indon
108A2 Balaklava Aust
61G3 Balakovo Russian Fed
86A2 Balāngir India
61F3 Balashov Russian Fed
86B2 Balasore India
86A3 Balāt Egypt
52C1 Balaton L Hung
45C2 Balbriggan Irish Rep
29E3 Balcarce Arg
54C2 Balchik Bulg
111B3 Balclutha NZ
18B2 Bald Knob USA
17B1 Baldwin USA
9C3 Baldy Peak Mt USA
Balearic Is = Islas Baleares
78C2 Baleh R Malay
79B2 Baler Phil
61H2 Balezino Russian Fed
106A1 Bali I Indon
92A2 Balıkesir Turk
93C2 Balikh R Syria
78D3 Balikpapan Indon
79B2 Baliungan Chan Phil
79A2 Bali S Indon
35A1 Baliza Brazil
84B1 Balkh Afghan
65J5 Balkhash Kazakhstan
44B3 Ballachulish Scot
45B2 Ballaghaderreen Irish Rep
42B2 Ballantrae Scot
4G2 Ballantyne Str Can
87B2 Ballapur India
107D4 Ballarat Aust
44C3 Ballater Scot
112C7 Balleny Is Ant
86A1 Ballia India
109D1 Ballina Aust
41B3 Ballina Irish Rep
45B2 Ballinasloe Irish Rep
45B2 Ballinrobe Irish Rep
55A2 Ballsh Alb
45B1 Ballycastle Irish Rep
45C1 Ballycastle N Ire
45B1 Ballymena N Ire
45C1 Ballymoney N Ire
45B1 Ballyshannon Irish Rep
45B1 Ballyvaghan Irish Rep
108B3 Balmoral Aust
34C2 Balnearia Arg
84B3 Balochistān Region, Pak
100A2 Balombo Angola
109C1 Balonn R Aust
85C3 Bālotra India
86A1 Balrāmpur India
107D4 Balranald Aust
31B3 Balsas Brazil
23B2 Balsas Mexico
24B3 Balsas R Mexico
60C4 Balta Ukraine
39H7 Baltic S N Europe

92B3 Baltim Egypt
45B3 Baltimore Irish Rep
10C3 Baltimore USA
86B1 Bālurghāt India
61H4 Balykski Kazakhstan
91C4 Bam Iran
98B1 Bama Nig
97B3 Bamako Mali
98C2 Bambari CAR
17B1 Bamberg USA
57C3 Bamberg Germany
98C2 Bambili Zaire
35B2 Bambui Brazil
98B2 Bamenda Cam
13C3 Bamfield Can
98B2 Bamingui R CAR
98B2 Bamingui Bangoran National Park CAR
84B2 Bamiyan Afghan
91D4 Bampur Iran
91D4 Bampur R Iran
98C2 Banalia Zaire
97B3 Banamba Mali
76C3 Ban Aranyaprathet Thai
76C2 Ban Ban Laos
77C4 Ban Betong Thai
45C1 Banbridge N Ire
43D3 Banbury Eng
44C3 Banchory Scot
25D3 Banco Chinchorro Is Mexico
15C1 Bancroft Can
86A1 Bānda India
70A3 Banda Aceh Indon
97B4 Bandama R Ivory Coast
91C4 Bandar Abbās Iran
90A2 Bandar Anzali Iran
99F2 Bandarbeyla Somalia
91B4 Bandar-e Daylam Iran
91B4 Bandar-e Lengheh Iran
91B4 Bandar-e Māqām Iran
91B4 Bandar-e Rig Iran
90B2 Bandar-e Torkoman Iran
91A3 Bandar Khomeyni Iran
78C2 Bandar Seri Begawan Brunei
71D4 Banda S Indon
91C4 Band Boni Iran
35C2 Bandeira Mt Brazil
97B3 Bandiagara Mali
60C5 Bandirma Turk
45B3 Bandon Irish Rep
98B3 Bandundu Zaire
78B4 Bandung Indon
25E2 Banes Cuba
13D2 Banff Can
44C3 Banff Scot
5G4 Banff R Can
13D2 Banff Nat Pk Can
87B2 Bangalore India
98C2 Bangassou CAR
70C3 Banggi I Malay
95B1 Banghāzi Libya
76D2 Bang Hieng R Laos
78B3 Bangka I Indon
78A3 Bangko Indon
76C3 Bangkok Thai
82C3 Bangladesh Republic, Asia
84D2 Bangong Co L China
10D2 Bangor Maine, USA
45D1 Bangor N Ire
16B2 Bangor Pennsylvania, USA
42B3 Bangor Wales
78D3 Bangsalsembera Indon
76B3 Bang Saphan Yai Thai
79B2 Bangued Phil
98B2 Bangui CAR
100C2 Bangweulu L Zambia
77C4 Ban Hat Yai Thai
76C2 Ban Hin Heup Laos
76C1 Ban Houei Sai Laos
76B3 Ban Hua Hin Thai

97B3 Bani R Mali
97C3 Bani Bangou Niger
95A1 Bani Walid Libya
92C2 Bāniyās Syria
94B2 Bāniyas Syria
52C2 Banja Luka Bosnia-Herzegovina
78C3 Banjarmasin Indon
97A3 Banjul The Gambia
77B4 Ban Kantang Thai
76D2 Ban Khemmarat Laos
77B4 Ban Khok Kloi Thai
71F5 Banks I Aust
5E4 Banks I British Columbia, Can
4F2 Banks I Northwest Territories, Can
20C1 Banks L USA
111B2 Banks Pen NZ
109C4 Banks Str Aust
86B2 Bankura India
76B2 Ban Mae Sariang Thai
76B2 Ban Mae Sot Thai
76D3 Ban Me Thuot Viet
45C1 Bann R N Ire
77B4 Ban Na San Thai
84C2 Bannu Pak
34A3 Baños Maule Chile
76C2 Ban Pak Neun Laos
77C4 Ban Pak Phanang Thai
76D3 Ban Ru Kroy Camb
76B3 Ban Sai Yok Thai
76C3 Ban Sattahip Thai
59B3 Banská Bystrica Slovakia
85C4 Bānswāra India
77B4 Ban Tha Kham Thai
76D2 Ban Thateng Laos
76C2 Ban Tha Tum Thai
41B3 Bantry Irish Rep
41A3 Bantry B Irish Rep
76D3 Ban Ya Soup Viet
78C4 Banyuwangi Indon
72C3 Baofeng China
76C1 Bao Ha Viet
72B3 Baoji China
76D3 Bao Loc Viet
68B4 Baoshan China
72C1 Baotou China
87C1 Bāpatla India
46B1 Bapaume France
93D3 Ba'Qūbah Iraq
32J7 Baquerizo Moreno Ecuador
54A2 Bar Montenegro, Yugos
99D1 Bara Sudan
99E2 Baraawe Somalia
78D3 Barabai Indon
86A1 Bāra Banki India
65J4 Barabinsk Russian Fed
65J4 Barabinskaya Step Steppe Kazakhstan/Russian Fed
50B1 Baracaldo Spain
26C2 Baracoa Cuba
94C2 Baradá R Syria
109C2 Baradine Aust
87A1 Bārāmati India
84C2 Baramula Pak
85D3 Bārān India
79B3 Barangas Phil
4E4 Baranof I USA
60C3 Baranovichi Belorussia
108A2 Baratta Aust
86B1 Barauni India
31C6 Barbacena Brazil
27F4 Barbados I Caribbean S
51C1 Barbastro Spain
101H1 Barberton S Africa
48B2 Barbezieux France
32C2 Barbòsa Colombia
27E3 Barbuda I Caribbean S
107D3 Barcaldine Aust
53C3 Barcellona Italy
51C1 Barcelona Spain

33E1 Barcelona Ven
107D3 Barcoo R Aust
34B3 Barda del Medio Arg
95A2 Bardai Chad
29C3 Bardas Blancas Arg
86B2 Barddhamān India
59C3 Bardejov Slovakia
47C2 Bardi Italy
47B2 Bardonecchia Italy
43B3 Bardsey I Wales
84D3 Bareilly India
64D2 Barentsoya I Barents S
64E2 Barents S Russian Fed
95C3 Barentu Eritrea
86A2 Bargarh India
47B2 Barge Italy
63D2 Barguzin Russian Fed
63D2 Barguzin R Russian Fed
86B2 Barhi India
53C2 Bari Italy
51D2 Barika Alg
32C2 Barinas Ven
86B2 Bāripāda India
85C4 Bāri Sādri India
86C2 Barisal Bang
78C3 Barito R Indon
95A2 Barjuj Watercourse Libya
73A3 Barkam China
18C2 Barkley,L USA
13B3 Barkley Sd Can
100B4 Barkly East S Africa
106C2 Barkly Tableland Mts Aust
46C2 Bar-le-Duc France
106A3 Barlee,L Aust
106A3 Barlee Range Mts Aust
53C2 Barletta Italy
79B1 Barmer India
108B2 Barmera Aust
43B3 Barmouth Wales
42D2 Barnard Castle Eng
6C4 Barnaul Russian Fed
16B3 Barnegat USA
16B3 Barnegat B USA
6C2 Barnes Icecap Can
17B1 Barnesville Georgia, USA
14B3 Barnesville Ohio, USA
42D3 Barnsley Eng
43B4 Barnstaple Eng
97C4 Baro Nig
86C1 Barpeta India
32D1 Barquisimeto Ven
31C4 Barra Brazil
44A3 Barra I Scot
109D2 Barraba Aust
23A2 Barra de Navidad Mexico
35C2 Barra de Pirai Brazil
35A1 Barragem de São Simão Res Brazil
35A1 Barra do Garças Brazil
35B1 Barragem Agua Vermelha Res Brazil
50A2 Barragem do Castelo do Bode Res Port
50A2 Barragem do Maranhão Res Port
35A2 Barragem Três Irmãos Res Brazil
44A3 Barra Head Pt Scot
31C6 Barra Mansa Brazil
32B6 Barranca Peru
32C2 Barrancabermeja Colombia
33E2 Barrancas Ven
30E4 Barranqueras Arg
32C1 Barranquilla Colombia
44A3 Barra,Sound of Chan Scot
16C1 Barre USA
34B2 Barreal Arg
31C4 Barreiras Brazil
50A2 Barreiro Port

31D3 Barreiros Brazil
107D5 Barren,C Aust
12D3 Barren Is USA
31B6 Barretos Brazil
13E2 Barrhead Can
14C2 Barrie Can
13C2 Barrière Can
108B2 Barrier Range Mts Aust
107E4 Barrington,Mt Aust
27N2 Barrouaillie St Vincent and the Grenadines
4C2 Barrow USA
45C2 Barrow R Irish Rep
106C3 Barrow Creek Aust
106A3 Barrow I Aust
42C2 Barrow-in-Furness Eng
4C2 Barrow,Pt USA
6A2 Barrow Str Can
15C1 Barry's Bay Can
87B1 Barsi India
9B3 Barstow USA
49C2 Bar-sur-Aube France
33F2 Bartica Guyana
92B1 Bartin Turk
107D2 Bartle Frere,Mt Aust
9D3 Bartlesville USA
101C3 Bartolomeu Dias Mozam
58C2 Bartoszyce Pol
78C4 Barung I Indon
85D4 Barwāh India
85C4 Barwāni India
109C1 Barwon R Aust
61G3 Barysh Russian Fed
98B2 Basankusu Zaire
34D2 Basavilbasa Arg
79B1 Basco Phil
52A1 Basel Switz
53C2 Basento R Italy
13E2 Bashaw Can
79B1 Bashi Chan Phil
61H3 Bashkortostan Russian Fed
79B4 Basilan I Phil
43E4 Basildon Eng
43D4 Basingstoke Eng
8B2 Basin Region USA
93E3 Basra Iraq
46D2 Bas-Rhin Department, France
76D3 Bassac R Camb
13E2 Bassano Can
52B1 Bassano Italy
47D2 Bassano del Grappa Italy
97C4 Bassari Togo
101C3 Bassas da India I Mozam Chan
76A2 Bassein Burma
27E3 Basse Terre Guadeloupe
97C4 Bassila Benin
22C2 Bass Lake USA
107D4 Bass Str Aust
39G7 Bästad Sweden
91B4 Bastak Iran
86A1 Basti India
52A2 Bastia Corse
57B3 Bastogne Belg
19B3 Bastrop Louisiana, USA
19A3 Bastrop Texas, USA
98A2 Bata Eq Guinea
78D3 Batakan Indon
84D2 Batala India
68B3 Batang China
98B2 Batangafo CAR
79B1 Batan Is Phil
35B2 Batatais Brazil
15C2 Batavia USA
109D3 Batemans Bay Aust
17B1 Batesburg USA
18B2 Batesville Arkansas, USA
19C3 Batesville Mississippi, USA
43C4 Bath Eng
15C2 Bath New York, USA
98B1 Batha R Chad
107D4 Bathurst Aust
7D5 Bathurst Can

Bathurst,C

4F2 Bathurst,C Can
106C2 Bathurst I Aust
4H2 Bathurst I Can
4H3 Bathurst Inlet *B* Can
97B3 Batié Burkina
90B3 Bātlāq-e-Gavkhūni
   Salt Flat Iran
109C3 Batlow Aust
93D2 Batman Turk
96C1 Batna Alg
11A3 Baton Rouge USA
94B1 Batroun Leb
76C3 Battambang Camb
87C3 Batticaloa Sri Lanka
13F2 Battle *R* Can
10B2 Battle Creek USA
7E4 Battle Harbour Can
20C2 Battle Mountain USA
78D2 Botukelau Indon
65F5 Batumi Georgia
77C5 Batu Pahat Malay
78A3 Baturaja Indon
94B2 Bat Yam Israel
71D4 Baubau Indon
97C3 Bauchi Nig
47B2 Bauges *Mts* France
7E4 Bauld,C Can
47B1 Baumes-les-Dames
   France
63D2 Baunt Russian Fed
31B6 Bauru Brazil
35A1 Baus Brazil
57C2 Bautzen Germany
78C4 Baween *I* Indon
95B2 Bawiti Egypt
97B3 Bawku Ghana
76B2 Bawlake Burma
108A2 Bawlen Aust
17B1 Baxley USA
25E2 Bayamo Cuba
78D4 Bayan Indon
68C2 Bayandzürh
   Mongolia
68B3 Bayan Har Shan *Mts*
   China
72A1 Bayan Mod China
72B1 Bayan Obo China
47A2 Bayard *P* France
12J3 Bayard,Mt Can
63D3 Bayasgalant
   Mongolia
79B3 Baybay Phil
93D1 Bayburt Turk
10B2 Bay City Michigan,
   USA
19A4 Bay City Texas, USA
92B2 Bay Dağlari Turk
64H3 Baydaratskaya Guba
   B Russian Fed
99E2 Baydhabo Somalia
48B2 Bayeux France
47D1 Bayerische Alpen
   Mts Germany
57C3 Bayern State,
   Germany
92C3 Bāyir Jordan
63C2 Baykalskiy Khrebet
   Mts Russian Fed
63B1 Baykit Russian Fed
63B3 Baylik Shan *Mts*
   China/Mongolia
61J3 Baynak Russian Fed
79B2 Bayombong Phil
48B3 Bayonne France
57C3 Bayreuth Germany
19C3 Bay St Louis USA
15D2 Bay Shore USA
15C1 Bays,L of Can
68A2 Baytik Shan *Mts*
   China
   Bayt Lahm =
   Bethlehem
19B4 Baytown USA
50B2 Baza Spain
59D3 Bazaliya Ukraine
48B3 Bazas France
73B3 Bazhong China
91D4 Bazmān Iran
16C1 Bcharre Leb
16B3 Beach Haven USA
43E4 Beachy Head Eng
16C2 Beacon USA
101D2 Bealanana Madag
18B1 Beardstown USA

Bear *I* = Bjørnøya
22B1 Bear Valley USA
8D2 Beatrice USA
44C2 Beatrice *Oilfield* N
   Sea
13C1 Beatton *R* Can
5F4 Beatton River Can
29E6 Beauchene Is
   Falkland Is
109D1 Beaudesert Aust
1B5 Beaufort *S* Can
100B4 Beaufort West
   S Africa
15D1 Beauharnois Can
44B3 Beauly Scot
21B3 Beaumont California,
   USA
11A3 Beaumont Texas,
   USA
49C2 Beaune France
48C2 Beauvais France
13F1 Beauval Can
12E1 Beaver Alaska, USA
13F2 Beaver *R*
   Saskatchewan, Can
4D3 Beaver Creek Can
12E1 Beaver Creek USA
18C2 Beaver Dam
   Kentucky, USA
13E2 Beaverhill L Can
14A1 Beaver I USA
18B2 Beaver L USA
13D1 Beaverlodge Can
85C3 Bebear Indon
34B2 Beazley Arg
35B2 Bebedouro Brazil
43E3 Beccles Eng
54B1 Bečej Serbia, Yugos
96B1 Béchar Alg
12C3 Becharof L USA
11B3 Beckley USA
43D3 Bedford County, Eng
43D3 Bedford Eng
14A3 Bedford Indiana,
   USA
27M2 Bedford Pt Grenada
4D2 Beechey Pt USA
109C3 Beechworth Aust
109D1 Beenleigh Aust
92B3 Beersheba Israel
   Beër Sheva =
   Beersheba
94B3 Beër Sheva *R* Israel
9D4 Beeville USA
98C2 Befale Zaïre
101D2 Befandriana Madag
109C3 Bega Aust
91B3 Behbehān Iran
12H3 Behm Canal *Sd* USA
90B2 Behshahr Iran
84B2 Behsūd Afghan
69E2 Bei'an China
73B5 Beihai China
72D2 Beijing China
76E1 Beiliu China
73B4 Beipan Jiang *R*
   China
72E1 Beipiao China
   Beira = Sofala
92C3 Beirut Leb
68B2 Bei Shan *Mts* China
94B2 Beit ed Dine Leb
94B3 Beit Jala Israel
50A2 Beja Port
96C1 Beja Tunisia
96C1 Bejaïa Alg
50A1 Béjar Spain
90C3 Bejestān Iran
59B3 Békéscsaba Hung
101D3 Bekily Madag
86A1 Bela India
85B3 Bela Pak
78C2 Belaga Malay
16A3 Bel Air USA
87B1 Belamoalli India
71D3 Belang Indon
70A3 Belangpidie Indon
   Belarus = Belorussia
   Belau = Palau Is.
101C3 Béla Vista Mozam
70A3 Belawan Indon
61J2 Belaya *R* Ukraine
6A2 Belcher Chan Can
7C4 Belcher Is Can

84B1 Belchiragh Afghan
61H3 Belebey Russian Fed
99E2 Beled Weyne
   Somalia
31B2 Belém Brazil
32B3 Belén Colombia
34D2 Belén Urug
9C3 Belen USA
45D1 Belfast N Ire
101H1 Belfast S Africa
45D1 Belfast Lough
   Estuary N Ire
97D1 Bèlfodiyo Eth
42D2 Belford Eng
49D2 Belfort France
87A1 Belgaum India
56A2 Belgium Kingdom,
   N W Europe
60E3 Belgorod
   Russian Fed
60D4 Belgorod
   Dnestrovskiy Ukraine
   Belgrade = Beograd
95A2 Bel Hedan Libya
78B3 Belinyu Indon
78B3 Belitung *I* Indon
25D3 Belize Belize
25D3 Belize Republic,
   Cent America
48C2 Bellac France
5F4 Bella Coola Can
47C2 Bellagio Italy
19A4 Bellaire USA
47C1 Bellano Italy
87B1 Bellary India
109C1 Bellata Aust
47B2 Belledonne *Mts*
   France
8C2 Belle Fourche USA
49D2 Bellegarde France
17B2 Belle Glade USA
7E4 Belle I Can
7E4 Belle Isle *I* France
7E4 Belle Isle,Str of Can
7C5 Belleville Can
18A2 Belleville Kansas,
   USA
20B1 Bellevue
   Washington, USA
109D2 Bellingen Aust
8A2 Bellingham USA
112C2 Bellingshausen *Base*
   Ant
112C3 Bellingshausen S
   Ant
52A1 Bellinzona Switz
32B2 Bello Colombia
107E3 Bellona Reefs
   Nouvelle Calédonie
22B1 Bellota USA
15D2 Bellows Falls USA
6B3 Bell Pen Can
52B1 Belluno Italy
29D2 Bell Ville Arg
31Db Belmonte Brazil
25D3 Belmopan Belize
45B1 Belmullet Irish Rep
69E1 Belogorsk
   Russian Fed
101D3 Beloha Madag
31Cb Belo Horizonte Brazil
10B2 Beloit Wisconsin,
   USA
64E3 Belomorsk
   Russian Fed
61J3 Beloretsk
   Russian Fed
   Belorussia Republic,
   Europe
101D2 Belo-Tsiribihina
   Madag
64E3 Beloye More *S*
   Russian Fed
60C3 Beloye Ozero *L*
   Russian Fed
60E1 Belozersk
   Russian Fed
14B3 Belpre USA
108A2 Beltana Aust
19A3 Belton USA
59D3 Bel'tsy Moldova
16B2 Belvidere New
   Jersey, USA
98B3 Bembe Angola

97C3 Bembéréke Benin
10A2 Bemidji USA
39G6 Bena Nor
98C3 Bena Dibele Zaïre
108C3 Benalla Aust
44B3 Ben Attow *Mt* Scot
50A1 Benavente Spain
44A3 Benbecula *I* Scot
106A4 Bencubbin Aust
8A2 Bend USA
84B3 Ben Dearg *Mt* Scot
60C4 Bendery Moldova
107D4 Bendigo Aust
57C3 Benešov
   Czech Republic
53B2 Benevento Italy
83C4 Bengal,B of Asia
96D1 Ben Gardane Tunisia
72D3 Bengbu China
78A2 Bengkalis Indon
78A3 Bengkulu Indon
100A2 Benguela Angola
92B3 Benha Egypt
84B2 Ben Hope *Mt* Scot
99C2 Beni Zaïre
32D6 Beni *R* Bol
96B1 Beni Abbes Alg
51C1 Benicarló Spain
7A5 Benidji USA
51B2 Benidorm Spain
51C2 Beni Mansour Alg
95C2 Beni Mazâr Egypt
96B1 Beni Mellal Mor
97C4 Benin Republic,
   Africa
97C4 Benin City Nig
95C2 Beni Suef Egypt
44B2 Ben Kilbreck *Mt* Scot
44B3 Ben Lawers *Mt* UK
109C4 Ben Lomond *Mt*
   Aust
44C3 Ben Macdui *Mt* Scot
44A3 Ben More Assynt *Mt*
   Scot
111B2 Benmore,L NZ
44B3 Ben Nevis *Mt* Scot
15D2 Bennington USA
94B2 Bennt Jbail Leb
98B2 Benoué *R* Cam
9B3 Benson Arizona, USA
99C2 Bentiu Sudan
19B3 Benton Arkansas,
   USA
18C2 Benton Kentucky,
   USA
14A2 Benton Harbor USA
97C4 Benue *R* Nig
45B1 Benwee Hd *C*
   Irish Rep
44B3 Ben Wyvis *Mt* Scot
72E1 Benxi China
54B2 Beograd Serbia,
   Yugos
86A2 Beohāri India
74C4 Beppu Japan
55A2 Berat Alb
95C3 Berber Sudan
99E1 Berbera Somalia
98B2 Berbérati CAR
   Berck France
60L4 Berdichev Ukraine
60E4 Berdyansk Ukraine
97B4 Berekum Ghana
22B2 Berenda USA
5J4 Berens *R* Can
5J4 Berens River Can
108A1 Beresford Aust
59C3 Berettyóújfalu Hung
59C3 Bereza Belorussia
59C3 Berezhany Ukraine
65G4 Berezniki
   Russian Fed
60D4 Berezovka Ukraine
64H3 Berezovo
   Russian Fed
92A2 Bergama Turk
52A1 Bergamo Italy
39F6 Bergen Nor
46C1 Bergen op Zoom
   Neth
48C3 Bergerac France
46D1 Bergisch-Gladbach
   Germany
12F2 Bering Gl USA

1C6 Bering Str USA/
Russian Fed
91C4 Berizak Iran
50B2 Berja Spain
8A3 Berkeley USA
112B2 Berkner I Ant
54B2 Berkovitsa Bulg
43D4 Berkshire County,
Eng
16C1 Berkshire Hills USA
13D2 Berland R Can
56C2 Berlin Germany
56C2 Berlin State,
Germany
15D2 Berlin New
Hampshire, USA
30D3 Bermejo Bol
30D4 Bermejo R Arg
3M5 Bermuda I Atlantic O
52A1 Bern Switz
16B2 Bernardsville USA
34C3 Bernasconi Arg
56C2 Bernburg Germany
47B1 Berner Oberland Mts
Switz
6B2 Bernier B Can
57C3 Berounka R
Czech Republic
108B2 Berri Aust
96C1 Berriane Alg
48C2 Berry Region, France
22A1 Berryessa,L USA
11C4 Berry Is The
Bahamas
98B2 Bertoua Cam
45B2 Bertraghboy B
Irish Rep
15C2 Berwick USA
42C2 Berwick-upon-Tweed
Eng
43C3 Berwyn Mts Wales
101D2 Besalampy Madag
49D2 Besançon France
59C3 Beskidy Zachodnie
Mts Pol
93C2 Besni Turk
94B3 Besor R Israel
11B3 Bessemer USA
101D2 Betafo Madag
50A1 Betanzos Spain
94B3 Bet Guvrin Israel
101G1 Bethal S Africa
100A3 Bethanie Namibia
18B1 Bethany Missouri,
USA
18A2 Bethany Oklahoma,
USA
4B3 Bethel Alaska, USA
16C2 Bethel Connecticut,
USA
14B2 Bethel Park USA
15C3 Bethesda USA
94B3 Bethlehem Israel
101G1 Bethlehem S Africa
15C2 Bethlehem USA
48C1 Bethune France
101D3 Betioky Madag
108B1 Betoota Aust
98B2 Betou Congo
82A1 Betpak Dala Steppe
Kazakhstan
101D3 Betroka Madag
7D5 Betsiamites Can
86A1 Bettiah India
12D1 Bettles USA
47C2 Béttola Italy
85D4 Bétul India
85D3 Betwa R India
46D1 Betzdorf Germany
12C3 Beverley,L USA
16D1 Beverly USA
21B3 Beverly Hills USA
97B4 Beyla Guinea
87B2 Beypore India
Beyrouth = Beirut
92B2 Beysehir Turk
92B2 Beysehir Gölü L Turk
94B2 Beyt Shean Israel
47C1 Bezau Austria
60E2 Bezhetsk
Russian Fed
49C3 Béziers France
90C2 Bezmein
Turkmenistan

63C2 Beznosova
Russian Fed
86B1 Bhadgaon Nepal
87C1 Bhadrāchalam India
86B2 Bhadrakh India
87B2 Bhadra Res India
87B2 Bhadravati India
84B3 Bhag Pak
86B1 Bhāgalpur India
84C2 Bhakkar Pak
82D3 Bhamo Burma
85D4 Bhandāra India
85D3 Bharatpur India
85C4 Bharūch India
86B2 Bhatiāpāra Ghat
Bang
84C2 Bhatinda India
87A2 Bhatkal India
86B2 Bhātpāra India
85C4 Bhāvnagar India
84C2 Bhera Pak
86A1 Bheri R Nepal
86A2 Bhilai India
85C3 Bhilwāra India
87C1 Bhimavaram India
85D3 Bhind India
84D3 Bhiwāni India
87B1 Bhongir India
85D4 Bhopal India
86B2 Bhubaneshwar India
85B4 Bhuj India
85D4 Bhusāwal India
82C3 Bhutan Kingdom,
Asia
71E4 Biak I Indon
58C2 Biala Podlaska Pol
58B2 Bialograd Pol
58B2 Bialystok Pol
38A1 Biargtangar C
Iceland
90C2 Biarjmand Iran
48B3 Biarritz France
47C1 Biasca Switz
92B4 Biba Egypt
74E2 Bibai Japan
100A2 Bibala Angola
57B3 Biberach Germany
97B4 Bibiani Ghana
54C1 Bicaz Rom
97C4 Bida Nig
87B1 Bidar India
91C5 Bidbid Oman
43B4 Bideford Eng
43B4 Bideford B Eng
96C2 Bidon 5 Alg
58C2 Biebrza Pol
52A1 Biel Switz
59B2 Bielawa Pol
56B2 Bielefeld Germany
47B1 Bieler See L Switz
52A1 Biella Italy
58C2 Bielsk Podlaski Pol
76D3 Bien Hoa Viet
53B2 Biferno R Italy
52A1 Biga Türk
55C3 Bigadiç Turk
19C3 Big Black R USA
18A1 Big Blue R USA
17B2 Big Cypress Swamp
USA
4D3 Big Delta USA
49D2 Bigent Germany
13F2 Biggar Can
5H4 Biggar Kindersley
Can
109D1 Biggenden Aust
12G3 Bigger,Mt Can
8C2 Bighorn R USA
76C3 Bight of Bangkok B
Thai
97C4 Bight of Benin B W
Africa
97C4 Bight of Biafra B
Cam
6C3 Big I Can
47C1 Bignasco Switz
97A3 Bignona Sen
21B2 Big Pine USA
17B2 Big Pine Key USA
22C3 Big Pine Mt USA
14A2 Big Rapids USA
5H4 Big River Can
9C3 Big Spring USA
7A4 Big Trout L Can

7B4 Big Trout Lake Can
52C2 Bihać Bosnia-
Herzegovina
86B1 Bihār India
86B2 Bihar State, India
99D3 Biharamulo Tanz
60B4 Bihor Mt Rom
87B1 Bijāpur India
87C1 Bijāpur India
90A2 Bijar Iran
86A1 Bijauri Nepal
54A2 Bijeljina Bosnia-
Herzegovina
73B4 Bijie China
84D3 Bijnor India
84C3 Bijnot Pak
84C3 Bikāner India
94B2 Bikfaya Leb
69F2 Bikin Russian Fed
98B3 Bikoro Zaire
85C3 Bilara India
84D2 Bilaspur India
86A2 Bilāspur India
76B3 Bilauktaung Range
Mts Thai
50B1 Bilbao Spain
Bilbao = Bilbao
59B3 Bílé R
Czech Republic
54A2 Bileca Bosnia-
Herzegovina
92B1 Bilecik Turk
99C2 Bili R Zaire
79B3 Biliran I Phil
8C2 Billings USA
95A3 Bilma Niger
11B3 Biloxi USA
98C1 Biltine Chad
85D4 Bina-Etawa India
79B3 Binalbagan Phil
101C2 Bindura Zim
100B2 Binga Zim
101C2 Binga Mt Zim
109D1 Bingara Aust
57B3 Bingen Germany
10C2 Binghamton USA
78D1 Bingkor Malay
93D2 Bingöl Turk
72D3 Binhai China
78A2 Bintan I Indon
78A3 Bintulun Indon
78C2 Bintulu Malay
29B3 Bió Bió R Chile
102J4 Bioko I Atlantic O
87B1 Bir India
95B2 Bir Abu Husein Well
Egypt
95B2 Bir al Harash Well
Libya
98C1 Birao CAR
86B1 Biratnagar Nepal
12E1 Birch Creek USA
108B3 Birchip Aust
5G4 Birch Mts Can
7A4 Bird Can
106C3 Birdsville Aust
106C2 Birdum Aust
86A1 Birganj Nepal
94A3 Bir Gifgâfa Well
Egypt
94A3 Bir Hasana Well
Egypt
35A2 Birigui Brazil
90C3 Birjand Iran
92B4 Birkat Qarun L Egypt
46D2 Birkenfeld Germany
42C3 Birkenhead Eng
60C4 Birlad Rom
94A3 Bîr Lahfân Well
Egypt
43C3 Birmingham Eng
11B3 Birmingham USA
95B2 Bir Misâha Well
Egypt
96A2 Bir Moghrein Maur
97C3 Birnin Kebbi Nig
97C3 Birni N'Konni Nig
69F2 Birobidzhan
Russian Fed
54C2 Birr Irish Rep
51C2 Bir Rabalou Alg
109C1 Birrie R Aust
44C2 Birsay Scot
61J2 Birsk Russian Fed

95B3 Bir Tarfâwi Well
Egypt
63B2 Biryusa Russian Fed
39J7 Biržai Lithuania
96B2 Bir Zreigat Well
Maur
48A2 Biscay,B of France/
Spain
17B2 Biscayne B USA
46D2 Bischwiller France
73B4 Bishan China
82B1 Bishkek Kirghizia
8B3 Bishop USA
42D2 Bishop Auckland Eng
43E4 Bishop's Stortford
Eng
86A2 Bishrāmpur India
96C1 Biskra Alg
79C4 Bislig Phil
8C2 Bismarck USA
90A3 Bisotûn Iran
97A3 Bissau Guinea-
Bissau
10A1 Bissett Can
5G4 Bistcho L Can
54C1 Bistrita R Rom
98B2 Bitam Gabon
57B3 Bitburg Germany
46D2 Bitche France
93D2 Bitlis Turk
55B2 Bitola Macedonia
56C2 Bitterfeld Germany
100A4 Bitterfontein S Africa
92B3 Bitter Lakes Egypt
8B2 Bitteroot Range Mts
USA
74D3 Biwa-ko L Japan
99E1 Biyo Kaboba Eth
65K4 Biysk Russian Fed
96C1 Bizerte Tunisia
51C2 Bj bou Arrérídj Alg
52C1 Bjelovar Croatia
96B2 Bj Flye Ste Marie Alg
64C2 Bjørnøya I Barents S
12F1 Black R USA
18B2 Black R USA
107D3 Blackall Aust
42C3 Blackburn Eng
4D3 Blackburn,Mt USA
13E2 Black Diamond Can
5H5 Black Hills USA
44B3 Black Isle Pen Scot
27H3 Blackman's
Barbados
43C4 Black Mts Wales
45A1 Blackpool Eng
27H1 Black River Jamaica
8B2 Black Rock Desert
USA
65E5 Black S Asia/Europe
45A1 Blacksod B Irish Rep
109D2 Black Sugarloaf Mt
Aust
97B3 Black Volta R Ghana
41B3 Blackwater R
Irish Rep
18A2 Blackwell USA
54B2 Blagoevgrad Bulg
63E2 Blagoveshchensk
Russian Fed
20B1 Blaine USA
44C3 Blair Atholl Scot
44C3 Blairgowrie Scot
17B1 Blakely USA
108A1 Blanche,L Aust
34A2 Blanco R Arg
34B1 Blanco R Arg
8A2 Blanco,C USA
7E4 Blanc Sablon Can
43C4 Blandford Forum
Eng
46A2 Blangy-sur-Bresle
France
46B1 Blankenberge Belg
101C2 Blantyre Malawi
48B2 Blaye France
109C2 Blayney Aust
111B2 Blenheim NZ
96C1 Blida Alg
14B1 Blind River Can
108C2 Blinman Aust
78C4 Blitar Indon
15D2 Block I USA
16D2 Block Island Sd USA

121

Bloemfontein

101G1 **Bloemfontein**
　　　S Africa
101G1 **Bloemhof** S Africa
101G1 **Bloemhof Dam** Res
　　　S Africa
33F3 **Blommesteinmeer** L
　　　Surinam
38A1 **Blonduós** Iceland
45B1 **Bloody Foreland** C
　　　Irish Rep
14A3 **Bloomfield** Indiana,
　　　USA
18B1 **Bloomfield** Iowa,
　　　USA
10B2 **Bloomington** Illinois,
　　　USA
14A3 **Bloomington**
　　　Indiana, USA
16A2 **Bloomsburg** USA
78C4 **Blora** Indon
6H3 **Blosseville Kyst** Mts
　　　Greenland
57B3 **Bludenz** Austria
11B3 **Bluefield** USA
32A1 **Bluefields** Nic
26B3 **Blue Mountain Peak**
　　　Mt Jamaica
16A2 **Blue Mt** USA
109D2 **Blue Mts** Aust
27J1 **Blue Mts** Jamaica
8A2 **Blue Mts** USA
　　　Blue Nile = Bahr el
　　　Azraq
99D1 **Blue Nile** R Sudan
4G3 **Bluenose L** Can
11B3 **Blue Ridge Mts** USA
13D2 **Blue River** Can
45B1 **Blue Stack** Mt
　　　Irish Rep
111A3 **Bluff** NZ
106A4 **Bluff Knoll** Mt Aust
30G4 **Blumenau** Brazil
49D2 **Blundez** Austria
20B2 **Bly** USA
12E3 **Blying Sd** USA
42D2 **Blyth** Eng
9B3 **Blythe** USA
11B3 **Blytheville** USA
97A4 **Bo** Sierra Leone
79B3 **Boac** Phil
72D2 **Boading** China
14B2 **Boardman** USA
63C3 **Boatou** China
33E3 **Boa Vista** Brazil
97A4 **Boa Vista** I Cape
　　　Verde
76E1 **Bobai** China
47C2 **Bóbbio** Italy
97B3 **Bobo Dioulasso**
　　　Burkina
60C3 **Bobruysk** Belorussia
17B2 **Boca Chica Key** I
　　　USA
22D6 **Bôca do Acre** Brazil
35C1 **Bocaiúva** Brazil
98B2 **Bocaranga** CAR
17B2 **Boca Raton** USA
59C3 **Bochnia** Pol
56B2 **Bocholt** Germany
56D1 **Bochum** Germany
100A2 **Bocoio** Angola
98B2 **Boda** CAR
63D2 **Bodaybo**
　　　Russian Fed
21A2 **Bodega Head** Pt
　　　USA
95A3 **Bodélé** Region Chad
38J5 **Boden** Sweden
47C1 **Bodensee** L Switz/
　　　Germany
87B1 **Bodhan** India
87B2 **Bodinàyakkanūr**
　　　India
43B4 **Bodmin** Eng
43B4 **Bodmin Moor**
　　　Upland Eng
38G5 **Bodø** Nor
55C3 **Bodrum** Turk
54C3 **Boende** Zaire
97A3 **Boffa** Guinea
76B2 **Bogale** Burma
19C3 **Bogalusa** USA
109C2 **Bogan** R Aust
97B3 **Bogandé** Burkina

6H3 **Bogarnes** Iceland
92C2 **Boğazlıyan** Turk
61K2 **Bogdanovich**
　　　Russian Fed
68A2 **Bogda Shan** Mt
　　　China
100A3 **Bogenfels** Namibia
109D1 **Boggabilla** Aust
109C2 **Boggabri** Aust
45B2 **Boggeragh Mts**
　　　Irish Rep
79B3 **Bogo** Phil
109C3 **Bogong,Mt** Aust
78B4 **Bogor** Indon
61H2 **Bogorodskoye**
　　　Russian Fed
32C3 **Bogotá** Colombia
63A2 **Bogotol** Russian Fed
86B2 **Bogra** Bang
72D2 **Bo Hai** B China
46B2 **Bohain-en-**
　　　Vermandois France
72D2 **Bohai Wan** B China
57C3 **Böhmer-Wald**
　　　Upland Germany
79B4 **Bohol** I Phil
79B4 **Bohol S** Phil
35A1 **Bois** R Brazil
14B1 **Bois Blanc I** USA
8B2 **Boise** USA
96A2 **Bojador,C** Mor
79B2 **Bojeador,C** Phil
90C2 **Bojnūrd** Iran
97A3 **Boké** Guinea
109C1 **Bokhara** R Aust
39F7 **Boknafjord** Inlet Nor
98B3 **Boko** Congo
76C3 **Bokor** Camb
98C3 **Bokungu** Zaire
98B1 **Bol** Chad
23A1 **Bolaānos** Mexico
97A3 **Bolama** Guinea-
　　　Bissau
23A1 **Bolanos** R Mexico
48C2 **Bolbec** France
97B4 **Bole** Ghana
59B2 **Bolesławiec** Pol
97B3 **Bolgatanga** Ghana
60C4 **Bolgrad** Ukraine
34C3 **Bolivar** Arg
18B2 **Bolivar** Missouri,
　　　USA
18C2 **Bolivar** Tennessee,
　　　USA
30C2 **Bolivia** Republic,
　　　S America
38H6 **Bollnas** Sweden
109C1 **Bollon** Aust
32C2 **Bollvar** Mt Ven
52B2 **Bologna** Italy
60D2 **Bologoye**
　　　Russian Fed
69F2 **Bolon'** Russian Fed
61G3 **Bol'shoy Irgiz** R
　　　Russian Fed
74C2 **Bol'shoy Kamen**
　　　Russian Fed
　　　Bol'shoy Kavkaz
　　　=Caucasus
01O4 **Bol'shoy Uzen** R
　　　Kazakhstan
9C4 **Bolson de Mapimi**
　　　Desert Mexico
43C3 **Bolton** Eng
92B1 **Bolu** Turk
38A1 **Bolungarvik** Iceland
92B2 **Bolvadin** Turk
52B1 **Bolzano** Italy
98B3 **Boma** Zaire
107D4 **Bombala** Aust
87A1 **Bombay** India
99D2 **Bombo** Uganda
33E5 **Bom Despacho** Brazil
86C1 **Bomdila** India
97A4 **Bomi Hills** Lib
31C4 **Bom Jesus da Lapa**
　　　Brazil
63E2 **Bomnak** Russian Fed
98C2 **Bomokandi** R Zaire
98C2 **Bomu** R CAR/Zaire
27D4 **Bonaire** I
　　　Caribbean S
12F2 **Bona,Mt** USA
25D3 **Bonanza** Nic

7E5 **Bonavista** Can
108A2 **Bon Bon** Aust
98C2 **Bondo** Zaire
97B4 **Bondoukou** Ivory
　　　Coast
　　　Bône = 'Annaba
33E3 **Bonfim** Guyana
98C2 **Bongandanga** Zaire
98B1 **Bongor** Chad
19A3 **Bonham** USA
53A2 **Bonifacio** Corse
52A2 **Bonifacio,Str of** Chan
　　　Medit S
　　　Bonin Is = Ogasawara
　　　Gunto
17B2 **Bonita Springs** USA
57B2 **Bonn** Germany
20C1 **Bonners Ferry** USA
12H1 **Bonnet Plume** R Can
13E2 **Bonnyville** Can
47B2 **Bonorva** Sardegna
97A4 **Bonthe** Sierra Leone
99E1 **Booaaso** Somalia
108B2 **Booligal** Aust
100D1 **Boonah** Aust
15C2 **Boonville** USA
109C2 **Boorowa** Aust
6A2 **Boothia,G of** Can
6A2 **Boothia Pen** Can
98B3 **Booué** Gabon
108A1 **Bopeechee** Aust
99D2 **Bor** Sudan
92B2 **Bor** Turk
54B2 **Bor** Serbia, Yugos
8B2 **Borah Peak** Mt USA
39G7 **Borås** Sweden
91B4 **Boräzjän** Iran
108A3 **Borda,C** Aust
48B3 **Bordeaux** France
4G2 **Borden I** Can
6B2 **Borden Pen** Can
16B2 **Bordentown** USA
42C2 **Borders** Region, Scot
108B3 **Bordertown** Aust
96C2 **Bordj Omar Dris** Alg
8D1 **Borens River** Can
38A2 **Borgarnes** Iceland
9C3 **Borger** USA
39H7 **Borgholm** Sweden
47C2 **Borgosia** Italy
47D1 **Borgo Valsugana**
　　　Italy
59C3 **Borislav** Ukraine
61F3 **Borisoglebsk**
　　　Russian Fed
60C3 **Borisov** Belorussia
60E3 **Borisovka**
　　　Russian Fed
95A3 **Borkou** Region Chad
39H6 **Borlänge** Sweden
47C2 **Bormida** Italy
47D1 **Bormio** Italy
67F5 **Borneo** I Malay/
　　　Indon
39H7 **Bornholm** I Denmark
55C3 **Bornova** Turk
98C2 **Boro** R Sudan
97B3 **Boromo** Burkina
60D2 **Borovichi**
　　　Russian Fed
106C2 **Borroloola** Aust
54D1 **Borsa** Rom
90A3 **Borüjed** Iran
90B3 **Borüjen** Iran
58B2 **Bory Tucholskie**
　　　Region, Pol
63D2 **Borzya** Russian Fed
73B5 **Bose** China
101G1 **Boshof** S Africa
54A2 **Bosna** R Bosnia-
　　　Herzegovina
37E4 **Bosnia-Herzegovina**
　　　Republic, Europe
75C1 **Bösö-hantö** B Japan
　　　Bosporus = Karadeniz
　　　Boğazi
51C2 **Bosquet** Alg
98B2 **Bossangoa** CAR
98B2 **Bossèmbélé** CAR
19B3 **Bossier City** USA
65K5 **Bosten Hu** L China
43D3 **Boston** Eng
10C2 **Boston** USA
11A3 **Boston Mts** USA
85C4 **Botäd** India

54B2 **Botevgrad** Bulg
101G1 **Bothaville** S Africa
64C3 **Bothnia,G of**
　　　Sweden/Fin
100B3 **Botletli** R Botswana
60C4 **Botosani** Rom
100B3 **Botswana** Republic,
　　　Africa
53C3 **Botte Donato** Mt
　　　Italy
46D1 **Bottrop** Germany
35B2 **Botucatu** Brazil
7E5 **Botwood** Can
89D7 **Bouaké** Ivory Coast
98B2 **Bouar** CAR
96B1 **Bouärfa** Mor
98B2 **Bouca** CAR
51C2 **Doufarik** Alg
　　　Bougie = Bejaïa
98B3 **Bougouni** Mali
46C2 **Bouillon** France
96B2 **Bou Izakarn** Mor
46D2 **Boulay-Moselle**
　　　France
8C2 **Boulder** Colorado,
　　　USA
9B3 **Boulder City** USA
22A2 **Boulder Creek** USA
48C1 **Boulogne** France
98B2 **Boumba** R CAR
97B4 **Bouna** Ivory Coast
8B3 **Boundary Peak** Mt
　　　USA
97B4 **Boundiali** Ivory Coast
107F3 **Bourail** Nouvelle
　　　Calédonie
97B3 **Bourem** Mali
49D2 **Bourg** France
49D2 **Bourg de Péage**
　　　France
48C2 **Bourges** France
48C3 **Bourg-Madame**
　　　France
49C2 **Bourgogne** Region,
　　　France
47B2 **Bourg-St-Maurice**
　　　France
108C2 **Bourke** Aust
43D4 **Bournemouth** Eng
96C1 **Bou Saâda** Alg
98B1 **Bousso** Chad
97A3 **Boutilimit** Maur
103J7 **Bouvet I** Atlantic O
34D2 **Bovril** Arg
13E2 **Bow** R Can
107D2 **Bowen** Aust
19A3 **Bowie** Texas, USA
13E2 **Bow Island** Can
11B3 **Bowling Green**
　　　Kentucky, USA
18B2 **Bowling Green**
　　　Missouri, USA
14B2 **Bowling Green** Ohio,
　　　USA
15C3 **Bowling Green**
　　　Virginia, USA
15C2 **Bowmanville** Can
103D2 **Bowral** Aust
13C2 **Bowron** R Can
72D3 **Bo Xian** China
72D2 **Boxing** China
92B1 **Boyabat** Turk
98B2 **Boyali** CAR
5J4 **Boyd** Can
16B2 **Boyertown** USA
13E2 **Boyle** Can
45B2 **Boyle** Irish Rep
45C2 **Boyne** R Irish Rep
17B2 **Boynton Beach**
　　　USA
98C2 **Boyoma Falls** Zaire
55C3 **Bozca Ada** I Turk
55C3 **Boz Dağlari** Mts
　　　Turk
8B2 **Bozeman** USA
　　　Bozen = Bolzano
98B2 **Bozene** Zaire
98B2 **Bozoum** CAR
52C2 **Brač** I Croatia
15C1 **Bracebridge** Can
95A2 **Brack** Libya
38H6 **Bräcke** Sweden
17B2 **Bradenton** USA

42D3 **Bradford** Eng
44E1 **Brae** Scot
44C3 **Braemar** Scot
50A1 **Braga** Port
34C3 **Bragado** Arg
50A1 **Bragana** Port
31B2 **Bragança** Brazil
35B2 **Bragança Paulista** Brazil
86C2 **Brahman-Baria** Bang
86B2 **Brāhmani** R India
86C1 **Brahmaputra** R India
7E5 **Braie Verte** Can
60C4 **Brăila** Rom
10A2 **Brainerd** USA
97A3 **Brakna** Region, Maur
5F4 **Bralorne** Can
14C2 **Brampton** Can
33E3 **Branco** R Brazil
100A3 **Brandberg** Mt Namibia
56C2 **Brandenburg** Germany
56C2 **Brandenburg** State, Germany
101G1 **Brandfort** S Africa
8D2 **Brandon** Can
100B4 **Brandvlei** S Africa
57C2 **Brandys nad Lebem** Czech Republic
58B2 **Braniewo** Pol
10B2 **Brantford** Can
108B3 **Branxholme** Aust
7D5 **Bras D'Or L** Can
35C1 **Brasila de Minas** Brazil
32D6 **Brasiléia** Brazil
31B5 **Brasília** Brazil
54C1 **Brasov** Rom
78D1 **Brassay Range** Mts Malay
59B3 **Bratislava** Slovakia
63C2 **Bratsk** Russian Fed
15D2 **Brattleboro** USA
56C2 **Braunschweig** Germany
97A4 **Brava** I Cape Verde
9B3 **Brawley** USA
45C2 **Bray** Irish Rep
6C3 **Bray I** Can
13D2 **Brazeau** R Can
13D2 **Brazeau,Mt** Can
28D4 **Brazil** Republic, S America
103G5 **Brazil Basin** Atlantic O
9D3 **Brazos** R USA
98B3 **Brazzaville** Congo
57C3 **Brdy** Upland Czech Republic
111A3 **Breaksea Sd** NZ
110B1 **Bream B** NZ
78B4 **Brebes** Indon
44C1 **Brechin** Scot
46C1 **Brecht** Belg
59B3 **Břeclav** Czech Republic
43C4 **Brecon** Wales
43C4 **Brecon Beacons** Mts Wales
43B3 **Brecon Beacons Nat Pk** Wales
56A2 **Breda** Neth
100B4 **Bredasdorp** S Africa
38H6 **Bredbyn** Sweden
61J3 **Bredy** Russian Fed
15C2 **Breezewood** USA
47C1 **Bregenz** Austria
47C1 **Bregenzer Ache** R Austria
38A1 **Breiðafjörður** B Iceland
47C2 **Brembo** R Italy
17A1 **Bremen** USA
56B2 **Bremen** Germany
56B2 **Bremerhaven** Germany
20B1 **Bremerton** USA
19A3 **Brenham** USA
57C3 **Brenner** P Austria/ Italy
47D2 **Breno** Italy
47D2 **Brenta** R Italy
22B2 **Brentwood** USA

52B1 **Brescia** Italy
   Breslau = Wrocław
47D1 **Bressanone** Italy
44E1 **Bressay** I Scot
48B2 **Bressuire** France
58C2 **Brest** Belorussia
48B2 **Brest** France
48B2 **Bretagne** Region, France
46B2 **Breteuil** France
16B2 **Breton Woods** USA
110B1 **Brett,C** NZ
109C1 **Brewarrina** Aust
16C2 **Brewster** New York, USA
20C1 **Brewster** Washington, USA
101G1 **Breyten** S Africa
52C1 **Brežice** Slovenia
98C2 **Bria** CAR
49D3 **Briancon** France
49C2 **Briare** France
21B2 **Bridgeport** California, USA
15D2 **Bridgeport** Connecticut, USA
19A3 **Bridgeport** Texas, USA
16B3 **Bridgeton** USA
27F4 **Bridgetown** Barbados
7D5 **Bridgewater** Can
16D2 **Bridgewater** USA
43C4 **Bridgwater** Eng
43C4 **Bridgwater B** Eng
42D2 **Bridlington** Eng
109C4 **Bridport** Aust
47B1 **Brienzer See** L Switz
46C2 **Briey** France
52A1 **Brig** Switz
8B2 **Brigham City** USA
109C3 **Bright** Aust
43D4 **Brighton** Eng
46E1 **Brilon** Germany
55A2 **Brindisi** Italy
19B3 **Brinkley** USA
107E3 **Brisbane** Aust
15D2 **Bristol** Connecticut, USA
43C4 **Bristol** Eng
15D2 **Bristol** Pennsylvania, USA
16D2 **Bristol** Rhode Island, USA
11B3 **Bristol** Tennessee, USA
12B3 **Bristol B** USA
43B4 **Bristol Chan** Eng/ Wales
4D3 **British** Mts USA
5F4 **British Columbia** Province, Can
6B1 **British Empire Range** Mts Can
101G1 **Brits** S Africa
100B4 **Britstown** S Africa
48C2 **Brive** France
59B3 **Brno** Czech Republic
17B1 **Broad** R USA
7C4 **Broadback** R Can
44A2 **Broad Bay** Inlet Scot
44B3 **Broadford** Scot
5H4 **Brochet** Can
4G2 **Brock I** Can
15C2 **Brockport** USA
16D1 **Brockton** USA
15C2 **Brockville** Can
6B2 **Brodeur Pen** Can
42B2 **Brodick** Scot
58B2 **Brodnica** Pol
60C3 **Brody** Ukraine
19B3 **Broken Bow** Oklahoma, USA
19B3 **Broken Bow L** USA
107D4 **Broken Hill** Aust
47C2 **Broni** Italy
38G5 **Brønnøysund** Nor
16C2 **Bronx** Borough, New York, USA
79A4 **Brooke's Point** Phil
18B2 **Brookfield** Missouri, USA
11A3 **Brookhaven** USA

20B2 **Brookings** Oregon, USA
8D2 **Brookings** South Dakota, USA
16D1 **Brookline** USA
16C2 **Brooklyn** Borough, New York, USA
5G4 **Brooks** Can
12C3 **Brooks,L** USA
12A1 **Brooks Mt** USA
4C3 **Brooks Range** Mts USA
17B2 **Brooksville** USA
109D1 **Brooloo** Aust
106B2 **Broome** Aust
44C2 **Brora** Scot
20B2 **Brothers** USA
95A3 **Broulkou** Chad
13E3 **Browning** USA
9D4 **Brownsville** USA
9D3 **Brownwood** USA
46B1 **Bruay-en-Artois** France
106A3 **Bruce,Mt** Aust
14B1 **Bruce Pen** Can
59B3 **Brück an der Mur** Austria
   Bruges = Brugge
46B1 **Brugge** Belg
46D1 **Brühl** Germany
77A2 **Brunei** Sultanate, S E Asia
52B1 **Brunico** Italy
111B2 **Brunner,L** NZ
11B3 **Brunswick** Georgia, USA
18B2 **Brunswick** Mississippi, USA
29B6 **Brunswick,Pen de** Chile
109C4 **Bruny I** Aust
61F1 **Brusenets** Russian Fed
26A3 **Brus Laguna** Honduras
   Brüssel = Bruxelles
56A2 **Bruxelles** Belg
19B3 **Bryan** USA
108A2 **Bryan,Mt** Aust
60D3 **Bryansk** Russian Fed
19B3 **Bryant** USA
59B2 **Brzeg** Pol
93E4 **Būbiyan** I Kuwait/ Iraq
99D3 **Bubu** R Tanz
32C2 **Bucaramanga** Colombia
44D3 **Buchan** Oilfield N Sea
97A4 **Buchanan** Lib
44D3 **Buchan Deep** N Sea
6C2 **Buchan G** Can
40C2 **Buchan Ness** Pen Scot
7E5 **Buchans** Can
34C2 **Buchardo** Arg
   Bucharest = București
47C1 **Buchs** Switz
43D3 **Buckingham** Eng
12B1 **Buckland** USA
12B1 **Buckland** R USA
108A2 **Buckleboo** Aust
98B3 **Buco Zau** Congo
54C2 **București** Rom
59B3 **Budapest** Hung
84D3 **Budaun** India
43B4 **Bude** Eng
19B3 **Bude** USA
61F5 **Budennovsk** Russian Fed
54A2 **Budva** Montenegro, Yugos
98A2 **Buéa** Cam
22B3 **Buellton** USA
34B2 **Buena Esperanza** Arg
32B3 **Buenaventura** Colombia
23A2 **Buenaventura** Mexico
29E2 **Buenos Aires** Arg
29D3 **Buenos Aires** State, Arg
18B2 **Buffalo** Mississipi, USA

10C2 **Buffalo** New York, USA
8C2 **Buffalo** South Dakota, USA
19A3 **Buffalo** Texas, USA
8C2 **Buffalo** Wyoming, USA
101H1 **Buffalo** R S Africa
13E2 **Buffalo L** Alberta, Can
5G3 **Buffalo L** Northwest Territories, Can
5H4 **Buffalo Narrows** Can
17B1 **Buford** USA
54C2 **Buftea** Rom
59C2 **Bug** R Pol/Ukraine
32B3 **Buga** Colombia
90B2 **Bugdayli** Turkmenistan
61H3 **Bugulma** Russian Fed
61H3 **Buguruslan** Russian Fed
93C2 **Buhayrat al Asad** Res Syria
41C3 **Builth Wells** Wales
34A2 **Buin** Chile
99C3 **Bujumbura** Burundi
98C3 **Bukama** Zaire
99C3 **Bukavu** Zaire
80E2 **Bukhara** Uzbekistan
78C2 **Bukit Batubrok** Mt Indon
70B4 **Bukittinggi** Indon
99D3 **Bukoba** Tanz
78D3 **Buku Gandadiwata** Mt Indon
71E4 **Bula** Indon
79B3 **Bulan** Phil
84D3 **Bulandshahr** India
100B3 **Bulawayo** Zim
55C3 **Buldan** Turk
80D4 **Buldana** India
68C2 **Bulgan** Mongolia
54B2 **Bulgaria** Republic, Europe
47B1 **Bulle** Switz
111B2 **Buller** R NZ
109C3 **Buller,Mt** Aust
106A4 **Bullfinch** Aust
108B1 **Bulloo** R Aust
108B1 **Bulloo Downs** Aust
108B1 **Bulloo L** Aust
18B2 **Bull Shoals Res** USA
34A3 **Bulnes** Chile
71F4 **Bulolo** PNG
101G1 **Bultfontein** S Africa
98C2 **Bumba** Zaire
76B2 **Bumphal Dam** Thai
99D2 **Buna** Kenya
106A4 **Bunbury** Aust
45C1 **Buncrana** Irish Rep
107E3 **Bundaberg** Aust
109D2 **Bundarra** Aust
85D3 **Bündi** India
45B1 **Bundoran** Irish Rep
109C1 **Bungil** R Aust
98B3 **Bungo** Angola
75A2 **Bungo-suidō** Str Japan
70B3 **Bunguran** I Ind
99D2 **Bunia** Zaire
18B2 **Bunker** USA
19B3 **Bunkie** USA
17B2 **Bunnell** USA
78C3 **Buntok** Indon
71D3 **Buol** Indon
94C2 **Buräq** Syria
98C1 **Buram** Sudan
99E2 **Burao** Somalia
79B3 **Burauen** Phil
80C3 **Buraydah** S Arabia
21B3 **Burbank** USA
109C2 **Burcher** Aust
92B2 **Burdur** Turk
61K3 **Bureinskiy Khrebet** Mts Russian Fed
56C2 **Burg** Germany
54C2 **Burgas** Bulg
17C1 **Burgaw** USA
47B1 **Burgdorf** Switz
100B4 **Burgersdorp** S Africa
50B1 **Burgos** Spain
58B1 **Burgsvik** Sweden

Burhaniye

55C3 **Burhaniye** Turk
85D4 **Burhānpur** India
79B3 **Burias** I Phil
76C2 **Buriram** Thai
35B1 **Buritis** Brazil
13B2 **Burke Chan** Can
106C2 **Burketown** Aust
97B3 **Burkina** Republic, Africa
15C1 **Burks Falls** Can
8B2 **Burley** USA
10A2 **Burlington** Iowa, USA
16B2 **Burlington** New Jersey, USA
10C2 **Burlington** Vermont, USA
20B1 **Burlington** Washington, USA
83D3 **Burma** Republic, Asia
20A2 **Burney** USA
16A2 **Burnham** USA
107D5 **Burnie** Aust
42C3 **Burnley** Eng
20C2 **Burns** USA
5F4 **Burns Lake** Can
82C1 **Burqin** China
108A2 **Burra** Aust
109C2 **Burragorang,L** Aust
44C2 **Burray** I Scot
109C2 **Burren Junction** Aust
109C2 **Burrinjuck Res** Aust
60C5 **Bursa** Turk
80B3 **Bûr Safâga** Egypt
       Bûr Sa'îd = Port Said
14B2 **Burton** USA
43D3 **Burton upon Trent** Eng
38J6 **Burtrask** Sweden
108B2 **Burtundy** Aust
71D4 **Buru** Indon
99C3 **Burundi** Republic, Africa
78A2 **Burung** Indon
63D2 **Buryatskaya Respublika,** Russian Fed
99D1 **Burye** Eth
61H4 **Burynshik** Kazakhstan
43E3 **Bury St Edmunds** Eng
91B4 **Büshehr** Iran
98B3 **Busira** R Zaire
58C2 **Buskozdroj** Pol
94C2 **Busrá ash Shām** Syria
106A4 **Busselton** Aust
49D2 **Busto** Italy
52A1 **Busto Arsizio** Italy
79A3 **Busuanga** I Phil
98C2 **Buta** Zaire
34B3 **Buta Ranquil** Arg
99C3 **Butare** Rwanda
42B2 **Bute** I Scot
69E2 **Butha Qi** China
14C2 **Butler** USA
8B2 **Butte** USA
77C4 **Butterworth** Malay
40B2 **Butt of Lewis** C Scot
6D3 **Button Is** Can
79C4 **Butuan** Phil
71D4 **Butung** I Indon
61F3 **Buturlinovka** Russian Fed
86A1 **Butwal** Nepal
99E2 **Buulo Barde** Somalia
99E2 **Buur Hakaba** Somalia
61F2 **Buy** Russian Fed
72B1 **Buyant Ovvo** Mongolia
61G5 **Buynaksk** Russian Fed
63D3 **Buyr Nuur** L Mongolia
93D2 **Büyük Ağri** Mt Turk
92A2 **Büyük Menderes** R Turk
54C1 **Buzău** Rom
54C1 **Buzau** R Rom
61H3 **Buzuluk** Russian Fed

16D2 **Buzzards B** USA
54C2 **Byala** Bulg
54B2 **Byala Slatina** Bulg
4H2 **Byam Martin** Chan Can
4H2 **Byam Martin I** Can
       Byblos = Jubail
94B1 **Byblos** Hist Site, Leb
58B2 **Bydgoszcz** Pol
39F7 **Bygland** Nor
6C2 **Bylot I** Can
109C2 **Byrock** Aust
22B2 **Byron** USA
109D1 **Byron,C** Aust
59B2 **Bytom** Pol

C

30F4 **Caacupé** Par
100A2 **Caála** Angola
13B2 **Caamano Sd** Can
30E4 **Caazapá** Par
79B2 **Cabanatuan** Phil
31E3 **Cabedelo** Brazil
50A2 **Cabeza del Buey** Spain
34C3 **Cabildo** Arg
34A2 **Cabildo** Chile
32C1 **Cabimas** Ven
100A2 **Cabinda** Angola
98B3 **Cabinda** Province, Angola
27C3 **Cabo Beata** Dom Rep
51C2 **Cabo Binibeca** C Spain
53A3 **Cabo Carbonara** C Sardegna
34A3 **Cabo Carranza** C Chile
50A2 **Cabo Carvoeiro** C Port
9B3 **Cabo Colnett** C Mexico
32B2 **Cabo Corrientes** C Colombia
24B2 **Cabo Corrientes** C Mexico
26B3 **Cabo Cruz** C Cuba
50B1 **Cabo de Ajo** C Spain
51C1 **Cabo de Caballeria** C Spain
51C1 **Cabo de Creus** C Spain
50B2 **Cabo de Gata** C Spain
29C7 **Cabo de Hornos** C Chile
51C2 **Cabo de la Nao** C Spain
50A1 **Cabo de Peñas** C Spain
50A2 **Cabo de Roca** C Port
51C2 **Cabo de Salinas** C Spain
35C2 **Cabo de São Tomé** C Brazil
50A2 **Cabo de São Vicente** C Port
50A2 **Cabo de Gines** C Spain
51C1 **Cabo de Tortosa** C Spain
29C4 **Cabo Dos Bahias** C Arg
50A2 **Cabo Espichel** C Port
9B4 **Cabo Falso** C Mexico
51B2 **Cabo Ferrat** C Alg
50A1 **Cabo Finisterre** C Spain
51C1 **Cabo Formentor** C Spain
35C2 **Cabo Frio** Brazil
35C2 **Cabo Frio** C Brazil
26A4 **Cabo Gracias à Dios** Honduras
31B2 **Cabo Maguarinho** C Brazil
50A2 **Cabo Negro** C Mor
109D1 **Caboolture** Aust
33G3 **Cabo Orange** C Brazil
21B3 **Cabo Punta Banda** C Mexico
101C2 **Cabora Bassa Dam** Mozam

24A1 **Caborca** Mexico
24C2 **Cabo Rojo** C Mexico
23B1 **Cabos** Mexico
29C6 **Cabo San Diego** C Arg
32A4 **Cabo San Lorenzo** C Ecuador
53A3 **Cabo Teulada** C Sardegna
50A2 **Cabo Trafalgar** C Spain
50B2 **Cabo Tres Forcas** C Mor
29C5 **Cabo Tres Puntas** C Arg
7D5 **Cabot Str** Can
50B2 **Cabra** Spain
50A1 **Cabreira** Mt Port
51C2 **Cabrera** I Spain
34A3 **Cabrero** Chile
51B2 **Cabriel** R Spain
23B2 **Cacahuamilpa** Mexico
54B2 **Čačak** Serbia, Yugos
33C2 **C A Carillo** Mexico
50A2 **Cáceres** Brazil
50A2 **Caceres** Spain
18B2 **Cache** R USA
13C2 **Cache Creek** Can
30C4 **Cachi** Arg
33D3 **Cachimbo** Brazil
31D4 **Cachoeira** Brazil
35A1 **Cachoeira Alta** Brazil
31D3 **Cachoeira de Paulo Alfonso** Waterfall Brazil
29F2 **Cachoeira do Sul** Brazil
31C6 **Cachoeiro de Itapemirim** Brazil
22C3 **Cachuma,L** USA
100A2 **Cacolo** Angola
100A2 **Caconda** Angola
35A1 **Caçu** Brazil
100A2 **Çaculuvar** R Angola
59B3 **Cadca** Slovakia
43C3 **Cader Idris** Mts Wales
18D2 **Cadillac** USA
79B3 **Cadiz** Phil
50A2 **Cadiz** Spain
68B2 **Caen** France
42B3 **Caernarfon** Wales
43B3 **Caernarfon B** Wales
94B2 **Caesarea** Hist Site Israel
31C4 **Caetité** Brazil
30C4 **Cafayate** Arg
92B2 **Caga Tepe** Turk
79B2 **Cagayan** R Phil
79B4 **Cagayan de Oro** Phil
79B4 **Cagayan Is** Phil
53A3 **Cagliari** Sardegna
27D3 **Caguas** Puerto Rico
45B3 **Caha Mts** Irish Rep
45A3 **Cahersiveen** Irish Rep
45C2 **Cahir** Irish Rep
45C2 **Cahone Pt** Irish Rep
48C3 **Cahors** France
101C2 **Caia** Mozam
100B2 **Caianda** Angola
35A1 **Caiapó** R Brazil
35A1 **Caiapônia** Brazil
31D3 **Caicó** Brazil
26C2 **Caicos Is** Caribbean S
11C4 **Caicos Pass** The Bahamas
45C2 **Cairn Mt** USA
44C3 **Cairngorms** Mts Scot
107D2 **Cairns** Aust
92B3 **Cairo** Egypt
11B3 **Cairo** USA
108B1 **Caiwarro** Aust
32B5 **Cajabamba** Peru
32B5 **Cajamarca** Peru
32B2 **Cabozo** Ven
54B2 **Čakat'** Rom
29B6 **Calafate** Arg
79B3 **Calagua Is** Phil
51B1 **Calahorra** Spain
48C1 **Calais** France

30C3 **Calama** Chile
32C3 **Calamar** Colombia
79A3 **Calamian Group** Is Phil
98B3 **Calandula** Angola
70A3 **Calang** Indon
95B2 **Calanscio Sand Sea** Libya
79B3 **Calapan** Phil
54C2 **Calarasi** Rom
51B1 **Calatayud** Spain
22B2 **Calaveras Res** USA
79B3 **Calbayog** Phil
19B4 **Calcasieu L** USA
86B2 **Calcutta** India
50A2 **Caldas da Rainha** Port
31B5 **Caldas Novas** Brazil
30B4 **Caldera** Chile
8B2 **Caldwell** USA
29C5 **Caleta Olivia** Arg
9B3 **Calexico** USA
5G4 **Calgary** Can
17B1 **Calhoun** USA
11B1 **Calhoun Falls** USA
32B3 **Cali** Colombia
87B2 **Calicut** India
8B3 **Caliente** Nevada, USA
8A3 **California** State, USA
22C3 **California Aqueduct** USA
87B2 **Calimera,Pt** India
34B2 **Calingasta** Arg
22A1 **Calistoga** USA
108B1 **Callabonna** L Aust
108A1 **Callabonna,L** Aust
15C1 **Callander** Can
44B3 **Callander** Scot
108A1 **Callanna** Aust
32B6 **Callao** Peru
13E1 **Calling L** Can
23B1 **Calmalli** Mexico
17B2 **Caloosahatchee** R USA
109D1 **Caloundra** Aust
23B2 **Calpulalpan** Mexico
53B3 **Caltanissetta** Italy
98B3 **Caluango** Angola
100A2 **Calulo** Angola
100A2 **Calunganne** Angola
99F1 **Caluula** Somalia
13B2 **Calvert I** Can
52A2 **Calvi** Corse
23A1 **Calvillo** Mexico
100A4 **Calvinia** S Africa
25E2 **Camagüey** Cuba
25E2 **Camagüey,Arch de** Is Cuba
30B2 **Camaná** Peru
30C3 **Camargo** Bol
22C3 **Camarillo** USA
29L4 **Camarones** Arg
20B1 **Camas** USA
98B3 **Camaxilo** Angola
98B3 **Cambatela** Angola
76C3 **Cambodia** Republic, S E Asia
43B4 **Camborne** Eng
49C1 **Cambrai** France
43C3 **Cambrian Mts** Wales
14B2 **Cambridge** Can
43D3 **Cambridge** County, Eng
43E3 **Cambridge** Eng
27H1 **Cambridge** Jamaica
15C3 **Cambridge** Maryland, USA
15D2 **Cambridge** Massachussets, USA
110C1 **Cambridge** NZ
14B2 **Cambridge** Ohio, USA
4H3 **Cambridge Bay** Can
60E5 **Cam Burun** Pt Turk
11A3 **Camden** Arkansas, USA
109D2 **Camden** Aust
15D3 **Camden** New Jersey, USA
11B1 **Camden** South Carolina, USA
18B2 **Cameron** Missouri, USA

19A3	**Cameron** Texas, USA
4H2	**Cameron I** Can
111A3	**Cameron Mts** NZ
98A2	**Cameroon Federal Republic**, Africa
98A2	**Cameroun** M Cam
31B2	**Cametá** Brazil
79B4	**Camiguin** I Phil
79B2	**Camiling** Phil
17B1	**Camilla** USA
22B1	**Camino** USA
30D3	**Camiri** Bol
31C2	**Camocim** Brazil
98C3	**Camissombo** Angola
106C2	**Camooweal** Aust
34D2	**Campana** Arg
29A5	**Campana I** Chile
13B2	**Campana I** Can
111B2	**Campbell,C** NZ
13B2	**Campbell I** Can
105G6	**Campbell I** NZ
4E3	**Campbell,Mt** Can
84C2	**Campbellpore** Pak
5F5	**Campbell River** Can
7D5	**Campbellton** Can
109D2	**Campbelltown** Aust
42B2	**Campbeltown** Scot
25C3	**Campeche** Mexico
108B3	**Camperdown** Aust
31D3	**Campina Grande** Brazil
31B6	**Campinas** Brazil
35B1	**Campina Verde** Brazil
98A2	**Campo** Cam
53B2	**Campobasso** Italy
35B1	**Campo Belo** Brazil
35B1	**Campo Florido** Brazil
30D4	**Campo Gallo** Arg
30F3	**Campo Grande** Brazil
31C2	**Campo Maior** Brazil
30F3	**Campo Mourão** Brazil
35C2	**Campos** Brazil
35B1	**Campos Altos** Brazil
47D1	**Campo Tures** Italy
76D3	**Cam Ranh** Viet
5G4	**Camrose** Can
100A2	**Camucuio** Angola
27K1	**Canaan** Tobago
31B2	**Canaan** USA
100A2	**Canacupa** Angola
2F3	**Canada** Dominion, N America
29D2	**Cañada de Gomez** Arg
9C3	**Canadian** R USA
60C5	**Canakkale** Turk
34B3	**Canalejas** Arg
13D2	**Canal Flats** Can
24A1	**Cananea** Mexico
102G3	**Canary Basin** Atlantic O
	Canary Is = Islas Canarias
23A2	**Canas** Mexico
24B2	**Canatlán** Mexico
11B4	**Canaveral,C** USA
31D5	**Canavieiras** Brazil
107D4	**Canberra** Aust
20B2	**Canby** California, USA
55C3	**Çandarli Körfezi** B Turk
16C2	**Candlewood,L** USA
29E2	**Canelones** Urug
18A2	**Caney** USA
100A2	**Cangamba** Angola
100B2	**Cangombe** Angola
72D2	**Cangzhou** China
7D4	**Caniapiscau** R Can
53B3	**Canicatti** Italy
31D2	**Canindé** Brazil
92B1	**Çankiri** Turk
13D2	**Canmore** Can
44A3	**Canna I** Scot
87B2	**Cannanore** India
49D3	**Cannes** France
109C3	**Cann River** Aust
30F4	**Canôas** Brazil
13F1	**Canoe L** Can
9C3	**Canon City** USA
108B2	**Canopus** Aust
5H4	**Canora** Can
109C2	**Canowindra** Aust
45C2	**Cansore Pt** Irish Rep
43E4	**Canterbury** Eng
111B2	**Canterbury Bight** B NZ
111B2	**Canterbury Plains** NZ
77D4	**Can Tho** Viet
	Canton = Guangzhou
19C3	**Canton** Mississippi, USA
18B1	**Canton** Missouri, USA
10B2	**Canton** Ohio, USA
12E2	**Cantwell** USA
20C2	**Canyon City** USA
12J2	**Canyon Range** Mts USA
20B2	**Canyonville** USA
98C3	**Canzar** Angola
76D1	**Cao Bang** Viet
31B2	**Capanema** Brazil
35B2	**Capão Bonito** Brazil
48B3	**Capbreton** France
24B2	**Cap Corrientes** C Mexico
49B2	**Cap Corse** C Corse
48B2	**Cap de la Hague** C France
15D1	**Cap-de-la-Madeleine** Can
6C3	**Cap de Nouvelle-France** C Can
51C2	**Capdepera** Spain
23A2	**Cap de Tancitiario** C Mexico
109C4	**Cape Barren I** Aust
103J6	**Cape Basin** Atlantic O
7E5	**Cape Breton I** Can
97B4	**Cape Coast** Ghana
15D2	**Cape Cod B** USA
6C3	**Cape Dorset** Can
17C1	**Cape Fear** R USA
18C2	**Cape Girardeau** Can
6B3	**Cape Henrietta Maria** Can
	Cape Horn = Cabo de Hornos
104E3	**Cape Johnston Depth** Pacific O
35C1	**Capelinha** Brazil
4B3	**Cape Lisburne** Can
100A2	**Capelongo** Angola
15D3	**Cape May** USA
6C3	**Cape Mendocino** USA
98B3	**Capenda Camulemba** Angola
4F2	**Cape Perry** Can
100B4	**Cape Province** S Africa
7A4	**Cape Tatnam** Can
100A4	**Cape Town** S Africa
102G4	**Cape Verde Is** Atlantic O
102G4	**Cape Verde Basin** Atlantic O
12F3	**Cape Yakataga** USA
107D2	**Cape York Pen** Aust
46A1	**Cap Gris Nez** C France
26C3	**Cap-Haitien** Haiti
31B2	**Capim** R Brazil
112C2	**Capitán Arturo Prat** Base Ant
27P2	**Cap Moule à Chique** C St Lucia
53C3	**Capo Isola de Correnti** C Italy
53C3	**Capo Rizzuto** C Italy
55A3	**Capo Santa Maria di Leuca** C Italy
53B3	**Capo San Vito** Italy
53C3	**Capo Spartivento** C Italy
27P2	**Cap Pt** St Lucia
53B3	**Capri I** Italy
100B2	**Caprivi Strip** Region, Namibia
52A2	**Cap Rosso** C Corse
102H4	**Cap Vert** C Sen
32C4	**Caquetá** R Colombia
54B2	**Caracal** Rom
33E3	**Caracaraí** Brazil
32D1	**Caracas** Ven
35B2	**Caraguatatuba** Brazil
29B3	**Carahue** Chile
35C1	**Caraí** Brazil
35C2	**Carandaí** Brazil
31C6	**Carangola** Brazil
54B1	**Caransebeş** Rom
108A2	**Carappee Hill** Mt Aust
26A3	**Caratasca** Honduras
35C1	**Caratinga** Brazil
51B2	**Caravaca** Spain
35D1	**Caravelas** Brazil
18C2	**Carbondale** Illinois, USA
53A3	**Carbonia** Sardegna
7E5	**Carborear** Can
99E1	**Carcar Mts** Somalia
48C3	**Carcassonne** France
4E3	**Carcross** Can
23B2	**Cardel** Mexico
25D2	**Cárdenas** Cuba
23B1	**Cárdenas** Mexico
43C4	**Cardiff** Wales
43B3	**Cardigan** Wales
43B3	**Cardigan B** Wales
13E2	**Cardston** Can
54B1	**Carei** Rom
33F4	**Carenó** Brazil
34A2	**Carén** Chile
14B2	**Carey** USA
48B2	**Carhaix-Plouguer** France
29D3	**Carhué** Arg
31C6	**Cariacica** Brazil
5J4	**Caribou** Can
5G4	**Caribou Mts** Alberta, Can
5F4	**Caribou Mts** British Columbia, Can
79B3	**Carigara** Phil
46C2	**Carignan** France
33E1	**Caripito** Ven
101G1	**Carleton Place** Can
101G1	**Carletonville** S Africa
18C2	**Carlinville** USA
42C2	**Carlisle** Eng
15C2	**Carlisle** USA
34C3	**Carlos** Arg
35C1	**Carlos Chagas** Brazil
45C2	**Carlow** County, Irish Rep
45C2	**Carlow** Irish Rep
21B3	**Carlsbad** California, USA
9C3	**Carlsbad** New Mexico, USA
5H5	**Carlyle** Can
12G2	**Carmacks** Can
47B2	**Carmagnola** Italy
43B4	**Carmarthen** Wales
43B4	**Carmarthen B** Wales
22B2	**Carmel** California, USA
16C2	**Carmel** New York, USA
94B2	**Carmel,Mt** Israel
34D2	**Carmelo** Urug
22B2	**Carmel Valley** USA
9B4	**Carmen I** Mexico
29D4	**Carmen de Patagones** Arg
18C2	**Carmi** USA
21A2	**Carmichael** USA
35B1	**Carmo do Paranaiba** Brazil
50A2	**Carmona** Spain
106A3	**Carnarvon** Aust
100B4	**Carnarvon** S Africa
35D1	**Carncacá** Brazil
45C1	**Carndonagh** Irish Rep
106B3	**Carnegi,L** Aust
98B2	**Carnot** CAR
108A2	**Carnot,C** Aust
17B2	**Carol City** USA
31B3	**Carolina** Brazil
101H1	**Carolina** S Africa
17C1	**Carolina Beach** USA
104F3	**Caroline Is** Pacific O
60B4	**Carpathians** Mts E Europe
59D3	**Carpatii Orientali** Mts Rom
106C2	**Carpentaria,G of** Aust
83C5	**Carpenter Ridge** Indian O
49D3	**Carpentras** France
52B2	**Carpi** Italy
22C3	**Carpinteria** USA
17B2	**Carrabelle** USA
52B2	**Carrara** Italy
41B3	**Carrauntoohill** Mt Irish Rep
45C2	**Carrickmacross** Irish Rep
45B2	**Carrick on Shannon** Irish Rep
45C2	**Carrick-on-Suir** Irish Rep
108A2	**Carrieton** Aust
8D2	**Carrington** USA
50B1	**Carrión** R Spain
10A2	**Carroll** USA
17A1	**Carrollton** Georgia, USA
14A3	**Carrollton** Kentucky, USA
18B2	**Carrollton** Missouri, USA
18C2	**Carruthersville** USA
60E5	**Carsamba** Turk
92B2	**Carsamba** R Turk
8B3	**Carson City** USA
14B2	**Carsonville** USA
26B4	**Cartagena** Colombia
51B2	**Cartagena** Spain
32B3	**Cartago** Colombia
25D4	**Cartago** Costa Rica
111C2	**Carterton** NZ
18B2	**Carthage** Missouri, USA
15C2	**Carthage** New York, USA
19B3	**Carthage** Texas, USA
106B2	**Cartier I** Timor S
7E4	**Cartwright** Can
31D3	**Caruaru** Brazil
33E1	**Carúpano** Ven
46B1	**Carvin** France
34A2	**Casablanca** Chile
96B1	**Casablanca** Mor
38C3	**Casa Branca** Brazil
9B3	**Casa Grande** USA
52A1	**Casale Monferrato** Italy
47D2	**Casalmaggiore** Italy
34C3	**Casares** Arg
13C3	**Cascade** Arg Can/ USA
111A2	**Cascade Pt** NZ
8A2	**Cascade Range** Mts USA
30F3	**Cascavel** Brazil
53B2	**Caserta** Italy
112C9	**Casey** Base Ant
54B1	**Cashel** Irish Rep
34C2	**Casilda** Arg
107E3	**Casino** Aust
32B5	**Casma** Peru
51B1	**Caspe** Spain
61G4	**Caspian Depression** Region Kazakhstan
65G6	**Caspian S** Asia/ Europe
14C3	**Cass** USA
100B2	**Cassamba** Angola
46B1	**Cassel** France
12J3	**Cassiar** Can
34E2	**Cassiar Mts** Can
35A1	**Cassilândia** Brazil
53B2	**Cassino** Italy
22C3	**Castaic** USA
34B2	**Castaño** R Arg
47D2	**Castelfranco** Italy
49D3	**Castellane** France
34D3	**Castelli** Arg
51B2	**Castellon de la Plana** Spain
31C3	**Casteló** Brazil
50A2	**Castelo Branco** Port
48C3	**Castelsarrasin** France
53B3	**Castelvetrano** Italy
108B3	**Casterton** Aust

Castilla La Nueva

50B2 **Castilla La Nueva**
Region, Spain
50B1 **Castilla La Vieja**
Region, Spain
41B3 **Castlebar** Irish Rep
44A3 **Castlebay** Scot
42C2 **Castle Douglas** Scot
20C1 **Castlegar** Can
45B2 **Castleisland**
Irish Rep
108B3 **Castlemain** Aust
45B2 **Castlerea** Irish Rep
109C2 **Castlereagh** Aust
48C3 **Castres-sur-l'Agout**
France
27E4 **Castries** St Lucia
29B4 **Castro** Arg
30F3 **Castro** Brazil
31D4 **Castro Alves** Brazil
53C3 **Castrovillari** Italy
22B2 **Castroville** USA
111A2 **Caswell Sd** NZ
25E2 **Cat** / The Bahamas
79B3 **Catabalogan** Phil
32A5 **Catacaos** Peru
35C2 **Cataguases** Brazil
19B3 **Catahoula L** USA
35B1 **Catalão** Brazil
51C1 **Cataluña** Region,
Spain
30C4 **Catamarca** Arg
30C4 **Catamarca** State, Arg
101C1 **Catanduanes** Mcoum
79B3 **Catanduanes** / Phil
31B6 **Catanduva** Brazil
53C3 **Catania** Italy
53C3 **Catanzaro** Italy
79B3 **Catarman** Phil
108A2 **Catastrophe,C** Aust
26C5 **Catatumbo** R Ven
16A2 **Catawissa** USA
23B2 **Catemaco** Mexico
49D3 **Cater** Corse
52A2 **Cateraggio** Corse
98B3 **Catete** Angola
97A3 **Catio** Guinea-Bissau
7A4 **Cat Lake** Can
13D3 **Catlegar** Can
107E3 **Cato** / Aust
25D2 **Catoche,C** Mexico
16A3 **Catoctin Mt** USA
15C3 **Catonsville** USA
34C3 **Catrilo** Arg
15D2 **Catskill** USA
15D2 **Catskill Mts** USA
32C2 **Cauca** R Colombia
31D2 **Caucaia** Brazil
32B2 **Caucasia** Colombia
65F5 **Caucasus** Mts
Georgia
46B1 **Caudry** France
98B3 **Caungula** Angola
29B3 **Cauquenes** Chile
87B2 **Cauvery** R India
49D2 **Cavaillon** France
47D1 **Cavalese** Italy
97B4 **Cavally** R Lib
45C2 **Cavan** County,
Irish Rep
45C2 **Cavan** Irish Rep
79B3 **Cavite** Phil
31C2 **Caxias** Brazil
32C4 **Caxias** Brazil
30F4 **Caxias do Sul** Brazil
98B3 **Caxito** Angola
17B1 **Cayce** USA
93D1 **Çayeli** Turk
33G3 **Cayenne** French
Guiana
46A1 **Cayeux-sur-Mer**
France
25E3 **Cayman Brac** /
Caribbean S
26A3 **Cayman Is**
Caribbean S
26A3 **Cayman Trench**
Caribbean S
99E2 **Caynabo** Somalia
25E2 **Cayo Romana** / Cuba
25D3 **Cayos Miskitos** /s
Nic
26A2 **Cay Sal** /
Caribbean S
100B2 **Cazombo** Angola

Ceará = Fortaleza
31C3 **Ceara** State, Brazil
79B3 **Cebu** Phil
79B3 **Cebu** / Phil
16B3 **Cecilton** USA
52B2 **Cecina** Italy
8B3 **Cedar City** USA
19A3 **Cedar Creek Res**
USA
5J4 **Cedar L** Can
10A2 **Cedar Rapids** USA
17A1 **Cedartown** USA
24A2 **Cedros** / Mexico
106C4 **Ceduna** Aust
99E2 **Ceelbuur** Somalia
99E1 **Ceerigaabo** Somalia
53B3 **Cefalu** Italy
59B3 **Cegléd** Hung
100A2 **Cela** Angola
24B2 **Celaya** Mexico
Celebes = Sulawesi
70C3 **Celebes S** S E Asia
16B2 **Celina** USA
52C1 **Celje** Slovenia
56C2 **Celle** Germany
71E4 **Cendrawasih** Pen
Indon
47C2 **Ceno** R Italy
19B3 **Center** USA
16C2 **Center Moriches**
USA
17A1 **Center Point** USA
47D2 **Cento** Italy
44B3 **Central** Region,
Scot
98B2 **Central African
Republic** Africa
16D2 **Central Falls** USA
18C2 **Centralia** Illinois,
USA
8A2 **Centralia**
Washington, USA
20B2 **Central Point** USA
71F4 **Central Range** Mts
PNG
16A3 **Centreville** Maryland,
USA
78C4 **Cepu** Indon
Ceram = Seram
71D4 **Ceram Sea** Indon
34C3 **Cereales** Arg
31B5 **Ceres** Brazil
100A4 **Ceres** S Africa
22B2 **Ceres** USA
48C2 **Cergy-Pontoise**
France
53C2 **Cerignola** Italy
60C5 **Cernavodă** Rom
9C4 **Cerralvo** / Mexico
23A1 **Cerritos** Mexico
34B2 **Cerro Aconcagua** R
Arg
23B1 **Cerro Azul** Mexico
34A3 **Cerro Campanario**
Mt Chile
34C2 **Cerro Champaqui** Mt
Arg
23A2 **Cerro Cuachaia** Mt
Mexico
23B1 **Cerro de Astillero**
Mexico
34B2 **Cerro de Olivares** Mt
Arg
32B6 **Cerro de Pasco** Peru
27D3 **Cerro de Punta** Mt
Puerto Rico
23A2 **Cerro El Cantado** Mt
Mexico
34B3 **Cerro El Nevado** Mt
Arg
23A2 **Cerro Grande** Mts
Mexico
34A2 **Cerro Juncal** Mt Arg/
Chile
23A1 **Cerro la Ardilla** Mts
Mexico
34B1 **Cerro las Tortolas** Mt
Chile
23A2 **Cerro Laurel** Mt
Mexico
34A2 **Cerro Mercedario** Mt
Arg
34A3 **Cerro Mora** Mt Chile
27C4 **Cerron** Mt Ven

34B3 **Cerro Payún** Mt Arg
23B2 **Cerro Penón del
Rosario** Mt Mexico
34B2 **Cerro Sosneado** Mt
Arg
23A2 **Cerro Teotepec** Mt
Mexico
34B2 **Cerro Tupungato** Mt
Arg
23B2 **Cerro Yucuyacau** Mt
Mexico
47C2 **Cervo** R Italy
52B2 **Cesena** Italy
60B2 **Cēsis** Latvia
57C3 **České Budejovice**
Czech Republic
59B3 **Českomoravská
Vysocina** Mts
Czech Republic
55C3 **Çeşme** Turk
107E4 **Cessnock** Aust
52C2 **Cetina** R Croatia
96B1 **Ceuta** N W Africa
92C2 **Ceyhan** Turk
92C2 **Ceyhan** R Turk
93C2 **Ceylanpinar** Turk
Ceylon = Sri Lanka
63B2 **Chaa-Khol**
Russian Fed
48C2 **Chaâteaudun** France
47B1 **Chablais** Region,
France
34C2 **Chacabuco** Arg
32B5 **Chachapoyas** Peru
84C3 **Chacharran** R India
84C3 **Chachran** Pak
30D4 **Chaco** State, Arg
98B1 **Chad** Republic,
Africa
98B1 **Chad** L C Africa
34B3 **Chadileuvu** R Arg
8C2 **Chadron** USA
18C2 **Chaffee** USA
85B3 **Chagai** Pak
63F2 **Chagda** Russian Fed
76C2 **Chagharcharan** Afghan
104B4 **Chagos Arch**
Indian O
27L1 **Chaguanas** Trinidad
91D4 **Chāh Bahār** Iran
76C2 **Chai Badan** Thai
76C3 **Chaine des
Cardamomes** Mts
Camb
98C4 **Chaine des Mitumba**
Mts Zaïre
76C2 **Chaiyaphum** Thai
34D2 **Chajari** Arg
84C2 **Chakwal** Pak
30B2 **Chala** Peru
100C2 **Chalabesa** Zambia
84A2 **Chalap Dalam** Mts
Afghan
73C4 **Challuy** China
85C4 **Chalisgaon** India
12F1 **Chalkyitsik** USA
46C2 **Challerange** France
46C2 **Châlons sur Marne**
France
40C2 **Chalun sur Saône**
France
57C3 **Cham** Germany
84B2 **Chaman** Pak
84B3 **Chamba** India
85D3 **Chambal** R India
15C3 **Chambersburg** USA
49D2 **Chambéry** France
46B2 **Chambly** France
85A3 **Chambor Kalat** Pak
90B3 **Chamgordan** Iran
34B2 **Chamical** Arg
47B2 **Chamonix** France
86A2 **Chamrajnagar** India
46C2 **Champagne** Region,
France
101G1 **Champagne Castle**
Mt Lesotho
47A1 **Champagnole** France
10B2 **Champaign** USA
76D3 **Champassak** Laos
10C2 **Champlain,L** USA
87B2 **Chamrajnagar** India
30B4 **Chañaral** Chile
34A3 **Chanco** Chile

4D3 **Chandalar** USA
4D3 **Chandalar** R USA
84D2 **Chandigarh** India
86C2 **Chandpur** Bang
85D5 **Chandrapur** India
91D4 **Chānf** Iran
101C2 **Changara** Mozam
74B2 **Changbai** China
69E2 **Changchun** China
73C4 **Changde** China
68E4 **Chang-hua** Taiwan
76D2 **Changjiang** China
73D3 **Chang Jiang** R
China
74B2 **Changjin** N Korea
73C4 **Changsha** China
72E3 **Changshu** China
74A2 **Changtu** China
73C4 **Changwu** China
74B3 **Changyón** N Korea
72C2 **Changzhi** China
73E3 **Changzhou** China
48B2 **Channel Is** Europe
9B3 **Channel Is** USA
7E5 **Channel Port-aux-
Basques** Can
76C3 **Chanthaburi** Thai
46B2 **Chantilly** France
18A2 **Chanute** USA
73D5 **Chaoàn** China
72D5 **Chao'an** China
73D3 **Chao Hu** L China
76C3 **Chao Phraya** R Thai
72E1 **Chaoyang** China
31C4 **Chapada Diamantina**
Mts Brazil
31C2 **Chapadinha** Brazil
23A1 **Chapala** Mexico
23A1 **Chapala,Lac de** L
Mexico
61H3 **Chapayevo**
Kazakhstan
30F4 **Chapecó** Brazil
27H1 **Chapelton** Jamaica
7B5 **Chapleau** Can
61E3 **Chaplygin**
Russian Fed
112C3 **Charcot I** Ant
80E2 **Chardzhou**
Turkmenistan
48C2 **Charente** R France
98B1 **Chari** R Chad
98B1 **Chari Baguirmi**
Region, Chad
84B1 **Charikar** Afghan
18B1 **Chariton** R USA
33F2 **Charity** Guyana
85D3 **Charkhāri** India
46C1 **Charleroi** Belg
18C2 **Charleston** Illinois,
USA
18C2 **Charleston** Missouri,
USA
11C3 **Charleston** S
Carolina, USA
10B3 **Charleston** W
Virginia, USA
98C3 **Charlesville** Zaïre
107D3 **Charleville** Auot
49C2 **Charleville-Mézières**
France
14A1 **Charlevoix** USA
14B2 **Charlotte** Michigan,
USA
11B3 **Charlotte** N Carolina,
USA
17B2 **Charlotte Harbor** B
USA
10C3 **Charlottesville** USA
7D5 **Charlottetown** Can
27K1 **Charlotteville**
Tobago
108B3 **Charlton** Aust
10C1 **Charlton I** Can
84C2 **Charsadda** Pak
107D3 **Charters Towers**
Aust
48C2 **Chartres** France
29E3 **Chascomús** Arg
13D2 **Chase** Can
48B2 **Châteaubriant**
France
48C2 **Châteaudun** France
48B2 **Châteaulin** France

48C2 Châteauroux France
46D2 Château-Salins France
49C2 Château-Thierry France
46C1 Châtelet Belg
48C2 Châtellerault France
43E4 Chatham Eng
7D5 Chatham New Brunswick, Can
16C1 Chatham New York, USA
14B2 Chatham Ontario, Can
13A2 Chatham Sd Can
12H3 Chatham Str USA
49C2 Châtillon France
47B2 Châtillon Italy
16B3 Chatsworth USA
17B1 Chattahoochee USA
17A1 Chattahoochee R USA
11B3 Chattanooga USA
76A1 Chauk Burma
49D2 Chaumont France
46B2 Chauny France
77D3 Chau Phu Viet
50A1 Chaves Port
61H2 Chaykovskiy Russian Fed
50B2 Chazaouet Alg
34C2 Chazón Arg
32C2 Checontá Colombia
57C2 Cheb Czech Republic
65F4 Cheboksary Russian Fed
10B2 Cheboygan USA
74B3 Chech'on S Korea
85C3 Chechro Pak
18A2 Checotah USA
76A2 Cheduba I Burma
108B1 Cheepie Aust
96B2 Chegga Maur
100C2 Chegutu Zim
20B1 Chehalis USA
74B4 Cheju S Korea
74B4 Cheju do I S Korea
74B4 Cheju-haehyöp Str S Korea
63F2 Chekunda Russian Fed
20B1 Chelan,L USA
90B2 Cheleken Turkmenistan
34B3 Chelforo Arg
80D1 Chelkar Kazakhstan
59C2 Chelm Pol
58B2 Chelmno Pol
43E4 Chelmsford Eng
43C4 Cheltenham Eng
65H4 Chelyabinsk Russian Fed
101C2 Chemba Mozam
57C2 Chemnitz Germany
84D2 Chenab R India/Pak
96B2 Chenachane Alg
20C1 Cheney USA
18A2 Cheney Res USA
72D1 Chengda China
73A3 Chengdu China
72E2 Chengshan Jiao Pt China
73C4 Chenxi China
73C4 Chen Xian China
73D3 Cheo Xian China
32B5 Chepén Peru
34B2 Chepes Arg
48C2 Cher R France
23A2 Cheran Mexico
17C1 Cheraw USA
48B2 Cherbourg France
96C1 Cherchell Alg
63C2 Cheremkhovo Russian Fed
60E2 Cherepovets Russian Fed
60D4 Cherkassy Ukraine
61F5 Cherkessk Russian Fed
60D3 Chernigov Ukraine
60D2 Chernobyl Ukraine
60C4 Chernovtsy Ukraine
61J2 Chernushka Russian Fed

60B3 Chernyakhovsk Russian Fed
61G4 Chernyye Zemli Region, Russian Fed
18A2 Cherokees,L o'the USA
34A3 Cherquenco Chile
86C1 Cherrapunji India
60C3 Cherven' Belorussia
59C2 Chervonograd Ukraine
10C3 Chesapeake B USA
42C3 Cheshire County, Eng
16C1 Cheshire USA
64F3 Chëshskaya Guba B Russian Fed
21A1 Chester California, USA
42C3 Chester Eng
18C2 Chester Illinois, USA
16C1 Chester Massachusets, USA
15C3 Chester Pennsylvania, USA
17B1 Chester S Carolina, USA
16A3 Chester R USA
42D3 Chesterfield Eng
6A3 Chesterfield Inlet Can
16A3 Chestertown USA
25D3 Chetumal Mexico
13C1 Chetwynd Can
12A2 Chevak USA
111B2 Cheviot NZ
40C2 Cheviots Hills Eng/Scot
13D3 Chewelah USA
8C2 Cheyenne USA
86A1 Chhapra India
86C1 Chhatak Bang
85D4 Chhatarpur India
85D4 Chhindwâra India
86B1 Chhuka Bhutan
73E5 Chia'i Taiwan
100A2 Chiange Angola
76C2 Chiang Kham Thai
76B2 Chiang Mai Thai
47C1 Chiavenna Italy
74E3 Chiba Japan
86B2 Chibâsa India
100A2 Chibia Angola
7C4 Chibougamou Can
75A1 Chiburi-jima I Japan
101C3 Chibuto Mozam
10B2 Chicago USA
14A2 Chicago Heights USA
12G3 Chichagof I USA
43D4 Chichester Eng
75B1 Chichibu Japan
69G4 Chichi-jima I Japan
11B3 Chickamauga L USA
19C3 Chickasawhay R USA
9D3 Chickasha USA
12F2 Chicken USA
32A5 Chiclayo Peru
8A3 Chico USA
29C4 Chico R Arg
101C2 Chicoa Mozam
15D2 Chicopee USA
7C5 Chicoutimi Can
101C3 Chicualacuala Mozam
87B2 Chidambaram India
6D3 Chidley,C Can
17B2 Chiefland USA
99C3 Chiengi Zambia
47B2 Chieri Italy
46C2 Chiers R France
47C1 Chiesa Italy
47D2 Chiese R Italy
72D1 Chifeng China
12C3 Chiginigak,Mt USA
4C3 Chignik USA
23B2 Chignahuapán Mexico
12C3 Chignik USA
24B2 Chihuahua Mexico
87B2 Chik Ballapur India
87B2 Chikmagalür India

12C2 Chikuminuk L USA
101C2 Chikwawa Malawi
76A1 Chi-kyaw Burma
87C1 Chilakalürupet India
23B2 Chilapa Mexico
87B3 Chilaw Sri Lanka
28B6 Chile Republic
34B2 Chilecito Mendoza, Arg
100B2 Chililabombwe Zambia
86B2 Chilka L India
13C2 Chilko R Can
5F4 Chilko L Can
13C2 Chilkotin R Can
34A3 Chillán Chile
34D3 Chillar Arg
18B2 Chillicothe Missouri, USA
14B3 Chillicothe Ohio, USA
13C3 Chilliwack Can
86B1 Chilmari India
101C2 Chilongozi Zambia
20B2 Chiloquin USA
24C3 Chilpancingo Mexico
43D4 Chiltern Hills Upland Eng
14A2 Chilton USA
101C2 Chilumba Malawi
69E4 Chi-lung Taiwan
101C2 Chilwa L Malawi
100C2 Chimanimani Zim
46C1 Chimay Belg
65G5 Chimbay Uzbekistan
32B4 Chimborazo Mt Ecuador
32B5 Chimbote Peru
65H5 Chimkent Kazakhstan
101C2 Chimoio Mozam
67E3 China Republic, Asia
China National Republic = Taiwan
25D3 Chinandega Nic
32B6 Chincha Alta Peru
109D1 Chinchilla Aust
101C2 Chinde Mozam
86C2 Chindwin R Burma
100B2 Chingola Zambia
100A2 Chinguar Angola
96A2 Chinguetti Maur
74B3 Chinhae S Korea
100C2 Chinhoyi Zim
12D3 Chiniak,C USA
84C2 Chiniot Pak
74B3 Chinju S Korea
98C2 Chinko R CAR
75B1 Chino Japan
101C2 Chinsali Zambia
52B1 Chioggia Italy
101C2 Chipata Zambia
101C3 Chipinge Zim
87A1 Chiplün India
43C4 Chippenham Eng
10A2 Chippewa Falls USA
32A4 Chira R Peru
87C1 Chirâla India
101C3 Chiredzi Zim
95A2 Chirfa Niger
32A2 Chiriqui Mt Panama
54C2 Chirpan Bulg
32A2 Chirripo Grande Mt Costa Rica
100B2 Chirundu Zim
100B2 Chisamba Zambia
7C4 Chisasibi Can
73B4 Chishui He R China
Chişinäu = Kishinev
47B2 Chisone R Italy
61H2 Chistopol Russian Fed
68D1 Chita Russian Fed
100A2 Chitado Angola
100A2 Chitembo Angola
12F2 Chitina USA
12F2 Chitina R USA
87B2 Chitradurga India
84C1 Chitral Pak
32A2 Chitré Panama
86C2 Chittagong Bang
85C4 Chittaurgarh India
87B2 Chittoor India
100B2 Chiume Angola

47D1 Chiusa Italy
47B2 Chivasso Italy
100C2 Chivhu Zim
29D2 Chivilcoy Arg
100C2 Chivu Zim
75A1 Chizu Japan
29C3 Choele Choel Arg
34C3 Choique Arg
24B2 Choix Mexico
58B2 Chojnice Pol
99D1 Choke Mts Eth
48B2 Cholet France
23B2 Cholula Mexico
100B2 Choma Zambia
86B1 Chomo Yummo Mt China/India
57C2 Chomutov Czech Republic
63C1 Chona R Russian Fed
74B3 Ch'ŏnan S Korea
76C3 Chon Buri Thai
32A4 Chone Ecuador
74B3 Ch'ŏngjin N Korea
74B3 Chongju N Korea
74B3 Ch'ŏngju S Korea
100A2 Chongoroi Angola
73B4 Chongqing China
74B3 Chŏngŭp S Korea
74B3 Chŏnju S Korea
86B1 Chooyu Mt China/Nepal
59D3 Chortkov Ukraine
74B3 Ch'ŏrwŏn N Korea
59B2 Chorzow Pol
74E3 Choshi Japan
34A3 Chos-Malal Arg
58B2 Choszczno Pol
86A2 Chotanägpur Region, India
96C1 Chott Melrhir Alg
22B2 Chowchilla USA
63D3 Choybalsan Mongolia
6A3 Chrantrey Inlet B Can
111B2 Christchurch NZ
101G1 Christiana S Africa
6D2 Christian,C Can
12H3 Christian Sd USA
6E3 Christianshab Greenland
104D4 Christmas I Indian O
65J5 Chu Kazakhstan
65J5 Chu R Kazakhstan
29C4 Chubut State, Arg
29C4 Chubut R Arg
60D2 Chudovo Russian Fed
Chudskoye Ozero = Peipus, Lake
4D3 Chugach Mts USA
12E2 Chugiak USA
75A1 Chūgoku-sanchi Mts Japan
29F2 Chui Brazil
29B3 Chuillán Chile
77C5 Chukai Malay
76D2 Chu Lai Viet
21B3 Chula Vista USA
12E2 Chulitna USA
63E2 Chulman Russian Fed
32A5 Chulucanas Peru
32A6 Chulumani Bol
65K4 Chulym Russian Fed
63A2 Chulym R Russian Fed
63B2 Chuma R Russian Fed
84D2 Chumar India
63F2 Chumikan Russian Fed
77B3 Chumphon Thai
74B3 Ch'unch'ŏn S Korea
86B2 Chunchura India
74B3 Ch'ungju S Korea
Chungking = Chongqing
99D3 Chunya Tanz
63C1 Chunya R Russian Fed
27L1 Chupara Pt Trinidad
30C3 Chuquicamata Chile
52A1 Chur Switz

86C2 **Churāchāndpur** India
7A4 **Churchill** Can
7D4 **Churchill** *R*
  Labrador, Can
7A4 **Churchill** *R*
  Manitoba, Can
7A4 **Churchill,C** Can
7D4 **Churchill Falls** Can
5H4 **Churchill L** Can
84C3 **Chūru** India
23A2 **Churumuco** Mexico
61J2 **Chusovoy**
  Russian Fed
61G2 **Chuvashskaya**
  Respublika,
  Russian Fed
68B4 **Chuxiong** China
76D3 **Chu Yang Sin** *Mt*
  Viet
78B4 **Ciano d'Enza** Italy
47D2 **Ciano** Indon
35A2 **Cianorte** Brazil
58C2 **Ciechanów** Pol
25E2 **Ciego de Avila** Cuba
32C1 **Ciénaga** Colombia
25D2 **Cienfuegos** Cuba
59B3 **Cieszyn** Pol
51B2 **Cieza** Spain
92B2 **Cihanbeyli** Turk
23A2 **Cihuatlan** Mexico
78R4 **Cijulang** Indon
78B4 **Cilacap** Indon
54C1 **Cimpina** Rom
51C1 **Çinca** *R* Spain
52C2 **Činčer** *Mt* Bosnia-
  Herzegovina
10B3 **Cincinnati** USA
54B1 **Cindrelu** *Mt* Rom
55C3 **Cine** *R* Turk
46C1 **Ciney** Belg
34B3 **Cipolletti** Arg
4D3 **Circle** Alaska, USA
14B3 **Circleville** USA
78B4 **Cirebon** Indon
43D4 **Cirencester** Eng
47D2 **Citadella** Italy
24C3 **Citlaltepetl** *Mt*
  Mexico
100A4 **Citrusdal** S Africa
52B2 **Citta del Vaticano**
  Italy
52B2 **Città di Castello** Italy
24B2 **Ciudad Acuña**
  Mexico
23A2 **Ciudad Altamirano**
  Mexico
33E2 **Ciudad Bolivar** Ven
24B2 **Ciudad Camargo**
  Mexico
25C3 **Ciudad del Carmen**
  Mexico
23B1 **Ciudad del Maiz**
  Mexico
51C1 **Ciudadela** Spain
33E2 **Ciudad Guayana**
  Ven
24B3 **Ciudad Guzman**
  Mexico
23A2 **Ciudad Hidalgo**
  Mexico
24D1 **Ciudad Juárez**
  Mexico
9C4 **Ciudad Lerdo** Mexico
24C2 **Ciudad Madero**
  Mexico
23B2 **Ciudad Mendoza**
  Mexico
24B2 **Ciudad Obregon**
  Mexico
27C4 **Ciudad Ojeda** Ven
33E2 **Ciudad Piar** Ven
50B2 **Ciudad Real** Spain
50A1 **Ciudad Rodrigo**
  Spain
24C2 **Ciudad Valles**
  Mexico
24C2 **Ciudad Victoria**
  Mexico
52B2 **Civitavecchia** Italy
93D2 **Cizre** Turk
43E4 **Clacton-on-Sea** Eng
5G4 **Claire,L** Can
14C2 **Clairton** USA
47A1 **Clairvaux** France

17A1 **Clanton** USA
100A4 **Clanwilliam** S Africa
45C2 **Clara** Irish Rep
34D3 **Claraz** Arg
45B2 **Clare** County,
  Irish Rep
14B2 **Clare** USA
45A2 **Clare** *I* Irish Rep
15D2 **Claremont** USA
18A2 **Claremore** USA
45B2 **Claremorris** Irish Rep
109D1 **Clarence** *R* Aust
111B2 **Clarence** *R* NZ
106C2 **Clarence Str** Aust
12H3 **Clarence Str** USA
19B3 **Clarendon** USA
7E5 **Clarenville** Can
5G4 **Claresholm** Can
18A1 **Clarinda** USA
15C2 **Clarion**
  Pennsylvania, USA
24A3 **Clarión** *I* Mexico
15C2 **Clarion** *R* USA
105J3 **Clarion Fracture Zone**
  Pacific O
11B3 **Clark Hill Res** USA
14B2 **Clark,Pt** Can
14B3 **Clarksburg** USA
11B3 **Clarksdale** USA
12C3 **Clarks Point** USA
20C1 **Clarkston** USA
10D3 **Clarksville** Arkansas,
  USA
35A1 **Claro** *R* Brazil
29D3 **Claromecó** Arg
18A2 **Clay Center** USA
44D2 **Claymore** *Oilfield*
  N Sea
13B3 **Clayoquot Sd** Can
9C3 **Clayton** New Mexico,
  USA
15C2 **Clayton** New York,
  USA
41B3 **Clear** Irish Rep
12E3 **Cleare,C** USA
13D1 **Clear Hills** *Mts* Can
21A2 **Clear L** USA
20B2 **Clear Lake Res** USA
13D2 **Clearwater** Can
11B4 **Clearwater** USA
13E1 **Clearwater** *R* Can
13C2 **Clearwater L** Can
9D3 **Clebune** USA
42E2 **Cleeton** *Oilfield*
  North Sea
22B1 **Clements** USA
79A3 **Cleopatra Needle** *Mt*
  Phil
107D3 **Clermont** Aust
46B2 **Clermont** France
46C2 **Clermont-en-Argonne**
  France
49C2 **Clermont-Ferrand**
  France
46D1 **Clervaux** Germany
47D1 **Cles** Italy
108A2 **Cleve** Aust
42D2 **Cleveland** County,
  Eng
19B3 **Cleveland**
  Mississippi, USA
10B2 **Cleveland** Ohio, USA
11B3 **Cleveland**
  Tennessee, USA
19A3 **Cleveland** Texas,
  USA
41B3 **Clew** *B* Irish Rep
45A2 **Clifden** Irish Rep
109D1 **Clifton** Aust
16B2 **Clifton** New Jersey,
  USA
108A1 **Clifton Hills** Aust
13F3 **Climax** Can
18B2 **Clinton** Arkansas,
  USA
5F4 **Clinton** Can
16C2 **Clinton** Connecticut,
  USA
16D1 **Clinton**
  Massachusetts, USA
19B3 **Clinton** Mississippi,
  USA
18B2 **Clinton** Missouri,
  USA

16B2 **Clinton** New Jersey,
  USA
4H3 **Clinton-Colden L** Can
24B3 **Clipperton I** Pacific O
30C2 **Cliza** Bol
45B3 **Clonakilty** Irish Rep
107D3 **Cloncurry** Aust
45C1 **Clones** Irish Rep
45C2 **Clonmel** Irish Rep
10A2 **Cloquet** USA
12C2 **Cloudy Mt** USA
22C2 **Clovis** California,
  USA
9C3 **Clovis** New Mexico,
  USA
60B4 **Cluj** Rom
54B1 **Cluj-Napoca** Rom
47B1 **Cluses** France
47C2 **Clusone** Italy
111A3 **Clutha** *R* NZ
43C3 **Clwyd** County, Wales
6D2 **Clyde** Can
111A3 **Clyde** NZ
42B2 **Clyde** *R* Scot
23A2 **Coahuayana** Mexico
23A2 **Coalcomán** Mexico
13E2 **Coaldale** Can
21B2 **Coaldale** USA
21A2 **Coalinga** USA
33E5 **Coari** *R* Brazil
17A1 **Coastal Plain** USA
4F4 **Coast Mts** Can
8A2 **Coast Ranges** *Mts*
  USA
42B2 **Coatbridge** Scot
23B2 **Coatepec** Mexico
16B3 **Coatesville** USA
15D1 **Coaticook** Can
6B3 **Coats I** Can
112B1 **Coats Land** Region,
  Ant
25C3 **Coatzacoalcos**
  Mexico
7C5 **Cobalt** Can
25C3 **Cobán** Guatemala
109C2 **Cobar** Aust
45B3 **Cobh** Irish Rep
32D6 **Cobija** Bol
16B1 **Cobleskill** USA
51B2 **Cobo de Palos** *C*
  Spain
7C5 **Cobourg** Can
106C2 **Cobourg Pen** Aust
57C2 **Coburg** Germany
32B4 **Coca** Ecuador
17B2 **Coca** USA
30C2 **Cochabamba** Bol
46D1 **Cochem** Germany
87B3 **Cochin** India
13E2 **Cochrane** Alberta,
  Can
7B5 **Cochrane** Ontario,
  Can
108B2 **Cockburn** Aust
16A3 **Cockeysville** USA
27H1 **Cockpit Country,The**
  Jamaica
25D3 **Coco** *R* Honduras/
  Nic
98A2 **Cocobeach** Gabon
27L1 **Cocos B** Trinidad
104C4 **Cocos Is** Indian O
23A1 **Cocula** Mexico
10C2 **Cod,C** USA
111A3 **Codfish I** NZ
7D4 **Cod I** Can
47E2 **Codigoro** Italy
31C2 **Codó** Brazil
47C2 **Codogno** Italy
8C2 **Cody** USA
56B2 **Coesfeld** Germany
8B2 **Coeur d'Alene** USA
109D1 **Coffin B** Aust
109D2 **Coff's Harbour** Aust
23B2 **Cofre de Perote** *Mt*
  Mexico
48B2 **Cognac** France
15D2 **Cohoes** USA
108B3 **Cohuna** Aust
29B5 **Coihaique** Chile
87B2 **Coimbatore** India
50A1 **Coimbra** Port

32A3 **Cojimies** Ecuador
107D4 **Colac** Aust
31C5 **Colatina** Brazil
112B6 **Colbeck,C** Ant
43E4 **Colchester** Eng
16C2 **Colchester** USA
47B1 **Col de la Faucille**
  France
12E2 **Cold L** Can
52A1 **Col du Grand St
  Bernard** *P*
  Italy/Switz
47B2 **Col du Lautaret** *P*
  France
52A1 **Col du Mont Cenis** *P*
  France/Italy
14B2 **Coldwater** USA
12F1 **Coleen** *R* USA
14B2 **Coleman** Michigan,
  USA
101G1 **Colenso** S Africa
45C1 **Coleraine** N Ire
111B2 **Coleridge,L** NZ
100B4 **Colesberg** S Africa
22C1 **Coleville** USA
21A2 **Colfax** California,
  USA
19B3 **Colfax** Louisiana,
  USA
20C1 **Colfax** Washington,
  USA
24B3 **Colima** Mexico
23A2 **Colima** State, Mexico
34A2 **Colina** Chile
44A3 **Coll** *I* Scot
109C1 **Collarenebri** Aust
52A2 **Colle de Tende** *P*
  France/Italy
12E2 **College** USA
17B1 **College Park**
  Georgia, USA
16A3 **College Park**
  Washington, USA
19A3 **College Station** USA
106A4 **Collie** Aust
106B2 **Collier B** Aust
46A1 **Collines de L'Artois**
  Mts France
46B2 **Collines De Thiérache**
  France
14B2 **Collingwood** Can
110B2 **Collingwood** NZ
19C3 **Collins** Mississippi,
  USA
4H2 **Collinson Pen** Can
107D3 **Collinsville** Aust
18C2 **Collinsville** Illinois,
  USA
18A2 **Collinsville**
  Oklahoma, USA
34A3 **Collipulli** Chile
49D2 **Colmar** France
  Cologne = Köln
35B2 **Colômbia** Brazil
32B3 **Colombia** Republic,
  S America
15C3 **Colombia** USA
87B3 **Colombo** Sri Lanka
25D2 **Colón** Cuba
32B2 **Colón** Panama
29C2 **Colonia** Urug
34D2 **Colonia del
  Sacramento** Urug
34B3 **Colonia 25 de Mayo**
  Arg
29C5 **Colonia Las Heras**
  Arg
44A3 **Colonsay** *I* Scot
23A1 **Colontlán** Mexico
27E5 **Coloradito** Ven
8C3 **Colorado** State, USA
9B3 **Colorado** *R* Arizona,
  USA
29D3 **Colorado** *R*
  Buenos Aires, Arg
9D3 **Colorado** *R* Texas,
  USA
9B3 **Colorado Plat** USA
8C3 **Colorado Springs**
  USA
22D3 **Colton** USA
16A3 **Columbia** Maryland,
  USA

19C3	**Columbia** Mississippi, USA
10A3	**Columbia** Missouri, USA
15C2	**Columbia** Pennsylvania, USA
11B3	**Columbia** S Carolina, USA
11B3	**Columbia** Tennessee, USA
13D2	**Columbia** *R* Can
8A2	**Columbia** *R* Can
5G4	**Columbia,Mt** Can
20C1	**Columbia Plat** USA
11B3	**Columbus** Georgia, USA
14A3	**Columbus** Indiana, USA
11B3	**Columbus** Mississippi, USA
8D2	**Columbus** Nebraska, USA
10B2	**Columbus** Ohio, USA
19A4	**Columbus** Texas, USA
20C1	**Colville** USA
4C3	**Colville** *R* USA
110C1	**Colville,C** NZ
4F3	**Colville** *L* Can
42C3	**Colwyn Bay** Wales
47E2	**Comacchio** Italy
22B1	**Comanche Res** USA
112C2	**Comandante Ferraz** *Base* Ant
25D3	**Comayagua** Honduras
34A2	**Combarbalá** Chile
45C2	**Comeragh** *Mts* Irish Rep
86C2	**Comilla** Bang
25C3	**Comitán** Mexico
46C2	**Commercy** France
6B3	**Committees B** Can
52A1	**Como** Italy
29C5	**Comodoro Rivadavia** Arg
23A1	**Comonfort** Mexico
87B3	**Comorin,C** India
101D2	**Comoros** *Is* Indian O
49C2	**Compiègne** France
23A1	**Compostela** Mexico
34B2	**Comte Salas** Arg
86C1	**Cona** China
97A4	**Conakry** Guinea
34B2	**Concarán** Arg
48B2	**Concarneau** France
35D1	**Conceição da Barra** Brazil
31B3	**Conceição do Araguaia** Brazil
35C1	**Conceição do Mato Dentro** Brazil
29B3	**Concepción** Chile
30E3	**Concepción** Par
29E2	**Concepción** *P* Arg
24B2	**Concepción del Oro** Mexico
34D2	**Concepcion del Uruguay** Arg
9A3	**Conception,Pt** USA
35B2	**Conchas** Brazil
9C4	**Conchos** *R* Mexico
21A2	**Concord** California, USA
10C2	**Concord** New Hampshire, USA
29E2	**Concordia** Arg
8D3	**Concordia** USA
20B1	**Concrete** USA
109D1	**Condamine** Aust
107D4	**Condobolin** Aust
20B1	**Condon** USA
46C1	**Condroz** *Mts* Belg
17A1	**Conecuh** *R* USA
47E2	**Conegliano** Italy
89F8	**Congo** Republic, Africa
89F8	**Congo** *R* Congo
	Congo,R = Zaïre
14B1	**Coniston** Can
45B2	**Connaught** Region, Irish Rep
14B2	**Conneaut** USA
10C2	**Connecticut** State, USA
15D2	**Connecticut** *R* USA
15C2	**Connellsville** USA
45B2	**Connemara,Mts of** Irish Rep
14A3	**Connersville** USA
108B2	**Conoble** Aust
19A3	**Conroe** USA
35C2	**Conselheiro Lafaiete** Brazil
77D4	**Con Son** *Is* Viet
	Constance,L = Bodensee
60C5	**Constanta** Rom
96C1	**Constantine** Alg
12C3	**Constantine,C** USA
29B3	**Constitución** Chile
13F3	**Consul** Can
47E2	**Contarina** Italy
31C4	**Contas** *R* Brazil
23B2	**Contreras** Mexico
4H3	**Contuoyto L** Can
11A3	**Conway** Arkansas, USA
15D2	**Conway** New Hampshire, USA
17C1	**Conway** South Carolina, USA
108A1	**Conway,L** Aust
42C3	**Conwy** Wales
106C3	**Coober Pedy** Aust
110B2	**Cook** *Str* NZ
13B2	**Cook,C** Can
4C3	**Cook Inlet** *B* USA
111B2	**Cook Is** Pacific O
111B2	**Cook,Mt** NZ
107D2	**Cooktown** Aust
109C2	**Coolabah** Aust
108C1	**Cooladdi** Aust
109C2	**Coolah** Aust
109C2	**Coolamon** Aust
106B4	**Coolgardie** Aust
109C3	**Cooma** Aust
109C2	**Coonabarabran** Aust
109C2	**Coonamble** Aust
108A2	**Coondambo** Aust
108C1	**Coongoola** Aust
87B2	**Coonoor** India
108B1	**Cooper Basin** Aust
106C3	**Cooper Creek** Aust
108B1	**Cooper Creek** *R* Aust
108A3	**Coorong,The** Aust
109D1	**Cooroy** Aust
20B2	**Coos B** USA
20B2	**Coos Bay** USA
107D4	**Cootamundra** Aust
45C1	**Cootehill** Irish Rep
23B2	**Copala** Mexico
23B2	**Copalillo** Mexico
	Copenhagen = København
30B4	**Copiapó** Chile
47D2	**Copparo** Italy
12F2	**Copper** *R* USA
4D3	**Copper Centre** USA
14B1	**Copper Cliff** Can
	Coppermine = Qurlurtuuq
4G3	**Coppermine** *R* Can
	Coquilhatville = Mbandaka
30B4	**Coquimbo** Chile
54B2	**Corabia** Rom
17B2	**Coral Gables** USA
6B3	**Coral Harbour** Can
107D2	**Coral S** Aust/PNG
104F4	**Coral Sea Basin** Pacific O
107E2	**Coral Sea Island Territories** Aust
108B3	**Corangamite,L** Aust
33F3	**Corantijn** *R* Surinam/Guyana
46B2	**Corbeil-Essonnes** France
50A1	**Corcubion** Spain
11B3	**Cordele** USA
50A1	**Cordillera Cantabrica** *Mts* Spain
26C3	**Cordillera Central** *Mts* Dom Rep
79B2	**Cordillera Central** *Mts* Phil
34B2	**Cordillera de Ansita** *Mts* Arg
32B5	**Cordillera de los Andes** *Mts* Peru
30C4	**Cordillera del Toro** *Mt* Arg
32C2	**Cordillera de Mérida** Ven
34A3	**Cordillera de Viento** *Mts* Arg
25D3	**Cordillera Isabelia** *Mts* Nic
32B3	**Cordillera Occidental** *Mts* Colombia
32B3	**Cordillera Oriental** *Mts* Colombia
108B1	**Cordillo Downs** Aust
29D2	**Córdoba** Arg
24C3	**Córdoba** Mexico
50B2	**Córdoba** Spain
29D2	**Córdoba** State, Arg
4D3	**Cordova** USA
	Corfu = Kérkira
109D2	**Coricudgy,Mt** Aust
53C3	**Corigliano Calabro** Italy
11B3	**Corinth** Mississippi, USA
31C5	**Corinto** Brazil
45B2	**Cork** County, Irish Rep
41B3	**Cork** Irish Rep
92A1	**Çorlu** Turk
31C5	**Cornel Fabriciano** Brazil
35A2	**Cornelio Procópio** Brazil
7E5	**Corner Brook** Can
109C3	**Corner Inlet** *B* Aust
7C5	**Corning** USA
43B4	**Cornwall** County, Eng
43B4	**Cornwall,C** Eng
43B4	**Cornwall I** Can
6A2	**Cornwallis I** Can
32D1	**Coro** Ven
31C2	**Coroatá** Brazil
32C2	**Coroico** Bol
35B1	**Coromandel** Brazil
87C2	**Coromandel Coast** India
110C1	**Coromandel Pen** NZ
110C1	**Coromandel Range** *Mts* NZ
22D4	**Corona** California, USA
13E2	**Coronation** Can
4G3	**Coronation G** Can
29B3	**Coronel** Chile
34D3	**Coronel Brandsen** Arg
34C3	**Coronel Dorrego** Arg
35C1	**Coronel Fabriciano** Brazil
30E4	**Coronel Oviedo** Par
29D3	**Coronel Pringles** Arg
34C3	**Coronel Suárez** Arg
34D3	**Coronel Vidal** Arg
30B2	**Coropuna** *Mt* Peru
109C3	**Corowa** Aust
49D3	**Corps** France
9D4	**Corpus Christi** USA
9D4	**Corpus Christi,L** USA
79B3	**Corregidor** *I* Phil
35A1	**Corrente** *R* Mato Grosso, Brazil
30E4	**Corrientes** Arg
30E4	**Corrientes** State, Arg
19B3	**Corrigan** USA
106A4	**Corrigin** Aust
107E2	**Corringe Is** Aust
109C3	**Corryong** Aust
52A2	**Corse** *I* Medit S
42B2	**Corsewall** *Pt* Scot
	Corsica = Corse
9D3	**Corsicana** USA
52A2	**Corte** Corse
9C3	**Cortez** USA
52B1	**Cortina d'Ampezzo** Italy
15C2	**Cortland** USA
23A2	**Coruca de Catalan** Mexico
93D1	**Çoruh** *R* Turk
60E5	**Çorum** Turk
30E2	**Corumbá** Brazil
35B1	**Corumba** *R* Brazil
35B1	**Corumbaíba** Brazil
20B2	**Corvallis** USA
96A1	**Corvo** *I* Açores
43C3	**Corwen** Wales
23B2	**Coscomatopec** Mexico
53C3	**Cosenza** Italy
101D1	**Cosmoledo** *Is* Seychelles
34C2	**Cosquin** Arg
51B2	**Costa Blanca** Region, Spain
51C1	**Costa Brava** Region, Spain
50B2	**Costa de la Luz** Region, Spain
50B2	**Costa del Sol** Region, Spain
22D4	**Costa Mesa** USA
25D3	**Costa Rica** Republic, Cent America
79B4	**Cotabato** Phil
30C3	**Cotagaita** Bol
49D3	**Côte d'Azur** Region, France
46C2	**Côtes de Meuse** *Mts* France
97C4	**Cotonou** Benin
32B4	**Cotopaxi** *Mt* Ecuador
43C4	**Cotswold Hills** *Upland* Eng
20B2	**Cottage Grove** USA
56C2	**Cottbus** Germany
108A3	**Couedic,C du** Aust
20C1	**Couer d'Alene L** USA
46B2	**Coulommiers** France
15C1	**Coulonge** *R* Can
22B2	**Coulterville** USA
4B3	**Council** USA
8D2	**Council Bluffs** USA
58C1	**Courland Lagoon** *Lg* Lithuania/Russian Fed
47B2	**Courmayeur** Italy
13B3	**Courtenay** Can
	Courtrai = Kortrijk
48B2	**Coutances** France
43D3	**Coventry** Eng
50A1	**Covilhã** Spain
17B1	**Covington** Georgia, USA
19B3	**Covington** Louisiana, USA
109C2	**Cowal,L** Aust
108B3	**Cowangie** Aust
15D1	**Cowansville** Can
108A1	**Coward Springs** Aust
108C3	**Cowell** Aust
108C3	**Cowes** Aust
20B1	**Cowichan L** Can
20B1	**Cowlitz** *R* USA
109C2	**Cowra** Aust
30F2	**Coxim** Brazil
16C1	**Coxsackie** USA
86C2	**Cox's Bazar** Bang
22B2	**Coyote** USA
23A2	**Coyuca de Benitez** Mexico
59B2	**Cracow** Pol
100B4	**Cradock** S Africa
8C2	**Craig** USA
57C3	**Crailsheim** Germany
54B2	**Craiova** Rom
15D2	**Cranberry L** USA
5G5	**Cranbrook** Can
20C2	**Crane** Oregon, USA
16D2	**Cranston** USA
20B2	**Crater L** USA
20B2	**Crater Lake Nat Pk** USA
31C3	**Crateus** Brazil
31D3	**Crato** Brazil
14A2	**Crawfordsville** USA
17B1	**Crawfordville** USA
43D4	**Crawley** Eng
5H4	**Cree L** Can
46B2	**Creil** France

129

Crema

47C2 Crema Italy
52B1 Cremona Italy
46B2 Crépy-en-Valois France
52B2 Cres / Yugos
20B2 Crescent City USA
34C2 Crespo Arg
13D3 Creston Can
18B1 Creston USA
17A1 Crestview USA
108B3 Creswick Aust
47A1 Crêt de la Neige Mt France
    Crete = Kriti
18A1 Crete USA
55B3 Crete,S of Greece
48C2 Creuse R France
43C3 Crewe Eng
44B3 Crianlarich Scot
30G4 Criciuma Brazil
44C3 Crieff Scot
12G3 Crillon,Mt USA
35B1 Cristalina Brazil
52C1 Croatia Republic, Europe
78D1 Crocker Range Mts Malay
19A3 Crockett USA
106C2 Croker I Aust
44C3 Cromarty Scot
43E3 Cromer Eng
111A3 Cromwell NZ
11C4 Crooked I The Bahamas
13C2 Crooked R Can
8D2 Crookston USA
100A2 Crookwell Aust
109D1 Croppa Creek Aust
11A3 Crossett USA
12G3 Cross Sd USA
53C3 Crotone Italy
19B3 Crowley USA
27K1 Crown Pt Tobago
109D1 Crows Nest Aust
107D2 Croydon Aust
43D4 Croydon Eng
104B5 Crozet Basin Indian O
4F2 Crozier Chan Can
30F4 Cruz Alta Brazil
25E3 Cruz,C Cuba
29D2 Cruz del Eje Arg
35C2 Cruzeiro Brazil
32C5 Cruzeiro do Sul Brazil
13C1 Crysdale,Mt Can
108A2 Crystal Brook Aust
18B2 Crystal City Missouri, USA
14A1 Crystal Falls USA
101C2 Cuamba Mozam
100B2 Cuando R Angola
100A2 Cuangar Angola
    Cuango,n = Kwango,R
34C2 Cuarto R Arg
24B2 Cuauhtémoc Mexico
23B2 Cuautla Mexico
25D2 Cuba Republic, Caribbean S
100A2 Cubango R Angola
100A2 Cuchi R Angola
100A2 Cuchi R Angola
34C3 Cuchillo Co Arg
32D3 Cucuí Brazil
32C2 Cúcuta Colombia
87B2 Cuddalore India
87B2 Cuddapah India
106A3 Cue Aust
32B4 Cuenca Ecuador
51B1 Cuenca Spain
24C3 Cuernavaca Mexico
19A4 Cuero USA
30E2 Cuiabá Brazil
30E2 Cuiabá R Brazil
23B2 Cuicatlan Mexico
35C1 Cuieté R Brazil
44A3 Cuillin Hills Mts Scot
98B3 Cuilo R Angola
100A2 Cuito R Angola
100A2 Cuito Cunavale Angola
23A2 Cuitzeo Mexico
77D3 Cu Lao Hon / Viet

109C3 Culcairn Aust
109C1 Culgoa R Aust
24B2 Culiacán Mexico
79A3 Culion / Phil
17A1 Cullman USA
47A2 Culoz France
15C3 Culpeper USA
32J7 Culpepper / Ecuador
17B2 Culter Ridge USA
111B2 Culverden NZ
33E1 Cumaná Ven
10C3 Cumberland Maryland, USA
11B3 Cumberland R USA
6D3 Cumberland Pen Can
6D3 Cumbernauld Sd Can
42C2 Cumbria Eng
21A2 Cummings USA
108A2 Cummins Aust
42B2 Cumnock Scot
34A3 Cunco Chile
100A2 Cunene R Angola/Namibia
52A2 Cuneo Italy
107D3 Cunnamulla Aust
44C3 Cupar Scot
54B2 Cuprija Serbia,Yugos
27D4 Curaçao / Caribbean S
34A3 Curacautin Chile
34A3 Curacö R Arg
34A3 Curanilahue Chile
34A3 Curepto Chile
29B2 Curicó Chile
30G4 Curitiba Brazil
108A2 Curnamona Aust
100A2 Curoca R Angola
31C5 Curvelo Brazil
18A2 Cushing USA
13D2 Cutbank R Can
17B1 Cuthbert USA
34B3 Cutral-Có Arg
86B2 Cuttack India
100A2 Cuvelai Angola
56B2 Cuxhaven Germany
14B2 Cuyahoga Falls USA
79B3 Cuyo Is Phil
32C6 Cuzco Peru
99C3 Cyangugu Zaïre
    Cyclades = Kikládhes
13F3 Cypress Hills Mts Can
92B3 Cyprus Republic, Medit S
6D3 Cyrus Field B Can
59B2 Czech Republic Republic, Europe
59B2 Częstochowa Pol

D

76C1 Da R Viet
69E2 Da'an China
94C3 Dab'a Jordan
27C4 Dabajuro Ven
99E2 Dabaro Somalia
73B3 Daba Shan Mts China
99D1 Dabat Eth
86A1 Dabhoi India
73C3 Dabie Shan Mts China
97A3 Dabola Guinea
97B4 Dabou Ivory Coast
59B2 Dabrowa Gorn Pol
57C3 Dachau Germany
52B1 Dachstein Mt Austria
73A3 Dada He R China
17B2 Dade City USA
84B3 Dadhar Pak
85B3 Dadu Pak
68C3 Dadu He R China
79B3 Daet Phil
73B4 Dafang China
76B2 Daga R Burma
99E2 Dagabur Eth
97A3 Dagana Sen
65F5 Dagestanskaya Respublic, Russian Fed
79B2 Dagupan Phil
92B4 Dahab Egypt
63E3 Da Hinggan Ling Mts China

17B1 Dahlonega USA
85C4 Dāhod India
86A1 Dailekh Nepal
34C3 Daireaux Arg
69F4 Daitō Is Pacific O
106C3 Dajarra Aust
97A3 Dakar Sen
95B2 Dakhla Oasis Egypt
97C3 Dakoro Niger
54B2 Dakovica Serbia, Yugos
54A1 Dakovo Croatia
100B2 Dala Angola
97A3 Dalaba Guinea
72D1 Dalai Nur L China
68C2 Dalandzadgad Mongolia
79B3 Dalanganem Is Phil
76D3 Da Lat Viet
72A1 Dalay Mongolia
107E3 Dalby Aust
39F7 Dalen Nor
72A1 Dales,The Upland Eng
17A1 Daleville USA
9C3 Dalhart USA
4E2 Dalhousie,C Can
72E2 Dalian China
9D3 Dallas USA
20B1 Dalles,The USA
6E4 Dall I USA
84D2 Dalli Rajhara India
97C3 Dallol R Niger
97C3 Dallol Bosso R Niger
52C2 Dalmatia Region Bosnia-Herzegovina
69F2 Dal'nerechensk Russian Fed
97B4 Daloa Ivory Coast
73B4 Dalou Shan Mts China
86A2 Dāltenganj India
17B1 Dalton Georgia, USA
16C1 Dalton Massachusetts, USA
106C2 Daly R Aust
21A2 Daly City USA
106C2 Daly Waters Aust
79B4 Damaguete Phil
85C4 Daman India
92B3 Damanhûr Egypt
71D4 Damar / Indon
98B2 Damara CAR
92C3 Damascus Syria
16A3 Damascus USA
97D3 Damaturu Nig
90B2 Damavand Iran
98B3 Damba Angola
87C3 Dambulla Sri Lanka
90B2 Damghan Iran
85D4 Damoh India
99E2 Damot Eth
94B2 Damour Leb
106A3 Dampier Aust
84B3 Daná Jordan
22C2 Dana,Mt USA
97B4 Danané Lib
76D2 Da Nang Viet
79B3 Danau Poso L Indon
70A3 Danau Tobu L Indon
71D4 Danau Tuwuti L Indon
73A3 Danbu China
15D2 Danbury USA
86A1 Dandeldhura Nepal
87A1 Dandeli India
108C3 Dandenong Aust
74A2 Dandong China
100A4 Danger Pt S Africa
99D1 Dangila Eth
6D1 Danguard Jenson Land Region Can
7E4 Daniels Harbour Can
6G3 Dannebrogs Øy / Greenland
110C2 Dannevirke NZ
87C1 Dantewära India
    Danube = Donau
10B2 Danville Illinois, USA
11B3 Danville Kentucky, USA
16A2 Danville Pennsylvania, USA

11C3 Danville Virginia, USA
    Danzig = Gdańsk
73C4 Dao Xian China
73B4 Daozhen China
79B4 Dapaab,Mt Phil
79B4 Dapitan Phil
68B3 Da Qaidam China
69E2 Daqing China
94C2 Dar'a Syria
91B4 Dārāb Iran
95A1 Daraj Libya
90B3 Dārān Iran
92C3 Dar'ā Salkhad Syria
86B1 Darbhanga India
22C1 Dardanelle USA
18B2 Dardanelle,L USA
    Dar-el-Beïda = Casablanca
99D3 Dar es Salaam Tanz
110B1 Dargaville NZ
17B1 Darien USA
    Darjeeling = Därjiling
86B1 Därjiling India
107D4 Darling R Aust
109C1 Darling Downs Aust
6C1 Darling Pen Can
72D1 Darlington Aust
42D2 Darlington Eng
17C1 Darlington USA
57B3 Darmstadt Germany
95B1 Darnah Libya
22B2 Darnick Aust
112C10 Darnley,C Ant
51B1 Daroca Spain
98C2 Dar Rounga Region, CAR
43C4 Dart R Eng
41C3 Dartmoor Moorland Eng
43C4 Dartmoor Nat Pk Eng
7D5 Dartmouth Can
43C4 Dartmouth Eng
107D1 Daru PNG
72A2 Daruvar Croatia
106C2 Darwin Aust
91B4 Daryācheh-ye Bakhtegan L Iran
91B4 Daryācheh-ye Mahārlū L Iran
90B3 Daryācheh-ye Namak Salt Flat Iran
90D3 Daryācheh-ye-Sistan Salt L Iran/Afghan
91B4 Daryācheh-ye Tashk L Iran
80C2 Daryācheh-ye Urūmīyeh L Iran
91C4 Dārzīn Iran
91B4 Das / UAE
73C3 Dashennonglia Mt China
90C2 Dasht Iran
90B3 Dasht-e-Kavir Salt Desert Iran
90C3 Dasht-e Lut Salt Desert Iran
90D3 Dasht-e Naomid Desert Region Iran
85D3 Datia India
72A2 Datong China
72A2 Datong He R China
79B4 Datu Piang Phil
39K7 Daugava R Latvia
60C2 Daugavpils Latvia
6D1 Dauguard Jensen Land Greenland
84A1 Daulatabad Afghan
85D3 Daulpur India
46D1 Daun Germany
87A1 Daund India
5H4 Dauphin Can
16A2 Dauphin USA
49D2 Dauphiné Region, France
97C3 Daura Nig
85D3 Dausa India
87B2 Dāvangere India
79C4 Davao Phil
79C4 Davao G Phil
22A2 Davenport California, USA

10A2 **Davenport** Iowa, USA
32A2 **David** Panama
4D3 **Davidson Mts** USA
21A2 **Davis** USA
112C10 **Davis** *Base* Ant
7D4 **Davis Inlet** Can
6E3 **Davis Str** Greenland/ Can
61J3 **Davlekanovo** Russian Fed
47C1 **Davos** Switz
99E2 **Dawa** *R* Eth
73A4 **Dawan** China
84B2 **Dawat Yar** Afghan
Dawei = Tavoy
91B4 **Dawḥat Salwah** *B* Qatar/S Arabia
76B2 **Dawna Range** *Mts* Burma
4E3 **Dawson** Can
17B1 **Dawson** Georgia, USA
107D3 **Dawson** *R* Aust
5F4 **Dawson Creek** Can
13D2 **Dawson,Mt** Can
12G2 **Dawson Range** *Mts* Can
73A3 **Dawu** China
73C3 **Dawu** China
48B3 **Dax** France
73B2 **Daxian** China
73A3 **Daxin** China
73A3 **Daxue Shan** *Mts* China
73C4 **Dayong** China
94C2 **Dayr 'Ali** Syria
94C1 **Dayr 'Atiyah** Syria
93D2 **Dayr az Zawr** Syria
10B3 **Dayton** Ohio, USA
19B4 **Dayton** Texas, USA
20C1 **Dayton** Washington, USA
11B4 **Daytona Beach** USA
73C4 **Dayu** China
78D3 **Dayu** Indon
72D2 **Da Yunhe** *R* China
20C2 **Dayville** USA
73A3 **Dazhu** China
100B4 **De Aar** S Africa
26C2 **Deadman's Cay** The Bahamas
92C3 **Dead S** Israel/Jordan
46A1 **Deal** Eng
101G1 **Dealesville** S Africa
13B2 **Dean** *R* Can
13B2 **Dean Chan** Can
34C2 **Deán Funes** Arg
14B2 **Dearborn** USA
4F3 **Dease Arm** *B* Can
4E4 **Dease Lake** Can
9B3 **Death V** USA
48C2 **Deauville** France
97B4 **Debakala** Ivory Coast
12B2 **Debauch Mt** USA
27L1 **Débé** Trinidad
59C2 **Debica** Pol
58C2 **Deblin** Pol
97B3 **Débo,L** Mali
59C3 **Debrecen** Hung
99D2 **Debre Birhan** Eth
99D1 **Debre Markos** Eth
99D1 **Debre Tabor** Eth
11B3 **Decatur** Alabama, USA
17B1 **Decatur** Georgia, USA
10B3 **Decatur** Illinois, USA
14B2 **Decatur** Indiana, USA
48C3 **Decazeville** France
73A4 **Dechang** China
97B3 **Dédougou** Burkina
101C2 **Dedza** Malawi
42B2 **Dee** *R* Dumfries and Galloway, Scot
42C3 **Dee** *R* Eng/Wales
44C3 **Dee** *R* Grampian, Scot
15C1 **Deep River** Can
16C2 **Deep River** USA
109D1 **Deepwater** Aust
7E5 **Deer Lake** Can
8B2 **Deer Lodge** USA

34D3 **Defferrari** Arg
17A1 **De Funiak Springs** USA
68B3 **Dêgê** China
99E1 **Degeh Bur** Eth
106A3 **De Grey** *R* Aust
91B3 **Deh Bid** Iran
84B1 **Dehi** Afghan
96D1 **Dehibat** Tunisia
87B3 **Dehiwala-Mt Lavinia** Sri Lanka
90A3 **Dehlorän** Iran
84D2 **Dehra Dün** India
86A2 **Dehri** India
98C2 **Deim Zubeir** Sudan
94B2 **Deir Abu Sa'id** Jordan
94C1 **Deir el Ahmar** Leb
60B4 **Dej** Rom
19B3 **De Kalb** Texas, USA
63G2 **De Kastri** Russian Fed
98C3 **Dekese** Zaire
98B2 **Dekoa** CAR
106B1 **Dekusi** Indon
9B3 **Delano** USA
10C3 **Delaware** State, USA
14B2 **Delaware** USA
15C2 **Delaware** *R* USA
10C3 **Delaware B** USA
109C3 **Delegate** Aust
47B1 **Delemont** Switz
101D2 **Delgado** *C* Mozam
84D3 **Delhi** India
15D2 **Delhi** New York, USA
92B1 **Delice** Turk
24B2 **Delicias** Mexico
90B3 **Delijän** Iran
47B1 **Delle** France
22D4 **Del Mar** USA
39F8 **Delmenhorst** Germany
4B3 **De Long** *Mts* USA
109C4 **Deloraine** Aust
5H5 **Deloraine** Can
17B2 **Delray Beach** USA
9C4 **Del Rio** USA
8B3 **Delta** USA
12E2 **Delta** *R* USA
12E2 **Delta Junction** USA
46C1 **Demer** *R* Belg
9C3 **Deming** USA
54C2 **Demirköy** Turk
49C1 **Denain** France
82A2 **Denau** Uzbekistan
42C3 **Denbigh** Wales
12B2 **Denbigh,C** USA
78B3 **Dendang** Indon
46C1 **Dendermond** Belg
99D2 **Dendi** *Mt* Eth
46B1 **Dêndre** *R* Belg
72B1 **Dengkou** China
72C3 **Deng Xian** China
Den Haag = 's-Gravenhage
27H1 **Denham,Mt** Jamaica
56A2 **Den Helder** Neth
51C2 **Denia** Spain
107D4 **Deniliquin** Aust
20C2 **Denio** USA
9D3 **Denison** Texas, USA
12D3 **Denison,Mt** USA
92A2 **Denizli** Turk
39F7 **Denmark** Kingdom, Europe
1C1 **Denmark Str** Greenland/Iceland
27P2 **Dennery** St Lucia
78D4 **Denpasar** Indon
16B3 **Denton** Maryland, USA
9D3 **Denton** Texas, USA
107E1 **D'Entrecasteaux Is** PNG
47B1 **Dents du Midi** *Mt* Switz
8C3 **Denver** USA
98B2 **Déo** *R* Cam
86B2 **Deoghar** India
85C5 **Deolāli** India
84D1 **Deosai Plain** India

95B3 **Dépression du Mourdi** Chad
19B3 **De Queen** USA
84C3 **Dera** Pak
84B3 **Dera Bugti** Pak
84C2 **Dera Ismail Khan** Pak
106B2 **Derby** Aust
16C2 **Derby** Connecticut, USA
43D3 **Derby** County, Eng
43D3 **Derby** Eng
18A2 **Derby** Kansas, USA
60E3 **Dergachi** Ukraine
19B3 **De Ridder** USA
Derna = Darnah
95C3 **Derudeb** Sudan
109C4 **Derwent Bridge** Aust
34B2 **Desaguadero** USA
34B2 **Desaguadero** *R* Arg
30C2 **Desaguadero** *R* Bol
21B3 **Descanso** Mexico
20B2 **Deschutes** *R* USA
99D1 **Desē** Eth
29C5 **Deseado** Arg
29C5 **Deseado** *R* Arg
47D2 **Desenzano** Italy
96A1 **Deserta Grande** *I* Medeira
30C4 **Desierto de Atacama** *Desert* Chile
18B2 **Desloge** USA
10A2 **Des Moines** Iowa, USA
60D3 **Desna** *R* Russian Fed
29B6 **Desolación** *I* Chile
14A2 **Des Plaines** USA
56C2 **Dessau** Germany
12G2 **Destruction Bay** Can
46A1 **Desvres** France
54B1 **Deta** Rom
100B2 **Dete** Zim
10B2 **Detroit** USA
76D3 **Det Udom** Thai
54B1 **Deva** Rom
56B2 **Deventer** Neth
44C3 **Deveron** *R* Scot
85C3 **Devikot** India
22C2 **Devil Postpile Nat Mon** USA
22C1 **Devils Gate** *P* USA
Devil's Island = Isla du Diable
8D2 **Devils Lake** USA
12H3 **Devils Paw** *Mt* Can
43D4 **Devizes** Eng
85D3 **Devoll** *R* Alb
55B2 **Devoll** *R* Alb
43B4 **Devon** County, Eng
6A2 **Devon I** Can
107D5 **Devonport** Aust
86C1 **Dewangiri** Bhutan
85D4 **Dewäs** India
101G1 **Dewetsdorp** S Africa
11B3 **Dewey Res** USA
19B3 **De Witt** USA
18C2 **Dexter** Missouri, USA
73A3 **Deyang** China
90C3 **Deyhuk** Iran
90A3 **Dezfül** Iran
72D2 **Dezhou** China
90A2 **Dezh Shähpür** Iran
91B4 **Dhahran** S Arabia
86C2 **Dhäkä** Bang
87B2 **Dhamavaram** India
86A2 **Dhamtari** India
86B2 **Dhanbäd** India
86A1 **Dhangarhi** Nepal
86B1 **Dhankuta** Nepal
85D4 **Dhär** India
87B2 **Dharmapuri** India
84D2 **Dharmshala** India
97B3 **Dhar Oualata** *Desert Region* Maur
86A1 **Dhaulagiri** *Mt* Nepal
86B2 **Dhenkänäl** India
94B3 **Dhibah** Jordan
55C3 **Dhíkti Óri** *Mt* Greece
55C3 **Dhodhekánisos** *Is* Greece
55B3 **Dhomokós** Greece
87B1 **Dhone** India

Discovery B

85C4 **Dhoraji** India
85C4 **Dhrängadhra** India
86B1 **Dhuburi** India
85C4 **Dhule** India
22B2 **Diablo,Mt** USA
21A2 **Diablo Range** *Mts* USA
34C2 **Diamante** Arg
34B2 **Diamante** *R* Arg
31C5 **Diamantina** Brazil
107D3 **Diamantina** *R* Aust
86B2 **Diamond Harbours** India
22B1 **Diamond Springs** USA
91C4 **Dibä** UAE
98C3 **Dibaya** Zaïre
86C1 **Dibrugarh** India
8C2 **Dickinson** USA
15C2 **Dickson City** USA
93D2 **Dicle** *R* Turk
13E2 **Didsbury** Can
85C3 **Didwäna** India
97B3 **Diébougou** Burkina
46D2 **Diekirch** Lux
97B3 **Diéma** Mali
76C1 **Dien Bien Phu** Viet
56B2 **Diepholz** Germany
48C2 **Dieppe** France
46C1 **Diest** Belg
46D2 **Dieuze** France
7D5 **Digby** Can
49D3 **Digne-les-Bains** France
49C2 **Digoin** France
79C4 **Digos** Phil
71E4 **Digul** *R* Indon
86C1 **Dihang** *R* India
Dijlah = Tigris
49C2 **Dijon** France
98B2 **Dik** Chad
99E1 **Dikhil** Djibouti
46B1 **Diksmuide** Belg
18B2 **Dikson** Russian Fed
82A2 **Dilaram** Afghan
106B1 **Dili** Indon
76D3 **Di Linh** Viet
46E1 **Dillenburg** Germany
99C1 **Dilling** Sudan
12C3 **Dillingham** USA
8B2 **Dillon** USA
16A2 **Dillsburg** USA
100B2 **Dilolo** Zaïre
Dimashq = Damascus
98C3 **Dimbelenge** Zaïre
97B4 **Dimbokro** Ivory Coast
54C2 **Dimitrovgrad** Bulg
61G3 **Dimitrovgrad** Russian Fed
94B3 **Dimona** Israel
86B1 **Dimäpur** India
79C3 **Dinagat** *I* Phil
86B1 **Dinajpur** India
48B2 **Dinan** France
46C1 **Dinant** Belg
92B2 **Dinar** Turk
99D1 **Dinder** *R* Sudan
82B2 **Dindigul** India
72B2 **Dingbian** China
81B3 **Dinggyê** China
41A3 **Dingle** Irish Rep
41A3 **Dingle B** Irish Rep
97A3 **Dinguiraye** Guinea
44B3 **Dingwall** Scot
72A2 **Dingxi** China
72D2 **Ding Xian** China
76D1 **Dinh Lap** Viet
22C2 **Dinuba** USA
97A3 **Diouloulou** Sen
86C1 **Diphu** India
99E2 **Dirê Dawa** Eth
106A3 **Dirk Hartog** *I* Aust
95A3 **Dirkou** Niger
109C1 **Dirranbandi** Aust
99E2 **Dirri** Somalia
29G8 **Disappointment,C** South Georgia
20B1 **Disappointment,C** USA
106B3 **Disappointment,L** Aust
108B3 **Discovery B** Aust

Discovery Tablemount

103J7 **Discovery Tablemount** Atlantic O
47C1 Disentis Muster Switz
6E3 Disko Greenland
6E3 Disko Bugt *B* Greenland
6E3 Diskorjord Greenland
58D1 Disna *R* Belorussia
35B1 Distrito Federal Federal Distrib, Brazil
85C4 Diu India
79C4 Diuat Mts Phil
31C6 Divinópolis Brazil
61F4 Divnoye Russian Fed
93C2 Divriği Turk
22B1 Dixon California, USA
5E4 Dixon Entrance *Sd* Can/USA
13D1 Dixonville Can
93E3 Diyālā *R* Iraq
65F6 Diyarbakir Turk
90A3 Diz *R* Iran
98B2 Dja *R* Cam
96C1 Djadi *R* Alg
95A2 Djado,Plat du Niger
98B3 Djambala Congo
96C2 Djanet Alg
50A2 Djebel Bouhalla *Mt* Mor
96C1 Djelfa Alg
98C2 Djéma CAR
97B3 Djenné Mali
97B3 Djibo Burkina
99E1 Djibouti Djibouti
99E1 Djibouti Republic, E Africa
98C2 Djolu Zaïre
97C4 Djougou Benin
99D2 Djugu Zaïre
38C2 Djúpivogur Iceland
51C2 Djurdjura Mts Alg
60E2 Dmitrov Russian Fed
Dnepr = Dnieper
60D4 Dneprodzerzhinsk Ukraine
60E4 Dnepropetrovsk Ukraine
60C3 Dneprovskaya Nizmennost' Region, Ukraine
Dnestr = Dniester
60D4 Dnieper *R* Ukraine
60D4 Dniester *R* Ukraine
60D2 Dno Russian Fed
98B2 Doba Chad
58C1 Dobele Latvia
34C3 Doblas Arg
71E4 Dobo Indon
54A2 Doboj Bosnia-Herzegovina
54B2 Dobreta-Turnu-Severin Rom
54C2 Dobrich Bulg
60D3 Dobrush Belorussia
31C5 Doce *R* Brazil
30D3 Doctor R P Peña Arg
87B2 Dod India
87B2 Doda Betta *Mt* India
Dodecanese = Sporádhes
9C3 Dodge City USA
99D3 Dodoma Tanz
75A1 Dógo *I* Japan
97C3 Dogondoutchi Niger
93D2 Doğubayazit Turk
91B4 Doha Qatar
7C5 Doilchau Can
49D2 Dôle France
43C3 Dolgellau Wales
47D1 Dolomitche Mts Italy
99E2 Dolo Odo Eth
29E3 Dolores Arg
34D2 Dolores Urug
23A1 Dolores Hidalgo Mexico
4G3 Dolphin and Union Str Can
29E6 Dolphin,C Falkland Is
71E4 Dom *Mt* Indon
65G4 Dombarovskiy Russian Fed

38F6 Dombas Nor
46D2 Dombasle-sur-Meurthe France
54A1 Dombóvár Hung
48B2 Domfront France
27E3 Dominica *I* Caribbean S
27C3 Dominican Republic Caribbean S
6C3 Dominion,C Can
7E4 Domino Can
68D1 Domna Russian Fed
52A1 Domodossola Italy
78D4 Dompu Indon
29B3 Domuyo *Mt* Arg
109D1 Domville,Mt Aust
44C3 Don *R* Scot
61F4 Don *R* Russian Fed
45C1 Donaghadee N Ire
57C3 Donau *R* Germany
57C3 Donauwörth Germany
50A2 Don Benito Spain
42D3 Doncaster Eng
98B3 Dondo Angola
101C2 Dondo Mozam
87C3 Dondra Head *C* Sri Lanka
45B1 Donegal County, Irish Rep
40B3 Donegal Irish Rep
40B3 Donegal *B* Irish Rep
45B1 Donegal Mts Irish Rep
60E4 Donetsk Ukraine
73C4 Dong'an China
106A3 Dongara Aust
73A4 Dongchuan China
76D2 Dongfang China
74B2 Dongfeng China
70C4 Donggala Indon
68B3 Donggi Cona *L* China
74A3 Donggou China
73C5 Donghai Dao *I* China
72A1 Dong He *R* China
76D2 Dong Hoi Viet
73C5 Dong Jiang *R* China
95C3 Dongola Sudan
73D5 Dongshan China
68D4 Dongsha Qundao *I* China
72C2 Dongsheng China
72E3 Dongtai China
73C4 Dongting Hu *L* China
73B5 Dongxing China
73D3 Dongzhi China
18B2 Doniphan USA
52C2 Donji Vakuf Bosnia-Herzegovina
38G5 Dönna *I* Nor
21A2 Donner P USA
46D2 Donnersberg *Mt* Germany
101G1 Donnybrook S Africa
Donostia = San Sebastian
22B2 Don Pedro Res USA
12D1 Doonerak,Mt USA
79R4 Dopolong Phil
73A3 Do Qu *R* China
47B2 Dora Baltea *R* Italy
49D2 Dorbirn Austria
43C4 Dorchester Eng
6C3 Dorchester,C Can
48C2 Dordogne *R* France
56A2 Dordrecht Neth
13F2 Dore *L* Can
13F2 Dore Lake Can
97B3 Dori Burkina
46B2 Dormans France
57B3 Dornbirn Austria
44B3 Dornoch Scot
44B3 Dornoch Firth Estuary Scot
38H6 Dorotea Sweden
109D2 Dorrigo Aust
20B2 Dorris USA
43C4 Dorset County, Eng
46D1 Dorsten Germany
56B2 Dortmund Germany
98C2 Doruma Zaïre
63D2 Dosatuy Russian Fed
84B1 Doshi Afghan

22B2 Dos Palos USA
97C3 Dosso Niger
65G5 Dossor Kazakhstan
11B3 Dothan USA
49C1 Douai France
98A2 Douala Cam
109D1 Double Island Pt Aust
49D2 Doubs *R* France
111A3 Doubtful Sd NZ
97B3 Douentza Mali
9C3 Douglas Arizona, USA
42B2 Douglas Eng
17B1 Douglas Georgia, USA
8C2 Douglas Wyoming, USA
12A1 Douglas,C USA
13B2 Douglas Chan Can
12D3 Douglas,Mt USA
46B1 Doullens France
45C1 Doun County, N Ire
30F3 Dourados Brazil
50A1 Douro *R* Port
15C3 Dover Delaware, USA
43E4 Dover Eng
15D2 Dover New Hampshire, USA
16B2 Dover New Jersey, USA
14B2 Dover Ohio, USA
43D3 Dover *R* Eng
41D3 Dover,Str of UK/France
16B3 Downington USA
42B2 Downpatrick N Ire
13C2 Downton,Mt Can
16B2 Doylestown USA
74B2 Dözen *I* Japan
96A2 Dr'aa *R* Mor
35A2 Dracena Brazil
16D1 Dracut USA
49D3 Draguignan France
101C3 Drakensberg Mts S Africa
101G1 Drakensberg *Mt* S Africa
103E7 Drake Pass Pacific/Atlantic O
55B2 Dráma Greece
39G7 Drammen Nor
38A1 Drangajökull Iceland
52C1 Drava *R* Slovenia
13D2 Drayton Valley Can
49C2 Dreaux France
57C2 Dresden Germany
48C2 Dreux France
20C2 Drewsey USA
54B2 Drina *R* Alb
54A2 Drina *R* Bosnia-Herzegovina/Serbia
58D1 Drissa *R* Belorussia
45C2 Drogheda Irish Rep
59C3 Drogobych Ukraine
112B12 Dronning Maud Land Region, Ant
30D3 Dr P.P. Penã Par
62J1 Drumheller Can
14B1 Drummond I USA
15D1 Drummondville Can
58C2 Druskininksi Lithuania
12G3 Dry B USA
7A5 Dryden Can
27H1 Dry Harbour Mts Jamaica
76B3 Duang *I* Burma
91C4 Dubai UAE
5H3 Dubawnt *R* Can
4H3 Dubawnt *L* Can
107D4 Dubbo Aust
45C2 Dublin County, Irish Rep
45C2 Dublin Irish Rep
17B1 Dublin USA
60E2 Dubna Russian Fed
60C3 Dubno Ukraine
15C2 Du Bois USA
13B2 Dubose,Mt Can
58D2 Dubrovica Ukraine
54A2 Dubrovnik Croatia
10A2 Dubuque USA

46D2 Dudelange Lux
1C10 Dudinka Russian Fed
43C3 Dudley Eng
97B4 Duekoué Ivory Coast
50B1 Duero *R* Spain
44C3 Dufftown Scot
52B2 Dugi Otok *I* Croatia
56B2 Duisburg Germany
93E3 Dükan Iraq
99D2 Duk Faiwil Sudan
91B4 Dukhan Qatar
73A4 Dukou China
68B3 Dulan China
34C2 Dulce *R* Arg
78C2 Dulit Range Mts Malay
86C2 Dullabchara India
10A2 Duluth USA
94C2 Dūmā Syria
78A2 Dumai Indon
79A3 Dumaran *I* Phil
9C3 Dumas USA
94C2 Dumayr Syria
42B2 Dumbarton Scot
42C2 Dumfries Eng
42B2 Dumfries and Galloway Region, Scot
86B2 Dumka India
15C1 Dumoine,L Can
112C8 Dumont d'Urville Base Ant
95C1 Dumyat Egypt
54C2 Dunărea *R* Rom
45B2 Dunary Head *Pt* Irish Rep
54C2 Dunav *R* Bulg
59D3 Dunayevtsy Ukraine
13C3 Duncan Can
16A2 Duncannon USA
44C2 Duncansby Head *Pt* Scot
45C1 Dundalk Irish Rep
16A3 Dundalk USA
45C2 Dundalk B Irish Rep
6D2 Dundas Greenland
4G2 Dundas Pen Can
7E5 Dundas Str Aust
101H1 Dundee S Africa
44C3 Dundee Scot
108B1 Dundoo Aust
44B2 Dundrum B N Ire
111B3 Dunedin NZ
17B2 Dunedin USA
109C2 Dunedoo Aust
44C3 Dunfermline Scot
45C2 Dungarvan Irish Rep
45C2 Dungarvan Irish Rep
43E4 Dungeness Eng
109D2 Dungog Aust
99C2 Dungu Zaïre
95C3 Dungunab Sudan
68B2 Dunhuang China
46B1 Dunkerque France
10C2 Dunkirk USA
9F8 Dunkwa Ghana
97B4 Dunkwa Ghana
41B3 Dun Laoghaire Irish Rep
45B3 Dunmanway Irish Rep
26B1 Dunmore Town The Bahamas
44C2 Dunnet Head *Pt* Scot
42C2 Duns Scot
20B2 Dunsmuir USA
111A2 Dunstan Mts NZ
46C2 Dun-sur-Meuse France
72D1 Duolun China
18C2 Du Quoin USA
93B3 Dura Israel
49D3 Durance *R* France
24B2 Durango Mexico
50B1 Durango Spain
9C3 Durango USA
29E2 Durano Urug
9D3 Durant USA
94C1 Duraykish Syria
101H1 Durban S Africa
46D1 Düren Germany
86A2 Durg India
86B2 Durgapur India
42D2 Durham County, Eng

42D2 **Durham** Eng
11C3 **Durham** N Carolina, USA
16D1 **Durham** New Hampshire, USA
108B1 **Durham Downs** Aust
54A2 **Durmitor** *Mt* Montenegro, Yugos
44B2 **Durness** Scot
55A2 **Durrës** Alb
108B1 **Durrie** Aust
45A3 **Dursey** *I* Irish Rep
55C3 **Dursunbey** Turk
110B2 **D'Urville I** NZ
90D2 **Dushak** Turkmenistan
73B4 **Dushan** China
82A2 **Dushanbe** Tajikistan
111A3 **Dusky Sd** NZ
56B2 **Düsseldorf** Germany
73B4 **Duyun** China
92B1 **Düzce** Turk
60C2 **Dvina** *R* Latvia
85B4 **Dwärka** India
6D3 **Dyer,C** Can
11B3 **Dyersburg** USA
43B3 **Dyfed** County, Wales
61F5 **Dykh Tau** *Mt* Russian Fed
108B1 **Dynevore Downs** Aust
68B2 **Dzag** Mongolia
63C3 **Dzamin Üüd** Mongolia
101D2 **Dzaoudzi** Mayotte
68C2 **Dzarnin Üüd** Mongolia
68B2 **Dzavhan Gol** *R* Mongolia
80E1 **Dzehezkazgan** Kazakhstan
61F2 **Dzerzhinsk** Russian Fed
63E2 **Dzhalinda** Russian Fed
65J5 **Dzhambul** Kazakhstan
60D4 **Dzhankoy** Ukraine
65H4 **Dzhezkazgan** Kazakhstan
84B1 **Dzhilikul'** Tajikistan
65J5 **Dzhungarskiy Alatau** *Mts* Kazakhstan
59B2 **Dzierzoniow** Pol
63B3 **Dzüyl** Mongolia
82C1 **Dzungaria** Basin, China

E

7B4 **Eabamet L** Can
12F2 **Eagle** Alaska, USA
20B2 **Eagle L** California, USA
19A3 **Eagle Mountain L** USA
9C4 **Eagle Pass** USA
4E3 **Eagle Plain** Can
12E2 **Eagle River** USA
21B2 **Earlimart** USA
17B1 **Easley** USA
15C2 **East Aurora** USA
43E4 **Eastbourne** Eng
14A2 **East Chicago** USA
69E3 **East China Sea** China/Japan
83B4 **Eastern Ghats** *Mts* India
29E6 **East Falkland** *I* Falkland Is
12E1 **East Fork** *R* USA
21B2 **Eastgate** USA
16C1 **Easthampton** USA
16C2 **East Hampton** USA
14A2 **East Lake** USA
14B2 **East Liverpool** USA
100B4 **East London** S Africa
7C4 **Eastmain** Can
7C4 **Eastmain** *R* Can
17B1 **Eastman** USA
15C3 **Easton** Maryland, USA
15C2 **Easton** Pennsylvania, USA
16B2 **East Orange** USA

105L4 **East Pacific Ridge** Pacific O
17B1 **East Point** USA
42D3 **East Retford** Eng
11A3 **East St Louis** USA
1B7 **East Siberian S** Russian Fed
43E4 **East Sussex** County, Eng
17B1 **Eatonton** USA
10A2 **Eau Claire** USA
71F3 **Eauripik** *I* Pacific O
23B1 **Ebano** Mexico
98B2 **Ebebiyin** Eq Guinea
56C2 **Eberswalde** Germany
73A4 **Ebian** China
65K5 **Ebinur** *L* China
53C2 **Eboli** Italy
98B2 **Ebolowa** Cam
51B1 **Ebro** *R* Spain
92A1 **Eceabat** Turk
96C1 **Ech Cheliff** Alg
72D2 **Eching** China
20C1 **Echo** USA
4G3 **Echo Bay** Can
46D2 **Echternach** Lux
108B3 **Echuca** Aust
50A2 **Ecija** Spain
6B2 **Eclipse Sd** Can
32B4 **Ecuador** Republic, S America
99E1 **Ed** Eritrea
44C2 **Eday** *I* Scot
98C1 **Ed Da'ein** Sudan
95C3 **Ed Damer** Sudan
95C3 **Ed Debba** Sudan
44B2 **Edderachilis** *B* Scot
99D1 **Ed Dueim** Sudan
109C4 **Eddystone Pt** Aust
98A2 **Edea** Cam
109C3 **Eden** Aust
42C2 **Eden** *R* Eng
101G1 **Edenburg** S Africa
111A3 **Edendale** NZ
46E2 **Edenkoben** Germany
46E1 **Eder** *R* Germany
6D3 **Edgell I** Can
64D2 **Edgeøya** *I* Barents S
16A3 **Edgewood** USA
94B3 **Edh Dhahiriya** Israel
55B2 **Edhessa** Greece
44C3 **Edinburgh** Scot
60C5 **Edirne** Turk
17B1 **Edisto** *R* USA
13D2 **Edith Cavell,Mt** Can
20B1 **Edmonds** USA
5G4 **Edmonton** Can
7D5 **Edmundston** Can
19A4 **Edna** USA
12H3 **Edna Bay** USA
52B1 **Edolo** Italy
94B3 **Edom** Region, Jordan
92A2 **Edremit** Turk
55C3 **Edremit Körfezi** *B* Turk
68B2 **Edrengiyn Nuruu** *Mts* Mongolia
5G4 **Edson** Can
34C3 **Eduardo Castex** Arg
12J2 **Eduni,Mt** Can
108B3 **Edward** *R* Aust
99C3 **Edward,L** Uganda/Zaire
108A1 **Edwards Creek** Aust
9C3 **Edwards Plat** USA
18C2 **Edwardsville** USA
12H3 **Edziza,Mt** Can
12B2 **Eek** USA
46B1 **Eeklo** Belg
10B3 **Effingham** USA
6E3 **Egedesminde** Greenland
12C3 **Egegik** USA
59C3 **Eger** Hung
39F7 **Egersund** Nor
16B3 **Egg Harbor City** USA
4G2 **Eglinton I** Can
110B1 **Egmont,C** NZ
110B1 **Egmont,Mt** NZ
92B2 **Eğridir Gölü** *L* Turk
95B2 **Egypt** Republic, Africa

50B1 **Eibar** Spain
49C2 **Eibeuf** France
46D1 **Eifel** Region, Germany
44A3 **Eigg** *I* Scot
83B5 **Eight Degree Chan** Indian O
106B2 **Eighty Mile Beach** Aust
108C3 **Eildon,L** Aust
52B2 **Eindhoven** Neth
47C1 **Einsiedeln** Switz
94B3 **Ein Yahav** Israel
57C2 **Eisenach** Germany
57C3 **Eisenerz** Austria
46D1 **Eitorf** Germany
72A1 **Ejin qi** China
23B2 **Ejutla** Mexico
110C2 **Eketahuna** NZ
65J4 **Ekibastuz** Kazakhstan
63F2 **Ekimchan** Russian Fed
92B3 **Ek Mahalla el Kubra** Egypt
39H7 **Eksjo** Sweden
10B1 **Ekwen** *R* Can
92A3 **El'Alamein** Egypt
92B3 **El'Arish** Egypt
92B4 **Elat** Israel
95B3 **El'Atrun Oasis** Sudan
93C2 **Elazig** Turk
92C3 **El Azraq** Jordan
52B2 **Elba** *I* Italy
95C2 **El Balyana** Egypt
32C2 **El Banco** Colombia
55B2 **Elbasan** Alb
27D5 **El Baúl** Ven
57C2 **Elbe** *R* Germany
94C1 **El Bega'a** *R* Leb
14A2 **Elberta** USA
8C3 **Elbert,Mt** USA
17B1 **Elberton** USA
92C2 **Elbistan** Turk
58B2 **Elblag** Pol
29B4 **El Bolson** Arg
61F5 **Elbrus** *Mt* Russian Fed
Elburz Mts = Reshteh-ye Alborz
21B3 **El Cajon** USA
19A4 **El Campo** USA
51B2 **Elche** Spain
51B2 **Elda** Spain
32B3 **El Diviso** Colombia
96B2 **El Djouf** *Desert Region* Maur
18B2 **Eldon** USA
11A3 **El Dorado** Arkansas, USA
35B2 **Eldorado** Brazil
9D3 **El Dorado** Kansas, USA
24B2 **El Dorado** Mexico
33E2 **El Dorado** Ven
97D2 **Eldoret** Kenya
22C1 **Eleanor,L** USA
96B2 **El Eglab** Region, Alg
50B1 **El Escorial** Spain
93D2 **Eleskirt** Turk
11C4 **Eleuthera** *I* The Bahamas
92B4 **El Faiyûm** Egypt
98B2 **El Farsia** *Well* Mor
98C1 **El Fasher** Sudan
92B4 **El Fashn** Egypt
50A1 **El Ferrol del Caudillo** Spain
95C1 **El Fula** Sudan
96C1 **El Gassi** Alg
99D1 **El Geteina** Sudan
99D1 **El Gezira** Region, Sudan
94B3 **El Ghor** *V* Israel/Jordan
10B2 **Elgin** Illinois, USA
44C3 **Elgin** Scot
92B3 **El Giza** Egypt
96C1 **El Golea** Alg
99D2 **Elgon,Mt** Uganda/Kenya
99E2 **El Goran** Eth
23A2 **El Grullo** Mexico

96B2 **El Guettara** *Well* Mali
96B2 **El Haricha** *Desert Region* Mali
92A4 **El Harra** Egypt
51C2 **El Harrach** Alg
99D1 **El Hawata** Sudan
23B1 **El Higo** Mexico
34A3 **El Huecu** Arg
92B4 **El'Igma** *Desert Region* Egypt
12B2 **Elim** USA
4H2 **Elira,C** Can
Elisabethville = Lubumbashi
39K6 **Elisenvaara** Fin
El Iskandariya = Alexandria
61F4 **Elista** Russian Fed
106C4 **Elizabeth** Aust
15D2 **Elizabeth** USA
11C3 **Elizabeth City** USA
17C1 **Elizabethtown** N Carolina, USA
16A2 **Elizabethtown** Pennsylvania, USA
96B1 **El Jadida** Mor
92C3 **El Jafr** Jordan
99D1 **El Jebelein** Sudan
96D1 **El Jem** Tunisia
58C2 **Elk** Pol
16B3 **Elk** *R* Maryland, USA
14B3 **Elk** *R* W Virginia, USA
95C3 **El Kamlin** Sudan
22B1 **Elk Grove** USA
El Khalil = Hebron
80B3 **El Khârga** Egypt
80B3 **El-Khârga Oasis** Egypt
14A2 **Elkhart** USA
96B2 **El Khenachich** *Desert Region* Mali
54C2 **Elkhovo** Bulg
14C3 **Elkins** USA
8B2 **Elko** USA
16B3 **Elkton** USA
92B3 **El Kuntilla** Egypt
99C1 **El Lagowa** Sudan
4H2 **Ellef Ringnes I** Can
8A2 **Ellensburg** USA
16B2 **Ellenville** USA
6B2 **Ellesmere I** Can
111B2 **Ellesmere,L** NZ
16A3 **Ellicott City** USA
100B4 **Elliot** S Africa
7B5 **Elliot Lake** Can
94B3 **El Lisan** *Pen* Jordan
112B3 **Ellsworth Land** *Region* Ant
95B1 **El Maghra** *L* Egypt
92B3 **El Mansûra** Egypt
16B3 **Elmer** USA
96B3 **El Merelé** *Desert Region* Maur
34B2 **El Milagro** Arg
94B1 **El Mina** Leb
92B4 **El Minya** Egypt
22B1 **Elmira** California, USA
10C2 **Elmira** New York, USA
96B2 **El Mreïti** *Well* Maur
56B2 **Elmshorn** Germany
98C1 **El Muglad** Sudan
96B2 **El Mzereb** *Well* Mali
79A3 **El Nido** Phil
99D1 **El Obeid** Sudan
23A2 **El Oro** Mexico
96C1 **El Oued** Alg
9C3 **El Paso** USA
21A2 **El Porta** USA
22C2 **El Portal** USA
50A2 **El Puerto del Sta Maria** Spain
El Qâhira = Cairo
El Quds = Jerusalem
94B3 **El Quseima** Egypt
9D3 **El Reno** USA
4E3 **Elsa** Can
25D3 **El Salvador** Republic, Cent America
22D4 **Elsinore L** USA
34B3 **El Sosneade** Arg

Elsterwerde

57C2 Elsterwerde Germany
El Suweis = Suez
50A1 El Teleno *Mt* Spain
110B1 Eltham NZ
33E2 El Tigre Ven
92B4 El Tih *Desert Region* Egypt
34C2 El Tio Arg
20C1 Ettopia USA
92B4 El Tûr Egypt
87C1 Elûru India
32C5 Elva Port
32C5 Elvira Brazil
34A2 El Volcán Chile
14A2 Elwood USA
43E3 Ely Eng
10A2 Ely Minnesota, USA
8B3 Ely Nevada, USA
14B2 Elyria USA
90B2 Emämrud Iran
84B1 Emām Sāheb Afghan
58B1 Eman *R* Sweden
61J4 Emba Kazakhstan
61J4 Emba *R* Kazakhstan
29C3 Embalse Cerros Colorados *L* Arg
51B2 Embalse de Alarcón *Res* Spain
50A2 Embalse de Alcántara *Res* Spain
50A1 Embalse de Almendra *Res* Spain
50A2 Embalse de Garcia de Sola *Res* Spain
33E2 Embalse de Guri *L* Ven
51B1 Embalse de Mequinenza *Res* Spain
50A1 Embalse de Ricobayo *Res* Spain
29E2 Embalse de Rio Negro *Res* Urug
29C3 Embalse El Chocón *L* Arg
29C4 Embalse Florentine Ameghino *L* Arg
50A1 Embalse Gabriel y Galan *Res* Spain
30D3 Embarcación Arg
5G4 Embarras Portage Can
47B2 Embrun France
99D3 Embu Kenya
56B2 Emden Germany
73A4 Emei China
107D3 Emerald Aust
7D4 Emeri Can
5J5 Emerson Can
21B1 Emigrant P USA
95A3 Emi Koussi *Mt* Chad
34B3 Emilo Mitre Arg
92B2 Emirdağ Turk
16B2 Emmaus USA
56B2 Emmen Neth
20C2 Emmett USA
16A3 Emmitsburg USA
12B2 Emmonak USA
9C4 Emory Peak *Mt* USA
24A2 Empalme Mexico
101H1 Empangeni S Africa
30E4 Empedrado Arg
105G1 Emperor Seamount Chain Pacific O
18A2 Emporia Kansas, USA
56B2 Ems *R* Germany
44B2 Enard B Scot
23A1 Encarnacion Mexico
30E4 Encarnación Par
97B4 Enchi Ghana
22D4 Encinitas USA
35C1 Encruzilhada Brazil
106B1 Endeh Indon
13D2 Enderby Can
112C11 Enderby Land Region, Ant
15C2 Endicott USA
12D1 Endicott Mts USA
47D1 Engadin Mts Switz
79B2 Engaño,C Phil
94B3 En Gedi Israel

47C1 Engelberg Switz
78A4 Enggano *I* Indon
41C3 England Country, UK
7E4 Englee Can
41C3 English Channel Eng/France
97B3 Enji *Well* Maur
39H7 Enkoping Sweden
53B3 Enna Italy
99C1 En Nahud Sudan
95B3 Ennedi *Region* Chad
109C1 Enngonia Aust
41B3 Ennis Irish Rep
19A3 Ennis Texas, USA
45C2 Enniscorthy Irish Rep
45C1 Enniskillen N Ire
45B2 Ennistimon Irish Rep
94B2 Enn Nâqoûra Leb
57C3 Enns *R* Austria
39F8 Enschede Neth
24A1 Ensenada Mexico
73B3 Enshi China
99D2 Entebbe Uganda
17A1 Enterprise Alabama, USA
20C1 Enterprise Oregon, USA
97C4 Enugu Nig
75B1 Enzan Japan
49C2 Epernay France
16A2 Ephrata Pennsylvania, USA
20C1 Ephrata Washington, USA
49D2 Epinal France
46A2 Epte *R* France
100A3 Epukiro Namibia
34C3 Epu pel Arg
90B3 Eqlid Iran
89D7 Equator
98A2 Equatorial Guinea Republic, Africa
47C2 Erbe Italy
46D2 Erbeskopf *Mt* Germany
34A3 Ercilla Chile
93D2 Ercis Turk
92C2 Erciyas Daglari *Mt* Turk
74B2 Erdaobaihe China
72C1 Erdene Mongolia
72C1 Erdenet Mongolia
95B3 Erdi *Region* Chad
30F4 Erechim Brazil
92B1 Ereğli Turk
92B2 Ereğli Turk
68D2 Erenhot China
50B1 Eresma *R* Spain
46D1 Erft *R* Germany
57C2 Erfurt Germany
93C2 Ergani Turk
96B2 Erg Chech *Desert Region* Alg
95A3 Erg du Djourab *Desert* Chad
97D3 Erg Du Ténéré *Desert Region* Niger
92A1 Ergene *R* Turk
96B2 Erg Iguidi *Region* Alg
58B1 Ergli Latvia
97B3 Erguig *R* Chad
68D1 Ergun' *R* China/Russian Fed
63E2 Ergun Zuoqi China
95C3 Eriba Sudan
10C2 Erie USA
10B2 Erie,L Can/USA
42B2 Erin Port Eng
44A3 Eriskay *I* Scot
99D1 Eritrea Republic,Africa
46D1 Erkelenz Germany
57C3 Erlangen Germany
19B3 Erling,L USA
101G1 Ermelo S Africa
87B3 Ernäkulam India
87B2 Erode India
108B1 Eromanga Aust
96B1 Er Rachidia Mor
99D1 Er Rahad Sudan
101C2 Errego Mozam
40B2 Errigal *Mt* Irish Rep
41A3 Erris Head *Pt* Irish Rep

99D1 Er Roseires Sudan
94B2 Er Rummân Jordan
57C2 Erzgebirge *Upland* Germany
93C2 Erzincan Turk
65F6 Erzurum Turk
48C3 Esara *R* Spain
56B1 Esbjerg Den
9C4 Escalón Mexico
10B2 Escanaba USA
25C3 Escárcega Mexico
46C2 Esch Lux
21B3 Escondido USA
24B2 Escuinapa Mexico
25C3 Escuintla Guatemala
98B2 Eséka Cam
51C1 Esera *R* Spain
90B3 Esfahân Iran
101H1 Eshowe S Africa
110C1 Eskdale NZ
38C1 Eskifjörður Iceland
39H7 Eskilstuna Sweden
4E3 Eskimo L Can
35C1 Eskimo Point Can
92B2 Eskisehir Turk
50A1 Esla *R* Spain
29A5 Esmeralda *I* Chile
32B3 Esmeraldas Ecuador
26B2 Esmeralda Cuba
49C3 Espalion France
14B1 Espanola Can
32J7 Español *I* Ecuador
106B4 Esperance Aust
34C2 Esperanza Arg
112C2 Esperanza *Base* Ant
35C1 Espírito Santo State, Brazil
101C3 Espungabera Mozam
29B4 Esquel Arg
20B1 Esquimalt Can
34D2 Esquina Arg
94C2 Es Samra Jordan
96B1 Essaouira Mor
96A2 Es Semara Mor
56B2 Essen Germany
33F3 Essequibo *R* Guyana
43E4 Essex County, Eng
14B2 Essexville USA
57B3 Esslingen Germany
46B2 Essonne France
31D4 Estância Brazil
10G1 Estcourt S Africa
47D2 Este Italy
46B2 Esternay France
30D3 Esteros Par
5H5 Estevan Can
17B1 Estill USA
60B2 Estonia Republic, Europe
29B6 Estrecho de Magallanes *Str* Chile
50A2 Estremoz Port
59B3 Esztergom Hung
108A1 Etadunna Aust
12H4 Etah Greenland
48C2 Étampes France
46A1 Etamunbanie,L Aust
46A1 Etaples France
85D3 Etäwah India
99D2 Ethiopia Republic, Africa
23B2 Etla Mexico
53B3 Etna *Mt* Italy
12H3 Etolin *I* USA
12A3 Etolin Str USA
6C2 Eton Can
100A2 Etosha Nat Pk Namibia
100A2 Etosha Pan *Salt L* Namibia
17B1 Etowah *R* USA
46D2 Ettelbruck Lux
109C2 Euabalong Aust
14B2 Euclid USA
109C3 Eucumbene,L Aust
108A2 Eudunda Aust
19A2 Eufala L USA
17A1 Eufaula USA
8A2 Eugene USA
19B3 Eunice Louisiana, USA
46D1 Eupen Germany
93D3 Euphrates *R* Iraq

19C3 Eupora USA
48C2 Eure *R* France
20B2 Eureka California, USA
6B1 Eureka Can
108C3 Eureka Nevada, USA
6B2 Eureka Sd Can
108C3 Euroa Aust
109C1 Eurombah *R* Aust
101D3 Europa *I* Mozam Chan
57B2 Euskirchen Germany
13B2 Eutsuk L Can
13D2 Evansburg Can
6B1 Evans,C Can
7C4 Evans,L Can
6B3 Evans Str Can
14A2 Evanston Illinois, USA
8B2 Evanston Wyoming, USA
11B3 Evansville Indiana, USA
101G1 Evaton S Africa
106C4 Everard,L Aust
82C3 Everest,Mt China/Nepal
8A2 Everett Washington, USA
16C1 Everett,Mt USA
11B4 Everglades,The *Swamp* USA
43D3 Evesham Eng
98B2 Evinayong Eq Guinea
39F7 Evje Nor
47B1 Evolène Switz
50A2 Evora Port
48C2 Evreux France
55B3 Evvoia *I* Greece
98B3 Ewo Congo
22C1 Excelsior Mt USA
18B2 Excelsior Springs USA
21B2 Exeter California, USA
43C4 Exeter Eng
15D2 Exeter New Hampshire, USA
43C4 Exmoor Nat Pk Eng
43C4 Exmouth Eng
50A2 Extremadura Region, Spain
25C2 Exuma Sd The Bahamas
99D3 Eyasi L Tanz
42C2 Eyemouth Scot
99E2 Eyl Somalia
106B4 Eyre Aust
106C3 Eyre Creek *R* Aust
106C3 Eyre,L Aust
106C4 Eyre Pen Aust
79B3 Eyte *I* Phil
23A1 Eztatlan Mexico
55C3 Ezine Turk

F
4G3 Faber L Can
39G7 Fåborg Den
52B2 Fabriano Italy
95A3 Fachi Niger
95B3 Fada Chad
97C3 Fada N'Gourma Burkina
52B2 Faenza Italy
63E2 Faeringehavn Greenland
88B2 Fafa *R* CAR
99E2 Fafan *R* Eth
46C1 Fagnes Region, Belg
97B3 Faguibine,L *L* Mali
91C5 Fahud Oman
96A1 Faiol *I* Açores
4D3 Fairbanks USA
14B3 Fairborn USA
8D2 Fairbury USA
16A3 Fairfax USA
21A2 Fairfield California, USA
16C2 Fairfield Connecticut, USA
14B3 Fairfield Ohio, USA
45C1 Fair Head *Pt* N Ire
40C2 Fair Isle *I* Scot

111B2 Fairlie NZ
14B3 Fairmont W Virginia, USA
13D1 Fairview Can
4E4 Fairweather,Mt USA
71F3 Fais / Pacific O
84C2 Faisalabad Pak
8C2 Faith USA
44E1 Faither,The Pen Scot
86A1 Faizābād India
43E3 Fakenham Eng
39G7 Faköping Sweden
86C2 Falam Burma
24C2 Falcon Res Mexico/ USA
97A3 Falémé R Mali/Sen
39G7 Falkenberg Sweden
42C2 Falkirk Scot
29D6 Falkland Is Dependency, S Atlantic
29E6 Falkland Sd Falkland Is
22D4 Fallbrook USA
8B3 Fallon USA
15D2 Fall River USA
18A1 Falls City USA
43B4 Falmouth Eng
27H1 Falmouth Jamaica
16D2 Falmouth Massachusetts, USA
100A4 False B S Africa
24A2 Falso,C Mexico
56C2 Falster / Den
54C1 Fălticeni Rom
39H6 Falun Sweden
92B2 Famagusta Cyprus
46C1 Famenne Region, Belg
76B2 Fang Thai
99D2 Fangak Sudan
35C3 Fang liao Taiwan
52B2 Fano Italy
112C3 Faraday Base Ant
99C2 Faradje Zaire
101D3 Farafangana Madag
95B2 Farafra Oasis Egypt
80E2 Farah Afghan
71F2 Farallon de Medinilla / Pacific O
97A3 Faranah Guinea
71F3 Faraulep / Pacific O
43D4 Fareham Eng
Farewell,C = Kap Farvel
107G5 Farewell,C NZ
110B2 Farewell Spit Pt NZ
8D2 Fargo USA
94B2 Fari'a R Israel
10A2 Faribault USA
86B2 Faridpur Bang
90C2 Fariman Iran
18B2 Farmington Missouri, USA
9C3 Farmington New Mexico, USA
22B2 Farmington Res USA
42D2 Farne Deep N Sea
13D2 Farnham,Mt Can
12H2 Faro Can
50A2 Faro Port
39H7 Fåro / Sweden
89K9 Farquhar Is Indian O
44B3 Farrar R Scot
14B2 Farrell USA
55B3 Fársala Greece
91B4 Fasā Iran
45B3 Fastnet Rock Irish Rep
60C3 Fastov Ukraine
86A1 Fatehpur India
13D1 Father Can
30F2 Fatima do Sul Brazil
101G1 Fauresmith S Africa
47B2 Faverges France
7B4 Fawn R Can
38H6 Fax R Sweden
38A2 Faxaflói B Iceland
95A3 Faya Chad
11A3 Fayetteville Arkansas, USA
11C3 Fayetteville N Carolina, USA

93E4 Faylakah / Kuwait
84C2 Fāzilka India
96A2 Fdérik Maur
11C3 Fear,C USA
21A2 Feather Middle Fork R USA
48C2 Fécamp France
34D2 Federación Arg
34D2 Federal Arg
71F3 Federated States of Micronesia Is Pacific O
56C2 Fehmarn / Germany
32C5 Feijó Brazil
73C5 Feilai Xai Bei Jiang R China
110C2 Feilding NZ
100C2 Feira Zambia
31D4 Feira de Santan Brazil
92C2 Feke Turk
57B3 Feldkirch Austria
34D2 Feliciano R Arg
41D3 Felixstowe Eng
47D1 Feltre Italy
38G6 Femund L Nor
74A2 Fengcheng China
73B4 Fengdu China
72D1 Fenging China
73B3 Fengjie China
73B3 Feng Xian China
72C1 Fengzhen China
72C2 Fen He R China
101D2 Fenoarivo Atsinanana Madag
60E5 Feodosiya Ukraine
90C3 Ferdow Iran
46B2 Fère-Champenoise France
82B2 Fergana Uzbekistan
45C1 Fermanagh County, N Ire
45B2 Fermoy Irish Rep
47D1 Fern Mt Austria
32J7 Fernandina / Ecuador
17B1 Fernandina Beach USA
103G5 Fernando de Noronha / Atlantic O
35A2 Fernandópolis Brazil
20B1 Ferndale USA
21B2 Fernley USA
52B2 Ferrara Italy
32B5 Ferreñafe Peru
19B3 Ferriday USA
96B1 Fès Mor
18B2 Festus USA
54C2 Feteşti Rom
92A2 Fethiye Turk
61H5 Fetisovo Kazakhstan
44E1 Fetlar / Scot
84C1 Feyzabad Afghan
101D3 Fianarantsoa Madag
99D2 Fichē Eth
101G1 Ficksburg S Africa
47D2 Fidenza Italy
55A2 Fier Alb
47D1 Fiera Di Primeiro Italy
44C3 Fife Region, Scot
44C3 Fife Ness Pen Scot
48C3 Figeac France
50A1 Figueira da Foz Port
51C1 Figueras Spain
Figueres = Figueras
96B1 Figuig Mor
105G4 Fiji Is Pacific O
30D3 Filadelfia Par
54B2 Filiaşi Rom
55B3 Filiatrá Greece
53B3 Filicudi / Italy
21B3 Fillmore California, USA
44B3 Findhorn R Scot
10B2 Findlay USA
13D2 Findlay,Mt Can
15C2 Finger Lakes USA
101C2 Fingoè Mozam
92B2 Finike Turk
106C3 Finke R Aust
108A1 Finke Flood Flats Aust
64D3 Finland Republic, N Europe

39J7 Finland,G of N Europe
5F4 Finlay R Can
5F4 Finlay Forks Can
108C3 Finley Aust
38H5 Finnsnes Nor
71F4 Finschhafen PNG
47C1 Finsteraarhorn Mt Switz
56C2 Finsterwalde Germany
45C1 Fintona N Ire
111A3 Fiordland Nat Pk NZ
94B2 Fiq Syria
93C2 Firat R Turk
22B2 Firebaugh USA
52B2 Firenze Italy
34C2 Firmat Arg
85D3 Firozābād India
84C2 Firozpur India
39H7 Firspäng Sweden
42B2 Firth of Clyde Estuary Scot
44C3 Firth of Forth Estuary Scot
44A3 Firth of Lorn Estuary Scot
40C2 Firth of Tay Estuary Scot
91B4 Firūzābād Iran
100A3 Fish R Namibia
22C2 Fish Camp USA
16C2 Fishers I USA
6B3 Fisher Str Can
43B4 Fishguard Wales
6E3 Fiskenaesset Greenland
46B2 Fismes France
15D2 Fitchburg USA
44E2 Fitful Head Pt Scot
17B1 Fitzgerald USA
106B2 Fitzroy R Aust
106B2 Fitzroy Crossing Aust
14B1 Fitzwilliam I Can
Fiume = Rijeka
99C3 Fizi Zaire
9B3 Flagstaff USA
42D2 Flamborough Head C Eng
8C2 Flaming Gorge Res USA
44A2 Flannan Isles Is Scot
12J2 Flat R Can
13C3 Flathead R USA
8B2 Flathead L USA
18A2 Flat River USA
42C3 Fleetwood Eng
39F7 Flekkefjord Nor
69G4 Fleming Deep Pacific O
16B2 Flemington USA
56B2 Flensburg Germany
47B1 Fleurier Switz
106C4 Flinders R Aust
107D4 Flinders I Aust
107D2 Flinders R Aust
106C4 Flinders Range Mts Aust
5H4 Flin Flon Can
10B2 Flint USA
42C3 Flint Wales
11B3 Flint R USA
46B1 Flixecourt France
17A1 Florala USA
Florence = Firenze
11B3 Florence Alabama, USA
18A2 Florence Kansas, USA
20B2 Florence Oregon, USA
11C3 Florence S Carolina, USA
32B3 Florencia Colombia
46C2 Florenville Belg
25D3 Flores Guatemala
96A1 Flores / Açores
96A1 Flores / Indon
34D3 Flores R Arg
70C4 Flores S Indon
31C3 Floriano Brazil
30G4 Florianópolis Brazil
25D2 Florida State, USA

29E2 Florida Urug
17B2 Florida B USA
17B2 Florida City USA
107E1 Florida Is Solomon Is
11B4 Florida Keys Is USA
11B4 Florida,Strs of USA
55B2 Flórina Greece
38F6 Florø Nor
47D1 Fluchthorn Mt Austria
54C1 Focsani Rom
53C2 Foggia Italy
97A4 Fogo / Cape Verde
48C3 Foix France
6C3 Foley I Can
52B2 Foligno Italy
43E4 Folkestone Eng
17B1 Folkston USA
52B2 Follonica Italy
22B1 Folsom USA
22B1 Folsom L USA
5H4 Fond-du-Lac Can
10B2 Fond du Lac USA
48C2 Fontainebleau France
18B2 Fontenac USA
48B2 Fontenay-le-Comte France
52C1 Fonyod Hung
Foochow = Fuzhou
12D2 Forbes,Mt USA
46D2 Forbach France
109C2 Forbes Aust
97C4 Forcados Nig
38F6 Forde Nor
108C1 Fords Bridge Aust
19B3 Fordyce USA
97A4 Forécariah Guinea
6G3 Forel,Mt Greenland
14B2 Forest Can
17B1 Forest Park USA
22A1 Forestville USA
44C3 Forfar Scot
46A2 Forges-les-Eaux France
20B1 Forks USA
52B2 Forlì Italy
51C2 Formentera / Spain
53B2 Formia Italy
96A1 Formigas / Açores
Formosa = Taiwan
30E4 Formosa Arg
31B5 Formosa Brazil
30D3 Formosa State, Arg
73D5 Formosa Str Taiwan/ China
47D2 Fornovo di Taro Italy
38D3 Føroyar Is N Atlantic O
44C3 Forres Scot
106B4 Forrest Aust
11A3 Forrest City USA
107D2 Forsayth Can
39J6 Forssa Fin
109D2 Forster Aust
18B2 Forsyth Missouri, USA
84C3 Fort Abbas Pak
7B4 Fort Albany Can
31D2 Fortaleza Brazil
44B3 Fort Augustus Scot
100B4 Fort Beaufort S Africa
21A2 Fort Bragg USA
8C2 Fort Collins USA
15C1 Fort Coulogne Can
27E4 Fort de France Martinique
17A1 Fort Deposit USA
10A2 Fort Dodge USA
106A3 Fortescue R Aust
7A5 Fort Frances Can
4F3 Fort Franklin Can
6G4 Fort Good Hope Can
108B1 Fort Grey Aust
44B3 Forth R Scot
7B4 Fort Hope Can
34B3 Fortin Uno Arg
4F3 Fort Laird Can
96C1 Fort Lallemand Alg
Fort Larny = Ndjamena
11B4 Fort Lauderdale USA
4F3 Fort Liard Can

Fort Mackay

5G4 **Fort Mackay** Can
5G5 **Fort Macleod** Can
5G4 **Fort McMurray** Can
4E3 **Fort McPherson** Can
18B2 **Fort Madison** USA
8C2 **Fort Morgan** USA
11B4 **Fort Myers** USA
5F4 **Fort Nelson** Can
4F3 **Fort Norman** Can
17A1 **Fort Payne** USA
8C2 **Fort Peck Res** USA
11B4 **Fort Pierce** USA
4G3 **Fort Providence** Can
5G3 **Fort Resolution** Can
98B3 **Fort Rousset** Congo
5F4 **Fort St James** Can
13C1 **Fort St John** Can
13E2 **Fort Saskatchewan**
     Can
18B2 **Fort Scott** USA
4E3 **Fort Selkirk** Can
7B4 **Fort Severn** Can
61H5 **Fort Shevchenko**
     Kazakhstan
4F3 **Fort Simpson** Can
5G3 **Fort Smith** Can
4G3 **Fort Smith** Region,
     Can
11A3 **Fort Smith** USA
9C3 **Fort Stockton** USA
20B2 **Fortuna** California,
     USA
5G4 **Fort Vermillion** Can
17A1 **Fort Walton Beach**
     USA
10B2 **Fort Wayne** USA
44B3 **Fort William** Scot
9D3 **Fort Worth** USA
12F2 **Fortymile** R USA
12E1 **Fort Yukon** USA
73C5 **Foshan** China
47B2 **Fossano** Italy
12G3 **Foster,Mt** USA
98B3 **Fougamou** Gabon
48B2 **Fougères** France
44D1 **Foula** I Scot
43E4 **Foulness I** Eng
111B2 **Foulwind,C** NZ
98B2 **Foumban** Cam
49C1 **Fourmies** France
55C3 **Fournoi** I Greece
97A3 **Fouta Djallon** Mts
     Guinea
111B3 **Foveaux** Str NZ
43B4 **Fowey** Eng
13D2 **Fox Creek** Can
6B3 **Foxe Basin** G Can
6B3 **Foxe Chan** Can
6C3 **Foxe Pen** Can
110C2 **Foxton** NZ
13F2 **Fox Valley** Can
45B2 **Foynes** Irish Rep
100A2 **Foz do Cuene**
     Angola
30F4 **Foz do Iguaçu** Brazil
16A2 **Frackville** USA
34B2 **Fraga** Arg
16D1 **Framingham** USA
31B6 **Franca** Brazil
49C2 **France**
     Republic, Europe
10A2 **Frances** Can
12J2 **Frances** R Can
49D2 **Franche Comté**
     Region, France
100B3 **Francistown**
     Botswana
13B2 **Francois L** Can
14A2 **Frankfort** Indiana,
     USA
11B3 **Frankfort** Kentucky,
     USA
101G1 **Frankfort** S Africa
57B2 **Frankfurt** Germany
46E1 **Frankfurt am Main**
     Germany
56C2 **Frankfurt-an-der-Oder**
     Germany
57C3 **Fränkischer Alb**
     Upland Germany
14A3 **Franklin** Indiana,
     USA
19B4 **Franklin** Louisiana,
     USA

16D1 **Franklin**
     Massachusetts, USA
16B2 **Franklin** New Jersey,
     USA
14C2 **Franklin**
     Pennsylvania, Can
4F2 **Franklin B** Can
20C1 **Franklin D Roosevelt**
     L USA
4F3 **Franklin Mts** Can
4J2 **Franklin Str** Can
111B2 **Franz Josef Glacier**
     NZ
     Franz-Joseph-Land =
     Zemlya Frantsa Iosifa
5F5 **Fraser** R Can
44C3 **Fraserburgh** Scot
107E3 **Fraser I** Aust
13B2 **Fraser L** Can
47B1 **Frasne** France
47C1 **Frauenfeld** Switz
34D2 **Fray Bentos** Urug
44B3 **Frazerburgh** Scot
16B3 **Frederica** USA
56B1 **Fredericia** Den
15C3 **Frederick** Maryland,
     USA
15C3 **Fredericksburg**
     Virginia, USA
12H3 **Frederick Sd** USA
18B2 **Fredericktown** USA
7D5 **Fredericton** Can
6E3 **Frederikshåb**
     Greenland
39G7 **Frederikshavn** Den
15C2 **Fredonia** USA
16B2 **Fredrikstad** Nor
16B2 **Freehold** USA
26B1 **Freeport** The
     Bahamas
19A4 **Freeport** Texas, USA
97A4 **Freetown** Sierra
     Leone
57B3 **Freiburg** Germany
57C3 **Freistadt** Austria
106A4 **Fremantle** Aust
22B2 **Fremont** California,
     USA
18A1 **Fremont** Nebraska,
     USA
14B2 **Fremont** Ohio, USA
33G3 **French Guiana**
     Dependency,
     S America
109C4 **Frenchmans Cap** Mt
     Aust
105J4 **French Polynesia** Is
     Pacific O
24B2 **Fresnillo** Mexico
8B3 **Fresno** USA
22C2 **Fresno** R USA
47A1 **Fretigney** France
46B1 **Frévent** France
109C4 **Freycinet Pen** Aust
97A3 **Fria** Guinea
22C2 **Friant** USA
22C2 **Friant Dam** USA
52A1 **Fribourg** Switz
57B3 **Friedrichshafen**
     Germany
6D3 **Frobisher B** Can
6D3 **Frobisher Bay** Can
13B2 **Frobisher L** Can
61F4 **Frolovo** Russian Fed
43C4 **Frome** Eng
108A1 **Frome** R Aust
43C4 **Frome** R Eng
16C4 **Frome,L** Aust
25C3 **Frontera** Mexico
15C3 **Front Royal** USA
53B2 **Frosinone** Italy
73C5 **Fuchuan** China
73E4 **Fuding** China
24B2 **Fuerte** R Mexico
30E3 **Fuerte Olimpo** Par
96A2 **Fuerteventura** I
     Canary Is
72C2 **Fugu** China
68A2 **Fuhai** China
91C4 **Fujairah** UAE
75B1 **Fuji** Japan
73D4 **Fujian** Province,
     China
69F2 **Fujin** China

75B1 **Fujinomiya** Japan
74D3 **Fuji-san** Mt Japan
75B1 **Fujisawa** Japan
75B1 **Fuji-Yoshida** Japan
63A3 **Fukang** China
74C3 **Fukuchiyima** Japan
74D3 **Fukui** Japan
74C4 **Fukuoka** Japan
74E3 **Fukushima** Japan
74C4 **Fukuyama** Japan
57B2 **Fulda** Germany
57B2 **Fulda** R Germany
73B4 **Fuling** China
27L1 **Fullarton** Trinidad
22D4 **Fullerton** USA
18C2 **Fulton** Kentucky,
     USA
15C2 **Fulton** New York,
     USA
46C1 **Furnay** France
75C1 **Funabashi** Japan
96A1 **Funchal** Medeira
35C1 **Fundão** Brazil
7D5 **Fundy,B of** Can
101C3 **Funhalouro** Mozam
72D3 **Funing** China
73B5 **Funing** China
97C3 **Funtua** Nig
73D4 **Fuqing** China
101C2 **Furancungo** Mozam
91C4 **Fürg** Iran
47C1 **Furka** P Switz
107D5 **Furneaux Group** Is
     Aust
56C2 **Fürstenwalde**
     Germany
57C3 **Fürth** Germany
74D3 **Furukawa** Japan
6B3 **Fury and Hecla St**
     Can
74A2 **Fushun** Liaoning,
     China
73A4 **Fushun** Sichuan,
     China
74B2 **Fusong** China
57C3 **Füssen** Germany
72E2 **Fu Xian** China
72E1 **Fuxin** China
72D3 **Fuyang** China
72E1 **Fuyuan** Liaoning,
     China
73A4 **Fuyuan** Yunnan,
     China
68A2 **Fuyun** China
73D4 **Fuzhou** China
56C1 **Fyn** I Den

G

99E2 **Gaalkacyo** Somalia
21B2 **Gabbs** USA
100A2 **Gabela** Angola
96D1 **Gabe's** Tunisia
22B2 **Gabilan Range** Mts
     USA
98B3 **Gabon** Republic,
     Africa
100B3 **Gaborone** Botswana
54C2 **Gabrovo** Bulg
91B3 **Gach Sãrãn** Iran
17A1 **Gadsden** Alabama,
     USA
10A1 **Gads L** Can
53B2 **Gaeta** Italy
71F3 **Gaferut** I Pacific O
96C1 **Gafsa** Tunisia
60D2 **Gagarin** Russian Fed
97B4 **Gagnoa** Ivory Coast
7D4 **Gagnon** Can
61F5 **Gagra** Georgia
86B1 **Gaibanda** India
29C4 **Gaimán** Arg
17B2 **Gainesville** Florida,
     USA
17B1 **Gainesville** Georgia,
     USA
19A3 **Gainesville** Texas,
     USA
42D3 **Gainsborough** Eng
108A2 **Gairdner,L** Aust
44B3 **Gairloch** Scot
16A3 **Gaithersburg** USA
87B1 **Gajendragarh** India
73D4 **Ga Jiang** R China
99D3 **Galana** R Kenya

103D5 **Galapagos Is**
     Pacific O
42C2 **Galashiels** Scot
54C1 **Galaţi** Rom
4C3 **Galena** USA
18B2 **Galena** Kansas, USA
27L1 **Galeota Pt** Trinidad
27L1 **Galera Pt** Trinidad
10A2 **Galesburg** USA
15C2 **Galeton** USA
61F2 **Galich** Russian Fed
50A1 **Galicia** Region, Spain
     Galilee,S of =
     Tiberias,L
27J1 **Galina Pt** Jamaica
99D1 **Gallabat** Sudan
47C2 **Gallarate** Italy
87C3 **Galle** Sri Lanka
51B1 **Gállego** R Spain
     Gallipoli = **Gelibolu**
55A2 **Gallipoli** Italy
38J5 **Gällivare** Sweden
42B2 **Galloway** District
42B2 **Galloway,Mull of** C
     Scot
8C3 **Gallup** USA
22B1 **Galt** USA
96A2 **Galtat Zemmour** Mor
25C2 **Galveston** USA
11A4 **Galveston B** USA
34C2 **Gálvez** Arg
49D3 **Galvi** Corse
45B2 **Galway** County,
     Irish Rep
41B3 **Galway** Irish Rep
41B3 **Galway** B Irish Rep
86B1 **Gamba** China
97B3 **Gambaga** Ghana
4A3 **Gambell** USA
97A3 **Gambia** R The
     Gambia/Sen
97A3 **Gambia,The**
     Republic, Africa
98B3 **Gamboma** Congo
100A2 **Gambos** Angola
87C3 **Gampola** Sri Lanka
99E2 **Ganale Dorya** R Eth
15C2 **Gananoque** Can
     Gand = **Gent**
100A2 **Ganda** Angola
98C3 **Gandajika** Zaire
84B3 **Gandava** Pak
7E5 **Gander** Can
85C4 **Gandhidham** India
85C4 **Gåndhinagar** India
85D4 **Gandhi Sagar** L
     India
51B2 **Gandia** Spain
86B2 **Ganga** R India
85C3 **Ganganar** India
86C2 **Gangaw** Burma
72A2 **Gangca** China
02C2 **Gangdisê Shan** Mts
     China
     Ganges = Ganga
86B1 **Gangtok** India
72B3 **Gangu** China
8C2 **Gannett Peak** Mt
     USA
77B2 **Ganquan** China
108A3 **Gantheaume** C Aust
39K8 **Gantsevichi**
     Belorussia
73D4 **Ganzhou** China
97C3 **Gao** Mali
72A2 **Gaolan** China
72B2 **Gaoping** China
97B3 **Gaoua** Burkina
97A3 **Gaoual** Guinea
72D3 **Gaoyou Hu** L China
73C5 **Gaozhou** China
49D3 **Gap** France
79B2 **Gapan** Phil
84D2 **Gar** China
109C1 **Garah** Aust
31D3 **Garanhuns** Brazil
21A1 **Garberville** USA
35B2 **Garça** Brazil
35A2 **Garcias** Brazil
47D2 **Garda** Italy
9C3 **Garden City** USA
14A1 **Garden Pen** USA
34D3 **Gardey** Arg
84B2 **Gardez** Afghan

16C2 **Gardiners I** USA
16D1 **Gardner** USA
47D2 **Gardone** Italy
47D2 **Gargano** Italy
85D4 **Garhākota** India
61K2 **Gari** Russian Fed
100A4 **Garies** S Africa
99D3 **Garissa** Kenya
19A3 **Garland** USA
57C3 **Garmisch-**
       Partenkirchen
       Germany
90B2 **Garmsar** Iran
18A2 **Garnett** USA
8B2 **Garnett Peak** Mt
       USA
48C3 **Garonne** R France
44B3 **Garry** R Scot
78B4 **Garut** Indon
86A2 **Garwa** India
14A2 **Gary** USA
82C2 **Garyarsa** China
4H3 **Gary L** Can
19A3 **Garza-Little Elm** Res
       USA
90B2 **Gasan Kuli**
       Turkmenistan
48B3 **Gascogne** Region,
       France
18B2 **Gasconade** R USA
106A3 **Gascoyne** R Aust
98B2 **Gashaka** Nig
97D3 **Gashua** Nig
10D2 **Gaspé** Can
10D2 **Gaspé,C. de** Can
94A1 **Gata,C** Cyprus
60C2 **Gatchina**
       Russian Fed
42D2 **Gateshead** Eng
19A3 **Gatesville** USA
15C1 **Gatineau** Can
15C1 **Gatineau** R Can
109D1 **Gatton** Aust
86C1 **Gauhāti** India
58C1 **Gauja** R Latvia
86A1 **Gauri Phanta** India
22B3 **Gaviota** USA
39H6 **Gävle** Sweden
108A2 **Gawler Ranges** Mts
       Aust
72A1 **Gaxun Nur** L China
86A2 **Gaya** India
97C3 **Gaya** Niger
14B1 **Gaylord** USA
109D1 **Gayndah** Aust
61H1 **Gayny** Russian Fed
60C4 **Gaysin** Ukraine
92B3 **Gaza** Israel
92C2 **Gaziantep** Turk
97B4 **Gbaringa** Lib
58B2 **Gdańsk** Pol
58B2 **Gdańsk,G of** Pol
39K7 **Gdov** Russian Fed
58B2 **Gdynia** Pol
94A3 **Gebel Halâl** Mt
       Egypt
95C2 **Gebel Hamata** Mt
       Egypt
92B4 **Gebel Katherina** Mt
       Egypt
94A3 **Gebel Libni** Mt
       Egypt
94A3 **Gebel Maghâra** Mt
       Egypt
99D1 **Gedaref** Sudan
55C3 **Gediz** R Turk
56C2 **Gedser** Den
46C1 **Geel** Belg
108B3 **Geelong** Aust
109C4 **Geeveston** Aust
97D3 **Geidam** Nig
46D1 **Geilenkirchen**
       Germany
99D3 **Geita** Tanz
73A5 **Gejiu** China
53B3 **Gela** Italy
99E2 **Geladi** Eth
46D1 **Geldern** Germany
55C2 **Gelibolu** Turk
92B2 **Gelidonya Burun**
       Turk
46D1 **Gelsenkirchen**
       Germany
39F8 **Gelting** Germany

77C5 **Gemas** Malay
46C1 **Gembloux** Belg
98B2 **Gemena** Zaïre
92C2 **Gemerek** Turk
92A1 **Gemlik** Turk
52B1 **Gemona** Italy
100B3 **Gemsbok** Nat Pk
       Botswana
98C1 **Geneina** Sudan
34C3 **General Acha** Arg
34C3 **General Alvear**
       Buenos Aires, Arg
34B2 **General Alvear**
       Mendoza, Arg
34C2 **General Arenales** Arg
34D3 **General Belgrano**
       Arg
112B2 **General Belgrano**
       Base Ant
112C2 **General Bernardo**
       O'Higgins Base Ant
34D3 **General Conesa**
       Buenos Aires, Arg
30D3 **General Eugenio A**
       Garay Par
34D3 **General Guido** Arg
34C3 **General La Madrid**
       Arg
34C2 **General Levalle** Arg
30C4 **General Manuel**
       Belgrano Mt Arg
34D3 **General Paz**
       Buenos Aires, Arg
34C3 **General Pico** Arg
34C2 **General Pinto** Arg
34D3 **General Pirán** Arg
29C3 **General Roca** Arg
112C3 **General San Martín**
       Base Ant
79C4 **General Santos** Phil
34C3 **General Viamonte**
       Arg
34C3 **General Villegas** Arg
15C2 **Genesee** R USA
15C2 **Geneseo** USA
18A1 **Geneva = Genève**
15C2 **Geneva** Nebraska,
       USA
15C2 **Geneva** New York,
       USA
       Geneva,L of =
       LacLéman
52A1 **Genève** Switz
50B2 **Genil** R Spain
       Genoa = Genova
109C3 **Genoa** Aust
52A2 **Genova** Italy
32J7 **Genovesa** I Ecuador
46B1 **Gent** Belg
78B4 **Genteng** Indon
56C2 **Genthin** Germany
93E1 **Geokchay**
       Azerbaijan
100B4 **George** S Africa
7D4 **George** R Can
109C2 **George,L** Aust
17B2 **George,L** Florida,
       USA
15D2 **George,L** New York,
       USA
111A2 **George Sd** NZ
109C4 **George Town** Aust
15C3 **Georgetown**
       Delaware, USA
33F2 **Georgetown** Guyana
14B3 **Georgetown**
       Kentucky, USA
77C4 **George Town** Malay
27N2 **Georgetown**
       St Vincent and the
       Grenadines
17C1 **Georgetown** S
       Carolina, USA
19A3 **Georgetown** Texas,
       USA
97A3 **Georgetown** The
       Gambia
112C8 **George V Land**
       Region, Ant
65F5 **Georgia** Republic,
       Europe
112C12 **Georg Forster** Base
       Ant
17B1 **Georgia** State, USA

14B1 **Georgian B** Can
13C3 **Georgia,Str of** Can
106C3 **Georgina** R Aust
61F5 **Georgiyevsk**
       Russian Fed
57C2 **Gera** Germany
46B1 **Geraardsbergen** Belg
111B2 **Geraldine** NZ
106A3 **Geraldton** Aust
10B2 **Geraldton** Can
94B3 **Gerar** R Israel
4C3 **Gerdine,Mt** USA
12E2 **Gerdova Peak** Mt
       USA
77C4 **Gerik** Malay
60B4 **Gerlachovsky** Mt Pol
13C1 **Germanson Lodge**
       Can
56C2 **Germany**
       Republic, Europe
101G1 **Germiston** S Africa
46D1 **Gerolstein** Germany
57C1 **Gerona** R Eth
50B1 **Getafe** Spain
16A3 **Gettysburg**
       Pennsylvania, USA
93D2 **Gevaş** Turk
55B2 **Gevgelija**
       Macedonia
47B1 **Gex** France
94C2 **Ghabāghib** Syria
96C1 **Ghadamis** Libya
90B2 **Ghaem Shahr** Iran
86A1 **Ghāghara** R India
97B4 **Ghana** Republic,
       Africa
100B3 **Ghanzi** Botswana
96C1 **Ghardaïa** Alg
95A1 **Gharyan** Libya
95A2 **Ghat** Libya
84D3 **Ghāziābād** India
84C3 **Ghazi Khan** Pak
84B2 **Ghazni** Afghan
84C1 **Gheorgheni** Rom
88E4 **Ghudamis** Alg
90D3 **Ghurian** Afghan
95B2 **Gialo** Libya
99E2 **Giamame** Somalia
53C3 **Giarre** Italy
100A3 **Gibeon** Namibia
50A2 **Gibraltar** Colony,
       SW Europe
50A2 **Gibraltar,Str of**
       Spain/Africa
106B3 **Gibson Desert** Aust
20B1 **Gibsons** Can
87B1 **Giddalūr** India
99D2 **Gīdolē** Eth
57B2 **Giessen** Germany
17B2 **Gifford** USA
74D3 **Gifu** Japan
42B2 **Gigha** I Scot
52B2 **Giglio** I Italy
50A1 **Gijón** Spain
107D2 **Gilbert** R Aust
13C2 **Gilbert,Mt** Can
101C2 **Gilé** Mozam
94B2 **Gilead** Region,
       Jordan
95B2 **Gilf Kebir Plat** Egypt
109C2 **Gilgandra** Aust
84C1 **Gilgit** Pak
84C1 **Gilgit** R Pak
108C2 **Gilgunnia** Aust
7A4 **Gillam** Can
34C2 **Gilles** L Aust
13B2 **Gill I** Can
14A1 **Gills Rock** USA
14A2 **Gilman** USA
22B2 **Gilroy** USA
62D1 **Gimli** Can
101H1 **Gingindlovu** S Africa
79C4 **Gingoog** Phil
99E2 **Ginir** Eth
55B3 **Gióna** Mt Greece
109C3 **Gippsland** Mts Aust
14B2 **Girard** USA
32C3 **Girardot** Colombia
44C3 **Girdle Ness** Pen
       Scot
93C1 **Giresun** Turk
85C4 **Gir Hills** India

98B2 **Giri** R Zaïre
86B2 **Giridih** India
       Girona = Gerona
48B2 **Gironde** R France
42B2 **Girvan** Scot
111C2 **Gisborne** NZ
46A2 **Gisors** France
99C3 **Gitega** Burundi
       Giuba,R = Juba,R
54C2 **Giurgiu** Rom
46C1 **Givet** Belg
58C2 **Gizycko** Pol
55B2 **Gjirokastër** Alb
4J3 **Gjoatlaven** Can
39G6 **Gjøvik** Nor
7D5 **Glace Bay** Can
12G3 **Glacier Bay Nat Mon**
       USA
13E3 **Glacier Nat Pk** USA/
       Can
20B1 **Glacier Peak** Mt USA
6B2 **Glacier Str** Can
107E3 **Gladstone**
       Queensland, Aust
108A2 **Gladstone** S Aust,
       Aust
109C4 **Gladstone** Tasmania,
       Aust
14A1 **Gladstone** USA
38A1 **Gláma** Mt Iceland
39G6 **Gláma** R Nor
46D2 **Glan** R Germany
47C1 **Glärner** Mts Switz
47C1 **Glarus** Switz
18A2 **Glasco** USA
8C2 **Glasgow** Montana,
       USA
42B2 **Glasgow** Scot
16B3 **Glassboro** USA
43C4 **Glastonbury** Eng
61H2 **Glazov** Russian Fed
59B3 **Gleisdorf** Austria
110C1 **Glen Afton** NZ
16A3 **Glen Burnie** USA
101H1 **Glencoe** S Africa
9B3 **Glendale** Arizona, USA
22C3 **Glendale** California,
       USA
12E2 **Glenhallen** USA
109D1 **Glen Innes** Aust
109C1 **Glenmorgan** Aust
109D2 **Glenreagh** Aust
16A3 **Glen Rock** USA
19A3 **Glen Rose** USA
44C3 **Glenrothes** UK
15D2 **Glens Falls** USA
45B1 **Glenties** Irish Rep
19B3 **Glenwood** Arkansas,
       USA
8C3 **Glenwood Springs**
       USA
39F6 **Glittertind** Mt Nor
59B2 **Gliwice** Pol
8B2 **Globe** USA
58B2 **Głogów** Pol
38G5 **Glomfjord** Nor
107D2 **Gloucester** Aust
43C4 **Gloucester** Eng
16D1 **Gloucester** USA
58D1 **Glubokoye**
       Belorussia
60D3 **Glukhov** Russian Fed
59B3 **Gmünd** Austria
57C3 **Gmunden** Austria
58B2 **Gniezno** Pol
100A3 **Goabeg** Namibia
87A1 **Goa, Daman and Du**
       Union Territory, India
86C1 **Goālpāra** India
99D2 **Goba** Eth
100A3 **Gobabis** Namibia
34C2 **Gobernador Crespo**
       Arg
34B3 **Gobernador Duval**
       Arg
72B1 **Gobi** Desert China/
       Mongolia
75B2 **Gobo** Japan
87B1 **Godag** India
87B1 **Godāvari** R India
14B2 **Goderich** Can
6E3 **Godhavn** Greenland
85C4 **Godhra** India
34B2 **Godoy Cruz** Arg

137

Gods L

7A4 Gods L Can
6E3 Godthåb Greenland
Godwin Austen = K2
35B1 Goiandira Brazil
35B1 Goianésia Brazil
35B1 Goiânia Brazil
35A1 Goiás Brazil
31B4 Goiás State, Brazil
35A2 Goio-Erê Brazil
99D2 Gojab R Eth
55C2 Gökçeada I Turk
55C3 Gökova Körfezi B Turk
92C2 Göksun Turk
63C3 Gol R Mongolia
86C1 Golāghāt India
93C2 Gölbaşi Turk
20C2 Golconda USA
20B2 Gold Beach USA
109D1 Gold Coast Aust
13D2 Golden Can
110B2 Golden B NZ
20B1 Goldendale USA
22A2 Golden Gate Chan USA
19B4 Golden Meadow USA
21B2 Goldfield USA
13B3 Gold River Can
56C2 Goleniów Pol
22C3 Goleta USA
52A2 Golfe d'Ajaccio G Corse
96D1 Golfe de Gabes G Tunisia
Golfe de Gascogne = Biscay,Bay of
52A2 Golfe de St Florent G Corse
48B2 Golfe de St-Malo B France
49C3 Golfe du Lion G France
29B4 Golfo Corcovado G Chile
50B2 Golfo de Almeira G Spain
29B4 Golfo de Ancud G Chile
25D2 Golfo de Batabano G Cuba
50A2 Golfo de Cadiz G Spain
53A2 Golfo de Cagliari G Sardegna
24A1 Golfo de California G Mexico
25D4 Golfo de Chiriqui G Panama
25D3 Golfo de Fonseca Honduras
26B2 Golfo de Guacanayabo G Cuba
32A4 Golfo de Guayaquil G Ecuador
26B5 Golfo del Darien G Colombia/Panama
32A2 Golfo de los Mosquitos G Panama
25D3 Golfo del Papagaya G Nic
51B2 Golfo de Mazarrón G Spain
25D4 Golfo de Nicoya G Costa Rica
53A3 Golfo de Oristano G Sardegna
25E4 Golfo de Panamá G Panama
25D3 Golfo de Papagayo G Costa Rica
27E4 Golfo de Paria G Ven
29B5 Golfo de Penas G Chile
49D3 Golfo de St Florent G Corse
51C1 Golfo de San Jorge G Spain
24C3 Golfo de Tehuantepec G Mexico

32B3 Golfo de Torugas G Colombia
32B2 Golfo de Uraba G Colombia
51C2 Golfo de Valencia G Spain
27C4 Golfo de Venezuela G Ven
52A2 Golfo di Genova G Italy
53C3 Golfo di Policastro G Italy
53C3 Golfo di Squillace G Italy
53C2 Golfo di Taranto G Italy
52B1 Golfo di Venezia G Italy
25D4 Golfo Dulce G Costa Rica
29C5 Golfo San Jorge G Arg
29D4 Golfo San Matias G Arg
68B3 Golmud China
99E2 Golocha Eth
12B2 Golovin B USA
74F2 Golovnino Russian Fed
99C3 Goma Zaire
97D3 Gombe Nig
60D2 Gomel Belorussia
96A2 Gomera I Canary Is
24B2 Gomez Palacio Mexico
63E2 Gonam R Russian Fed
90C2 Gonbad-e Kāvūs Iran
86A1 Gonda India
85C4 Gondal India
99D1 Gonder Eth
92A1 Gönen Turk
55C3 Gonen R Turk
73A4 Gongga Shan Mt China
72A2 Gonghe China
97D3 Gongola R Nig
22B2 Gonzales California, USA
19A4 Gonzales Texas, USA
34C3 Gonzalez Chaves Arg
13C2 Good Hope Mt Can
8C2 Goodland USA
12B3 Goodnews Bay USA
109C1 Goodooga R Aust
42D3 Goole Eng
108C2 Goolgowi Aust
108A3 Goolwa Aust
106A4 Goomalling Aust
108C2 Goombalie Aust
109D1 Goomeri Aust
109D1 Goondiwindi Aust
7E4 Goose Bay Can
17C1 Goose Creek USA
20B2 Goose L USA
87B1 Gooty India
63C2 Gora Munku Sardyk Mt Mongolia/Russian Fed
64H3 Gora Narodnaya R Russian Fed
64G3 Gora Tel'pos-iz Russian Fed
54A2 Goražde Bosnia-Herzegovina
4D3 Gordon USA
13E1 Gordon L Can
15C3 Gordonsville USA
98B2 Goré Chad
99D2 Goré Eth
111A3 Gore NZ
63F2 Gore Topko Mt Russian Fed
45C2 Gorey Irish Rep
90B2 Gorgān Iran
93E2 Goris Armenia
52B1 Gorizia Italy
Gor'kiy = Nizniy Novgorod
61F2 Gor'kovskoye Vodokhranilishche Res Russian Fed

57C2 Gorlitz Germany
60E4 Gorlovka Ukraine
22C3 Gorman USA
54C2 Gorna Orjahovica Bulg
68A1 Gorno-Altaysk Russian Fed
69G2 Gornozavodsk Russian Fed
61F2 Gorodets Russian Fed
59C3 Gorodok Ukraine
59D3 Gorodok Ukraine
71F4 Goroka PNG
86A1 Gorokhpur India
101C2 Gorongosa Mozam
71D3 Gorontalo Indon
61K2 Goro Yurma Mt Russian Fed
45B2 Gort Irish Rep
63C2 Goryachinsk Russian Fed
59D3 Goryn' R Ukraine
59C2 Góry Swietokrzyskie Upland Pol
64G3 Gory Tel'pos-iz' Mt Russian Fed
39H8 Gorzów Wielkopolski Pol
74E2 Goshogawara Japan
52C2 Gospic Croatia
54B2 Gostivar Macedonia
58B2 Gostynin Pol
39G7 Göteborg Sweden
98B2 Gotel Mts Nig
39H7 Gotland I Sweden
74B4 Goto-retto I Japan
39H7 Gotska Sandön I Sweden
74C3 Götsu Japan
98B1 Goudoumaria Niger
103H7 Gough I Atlantic O
109C2 Goulburn Aust
97B3 Goumbou Mali
97B3 Goundam Mali
98B1 Gouré Niger
97B3 Gourma Rharous Mali
46A2 Gournay-en-Bray France
95A3 Gouro Chad
71E5 Gove Pen Aust
60E4 Goverla Mt Ukraine
35C1 Governador Valadares Brazil
86A2 Govind Ballabh Paht Sāgar L India
15C2 Gowanda USA
84B3 Gowārān Afghan
30E4 Goya Arg
98C1 Goz-Beida Chad
53B3 Gozo I Medit S
95C3 Goz Regeb Sudan
100B4 Graaff-Reinet S Africa
51C1 Gracefield Can
109D1 Grafton Aust
8D2 Grafton N Dakota, USA
14B3 Grafton W Virginia, USA
5E4 Graham I Can
13C1 Graham R Can
13E1 Graham L Can
100B4 Grahamstown S Africa
31B3 Grajaú Brazil
58C2 Grajewo Pol
55B2 Grámmos Mt Greece/Alb
44B3 Grampian Mts Scot
32C3 Granada Colombia
25D3 Granada Nic
50B2 Granada Spain
15D1 Granby Can
96A2 Gran Canaria I Canary Is
30D4 Gran Chaco Region Arg
14A2 Grand R Michigan, USA

18B1 Grand R Missouri, USA
27Q2 Grand B Dominica
11C4 Grand Bahama I The Bahamas
7E5 Grand Bank Can
102F2 Grand Banks Atlantic O
11C4 Grand Bassam Ivory Coast
9B3 Grand Canyon USA
26A3 Grand Cayman I Caribbean S
13E2 Grand Centre Can
20C1 Grand Coulee USA
34B3 Grande R Arg
31C4 Grande R Bahia, Brazil
35B1 Grande R Minas Gerais/São Paulo, Brazil
13D2 Grande Cache Can
47A2 Grande Chartreuse Region, France
101D2 Grande Comore I Comoros
13D1 Grande Prairie Can
19A3 Grande Prairie USA
95A3 Grand Erg de Bilma Desert Niger
96B2 Grand erg Occidental Mts Alg
96C2 Grand erg Oriental Mts Alg
7C4 Grande Rivière de la Baleine R Can
20C1 Grande Ronde R USA
7D5 Grand Falls New Brunswick, Can
7E5 Grand Falls Newfoundland, Can
20C1 Grand Forks Can
8D2 Grand Forks USA
16B1 Grand Gorge USA
14A2 Grand Haven USA
19C3 Grand Isle USA
19B4 Grand L USA
15D1 Grand Mère Can
50A2 Grândola Port
5J4 Grand Rapids Can
20C1 Grand Rapids Michigan, USA
10A2 Grand Rapids Minnesota, USA
47B2 Grand St Bernard P Italy/Switz
8B2 Grand Teton Mt USA
8B2 Grand Teton Nat Pk USA
46A2 Grandvilliers France
25D1 Grangeburg USA
51C1 Granollers Spain
52A1 Gran Paradiso Mt Italy
47D1 Gran Pilastro Mt Austria/Italy
43D3 Grantham Eng
21B2 Grant,Mt USA
44C3 Grantown-on-Spey Scot
9C3 Grants USA
20B2 Grants Pass USA
48B2 Granville France
5H4 Granville L Can
35C1 Grão Mogol Brazil
49D3 Grasse France
21A2 Grass Valley USA
5H5 Gravelbourg Can
46B1 Gravelines France
100C3 Gravelotte S Africa
15C2 Gravenhurst Can
109D1 Gravesend Aust
12H3 Gravina I USA
12B2 Grayling USA
20B1 Grays Harbor B USA
14B3 Grayson USA
18C2 Grayville USA
59B3 Graz Austria
27H1 Great R Jamaica
11C4 Great Abaco I The Bahamas

106B4 Great Australian Bight, *G* Aust
16B3 Great B New Jersey, USA
25E2 Great Bahama Bank The Bahamas
110C1 Great Barrier I NZ
107D2 Great Barrier Reef *Is* Aust
16C1 Great Barrington USA
4F3 Great Bear L Can
9D2 Great Bend USA
107D3 Great Dividing Range *Mts* Aust
42D2 Great Driffield Eng
16B3 Great Egg Harbor *B* USA
112B10 Greater Antarctic Region, Ant
26B2 Greater Antilles *Is* Caribbean S
43D4 Greater London Metropolitan County, Eng
43C3 Greater Manchester County, Eng
25E2 Great Exuma I The Bahamas
8B2 Great Falls USA
44B3 Great Glen *V* Scot
86B1 Great Himalayan Range *Mts* Asia
11C4 Great Inagua I The Bahamas
100B4 Great Karroo *Mts* S Africa
109C4 Great L Aust
100A3 Great Namaland Region, Namibia
42C3 Great Ormes Head *C* Wales
11C4 Great Ragged I The Bahamas
99D3 Great Ruaha *R* Tanz
15D2 Great Sacandaga L USA
8B2 Great Salt L USA
95B2 Great Sand Sea Libya/Egypt
106B3 Great Sandy Desert Aust
8A2 Great Sandy Desert USA
Great Sandy I = Fraser I
4G3 Great Slave L Can
16C2 Great South B USA
106B3 Great Victoria Desert Aust
112C2 Great Wall *Base* Ant
72B2 Great Wall China
43E3 Great Yarmouth Eng
94B1 Greco,C Cyprus
55B3 Greece Republic, Europe
15C2 Greeley USA
8C2 Greeley USA
6B1 Greely Fjord Can
14A1 Green B USA
14A2 Green Bay USA
14A3 Greencastle Indiana, USA
16C1 Greenfield Massachusetts, USA
14A2 Greenfield Wisconsin, USA
13F2 Green Lake Can
6F2 Greenland Dependency, N Atlantic O
102H1 Greenland Basin Greenland S
1B1 Greenland S Greenland
42B2 Greenock Scot
16C2 Greenport USA
21A2 Greensboro Maryland, USA
11C3 Greensboro N Carolina, USA
15C2 Greensburg Pennsylvania, USA
44B3 Greenstone *Pt* Scot

18C2 Greenup USA
17A1 Greenville Alabama, USA
97B4 Greenville Lib
19B3 Greenville Mississippi, USA
16D1 Greenville N Hampshire, USA
14B2 Greenville Ohio, USA
17B1 Greenville S Carolina, USA
19A3 Greenville Texas, USA
43E4 Greenwich Eng
16C2 Greenwich USA
16B3 Greenwood Delaware, USA
19B3 Greenwood Mississippi, USA
17B1 Greenwood S USA
18B2 Greers Ferry L USA
108A1 Gregory,L Aust
107D2 Gregory Range *Mts* Aust
56C2 Greifswald Germany
64F3 Gremikha Russian Fed
56C1 Grenå Den
26B2 Grenada USA
27E4 Grenada I Caribbean S
109C2 Grenfell Aust
49D2 Grenoble France
27M2 Grenville Grenada
107D2 Grenville,C Aust
20B1 Gresham USA
78C4 Gresik Jawa, Indon
78A3 Gresik Sumatera, Indon
19B4 Gretna USA
111B2 Grey *R* NZ
12G2 Grey Hunter Pk *Mt* Can
7E4 Grey Is Can
16C1 Greylock,Mt USA
111B2 Greymouth NZ
107D3 Grey Range *Mts* Aust
45C2 Greystones Irish Rep
101H1 Greytown S Africa
101F1 Griekwastad S Africa
17B1 Griffin USA
108C2 Griffith Aust
107D5 Grim,C Aust
15C2 Grimsby Can
42D3 Grimsby Eng
38B1 Grímsey I Iceland
13D1 Grimshaw Can
39F7 Grimstad Nor
47C1 Grindelwald Switz
6A2 Grinnell Pen Can
6B2 Grise Fjord Can
61H1 Griva Russian Fed
39J7 Grobina Latvia
58C2 Grodno Belorussia
86A1 Gromati *R* India
56B2 Groningen Neth
106C2 Groote Eylandt I Aust
100A2 Grootfontein Namibia
100B3 Grootvloer *Salt L* S Africa
27P2 Gros Islet St Lucia
46E1 Grosser Feldberg *Mt* Germany
52B2 Grosseto Italy
46E2 Gross-Gerau Germany
57C3 Grossglockner *Mt* Austria
47E1 Gross Venediger *Mt* Austria
12C3 Grosvenor,L USA
22B2 Groveland USA
21A2 Grover City USA
15D2 Groveton USA
61G5 Groznyy Russian Fed
58B2 Grudziadz Pol
100A3 Grünau Namibia
44E2 Grutness Scot
61F3 Gryazi Russian Fed

61E2 Gryazovets Russian Fed
29G8 Grytviken South Georgia
45A2 Gt Blasket I Irish Rep
35C2 Guaçui Brazil
23A1 Guadalajara Mexico
50B1 Guadalajara Spain
107E1 Guadalcanal I Solomon Is
50B2 Guadalimar *R* Spain
51B1 Guadalope *R* Spain
50B2 Guadalqivir *R* Spain
24B2 Guadalupe Mexico
3G6 Guadalupe I Mexico
27E3 Guadeloupe I Caribbean S
50B2 Guadian *R* Spain
50A2 Guadiana *R* Port
50B2 Guadix Spain
32D6 Guajará Mirim Brazil
32C1 Guajira,Pen de Colombia
32B4 Gualaceo Ecuador
34D2 Gualeguay Arg
34D2 Gualeguaychú Arg
71F2 Guam I Pacific O
34C3 Guamini Arg
77C5 Gua Musang Malay
23A1 Guanajuato Mexico
23A1 Guanajuato State, Mexico
32D2 Guanare Ven
25D2 Guane Cuba
73C5 Guangdong Province, China
73A3 Guanghan China
72C3 Guanghua China
73A4 Guangmao Shan *Mt* China
73B5 Guangnan China
72B3 Guangyuan China
73D4 Guangze China
67F3 Guangzhou China
35C1 Guanhães Brazil
32D3 Guania *R* Colombia
27E6 Guanipa *R* Ven
26B2 Guantánamo Cuba
72D1 Guanting Shuiku *Res* China
73B5 Guanxi Province, China
73A3 Guan Xian China
32B2 Guapa Colombia
33E6 Guaporé *R* Brazil/Bol
30C2 Guaqui Bol
32B4 Guaranda Ecuador
30F4 Guarapuava Brazil
35B2 Guaratinguetá Brazil
50A1 Guarda Port
35B1 Guarda Mor Brazil
9C4 Guasave Mexico
47D2 Guastalla Italy
25C3 Guatemala Guatemala
25C3 Guatemala Republic, Cent America
34C3 Guatrache Arg
32C3 Guavrare *R*
35B2 Guaxupé Brazil
27L1 Guayaguayare Trinidad
32A4 Guayaquil Ecuador
24A2 Guaymas Mexico
34D2 Guayquiraro *R* Arg
100B2 Guba Zaire
99E2 Guban *Region* Somalia
79B3 Gubat Phil
56C2 Gubin Pol
87B2 Güdür India
14B2 Guelpho Can
26A2 Guenabacoa Cuba
98C1 Guéréda Chad
48C2 Guéret France
48B2 Guernsey I UK
23A2 Guerrero State, Mexico
99D2 Gughe *Mt* Eth
63E2 Gugigu China
71F2 Guguan I Pacific O
109C2 Guiargambone Aust

73C4 Guidong China
97B4 Guiglo Ivory Coast
73C5 Gui Jiang *R* China
43D4 Guildford Eng
73C4 Guilin China
47B2 Guillestre France
72A2 Guinan China
97A3 Guinea Republic, Africa
102H4 Guinea Basin Atlantic O
97A3 Guinea-Bissau Republic, Africa
97C4 Guinea,G of W Africa
26A2 Güines Cuba
97B3 Guir *Well* Mali
84C2 Guiranwala Pak
33E1 Güiria Ven
46B2 Guise France
79C3 Guiuan Phil
73B5 Gui Xian China
73B4 Guiyang China
73B4 Guizhou Province, China
85C4 Gujarát State, India
84C2 Gujrat Pak
87B1 Gulbarga India
58D1 Gulbene Latvia
80D3 Gulf,The S W Asia
109C2 Gulgong Aust
73B4 Gulin China
12E2 Gulkana USA
12E2 Gulkana *R* USA
13E2 Gull L Can
13F2 Gull Lake Can
55C3 Güllük Körfezi *B* Turk
99D2 Gulu Uganda
109C1 Guluguba Aust
97C3 Gumel Nig
46D1 Gummersbach Germany
86A2 Gumpla India
93C1 Gümüşhane Turk
85D4 Guna India
99D1 Guna *Mt* Eth
109C3 Gundagai Aust
98B3 Gungu Zaire
6H3 Gunnbjørn Fjeld *Mt* Greenland
109D2 Gunnedah Aust
87B1 Guntakal India
17A1 Guntersville USA
17A1 Guntersville L USA
87C1 Guntúr India
78D3 Gunung Batu Putch *Mt* Malay
78D2 Gunung Besar *Mt* Indon
78D2 Gunung Bulu *Mt* Indon
78A3 Gunung Gedang *Mt* Indon
78C2 Gunung Lawit *Mt* Malay
78C4 Gunung Lawu *Mt* Indon
78D2 Gunung Menyapa *Mt* Indon
78D2 Gunung Niapa *Mt* Indon
78A3 Gunung Patah *Mt* Indon
78C4 Gunung Raung *Mt* Indon
78A3 Gunung Resag *Mt* Indon
78D3 Gunung Sarempaka *Mt* Indon
78C4 Gunung Sumbing *Mt* Indon
77C5 Gunung Tahan *Mt* Malay
78A2 Gunung Talakmau *Mt* Indon
100A2 Gunza Angola
72D3 Guoyang China
84C2 Gurdáspur India
84D3 Gurgaon India
86A1 Gurkha Nepal
92C2 Gürün Turk
31B2 Gurupi *R* Brazil

Guruve

100C2 **Guruve** Zim
72A1 **Gurvan Sayhan Uul**
  Upland Mongolia
61H4 **Gur'yev** Kazakhstan
97C3 **Gusau** Nig
58C2 **Gusev** Russian Fed
74A3 **Gushan** China
61F2 **Gus'khrustalnyy**
  Russian Fed
12G3 **Gustavus** USA
22B2 **Gustine** USA
11B3 **Guston** USA
56B2 **Gütersloh** Germany
18C2 **Guthrie** Kentucky,
  USA
18A2 **Guthrie** Oklahoma,
  USA
23B1 **Gutiérrez Zamora**
  Mexico
33F3 **Guyana** Republic,
  S America
102F4 **Guyana Basin**
  Atlantic O
72C1 **Guyang** China
48B3 **Guyenne** Region,
  France
9C3 **Guymon** USA
109D2 **Guyra** Aust
72B2 **Guyuan** China
109C2 **Gwabegar** Aust
85B3 **Gwalior** India
100B3 **Gwanda** Zim
98C2 **Gwane** Zaire
82A3 **Gwardar** Pak
45B1 **Gweebarra B**
  Irish Rep
89G9 **Gwelo** Zim
43C4 **Gwent** County,
  Wales
100B2 **Gweru** Zim
109C1 **Gwydir** R Aust
43C3 **Gwynedd** Wales
65F5 **Gyandzha**
  Azerbaijan
86B1 **Gyangzê** China
68B3 **Gyaring Hu** L China
64J2 **Gydanskiy Poluostrov**
  Pen Russian Fed
86B1 **Gyirong** China
6F3 **Gyldenløues**
  Greenland
109D1 **Gympie** Aust
59B3 **Gyöngyös** Hung
59B3 **Györ** Hung

H

38K6 **Haapajärvi** Fin
60B2 **Haapsalu** Estonia
56A2 **Haarlem** Neth
46D1 **Haarstrang** Region,
  Germany
25D2 **Habana** Cuba
06C2 **Habiganj** Bang
74D4 **Hachijo-jima** I Japan
75B1 **Hachiman** Japan
74E2 **Hachinohe** Japan
75B1 **Hachioji** Japan
16B2 **Hackettstown** USA
100A2 **Hack,Mt** Mt Aust
42C2 **Haddington** Scot
108B1 **Haddon Corner** Aust
108B1 **Haddon Downs** Aust
97D3 **Hadejia** Nig
97C3 **Hadejia** R Nig
94B2 **Hadera** Israel
56B1 **Hadersleve** Den
81D4 **Hadiboh** Socotra
4H2 **Hadley B** Can
73B5 **Hadong** China
81C4 **Hadramawt** Region,
  Yemen
56C1 **Hadsund** Den
74B3 **Haeju** N Korea
91A4 **Hafar al Bātin**
  S Arabia
6D2 **Haffners Bjerg** Mt
  Greenland
84C2 **Hafizabad** Pak
86C1 **Hāflong** India
38A2 **Hafnafjörður** Iceland
12B3 **Hageneister** I USA
56B2 **Hagen** Germany
15C3 **Hagerstown** USA
75A2 **Hagi** Japan

73A5 **Ha Giang** Vietnam
46D2 **Hagondange** France
45B2 **Hags Hd** C Irish Rep
46D2 **Haguenan** France
96A2 **Hagunia** Well Mor
69G4 **Haha-jima** I Japan
68B3 **Hah Xil Hu** L China
74A2 **Haicheng** China
76D1 **Hai Duong** Viet
94B2 **Haifa** Israel
94B2 **Haifa,B of** Israel
72D2 **Hai He** R China
73C5 **Haikang** China
76E1 **Haikou** China
80C3 **Ha'il** S Arabia
86C2 **Hailäkändi** India
63D3 **Hailar** China
74B2 **Hailong** China
69E2 **Hailun** China
38J5 **Hailuoto** I Fin
76D2 **Hainan** I China
12G3 **Haines** USA
12G2 **Haines Junction**
  Can
59B3 **Hainfeld** Austria
73B5 **Haiphong** Vietnam
26C3 **Haiti** Republic,
  Caribbean S
95C3 **Haiya** Sudan
72A2 **Haiyan** China
72B2 **Haiyuan** China
72D3 **Haizhou Wan** B
  China
59C3 **Hajdúböszörmény**
  Hung
75B1 **Hajiki-saki** Pt Japan
86C2 **Haka** Burma
21C4 **Hakalau** Hawaiian Is
93D2 **Hakkâri** Turk
74E2 **Hakodate** Japan
  Hakwa = Haka
75B1 **Hakui** Japan
75B1 **Haku-san** Mt Japan
92C2 **Halab** Syria
93E3 **Halabja** Iraq
95C2 **Halaib** Sudan
94C1 **Halba** Leb
68B2 **Halban** Mongolia
56C2 **Halberstadt**
  Germany
79B3 **Halcon,Mt** Phil
39G7 **Halden** Nor
88B2 **Haldia** India
84D3 **Haldwāni** India
13C1 **Halfway** R Can
7D5 **Halifax** Can
42D3 **Halifax** Eng
6D1 **Hall Basin** Sd Can
6B3 **Hall Beach** Can
46C1 **Halle** Belg
56C2 **Halle** Germany
112B1 **Halley** Base Ant
39F6 **Hallingdal** R Nor
6D3 **Hall Pen** Can
106B2 **Hall's Creek** Aust
71D3 **Halmahera** I Indon
39G7 **Halmstad** Sweden
56B2 **Haltern** Germany
38J5 **Halti** Mt Nor
42C2 **Haltwhistle** Eng
91H4 **Haluf** I Oman
94B3 **Haluza** Hist Site
  Israel
75A2 **Hamada** Japan
96C2 **Hamada de Tinrhert**
  Desert Region Alg
96B2 **Hamada du Dra**
  Upland Alg
90A3 **Hamadān** Iran
96B2 **Hamada Tounassine**
  Region, Alg
92C2 **Hamāh** Syria
75B2 **Hamamatsu** Japan
39G6 **Hamar** Nor
87C3 **Hambantota**
  Sri Lanka
19B3 **Hamburg** Arkansas,
  USA
18A1 **Hamburg** Iowa, USA
16B2 **Hamburg**
  Pennsylvania, USA
56B2 **Hamburg** Germany
16C2 **Hamden** USA
39J6 **Hämeenlinna** Fin

106A3 **Hamersley Range**
  Mts Aust
74B2 **Hamgyong Sanmaek**
  Mts N Korea
74B2 **Hamhŭng** N Korea
68B2 **Hami** China
94B1 **Hamidiyah** Syria
108B3 **Hamilton** Aust
14C2 **Hamilton** Can
110C1 **Hamilton** NZ
14B3 **Hamilton** Ohio, USA
42B2 **Hamilton** Scot
22B2 **Hamilton,Mt** USA
38K6 **Hamina** Fin
86A1 **Hamirpur** India
56B2 **Hamm** Germany
95A2 **Hammādah al Hamra**
  Upland Libya
38H6 **Hammerdal** Sweden
38J4 **Hammerfest** Nor
14A2 **Hammond** Illinois,
  USA
19B3 **Hammond** Louisiana,
  USA
16B3 **Hammonton** USA
111B3 **Hampden** NZ
43D4 **Hampshire** County,
  Eng
19B3 **Hampton** Arkansas,
  USA
91C4 **Hāmūn-e Jaz Mūrian**
  L Iran
84B3 **Hamun-i-Lora** Salt L
  Pak
21C4 **Hana** Hawaiian Is
21C4 **Hanalei** Hawaiian Is
74E2 **Hanamaki** Japan
72C2 **Hanchuan** China
73C3 **Hanchuan** China
15C3 **Hancock** Maryland,
  USA
10B2 **Hancock** Michigan,
  USA
75B2 **Handa** Japan
72C2 **Handan** China
99D3 **Handeni** Tanz
72B2 **Hanggin Qi** China
39J7 **Hangö** Fin
73E3 **Hangzhou** China
73E3 **Hangzhou Wan** B
  China
111B2 **Hanmer Springs** NZ
13E2 **Hanna** Can
18E2 **Hannibal** USA
56B2 **Hannover** Germany
39G7 **Hanöbukten** B
  Sweden
76D1 **Hanoi** Viet
14A3 **Hanover** USA
29B6 **Hanover** I Chile
72B3 **Han Shui** China
73C3 **Han Shui** R China
85D3 **Hānsi** India
68C2 **Hantay** Mongolia
72B3 **Hanzhong** China
86B2 **Haora** India
38J5 **Haparanda** Sweden
86C1 **Hāpoli** India
92C4 **Haql** S Arabia
80C2 **Haradh** S Arabia
80C2 **Hara Fanna** Eth
75C1 **Haramachi** Japan
101C2 **Harare** Zim
98C1 **Harazé** Chad
14B2 **Harbor Beach** USA
85D4 **Harda** India
39F6 **Hardangerfjord** Inlet
  Nor
46D2 **Hardt** Region,
  Germany
108A2 **Hardwicke B** Aust
18B2 **Hardy** USA
99E2 **Harer** Eth
99E2 **Hargeysa** Somalia
94B3 **Har Hakippa** Mt
  Israel
84B1 **Hari** R Indon
78A3 **Hari** R Indon
87A2 **Harīna-nada** B
  Japan
56B2 **Harlingen** Neth
9D4 **Harlingen** USA
43E4 **Harlow** Eng
94B2 **Har Meron** Mt Israel

20C2 **Harney Basin** USA
20C2 **Harney L** USA
38H6 **Harnösand** Sweden
63B3 **Har Nuur** L
  Mongolia
97B4 **Harper** Lib
12F2 **Harper,Mt** USA
15C3 **Harpers Ferry** USA
94B3 **Har Ramon** Mt Israel
7C4 **Harricanaw** R Can
16B3 **Harrington** USA
7E4 **Harrington Harbour**
  Can
44A3 **Harris** District Scot
18C2 **Harrisburg** Illinois,
  USA
16A2 **Harrisburg**
  Pennsylvania, USA
101G1 **Harrismith** S Africa
18B2 **Harrison** USA
15C3 **Harrisonburg** USA
7E4 **Harrison,C** Can
13C3 **Harrison L** Can
18B2 **Harrisonville** USA
44A3 **Harris,Sound of** Chan
  Scot
42D3 **Harrogate** Eng
94B3 **Har Saggi** Mt Israel
38H5 **Harstad** Nor
12G2 **Hart** R Can
38G6 **Hårteigen,Mt** Nor
16C2 **Hartford** Connecticut,
  USA
14A2 **Hartford** Michigan,
  USA
38G6 **Hartkjølen** Mt Nor
108A2 **Hart,L** Aust
43B4 **Hartland Pt** Eng
42D2 **Hartlepool** Eng
19A3 **Hartshorne** USA
17B1 **Hartwell Res** USA
101F1 **Hartz** R S Africa
68B2 **Har Us Nuur** L
  Mongolia
43E4 **Harwich** Eng
84D3 **Haryāna** State, India
56B2 **Hase** Germany
90A2 **Hashtpar** Iran
90A2 **Hashtrud** Iran
87B2 **Hassan** India
56B2 **Hasselt** Belg
96C2 **Hassi Inifel** Alg
96B2 **Hassi Mdakane** Well
  Alg
96C1 **Hassi Messaoud** Alg
108C3 **Hastings** Aust
43E4 **Hastings** Eng
8D2 **Hastings** Nebraska,
  USA
110C1 **Hastings** NZ
108B2 **Hatfield** Aust
12B1 **Hatham Inlet** USA
85D3 **Hāthras** India
76D2 **Ha Tinh** Viet
108B2 **Hattah** Aust
19C3 **Hatteras,C** USA
19C3 **Hatteras Inlet** USA
59B3 **Hatvan** Hung
76D3 **Hau Bon** Viet
99E2 **Haud** Region, Eth
39F7 **Haugesund** Nor
110C1 **Hauhungaroa Range**
  Mts NZ
13F1 **Haultain** R Can
110B1 **Hauraki G** NZ
111A3 **Hauroko,L** NZ
47C1 **Hausstock** Mt Switz
96B1 **Haut Atlas** Mts Mor
98C2 **Haute Kotto** Region,
  CAR
46C1 **Hautes Fagnes** Mts
  Belg
46B1 **Hautmont** Belg
96B1 **Hauts Plateaux** Mts
  Alg
90D3 **Hauzdar** Iran
18B1 **Havana** USA
  Havana = Habana
87B3 **Havankulam**
  Sri Lanka

110C1 **Havelock North** NZ
43B4 **Haverfordwest** Wales
16D1 **Haverhill** USA
87B2 **Häveri** India
16C2 **Haverstraw** USA
59B3 **Havlíčkův Brod** Czech Republic
8C2 **Havre** USA
16A3 **Havre de Grace** USA
7D4 **Havre-St-Pierre** Can
54C2 **Havsa** Turk
21C4 **Hawaii** / Hawaiian Is
21C4 **Hawaii Volcanoes Nat Pk** Hawaiian Is
111A2 **Hawea,L** NZ
110B1 **Hawera** NZ
42C2 **Hawick** Scot
111A2 **Hawkdun Range** *Mts* NZ
110C1 **Hawke B** NZ
109D2 **Hawke,C** Aust
108A2 **Hawker** Aust
76B1 **Hawng Luk** Burma
93D3 **Hawr al Habbaniyah** *L* Iraq
93E3 **Hawr al Hammār** *L* Iraq
21B2 **Hawthorne** USA
108B2 **Hay** Aust
5G3 **Hay** *R* Can
46D2 **Hayange** France
4B3 **Haycock** USA
7A4 **Hayes** *R* Can
6D2 **Hayes Halvø** *Region* Greenland
12E2 **Hayes,Mt** USA
5G3 **Hay River** Can
18A2 **Haysville** USA
22A2 **Hayward** California, USA
86B2 **Hazārībāg** India
46B1 **Hazebrouck** France
19B3 **Hazelhurst** USA
4G2 **Hazel Str** Can
5F4 **Hazelton** Can
13B1 **Hazelton Mts** Can
6C1 **Hazen L** Can
9A83 **Hazeva** Israel
16B2 **Hazleton** USA
22A1 **Healdsburg** USA
108C3 **Healesville** Aust
12E2 **Healy** USA
6B8 **Heard I** Indian O
19A3 **Hearne** USA
10B2 **Hearst** Can
72D2 **Hebei** Province, China
109C1 **Hebel** Aust
72C2 **Hebi** China
72C2 **Hebian** China
7D4 **Hebron** Can
9A83 **Hebron** Israel
18A1 **Hebron** Nebraska, USA
5E4 **Hecate** *Str* Can
12H3 **Heceta I** USA
73B5 **Hechi** China
4G2 **Hecla and Griper B** Can
111C2 **Hector,Mt** NZ
38G6 **Hede** Sweden
39H6 **Hedemora** Sweden
20C1 **He Devil Mt** USA
56B2 **Heerenveen** Neth
46C1 **Heerlen** Neth
  Hefa = Haifa
73D3 **Hefei** China
73B4 **Hefeng** China
69F2 **Hegang** China
75B1 **Hegura-jima** / Japan
94B3 **Heidan** *R* Jordan
56B2 **Heide** Germany
101G1 **Heidelberg** Transvaal, S Africa
57B3 **Heidelberg** Germany
62E3 **Heihe** China
101G1 **Heilbron** S Africa
57B3 **Heilbronn** Germany
56C2 **Heiligenstadt** Germany
38K6 **Heinola** Fin
73B4 **Hejiang** China
6J3 **Hekla** *Mt* Iceland

76C1 **Hekou** Viet
73A5 **Hekou Yaozou Zizhixian** China
72B1 **Helan** China
72B2 **Helan Shan** *Mt* China
19B3 **Helena** Arkansas, USA
8B2 **Helena** Montana, USA
22D3 **Helendale** USA
71E3 **Helen Reef** / Pacific O
44B3 **Helensburgh** Scot
91B4 **Helleh** *R* Iran
51B2 **Hellín** Spain
20C1 **Hells Canyon** *R* USA
46D1 **Hellweg** Region, Germany
22B2 **Helm** USA
80E2 **Helmand** *R* Afghan
100A3 **Helmeringhausen** Namibia
46C1 **Helmond** Neth
44C2 **Helmsdale** Scot
74B2 **Helong** China
39G7 **Helsingborg** Sweden
  Helsingfors = Helsinki
56C1 **Helsingør** Den
38J6 **Helsinki** Fin
43B4 **Helston** Eng
92B4 **Helwân** Egypt
19A3 **Hempstead** USA
39H7 **Hemse** Sweden
72A3 **Henan** China
72C3 **Henan** Province, China
110B1 **Hen and Chicken Is** NZ
14A3 **Henderson** Kentucky, USA
9B3 **Henderson** Nevada, USA
19B3 **Henderson** Texas, USA
73E5 **Heng-ch'un** Taiwan
68B4 **Hengduan Shan** *Mts* China
56B2 **Hengelo** Neth
72B2 **Hengshan** China
72D2 **Hengshui** China
72D1 **Heng Xian** China
73C4 **Hengyang** China
77A4 **Henhoaha** Nicobar Is
43D4 **Henley-on-Thames** Eng
16B3 **Henlopen,C** USA
7B4 **Henrietta Maria,C** Can
18A2 **Henryetta** USA
112C2 **Henryk Arctowski** *Base* Ant
6D3 **Henry Kater Pen** Can
68C2 **Hentiyn Nuruu** *Mts* Mongolia
76B2 **Henzada** Burma
73B5 **Hepu** China
80E2 **Herat** Afghan
5H4 **Herbert** Can
110C2 **Herbertville** NZ
46E1 **Herborn** Germany
26A4 **Heredia** Costa Rica
43C3 **Hereford** Eng
43C3 **Hereford & Worcester** County, Eng
46C1 **Herentals** Belg
47B1 **Héricourt** France
18A2 **Herington** USA
111A3 **Heriot** NZ
47C1 **Herisau** Switz
15D2 **Herkimer** USA
44E1 **Herma Ness** *Pen* Scot
109C2 **Hermidale** Aust
111B2 **Hermitage** NZ
  Hermon,Mt = Jebel ash Shaykh
24A2 **Hermosillo** Mexico
16A2 **Herndon** Pennsylvania, USA
22C2 **Herndon** California, USA
46D1 **Herne** Germany
56B1 **Herning** Den

90A2 **Herowäbad** Iran
50A2 **Herrera del Duque** Spain
16A2 **Hershey** USA
43D4 **Hertford** County, Eng
94B2 **Herzliyya** Israel
46C1 **Hesbaye** Region, Belg
46B1 **Hesdin** France
72B2 **Heshui** China
22D3 **Hesperia** USA
12H2 **Hess** *R* Can
57B2 **Hessen** State, Germany
22C2 **Hetch Hetchy Res** USA
42C2 **Hexham** Eng
73C5 **He Xian** China
73C5 **Heyuan** China
108B3 **Heywood** Aust
72D2 **Heze** China
17B2 **Hialeah** USA
10A2 **Hibbing** USA
110C1 **Hicks Bay** NZ
109C3 **Hicks,Pt** Aust
23B1 **Hidalgo** State, Mexico
24B2 **Hidalgo del Parral** Mexico
35B1 **Hidrolândia** Brazil
96A2 **Hierro** / Canary Is
75C1 **Higashine** Japan
74B4 **Higashi-suidō** *Str* Japan
20B2 **High Desert** USA
19B4 **High Island** USA
44B3 **Highland** Region, Scot
22D3 **Highland Peak** *Mt* USA
16B2 **Highlands Falls** USA
11B3 **High Point** USA
13D1 **High Prairie** Can
5G4 **High River** Can
17B2 **High Springs** USA
16B2 **Hightstown** USA
43D4 **High Wycombe** Eng
39J7 **Hiiumaa** / Estonia
80B3 **Hijaz** Region, S Arabia
75B2 **Hikigawa** Japan
75B1 **Hikone** Japan
110B1 **Hikurangi** NZ
9C4 **Hildago** Mexico
9C4 **Hildago del Parral** Mexico
56B2 **Hildesheim** Germany
27R3 **Hillaby,Mt** Barbados
56C1 **Hillerød** Den
14B3 **Hillsboro** Ohio, USA
20B1 **Hillsboro** Oregon, USA
19A3 **Hillsboro** Texas, USA
108C2 **Hillston** Aust
44E1 **Hillswick** Scot
21C4 **Hilo** Hawaiian Is
93C2 **Hilvan** Turk
56B2 **Hilversum** Neth
84D2 **Himachal Pradesh** State, India
82B3 **Himalaya** *Mts* Asia
85C4 **Himatnagar** India
74C4 **Himeji** Japan
92C3 **Hims** Syria
12E2 **Hinchinbrook Entrance** USA
12E2 **Hinchinbrook I** USA
85D3 **Hindaun** India
84B1 **Hindu Kush** *Mts* Afghan
87B2 **Hindupur** India
13D1 **Hines Creek** Can
85D4 **Hinganghāt** India
72B2 **Hinggan Ling** *Upland* China
85B3 **Hingol** *R* Pak
85B3 **Hingoli** India
38H5 **Hinnøya** / Nor
16C1 **Hinsdale** USA
13D2 **Hinton** Can
34B2 **Hipolito Itrogoyen** Arg

86A2 **Hirakud Res** India
92B2 **Hirfanli Baraji** *Res* Turk
87B2 **Hīrīhar** India
74E2 **Hirosaki** Japan
74C4 **Hiroshima** Japan
46C2 **Hirson** France
54C2 **Hîrşova** Rom
56B1 **Hirtshals** Den
84D3 **Hisār** India
26C3 **Hispaniola** / Caribbean S
94C1 **Hisyah** Syria
93D3 **Hīt** Iraq
74E3 **Hitachi** Japan
75C1 **Hitachi-Ōta** Japan
43D4 **Hitchin** Eng
38F6 **Hitra** / Nor
75A2 **Hiuchi-nada** *B* Japan
75A2 **Hiwasa** Japan
56B1 **Hjørring** Den
76B1 **Hka** *R* Burma
97C4 **Ho** Ghana
76D1 **Hoa Binh** Viet
76D3 **Hoa Da** Viet
109C4 **Hobart** Aust
9C3 **Hobbs** USA
56B1 **Hobro** Den
13C2 **Hobson L** Can
99E2 **Hobyo** Somalia
76D3 **Ho Chi Minh** Viet
57C3 **Hochkönig** *Mt* Austria
54B1 **Hódmező'hely** Hung
59B3 **Hodonín** Czech Republic
74B2 **Hoeryong** N Korea
57C2 **Hof** Germany
38B2 **Hofsjökull** *Mts* Iceland
74C4 **Hōfu** Japan
96C2 **Hoggar** *Upland* Alg
46D1 **Hohe Acht** *Mt* Germany
72C1 **Hohhot** China
6J3 **Höhn** Iceland
68B3 **Hoh Sai Hu** *L* China
82C2 **Hoh Xil Shan** *Mts* China
99D2 **Hoima** Uganda
86C1 **Hojāī** India
75A2 **Hojo** Japan
110B1 **Hokianga Harbour** *B* NZ
111B2 **Hokitika** NZ
74E2 **Hokkaidō** Aust
90C2 **Hokmābād** Iran
109C3 **Holbrook** Aust
9B3 **Holbrook** USA
19A2 **Holdenville** USA
87B2 **Hole Narsipur** India
27R3 **Holetown** Barbados
26B2 **Holguín** Cuba
111B2 **Holitika** NZ
12C2 **Holitna** *R* USA
59B3 **Hollabrunn** Austria
14A2 **Holland** USA
22B2 **Hollister** USA
19C3 **Holly Springs** USA
22C3 **Hollywood** California, USA
17B2 **Hollywood** Florida, USA
4G2 **Holman Island** Can
38J6 **Holmsund** Sweden
94B2 **Holon** Israel
56B1 **Holstebro** Den
6E3 **Holsteinborg** Greenland
14B2 **Holt** USA
18A2 **Holton** USA
12C2 **Holy Cross** USA
42B3 **Holyhead** Wales
42D2 **Holy I** Eng
43B3 **Holy I** Wales
16C1 **Holyoke** Massachusetts, USA
86C2 **Homalin** Burma
6D3 **Home B** Can
12D3 **Homer** Alaska, USA
19B3 **Homer** Louisiana, USA
111A2 **Homer Tunnel** NZ
17B1 **Homerville** USA

Homestead

17B2 Homestead USA
17A1 Homewood USA
87B1 Homnábád India
101C3 Homoine Mozam
25D3 Hondo R Mexico
25D3 Honduras Republic, Cent America
25D3 Honduras,G of Honduras
39G6 Honefoss Nor
15C2 Honesdale USA
21A1 Honey L USA
76C1 Hong R Viet
76D1 Hon Gai Viet
73A4 Hongguo China
73C4 Hong Hu L China
72B2 Honghui China
73C4 Hongjiang China
73C5 Hong Kong Colony, China
68D2 Hongor Mongolia
73B5 Hongshui He R China
72A3 Hongyuan China
72D3 Hongze Hu L China
107E1 Honiara Solomon Is
77C4 Hon Khoai I Camb
76D3 Hon Lan I Viet
38K4 Honningsvag Nor
21C4 Honolulu Hawaiian Is
77C4 Hon Panjang I Viet
74D3 Honshu I Japan
20B1 Hood,Mt USA
20B1 Hood River USA
45C2 Hook Head C Irish Rep
12G3 Hoonah USA
12A2 Hooper Bay USA
101G1 Hoopstad S Africa
56A2 Hoorn Neth
9B3 Hoover Dam USA
12E2 Hope Alaska, USA
19B3 Hope Arkansas, USA
13C3 Hope Can
7D4 Hopedale Can
64D2 Hopen I Barents S
6D3 Hopes Advance,C Can
108B3 Hopetoun Aust
100B3 Hopetown S Africa
18C2 Hopkinsville USA
20B1 Hoquiam USA
93D1 Horasan Turk
99F1 Hordiyo Somalia
47C1 Horgen Switz
105H5 Horizon Depth Pacific O
91C4 Hormuz,Str of Oman/Iran
59B3 Horn Austria
6H3 Horn C Iceland
38H5 Hornavan L Sweden
19B3 Hornbeck USA
20B2 Hornbrook USA
111B2 Hornby NZ
7B5 Hornepayne Can
4F3 Horn Mts Can
42D3 Hornsea Eng
72B1 Horn Uul Mt Mongolia
30E3 Horqueta Par
15C2 Horseheads USA
56C1 Horsens Den
20B1 Horseshoe Bay Can
108B3 Horsham Aust
43D4 Horsham Eng
39G7 Horten Nor
4F3 Horton R Can
78C2 Hose Mts Malay
85D4 Hoshangábád India
84D2 Hoshiárpur India
87B1 Hospet India
7C2 Hoste I Chile
82B2 Hotan China
19B3 Hot Springs Arkansas, USA
8C2 Hot Springs S. Dakota, USA
4G3 Hottah Can
46A2 Houdan France
72C2 Houma China
19B4 Houma USA
16C2 Housatonic R USA
13B2 Houston Can

19C3 Houston Mississippi, USA
19A4 Houston Texas, USA
106A3 Houtman Is Aust
68B2 Hovd Mongolia
68C1 Hövsgöl Nuur L Mongolia
14A2 Howard City USA
12C1 Howard P USA
109C3 Howe,C Aust
101H1 Howick S Africa
44C2 Hoy I Scot
39F6 Høyanger Nor
59B2 Hradeç-Králové Czech Republic
59B3 Hranice Czech Republic
59D3 Hron R Slovakia
73E5 Hsin-chu Taiwan
73E5 Hsüeh Shan Mt Taiwan
72B2 Huachi China
32B6 Huacho Peru
72C1 Huade China
72D3 Huaibin China
72D3 Huai He R China
73C4 Huaihua China
73C5 Huaiji China
72D3 Huainan China
69E1 Hua lian Taiwan
32B5 Huallaga R Peru
32B5 Huallanca Peru
32B5 Huamachuco Peru
100A2 Huambo Angola
30C2 Huanay Bol
32B5 Huancabamba Peru
32B6 Huancavelica Peru
32B6 Huancayo Peru
73D3 Huangchuan China
Huang Hai = Yellow S
72D2 Huang He R China
72B2 Huangling China
76D2 Huangliu China
73C3 Huangpi China
73C4 Huangshan China
73D3 Huangshi China
34C3 Huanguelén Arg
73E4 Huangyan China
74B2 Huanren China
32B5 Huánuco Peru
30C2 Huanuni Bol
72B2 Huan Xian China
32B5 Huaráz Peru
32B6 Huarmey Peru
32B5 Huascarán Mt Peru
30B4 Huasco Chile
23B2 Huatusco Mexico
23B1 Huauchinango Mexico
23B2 Huautla Mexico
72C2 Hua Xian China
24B2 Huayapan R Mexico
73C3 Hubei Province, China
87B1 Hubli India
34C3 Hucal Arg
74B2 Huch'ang N Korea
42D3 Huddersfield Eng
39H6 Hudiksvall Sweden
14D2 Hudson Florida, USA
14B2 Hudson Michigan, USA
16C1 Hudson New York, USA
16C1 Hudson R USA
7B4 Hudson B Can
5H4 Hudson Bay Can
13C1 Hudson's Hope Can
6C3 Hudson Str Can
76D2 Hue Viet
23B1 Huejutla Mexico
50A2 Huelva Spain
23A2 Hueramo Mexico
51B2 Húercal Overa Spain
51B1 Huesca Spain
23B2 Huexotla Hist Site Mexico
107D3 Hughenden Aust
12D1 Hughes USA
86B2 Hugli R India
19A3 Hugo USA
73D4 Hui'an China

110C1 Huiarau Range Mts NZ
74B2 Huich'ŏn N Korea
74B2 Huifa He R China
32B3 Huila Mt Colombia
73D5 Huilai China
73A4 Huili China
74B2 Huinan China
34C2 Huinca Renancó Arg
25C3 Huixtla Mexico
73A4 Huize China
73C5 Huizhou China
23B2 Hujuápan de Léon Mexico
69F2 Hulin China
15C1 Hull Can
42D3 Hull Eng
58B1 Hultsfred Sweden
63D3 Hulun Nur L China
69E1 Huma China
33E5 Humaitá Brazil
100B4 Humansdorp S Africa
42D3 Humber R Eng
42D3 Humberside County, Eng
5H4 Humboldt Can
20C2 Humboldt R USA
20B2 Humboldt B USA
6D2 Humboldt Gletscher Gl Greenland
21D2 Humboldt L USA
108C1 Humeburn Aust
109C3 Hume,L Aust
100A2 Humpata Angola
22C2 Humphreys USA
38A1 Húnaflói B Iceland
73C4 Hunan Province, China
74C2 Hunchun China
13C2 Hundred Mile House Can
54B1 Hunedoara Rom
59B3 Hungary Republic, Europe
108B1 Hungerford Aust
74B2 Hüngnam N Korea
74B2 Hunjiang China
46D2 Hunsrück Mts, Germany
109D2 Hunter R Aust
13B2 Hunter I Can
109C4 Hunter Is Aust
12D2 Hunter,Mt USA
14A3 Huntingburg USA
43D3 Huntingdon Eng
14B3 Huntingdon Indiana, USA
14B3 Huntington W Virginia, USA
22C4 Huntington Beach USA
22C4 Huntington Park USA
110C1 Huntly NZ
44C3 Huntly Scot
12J2 Hunt,Mt Can
108A1 Hunt Pen Aust
14B1 Huntsville Alabama, USA
15C1 Huntsville Can
19A3 Huntsville Texas, USA
76D2 Huong Khe Viet
71F4 Huon Peninsula Pen PNG
109C4 Huonville Aust
14B1 Hurd,C Can
80B3 Hurghada Egypt
8D2 Huron S. Dakota, USA
14B1 Huron,L Can/USA
34A2 Hurtado Chile
111B2 Hurunui R NZ
38B1 Húsavík Iceland
54C1 Huşi Rom
39G7 Huskvarna Sweden
12C1 Huslia USA
94B2 Husn Jordan
56B2 Husum Germany
109C1 Hutton,Mt Aust
72D2 Hutuo He R China
46C1 Huy Belg
72A2 Huzhu China
52C2 Hvar I Croatia
100B2 Hwange Zim

100B2 Hwange Nat Pk Zim
15D2 Hyannis USA
68B2 Hyargas Nuur L Mongolia
5E4 Hydaburg Can
16C2 Hyde Park USA
87B1 Hyderäbäd India
85B3 Hyderabad Pak
49D3 Hyères France
12J2 Hyland R Can
8B2 Hyndman Peak Mt USA
38K6 Hyrynsalmi Fin
13D1 Hythe Can
74C4 Hyuga Japan
39J6 Hyvikää Fin

I

31C4 Iaçu Brazil
54C2 Ialomiţa R Rom
54C1 Iaşi Rom
97C4 Ibadan Nig
32B3 Ibagué Colombia
54B2 Ibar R Montenegro/Serbia, Yugos
32B3 Ibarra Ecuador
35B1 Ibiá Brazil
30E4 Ibicuí R Brazil
34D2 Ibicuy Arg
51C2 Ibiza Spain
51C2 Ibiza I Spain
101D2 Ibo Mozam
31C4 Ibotirama Brazil
91C5 'Ibri Oman
32B6 Ica Peru
32D4 Icá R Brazil
32D3 Icana Brazil
38A1 Iceland Republic, N Atlantic O
13C2 Ice Mt Can
87A1 Ichalkaranji India
74E3 Ichihara Japan
75B1 Ichinomiya Japan
74E3 Ichinoseki Japan
12F3 Icy B USA
4B2 Icy C USA
19B3 Idabell USA
8B2 Idaho Falls USA
20B2 Idanha USA
46D2 Idar Oberstein Germany
95A2 Idehan Marzūg Desert Libya
95A2 Idehan Ubari Desert Libya
96C2 Idelès Alg
68B2 Iderlym Gol R Mongolia
95C2 Idfu Egypt
55B3 Idhi Oros Mt Greece
55B3 Idhra I Greece
98B3 Idiofa Zaïre
12C2 Iditarod R USA
92C2 Idlib Syria
39K7 Idritsa Russian Fed
100B4 Idutywa S Africa
55C3 Ierápetra Greece
10D1 Ieper Belg
63D2 Iet Oktyabr'ya Russian Fed
99D3 Ifakara Tanz
71F3 Ifalik I Pacific O
101D3 Ifanadiana Madag
97C4 Ife Nig
97C3 Iférouane Niger
78C2 Igan Malay
35B2 Igaranava Brazil
93E2 Igdir Iran
39H6 Iggesund Sweden
34B2 Iglésia Arg
53A3 Iglésias Sardegna
6B3 Igloolik Can
10A2 Ignace Can
55B3 Igoumenítsa Greece
61H2 Igra Russian Fed
23B2 Iguala Mexico
35B2 Iguape Brazil
35B2 Iguatama Brazil
31D3 Iguatu Brazil
98A3 Iguéla Gabon
101D3 Ihosy Madag
74D3 Iida Japan
75B1 Iide-san Mt Japan
38K6 Iisalmi Fin

75A2 Iizuka Japan
97C4 Ijebu Ode Nig
56B2 Ijsselmeer S Neth
55C3 Ikaria I Greece
74E2 Ikeda Japan
98C3 Ikela Zaire
54B2 Ikhtiman Bulg
12D3 Ikolik,C USA
101D2 Ikopa R Madag
79B2 Ilagan Phil
90A3 Ilām Iran
47C1 Ilanz Switz
13F1 Ile à la Crosse Can
13F1 Ile à la Crosse,L Can
89G8 Ilebo Zaire
96D1 Ile de Jerba I Tunisia
48B2 Ile de Noirmoutier I France
48B2 Ile de Ré I France
107F3 Ile des Pins I Nouvelle Calédonie
48A2 Ile d'Ouessant I France
48B2 Ile d'Yeu I France
61J3 Ilek R Russian Fed
107F2 Iles Bélep Nouvelle Calédonie
107E2 Iles Chesterfield Nouvelle Calédonie
49D3 Iles d'Hyères Is France
43B4 Ilfracombe Eng
92B1 Ilgaz Dağları Mts Turk
101C3 Ilha Bazaruto I Mozam
33G3 Ilha De Maracá I Brazil
33G4 Ilha de Marajó I Brazil
35B2 Ilha da São Sebastião I Brazil
33G6 Ilha do Bananal Region Brazil
35C2 Ilha Grande I Brazil
35B2 Ilha Santo Amaro I Brazil
96A1 Ilhas Selvegens I Atlantic O
35A2 Ilha Solteira Dam Brazil
31D4 Ilhéus Brazil
12C3 Iliamna L USA
12D2 Iliamna V USA
79B4 Iligan Phil
63C2 Ilim R Russian Fed
63C2 Ilim Russian Fed
63G3 Il'inskiy Russian Fed
55B3 Iliodhrómia I Greece
79B4 Ilana B Phil
34A2 Illapel Chile
34A2 Illapel R Chile
97C3 Illéla Niger
47D1 Iller R Germany
4C4 Illiamna L USA
10A2 Illinois State, USA
18B2 Illinois R USA
96C2 Illizi Alg
30B2 Ilo Peru
79B3 Iloilo Phil
38L6 Ilomantsi Fin
97C4 Ilorin Nig
75A2 Imabari Japan
75B1 Imalchi Japan
60C1 Imatra Fin
30G4 Imbituba Brazil
99E2 Imi Eth
20C2 Imlay USA
47D1 Immenstadt Germany
52B2 Imola Italy
31B3 Imperatriz Brazil
52A2 Imperia Italy
98B2 Impfondo Congo
86D2 Imphäl India
47D1 Imst Austria
12B1 Imuruk L USA
75B1 Ina Japan
96C2 In Afahleleh Well Alg
75B2 Inamba-jima I Japan
96C2 In Amenas Alg
38K5 Inari Fin
38K5 Inarijärvi L Fin

75C1 Inawashiro-ko L Japan
96C2 In Belbel Alg
60E5 Ince Burun Pt Turk
92B2 Incekum Burun Pt Turk
74B3 Inch'ŏn S Korea
96B2 In Dagouber Well Mali
35B1 Indaia R Brazil
38H6 Indals R Sweden
21B2 Independence California, USA
18A2 Independence Kansas, USA
18B2 Independence Missouri, USA
78A3 Inderagiri R Indon
61H4 Inderborsky Kazakhstan
83B3 India Federal Republic, Asia
14A2 Indiana State, USA
15C2 Indiana USA
104C6 Indian-Antarctic Ridge Indian O
14A3 Indianapolis USA
      Indian Desert = Thar Desert
7E4 Indian Harbour Can
104B4 Indian O
18B1 Indianola Iowa, USA
19B3 Indianola Mississippi, USA
35B1 Indianópolis Brazil
76D2 Indo China Region, S E Asia
70C4 Indonesia Republic, S E Asia
85D4 Indore India
78B4 Indramayu Indon
48C2 Indre R France
85B3 Indus R Pak
60D5 Inebulu Turk
96C2 In Ebeggi Well Alg
96C2 In Ecker Alg
92A1 Inegöl Turk
96D2 In Ezzane Alg
97C3 Ingal Niger
14B2 Ingersoll Can
107D2 Ingham Aust
6D2 Inglefield Land Region Can
110B1 Inglewood NZ
109D7 Inglewood Queensland, Aust
22C4 Inglewood Victoria, Aust
38B2 Ingólfshöfði I Iceland
57C3 Ingolstadt Germany
86B2 Ingrãj Bãzãr India
96C3 In-Guezzam Well Alg
101C3 Inhambane Mozam
101C3 Inharrime Mozam
35B1 Inhumas Brazil
32D3 Inirida R Colombia
45A2 Inishbofin I Irish Rep
45A1 Inishkea I Irish Rep
45B2 Inishmaan I Irish Rep
45B2 Inishmore I Irish Rep
45B1 Inishmurray I Irish Rep
45C1 Inishowen District, Irish Rep
45B3 Inishshark I Irish Rep
45A2 Inishturk I Irish Rep
109C1 Injune Aust
12H3 Inklin USA
12H3 Inklin R Can
12C1 Inland L USA
47D1 Inn R Austria
108B1 Innamincka Aust
68C2 Inner Mongolia Autonomous Region, China
107D2 Innisfail Aust
12C2 Innoko R USA
57C3 Innsbruck Austria
98B3 Inongo Zaire
58B2 Inowrocław Pol
96C2 In Salah Alg
47B1 Interlaken Switz

24C3 Intexpec Mexico
47C2 Intra Italy
78D3 Intu Indon
75C1 Inubo-saki C Japan
7C4 Inukjuak Can
4E3 Inuvik Can
4F3 Inuvik Region Can
44B3 Inveraray Scot
111A3 Invercargill NZ
109D1 Inverell Aust
13D2 Invermere Can
44B3 Inverness Scot
44C3 Inverurie Scot
108A3 Investigator Str Aust
68A1 Inya Russian Fed
21B2 Inyokern USA
98B3 Inzia R Zaire
55B3 Ioánnina Greece
18A2 Iola USA
44A3 Iona I Scot
100A2 Iôna Nat Pk Angola
20C1 Ione USA
      Ionian Is = Ioníoi Nísoi
55A3 Ionian S Italy/Greece
55B3 Ioníoi Nísoi Is Greece
55C3 Ios I Greece
10A2 Iowa R USA
10A2 Iowa City USA
35B1 Ipameri Brazil
35C1 Ipanema Brazil
61F4 Ipatovo Russian Fed
32B3 Ipiales Colombia
77C5 Ipoh Malay
30F2 Iporá Brazil
55C2 Ipsala Turk
109D1 Ipswich Aust
43E3 Ipswich Eng
16D1 Ipswich USA
30B3 Iquique Chile
32B4 Iquitos Peru
55C3 Iráklion Greece
80D2 Iran Republic, S W Asia
91D4 Iränshahr Iran
23A1 Irapuato Mexico
93D3 Iraq Republic, S W Asia
95A2 Irä Wan Watercourse Libya
94B2 Irbid Jordan
61K2 Irbit Russian Fed
36C3 Ireland Republic, NW Europe
33F3 Ireng R Guyana
74B3 Iri S Korea
71E4 Irian Jaya Province, Indon
95B3 Iriba Chad
79B3 Iriga Phil
99D3 Iringa Tanz
69E4 Iriomote I Japan
33G5 Iriri R Brazil
42B3 Irish S Eng/Irish Rep
12D1 Irkillik R USA
63C2 Irkutsk Russian Fed
65J4 Irlysh R Kazakhstan
108A2 Iron Knob Aust
14A3 Iron Mountain USA
107D2 Iron Range Aust
14A1 Iron River USA
14B3 Irontown USA
10B2 Ironwood USA
10B2 Iroquois Falls Can
75B2 Iro-zaki C Japan
76A2 Irrawaddy,Mouths of the Burma
65H4 Irtysh R Russian Fed
51B1 Irun Spain
42B2 Irvine Scot
19A3 Irving USA
79B4 Isabela Phil
32J7 Isabela I Ecuador
4H2 Isachsen Can
4H2 Isachsen,C Can
6H3 Isafjörður Iceland
74C4 Isahaya Japan
98C2 Isangi Zaire
47D1 Isar R Germany
47D1 Isarco R Italy
44E1 Isbister Scot
47D1 Ischgl Austria
53B2 Ischia I Italy
75B2 Ise Japan

47D2 Iseo Italy
46D1 Iserlohn Germany
53B2 Isernia Italy
75B2 Ise-wan B Japan
69E4 Ishigaki I Japan
74E2 Ishikari R Japan
74E2 Ishikari-wan B Japan
65H4 Ishim Russian Fed
65H4 Ishim R Kazakhstan
74E3 Ishinomaki Japan
75C1 Ishioka Japan
84C1 Ishkashim Afghan
14A1 Ishpeming USA
65J4 Isil'Kul Russian Fed
99D2 Isiolo Kenya
98C2 Isiro Zaire
92C2 Iskenderun Turk
92C2 Iskenferun Körfezi B Turk
92B1 Iskilip Turk
65K4 Iskitim Russian Fed
54B2 Iskur R Bulg
12H3 Iskut R Can/USA
23B2 Isla Mexico
34C3 Isla Bermejo I Arg
27E4 Isla Blanquilla Ven
32A2 Isla Coiba I Panama
29B4 Isla de Cedros I Mexico
29B4 Isla de Chiloé I Chile
25D2 Isla de Cozumel I Mexico
26C3 Isla de la Gonâve Cuba
26A2 Isla de la Juventud I Cuba
34D2 Isla de las Lechiguanas I Arg
3K8 Isla del Coco I Costa Rica
25D3 Isla del Maíz I Caribbean S
23B1 Isla de Lobos I Mexico
29D6 Isla de los Estados I Arg
28E2 Isla de Marajó I Brazil
105L5 Isla de Pascua I Pacific O
26A4 Isla de Providencia I Caribbean S
26A4 Isla de San Andres I Caribbean S
30G4 Isla de Santa Catarina I Brazil
33G2 Isla du Diable I French Guiana
31E2 Isla Fernando de Noronha I Brazil
29C6 Isla Grande de Tierra del Fuego I Arg/Chile
27D4 Isla la Tortuga I Ven
84C2 Islamabad Pak
24A2 Isla Magdalena I Mexico
27E4 Isla Margarita Ven
14A3 Isla Mocha Chile
17B2 Islamorada USA
10A1 Island L Can
108A2 Island Lg Aust
110B1 Islands,B of NZ
32A4 Isla Puná I Ecuador
103D6 Isla San Ambrosia I Pacific O
103D6 Isla San Felix I Pacific O
24A2 Isla Santa Margarita I Mexico
34A3 Isla Santa Maria I Chile
51C2 Islas Baleares Is Spain
96A2 Islas Canarias Is Atlantic O
51C2 Islas Columbretes Is Spain
25D3 Islas de la Bahia Is Honduras
26A4 Islas del Maíz Is Caribbean S
33E1 Islas de Margarita Is Ven

Islas Diego Ramírez

29C7 **Islas Diego Ramírez** *Is* Chile
32J7 **Islas Galapagos** *Is* Pacific O
30H6 **Islas Juan Fernández** Chile
32D1 **Islas los Roques** *Is* Ven
Islas Malvinas = Falkland Is
105L3 **Islas Revilla Gigedo** *Is* Pacific O
29C7 **Islas Wollaston** *Is* Chile
97A3 **Isla Tidra** *I* Maur
29B5 **Isla Wellington** *I* Chile
48C2 **Isle** *R* France
104B5 **Isle Amsterdam** *I* Indian O
43D4 **Isle of Wight** *I* Eng
10B2 **Isle Royale** *I* USA
104B5 **Isle St Paul** *I* Indian O
104A6 **Isles Crozet** *I* Indian O
105J4 **Isles de la Société** Pacific O
105K5 **Isles Gambier** *Is* Pacific O
101D2 **Isles Glorieuses** *Io* Madag
104B6 **Isles Kerguelen** *Is* Indian O
105K4 **Isles Marquises** *Is* Pacific O
105J4 **Isles Tuamotu** *Is* Pacific O
105J5 **Isles Tubai** *Is* Pacific O
22B1 **Isleton** USA
92B3 **Ismâ'îlîya** Egypt
101D3 **Isoanala** Madag
101C2 **Isoka** Zambia
53B3 **Isola Egadi** *I* Italy
52B2 **Isola Ponziane** *I* Italy
53B3 **Isole Lipari** *Is* Italy
52C2 **Isoles Tremiti** *Is* Italy
75B1 **Isosaki** Japan
92B2 **Isparta** Turk
94B2 **Israel** Republic, S W Asia
51C2 **Isser** *R* Alg
48C2 **Issoire** France
49C2 **Issoudun** France
92A1 **Istanbul** Turk
55B3 **Istiáia** Greece
25C3 **Istmo de Tehuantepec** *Isthmus* Mexico
17B2 **Istokpoga,L** USA
52B1 **Istra** *Pen* Croatia
35B1 **Itaberai** Brazil
35C1 **Itabira** Brazil
35C2 **Itabirito** Brazil
31D4 **Itabuna** Brazil
33F4 **Itacoatiara** Brazil
32B2 **Itagui** Colombia
33F4 **Itaituba** Brazil
30G4 **Itajai** Brazil
35B2 **Itajuba** Brazil
52B2 **Italy** Repubic, Europe
35D1 **Itamaraju** Brazil
35C1 **Itamarandiba** Brazil
35C1 **Itambacuri** Brazil
35C1 **Itambé** *Mt* Brazil
86C1 **Itânagar** India
35B2 **Itanhaém** Brazil
35C1 **Itanhém** Brazil
35C1 **Itanhém** *R* Brazil
35C1 **Itaobím** Brazil
35B2 **Itapecerica** Brazil
35C2 **Itaperuna** Brazil
35B2 **Itapetinga** Brazil
35B2 **Itapetininga** Brazil
35B2 **Itapeva** Brazil
31D2 **Itapipoca** Brazil
35B2 **Itapuranga** Brazil
30E4 **Itaqui** Brazil
35C1 **Itarantim** Brazil
35B2 **Itararé** Brazil
35B2 **Itararé** *R* Brazil
35C2 **Itaúna** Brazil
33E6 **Iténez** *R* Brazil/Bol

15C2 **Ithaca** USA
98C2 **Itimbiri** *R* Zaire
35C1 **Itinga** Brazil
6E3 **Itivdleq** Greenland
75B2 **Ito** Japan
74D3 **Itoigawa** Japan
33E6 **Itonomas** *R* Bol
35B2 **Itu** Brazil
35B1 **Itumbiara** Brazil
35A1 **Iturama** Brazil
30C3 **Iturbe** Arg
35B1 **Iturutaba** Brazil
56B2 **Itzehoe** Germany
58D2 **Ivacevichi** Belorussia
35A2 **Ivai** *R* Brazil
38K5 **Ivalo** Fin
54A2 **Ivangrad** Montenegro, Yugos
108B2 **Ivanhoe** Aust
59C3 **Ivano-Frankovsk** Ukraine
61F2 **Ivanovo** Russian Fed
65H3 **Ivdel'** Russian Fed
98B2 **Ivindo** *R* Gabon
101D3 **Ivohibe** Madag
101D2 **Ivongo Soanierana** Madag
97B4 **Ivory Coast** Republic, Africa
52A1 **Ivrea** Italy
6C3 **Ivujivik** Can
74E3 **Iwaki** Japan
74C4 **Iwakuni** Japan
74E2 **Iwanai** Japan
97C4 **Iwo** Nig
69G4 **Iwo Jima** *I* Japan
23B1 **Ixmiquilpa** Mexico
23A2 **Ixtapa** Mexico
23A1 **Ixtlán** Mexico
75A2 **Iyo** Japan
74A2 **Iyo-nada** *B* Japan
65G4 **Izhevsk** Russian Fed
64G3 **Izhma** Russian Fed
91C5 **Izki** Oman
60C4 **Izmail** Ukraine
92A2 **Izmir** Turk
55C3 **Izmir Körfezi** *B* Turk
92A1 **Izmit** Turk
92A1 **Iznik** Turk
55C2 **Iznik Gölü** *L* Turk
94C2 **Izra'** Syria
23B2 **Izúcar de Matamoros** Mexico
75B2 **Izumi-sano** Japan
75A1 **Izumo** Japan
74D4 **Izu-shotō** *Is* Japan

J

95B1 **Jabal al Akhdar** *Mts* Libya
94C2 **Jabal al 'Arab** Syria
95A2 **Jabal as Sawdā** *Mts* Libya
91B5 **Jabal az Zannah** UAE
94C1 **Jabal Halimah** *Mt* Leb/Syria
83B3 **Jabalpur** India
59B2 **Jablonec nad Nisou** Czech Republic
31D3 **Jaboatão** Brazil
35B2 **Jaboticabal** Brazil
51B1 **Jaca** Spain
23B1 **Jacala** Mexico
33F5 **Jacareacanga** Brazil
35B2 **Jacarei** Brazil
30F3 **Jacarezinho** Brazil
29C2 **Jáchal** Arg
35C1 **Jacinto** Brazil
13F2 **Jackfish L** Can
109C1 **Jackson** Aust
22B1 **Jackson** California, USA
14B2 **Jackson** Michigan, USA
19B3 **Jackson** Mississippi, USA
18C2 **Jackson** Missouri, USA
14B3 **Jackson** Ohio, USA
11B3 **Jackson** Tennessee, USA
111B2 **Jackson,C** NZ
111A2 **Jackson Head** *Pt* NZ

19B3 **Jacksonville** Arkansas, USA
17B1 **Jacksonville** Florida, USA
18B2 **Jacksonville** Illinois, USA
17C1 **Jacksonville** N Carolina, USA
19A3 **Jacksonville** Texas, USA
17B1 **Jacksonville Beach** USA
26C3 **Jacmel** Haiti
84B3 **Jacobabad** Pak
31C4 **Jacobina** Brazil
23A2 **Jacona** Mexico
Jadotville = Likasi
32B5 **Jaén** Peru
50B2 **Jaén** Spain
Jaffa = Tel Aviv Yafo
84B3 **Jaffa,C** Aust
87B3 **Jaffna** Sri Lanka
86B2 **Jagannathganj Ghat** Bang
87C1 **Jagdalpur** India
91A4 **Jagin** *R* Iran
87B1 **Jagtial** India
29F2 **Jaguarão** *R* Brazil
35B2 **Jaguariaíva** Brazil
91B4 **Jahrom** Iran
85D5 **Jaina** India
72A2 **Jaincá** China
85D3 **Jaipur** India
85C3 **Jaisalmer** India
90C2 **Jajarm** Iran
52C2 **Jajce** Bosnia-Herzegovina
78B4 **Jakarta** Indon
6E3 **Jakobshavn** Greenland
38J6 **Jakobstad** Fin
23B2 **Jalaca** Mexico
84B2 **Jalai-Kut** Afghan
84D2 **Jalandhar** India
23B2 **Jalapa** Mexico
35A2 **Jales** Brazil
86B1 **Jaleswar** Nepal
85D4 **Jalgaon** India
97D4 **Jalingo** Nig
51B1 **Jalón** *R* Spain
85C3 **Jālor** India
23A1 **Jalostotitlan** Mexico
86B1 **Jalpāiguri** India
23B1 **Jalpan** Mexico
95B2 **Jālū Oasis** Libya
32A4 **Jama** Ecuador
26B3 **Jamaica** *I* Caribbean S
26B3 **Jamaica Chan** Caribbean S
86B2 **Jamalpur** Bang
78A3 **Jambi** Indon
95C1 **Jambuseer** India
7B4 **James B** Can
5J5 **Jameston** USA
108A2 **Jamestown** Aust
8D2 **Jamestown** N. Dakota, USA
15C2 **Jamestown** New Yrk USA
16D2 **Jamestown** Rhode Island, USA
23B2 **Jamiltepec** Mexico
85B1 **Jammu** India
84C2 **Jammu and Kashmir** State, India
85B4 **Jamnagar** India
84C3 **Jampur** Pak
38K6 **Jämsä** Fin
86B2 **Jamshedpur** India
86B1 **Janakpur** Nepal
35C1 **Janaúba** Brazil
90B3 **Jandaq** Iran
109D1 **Jandowae** Aust
1B1 **Jan Mayen** *I* Norwegian S
35D1 **Januária** Brazil
85D4 **Jaora** India
51 **Japan** Empire, E Asia
74C3 **Japan,S of** S E Asia
104F2 **Japan Trench** Pacific O

32D4 **Japurá** *R* Brazil
93C2 **Jarābulus** Syria
35B1 **Jaraguá** Brazil
50B1 **Jarama** *R* Spain
94B2 **Jarash** Jordan
30E3 **Jardim** Brazil
51B2 **Jardin** *R* Spain
26B2 **Jardines de la Reina** *Is* Cuba
Jargalant = Hovd
33G3 **Jari** *R* Brazil
86C1 **Jaria Jhánjail** Bang
46C2 **Jarny** France
58B2 **Jarocin** Pol
59C2 **Jaroslaw** Pol
38G6 **Järpen** Sweden
72R2 **Jartai** China
85C4 **Jasdan** India
97C4 **Jasikan** Ghana
91C4 **Jāsk** Iran
59C3 **Jaslo** Pol
29D6 **Jason Is** Falkland Is
18B2 **Jasper** Arkansas, USA
13D2 **Jasper** Can
17B1 **Jasper** Florida, USA
14A3 **Jasper** Indiana, USA
19B3 **Jasper** Texas, USA
13D2 **Jasper Nat Pk** Can
58B2 **Jastrowie** Pol
35A1 **Jataí** Brazil
51B2 **Játiva** Spain
33E6 **Jaú** Brazil
32B6 **Jauja** Peru
86A1 **Jaunpur** India
Java = Jawa
87B2 **Javadi Hills** India
Javari = Yavari
70B4 **Java S** Indon
106A2 **Java Trench** Indon
78B4 **Jawa** *I* Indon
94C2 **Jayrud** Syria
96B2 **Jbel Ouarziz** *Mts* Mor
96B1 **Jbel Sarhro** *Mt* Mor
19B4 **Jeanerette** USA
97C4 **Jebba** Nig
93D2 **Jebel 'Abd al 'Aziz** *Mt* Syria
95B3 **Jebel Abyad** Sudan
91C5 **Jebel Akhdar** *Mt* Oman
92C4 **Jebel al Lawz** *Mt* S Arabia
94B2 **Jebel ash Shaykh** *Mt* Syria
94B3 **Jebel Asoteriba** *Mt* Sudan
94B3 **Jebel Ed Dabab** *Mt* Jordan
94B3 **Jebel el Ata'ita** *Mt* Jordan
92C3 **Jebel esh Sharqi** *Mts* Leb/Syria
94C3 **Jebel Ithriyat** *Mt* Jordan
91C5 **Jebel Ja'lan** *Mt* Oman
94B2 **Jebel Liban** *Mts* Leb
94C2 **Jebel Ma'lūlā** *Mt* Syria
98C1 **Jebel Marra** *Mt* Sudan
94C3 **Jebel Mudeisisat** *Mt* Jordan
95C2 **Jebel Oda** *Mt* Sudan
94B3 **Jebel Qasr ed Deir** *Mt* Jordan
94B2 **Jebel Um ed Daraj** *Mt* Jordan
95B2 **Jebel Uweinat** *Mt* Sudan
42C2 **Jedburgh** Scot
Jedda = Jiddah
59C2 **Jedrzejów** Pol
19B3 **Jefferson** Texas, USA
11A3 **Jefferson City** USA
8B3 **Jefferson,Mt** USA
14A3 **Jeffersonville** USA
60C2 **Jekabpils** Latvia
59B2 **Jelena Góra** Pol
60B2 **Jelgava** Latvia

78C4 Jember Indon	73D4 Jinhua China	86C1 Jowal India
57C2 Jena Germany	72C1 Jining Nei Monggol, China	99E2 Jowhar Somalia
78B2 Jenaja I Indon	72D2 Jining Shandong, China	12H2 Joy,Mt Can
47D1 Jenbach Austria	99D2 Jinja Uganda	5F5 Juan de Fuca,Str of Can/USA
94B2 Jenin Israel	76C1 Jinping China	101D2 Juan de Nova I Mozam Chan
19B3 Jennings USA	73A4 Jinsha Jiang R China	34D3 Juárez Arg
59B2 Jenseníky Upland Czech Republic	73C4 Jinshi China	31C3 Juàzeiro Brazil
6F3 Jensen Nunatakker Mt Greenland	72E1 Jinxi China	31D3 Juazeiro do Norte Brazil
6B3 Jens Munk I Can	72E2 Jin Xian China	99D2 Juba Sudan
108B3 Jeparit Aust	72E1 Jinzhou China	99E2 Juba R Somalia
31D4 Jequié Brazil	33E5 Jiparaná R Brazil	94B1 Jubail Leb
35C1 Jequital R Brazil	32A4 Jipijapa Ecuador	93D3 Jubbah S Arabia
35C1 Jequitinhonha Brazil	23A2 Jiquilpan Mexico	96A2 Juby,C Mor
31C5 Jequitinhonha R Brazil	91C4 Jiroft Iran	51B2 Jucar R Spain
50A2 Jerez de la Frontera Spain	99E2 Jirriban Somalia	23B2 Juchatengo Mexico
50A2 Jerez de los Caballeros Spain	73B4 Jishou China	23A1 Juchipila R Mexico
94B3 Jericho Israel	92C2 Jisr ash Shughūr Syria	23A1 Juchitlan Mexico
108C3 Jerilderie Aust	54B2 Jiu R Rom	57C3 Judenburg Austria
48B2 Jersey I UK	73D4 Jiujiang China	30B2 Juilaca Peru
10C2 Jersey City USA	73A4 Jiulong China	73C4 Juiling Shan Hills China
15C2 Jersey Shore USA	73D4 Jiulong Jiang R China	31C6 Juiz de Fora Brazil
18B2 Jerseyville USA	69F2 Jixi China	30C3 Jujuy State, Arg
92C3 Jerusalem Israel	94B3 Jiza Jordan	30C2 Juli Peru
109D3 Jervis B Aust	81C4 Jīzan S Arabia	33F3 Julianatop Mt Surinam
13C2 Jervis Inlet Sd Can	97A3 Joal Sen	6F3 Julianehab Greenland
52B1 Jesenice Slovenia	35C1 João Monlevade Brazil	46D1 Jülich Germany
86B2 Jessore Bang	31E3 João Pessoa Brazil	86A1 Jumla Nepal
11B3 Jesup USA	35B1 João Pirheiro Brazil	94B3 Jum Ali Swamp Mt Jordan
34C2 Jesus Maria Arg	34B2 Jocoli Arg	85C4 Jūnāgadh India
16D2 Jewett City USA	85C3 Jodhpur India	72D2 Junan China
54A2 Jezerce Mt Alb	38K6 Joensuu Fin	9D3 Junction City USA
58C2 Jeziero Mamry L Pol	46C2 Joeuf France	31B6 Jundiaí Brazil
58C2 Jeziero Śniardwy L Pol	42B2 Joffre,Mt Can	4E4 Juneau USA
94B2 Jezzine Leb	86B1 Jogbani India	107D4 Junee Aust
85C4 Jhābua India	87A2 Jog Falls India	22C2 June Lake USA
85D4 Jhālāwār India	101G1 Johannesburg S Africa	52A1 Jungfrau Mt Switz
84C2 Jhang Maghiana Pak	21B2 Johannesburg USA	16A2 Juniata R USA
85D3 Jhānsi India	6C2 Johan Pen Can	29D2 Junín Arg
86A2 Jhārsuguda India	12D1 John R USA	73A4 Junllian China
84C2 Jhelum Pak	20C2 John Day USA	31B6 Juquiá Brazil
84C2 Jhelum R Pak	20B1 John Day R USA	99C2 Jur R Sudan
11C3 J H Kerr L USA	44C2 John O'Groats Scot	42B2 Jura I Scot
84D3 Jhunjhunūn India	18A2 John Redmond Res USA	49D2 Jura Mts France
69F2 Jiamusi China	11B3 Johnson City Tennessee, USA	44B3 Jura,Sound of Chan Scot
73C4 Ji'an Jiangxi, China	17B1 Johnston USA	94B3 Jurf ed Darāwish Jordan
74B2 Ji'an Jilin, China	27N2 Johnston Pt St Vincent and the Grenadines	65K4 Jurga Russian Fed
73D4 Jiande China	15C2 Johnstown Pennsylvania, USA	60B2 Jūrmala Latvia
73B4 Jiang'an China	77C5 Johor Bharu Malay	32D4 Juruá R Brazil
73D4 Jiangbiancun China	49C2 Joigny France	33F6 Juruena R Brazil
73A5 Jiangcheng China	30G4 Joinville Brazil	94C1 Jūsiyah Syria
73B3 Jiang Jiang R China	61H3 Jok R Russian Fed	34B2 Justo Daract Arg
73C5 Jiangmen China	38H5 Jokkmokk Sweden	32D4 Jutaí R Brazil
72D3 Jiangsu Province, China	93E2 Jolfa Iran	25D3 Juticalpa Honduras
73C4 Jiangxi Province, China	10B2 Joliet USA	90C3 Jūymand Iran
73A3 Jiangyou China	7C5 Joliette Can	56B1 Jylland Pen Den
72D1 Jianping China	79B4 Jolo Phil	38K6 Jyväskylä Fin
73C3 Jianshui China	79B4 Jolo I Phil	
73D4 Jian Xi R China	82D2 Joma Mt China	**K**
73D4 Jianyang China	58C1 Jonava Lithuania	82B2 K2 Mt China/India
72E2 Jiaonan China	72A3 Jonê China	90C2 Kaakhka Turkmenistan
72E2 Jiao Xian China	11A3 Jonesboro Arkansas, USA	101H1 Kaapmuiden S Africa
72E2 Jiaozhou Wan B China	19B3 Jonesboro Louisiana, USA	71D4 Kabaena I Indon
72C2 Jiaozuo China	6B2 Jones Sd Can	97A4 Kabala Sierra Leone
73C3 Jiaxiang China	58C1 Joniškis Lithuania	99D3 Kabale Rwanda
68B3 Jiayuguan China	39G7 Jönköping Sweden	98C3 Kabalo Zaïre
81B3 Jiddah S Arabia	11A3 Joplin USA	98C3 Kabambare Zaïre
72D3 Jieshou China	92C3 Jordan Kingdom, S W Asia	99D2 Kabarole Uganda
72C2 Jiexiu China	94B2 Jordan R Israel	98C3 Kabinda Zaïre
72A3 Jigzhi China	20C2 Jordan Valley USA	94B3 Kabir Kuh Mts Iran
59B3 Jihlava Czech Republic	86C1 Jorhāt India	100B2 Kabompo Zambia
99E2 Jilib Somalia	38J5 Jörn Sweden	100B2 Kabompo R Zambia
69E2 Jilin China	78C3 Jorong Indon	98C3 Kabongo Zaïre
51B1 Jiloca R Spain	39F7 Jørpeland Nor	84B2 Kabul Afghan
99D2 Jima Eth	79B3 Jose Pañganiban Phil	85B4 Kachchh,G of India
9C4 Jiménez Coahuila, Mexico	106B2 Joseph Bonaparte G Aust	61J2 Kachkanar Russian Fed
72D2 Jinan China	64B3 Jotunheimen Mt Nor	63C2 Kachug Russian Fed
84D3 Jind India	94B2 Jouai'ya Leb	78B3 Kadapongan I Indon
72B2 Jingbian China	94B2 Jounie Leb	85C4 Kadi India
73D4 Jingdezhen China		108A2 Kadina Aust
76C1 Jinghong China		92B2 Kadınhanı Turk
73C3 Jingmen China		87B2 Kadiri India
72B2 Jingning China		
73B4 Jing Xiang China		

60E4 Kadiyevka Ukraine
100B2 Kadoma Zim
99C1 Kadugli Sudan
97C3 Kaduna Nig
97C3 Kaduna R Nig
87B2 Kadūr India
54E6 Kaédi Maur
21C4 Kaena Pt Hawaiian Is
74B3 Kaesŏng N Korea
97C4 Kafanchan Nig
97A3 Kaffrine Sen
94C1 Kafrūn Bashūr Syria
100B2 Kafue Zambia
100B2 Kafue R Zambia
100B2 Kafue Nat Pk Zambia
74D3 Kaga Japan
65H6 Kagan Kazakhstan
93D1 Kağizman Turk
74C4 Kagoshima Japan
90C2 Kahak Iran
99D3 Kahama Tanz
84B3 Kahan Pak
78C3 Kahayan R Indon
98B3 Kahemba Zaïre
46E1 Kahler Asten Mt Germany
91C4 Kahnūj Iran
18B1 Kahoka USA
21C4 Kahoolawe I Hawaiian Is
92C2 Kahramanmaraş Turk
21C4 Kahuku Pt Hawaiian Is
111B2 Kaiapoi NZ
33F2 Kaieteur Fall Guyana
72C3 Kaifeng China
110B1 Kaikohe NZ
111B2 Kaikoura NZ
111B2 Kaikoura Pen NZ
111B2 Kaikoura Range Mts NZ
73B4 Kaili China
21C4 Kailua Hawaiian Is
16A1 Kaimana Indon
75B2 Kainan Japan
97C3 Kainji Res Nig
110B1 Kaipara Harbour B NZ
73C5 Kaiping China
96D1 Kairouan Tunisia
22C2 Kaiser Peak Mt USA
57B3 Kaiserslautern Germany
74B2 Kaishantun China
58D2 Kaisiadorys Lithuania
110B1 Kaitaia NZ
111A3 Kaitangata NZ
84D3 Kaithal India
21C4 Kaiwi Chan Hawaiian Is
73A4 Kai Xian China
73A5 Kaiyuan Liaoning, China
74A2 Kaiyuan Yunnan, China
12C2 Kaiyuh Mts USA
38K6 Kajaani Fin
84B2 Kajaki Afghan
99D3 Kajiado Kenya
75A2 Kake Japan
12H3 Kake USA
12D3 Kakhonak USA
65E5 Kakhovskoye Vodokhranilishche Res Ukraine
91B4 Kākī Iran
87C1 Kākināda India
75A2 Kakogawa Japan
4D2 Kaktovik USA
75C1 Kakuda Japan
Kalaallit Nunaat = Greenland
55B3 Kalábaka Greece
78D1 Kalabakan Malay
100B2 Kalabo Zambia
61F3 Kalach Russian Fed
61F4 Kalach-na-Donu Russian Fed
86C2 Kaladan R Burma
21C4 Ka Lae C Hawaiian Is

Kalahari Desert

100B3 **Kalahari Desert** Botswana
38J6 **Kalajoki** Fin
63D2 **Kalakan** Russian Fed
70A3 **Kalakepen** Indon
84C1 **Kalam** Pak
55B3 **Kálamai** Greece
10B2 **Kalamazoo** USA
84B3 **Kalat** Pak
92B1 **Kalecik** Turk
78D3 **Kalembau** *I* Indon
99C3 **Kalémié** Zaïre
38L5 **Kalevala** Russian Fed
86C2 **Kalewa** Burma
12D2 **Kalgin** *I* USA
106B4 **Kalgoorlie** Aust
78B4 **Kalianda** Indon
79B3 **Kalibo** Phil
98C3 **Kalima** Zaïre
78C3 **Kalimantan** Province, Indon
55C3 **Kálimnos** *I* Greece
86B1 **Kälimpang** India
60B3 **Kaliningrad** Russian Fed
60C3 **Kalinkovichi** Belorussia
8B2 **Kalispell** USA
58B2 **Kalisz** Pol
99D3 **Kaliua** Tanz
38J5 **Kalix** *R* Sweden
100A3 **Kalkfeld** Namibia
100A3 **Kalkrand** Namibia
108A1 **Kallakoopah** *R* Aust
38K6 **Kallávesi** *L* Fin
55C3 **Kallonis Kólpos** *B* Greece
39H7 **Kalmar** Sweden
61G4 **Kalmytskaya Respublika,** Russian Fed
100B2 **Kalomo** Zambia
18B1 **Kalona** USA
13B2 **Kalone Peak** *Mt* Can
87A2 **Kalpeni** *I* India
85D3 **Kälpi** India
53A3 **Kalat Khasba** Tunisia
12B2 **Kalskag** USA
12C2 **Kaltag** USA
60E3 **Kaluga** Russian Fed
39G7 **Kalundborg** Den
59C3 **Kalush** Ukraine
87B2 **Kalyandurg** India
60E2 **Kalyazin** Russian Fed
61H1 **Kama** *R* Russian Fed
74E3 **Kamaishi** Japan
84C2 **Kamalia** Pak
110C1 **Kamanawa Mts** NZ
100A2 **Kamanjab** Namibia
84F2 **Kamat** *Mt* India
87B3 **Kamban** India
61H2 **Kambarka** Russian Fed
07A4 **Kambia** Sierra Leone
59D3 **Kamenets Podolskiy** Ukraine
61F3 **Kamenka** Russian Fed
65K4 **Kamen-na-Obi** Russian Fed
61K2 **Kamensk Ural'skiy** Russian Fed
5H3 **Kamilukuak** *L* Can
98C3 **Kamina** Zaïre
7A3 **Kaminak** *L* Can
75C1 **Kaminoyama** Japan
5F4 **Kamloops** Can
93E1 **Kamo** Armenia
75C1 **Kamogawa** Japan
99D2 **Kampala** Uganda
77C5 **Kampar** Malay
78A2 **Kampar** *R* Indon
77C5 **Kampen** Neth
76B2 **Kamphaeng Phet** Thai
77C3 **Kampot** Camb
91D4 **Kamsaptar** Iran
61J2 **Kamskoye Vodokhranilishche** *Res* Russian Fed
85D4 **Kämthi** India
61G3 **Kamyshin** Russian Fed

61K2 **Kamyshlov** Russian Fed
7C4 **Kanaaupscow** *R* Can
98C3 **Kananga** Zaïre
61G2 **Kanash** Russian Fed
75B1 **Kanayama** Japan
74D3 **Kanazawa** Japan
4C3 **Kanbisha** USA
87B2 **Känchipuram** India
84B2 **Kandahar** Afghan
64E3 **Kandalaksha** Russian Fed
38L5 **Kandalakshskaya Guba** *B* Russian Fed
97C3 **Kandi** Benin
109C2 **Kandos** Aust
87C3 **Kandy** Sri Lanka
15C2 **Kane** USA
6C1 **Kane Basin** *B* Can
98B1 **Kanem** *Desert Region* Chad
97B3 **Kangaba** Mali
92C2 **Kangal** Turk
6E3 **Kangâmiut** Greenland
91B4 **Kangän** Iran
77C4 **Kangar** Malay
106C4 **Kangaroo I** Aust
6E3 **Kangâtsiaq** Greenland
90A3 **Kangavar** Iran
72C1 **Kangbao** China
82C3 **Kangchenjunga** *Mt* Nepal
73A4 **Kangding** China
6G3 **Kangerdlugssuaq** Greenland
6G3 **Kangerdlugssvatsaiq** *B* Greenland
99D2 **Kangetet** Kenya
74B2 **Kanggye** N Korea
7D4 **Kangiqsualujjuaq** Can
6C3 **Kangiqsujuaq** Can
72C1 **Kangirsuk** Can
74B3 **Kangnüng** S Korea
98B2 **Kango** Gabon
68B4 **Kangto** *Mt* China
72B3 **Kang Xian** China
77D4 **Kanh Hung** Viet
98C3 **Kaniama** Zaïre
87B1 **Käni Giri** India
39J6 **Kankaanpää** Fin
14A2 **Kankakee** USA
14A2 **Kankakee** *R* USA
97B3 **Kankan** Guinea
86A2 **Känker** India
87B3 **Kanniyäkumari** India
97C3 **Kano** Nig
74C4 **Kanoya** Japan
86A1 **Känpur** India
9C3 **Kansas** State, USA
18A2 **Kansas** *R* USA
10A3 **Kansas City** USA
73U6 **Kanshi** China
63B2 **Kansk** Russian Fed
97C3 **Kantchari** Burkina
86B2 **Känthi** India
12D2 **Kantishna** USA
12D2 **Kantishna** *R* USA
100B3 **Kanye** Botswana
68D4 **Kao-hsiung** Taiwan
100A2 **Kaoka Veld** *Plain* Namibia
97A3 **Kaolack** Sen
100B2 **Kaoma** Zambia
21C4 **Kapaau** Hawaiian Is
98C3 **Kapanga** Zaïre
6F3 **Kap Cort Adelaer** *C* Greenland
6H3 **Kap Dalton** *C* Greenland
39H7 **Kapellskär** Sweden
6F4 **Kap Farvel** *C* Greenland
6G3 **Kap Gustav Holm** *C* Greenland
100B2 **Kapiri** Zambia
78C2 **Kapit** Malay
19B3 **Kaplan** USA
57C3 **Kaplice** Czech Republic
77B4 **Kapoe** Thai
99C3 **Kapona** Zaïre

52C1 **Kaposvár** Hung
6C2 **Kap Parry** *C* Can
6H3 **Kap Ravn** *C* Greenland
78B3 **Kapuas** *R* Indon
108A2 **Kapunda** Aust
84D2 **Kapurthala** India
7B5 **Kapuskasing** Can
109D2 **Kaputar** *Mt* Aust
93E2 **Kapydzhik** *Mt* Armenia
6D2 **Kap York** *C* Greenland
92B1 **Karabük** Turk
55C2 **Karacabey** Turk
85B4 **Karachi** Pak
87A1 **Karäd** India
60E5 **Kara Daglari** *Mt* Turk
54C5 **Karadeniz Boğazi** *Sd* Turk
68D1 **Karaftit** Russian Fed
65J5 **Karaganda** Kazakhstan
65J5 **Karagayly** Kazakhstan
87B2 **Käraikäl** India
90B2 **Karaj** Iran
92C3 **Karak** Jordan
65G5 **Kara Kalpakskaya Respublika,** Uzbekistan
84D1 **Karakax He** *H* China
71D3 **Karakelong** *I* Indon
84D1 **Karakoram Mts** India
84D1 **Karakoram P** India/China
97A3 **Karakoro** *R* Maur/Sen
65G6 **Karakumy** *Desert* Russian Fed
94B3 **Karama** Jordan
92B2 **Karaman** Turk
65K5 **Karamay** China
111B2 **Karamea** NZ
111B2 **Karamea Bight** *B* NZ
85D4 **Karanja** India
92B2 **Karapinar** Turk
64H2 **Kara S** Russian Fed
100A3 **Karasburg** Namibia
38K5 **Karasjok** Nor
65J4 **Karasuk** Russian Fed
92C2 **Karataş** Turk
65H5 **Kara Tau** *Mts* Kazakhstan
76B3 **Karathuri** Burma
74B4 **Karatsu** Japan
91B4 **Karäz** Iran
93D3 **Karbalä'** Iraq
54C2 **Karcag** Hung
55B3 **Kardhítsa** Greece
64E3 **Karel'skaya Respublika,** Russian Fed
38J5 **Karesvando** Sweden
96B2 **Karet** *Desert Region* Maur
65K4 **Kargasok** Russian Fed
97D3 **Kari** Nig
100B3 **Kariba** Zim
100B2 **Kariba** *R* Zim/Zambia
100B2 **Kariba Dam** Zim/Zambia
95C3 **Karima** Sudan
78B3 **Karimata** *I* Indon
86C2 **Karimganj** Bang
87B1 **Karimnagar** India
99E1 **Karin** Somalia
39J6 **Karis** Fin
99C3 **Karishimbe** *Mt* Zaïre
55B3 **Káristos** Greece
87A2 **Kärkal** India
71F4 **Karkar** *I* PNG
90A3 **Karkheh** *R* Iran
60D4 **Karkinitskiy Zaliv** *B* Ukraine
63B3 **Karlik Shan** *Mt* China
58B2 **Karlino** Pol
52C2 **Karlobag** Croatia
52C1 **Karlovac** Croatia
54B2 **Karlovo** Bulg
57C2 **Karlovy Vary** Czech Republic

39G7 **Karlshamn** Sweden
39G7 **Karlskoga** Sweden
39H7 **Karlskrona** Sweden
57B3 **Karlsruhe** Germany
39G7 **Karlstad** Sweden
12D3 **Karluk** USA
86C2 **Karnafuli Res** Bang
84D3 **Karnal** India
87A1 **Karnataka** State, India
54C2 **Karnobat** Bulg
100B2 **Karoi** Zim
99D3 **Karonga** Malawi
95C3 **Karora** Sudan
78D3 **Karossa** Indon
55C3 **Kárpathos** *I* Greece
6E2 **Karrats Fjord** Greenland
93D1 **Kars** Turk
65H4 **Karsakpay** Kazakhstan
58D1 **Kärsava** Latvia
80E2 **Karshi** Uzbekistan
38J6 **Karstula** Fin
94B1 **Kartaba** Leb
54C2 **Kartal** Turk
61K3 **Kartaly** Russian Fed
90A3 **Kärün** *R* Iran
86B1 **Karwa** India
87A2 **Kärwär** India
68D1 **Karymskoye** Russian Fed
98B3 **Kasai** *R* Zaïre
100B2 **Kasaji** Zaïre
101C2 **Kasama** Zambia
99D3 **Kasanga** Tanz
87A2 **Käsaragod** India
5H3 **Kasba L** Can
100B2 **Kasempa** Zambia
100B2 **Kasenga** Zaïre
99D2 **Kasese** Zaïre
90B3 **Käshän** Iran
12C2 **Kashegelok** USA
82B2 **Kashi** China
84D3 **Käshipur** India
74D3 **Kashiwazaki** Japan
90C2 **Kashmar** Iran
66D3 **Kashmir** State, India
61F3 **Kasimov** Russian Fed
18C2 **Kaskaskia** *R* USA
38J6 **Kaskinen** Fin
61K2 **Kasli** Russian Fed
5G5 **Kaslo** Can
98C3 **Kasonga** Zaïre
99B3 **Kasongo-Lunda** Zaïre
55C3 **Kásos** *I* Greece
Kaspiysky = Lagan'
95C3 **Kassala** Sudan
56B2 **Kassel** Germany
96C1 **Kasserine** Tunisia
100A2 **Kassinga** Angola
92B1 **Kastamonu** Turk
55B3 **Kastélli** Greece
92A2 **Kastellórizon** *I* Greece
55B2 **Kastoría** Greece
55C3 **Kástron** Greece
74D3 **Kasugai** Japan
75A1 **Kasumi** Japan
101C2 **Kasungu** Malawi
84C2 **Kasur** Pak
100B2 **Kataba** Zambia
98C3 **Katako-kombe** Zaïre
4D3 **Katalla** USA
63G2 **Katangli** Russian Fed
106A4 **Katanning** Aust
55B2 **Katerini** Greece
5E4 **Kates Needle** *Mt* Can/USA
82D3 **Katha** Burma
106C2 **Katherine** Aust
85C4 **Käthiäwär** *Pen* India
86B1 **Kathmandu** Nepal
84D2 **Kathua** India
86B1 **Katihär** India
100B2 **Katima Mulilo** Namibia
4C4 **Katmai,Mt** USA
12D3 **Katnai Nat Mon** USA
86A2 **Katni** India
109D2 **Katoomba** Aust
59B2 **Katowice** Pol
39H7 **Katrineholm** Sweden

97C3 **Katsina** Nig
97C4 **Katsina Ala** Nig
75C1 **Katsuta** Japan
75C1 **Katsuura** Japan
75B1 **Katsuy** Japan
65H6 **Kattakurgan** Uzbekistan
39G7 **Kattegat** *Str* Den/Sweden
21C4 **Kauai** *I* Hawaiian Is
21C4 **Kauai Chan** Hawaiian Is
21C4 **Kaulakahi Chan** Hawaiian Is
21C4 **Kaunakaki** Hawaiian Is
60B3 **Kaunas** Lithuania
97C3 **Kaura Namoda** Nig
38J5 **Kautokeino** Nor
55B2 **Kavadarci** Macedonia
55A2 **Kavajë** Alb
87B2 **Kavali** India
55B2 **Kaválla** Greece
85B4 **Kávda** India
75B1 **Kawagoe** Japan
75B1 **Kawaguchi** Japan
110B1 **Kawakawa** NZ
99C3 **Kawambwa** Zambia
86A2 **Kawardha** India
15C2 **Kawartha Lakes** Can
74D3 **Kawasaki** Japan
110C1 **Kawerau** NZ
110B1 **Kawhia** NZ
97B3 **Kaya** Burkina
12F3 **Kayak I** USA
78D2 **Kayan** *R* Indon
87B3 **Kāyankulam** India
97A3 **Kayes** Mali
92C2 **Kayseri** Turk
1B8 **Kazach'ye** Russian Fed
93E1 **Kazakh** Azerbaijan
65G5 **Kazakhstan** Republic, Asia
61G2 **Kazan'** Russian Fed
54C2 **Kazanlŭk** Bulg
69G4 **Kazan Retto** *Is* Japan
91B4 **Kāzerün** Iran
61H1 **Kazhim** Russian Fed
93E1 **Kazi Magomed** Azerbaijan
59C3 **Kazincbarcika** Hung
55B3 **Kéa** *I* Greece
21C4 **Kealaikahiki Chan** Hawaiian Is
8D2 **Kearney** USA
93C2 **Keban Baraji** *Res* Turk
97A3 **Kébémer** Sen
96C1 **Kebili** Tunisia
94C1 **Kebir** *R* Leb/Syria
38H5 **Kebnekaise** *Mt* Sweden
59B3 **Kecskemét** Hung
58C1 **Kedainiai** Lithuania
97A3 **Kédougou** Sen
12J2 **Keele** *R* Can
12H2 **Keele Pk** *Mt* Can
21B2 **Keeler** USA
15D2 **Keene** New Hampshire, USA
100A3 **Keetmanshoop** Namibia
18C1 **Keewanee** USA
6A3 **Keewatin** *Region* Can
55B3 **Kefallinía** *I* Greece
94B2 **Kefar Sava** Israel
97C4 **Keffi** Nig
38A2 **Keflavik** Iceland
5G4 **Keg River** Can
76B1 **Kehsi Mansam** Burma
108B3 **Keith** Aust
44C3 **Keith** Scot
4F3 **Keith Arm** *B* Can
6D3 **Kekertuk** Can
85D3 **Kekri** India
77C5 **Kelang** Malay
97C4 **Kelantan** *R* Malay
84B1 **Kelif** Turkmenistan
92C1 **Kelkit** *R* Turk
98B3 **Kellé** Congo

4F2 **Kellet,C** Can
20C1 **Kellogg** USA
64D3 **Kelloselka** Fin
45C2 **Kells** Irish Rep
42B2 **Kells Range** *Hills* Scot
58C1 **Kelme** Lithuania
5G5 **Kelowna** Can
5F4 **Kelsey Bay** Can
42C2 **Kelso** Scot
20B1 **Kelso** USA
64E3 **Kem'** Russian Fed
38L6 **Kem'** *R* Russian Fed
97B3 **Ke Macina** Mali
13B2 **Kemano** Can
65K4 **Kemerovo** Russian Fed
38J5 **Kemi** Fin
38K5 **Kemi** *R* Fin
38K5 **Kemijärvi** Fin
46C1 **Kempen** Region, Belg
26B2 **Kemps Bay** The Bahamas
109D2 **Kempsey** Aust
57C3 **Kempten** Germany
12D2 **Kenai** USA
12D3 **Kenai Mts** USA
12D2 **Kenai Pen** USA
99D2 **Kenamuke Swamp** Sudan
42C2 **Kendal** Eng
109D2 **Kendall** Aust
71D4 **Kendari** Indon
78C3 **Kendawangan** Indon
86B2 **Kendrāpāra** India
20C1 **Kendrick** USA
97A4 **Kenema** Sierra Leone
76B1 **Kengtung** Burma
100B3 **Kenhardt** S Africa
97A3 **Kéniéba** Mali
96B1 **Kenitra** Mor
45B3 **Kenmare** Irish Rep
45B3 **Kenmare** *R* Irish Rep
19B4 **Kenner** USA
18C2 **Kennett** USA
16B3 **Kennett Square** USA
20C1 **Kennewick** USA
5F4 **Kenny Dam** Can
7A5 **Kenora** Can
10B2 **Kenosha** USA
43E4 **Kent** County, Eng
20B1 **Kent** Washington, USA
14A2 **Kentland** USA
14B2 **Kenton** USA
4H3 **Kent Pen** Can
11B3 **Kentucky** State, USA
11B3 **Kentucky L** USA
19B3 **Kentwood** Louisiana, USA
14A2 **Kentwood** Michigan, USA
99D2 **Kenya** Republic, Africa
Kenya,Mt = Kirinyaga
18B1 **Keokuk** USA
86A2 **Keonchi** India
86B2 **Keonjhargarh** India
71E4 **Kepalau Tanimbar** Indon
6H3 **Keplavik** Iceland
59B2 **Kepno** Pol
78B2 **Kepulauan Anambas** *Arch* Indon
71E4 **Kepulauan Aru** *Arch* Indon
78B2 **Kepulauan Badas** *Is* Indon
71E4 **Kepulauan Banda** *Arch* Indon
71D4 **Kepulauan Banggai** *I* Indon
78B2 **Kepulauan Bunguran Selatan** *Arch* Indon
71E4 **Kepulauan Kai** *Arch* Indon
71D4 **Kepulauan Leti** *I* Indon
78A3 **Kepulauan Lingga** *Is* Indon
70A4 **Kepulauan Mentawi** *Arch* Indon

78A2 **Kepulauan Riau** *Arch* Indon
78D4 **Kepulauan Sabalana** *Arch* Indon
71D3 **Kepulauan Sangihe** *Arch* Indon
71D4 **Kepulauan Sula** *I* Indon
71D3 **Kepulauan Talaud** *Arch* Indon
78B2 **Kepulauan Tambelan** *Is* Indon
71E4 **Kepulauan Tanimbar** *I* Indon
71D4 **Kepulauan Togian** *I* Indon
71D4 **Kepulauan Tukambesi** *Is* Indon
87B2 **Kerala** State, India
108B3 **Kerang** Aust
39K6 **Kerava** Fin
60E4 **Kerch'** Ukraine
71F4 **Kerema** PNG
20C1 **Keremeps** Can
95C3 **Keren** Eritrea
104B6 **Kerguelen Ridge** Indian O
99D3 **Kericho** Kenya
70B4 **Kerinci** *Mt* Indon
99D2 **Kerio** *R* Kenya
80E2 **Kerki** Turkmenistan
55A3 **Kérkira** Greece
55A3 **Kérkira** *I* Greece
91C3 **Kerman** Iran
22B2 **Kerman** USA
90A3 **Kermānshāh** Iran
21B2 **Kern** *R* USA
13F2 **Kerrobert** Can
45B2 **Kerry** County, Irish Rep
17B1 **Kershaw** USA
78B3 **Kertamulia** Indon
63D3 **Kerulen** *R* Mongolia
96C2 **Kerzaz** Alg
55C2 **Keşan** Turk
74E3 **Kesennuma** Japan
38L5 **Kesten 'ga** Russian Fed
42C2 **Keswick** Eng
65K4 **Ket** *R* Russian Fed
97C4 **Kéta** Ghana
78C3 **Ketapang** Indon
5E4 **Ketchikan** USA
97C3 **Ketia** Niger
85B4 **Keti Bandar** Pak
58C2 **Kętrzyn** Pol
43D3 **Kettering** Eng
14B3 **Kettering** USA
20C1 **Kettle** *R* Can
20C1 **Kettle River Range** *Mts* USA
7C3 **Kettlestone B** Can
90C3 **Kevir-i Namak** *Salt Flat* Iran
14A2 **Kewaunee** USA
14B1 **Key Harbour** Can
17B2 **Key Largo** USA
11B4 **Key West** USA
63C2 **Kezhma** Russian Fed
54A1 **K'felegháza** Hung
12B2 **Kgun L** USA
94C2 **Khabab** Syria
62H3 **Khabarovsk** Russian Fed
85B3 **Khairpur** Pak
85B3 **Khairpur** Region, Pak
100B3 **Khakhea** Botswana
55C3 **Khálki** *I* Greece
55B2 **Khalkidhikí** *Pen* Greece
55B3 **Khalkis** Greece
61G2 **Khalturin** Russian Fed
85C4 **Khambhāt,G of** India
85D4 **Khāmgaon** India
76C2 **Kham Keut** Laos
87C1 **Khammam** India
90A2 **Khamseh** *Mts* Iran
76C2 **Khan** *R* Laos
84B1 **Khanabad** Afghan
93E3 **Khānaqin** Iraq
85D4 **Khandwa** India
84C2 **Khanewal** Pak

94C3 **Khan ez Zabib** Jordan
77D4 **Khanh Hung** Viet
55B3 **Khaniá** Greece
84C3 **Khanpur** Pak
65H3 **Khanty-Mansiysk** Russian Fed
91B4 **Khan Yunis** Egypt
84D1 **Khapalu** India
68C2 **Khapcheranga** Russian Fed
61G4 **Kharabali** Russian Fed
86B2 **Kharagpur** India
91C4 **Khāran** Iran
84B3 **Kharan** Pak
90B3 **Kharānaq** Iran
91B4 **Khārg** *Is* Iran
95C2 **Khârga Oasis** Egypt
85D4 **Khargon** India
60E4 **Khar'kov** Ukraine
54C2 **Kharmanli** Bulg
61F2 **Kharovsk** Russian Fed
95C3 **Khartoum** Sudan
95C3 **Khartoum North** Sudan
74C2 **Khasan** Russian Fed
95C3 **Khashm el Girba** Sudan
86C1 **Khasi-Jaintia Hills** India
54C2 **Khaskovo** Bulg
1B9 **Khatanga** Russian Fed
76B3 **Khawsa** Burma
76C2 **Khe Bo** Viet
85C4 **Khed Brahma** India
51C2 **Khemis** Alg
96B1 **Khenifra** Mor
51C2 **Kherrata** Alg
60D4 **Kherson** Ukraine
63D2 **Khilok** Russian Fed
55C3 **Khios** Greece
55C3 **Khios** *I* Greece
60C4 **Khmel'nitskiy** Ukraine
59C3 **Khodorov** Ukraine
84B1 **Kholm** Afghan
76D3 **Khong** Laos
91B4 **Khonj** Iran
69F2 **Khor** Russian Fed
91A3 **Khoramshahr** Iran
91B5 **Khōr Duwayhin** *B* UAE
84C1 **Khorog** Tajikistan
90A3 **Khorramābād** Iran
90C3 **Khosf** Iran
84B2 **Khost** Pak
60C4 **Khotin** Ukraine
12C2 **Khotol** *Mt* USA
60C3 **Khoyniki** Belorussia
63F2 **Khrebet Dzhugdzhur** *Mts* Russian Fed
90C2 **Khrebet Kopet Dag** *Mts* Turkmenistan
64H3 **Khrebet Pay-khoy** *Mts* Russian Fed
82C1 **Khrebet Tarbagatay** *Mts* Kazakhstan
63E2 **Khrebet Tukuringra** *Mts* Russian Fed
82A1 **Khudzhand** Tajikistan
86B2 **Khulna** Bang
84D1 **Khunjerab** *P* China/India
90B3 **Khunsar** Iran
91A3 **Khurays** S Arabia
86B2 **Khurda** India
84D3 **Khurja** India
84C2 **Khushab** Pak
94B2 **Khushniyah** Syria
59C3 **Khust** Ukraine
99C1 **Khuwei** Sudan
85B3 **Khuzdar** Pak
90D3 **Khvaf** Iran
61G3 **Khvalynsk** Russian Fed
90C3 **Khvor** Iran
91B4 **Khvormūj** Iran
93D2 **Khvoy** Iran
84C1 **Khwaja Muhammad** *Mts* Afghan
84C2 **Khyber P** Afghan/Pak

Kiambi

99C3 **Kiambi** Zaire
19A3 **Kianichi** R USA
12B1 **Kiana** USA
98B3 **Kibangou** Congo
99D3 **Kibaya** Tanz
98C3 **Kibombo** Zaire
99D3 **Kibondo** Tanz
99D3 **Kibungu** Rwanda
55B2 **Kičevo** Macedonia
5G4 **Kicking Horse P** Can
97C3 **Kidal** Mali
43C3 **Kidderminster** Eng
97A3 **Kidira** Sen
110C1 **Kidnappers,C** NZ
56C2 **Kiel** Germany
59C2 **Kielce** Pol
56C2 **Kieler Bucht** B
Germany
Kiev = Kiyev
80E2 **Kifab** Uzbekistan
97A3 **Kiffa** Maur
89H8 **Kigali** Rwanda
12A2 **Kigluaik Mts** USA
99C3 **Kigoma** Tanz
75B2 **Kii-sanchi** Mts
Japan
74C4 **Kii-suido** B Japan
54B1 **Kikinda** Serbia,
Yugos
55B3 **Kikládhes** Is Greece
71F4 **Kikori** PNG
98B3 **Kikwit** Zaire
21C4 **Kilauea Crater** Mt
Hawaiian Is
4C3 **Kilbuck Mts** USA
74B2 **Kilchu** N Korea
109D1 **Kilcoy** Aust
45C2 **Kildare** County,
Irish Rep
45C2 **Kildare** Irish Rep
19B3 **Kilgore** USA
99D3 **Kilifi** Kenya
99D3 **Kilimanjaro** Mt Tanz
99D3 **Kilindoni** Tanz
92C2 **Kilis** Turk
45B2 **Kilkee** Irish Rep
45C2 **Kilkenny** County,
Irish Rep
45C2 **Kilkenny** Irish Rep
45B2 **Kilkieran B** Irish Rep
55B2 **Kilkis** Greece
45B1 **Killala B** Irish Rep
45B2 **Killaloe** Irish Rep
109D1 **Killarney** Aust
41B3 **Killarney** Irish Rep
19A3 **Killeen** USA
12D1 **Killik** R USA
44B3 **Killin** Scot
55B3 **Killíni** Mt Greece
45B1 **Killybegs** Irish Rep
42B2 **Kilmarnock** Scot
61H2 **Kil'mez** Russian Fed
99D3 **Kilosa** Tanz
41B3 **Kilrush** Irish Rep
99C3 **Kilwa** Zaire
99D3 **Kilwa Kisiwani** Tanz
99D3 **Kilwa Kivinje** Tanz
108A2 **Kimba** Aust
12F2 **Kimball,Mt** USA
13D3 **Kimberley** Can
101F1 **Kimberley** S Africa
100D2 **Kimberley** Plat Aust
74B2 **Kimch'aek** N Korea
74B3 **Kimch'ŏn** S Korea
55B3 **Kími** Greece
60E2 **Kimry** Russian Fed
70C3 **Kinabalu** Mt Malay
78D1 **Kinabatangan** R
Malay
14B2 **Kincardine** Can
13B1 **Kincolith** Can
19B3 **Kinder** USA
13F2 **Kindersley** Can
97A3 **Kindia** Guinea
98C3 **Kindu** Zaire
61H3 **Kinel'** Russian Fed
61F2 **Kineshma**
Russian Fed
109D1 **Kingaroy** Aust
21A2 **King City** USA
5F4 **Kingcome Inlet** Can
7C4 **King George Is** Can
107D4 **King I** Aust
13B2 **King I** Can

106B2 **King Leopold Range**
Mts Aust
9B3 **Kingman** USA
98C3 **Kingombe** Zaire
108A2 **Kingoonya** Aust
22C2 **Kingsburg** USA
21B2 **Kings Canyon Nat Pk**
USA
108A3 **Kingscote** Aust
106B2 **King Sd** Aust
112C2 **King Sejong** Base
Ant
14A1 **Kingsford** USA
17B1 **Kingsland** USA
43E3 **King's Lynn** Eng
16C2 **Kings Park** USA
8B2 **Kings Peak** Mt USA
107C4 **Kingston** Aust
7C5 **Kingston** Can
25E3 **Kingston** Jamaica
15D2 **Kingston** New York,
USA
111A3 **Kingston** NZ
27E4 **Kingstown**
St Vincent and the
Grenadines
9D4 **Kingsville** USA
44B3 **Kingussie** Scot
4J3 **King William I** Can
100B4 **King William's Town**
S Africa
98B3 **Kinkala** Congo
39G7 **Kinna** Sweden
44D3 **Kinnairds Head** Pt
Scot
75B1 **Kinomoto** Japan
44C3 **Kinross** Scot
45B3 **Kinsale** Irish Rep
98B3 **Kinshasa** Zaire
78D3 **Kintap** Indon
42B2 **Kintyre** Pen Scot
13D1 **Kinuso** Can
99D2 **Kinyeti** Mt Sudan
55B3 **Kiparissía** Greece
55B3 **Kiparissiakós Kólpos**
G Greece
15C1 **Kipawa,L** Can
99D3 **Kipili** Tanz
12B3 **Kipnuk** USA
45C2 **Kippure** Mt Irish Rep
100B2 **Kipushi** Zaire
63C2 **Kirensk** Russian Fed
65J5 **Kirghizia** Republic,
Asia
82B1 **Kirgizskiy Khrebet**
Mts Kirghizia
98B3 **Kiri** Zaire
105G4 **Kiribati** Is Pacific O
92B2 **Kırıkkale** Turk
99D3 **Kirinyaga** Mt Kenya
60D2 **Kirishi** Russian Fed
85B3 **Kirithar Range** Mts
Pak
55C3 **Kirkağaç** Turk
90A2 **Kirk Bulāg Dāgh** Mt
Iran
42C2 **Kirkby** Eng
44C3 **Kirkcaldy** Scot
42B2 **Kirkcudbright** Scot
38K5 **Kirkenes** Nor
7B5 **Kirkland Lake** Can
112A **Kirkpatrick,Mt** Ant
10A2 **Kirksville** USA
93D2 **Kirkūk** Iraq
18B2 **Kirkwood** USA
60D3 **Kirov** Russian Fed
61G2 **Kirov** Russian Fed
93D1 **Kirovakan** Armenia
61J2 **Kirovgrad**
Russian Fed
60D4 **Kirovograd** Ukraine
61H2 **Kirs** Russian Fed
92B2 **Kirşehir** Turk
56C2 **Kiruna** Sweden
75B1 **Kiryū** Japan
98C2 **Kisangani** Zaire
75B1 **Kisarazu** Japan
86B1 **Kishanganj** India
85C3 **Kishangarh** India
60C4 **Kishinev** Moldova
75B2 **Kishiwada** Japan
99D3 **Kisii** Kenya
99D3 **Kisiju** Tanz

59B3 **Kiskunhalas** Hung
65F5 **Kislovodsk**
Russian Fed
99E3 **Kismaayo** Somalia
75B1 **Kiso-sammyaku** Mts
Japan
97A4 **Kissidougou**
Guinea
17B2 **Kissimmee,L** USA
99D3 **Kisumu** Kenya
59C3 **Kisvárda** Hung
97B3 **Kita** Mali
65H6 **Kitab** Uzbekistan
75C1 **Kitakata** Japan
74C4 **Kita-Kyūshū** Japan
99D2 **Kitale** Kenya
69G4 **Kitalo** I Japan
74C2 **Kitami** Japan
7B5 **Kitchener** Can
99D2 **Kitgum** Uganda
55B3 **Kíthira** I Greece
55B3 **Kíthnos** I Greece
94A1 **Kiti,C** Cyprus
4H3 **Kitikmeot** Region
Can
5F4 **Kitimat** Can
38K5 **Kitnen** R Fin
75A2 **Kitsuki** Japan
15C2 **Kittanning** USA
38J5 **Kittilä** Fin
99D3 **Kitunda** Tanz
13B1 **Kitwanga** Can
100B2 **Kitwe** Zambia
57C3 **Kitzbühel** Austria
47E1 **Kitzbühler Alpen** Mts
Austria
57C3 **Kitzingen** Germany
98C3 **Kiumbi** Zaire
12B1 **Kivalina** USA
59D2 **Kivercy** Ukraine
99C3 **Kivu,L** Zaire/Rwanda
4B3 **Kiwalik** USA
60D3 **Kiyev** Ukraine
61J2 **Kizel** Russian Fed
92C2 **Kizil** R Turk
80D2 **Kizyl-Arvat**
Turkmenistan
90B2 **Kizyl-Atrek**
Turkmenistan
57C2 **Kladno**
Czech Republic
57C3 **Klagenfurt** Austria
60B2 **Klaipėda** Lithuania
8A2 **Klamath** USA
20B2 **Klamath** R USA
8A2 **Klamath Falls** USA
20B2 **Klamath Mts** USA
57C2 **Klatovy**
Czech Republic
12H3 **Klawak** USA
13B1 **Kleiat** Leb
101G1 **Klerksdorp** S Africa
60E2 **Klin** Russian Fed
60B2 **Klintehamn** Sweden
60D3 **Klintsy** Russian Fed
52C2 **Ključ** Bosnia-
Herzegovina
59B2 **Kłodzko** Pol
12G2 **Klondike** R Can/USA
4U3 **Klondike Plat** Can/
USA
59B3 **Klosterneuburg**
Austria
12G2 **Kluane** R Can
12G2 **Kluane** L Can
12G2 **Kluane Nat Pk** Can
59B2 **Kluczbork** Pol
12G2 **Klukwan** USA
12E2 **Klutina L** USA
12E2 **Knight I** USA
43C3 **Knighton** Wales
52A2 **Knin** Croatia
106A4 **Knob,C** Aust
46B1 **Knokke-Heist** Belg
112C9 **Knox Coast** Ant
11B3 **Knoxville** Tennessee,
USA
6H3 **Knud Ramsussens**
Land Region
Greenland
78B3 **Koba** Indon
6F3 **Kobbermirebugt**
Greenland
74D4 **Kobe** Japan

56C1 **København** Den
57B2 **Koblenz** Germany
60B3 **Kobrin** Russian Fed
71E4 **Kobroör** I Indon
12C1 **Kobuk** R USA
54B2 **Kočani** Macedonia
76C3 **Ko Chang** I Thai
86B1 **Koch Bihar** India
47D1 **Kochel** Germany
6C3 **Koch I** Can
Kochi = Cochin
74C4 **Kōchi** Japan
12D3 **Kodiak** USA
12D3 **Kodiak I** USA
87B2 **Kodiyakkari** India
99D2 **Kodok** Sudan
100A3 **Koes** Namibia
101G1 **Koffiefontein**
S Africa
97B4 **Koforidua** Ghana
74D3 **Kōfu** Japan
75B1 **Koga** Japan
39G7 **Køge** Den
84C2 **Kohat** Pak
84B2 **Koh-i-Baba** Mts
Afghan
84B1 **Koh-i-Hisar** Mts
Afghan
84B2 **Koh-i-Khurd** Mt
Afghan
86C1 **Kohima** India
84B1 **Koh-i-Mazar** Mt
Afghan
84B3 **Kohlu** Pak
62C2 **Kohtla Järve** Estonia
75B1 **Koide** Japan
12F2 **Koidern** Can
77A4 **Koihoa** Is Nicobar Is
74B4 **Koje-do** I S Korea
74B4 **Kokchetav**
Kazakhstan
39J6 **Kokemaki** L Fin
38J6 **Kokkola** Fin
107D1 **Kokoda** PNG
14A2 **Kokomo** USA
71E4 **Kokonau** Indon
65K5 **Kokpekty**
Kazakhstan
7D4 **Koksoak** R Can
100B4 **Kokstad** S Africa
76C3 **Ko Kut** I Thai
38L5 **Kola** Russian Fed
71D4 **Kolaka** Indon
77B4 **Ko Lanta** I Thai
Kollam = Quilon
87B2 **Kolār** India
87B2 **Kolār Gold Fields**
India
97A3 **Kolda** Sen
39F7 **Kolding** Den
87A1 **Kolhāpur** India
12C3 **Kolianek** USA
59R2 **Kolín** Czech Republic
57B2 **Köln** Germany
58B2 **Kolo** Pol
58B2 **Kołobrzeg** Pol
97B3 **Kokkani** Mali
60E2 **Kolomna**
Russian Fed
60C4 **Kolomyya** Ukraine
65K4 **Kolpashevo**
Russian Fed
55C3 **Kólpos Merabéllou** B
Greece
55B2 **Kólpos Singitikós** G
Greece
55B2 **Kólpos Strimonikós**
G Greece
55B2 **Kólpos Toronaíos** G
Greece
38L5 **Kol'skiy Poluostrov**
Pen Russian Fed
38G6 **Kolvereid** Nor
100B2 **Kolwezi** Zaire
1C7 **Kolyma** R
Russian Fed
54B2 **Kom** Mt Bulg/Serbia,
Yugos
99D2 **Koma** Eth
97D3 **Komadugu Gana** R
Nig
55C3 **Komárno** Slovakia
101H1 **Komati** R S Africa
74D3 **Komatsu** Japan

148

75A2	**Komatsushima** Japan
64G3	**Komi Respublika,** Russian Fed
70C4	**Komodo** I Indon
71E4	**Komoran** I Indon
75B1	**Komoro** Japan
55C2	**Komotini** Greece
76D3	**Kompong Cham** Camb
76C3	**Kompong Chhnang** Mts Camb
77C3	**Kompong Som** Camb
76D3	**Kompong Thom** Camb
76D3	**Kompong Trabek** Camb
63F2	**Komsomol'sk na Amure** Russian Fed
65H4	**Konda** R Russian Fed
99D3	**Kondoa** Tanz
87B1	**Kondukür** India
6G3	**Kong Karls Land** Is Barents S
78D2	**Kongkemul** Mt Indon
98C3	**Kongolo** Zaire
39F7	**Kongsberg** Den
39G6	**Kongsvinger** Nor
58B2	**Konin** Pol
54A2	**Konjic** Bosnia-Herzegovina
61F1	**Konosha** Russian Fed
75B1	**Konosu** Japan
60D3	**Konotop** Ukraine
59C2	**Końskie** Pol
49D2	**Konstanz** Germany
97C3	**Kontagora** Nig
76D3	**Kontum** Viet
92B2	**Konya** Turk
13D3	**Kootenay** R Can
85C5	**Kopargaon** India
6J3	**Köpasker** Iceland
38A2	**Kópavogur** Iceland
52B1	**Koper** Slovenia
80D2	**Kopet Dag** Mts Iran/Turkmenistan
61K2	**Kopeysk** Russian Fed
77C4	**Ko Phangan** I Thai
77B4	**Ko Phuket** I Thai
39H7	**Köping** Sweden
87B1	**Koppal** India
52C1	**Koprivnica** Croatia
85B4	**Korangi** Pak
87C1	**Koraput** India
86A2	**Korba** India
57B2	**Korbach** Germany
4B3	**Korbuk** R USA
55B2	**Korçë** Alb
52C2	**Korčula** I Croatia
72E2	**Korea B** China/Korea
74B4	**Korea Str** S Korea/Japan
59D2	**Korec** Ukraine
92B1	**Körğlu Tepesi** Mt Turk
97B4	**Korhogo** Ivory Coast
85B4	**Kori Creek** India
55B3	**Korinthiakós Kólpos** G Greece
55B3	**Kórinthos** Greece
74E3	**Köriyama** Japan
61K3	**Korkino** Russian Fed
92B2	**Korkuteli** Turk
82C1	**Korla** China
52C2	**Kornat** I Croatia
60D5	**Köroğlu Tepesi** Mt Turk
99D3	**Korogwe** Tanz
108B3	**Koroit** Aust
71E3	**Koror** Palau Is, Pacific O
59C3	**Körös** R Hung
60C3	**Korosten** Ukraine
95A3	**Koro Toro** Chad
12B3	**Korovin** I USA
69G2	**Korsakov** Russian Fed
39G7	**Korsør** Den
46B1	**Kortrijk** Belg
55C3	**Kós** I Greece
77C4	**Ko Samui** I Thai
58B2	**Koscierzyna** Pol
107D4	**Kosciusko** Mt Aust
12H3	**Kosciusko** I USA
74B4	**Koshikijima-retto** I Japan
59C3	**Košice** Slovakia
74B3	**Kosong** N Korea
54B2	**Kosovo** Aut Republic, Serbia, Yugos
97B4	**Kossou** L Ivory Coast
101G1	**Koster** S Africa
99D1	**Kosti** Sudan
59D2	**Kostopol'** Ukraine
61F2	**Kostroma** Russian Fed
56C2	**Kostrzyn** Pol
39H8	**Kosalin** Pol
85D3	**Kota** India
78A4	**Kotaagung** Indon
78C3	**Kotabaharu** Indon
78D3	**Kotabaru** Indon
77C4	**Kota Bharu** Malay
78A3	**Kotabum** Indon
84C2	**Kot Addu** Pak
78D1	**Kota Kinabulu** Malay
87C1	**Kotapad** India
61G2	**Kotel'nich** Russian Fed
61F4	**Kotel'nikovo** Russian Fed
39K6	**Kotka** Fin
64F3	**Kotlas** Russian Fed
12B2	**Kotlik** USA
54A2	**Kotor** Montenegro, Yugos
60C4	**Kotovsk** Ukraine
85B3	**Kotri** Pak
87C1	**Kottagüdem** India
87B3	**Kottayam** India
98C2	**Kotto** R CAR
87B2	**Kottūru** India
12B1	**Kotzebue** USA
4B3	**Kotzebue Sd** USA
97C3	**Kouande** Benin
98C2	**Kouango** CAR
97B3	**Koudougou** Burkina
98B3	**Koulamoutou** Gabon
97B3	**Koulikoro** Mali
97B3	**Koupéla** Burkina
33G2	**Kourou** French Guiana
97B3	**Kouroussa** Guinea
98B1	**Kousséri** Cam
39K6	**Kouvola** Fin
38L5	**Kovdor** Russian Fed
60B3	**Kovel'** Ukraine
	Kovno = Kaunas
61F2	**Kovrov** Russian Fed
61F3	**Kovylkino** Russian Fed
60E1	**Kovzha** R Russian Fed
77C4	**Ko Way** I Thai
73C5	**Kowloon** Hong Kong
84B2	**Kowt-e-Ashrow** Afghan
92A2	**Köyceğiz** Turk
38L5	**Koydor** Russian Fed
87A1	**Koyna Res** India
12B2	**Koyuk** USA
12B1	**Koyuk** R USA
12C2	**Koyukuk** USA
12C1	**Koyukuk** R USA
92C2	**Kozan** Turk
55B2	**Kozani** Greece
61G2	**Koz'modemyansk** Russian Fed
75B2	**Közu-shima** I Japan
39F7	**Kragerø** Nor
54B2	**Kragujevac** Serbia, Yugos
77B3	**Kra,Isthmus of** Burma/Malay
	Krakatau = Rakata
94C1	**Krak des Chevaliers** Hist Site Syria
	Kraków = Cracow
54B2	**Kraljevo** Serbia, Yugos
60E4	**Kramatorsk** Ukraine
38H6	**Kramfors** Sweden
52B1	**Kranj** Slovenia
61G1	**Krasavino** Russian Fed
64G2	**Krasino** Russian Fed
59C2	**Kraśnik** Pol
61G3	**Krasnoarmeysk** Russian Fed
60E5	**Krasnodar** Russian Fed
61J2	**Krasnokamsk** Russian Fed
61K2	**Krasnotur'insk** Russian Fed
61J2	**Krasnoufimsk** Russian Fed
61J3	**Krasnousol'-skiy** Russian Fed
65G3	**Krasnoshersk** Russian Fed
65G5	**Krasnovodsk** Turkmenistan
63B2	**Krasnoyarsk** Russian Fed
59C2	**Krasnystaw** Pol
61G3	**Krasnyy Kut** Russian Fed
60E4	**Krasnyy Luch** Ukraine
61G4	**Krasnyy Yar** Russian Fed
76D3	**Kratie** Camb
6E2	**Kraulshavn** Greenland
56B2	**Krefeld** Germany
60D4	**Kremenchug** Ukraine
60D4	**Kremenchugskoye Vodokhranilische** Res Ukraine
59D2	**Kremenets** Ukraine
98A2	**Kribi** Cam
60D3	**Krichev** Belorussia
47E1	**Krimml** Austria
87B1	**Krishna** R India
87B2	**Krishnagiri** India
86B2	**Krishnangar** India
39F7	**Kristiansand** Nor
39G7	**Kristianstad** Sweden
64B3	**Kristiansund** Nor
39G7	**Kristinehamn** Sweden
38J6	**Kristiinankaupunki** Fin
55B3	**Kriti** I Greece
60D4	**Krivoy Rog** Ukraine
52B1	**Krk** I Croatia
6G3	**Kronpris Frederik Bjerge** Mts Greenland
39K7	**Kronstadt** Russian Fed
101G1	**Kroonstad** S Africa
65F5	**Kropotkin** Russian Fed
101G1	**Krugersdorp** S Africa
78A4	**Krui** Indon
55A2	**Kruje** Alb
58D2	**Krupki** Belorussia
12B1	**Krusenstern,C** USA
54B2	**Kruševac** Serbia, Yugos
39K7	**Krustpils** Latvia
12G3	**Kruzof** I USA
60E5	**Krym** Pen Ukraine
60E5	**Krymsk** Russian Fed
58B2	**Krzyz** Pol
96C1	**Ksar El Boukhari** Alg
96B1	**Ksar el Kebir** Mor
70A3	**Kuala** Indon
77C5	**Kuala Dungun** Malay
77C4	**Kuala Kerai** Malay
77C5	**Kuala Kubu Baharu** Malay
77C5	**Kuala Lipis** Malay
77C5	**Kuala Lumpur** Malay
77C4	**Kuala Trengganu** Malay
78D1	**Kuamut** Malay
74A2	**Kuandian** China
77C5	**Kuantan** Malay
93E1	**Kuba** Azerbaijan
71F4	**Kubar** PNG
78C2	**Kuching** Malay
70C3	**Kudat** Malay
78C4	**Kudus** Indon
61H2	**Kudymkar** Russian Fed
57C3	**Kufstein** Austria
90C3	**Kuh Duren** Upland Iran
91C4	**Küh e Bazmān** Mt Iran
90B3	**Küh-e Dinar** Mt Iran
90C2	**Küh-e-Hazär Masjed** Mts Iran
91C4	**Küh-e Jebäl Barez** Mts Iran
90B3	**Küh-e Karkas** Mts Iran
91C4	**Küh-e Laleh Zar** Mt Iran
90A2	**Küh-e Sahand** Mt Iran
91D4	**Kuh e Taftän** Mt Iran
90A2	**Kühhaye Sabalan** Mts Iran
90A3	**Kühhä-ye Zägros** Mts Iran
38K6	**Kuhmo** Fin
90B3	**Kühpäyeh** Iran
90C3	**Kühpäyeh** Iran
91C4	**Küh ye Bashäkerd** Mts Iran
90A2	**Küh ye Sabalan** Mt Iran
100A3	**Kuibis** Namibia
4B4	**Kuigillingok** USA
100A2	**Kuito** Angola
12H3	**Kuiu** I USA
74E2	**Kuji** Japan
75A2	**Kuju-san** Mt Japan
12C3	**Kukaklek** L USA
55C3	**Kukës** Alb
77C5	**Kukup** Malay
91C4	**Kül** R Iran
55C3	**Kula** Turk
61J4	**Kulakshi** Kazakhstan
99D2	**Kulal,Mt** Kenya
55B2	**Kulata** Bulg
60B2	**Kuldiga** Latvia
61H4	**Kul'sary** Kazakhstan
84D2	**Kulu** India
92B2	**Kulu** Turk
65J4	**Kulunda** Russian Fed
108B2	**Kulwin** Aust
61G5	**Kuma** R Russian Fed
75B1	**Kumagaya** Japan
78C3	**Kumai** Indon
74C4	**Kumamoto** Japan
74C4	**Kumano** Japan
54B2	**Kumanovo** Macedonia
63E2	**Kumara** China
74B1	**Kumasi** Ghana
65F5	**Kumayri** Armenia
98A2	**Kumba** Cam
87B2	**Kumbakonam** India
61J3	**Kumertau** Russian Fed
74B3	**Kümhwa** S Korea
39H7	**Kumla** Sweden
87A2	**Kumta** India
82C1	**Kümüx** China
84C2	**Kunar** R Afghan
39K7	**Kunda** Estonia
87A2	**Kundäpura** India
85C4	**Kundla** India
84B1	**Kunduz** Afghan
89F9	**Kunene** R Angola
39G7	**Kungsbacka** Sweden
61J2	**Kungur** Russian Fed
76B1	**Kunhing** Burma
82B2	**Kunlun Shan** Mts China
73A4	**Kunming** China
74B3	**Kunsan** S Korea
38K6	**Kuopio** Fin
52C1	**Kupa** R Croatia/Bosnia-Herzegovina
106B2	**Kupang** Indon
107D2	**Kupiano** PNG
12H3	**Kupreanof I** USA

Kupyansk

60E4 **Kupyansk** Ukraine
82C1 **Kuqa** China
75B1 **Kurabe** Japan
74C4 **Kurashiki** Japan
75A1 **Kurayoshi** Japan
54C2 **Kürdzhali** Bulg
74C4 **Kure** Japan
60B2 **Kuressaare** Estonia
63A1 **Kureyka** R Russian Fed
65H4 **Kurgan** Russian Fed
88K6 **Kuria Muria Is** Oman
38J6 **Kurikka** Fin
Kuril Is = Kuril'skoye Osrova
69H2 **Kuril'skiye Ostrova** Russian Fed
87B1 **Kurnool** India
15C1 **Kuroiso** Japan
111B2 **Kurow** NZ
109D2 **Kurri Kurri** Aust
60E3 **Kursk** Russian Fed
Kurskiy Zaliv = Courland Lagoon
68A2 **Kuruktag** R China
100B3 **Kuruman** S Africa
74C4 **Kurume** Japan
87C3 **Kurunegala** Sri Lanka
65K5 **Kurunktag** R China
61J2 **Kusa** Russian Fed
55C3 **Kuşadasi Körfezi** B Turk
55C2 **Kus Golü** L Turk
74D4 **Kushimoto** Japan
74E2 **Kushiro** Japan
86B2 **Kushtia** Bang
61H3 **Kushum** R Kazakhstan
80E2 **Kushva** Afgan
65G4 **Kushva** Russian Fed
12B2 **Kuskokwim** R USA
12B3 **Kuskokwim B** USA
12C2 **Kuskokwim Mts** USA
86A1 **Kusma** Nepal
74E2 **Kussharo-ko** L Japan
65H4 **Kustanay** Kazakhstan
92A2 **Kütahya** Turk
78D3 **Kutai** R Indon
59B3 **Kutná Hora** Czech Republic
58B2 **Kutno** Pol
98B3 **Kutu** Zaire
86C2 **Kutubdia I** Bang
98C1 **Kutum** Sudan
7D4 **Kuujjuaq** Can
7C4 **Kuujjuarapik** Can
38K5 **Kuusamo** Fin
61J3 **Kuvandyk** Russian Fed
93E4 **Kuwait** Kuwait
80C3 **Kuwait** Sheikdom, S W Asia
75B1 **Kuwana** Japan
Kuybyshev = Samara
65J4 **Kuybyshev** Russian Fed
61G3 **Kuybyshevskoye Vodokhranilishche** Res Russian Fed
63C2 **Kuytun** Russian Fed
60E5 **Kuzey Anadolu Daglari** Mts Turk
61G3 **Kuznetsk** Russian Fed
38J4 **Kvaenangen** Sd Nor
12C3 **Kvichak** USA
12C3 **Kvichak** R USA
12C3 **Kvichak B** USA
38G5 **Kvigtind** Mt Nor
38H5 **Kvikkjokk** Sweden
99D3 **Kwale** Kenya
74B3 **Kwangju** S Korea
98B3 **Kwango** R Zaire
100B2 **Kwekwe** Zim
12B2 **Kwethluk** USA
12B2 **Kwethluk** R USA
58B2 **Kwidzyn** Pol
71E4 **Kwoka** Mt Indon
108C3 **Kyabram** Aust
76B2 **Kyaikkami** Burma
76B2 **Kyaikto** Burma

68C1 **Kyakhta** Russian Fed
108A2 **Kyancutta** Aust
76B1 **Kyaukme** Burma
76B1 **Kyauk-padaung** Burma
76A2 **Kyaukpyu** Burma
40B2 **Kyle of Lochalsh** Scot
46D1 **Kyll** R Germany
108B3 **Kyneton** Aust
99D2 **Kyoga** L Uganda
109D1 **Kyogle** Aust
74B3 **Kyongju** S Korea
74D3 **Kyoto** Japan
Kyrgyzstan = Kirghizia
65H4 **Kyshtym** Russian Fed
74C4 **Kyūshū** I Japan
104E3 **Kyushu-Palau Ridge** Pacific O
54B2 **Kyustendil** Bulg
68B1 **Kyzyl** Russian Fed
65H5 **Kyzylkum** Desert Uzbekistan
65H5 **Kzyl Orda** Kazakhstan

L

99E2 **Laascaanood** Somalia
46F1 **Laaspne** Germany
99E1 **Laasqoray** Somalia
33E1 **La Asunción** Ven
96A2 **Laâyoune** Mor
23A1 **La Barca** Mexico
97A3 **Labé** Guinea
59B2 **Labe** R Czech Republic
15D1 **Labelle** Can
17B2 **La Belle** USA
12G2 **Laberge,L** Can
78D1 **Labi** Brunei
13E2 **La Biche,L** Can
61F5 **Labinsk** Russian Fed
94C1 **Laboué** Leb
34C2 **Laboulaye** Arg
7D4 **Labrador** Region Can
7D4 **Labrador City** Can
7E4 **Labrador S** Greenland/Can
33E5 **Lábrea** Brazil
78D1 **Labuan** I Malay
78B4 **Labuhan** Indon
76A2 **Labutta** Burma
66H3 **Labytnangi** Russian Fed
7C4 **Lac à L'eau Claire** Can
46B2 **La Capelle** France
34C2 **La Carlota** Arg
79B3 **La Carlota** Phil
12J1 **Lac Belot** L Can
7C4 **Lac Bienville** L Can
83B4 **Laccadive Is** India
47B2 **Lac d'Annecy** L France
4G3 **Lac de Gras** L Can
47B1 **Lac de Joux** L Switz
47B1 **Lac de Neuchâtel** L Switz
23A2 **Lac de Patzcuaro** L Mexico
23A2 **Lac de Sayula** L Mexico
4F3 **Lac des Bois** L Can
47A2 **Lac du Bourget** L France
25D3 **La Ceiba** Honduras
108A3 **Lacepede B** Aust
48C2 **La Châtre** France
47B1 **La-Chaux-de-Fonds** Switz
94B3 **Lachish** Hist Site Israel
107D4 **Lachlan** R Aust
32B2 **La Chorrera** Panama
15D1 **Lachute** Can
7C4 **Lac Joseph** L Can
15C2 **Lackawanna** USA
5G4 **Lac la Biche** Can
4G3 **Lac la Martre** L Can
5H4 **Lac la Ronge** L Can

52A1 **Lac Léman** L Switz/ France
10C1 **Lac Manouane** L Can
15D1 **Lac Megantic** Can
7C4 **Lac Mistassini** L Can
13E2 **Lacombe** Can
15D2 **Laconia** USA
50A1 **La Coruña** Spain
10A2 **La Crosse** USA
9C3 **La Cruces** USA
7A4 **Lac Seul** L Can
18B2 **La Cygne** USA
84D2 **Ladākh Range** India
85C3 **Lādnūn** India
73B5 **Ladong** China
60D1 **Ladozhskoye Ozero** L Ukraino
6B2 **Lady Ann Str** Can
109C4 **Lady Barron** Aust
101G1 **Ladybrand** S Africa
13C3 **Ladysmith** Can
101G1 **Ladysmith** S Africa
71F4 **Lae** PNG
76C3 **Laem Ngop** Thai
56C1 **Laesø** I Den
10B2 **Lafayette** Indiana, USA
11A3 **Lafayette** Louisiana, USA
46B2 **La Fère** France
46B2 **La-Ferté-sous-Jouarre** France
97C4 **Lafia** Nig
97C4 **Lafiagi** Nig
48B2 **La Flèche** France
96C1 **La Galite** I Tunisia
61G4 **Lagan'** Russian Fed
96C1 **Lagan** R Sweden
31D4 **Lagarto** Brazil
96C1 **Laghouat** Alg
35C2 **Lagoa de Araruama** Brazil
29F2 **Lagoa dos Patos** Lg Brazil
35C2 **Lagoa Feia** Brazil
32B4 **Lago Agrio** Ecuador
35C1 **Lagoa Juparanã** L Brazil
29D2 **Lagoa mar Chiguita** L Arg
29F2 **Lagoa Mirim** L Brazil/Urug
29B6 **Lago Argentino** L Arg
29B5 **Lago Buenos Aires** L Arg
29B5 **Lago Cochrane** L Arg/Chile
29C5 **Lago Colhué Huapi** L Arg
24B2 **Lago de Chapala** L Mexico
32A2 **Lago de Chiriqui** L Panama
23A2 **Lago de Cuitzeo** L Mexico
29B3 **Lago de la Laja** L Chile
53A2 **Lago del Coghinas** L Sardegna
32C2 **Lago de Maracaibo** L Ven
25D3 **Lago de Nicaragua** L Nic
32A1 **Lago de Perlas** L Nic
52B2 **Lago di Bolsena** L Italy
52B2 **Lago di Bracciano** L Italy
52A1 **Lago di Como** L Italy
47D2 **Lago d'Idro** L Italy
52B1 **Lago di Garda** L Italy
47C2 **Lago di Lecco** L Italy
47C2 **Lago di Lugano** L Italy
47D2 **Lago d'Iseo** L Italy
47C2 **Lago d'Orta** L Italy
29B5 **Lago General Carrera** L Chile
52A1 **Lago Maggiore** L Italy
29C5 **Lago Musters** L Arg
48B3 **Lagon** France

29B4 **Lago Nahuel Haupi** L Arg
29B5 **Lago O'Higgins** L Chile
53A3 **Lago Omodeo** L Sardegna
30C2 **Lago Poopó** L Bol
29B4 **Lago Ranco** L Chile
32D6 **Lago Rogaguado** L Bol
97C4 **Lagos** Nig
50A2 **Lagos** Port
29B5 **Lago San Martin** L Arg/Chile
24B2 **Lagos de Moreno** Mexico
30C2 **Lago Titicaca** Bol/Peru
29B5 **Lago Viedma** L Arg
8B2 **La Grande** USA
106B2 **Lagrange** Aust
11B3 **La Grange** Georgia, USA
14A3 **La Grange** Kentucky, USA
19A4 **La Grange** Texas, USA
33E2 **La Gran Sabana** Mts Ven
47B2 **La Grave** France
48B3 **Lagroño** Spain
34A3 **Laguna Alumine** L Arg
21B3 **Laguna Beach** USA
34C3 **Laguna Colorada** Grande L Arg
79B3 **Laguna de Bay** Lg Phil
25D3 **Laguna de Caratasca** Lg Honduras
25D4 **Laguna de Chiriqui** L Panama
25D3 **Laguna de Managua** L Nic
25D3 **Laguna de Nicaragua** L Nic
26A4 **Laguna de Perlas** Lg Nic
23B1 **Laguna de Pueblo Viejo** L Mexico
24C2 **Laguna de Tamiahua** Lg Mexico
25C3 **Laguna de Términos** L Mexico
23A1 **Laguna de Yuriria** L Mexico
23B1 **Laguna le Altamira** Mexico
24C2 **Laguna Madre** Lg Mexico
34C2 **Laguna Mar Chiquita** L Arg
29B4 **Laguna Nahuel Huapi** L Arg
34C2 **Laguna Paiva** Arg
29B4 **Laguna Ranco** Chile
9C4 **Laguna Seca** Mexico
23B1 **Laguna Tortugas** L Mexico
70C3 **Lahad Datu** Malay
78A3 **Lahat** Indon
38J6 **Lahia** Fin
90B2 **Lāhījān** Iran
46D1 **Lahn** R Germany
46D1 **Lahnstein** Germany
84C2 **Lahore** Pak
39K6 **Lahti** Fin
23A2 **La Huerta** Mexico
98B2 **Laï** Chad
73B5 **Laibin** China
76C1 **Lai Chau** Viet
100B4 **Laingsburg** S Africa
44B2 **Lairg** Scot
78A3 **Lais** Indon
79C4 **Lais** Phil
72E2 **Laiyang** China
72D2 **Laizhou Wan** B China
34A3 **Laja** R Chile
30F4 **Lajes** Brazil
22D4 **La Jolla** USA
9C3 **La Junta** USA
109C2 **Lake Cargelligo** Aust
11A3 **Lake Charles** USA

17B1 **Lake City** Florida, USA
17C1 **Lake City** S Carolina, USA
42C2 **Lake District** Region, Eng
22D4 **Lake Elsinore** USA
106C3 **Lake Eyre Basin** Aust
15C2 **Lakefield** Can
6D3 **Lake Harbour** Can
22C3 **Lake Hughes** USA
16B2 **Lakehurst** USA
19A4 **Lake Jackson** USA
13E2 **Lake la Biche** Can
17B2 **Lakeland** USA
7A5 **Lake of the Woods** Can
20B1 **Lake Oswego** USA
21A2 **Lakeport** USA
19B3 **Lake Providence** USA
111B2 **Lake Pukaki** NZ
109C3 **Lakes Entrance** Aust
22C2 **Lakeshore** USA
108B1 **Lake Stewart** Aust
15C1 **Lake Traverse** Can
8A2 **Lakeview** USA
20B1 **Lakeview Mt** Can
19B3 **Lake Village** USA
17B2 **Lake Wales** USA
22C4 **Lakewood** California, USA
16B2 **Lakewood** New Jersey, USA
14B2 **Lakewood** Ohio, USA
17B2 **Lake Worth** USA
86A1 **Lakhimpur** India
85B4 **Lakhpat** India
84C2 **Lakki** Pak
55B3 **Lakonikós Kólpos** G Greece
97B4 **Lakota** Ivory Coast
38K4 **Laksefjord** Inlet Nor
38K4 **Lakselv** Nor
34C2 **La Laguna** Arg
32A4 **La Libertad** Ecuador
34A2 **La Ligua** Chile
50A2 **La Linea** Spain
85D4 **Lalitpur** India
5H4 **La Loche** Can
13F1 **la Loche,L** Can
46C1 **La Louvière** Belg
26A4 **La Luz** Nic
7C5 **La Malbaie** Can
23B2 **La Malinche** Mt Mexico
50B2 **La Mancha** Region, Spain
9C3 **Lamar** Colorado, USA
18B2 **Lamar** Missouri, USA
19A4 **La Marque** USA
98B3 **Lambaréné** Gabon
32A5 **Lambayeque** Peru
112B10 **Lambert Gl** Ant
16B2 **Lambertville** USA
4F2 **Lamblon,C** Can
47C2 **Lambro** R Italy
76C2 **Lam Chi** R Thai
50A1 **Lamego** Port
47B2 **La Meije** Mt France
32B6 **La Merced** Peru
21B3 **La Mesa** USA
55B3 **Lamía** Greece
42C2 **Lammermuir Hills** Scot
39G7 **Lammhult** Sweden
79B3 **Lamon B** Phil
18B1 **Lamoni** USA
71F3 **Lamotrek** I Pacific O
43B3 **Lampeter** Wales
99E3 **Lamu** Kenya
47D1 **Lana** I Italy
21C4 **Lanai** I Hawaiian Is
21C4 **Lanai City** Hawaiian Is
42C2 **Lanark** Scot
76B3 **Lanbi** I Burma
76C1 **Lancang** R China
42C3 **Lancashire** County, Eng
21B3 **Lancaster** California, USA

24C2 **Lancaster** Eng
18B1 **Lancaster** Mississippi, USA
15D2 **Lancaster** New Hampshire, USA
14B3 **Lancaster** Ohio, USA
10C3 **Lancaster** Pennsylvania, USA
17B1 **Lancaster** S Carolina, USA
6B2 **Lancaster Sd** Can
78B3 **Landak** R Indon
46E2 **Landau** Germany
57C3 **Landeck** Austria
8C2 **Lander** USA
34C2 **Landeta** Arg
57C3 **Landsberg** Germany
4F2 **Lands End** C Can
43B4 **Land's End** Pt Eng
57C3 **Landshut** Germany
39G7 **Landskrona** Sweden
17A1 **Lanett** USA
56B2 **Langenhagen** Germany
47B1 **Langenthal** Switz
42C2 **Langholm** Scot
38A2 **Langjökull** Mts Iceland
77B4 **Langkawi** I Malay
13C3 **Langley** Can
108C1 **Langlo** R Aust
47B1 **Langnau** Switz
49D2 **Langres** France
70A3 **langsa** Indon
68C2 **Lang Shan** Mts China
76D1 **Lang Son** Viet
48C3 **Languedoc** Region, France
29B3 **Lanin** Mt Arg
76B3 **Lanoa,L** I. Phil
16B2 **Lansdale** USA
7B4 **Lansdowne House** Can
16B2 **Lansford** USA
10B2 **Lansing** USA
47B2 **Lanslebourg** France
96A2 **Lanzarote** I Canary Is
72A2 **Lanzhou** China
47B2 **Lanzo Torinese** Italy
79B2 **Laoag** Phil
76C1 **Lao Cai** Viet
72D1 **Laoha He** R China
45C2 **Laois** County, Irish Rep
46B2 **Laon** France
32B6 **La Oroya** Peru
76C2 **Laos** Republic, S E Asia
49C2 **Lapalisse** France
32B2 **La Palma** Panama
96A2 **La Palma** I Canary Is
34B3 **La Pampa** State, Arg
33E2 **La Paragua** Ven
29E2 **La Paz** Arg
34B2 **La Paz** Arg
30C2 **La Paz** Bol
23A2 **La Paz** Mexico
69G2 **La Perouse Str** Japan/Russian Fed
23A1 **La Piedad** Mexico
20B2 **La Pine** USA
19B3 **Laplace** USA
23A2 **la Placita** Mexico
29E2 **La Plata** Arg
13F1 **La Plonge,L** Can
14A2 **La Porte** USA
39K6 **Lappeenranta** Fin
38H5 **Lappland** Region Sweden/Fin
34C3 **Laprida** Arg
1B8 **Laptev S** Russian Fed
38J6 **Lapua** Fin
79B3 **Lapu-Lapu** Phil
9B4 **La Purísma** Mexico
95B2 **Laqiya Arba'in** Well Sudan
30C3 **La Quiaca** Arg
52B2 **L'Aquila** Italy
91B4 **Lār** Iran
96B1 **Larache** Mor
8C2 **Laramie** USA

8C2 **Laramie Range** Mts USA
50B2 **Larca** Spain
9D4 **Laredo** USA
91B4 **Larestan** Region, Iran
47B2 **L'Argentière** France
17B2 **Largo** USA
42B2 **Largs** Scot
90A2 **Lāri** Iran
30C4 **La Rioja** Arg
30C4 **La Rioja** State, Arg
55B3 **Lárisa** Greece
85B3 **Larkana** Pak
92B3 **Larnaca** Cyprus
94A1 **Larnaca B** Cyprus
45D1 **Larne** N Ire
50A1 **La Robla** Spain
46C1 **La Roche-en-Ardenne** Belg
48B2 **La Rochelle** France
47B1 **La Roche-sur-Foron** France
48B2 **La Roche-sur-Yon** France
51B2 **La Roda** Spain
27D3 **La Romana** Dom Rep
5H4 **La Ronge** Can
5H4 **La Ronge,L** Can
39F7 **Larvik** Nor
65J3 **Laryak** Russian Fed
50B2 **La Sagra** Mt Spain
15D1 **La Salle** Can
18C1 **La Salle** USA
7C5 **La Sarre** Can
34C1 **Las Avispas** Arg
34A2 **Las Cabras** Chile
5G4 **Lascombe** Can
9C3 **Las Cruces** USA
26C3 **La Selle** Mt Haiti
72B2 **Lasengmia** China
30B4 **La Serena** Chile
29E3 **Las Flores** Arg
76B1 **Lashio** Burma
53C3 **La Sila** Mts Italy
90B2 **Lāsjerd** Iran
34A3 **Las Lajas** Chile
50A2 **Las Marismas** Marshland Spain
96A2 **Las Palmas de Gran Canaria** Canary Is
52A2 **La Spezia** Italy
29C4 **Las Plumas** Arg
34C2 **Las Rosas** Arg
20B2 **Lassen Peak** Mt USA
20B2 **Lassen Volcanic Nat Pk** USA
23B2 **las Tinai** Mexico
98B3 **Lastoursville** Gabon
52C2 **Lastovo** I Croatia
24B2 **Las Tres Marías** Is Mexico
34C2 **Las Varillas** Arg
9C3 **Las Vegas** USA
Latakia = Al Ladhiqiyah
53B2 **Latina** Italy
34B2 **La Toma** Arg
32D1 **La Tortuga** I Ven
79B2 **La Trinidad** Phil
109C4 **La Trobe** Aust
94B3 **Latrun** Israel
7C5 **La Tuque** Can
87B1 **Latūr** India
60B2 **Latvia** Republic, Europe
107D5 **Launceston** Aust
43B4 **Launceston** Eng
29B4 **La Unión** Chile
25D3 **La Unión** El Salvador
23A2 **La Unión** Peru
32B5 **La Unión** Peru
107D2 **Laura** Aust
15C3 **Laurel** Delaware, USA
16A3 **Laurel** Maryland, USA
11B3 **Laurel** Mississippi, USA
17B1 **Laurens** USA
17C1 **Laurinburg** USA
52A1 **Lausanne** Switz
78D3 **Laut** I Indon
29B5 **Lautaro** Mt Chile

46D2 **Lauterecken** Germany
15D1 **Laval** Can
48B2 **Laval** France
22B2 **Laveaga Peak** Mt USA
47C2 **Laveno** Italy
31B6 **Lavras** Brazil
4A3 **Lavrentiya** Russian Fed
101H1 **Lavumisa** Swaziland
78D1 **Lawas** Malay
76B1 **Lawksawk** Burma
18A2 **Lawrence** Kansas, USA
15D2 **Lawrence** Massachusetts, USA
111A3 **Lawrence** NZ
14A3 **Lawrenceville** Illinois, USA
9D3 **Lawton** USA
91A5 **Layla** S Arabia
99D2 **Laylo** Sudan
23A2 **Lázaro Cárdenas** Mexico
99E1 **Laz Daua** Somalia
79B4 **Lazi** Phil
8C2 **Lead** USA
13F2 **Leader** Can
18A2 **Leavenworth** USA
58B2 **Leba** Pol
18B2 **Lebanon** Missouri, USA
20B2 **Lebanon** Oregon, USA
15C2 **Lebanon** Pennsylvania, USA
92C3 **Lebanon** Republic, S W Asia
101C3 **Lebombo** Mts Mozam/S Africa/Swaziland
58B2 **Lebork** Pol
47A2 **Le Bourg-d'Oisans** France
47B1 **Le Brassus** Switz
29B3 **Lebu** Chile
47B1 **Le Buet** Mt France
46B1 **Le Cateau** France
55A2 **Lecce** Italy
52A1 **Lecco** Italy
47D1 **Lech** R Austria
47D1 **Lechtaler Alpen** Mts Austria
49C2 **Le Creusot** France
43C3 **Ledbury** Eng
13E2 **Leduc** Can
16C1 **Lee** USA
45B3 **Lee** R Irish Rep
41C3 **Leeds** Eng
43C3 **Leek** Eng
56B2 **Leer** Germany
17B2 **Leesburg** Florida, USA
16A3 **Leesburg** Virginia, USA
19B3 **Leesville** USA
109C2 **Leeton** Aust
56B2 **Leeuwarden** Neth
106A4 **Leeuwin,C** Aust
22C2 **Lee Vining** USA
27E3 **Leeward Is** Caribbean S
94A1 **Lefkara** Cyprus
79B3 **Legazpi** Phil
47D2 **Legnago** Italy
59B2 **Legnica** Pol
33F2 **Leguan Inlet** Guyana
32C4 **Leguizamo** Colombia
84D2 **Leh** India
48C2 **Le Havre** France
16B2 **Lehigh** R USA
16B2 **Lehighton** USA
84C2 **Leiah** Pak
59B3 **Leibnitz** Austria
43D3 **Leicester** County, Eng
43D3 **Leicester** Eng
107C2 **Leichhardt** R Aust
56A2 **Leiden** Neth
46B1 **Leie** R Belg
106C4 **Leigh Creek** Aust
43D4 **Leighton Buzzard** Eng

Leine

56B2 **Leine** R Germany
45C2 **Leinster** Region, Irish Rep
57C2 **Leipzig** Germany
50A2 **Leiria** Port
39F7 **Leirvik** Nor
45B1 **Leitrim** County, Irish Rep
73C4 **Leiyang** China
73B5 **Leizhou Bandao** Pen Burma
73C5 **Leizhou Wan** B China
56A2 **Lek** R Neth
96C1 **Le Kef** Tunisia
19B3 **Leland** USA
54A2 **Lelija** Mt Bosnia-Herzegovina
47B1 **Le Locle** France
48C2 **Le Mans** France
6D3 **Lemicux Is** Can
8C2 **Lemmon** USA
21B2 **Lemoore** USA
49C2 **Lempdes** France
86C2 **Lemro** R Burma
52C2 **Le Murge** Region, Italy
63C2 **Lena** R Russian Fed
38L6 **Lendery** Russian Fed
73C4 **Lengshujiang** China
Leningrad = Sankt-Peterburg
117B7 **Leningradskaya** Base Ant
61H3 **Leninogorsk** Tatarskaya Respublika, Russian Fed
68A1 **Leninogorsk** Kazakhstan
65K4 **Leninsk-Kuznetskiy** Russian Fed
69F2 **Leninskoye** Russian Fed
65F6 **Lenkoran'** Azerbaijan
46E1 **Lenne** R Germany
16C1 **Lenox** USA
46B1 **Lens** France
63D1 **Lensk** Russian Fed
53B3 **Lentini** Italy
76B3 **Lenya** R Burma
52B1 **Leoben** Austria
43C3 **Leominster** Eng
16D1 **Leominster** USA
24B2 **Leon** Mexico
25D3 **Leon** Nic
50A1 **Leon** Region, Spain
50A1 **León** Spain
100A3 **Leonardville** Namibia
106B3 **Leonora** Aust
35C2 **Leopoldina** Brazil
Léopoldville = Kinshasa
60C3 **Lepel'** Belorussia
73D4 **Leping** China
49C2 **Le Puy-en-Velay** France
98B2 **Léré** Chad
101G1 **Leribe** Lesotho
47C2 **Lerici** Italy
51C1 **Lérida** Spain
23A1 **Lerma** R Mexico
47D1 **Lermoos** Austria
55C3 **Léros** I Greece
44E1 **Lerwick** Scot
46A2 **Les Andelys** France
26C3 **Les Cayes** Haiti
47B2 **Les Ecrins** Mt France
73A4 **Leshan** China
54B2 **Leskovac** Serbia, Yugos
48B3 **Les Landes** Region, France
101G1 **Leslie** S Africa
61H2 **Lesnoy** Russian Fed
63B2 **Lesosibirsk** Russian Fed
101G1 **Lesotho** Kingdom, S Africa
69F2 **Lesozavodsk** Russian Fed
48B2 **Les Sables-d'Olonne** France

112A **Lesser Antarctica** Region, Ant
27D4 **Lesser Antilles** Is Caribbean S
65F5 **Lesser Caucasus** Mts Azerbaijan/Georgia
13E1 **Lesser Slave L** Can
55C3 **Lésvos** I Greece
58B2 **Leszno** Pol
86C2 **Letha Range** Mts Burma
5G5 **Lethbridge** Can
33F3 **Lethem** Guyana
59D3 **Letichev** Ukraine
63D2 **Let Oktyobr'ya** Russian Fed
78B2 **Letong** Indon
46A1 **Le Touquet-Paris-Plage** France
76B2 **Letpadan** Burma
48C1 **Le Tréport** France
47B1 **Leuk** Switz
57A2 **Leuven** Belg
55B3 **Levádhia** Greece
38G6 **Levanger** Nor
47B2 **Levanna** Mt Italy
71D5 **Lévêque,C** Aust
46D1 **Leverkusen** Germany
59B3 **Levice** Slovakia
47D1 **Levico** Italy
110C2 **Levin** NZ
7C1 **Lévis** Can
15D2 **Levittown** USA
55B3 **Lévka -ri** Mt Greece
55B3 **Levkás** Greece
55B3 **Levkás** I Greece
106B2 **Lévêque,C** Aust
54C2 **Levski** Bulg
43E4 **Lewes** Eng
40B2 **Lewis** I Scot
16A2 **Lewisburg** USA
11B2 **Lewis P** NZ
8B2 **Lewis Range** Mts USA
8B2 **Lewiston** Idaho, USA
10C2 **Lewiston** Maine, USA
8C2 **Lewistown** Montana, USA
15C2 **Lewistown** Pennsylvania, USA
19B3 **Lewisville** USA
11B3 **Lexington** Kentucky, USA
18B2 **Lexington** Missouri, USA
15C3 **Lexington Park** USA
79C3 **Leyte G** Phil
54A2 **Lezhe** Alb
82D3 **Lhasa** China
86B1 **Lhazê** China
70A3 **Lhokseumawe** Indon
86C1 **Lhozhag** China
86B4 **Lhünzê** China
Liancourt Rocks =Tok-do
79C4 **Lianga** Phil
72B3 **Liangdang** China
73C5 **Lianjiang** China
73C5 **Lianping** China
73C5 **Lian Xian** China
72D3 **Lianyungang** China
72E1 **Liaodong Bandao** Pen China
72E1 **Liaodong Wan** B China
72E1 **Liao He** R China
72E1 **Liaoning** Province, China
72E1 **Liaoyang** China
72E1 **Liaoyuan** China
72E1 **Liaoyuang** China
4F3 **Liard** R Can
4F4 **Liard River** Can
46C2 **Liart** France
98B2 **Liban** Leb
9C3 **Liberal** USA
57C2 **Liberec** Czech Republic
97A4 **Liberia** Republic, Africa
18B2 **Liberty** Missouri, USA

15D2 **Liberty** New York, USA
19D1 **Liberty** Texas, USA
48B3 **Libourne** France
23B2 **Libres** Mexico
98A2 **Libreville** Gabon
95A2 **Libya** Republic, Africa
95B2 **Libyan Desert** Libya
95B1 **Libyan Plat** Egypt
53B3 **Licata** Italy
43D3 **Lichfield** Eng
101C2 **Lichinga** Mozam
101G1 **Lichtenburg** S Africa
14B3 **Licking** R USA
22B2 **Lick Observatory** USA
60C3 **Lida** Belorussia
39G7 **Lidköping** Sweden
53B2 **Lido di Ostia** Italy
52A1 **Liechtenstein** Principality, Europe
57B2 **Liège** Belg
58C1 **Lielupe** R Latvia
98C2 **Lienart** Zaire
57C3 **Lienz** Austria
60B2 **Liepāja** Latvia
57B2 **Lier** Belg
47B1 **Liestal** Switz
15C1 **Lièvre** R Can
57C3 **Liezen** Austria
40C2 **Liffey** R Irish Rep
107F3 **Lifu** I Nouvelle Calédonie
109C1 **Lightning Ridge** Aust
46C2 **Ligny-en-Barrois** France
101C2 **Ligonha** R Mozam
47C2 **Liguria** Region, Italy
52A2 **Ligurian** S Italy
21C4 **Lihue** Hawaiian Is
100B2 **Likasi** Zaire
49C1 **Lille** France
39G6 **Lillehammer** Nor
46B1 **Lillers** France
79C3 **Lillestom** Nor
13C2 **Lillooet** Can
13C2 **Lillooet** R Can
101C2 **Lilongwe** Malawi
79B4 **Liloy** Phil
54A2 **Lim** R Montenegro/ Serbia, Yugos
32B6 **Lima** Peru
50A1 **Lima** Spain
10B2 **Lima** USA
92B3 **Limassol** Cyprus
45C1 **Limavady** N Ire
34B3 **Limay** R Arg
34B3 **Limay Mahuida** Arg
98A2 **Limbe** Cam
101C2 **Limbe** Malawi
57B2 **Limburg** W Gem
31B6 **Limeira** Brazil
45B2 **Limerick** County, Irish Rep
41B3 **Limerick** Irish Rep
56B1 **Limfjorden** L Den
106C2 **Limmen Bight** B Aust
55C3 **Limnos** I Greece
31D3 **Limoeiro** Brazil
48C2 **Limoges** France
25D4 **Limón** Costa Rica
8C3 **Limon** USA
48C2 **Limousin** Region, France
79A3 **Linapacan Str** Phil
29B3 **Linares** Chile
9D4 **Linares** Mexico
50B2 **Linares** Spain
68B4 **Lincang** China
29D2 **Lincoln** Arg
18A1 **Lincoln** California, USA
42D3 **Lincoln** County, Eng
42D3 **Lincoln** Eng
18C1 **Lincoln** Illinois, USA
18D2 **Lincoln** Nebraska, USA
15D2 **Lincoln** New Hampshire, USA
111B2 **Lincoln** NZ
80A **Lincoln** S Greenland

20B2 **Lincoln City** USA
14B2 **Lincoln Park** USA
52A2 **L'Incudina** Mt Corse
57B3 **Lindau** Germany
33F2 **Linden** Guyana
39F7 **Lindesnes** C Nor
99D3 **Lindi** Tanz
98C2 **Lindi** R Zaire
101G1 **Lindley** S Africa
55C3 **Lindos** Greece
15C2 **Lindsay** Can
105J3 **Line Is** Pacific O
72C2 **Linfen** China
76D2 **Lingao** China
79B2 **Lingayen** Phil
56B2 **Lingen** Germany
73C4 **Lingling** China
73B5 **Lingshan** China
72C2 **Lingshi** China
97A3 **Linguère** Sen
73E4 **Linhai** Rhejiang, China
31D5 **Linhares** Brazil
72B1 **Linhe** China
74B2 **Linjiang** China
39H7 **Linköping** Sweden
72D2 **Linqing** China
35B2 **Lins** Brazil
72A2 **Lintao** China
47C1 **Linthal** Switz
68D2 **Linxi** China
72A2 **Linxia** China
57C3 **Linz** Austria
79B3 **Lipa** Phil
53B3 **Lipari** I Italy
61E3 **Lipetsk** Russian Fed
54B1 **Lipova** Rom
56B2 **Lippe** R Germany
46E1 **Lippstadt** Germany
99D2 **Lira** Uganda
98B3 **Liranga** Congo
98C2 **Lisala** Zaire
50A2 **Lisboa** Port
Lisbon = Lisboa
45C1 **Lisburn** N Ire
45B2 **Liscannor B** Irish Rep
73D4 **Lishui** China
73C4 **Li Shui** R China
60E4 **Lisichansk** Ukraine
48C2 **Lisieux** France
61F3 **Liski** Russian Fed
46E2 **L'Isle-Adam** France
47B1 **L'Isle-sur-le-Doubs** France
107E3 **Lismore** Aust
45B2 **Listowel** Irish Rep
73B5 **Litang** China
94B2 **Litani** R Leb
33G3 **Litani** R Surinam
18C2 **Litchfield** USA
107E4 **Lithgow** Aust
60B2 **Lithuania** Republic, Europe
16B2 **Lititz** USA
69F2 **Litovko** Russian Fed
19A3 **Little** R USA
11C4 **Little Abaco** I The Bahamas
110C1 **Little Barrier I** NZ
13E2 **Little Bow** R Can
26D3 **Little Cayman** I Caribbean S
16B3 **Little Egg Harbor** B USA
26C2 **Little Inagua** I Caribbean S
77A4 **Little Nicobar** I Nicobar Is
11A3 **Little Rock** USA
22D3 **Littlerock** USA
13D2 **Little Smoky** Can
13D2 **Little Smoky** R Can
16A3 **Littlestown** USA
15D2 **Littleton** New Hampshire, USA
74B2 **Liuhe** China
73B5 **Liuzhou** China
55C3 **Livanátais** Greece
58D1 **Līvāni** Latvia
12E1 **Livengood** USA
17B1 **Live Oak** USA
21A2 **Livermore** USA
7D5 **Liverpool** Can
42C3 **Liverpool** Eng

4E2 **Liverpool B** Can
42C3 **Liverpool B** Eng
6C2 **Liverpool,C** Can
109D2 **Liverpool Range** *Mts* Aust
8B2 **Livingston** Montana, USA
19B3 **Livingston** Texas, USA
44C4 **Livingston** UK
Livingstone = Maramba
19A3 **Livingston,L** USA
52C2 **Livno** Bosnia-Herzegovina
60E3 **Livny** Russian Fed
14B2 **Livonia** USA
52B2 **Livorno** Italy
99D3 **Liwale** Tanz
52B1 **Ljubljana** Slovenia
38G6 **Ljungan** *R* Sweden
39G7 **Ljungby** Sweden
39H6 **Ljusdal** Sweden
38H6 **Ljusnan** *R* Sweden
43C4 **Llandeilo** Wales
43C4 **Llandovery** Wales
43C3 **Llandrindod Wells** Wales
42C3 **Llandudno** Wales
43B4 **Llanelli** Wales
43C3 **Llangollen** Wales
9C3 **Llano Estacado** *Plat* USA
32C2 **Llanos** Region, Colombia/Ven
30D2 **Llanos de Chiquitos** Region, Bol
Lleida = Lérida
50A2 **Llerena** Spain
43B3 **Lleyn** *Pen* Wales
89E7 **Llorin** Nig
5H4 **Lloydminster** Can
30C3 **Llullaillaco** *Mt* Arg/Chile
30C3 **Loa** *R* Chile
49C2 **Loan** France
98B3 **Loange** *R* Zaire
100B3 **Lobatse** Botswana
98B2 **Lobaye** *R* CAR
34D3 **Loberia** Arg
100A2 **Lobito** Angola
34D3 **Lobos** Arg
47B2 **Locano** Italy
47C1 **Locarno** Switz
44B3 **Loch Awe** *L* Scot
44A3 **Lochboisdale** Scot
44A3 **Loch Bracadale** *Inlet* Scot
44B3 **Loch Broom** *Estuary* Scot
42B2 **Loch Doon** *L* Scot
44B3 **Loch Earn** *L* Scot
44B2 **Loch Eriboll** *Inlet* Scot
44B3 **Loch Ericht** *L* Scot
48C2 **Loches** France
44B3 **Loch Etive** *Inlet* Scot
44B3 **Loch Ewe** *Inlet* Scot
44B3 **Loch Fyne** *Inlet* Scot
44B3 **Loch Hourn** *Inlet* Scot
44B2 **Lochinver** Scot
44B2 **Loch Katrine** *L* Scot
44C3 **Loch Leven** *L* Scot
44B3 **Loch Linnhe** *Inlet* Scot
44B3 **Loch Lochy** *L* Scot
44B3 **Loch Lomond** *L* Scot
44B3 **Loch Long** *Inlet* Scot
44A3 **Lochmaddy** Scot
44B3 **Loch Maree** *L* Scot
44C3 **Lochnagar** *Mt* Scot
44B3 **Loch Ness** *L* Scot
44B3 **Loch Rannoch** *L* Scot
44A2 **Loch Roag** *Inlet* Scot
44B3 **Loch Sheil** *L* Scot
44B2 **Loch Shin** *L* Scot
44A3 **Loch Snizort** *Inlet* Scot
44B3 **Loch Sunart** *Inlet* Scot
44B3 **Loch Tay** *L* Scot

44B3 **Loch Torridon** *Inlet* Scot
108A2 **Lock** Aust
42C2 **Lockerbie** Scot
15C2 **Lock Haven** USA
15C2 **Lockport** USA
76D3 **Loc Ninh** Viet
53C3 **Locri** Italy
94B3 **Lod** Israel
108B3 **Loddon** *R* Aust
60D1 **Lodeynoye Pole** Russian Fed
84C3 **Lodhran** Pak
52A1 **Lodi** Italy
21A2 **Lodi** USA
98C3 **Lodja** *R* Zaire
47B1 **Lods** France
99D2 **Lodwar** Kenya
58B2 **Łódź** Pol
38G5 **Lofoten** *Is* Nor
8B2 **Logan** Utah, USA
4D3 **Logan,Mt** Can
14A2 **Logansport** Indiana, USA
19B3 **Logansport** Louisiana, USA
86A2 **Lohārdaga** India
39J6 **Lohja** Fin
76B2 **Loikaw** Burma
39J6 **Loimaa** Fin
48C2 **Loir** *R* France
49C2 **Loire** *R* France
32B4 **Loja** Ecuador
50B2 **Loja** Spain
38K5 **Lokan Tekojärvi** *Res* Fin
46B1 **Lokeren** Belg
99D2 **Lokitaung** Kenya
58D1 **Loknya** Russian Fed
98C3 **Lokolo** *R* Zaire
98C3 **Lokoro** *R* Zaire
6D3 **Loks Land** *I* Can
56C2 **Lolland** *I* Den
54B2 **Lom** Bulg
98C3 **Lomami** *R* Zaire
97A4 **Loma Mts** Sierra Leone/Guinea
47C2 **Lombardia** Region, Italy
71D4 **Lomblen** *I* Indon
78D4 **Lombok** *I* Indon
97C4 **Lomé** Togo
98C3 **Lomela** *R* Zaire
98C3 **Lomela** *R* Zaire
60C2 **Lomonosov** Russian Fed
47B1 **Lomont** Region, France
21A3 **Lompoc** USA
58C2 **Łomża** Pol
87A1 **Lonavale** India
29B3 **Loncoche** Chile
7B5 **London** Can
43D4 **London** Eng
45C1 **Londonderry** County, N Ire
45C1 **Londonderry** N Ire
45C1 **Londonderry** *I* Chile
106B2 **Londonderry,C** Aust
30C4 **Londres** Arg
30F3 **Londrina** Brazil
21B2 **Lone Pine** USA
11C4 **Long** *I* The Bahamas
71F4 **Long** *I* PNG
78C2 **Long Akah** Malay
47E1 **Longarone** Italy
34A3 **Longavi** *Mt* Chile
27H2 **Longa B** Jamaica
17C1 **Long B** USA
9B3 **Long Beach** California, USA
15D2 **Long Beach** New York, USA
15D2 **Long Branch** USA
73D5 **Longchuan** China
20C2 **Long Creek** USA
109C4 **Longford** Aust
45C2 **Longford** County, Irish Rep
45C2 **Longford** Irish Rep
44D3 **Long Forties** *Region* N Sea
72D1 **Longhua** China

7C4 **Long I** Can
10C2 **Long I** USA
16C2 **Long Island Sd** USA
7B4 **Longlac** Can
73B5 **Longlin** China
8C2 **Longmont** USA
78D2 **Longnawan** Indon
29B3 **Longquimay** Chile
107D3 **Longreach** Aust
72A2 **Longshou Shan** *Upland* China
42C2 **Longtown** Eng
15D1 **Longueuil** Can
34A3 **Longuimay** Chile
46C2 **Longuyon** France
11A3 **Longview** Texas, USA
8A2 **Longview** Washington, USA
46C2 **Longwy** France
72A3 **Longxi** China
77D3 **Long Xuyen** Viet
73D4 **Longyan** China
73B5 **Longzhou** China
47D2 **Lonigo** Italy
49D2 **Lons-le-Saunier** France
11C3 **Lookout,C** USA
99D3 **Loolmalasin** *Mt* Tanz
13D1 **Loon** *R* Can
45B2 **Loop Hd** *C* Irish Rep
76C3 **Lop Buri** Thai
98A3 **Lopez** *C* Gabon
68B2 **Lop Nur** *L* China
50A2 **Lora del Rio** Spain
10B2 **Lorain** USA
84B2 **Loralai** Pak
90B3 **Lordegān** Iran
107E4 **Lord Howe** *I* Aust
105G5 **Lord Howe Rise** Pacific O
6A3 **Lord Mayor B** Can
9C3 **Lordsburg** USA
35B2 **Lorena** Brazil
47E2 **Loreo** Italy
23A1 **Loreto** Mexico
48B2 **Lorient** France
108B3 **Lorne** Aust
57B3 **Lörrach** Germany
49D2 **Lorraine** *Region* France
9C3 **Los Alamos** USA
34A2 **Los Andes** Chile
29B3 **Los Angeles** Chile
9B3 **Los Angeles** USA
21A2 **Los Banos** USA
34B2 **Los Cerrillos** Arg
21A2 **Los Gatos** USA
52B2 **Lošinj** *I* Croatia
29B3 **Los Lagos** Chile
24B2 **Los Mochis** Mexico
22B3 **Los Olivos** USA
34A3 **Los Sauces** Chile
44C3 **Lossiemouth** Scot
27E4 **Los Testigos** *Is* Ven
29B2 **Los Vilos** Chile
48C3 **Lot** *R* France
34A3 **Lota** Chile
42C2 **Lothian** Region, Scot
99D2 **Lotikipi Plain** Sudan/Kenya
98C3 **Loto** Zaire
47B1 **Lötschberg Tunnel** Switz
38K5 **Lotta** *R* Fin/Russian Fed
48B2 **Loudéac** France
97A3 **Louga** Sen
43B3 **Lough Allen** *L* Irish Rep
45C2 **Lough Boderg** *L* Irish Rep
43D3 **Loughborough** Eng
45C2 **Lough Bowna** *L* Irish Rep
45C1 **Lough Carlingford** *L* N Ire
41B3 **Lough Conn** *L* Irish Rep
41B3 **Lough Corrib** *L* Irish Rep
41B3 **Lough Derg** *L* Irish Rep

45C2 **Lough Derravaragh** *L* Irish Rep
4H2 **Loughead I** Can
45C2 **Lough Ennell** *L* Irish Rep
41B3 **Lough Erne** *L* N Ire
40B2 **Lough Foyle** *Estuary* N Ire/Irish Rep
40B3 **Lough Neagh** *L* N Ire
45C1 **Lough Oughter** *L* Irish Rep
45B2 **Loughrea** Irish Rep
45C2 **Lough Ree** *L* Irish Rep
45C2 **Lough Sheelin** *L* Irish Rep
42B2 **Lough Strangford** *L* Irish Rep
45C1 **Lough Swilly** *Estuary* Irish Rep
14B3 **Louisa** USA
70C3 **Louisa Reef** *I* S E Asia
12E2 **Louise,L** USA
107E2 **Louisiade Arch** Solomon Is
11A3 **Louisiana** State, USA
17B1 **Louisville** Georgia, USA
11B3 **Louisville** Kentucky, USA
38L5 **Loukhi** Russian Fed
48B3 **Lourdes** France
108C2 **Louth** Aust
45C2 **Louth** County, Irish Rep
42D3 **Louth** Eng
Louvain = Leuven
48C2 **Louviers** France
60D2 **Lovat** *R* Russian Fed
54B2 **Lovech** Bulg
21B1 **Loveland** USA
52B1 **Lovere** Italy
9C3 **Lovington** USA
38L5 **Lovozero** Russian Fed
6B3 **Low,C** Can
10C2 **Lowell** Massachusetts, USA
20B2 **Lowell** Oregon, USA
16D1 **Lowell** USA
111B2 **Lower Hutt** NZ
43E3 **Lowestoft** Eng
58B2 **Łowicz** Pol
108B2 **Loxton** Aust
5F4 **Loyd George,Mt** Can
54A2 **Loznica** Serbia, Yugos
23A2 **Loz Reyes** Mexico
65H3 **Lozva** *R* Russian Fed
100B2 **Luacano** Angola
98C3 **Luachimo** Angola
98C3 **Lualaba** *R* Zaire
100B2 **Luampa** Zambia
100B2 **Luân** Angola
73D3 **Lu'an** China
98B3 **Luanda** Angola
100A2 **Luando** *R* Angola
100B2 **Luanginga** *R* Angola
76C1 **Luang Namtha** Laos
76C2 **Luang Prabang** Laos
98B3 **Luangue** *R* Angola
100C2 **Luangwa** *R* Zambia
72D1 **Luan He** *R* China
72D1 **Luanping** China
100B2 **Luanshya** Zambia
100B2 **Luapula** *R* Zaire
50A1 **Luarca** Spain
98B3 **Lubalo** Angola
58D2 **L'uban** Belorussia
79B3 **Lubang Is** Phil
100A2 **Lubango** Angola
9C3 **Lubbock** USA
56C2 **Lübeck** Germany
98C3 **Lubefu** Zaire
98C3 **Lubefu** *R* Zaire
98C3 **Lubero** Zaire
98C3 **Lubilash** *R* Zaire
59C2 **Lublin** Pol
60D3 **Lubny** Ukraine
78C2 **Lubok Antu** Malay
98C3 **Lubudi** Zaire
98C3 **Lubudi** *R* Zaire

Lubuklinggau

78A3 **Lubuklinggau** Indon
100B2 **Lubumbashi** Zaire
98C3 **Lubutu** Zaire
79B3 **Lucban** Phil
52B2 **Lucca** Italy
42B2 **Luce** *B* Scot
19C3 **Lucedale** USA
79B3 **Lucena** Phil
59B3 **Lucenec** Slovakia
 Lucerne = Luzern
73C5 **Luchuan** China
56C2 **Luckenwalde**
 Germany
101F1 **Luckhoff** S Africa
86A1 **Lucknow** India
100B2 **Lucusse** Angola
46D1 **Lüdenscheid**
 Germany
100A3 **Lüderitz** Namibia
84D2 **Ludhiana** India
14A2 **Ludington** USA
43C3 **Ludlow** Eng
54C2 **Ludogorie** *Upland*
 Bulg
17B1 **Ludovici** USA
54B1 **Luduş** Rom
39H6 **Ludvika** Sweden
57B3 **Ludwigsburg**
 Germany
57B3 **Ludwigshafen**
 Germany
56C2 **Ludwigslust**
 Germany
98C3 **Luebo** Zaire
98C3 **Luema** *R* Zaire
98C3 **Luembe** *R* Angola
100A2 **Luena** Angola
100B2 **Luena** *R* Angola
72B3 **Lüeyang** China
73D5 **Lufeng** China
11A3 **Lufkin** USA
60C2 **Luga** Russian Fed
60C2 **Luga** *R* Russian Fed
52A1 **Lugano** Switz
60E4 **Lugansk** Ukraine
101C2 **Lugela** Mozam
101C2 **Lugenda** *R* Mozam
50A1 **Lugo** Spain
54B1 **Lugoj** Rom
72A3 **Luhuo** China
98B3 **Lui** *R* Angola
100B2 **Luiana** Angola
100B2 **Luiana** *R* Angola
 **Luichow Peninsula =
 Leizhou Bandao**
47C2 **Luino** Italy
98B2 **Luionga** *R* Zaire
72B2 **Luipan Shan** *Upland*
 China
100B2 **Luishia** Zaire
68B4 **Luixi** China
98C3 **Luiza** Zaire
34B2 **Luján** Arg
34D2 **Luján** Arg
73D3 **Lujiang** China
98B3 **Lukenie** *R* Zaire
64E4 **Luki** Russian Fed
98B3 **Lukolela** Zaire
101C2 **Lukulu** Zambia
43B4 **Lundy** *I* Eng
56C2 **Lüneburg** Germany
46D2 **Lunéville** France
100B2 **Lunga** *R* Zambia
86C2 **Lunglei** India

100A2 **Lungue Bungo** *R*
 Angola
58D2 **Luninec** Belorussia
98B3 **Luobomo** Congo
73B5 **Luocheng** China
73C5 **Luoding** China
72C3 **Luohe** China
72C3 **Luo He** *R* Henan,
 China
72B2 **Luo He** *R* Shaanxi,
 China
73C4 **Luoxiao Shan** *Hills*
 China
72C3 **Luoyang** China
98B3 **Luozi** Zaire
100B2 **Lupane** Zim
101C2 **Lupilichi** Mozam
 Lu Qu = Tao He
30E4 **Luque** Par
45C1 **Lurgan** N Ire
101C2 **Lurio** *R* Mozam
90A3 **Luristan** Region, Iran
100B2 **Lusaka** Zambia
98C3 **Lusambo** Zaire
55A2 **Lushnjë** Alb
99D3 **Lushoto** Tanz
68B4 **Lushui** China
72E2 **Lüshun** China
43D4 **Luton** Eng
60C3 **Lutsk** Ukraine
99E2 **Luuq** Somalia
99C3 **Luvua** *R* Zaire
99D3 **Luvegu** *R* Tanz
100C2 **Luwingu** Zambia
71D4 **Luwuk** Indon
46D2 **Luxembourg** Grand
 Duchy, N W Europe
49D2 **Luxembourg** Lux
73A5 **Luxi** China
95C2 **Luxor** Egypt
61G1 **Luza** Russian Fed
61G1 **Luza** *R* Russian Fed
52A1 **Luzern** Switz
73B5 **Luzhai** China
73B4 **Luzhi** China
73B4 **Luzhou** China
31B4 **Luziânia** Brazil
79B2 **Luzon** *I* Phil
79B1 **Luzon Str** Phil
59C3 **L'vov** Ukraine
44C2 **Lybster** Scot
38H6 **Lycksele** Sweden
100B3 **Lydenburg** S Africa
8B3 **Lyell,Mt** USA
16A2 **Lykens** USA
43C4 **Lyme B** Eng
43C4 **Lyme Regis** Eng
11C3 **Lynchburg** USA
108A2 **Lyndhurst** Aust
75D2 **Lynn** USA
12G3 **Lynn Canal** *Sd* USA
17A1 **Lynn Haven** USA
5H4 **Lynn Lake** Can
5H3 **Lynx L** Can
49C2 **Lyon** France
12G3 **Lyon Canal** *Sd* USA
17B1 **Lyons** Georgia, USA
106A3 **Lyons** *R* Aust
47B2 **Lys** *R* Italy
61J7 **Lysva** Russian Fed
11B2 **Lyttelton** NZ
18C2 **Lytton** Can
22A1 **Lytton** USA
58D2 **Lyubeshov** Ukraine
60E2 **Lyublino** Russian Fed

M
76C1 **Ma** *R* Viet
94B2 **Ma'agan** Jordan
94B2 **Ma'alot Tarshiha**
 Israel
92C3 **Ma'an** Jordan
73D3 **Ma'anshan** China
92C2 **Ma'arrat an Nu'mān**
 Syria
46C1 **Maas** *R* Neth
46C1 **Maaseik** Belg
79B3 **Maasin** Phil
57B2 **Maastricht** Neth
101C3 **Mabalane** Mozam
33F2 **Mabaruma** Guyana
42E3 **Mablethorpe** Eng
101C3 **Mabote** Mozam
58C2 **Mabrita** Belorussia

58D2 **M'adel** Belorussia
35C2 **Macaé** Brazil
9D3 **McAlester** USA
9D4 **McAllen** USA
101C2 **Macaloge** Mozam
33G3 **Macapá** Brazil
35C1 **Macarani** Brazil
32B4 **Macas** Ecuador
31D3 **Macaú** Brazil
73C5 **Macau** Dependency,
 China
98C2 **M'Bari** *R* CAR
13C2 **McBride** Can
12F2 **McCarthy** USA
13A2 **McCauley I** Can
42C3 **Macclesfield** Eng
6B1 **McClintock B** Can
4H2 **McClintock Chan**
 Can
16A2 **McClure** USA
22B2 **McClure,L** USA
4G2 **McClure Str** Can
19B3 **McComb** USA
8C2 **McCook** USA
6C2 **Macculloch,C** Can
13C1 **McCusker,Mt** Can
4F4 **McDame** Can
6C2 **McDermitt** USA
13E2 **Macdonald** *R* Can
106C3 **Macdonnell Ranges**
 Mts Aust
50A1 **Macedo de Cavaleiros**
 Port
55B2 **Macedonia** Republic,
 Europe
31D3 **Maceió** Brazil
97B4 **Macenta** Guinea
52B2 **Macerata** Italy
108A2 **Macfarlane,L** Aust
19B3 **McGehee** USA
45B3 **MacGillycuddys**
 Reeks *Mts* Irish Rep
4C3 **McGrath** USA
35B2 **Machado** Brazil
101C3 **Machaila** Mozam
99D3 **Machakos** Kenya
32B4 **Machala** Ecuador
101C3 **Machaze** Mozam
87B1 **Mācherla** India
94B2 **Machgharab** Leb
87C1 **Māchilīpatnam** India
32B1 **Machiques** Ven
32C6 **Machu-Picchu** *Hist
 Site* Peru
101C3 **Macia** Mozam
109C1 **MacIntyre** *R* Aust
107D3 **Mackay** Aust
106B3 **Mackay,L** Aust
14C2 **McKeesport** USA
13C1 **Mackenzie** Can
4E3 **Mackenzie** *R* Can
4E3 **Mackenzie B** Can
4G2 **Mackenzie King I** Can
4E3 **Mackenzie Mts** Can
14B1 **Mackinac,Str of** USA
12D2 **McKinley,Mt** USA
19A3 **McKinney** USA
6C2 **Mackinson Inlet** *B*
 Can
100D2 **Macksville** Aust
20B2 **Mclaoughlin,Mt** USA
109D1 **Maclean** Aust
100B4 **Maclear** S Africa
5G4 **McLennan** Can
13D2 **McLeod** *R* Can
4G3 **McLeod B** Can
106A3 **McLeod,L** Aust
13D1 **McLeod L** Can
4E3 **Macmillan** *R* Can
12H2 **Macmillan P** Can
20B1 **McMinnville** Oregon,
 USA
112B7 **McMurdo** *Base* Ant
13D2 **McNaughton L** Can
18B1 **Macomb** USA
53A2 **Macomer** Sardegna
101C2 **Macomia** Mozam
49C2 **Mâcon** France
11B3 **Macon** Georgia, USA
18B2 **Macon** Missouri,
 USA
100B2 **Macondo** Angola
18A2 **McPherson** USA

104F6 **Macquarie** *Is* Aust
109C2 **Macquarie** *R* Aust
109C4 **Macquarie Harbour** *B*
 Aust
109D2 **Macquarie,L** Aust
17B1 **McRae** USA
112B11 **Mac. Robertson Land**
 Region, Ant
45B3 **Macroom** Irish Rep
96C1 **M'Sila** Alg
4G3 **McTavish Arm** *B*
 Can
108A1 **Macumba** *R* Aust
47C2 **Macunaga** Italy
4F3 **McVicar Arm** *B* Can
59B3 **M'yarovár** Hung
94R3 **Mādabā** Jordan
95A3 **Madadi** *Well* Chad
89J10 **Madagascar** *I*
 Indian O
95A2 **Madama** Niger
71F4 **Madang** PNG
97C3 **Madaoua** Niger
86C2 **Madaripur** Bang
90B2 **Madau** Turkmenistan
15C1 **Madawaska** *R* Can
96A1 **Madeira** *I* Atlantic O
33E5 **Madeira** *R* Brazil
7D5 **Madeleine, Isle de la**
 Can
24B2 **Madera** Mexico
21A2 **Madera** USA
87A1 **Madgaon** India
86B1 **Madhubani** India
86A2 **Madhya Pradesh**
 State, India
87B2 **Madikeri** India
98B3 **Madimba** Zaire
98B3 **Madingo Kayes**
 Congo
98B3 **Madingou** Congo
10B3 **Madison** Indiana,
 USA
10B2 **Madison** Wisconsin,
 USA
12C2 **Madisonville**
 Kentucky, USA
19A3 **Madisonville** Texas,
 USA
78C4 **Madiun** Indon
99D2 **Mado Gashi** Kenya
47D1 **Madonna Di**
 Campiglio Italy
87C2 **Madras** India
20B2 **Madras** USA
29A6 **Madre de Dios** *I*
 Chile
32D6 **Madre de Dios** *R* Bol
50B1 **Madrid** Spain
50B2 **Madridejos** Spain
78C4 **Madura** *I* Indon
87B3 **Madurai** India
75D1 **Maebashi** Japan
76B3 **Mae Khlong** *R* Thai
77B4 **Mae Nam Lunang** *R*
 Thai
76C2 **Mae Nam Mun** *R*
 Thai
76B2 **Mae Nam Ping** *R*
 Thai
101C2 **Maevatanana** Madag
101G1 **Mafeteng** Lesotho
109C3 **Maffra** Aust
99D3 **Mafia** *I* Tanz
101G1 **Mafikeng** S Africa
30G4 **Mafra** Brazil
92C3 **Mafraq** Jordan
32C2 **Magangué** Colombia
34D3 **Magdalena** Arg
24A1 **Magdalena** Mexico
26C4 **Magdalena** *R*
 Colombia
78D1 **Magdalena,Mt** Malay
56C2 **Magdeburg** Germany
31C6 **Magé** Brazil
78C4 **Magelang** Indon
47C1 **Maggia** *R* Switz
92B4 **Maghâgha** Egypt
45C1 **Magherafelt** N Ire
52A2 **Magilie** Italy
61J3 **Magnitogorsk**
 Russian Fed
19B3 **Magnolia** USA
101C2 **Magoé** Mozam

15D1 Magog Can
23B1 Magosal Mexico
13E2 Magrath Can
7A3 Maguse River Can
76B1 Magwe Burma
90A2 Mahābād Iran
86B1 Mahabharat Range Mts Nepal
87A1 Mahād India
85D4 Mahadeo Hills India
101D2 Mahajanga Madag
100B3 Mahalapye Botswana
86A2 Mahānadi R India
101D2 Mahanoro Madag
16A2 Mahanoy City USA
87A1 Maharashtra State, India
86A2 Mahāsamund India
76C2 Maha Sarakham Thai
101D2 Mahavavy R Madag
87B1 Mahbūbnagar India
96D1 Mahdia Tunisia
87B2 Mahe India
85D4 Mahekar India
101D2 Maheli I Comoros
86A2 Mahendragarh India
99D3 Mahenge Tanz
85C4 Mahesāna India
110C1 Mahia Pen NZ
85D3 Mahoba India
51C2 Mahón Spain
12J1 Mahony L Can
96D1 Mahrès Tunisia
85C4 Mahuva India
32C1 Maicao Colombia
47B1 Maiche France
43E4 Maidstone Eng
98B1 Maiduguri Nig
86A2 Maihar India
86C2 Maijdi Bang
76B3 Mail Kyun I Burma
84A1 Maimana Afghan
14B1 Main Chan Can
98B3 Mai-Ndombe L Zaïre
10D2 Maine State, USA
48B2 Maine Region France
44C2 Mainland I Scot
85D3 Mainpuri India
46A2 Maintenon France
101D2 Maintirano Madag
57B2 Mainz Germany
97A4 Maio I Cape Verde
29C2 Maipó Mt Arg/Chile
34D3 Maipú Arg
32D1 Maiquetia Ven
47B2 Maira R Italy
86C1 Mairābāri India
86C2 Maiskhal I Bang
107E4 Maitland New South Wales, Aust
108A2 Maitland S Australia, Aust
112C12 Maitri Base Ant
74D3 Maizuru Japan
70C4 Majene Indon
30B2 Majes R Peru
99D2 Maji Eth
72D2 Majia He R China
Majunga = Mahajanga
70C4 Makale Indon
86B1 Makalu Mt China/Nepal
98B2 Makanza Zaïre
52C2 Makarska Croatia
61F2 Makaryev Russian Fed
Makassar = Ujung Pandang
78D3 Makassar Str Indon
61H4 Makat Kazakhstan
97A4 Makeni Sierra Leone
60E4 Makeyevka Ukraine
100B3 Makgadikgadi Salt Pan Botswana
61G5 Makhachkala Russian Fed
99D3 Makindu Kenya
88H5 Makkah S Arabia
7E4 Makkovik Can
59C3 Makó Hung
98B2 Makokou Gabon
110C1 Makorako,Mt NZ

98B2 Makoua Congo
85C3 Makrāna India
85A3 Makran Coast Range Mts Pak
96C1 Makthar Tunisia
93D2 Mākū Iran
98C3 Makumbi Zaïre
74C4 Makurazaki Japan
97C4 Makurdi Nig
79B4 Malabang Phil
87A2 Malabar Coast India
89E7 Malabo Bioko
77C5 Malacca,Str of S E Asia
32C2 Málaga Colombia
50B2 Málaga Spain
101D3 Malaimbandy Madag
107F1 Malaita I Solomon Is
99D2 Malakal Sudan
84C2 Malakand Pak
78C4 Malang Indon
98B3 Malange Angola
97C3 Malanville Benin
39H7 Mälaren L Sweden
34B3 Malargüe Arg
12F3 Malaspina Gl USA
93C2 Malatya Turk
101C2 Malawi Republic, Africa
Malawi,L = Nyasa,L
79C4 Malaybalay Phil
90A3 Malāyer Iran
70B3 Malaysia Federation, S E Asia
93D2 Malazgirt Turk
58B2 Malbork Pol
56C2 Malchin Germany
18C2 Malden I
83B5 Maldives Is Indian O
104B4 Maldives Ridge Indian O
29F2 Maldonado Urug
47D1 Male Italy
85C4 Malegaon India
59B3 Malé Karpaty Upland Slovakia
101C2 Malema Mozam
84B2 Mālestān Afghan
38H5 Malgomaj L Sweden
95B3 Malha Well Sudan
20C2 Malheur L USA
97B3 Mali Republic, Africa
78D1 Malinau Indon
99E3 Malindi Kenya
Malines = Mechelen
40B2 Malin Head Pt Irish Rep
86A2 Malkala Range Mts India
85D4 Malkāpur India
55C2 Malkara Turk
54C2 Malko Türnovo Bulg
44B3 Mallaig Scot
95C2 Mallawi Egypt
47D1 Mallés Venosta Italy
51C2 Mallorca I Spain
45B2 Mallow Irish Rep
38G6 Malm Nor
38J5 Malmberget Sweden
46D1 Malmédy Germany
43C4 Malmesbury Eng
100A4 Malmesbury S Africa
39G7 Malmö Sweden
61G2 Malmyzh Russian Fed
79B3 Malolos Phil
15D2 Malone USA
101S1 Maloti Mts Lesotho
38F6 Måløy Nor
28A2 Malpelo I Colombia
34A2 Malpo R Chile
85D3 Mālpura India
8C2 Malta Montana, USA
53B3 Malta Chan Malta/Italy
53B3 Malta I Medit S
100A3 Maltahöhe Namibia
42D2 Malton Eng
39G6 Malung Sweden
87A1 Mālvan India
19B3 Malvern USA
85D4 Malwa Plat India

61G4 Malyy Uzen' R Kazakhstan
63D2 Mama Russian Fed
61H2 Mamadysh Russian Fed
99C2 Mambasa Zaïre
71E4 Mamberamo R Indon
98B2 Mambéré R CAR
98A2 Mamfé Cam
33D6 Mamoré R Bol
97A3 Mamou Guinea
101D2 Mampikony Madag
97B4 Mampong Ghana
94B3 Mamshit Hist Site Israel
100B3 Mamuno Botswana
97B4 Man Ivory Coast
21C4 Mana Hawaiian Is
101D3 Manabo Madag
33E4 Manacapuru Brazil
51C2 Manacor Spain
70D3 Manado Indon
25D3 Managua Nic
101D3 Manakara Madag
101D2 Mananara Madag
101D3 Mananjary Madag
111A3 Manapouri NZ
111A3 Manapouri,L NZ
86C1 Manas Bhutan
82C1 Manas China
65K5 Manas Hu L China
86A1 Manaslu Mt Nepal
16B2 Manasquan USA
33F4 Manaus Brazil
92B2 Manavgat Turk
93C2 Manbij Syria
42C3 Man,Calf of I Eng
87B1 Mancheral India
15D2 Manchester Connecticut, USA
42C3 Manchester Eng
10C2 Manchester New Hampshire, USA
16A2 Manchester Pennsylvania, USA
69E2 Manchuria Hist Region, China
91B4 Mand R Iran
101C2 Manda Tanz
35A2 Mandaguari Brazil
39F7 Mandal Nor
76B1 Mandalay Burma
68C2 Mandalgovi Mongolia
8C2 Mandan USA
14A2 Mandeona USA
99E2 Mandera Eth
26B3 Mandeville Jamaica
101C2 Mandimba Mozam
86A2 Mandla India
101D2 Mandritsara Madag
85D4 Mandsaur India
53C2 Manduria Italy
85B4 Mandvi India
87B2 Mandya India
58D2 Manevichi Ukraine
42D3 Manfield Eng
53C2 Manfredonia Italy
98B1 Manga Desert Region Niger
110C1 Mangakino NZ
54C2 Mangalia Rom
98B1 Mangalmé Chad
87A2 Mangalore India
78B3 Manggar Indon
68B3 Mangnia China
101C2 Mangoche Malawi
101D3 Mangoky R Madag
71D4 Mangole I Indon
85B4 Māngral India
63E2 Mangui China
8D3 Manhattan USA
31C6 Manhuacu Brazil
101D2 Mania R Madag
101C2 Manica Mozam
7D5 Manicouagan R Can
91A4 Manifah S Arabia
79B3 Manila Phil
109D2 Manilla Aust
97B3 Maninian Ivory Coast
86C2 Manipur State, India
86C2 Manipur R Burma
92A2 Manisa Turk

41C3 Man,Isle of Irish S
14A2 Manistee USA
14A2 Manistee R USA
14A1 Manistique USA
5H4 Manitoba Province, Can
5J4 Manitoba,L Can
13F2 Manito L Can
14A1 Manitou Is USA
7B5 Manitoulin I Can
14A2 Manitowoc USA
15C1 Maniwaki Can
32B2 Manizales Colombia
101D3 Manja Madag
106A4 Manjimup Aust
87B1 Mānjra R India
10A2 Mankato USA
97B4 Mankono Ivory Coast
12D2 Manley Hot Springs USA
110B1 Manly NZ
85C4 Manmād India
78A3 Manna Indon
108A2 Mannahill Aust
87B3 Mannar Sri Lanka
87B3 Mannar,G of India
87B2 Mannārgudi India
57B3 Mannheim Germany
13D1 Manning Can
17B1 Manning USA
108A2 Mannum Aust
97A4 Mano Sierra Leone
71E4 Manokwari Indon
98C3 Manono Zaïre
76B3 Manoron Burma
75B1 Mano-wan B Japan
74B2 Man'po N Korea
84D3 Mānsa India
100B2 Mansa Zambia
6B3 Mansel I Can
19B2 Mansfield Arkansas, USA
108C3 Mansfield Aust
19B3 Mansfield Louisiana, USA
16D1 Mansfield Massachusetts, USA
10B2 Mansfield Ohio, USA
15C2 Mansfield Pennsylvania, USA
71E2 Mansyu Deep Pacific O
32A4 Manta Ecuador
79A4 Mantalingajan,Mt Phil
32B6 Mantaro R Peru
22B2 Manteca USA
48C2 Mantes France
52B1 Mantova Italy
38J6 Mänttä Fin
61F2 Manturovo Russian Fed
35A2 Manuel Ribas Brazil
79B4 Manukan Phil
110B1 Manukau NZ
71F4 Manus I Pacific O
50B2 Manzanares Spain
25E2 Manzanillo Cuba
24B3 Manzanillo Mexico
63D3 Manzhouli China
94C3 Manzil Jordan
101C3 Manzini Swaziland
98B1 Mao Chad
72A2 Maomao Shan Mt China
73C5 Maoming China
101C3 Mapai Madag
71E3 Mapia Is Pacific O
79B4 Mapin I Phil
5H5 Maple Creek Can
101H1 Maputo Mozam
101H1 Maputo R Mozam
Ma Qu = Huange He
72A3 Maqu China
86B1 Maquan He R China
98B3 Maquela do Zombo Angola
34B3 Maquinchao Arg
31B3 Marabá Brazil
32C1 Maracaibo Ven
32D1 Maracay Ven
95A2 Marādah Libya
97C3 Maradi Niger
90A2 Marāgheh Iran

Maralal

99D2 **Maralal** Kenya
107F1 **Maramasike** /
　　Solomon Is
100B3 **Maramba** Zambia
90A2 **Marand** Iran
31B2 **Maranhäo** State,
　　Brazil
109C1 **Maranoa** *R* Aust
32B4 **Marañón** *R* Peru
7B5 **Marathon** Can
17B2 **Marathon** Florida,
　　USA
78D2 **Maratua** / Indon
23A2 **Maravatío** Mexico
79B4 **Marawi** Phil
34B2 **Marayes** Arg
50B2 **Marbella** Spain
106A3 **Marble Bar** Aust
100B3 **Marblehall** S Africa
16D1 **Marblehead** USA
57B2 **Marburg** Germany
57B2 **Marche** Belg
50A2 **Marchean** Spain
46C1 **Marche-en-Famenne**
　　Belg
32J7 **Marchena** / Ecuador
17B2 **Marco** USA
34C2 **Marcos Juárez** Arg
12E2 **Marcus Baker,Mt**
　　USA
15D2 **Marcy,Mt** USA
04C7 **Mardan** Pak
29E3 **Mar del Plata** Arg
93D2 **Mardin** Turk
99D1 **Mareb** *R* Eritrea/Eth
16B1 **Margaretville** USA
43E4 **Margate** Eng
54B1 **Marghita** Rom
109C4 **Maria** I Aust
104F3 **Mariana** *Is* Pacific O
13E1 **Mariana Lake** Can
104F3 **Marianas Trench**
　　Pacific O
86C1 **Mariäni** India
19B3 **Marianna** Arkansas,
　　USA
17A1 **Marianna** Florida,
　　USA
7G4 **Maria Van Diemen,C**
　　NZ
59B3 **Mariazell** Austria
52C1 **Maribor** Slovenia
99C2 **Maridi** Sudan
112B5 **Marie Byrd Land**
　　Region, Ant
27E3 **Marie Galante** /
　　Caribbean S
39H6 **Mariehamn** Fin
46C1 **Mariembourg** Belg
33G2 **Mariënberg** Surinam
100A3 **Mariental** Namibia
39G7 **Mariestad** Sweden
17B1 **Marietta** Georgia,
　　USA
14B3 **Marietta** Ohio, USA
19A3 **Marietta** Oklahoma,
　　USA
27Q2 **Marigot** Dominica
60B3 **Marijampole**
　　Lithuania
31B6 **Marília** Brazil
98B3 **Marimba** Angola
79B3 **Marinduque** / Phil
10B2 **Marinette** USA
30F3 **Maringá** Brazil
98C2 **Maringa** *R* Zaire
18B2 **Marion** Arkansas,
　　USA
18C2 **Marion** Illinois, USA
10B2 **Marion** Indiana, USA
10B2 **Marion** Ohio, USA
17C1 **Marion** S Carolina,
　　USA
11B3 **Marion,L** USA
107E2 **Marion Reef** Aust
21B2 **Mariposa** USA
22B2 **Mariposa** *R* USA
22B2 **Mariposa Res** USA
60C5 **Marista** *R* Bulg
60E4 **Mariupol'** Ukraine
61G2 **Mariyskaya**
　　Respublika,
　　Russian Fed
94B2 **Marjayoun** Leb

58D2 **Marjina Gorki**
　　Belorussia
94B3 **Marka** Jordan
99E2 **Marka** Somalia
56C1 **Markaryd** Sweden
43C3 **Market Drayton** Eng
43D3 **Market Harborough**
　　Eng
112A **Markham,Mt** Ant
22C1 **Markleeville** USA
16D1 **Marlboro**
　　Massachusetts, USA
107D3 **Marlborough** Aust
46B2 **Marle** France
19A3 **Marlin** USA
48C3 **Marmande** France
55C2 **Marmara Adi** / Turk
92A1 **Marmara,S of** Turk
55C3 **Marmaris** Turk
14B3 **Marmet** USA
52B1 **Marmolada** *Mt* Italy
12D3 **Marmot B** USA
47A1 **Marnay** France
46B2 **Marne** Department,
　　France
46B2 **Marne** *R* France
98B2 **Maro** Chad
101D2 **Maroantsetra** Madag
101C2 **Marondera** Zim
33G3 **Maroni** *R* French
　　Guiana
109D1 **Maroochydore** Aust
98B1 **Maroua** Cam
101D2 **Marovoay** Madag
11B4 **Marquesas Keys** *Is*
　　USA
10B2 **Marquette** USA
46A1 **Marquise** France
109C2 **Marra** *R* Aust
101H1 **Marracuene** Mozam
96B1 **Marrakech** Mor
109C3 **Marree** Aust
19B4 **Marrero** USA
101C2 **Marromeu** Mozam
101C2 **Marrupa** Mozam
92C2 **Marsa Alam** Egypt
99D2 **Marsabit** Kenya
53B3 **Marsala** Italy
49D3 **Marseille** France
12B2 **Marshall** Alaska,
　　USA
14A3 **Marshall** Illinois, USA
14B2 **Marshall** Michigan,
　　USA
18B2 **Marshall** Missouri,
　　USA
11A3 **Marshall** Texas, USA
105G3 **Marshall Is** Pacific O
18B2 **Marshfield** Missouri,
　　USA
26B1 **Marsh Harbour**
　　The Bahamas
19B4 **Marsh I** USA
12I2 **Marsh L** Can
76B2 **Martaban,G of** Burma
78A3 **Martapura** Indon
78C3 **Martapura** Indon
15D2 **Martha's Vineyard** /
　　USA
49D2 **Martigny** Switz
49B3 **Martigues** France
111C2 **Martinborough** NZ
34B3 **Martin de Loyola** Arg
23B1 **Martínez de la Torre**
　　Mexico
27E4 **Martinique** /
　　Caribbean S
17A1 **Martin,L** USA
15C3 **Martinsburg** USA
14B2 **Martins Ferry** USA
103G6 **Martin Vaz** /
　　Atlantic O
49D3 **Martizay** France
110C2 **Marton** NZ
50B2 **Martos** Spain
78D1 **Marudi** Malay
84B2 **Maruf** Afghan
75A2 **Marugame** Japan
85C3 **Mārwār** India
65H6 **Mary** Turkmenistan
107E3 **Maryborough**
　　Queensland, Aust
108B3 **Maryborough**
　　Victoria, Aust

5F4 **Mary Henry,Mt** Can
10C3 **Maryland** State, USA
42C2 **Maryport** Eng
21A2 **Marysville** California,
　　USA
18A2 **Marysville** Kansas,
　　USA
20B1 **Marysville**
　　Washington, USA
10A2 **Maryville** Iowa, USA
18B1 **Maryville** Missouri,
　　USA
95A2 **Marzuq** Libya
　　Masada = Mezada
94B2 **Mas'adah** Syria
99D3 **Masai Steppe**
　　Upland Tanz
99D3 **Masaka** Uganda
93E2 **Masally** Azerbaijan
74B3 **Masan** S Korea
101C2 **Masasi** Tanz
25D3 **Masaya** Nic
79B3 **Masbate** Phil
79B3 **Masbate** / Phil
96C1 **Mascara** Alg
23A1 **Mascota** Mexico
35D1 **Mascote** Brazil
101G1 **Maseru** Lesotho
66C3 **Mashad** Iran
84B2 **Mashaki** Afghan
90C2 **Mashhad** Iran
98B3 **Masi-Manimba** Zaire
99D2 **Masindi** Uganda
99C3 **Masisi** Zaire
90A3 **Masjed Soleyman**
　　Iran
101E2 **Masoala** *C* Madag
10A2 **Mason City** USA
91C5 **Masqat** Oman
52B2 **Massa** Italy
10C2 **Massachusetts** State,
　　USA
15D2 **Massachusetts B**
　　USA
98B1 **Massakori** Chad
101C3 **Massangena** Mozam
101C3 **Massawa = Mits'iwa**
15D2 **Massena** USA
98B1 **Massénya** Chad
14B1 **Massey** Can
49C2 **Massif Central** *Mts*
　　France
26C3 **Massif de la Hotte**
　　Mts Haiti
101D3 **Massif de l'Isalo**
　　Upland Madag
98C2 **Massif des Bongo**
　　Upland CAR
49D2 **Massif du Pelvoux**
　　Mts France
101D2 **Massif du**
　　Tsaratanana *Mt*
　　Madag
14B2 **Massillon** USA
97B3 **Massina** Region, Mali
101C3 **Massinga** Mozam
101C3 **Massingir** Mozam
61H4 **Masteksay**
　　Kazakhstan
111C2 **Masterton** NZ
74C4 **Masuda** Japan
98B3 **Masuku** Gabon
100C3 **Masvingo** Zim
92C2 **Maşyāf** Syria
98B3 **Matadi** Zaire
25D3 **Matadalpa** Nic
7C4 **Matagami** Can
9D4 **Matagorda B** USA
110C1 **Matakana I** NZ
100A2 **Matala** Angola
87C3 **Matale** Sri Lanka
97A3 **Matam** Sen
97C3 **Matameye** Niger
24C2 **Matamoros** Mexico
95B2 **Ma'tan as Sarra** *Well*
　　Libya
7D5 **Matane** Can
25D2 **Matanzas** Cuba
34A2 **Mataquito** *R* Chile
87C3 **Matara** Sri Lanka
106A1 **Mataram** Indon

30B2 **Matarani** Peru
51C1 **Mataró** Spain
111A3 **Mataura** NZ
24B2 **Matehuala** Mexico
27L1 **Matelot** Trinidad
53C2 **Matera** Italy
59C3 **Mátészalka** Hung
85D3 **Mathura** India
79C4 **Mati** Phil
78D3 **Matisiri** / Indon
43D3 **Matlock** Eng
33F6 **Mato Grosso** Brazil
33F6 **Mato Grosso** State,
　　Brazil
30E2 **Mato Grosso do Sul**
　　State, Brazil
101H1 **Matola** Mozam
91C5 **Matrah** Oman
92A3 **Matrûh** Egypt
74C3 **Matsue** Japan
74E2 **Matsumae** Japan
74D3 **Matsumoto** Japan
74D4 **Matsusaka** Japan
74D3 **Matsuyama** Japan
7B5 **Mattagami** *R* Can
15C1 **Mattawa** Can
52A1 **Matterhorn** *Mt* Italy/
　　Switz
26C2 **Matthew Town**
　　The Bahamas
14B2 **Mattoon** USA
84B2 **Matun** Afghan
27L1 **Matura B** Trinidad
33E2 **Maturín** Ven
86A1 **Mau** India
101C2 **Maúa** Mozam
46B2 **Maubeuge** France
108B2 **Maude** Aust
103J8 **Maud Seamount**
　　Atlantic O
21C4 **Maui** / Hawaiian Is
34A3 **Maule** *R* Chile
14B2 **Maumee** USA
14B2 **Maumee** *R* USA
100B2 **Maun** Botswana
21C4 **Mauna Kea** *Mt*
　　Hawaiian Is
21C4 **Mauna Loa** *Mt*
　　Hawaiian Is
4F3 **Maunoir,L** Can
4F3 **Maunoir,L** Can
48C2 **Mauriac** France
96A2 **Mauritania** Republic,
　　Africa
100E3 **Mauritius** / Indian O
100B2 **Mavinga** Angola
86C2 **Mawlaik** Burma
　　Mawlamyine =
　　Moulmein
112C10 **Mawson** *Base* Ant
78B3 **Maya** / Indon
63F2 **Maya** *R* Russian Fed
93D2 **Mayädin** Syria
11C4 **Mayaguana** /
　　The Bahamas
27D3 **Mayagüez** Puerto
　　Rico
97C3 **Mayahi** Niger
98B3 **Mayama** Congo
90C2 **Mayamey** Iran
42B2 **Maybole** Scot
10C3 **May,C** USA
109C4 **Maydena** Aust
46D1 **Mayen** Germany
48B2 **Mayenne** France
13D2 **Mayerthorpe** Can
18C2 **Mayfield** USA
61E5 **Maykop** Russian Fed
65H6 **Maymaneh** Afghan
76B1 **Maymyo** Burma
4E3 **Mayo** Can
45B2 **Mayo** County,
　　Irish Rep
16A3 **Mayo** USA
45B1 **Mayo,Mts of**
　　Irish Rep
79B3 **Mayon** *Mt* Phil
51C2 **Mayor** *Mt* Spain
34C3 **Mayor Buratovich**
　　Arg
110C1 **Mayor I** NZ
30D2 **Mayor P Lagerenza**
　　Par

101D2 Mayotte *I* Indian O
27H2 May Pen Jamaica
16B3 May Point,C USA
47D1 Mayrhofen Austria
16B3 Mays Landing USA
14B3 Maysville USA
98B3 Mayumba Gabon
100B2 Mazabuka Zambia
84D1 Mazar China
94B3 Mazãr Jordan
53B3 Mazara del Vallo Italy
84B1 Mazar-i-Sharif Afghan
24B2 Mazatlán Mexico
60B2 Mazeikiai Lithuania
94B3 Mazra Jordan
101C3 Mbabane Swaziland
98B3 Mbaiki CAR
99D3 Mbala Zambia
100B3 Mbalabala Zim
99D2 Mbale Uganda
98B2 Mbalmayo Cam
98B2 Mbam *R* Cam
101C2 Mbamba Bay Tanz
98B3 Mbandaka Zaire
98B3 Mbanza Congo Angola
98B3 Mbanza-Ngungu Zaïre
99D3 Mbarara Uganda
98B2 Mbènza Congo
98B2 Mbère *R* Cam
99D3 Mbeya Tanz
98B3 Mbinda Congo
97A3 Mbout Maur
98C3 Mbuji-Mayi Zaïre
99D3 Mbulu Tanz
96B2 Mcherrah Region, Alg
101C2 Mchinji Malawi
76D3 Mdrak Viet
9B3 Mead,L USA
5H4 Meadow Lake Can
14B2 Meadville USA
7E4 Mealy Mts Can
109C1 Meandarra Aust
5G4 Meander River Can
45C2 Meath County, Irish Rep
49C2 Meaux France
16C1 Mechanicville USA
56A2 Mechelen Belg
96B1 Mecheria Alg
56C2 Mecklenburg-Vorpommern *State* Germany
56C2 Mecklenburger Bucht *B* Germany
101C2 Meconta Mozam
101C2 Mecubúri Mozam
101D2 Mecufi Mozam
101C2 Mecula Mozam
70A3 Medan Indon
34C3 Médanos Arg
34D2 Médanos Arg
13E2 Medecine Hat Can
32B2 Medellín Colombia
96D1 Medenine Tunisia
8A2 Medford USA
34B2 Medea Arg
54B1 Mediaş Rom
20C1 Medical Lake USA
5G5 Medicine Hat Can
35C1 Medina Brazil
80B3 Medina *S* Arabia
50B1 Medinaceli Spain
50B1 Medina del Campo Spain
50A1 Medina de Rio Seco Spain
86B2 Medinipur India
88E4 Mediterranean S Europe
13F2 Medley Can
61J3 Mednogorsk Russian Fed
86D1 Mêdog China
98B2 Médouneu Gabon
61F3 Medvedista *R* Russian Fed
64E3 Medvezh'yegorsk Russian Fed

106A3 Meekatharra Aust
84D3 Meerut India
99D2 Mega Eth
55B3 Megalópolis Greece
55B3 Mégara Greece
86C1 Meghálaya State, India
86C2 Meghna *R* Bang
94B2 Megiddo *Hist Site* Israel
91B4 Mehran *R* Iran
90B3 Mehriz Iran
35B1 Meia Ponte *R* Brazil
98B2 Meiganga Cam
76B1 Meiktila Burma
47C1 Meiringen Switz
73A4 Meishan China
57C2 Meissen Germany
73D5 Mei Xian China
73D5 Meizhou China
30B3 Mejillones Chile
98B2 Mekambo Gabon
99D1 Mek'elê Eth
96B1 Meknès Mor
76D3 Mekong *R* Camb
97C3 Mékrou *R* Benin
77C5 Melaka Malay
104F4 Melanesia *Region* Pacific O
78C3 Melawi *R* Indon
107D4 Melbourne Aust
11B4 Melbourne USA
9C4 Melchor Mužguiz Mexico
61J3 Meleuz Russian Fed
98B1 Melfi Chad
5H4 Melfort Can
96B1 Melilla N W Africa
29B4 Melimoyu *Mt* Chile
34C2 Melincué Arg
34A2 Melipilla Chile
60E4 Melitopol' Ukraine
6D2 Melville Bugt *B* Greenland
99D2 Melka Guba Eth
101H1 Melmoth S Africa
34C2 Melo Arg
29F2 Melo Urug
22B2 Melones Res USA
12D1 Melozitna *R* USA
47C1 Mels Switz
43D3 Melton Mowbray Eng
49C2 Melun France
5H4 Melville Can
27Q2 Melville,C Dominica
4F3 Melville Hills *Mts* Can
106C2 Melville I Aust
4G2 Melville I Can
7E4 Melville,L Can
6B3 Melville Pen Can
45B1 Melvin,L Irish Rep
101D2 Memba Mozam
106A1 Memboro Indon
57C3 Memmingen Germany
78B2 Mempawah Indon
11B3 Memphis Tennessee, USA
19B3 Mena USA
43B3 Menai Str Wales
97C3 Menaka Mali
14A2 Menasha USA
78C3 Mendawai *R* Indon
49C3 Mende France
99D2 Mendebo *Mts* Eth
43C4 Mendip Hills *Upland* Eng
20B2 Mendocino,C USA
105J2 Mendocino Seascarp Pacific O
22B2 Mendota California, USA
29C2 Mendoza Arg
29C3 Mendoza State, Arg
55C3 Menemen Turk
46B1 Menen Belg
72D3 Mengcheng China
78B3 Menggala Indon
76B1 Menghai China
73A5 Mengla China
76B1 Menglian China
73A5 Mengzi China
107D4 Meninee Aust

108B2 Menindee L Aust
108A3 Meningie Aust
14A1 Menominee USA
14A2 Menomonee Falls USA
100A2 Menongue Angola
51C1 Menorca *I* Spain
12F2 Mentasta Mts USA
78B3 Mentok Indon
14B2 Mentor USA
46B2 Menton France
72A2 Menyuan China
61H2 Menzelinsk Russian Fed
56B2 Meppen Germany
78D2 Merah Indon
18B2 Meramec *R* USA
52B1 Merano Italy
71F4 Merauke Indon
8A3 Merced USA
22B2 Merced *R* USA
29B2 Mercedario *Mt* Chile
29C2 Mercedes Arg
29E2 Mercedes Buenos Aires, Arg
30E4 Mercedes Corrientes, Arg
29E2 Mercedes Urug
110C1 Mercury B NZ
110C1 Mercury Is NZ
4F2 Mercy B Can
6D3 Mercy,C Can
99E2 Meregh Somalia
76B3 Mergui Burma
76B3 Mergui Arch Burma
25D2 Mérida Mexico
50A2 Mérida Spain
32C2 Mérida Ven
11B3 Meridian USA
109C3 Merimbula Aust
108B2 Meringur Aust
95C3 Merowe Sudan
106A4 Merredin Aust
42B2 Merrick *Mt* Scot
14A2 Merrillville USA
13C2 Merritt Can
17B2 Merritt Island USA
109D2 Merriwa Aust
99E1 Mersa Fatma Eritrea
51B2 Mers el Kebir Alg
42C3 Mersey *R* Eng
42C3 Merseyside Metropolitan County, Eng
92B2 Mersin Turk
77C5 Mersing Malay
85C3 Merta India
43C4 Merthyr Tydfil Wales
50A2 Mertola Port
99D3 Meru *Mt* Tanz
60E5 Merzifon Turk
57B3 Merzig Germany
9B3 Mesa USA
46E1 Meschede Germany
93D1 Mescit Dağ *Mt* Turk
12C3 Meshik USA
99C2 Meshra Er Req Sudan
47C1 Mesocco Switz
55B3 Mesolóngion Greece
19A3 Mesquite Texas, USA
101C2 Messalo *R* Mozam
53C3 Messina Italy
100B3 Messina S Africa
55B3 Messíni Greece
55B3 Messiniakós Kólpos *G* Greece
54B2 Mesta *R* Bulg
51B1 Mestre Italy
32C3 Meta *R* Colombia
60D2 Meta *R* Russian Fed
32D2 Meta *R* Ven
6C3 Meta Incognito Pen Can
19B4 Metairie USA
20C1 Metaline Falls USA
30D4 Metán Arg
101C2 Metangula Mozam
53C2 Metaponto Italy
44C3 Methil Scot
16D1 Methuen USA
111B2 Methven NZ
12H3 Metlakatla USA

18C2 Metropolis USA
87B2 Mettür India
49D2 Metz France
70A3 Meulaboh Indon
46A2 Meulan France
46C2 Meuse Department, France
49D2 Meuse *R* France
19A3 Mexia USA
24A1 Mexicali Mexico
24B2 Mexico Federal Republic, Cent America
24C3 México Mexico
23A2 México State, Mexico
18B2 Mexico USA
24C2 Mexico,G of Cent America
94B3 Mezada *Hist Site*
23B2 Mezcala Mexico
64F3 Mezen' Russian Fed
64G2 Mezhdusharskiy, Ostrov *I* Russian Fed
85D4 Mhow India
23B2 Miahuatlán Mexico
11B4 Miami Florida, USA
18B2 Miami Oklahoma, USA
11B4 Miami Beach USA
90A2 Miandowāb Iran
101D2 Miandrivazo Madag
90A2 Miãneh Iran
84C2 Mianwali Pak
73A3 Mianyang China
73C3 Mianyang China
73A3 Mianzhu China
72E2 Miaodao Qundao *Arch* China
73B4 Miao Ling *Upland* China
61K3 Miass Russian Fed
59C3 Michalovce Slovakia
27D3 Miches Dom Rep
10B2 Michigan State, USA
14A2 Michigan City USA
10B2 Michigan,L USA
7B5 Michipicoten I Can
23A2 Michoacan State, Mexico
54C2 Michurin Bulg
61F3 Michurinsk Russian Fed
104F3 Micronesia *Region* Pacific O
78B2 Midai *I* Indon
102F4 Mid Atlantic Ridge Atlantic O
46B1 Middelburg Neth
20B2 Middle Alkali L USA
16D2 Middleboro USA
100B4 Middleburg Cape Province, S Africa
16A2 Middleburg Pennsylvania, USA
101G1 Middleburg Transvaal, S Africa
16B1 Middleburgh USA
15D2 Middlebury USA
11B3 Middlesboro USA
42D2 Middlesbrough Eng
16C2 Middletown Connecticut, USA
16B3 Middletown Delaware, USA
15D2 Middletown New York, USA
14B3 Middletown Ohio, USA
16A2 Middletown Pennsylvania, USA
96B1 Midelt Mor
43C4 Mid Glamorgan County, Wales
104B4 Mid Indian Basin Indian O
104B4 Mid Indian Ridge Indian O
7C5 Midland Can
14B2 Midland Michigan, USA
9C3 Midland Texas, USA
101D3 Midongy Atsimo Madag

Mid Pacific Mts

105G2 **Mid Pacific Mts** Pacific O
20C2 **Midvale** USA
105H2 **Midway Is** Pacific O
18A2 **Midwest City** USA
93D2 **Midyat** Turk
54B2 **Midzör** *Mt* Serbia, Yugos
59B2 **Mielec** Pol
54C1 **Miercurea-Ciuc** Rom
50A1 **Mieres** Spain
16A2 **Mifflintown** USA
75A2 **Mihara** Japan
72D1 **Mijun Shuiku** *Res* China
54B2 **Mikhaylovgrad** Bulg
61F3 **Mikhaylovka** Russian Fed
65J4 **Mikhaylovskiy** Russian Fed
38K6 **Mikkeli** Fin
55C3 **Mikonos** *I* Greece
59B3 **Mikulov** Czech Republic
99D3 **Mikumi** Tanz
74D3 **Mikuni-sammyaku** *Mts* Japan
75B2 **Mikura-jima** *I* Japan
32B4 **Milagro** Ecuador
 Milan = **Milano**
51C2 **Milana** Alg
101C2 **Milange** Mozam
52A1 **Milano** Italy
92A2 **Milas** Turk
107D4 **Mildura** Aust
73A5 **Mile** China
93D3 **Mileh Tharthār** *L* Iraq
107E3 **Miles** Aust
8C2 **Miles City** USA
16C2 **Milford** Connecticut, USA
15C3 **Milford** Delaware, USA
15D2 **Milford** Massachusetts, USA
18A1 **Milford** Nebraska, USA
16B2 **Milford** Pennsylvania, USA
43B4 **Milford Haven** Wales
43B4 **Milford Haven** *Sd* Wales
18A2 **Milford L** USA
111A2 **Milford Sd** NZ
13E2 **Milk River** Can
49C3 **Millau** France
16C2 **Millbrook** USA
17B1 **Milledgeville** USA
12F2 **Miller,Mt** USA
61F4 **Millerovo** Russian Fed
16A2 **Millersburg** USA
108A1 **Millers Creek** Aust
10C1 **Millers Falls** USA
16C2 **Millerton** USA
22C2 **Millerton L** USA
108B3 **Millicent** Aust
109D1 **Millmerran** Aust
45B2 **Milltown Malbay** Irish Rep
22A2 **Mill Valley** USA
15D3 **Millville** USA
6H2 **Milne Land** *I* Greenland
21C4 **Miloli** Hawaiian Is
55B3 **Milos** *I* Greece
107D3 **Milparinka** Aust
16A2 **Milroy** USA
111A3 **Milton** NZ
16A2 **Milton** Pennsylvania, USA
10B2 **Milwaukee** USA
51C2 **Mina** *R* Alg
93E4 **Minā' al Ahmadī** Kuwait
91C4 **Mināb** Iran
74C4 **Minamata** Japan
78A2 **Minas** Indon
29E2 **Minas** Urug
31B5 **Minas Gerais** State, Brazil
35C1 **Minas Novas** Brazil
25C3 **Minatitlan** Mexico

76A1 **Minbu** Burma
76A1 **Minbya** Burma
34A2 **Mincha** Chile
44A3 **Minch,Little** *Sd* Scot
44A2 **Minch,North** *Sd* Scot
40B2 **Minch,The** *Sd* Scot
12D2 **Minchumina,L** USA
47D2 **Mincio** *R* Italy
79B4 **Mindanao** *I* Phil
19B3 **Minden** Louisiana, USA
56B2 **Minden** Germany
108B2 **Mindona L** Aust
79B3 **Mindoro** *I* Phil
79B3 **Mindoro Str** Phil
45C3 **Mine Hd** *C* Irish Rep
43C4 **Minehead** Eng
30F2 **Mineiros** Brazil
19A3 **Mineola** USA
23B1 **Mineral de Monte** Mexico
16A2 **Minersville** USA
108B2 **Mingary** Aust
72A2 **Minhe** China
87A3 **Minicoy** *I* India
73D4 **Min Jiang** *R* Fujian, China
73A4 **Min Jiang** *R* Sichuan, China
22C2 **Minkler** USA
108A2 **Minlaton** Aust
72A2 **Minle** China
97C4 **Minna** Nig
10A2 **Minneapolis** USA
5J4 **Minnedosa** Can
10A2 **Minnesota** State, USA
50A1 **Miño** *R* Spain
8C2 **Minot** USA
72A2 **Minqin** China
72A3 **Min Shan** *Upland* China
60C3 **Minsk** Belorussia
58C2 **Minsk Mazowiecki** Pol
12E2 **Minto** USA
4G2 **Minto Inlet** *B* Can
7C4 **Minto,L** Can
63B2 **Minusinsk** Russian Fed
72A3 **Min Xian** China
7E5 **Miquelon** Can
22D3 **Mirage L** USA
87A1 **Miraj** India
29E3 **Miramar** Arg
84B2 **Miram Shah** Pak
50B1 **Miranda de Ebro** Spain
47D2 **Mirandola** Italy
84B2 **Mir Bachchen Küt** Afghan
78D1 **Miri** Malay
96A3 **Mirik,C** Maur
63A1 **Mirnoye** Russian Fed
63D1 **Mirnyy** Russian Fed
112C9 **Mirnyy** *Base* Ant
84C2 **Mirpur** Pak
85B3 **Mirpur Khas** Pak
55B3 **Mirtoan S** Greece
74B3 **Miryang** S Korea
86A1 **Mirzāpur** India
23B2 **Misantla** Mexico
84C1 **Misgar** Pak
14A2 **Mishawaka** USA
12B1 **Misheguk Mt** USA
75A2 **Mi-shima** *I* Japan
107E2 **Misima** *I* Solomon Is
30F4 **Misiones** State, Arg
59C3 **Miskolc** Hung
94C2 **Mismiyah** Syria
71E4 **Misoöl** *I* Indon
95A1 **Misrātah** Libya
7B5 **Missinaibi** *R* Can
20B1 **Mission City** Can
15C2 **Mississauga** Can
11A3 **Mississippi** State, USA
11A3 **Mississippi** *R* USA
19C3 **Mississippi Delta** USA
8B2 **Missoula** Mor
96B1 **Missour** Mor
11A3 **Missouri** State, USA

10A2 **Missouri** *R* USA
10C1 **Mistassini,L** Can
89B3 **Misti** *Mt* Peru
109C1 **Mitchell** Aust
8D2 **Mitchell** USA
107D2 **Mitchell** *R* Aust
11B3 **Mitchell,Mt** USA
45B2 **Mitchelstown** Irish Rep
84C3 **Mithankot** Pak
55C3 **Mitilíni** Greece
23B2 **Mitla** Mexico
54B2 **Mitrovica** Serbia, Yugos
95C3 **Mits'iwa** Eritrea
32C3 **Mitú** Colombia
99C3 **Mitumbar** *Mts* Zaire
98C3 **Mitwaba** Zaire
98B2 **Mitzic** Gabon
75B1 **Miura** Japan
72C3 **Mi Xian** China
69F3 **Miyake** *I* Japan
75B2 **Miyake-jima** *I* Japan
69E4 **Miyako** *I* Japan
74C4 **Miyakonojō** Japan
74C4 **Miyazaki** Japan
75B1 **Miyazu** Japan
74C4 **Miyoshi** Japan
72D1 **Miyun** China
99D2 **Mizan Teferi** Eth
95A1 **Mizdah** Libya
45B3 **Mizen Hd** *C* Irish Rep
54C1 **Mizil** Rom
86C2 **Mizo Hills** India
86C2 **Mizoram** Union Territory, India
94B3 **Mizpe Ramon** Israel
112B11 **Mizuho** *Base* Ant
74E3 **Mizusawa** Japan
39H7 **Mjolby** Sweden
100B2 **Mkushi** Zambia
111C1 **Mkuzi** S Africa
57C2 **Mladá Boleslav** Czech Republic
58C2 **Mława** Pol
52C2 **Mljet** *I* Croatia
100B3 **Mmabatho** S Africa
84D2 **Mnaii** India
97A4 **Moa** *R* Sierra Leone
94B3 **Moab** Region, Jordan
9C3 **Moab** USA
98B3 **Moanda** Congo
98B3 **Moanda** Gabon
99C3 **Moba** Zaire
75C1 **Mobara** Japan
98C2 **Mobaye** CAR
98C2 **Mobayi** Zaire
10A3 **Moberly** USA
11B3 **Mobile** USA
11B3 **Mobile B** USA
8C2 **Mobridge** USA
101D2 **Moçambique** Mozam
76C1 **Moc Chau** Viet
100B3 **Mochudi** Botswana
101D2 **Mocímboa da Praia** Mozam
32B3 **Mocoa** Colombia
35B2 **Mococa** Brazil
34D2 **Mocoreta** *R* Arg
23B1 **Moctezuma** *R* Mexico
101C2 **Mocuba** Mozam
47B2 **Modane** France
101G1 **Modder** *R* S Africa
52B2 **Modena** Italy
46D2 **Moder** *R* France
8A3 **Modesto** USA
22B2 **Modesto Res** USA
53B3 **Modica** Italy
59B3 **Mödling** Austria
107D4 **Moe** Aust
47C1 **Moesa** *R* Switz
42C2 **Moffat** Scot
84D2 **Moga** India
35B2 **Mogi das Cruzes** Brazil
60C3 **Mogilev** Belorussia
60C4 **Mogilev Podolskiy** Ukraine
35B2 **Mogi-Mirim** Brazil
101D2 **Mogincual** Mozam
47E2 **Mogliano** Italy

34B2 **Mogna** Arg
68D1 **Mogocha** Russian Fed
65K4 **Mogochin** Russian Fed
50A2 **Moguer** Spain
110C1 **Mohaka** *R* NZ
86C2 **Mohanganj** Bang
15D2 **Mohawk** *R* USA
99D3 **Mohoro** Tanz
65J5 **Mointy** Kazakhstan
38G5 **Mo i Rana** Nor
48C3 **Moissac** France
21B2 **Mojave** USA
22D3 **Mojave** *R* USA
9B3 **Mojave Desert** USA
78C4 **Mojokerto** Indon
86B1 **Mokama** India
110B1 **Mokau** *R* NZ
22B1 **Mokelumne** *R* USA
 Mokelumne Aqueduct USA
22B1 **Mokelumne Hill** USA
22B1 **Mokelumne North Fork** *R* USA
101G1 **Mokhotlong** Lesotho
96D1 **Moknine** Tunisia
76B2 **Mokokchüng** India
98B1 **Mokolo** Cam
74B4 **Mokp'o** S Korea
61F3 **Moksha** *R* Russian Fed
23B1 **Molango** Mexico
55B3 **Molaoi** Greece
38F6 **Molde** Nor
60C4 **Moldova** Republic, Europe
54B1 **Moldoveanu** *Mt* Rom
100B3 **Molepolole** Botswana
53C2 **Molfetta** Italy
34A3 **Molina** Chile
30B2 **Mollendo** Peru
60C3 **Molodechno** Belorussia
112C11 **Molodezhnaya** *Base* Ant
21C4 **Molokai** *I* Hawaiian Is
61G2 **Moloma** *R* Russian Fed
109C2 **Molong** Aust
100B3 **Molopo** *R* Botswana
98B2 **Molounddou** Cam
8D1 **Molson L** Can
71D4 **Molucca** S Indon
71D4 **Moluccas** *Is* Indon
101C2 **Moma** Mozam
31C3 **Mombaca** Brazil
00D3 **Mumbasa** Kenya
98C2 **Mompono** Zaire
56C2 **Mon** *I* Den
44A3 **Monach** *Is* Scot
49D3 **Monaco** Principality, Europe
44B3 **Monadhliath** *Mts* Scot
45C1 **Monaghan** County, Irish Rep
45C1 **Monaghan** Irish Rep
27D3 **Mona Pass** Caribbean S
13B2 **Monarch Mt** Can
5G4 **Monashee Mts** Can
41B3 **Monastereven** Irish Rep
47B2 **Moncalieri** Italy
31B2 **Monção** Brazil
38L5 **Monchegorsk** Russian Fed
56B2 **Mönchen-gladbach** Germany
24B2 **Monclova** Mexico
7D5 **Moncton** Can
9C4 **Monctova** Mexico
50A1 **Mondego** *R* Port
52A2 **Mondovi** Italy
27H1 **Moneague** Jamaica
14C2 **Monessen** USA
18B2 **Monett** USA
52B1 **Monfalcone** Italy

50A1	**Monforte de Lemos** Spain
98C2	**Monga** Zaïre
98C2	**Mongala** *R* Zaïre
99D2	**Mongalla** Sudan
76D1	**Mong Cai** Viet
98B1	**Mongo** Chad
68B2	**Mongolia** Republic, Asia
100B2	**Mongu** Zambia
21B2	**Monitor Range** *Mts* USA
98C3	**Monkoto** Zaïre
43C4	**Monmouth** Eng
18B1	**Monmouth** USA
13C2	**Monmouth,Mt** Can
97C4	**Mono** *R* Togo
21B2	**Mono L** USA
53C2	**Monopoli** Italy
51B1	**Monreal del Campo** Spain
19B3	**Monroe** Louisiana, USA
14B2	**Monroe** Michigan, USA
20B1	**Monroe** Washington, USA
18B2	**Monroe City** USA
97A4	**Monrovia** Lib
20D3	**Monrovia** USA
56A2	**Mons** Belg
47D2	**Monselice** Italy
16C1	**Monson** USA
58B1	**Mönsterås** Sweden
101D2	**Montagne d'Ambre** *Mt* Madag
96C1	**Montagnes des Ouled Nail** *Mts* Alg
12E3	**Montague I** USA
49C3	**Mont Aigoual** *Mt* France
48B2	**Montaigu** France
53C3	**Montallo** *Mt* Italy
88B2	**Montana** State, USA
50A1	**Montañas de León** *Mts* Spain
49C2	**Montargis** France
48C3	**Montauban** France
15D2	**Montauk** USA
15D2	**Montauk Pt** USA
49D2	**Montbéliard** France
52A1	**Mont Blanc** *Mt* France/Italy
49C2	**Montceau les Mines** France
51C1	**Montceny** *Mt* Spain
49D3	**Mont Cinto** *Mt* Corse
46C2	**Montcornet** France
48B3	**Mont-de-Marsan** France
42D2	**Montdidier** France
30D2	**Monteagudo** Bol
33G4	**Monte Alegre** Brazil
52B2	**Monte Amiata** *Mt* Italy
47D2	**Monte Baldo** *Mt* Italy
15C1	**Montebello** Can
106A3	**Monte Bello Is** Aust
47E2	**Montebelluna** Italy
49D3	**Monte Carlo** Monaco
35B1	**Monte Carmelo** Brazil
34D2	**Monte Caseros** Arg
52B2	**Monte Cimone** *Mt* Italy
52A2	**Monte Cinto** *Mt* Corse
34B2	**Monte Coman** Arg
52B2	**Monte Corno** *Mt* Italy
27C3	**Montecristi** Dom Rep
52B2	**Montecristo I** Italy
23A1	**Monte Escobedo** Mexico
52C2	**Monte Gargano** *Mt* Italy
26B3	**Montego Bay** Jamaica
47D2	**Monte Grappa** *Mt* Italy
47C2	**Monte Lesima** *Mt* Italy
49C3	**Montélimar** France
53B2	**Monte Miletto** *Mt* Italy
50A2	**Montemo-o-Novo** Port
24C2	**Montemorelos** Mexico
26B5	**Montená** Colombia
54A2	**Montenegro** Republic, Yugos
35D1	**Monte Pascoal** *Mt* Brazil
34A2	**Monte Patria** Chile
53C3	**Monte Pollino** *Mt* Italy
101C2	**Montepuez** Mozam
8A3	**Monterey** California, USA
15C3	**Monterey** Virginia, USA
8A3	**Monterey B** USA
32B2	**Monteria** Colombia
30D2	**Montero** Bol
47B2	**Monte Rosa** *Mt* Italy/Switz
24B2	**Monterrey** Mexico
31C5	**Montes Claros** Brazil
50B2	**Montes de Toledo** *Mts* Spain
29E2	**Montevideo** Urug
52A2	**Monte Viso** *Mt* Italy
27P2	**Mont Gimie** *Mt* St Lucia
11B3	**Montgomery** Alabama, USA
96C2	**Mont Grébioun** Niger
46C2	**Montherme** France
47B1	**Monthey** Switz
19B3	**Monticello** Arkansas, USA
16B2	**Monticello** New York, USA
9C3	**Monticello** Utah, USA
53A2	**Monti del Gennargentu** *Mt* Sardegna
47D2	**Monti Lessini** *Mts* Italy
53B3	**Monti Nebrodi** *Mts* Italy
7C5	**Mont-Laurier** Can
48C2	**Montluçon** France
7C5	**Montmagny** Can
46C2	**Montmédy** France
49C3	**Mont Mézenc** *Mt* France
46B2	**Montmirail** France
50B2	**Montoro** Spain
49D3	**Mont Pelat** *Mt* France
14B2	**Montpelier** Ohio, USA
10C2	**Montpelier** Vermont, USA
49C3	**Montpellier** France
7C5	**Montréal** Can
48C1	**Montreuil** France
52A1	**Montreux** Switz
47B1	**Mont Risoux** *Mt* France
8C3	**Montrose** Colorado, USA
40C2	**Montrose** Scot
48B2	**Mont-St-Michel** France
96B1	**Monts des Ksour** *Mts* Alg
51C3	**Monts des Ouled Neil** *Mts* Alg
51C2	**Monts du Hodna** *Mts* Alg
27E3	**Montserrat I** Caribbean S
10C1	**Monts Otish** *Mts* Can
12B1	**Monument Mt** USA
9B3	**Monument V** USA
98C2	**Monveda** Zaïre
76B1	**Monywa** Burma
52A1	**Monza** Italy
100B2	**Monze** Zambia
101H1	**Mooi** *R* S Africa
101G1	**Mooi River** S Africa
108B1	**Moomba** Aust
109D2	**Moonbi Range** *Mts* Aust
108B1	**Moonda L** Aust
109D1	**Moonie** Aust
109C1	**Moonie** *R* Aust
108A2	**Moonta** Aust
106A4	**Moora** Aust
106A3	**Moore,L** Aust
42C2	**Moorfoot Hills** Scot
8D2	**Moorhead** USA
22C3	**Moorpark** USA
7B4	**Moose** *R* Can
5H4	**Moose Jaw** Can
5H4	**Moosomin** Can
7B4	**Moosonee** Can
16D2	**Moosup** USA
101C2	**Mopeia** Mozam
97B3	**Mopti** Mali
30B2	**Moquegua** Peru
39G6	**Mora** Sweden
31D3	**Morada** Brazil
84D3	**Morādābād** India
35B1	**Morada Nova de Minas** *L* Brazil
101D2	**Morafenobe** Madag
101D2	**Moramanga** Madag
27J2	**Morant Bay** Jamaica
27J2	**Morant Pt** Jamaica
87B3	**Moratuwa** Sri Lanka
59B3	**Morava** *R* Austria/Slovakia
54B2	**Morava** *R* Serbia, Yugos
90C2	**Moraveh Tappeh** Iran
40C2	**Moray Firth** *Estuary* Scot
47C1	**Morbegno** Italy
85C4	**Morbi** India
93D2	**Mor Dağ** *Mt* Turk
5J5	**Morden** Can
61F3	**Mordvodskaya Respublika,** Russian Fed
42C2	**Morecambe** Eng
42C2	**Morecambe B** Eng
107D3	**Moree** Aust
14B3	**Morehead** USA
47C1	**Mörel** Switz
24B3	**Morelia** Mexico
23B2	**Morelos** State, Mexico
85D3	**Morena** India
5E4	**Moresby I** Can
109D1	**Moreton I** Aust
46B2	**Moreuil** France
19B4	**Morgan City** USA
22B2	**Morgan Hill** USA
14C3	**Morgantown** USA
101G1	**Morgenzon** S Africa
47B1	**Morges** Switz
46D2	**Morhange** France
74E2	**Mori** Japan
27K1	**Moriatio** Tobago
13B2	**Morice L** Can
13E2	**Morinville** Can
74E3	**Morioka** Japan
109D2	**Morisset** Aust
63D1	**Morkoka** *R* Russian Fed
48B2	**Morlaix** France
27Q2	**Morne Diablotin** *Mt* Dominica
106C2	**Mornington I** Aust
85B3	**Moro** Pak
96B2	**Morocco** Kingdom, Africa
79B4	**Moro G** Phil
99D3	**Morogoro** Tanz
23A1	**Moroleon** Mexico
101D3	**Morombe** Madag
26B2	**Morón** Cuba
101D3	**Morondava** Madag
50A2	**Moron de la Frontera** Spain
101D2	**Moroni** Comoros
71D3	**Morotai I** Indon
99D2	**Moroto** Uganda
61F4	**Morozovsk** Russian Fed
42D2	**Morpeth** Eng
19B2	**Morrilton** USA
35B1	**Morrinhos** Brazil
110C1	**Morrinsville** NZ
16B2	**Morristown** New Jersey, USA
15C2	**Morristown** New York, USA
16B2	**Morrisville** Pennsylvania, USA
21A2	**Morro Bay** USA
23A2	**Morro de Papanoa** Mexico
23A2	**Morro de Petatlán** Mexico
101C2	**Morrumbala** Mozam
101C3	**Morrumbene** Mozam
61F3	**Morshansk** Russian Fed
47C2	**Mortara** Italy
34C2	**Morteros** Arg
33G6	**Mortes** *R* Mato Grosso, Brazil
35C2	**Mortes** *R* Minas Gerais, Brazil
108B3	**Mortlake** Aust
27L1	**Moruga** Trinidad
109D3	**Moruya** Aust
109C1	**Morven** Aust
44B3	**Morven** *Pen* Scot
109C3	**Morwell** Aust
76B3	**Moscos Is** Burma
	Moscow = Moskva
20C1	**Moscow** Idaho, USA
56B2	**Mosel** *R* Germany
46D2	**Moselle** Department, France
46D2	**Mosele** *R* France
20C1	**Moses Lake** USA
111B3	**Mosgiel** NZ
99D3	**Moshi** Tanz
38G5	**Mosjøen** Nor
63G2	**Moskal'vo** Russian Fed
64E4	**Moskva** Russian Fed
35C1	**Mosquito** *R* Brazil
39G7	**Moss** Nor
98B3	**Mossaka** Congo
100B4	**Mossel Bay** S Africa
98B3	**Mossendjo** Congo
109D2	**Mossgiel** Aust
31D3	**Mossoró** Brazil
57C2	**Most** Czech Republic
96C1	**Mostaganem** Alg
54A2	**Mostar** Bosnia-Herzegovina
58C2	**Mosty** Belorussia
	Mosul = Al Mawşil
39H7	**Motala** Sweden
42C2	**Motherwell** Scot
86A1	**Motihari** India
51B2	**Motilla del Palancar** Spain
50B2	**Motril** Spain
111B2	**Motueka** NZ
111B2	**Motueka** *R* NZ
47B1	**Moudon** Switz
98B3	**Mouila** Gabon
108B2	**Moulamein** Aust
4G2	**Mould Bay** Can
49C2	**Moulins** France
76B2	**Moulmein** Burma
96B1	**Moulouya** *R* Mor
17B1	**Moultrie** USA
17C1	**Moultrie,L** USA
12B2	**Mound City** Illinois, USA
18A1	**Mound City** Missouri, USA
98B2	**Moundou** Chad
14B3	**Moundsville** USA
12J1	**Mountain** *R* Can
17A1	**Mountain Brook** USA
18B2	**Mountain Grove** USA
18B2	**Mountain Home** Arkansas, USA
22A2	**Mountain View** USA
12B2	**Mountain Village** USA
16A3	**Mount Airy** Maryland, USA
16A2	**Mount Carmel** USA
108A1	**Mount Dutton** Aust
108A2	**Mount Eba** Aust
108B3	**Mount Gambier** Aust
16B3	**Mount Holly** USA

16A2 **Mount Holly Springs** USA
108A2 **Mount Hope** Aust
106C3 **Mount Isa** Aust
108A2 **Mount Lofty Range** *Mts* Aust
12D2 **Mount McKinley Nat Pk** USA
106A3 **Mount Magnet** Aust
108B2 **Mount Manara** Aust
107E3 **Mount Morgan** Aust
19B3 **Mount Pleasant** Texas, USA
20B1 **Mount Rainier Nat Pk** USA
43B4 **Mounts B** Eng
20B2 **Mount Shasta** USA
11B3 **Mount Vernon** Illinois, USA
19A3 **Mount Vernon** Kentucky, USA
20B1 **Mount Vernon** Washington, USA
45C1 **Mourne Mts** N Ire
98B1 **Moussoro** Chad
86B2 **Mouths of the Ganga** India/Bang
85B4 **Mouths of the Indus** Pak
77D4 **Mouths of the Mekong** Viet
31C4 **Mouths of the Niger** Nig
47B1 **Moûtier** Switz
47B2 **Moûtiers** France
96C2 **Mouydir** *Mts* Alg
98B3 **Mouyondzi** Congo
46C2 **Mouzon** France
59B3 **M'ovar** Hung
23A1 **Moyahua** Mexico
99D2 **Moyale** Kenya
97A4 **Moyamba** Sierra Leone
96B1 **Moyen Atlas** *Mts* Mor
100B4 **Moyeni** Lesotho
99D2 **Moyo** Uganda
32B5 **Moyobamba** Peru
84D1 **Moyu** China
101C3 **Mozambique** Republic, Africa
101C3 **Mozambique Chan** Mozam/Mad
61H2 **Mozhga** Russian Fed
60C3 **Mozyr'** Belorussia
99D3 **Mpanda** Tanz
101C2 **Mpika** Zambia
99D3 **Mporokoso** Zambia
100B2 **Mposhi** Zambia
99D3 **Mpulungu** Zambia
99D3 **Mpwapwa** Tanz
60E3 **Mtsensk** Russian Fed
101H1 **Mtubatuba** S Africa
101D2 **Mtwara** Tanz
76C2 **Muang Chainat** Thai
76C2 **Muang Chiang Rai** Thai
76C2 **Muang Kalasin** Thai
76C2 **Muang Khon Kaen** Thai
76B2 **Muang Lampang** Thai
76B2 **Muang Lamphun** Thai
76C2 **Muang Loei** Thai
76C2 **Muang Lom Sak** Thai
76C2 **Muang Nakhon Phanom** Thai
76B2 **Muang Nakhon Sawan** Thai
76C2 **Muang Nan** Thai
76C2 **Muang Phayao** Thai
76C2 **Muang Phetchabun** Thai
76C2 **Muang Phichit** Thai
76C2 **Muang Phitsanulok** Thai
76C2 **Muang Phrae** Thai
76C2 **Muang Roi Et** Thai
76C2 **Muang Sakon Nakhon** Thai
76C2 **Muang Samut Prakan** Thai

76C2 **Muang Uthai Thani** Thai
76C2 **Muang Yasothon** Thai
77C5 **Muar** Malay
78C2 **Muara** Brunei
70B4 **Muara** Indon
78A3 **Muaralakitan** Indon
78A3 **Muaratebo** Indon
78C3 **Muaratewah** Indon
78A3 **Muarenim** Indon
76A2 **Muaungmaya** Burma
99D2 **Mubende** Uganda
100C2 **Muchinga** *Mts* Zambia
44A3 **Muck** *I* Scot
109C1 **Muckadilla** Aust
100B2 **Muconda** Angola
35D1 **Mucuri** Brazil
35C1 **Mucuri** *R* Brazil
100B2 **Mucuri** Brazil
69E2 **Mudanjiang** China
109C2 **Mudgee** Aust
76B2 **Mudon** Burma
101C2 **Mueda** Mozam
107F3 **Mueo** Nouvelle Calédonie
100B2 **Mufulira** Zambia
73C4 **Mufu Shan** *Hills* China
Mukalla = [al Mukalla]
93C4 **Mughayra** S Arabia
92A2 **Mugla** Turk
65G5 **Mugodzhary** *Mts* Kazakhstan
73A3 **Muguaping** China
93D3 **Muhaywir** Iraq
57C3 **Mühldorf** Germany
57C2 **Mühlhausen** Germany
38K6 **Muhos** Fin
77C4 **Mui Bai Bung** *C* Camb
45C2 **Muine Bheag** Irish Rep
100B2 **Mujimbeji** Zambia
59B3 **Mukachevo** Ukraine
78C2 **Mukah** Malay
69G4 **Muko-jima** *I* Japan
86A1 **Muktinath** Nepal
84B2 **Mukur** Afghan
18B2 **Mulberry** USA
12C2 **Mulchatna** *R* USA
34A3 **Mulchén** Chile
56C2 **Mulde** *R* Germany
50B2 **Mulhacén** *Mt* Spain
46D1 **Mülheim** Germany
49D2 **Mulhouse** France
73A4 **Muli** China
44B3 **Mull** *I* Scot
87C3 **Mullaitvu** Sri Lanka
109C2 **Mullaley** Aust
106A3 **Mullewa** Aust
16B3 **Mullica** *R* USA
45C2 **Mullingar** Irish Rep
42B2 **Mull of Kintyre** *Pt* Scot
45C1 **Mull of Oa** *C* Scot
109D1 **Mullumbimby** Aust
100B2 **Mulobezi** Zambia
84C2 **Multan** Pak
Mumbai = Bombay
100B2 **Mumbwa** Zambia
61G4 **Mumra** Russian Fed
71D4 **Muna** *I* Indon
57C3 **München** Germany
14A2 **Muncie** USA
15C2 **Muncy** USA
56B2 **Münden** Germany
109D1 **Mundubbera** Aust
109C1 **Mungallala** Aust
109C1 **Mungallala** *R* Aust
99C2 **Mungbere** Zaire
86A2 **Mungeli** India
86B1 **Munger** India
109C1 **Mungindi** Aust
Munich = München
14A1 **Munising** USA
29B6 **Muñoz Gomero,Pen** Chile
45B2 **Munster** Region, Irish Rep

47C1 **Münster** Switz
56B2 **Münster** Germany
54B1 **Muntii Apuseni** *Mts* Rom
54B1 **Muntii Călimanilor** *Mts* Rom
54B1 **Muntii Carpatii Meridionali** *Mts* Rom
54B1 **Muntii Rodnei** *Mts* Rom
54B1 **Muntii Zarandului** *Mts* Rom
100B2 **Munyati** *R* Zim
93C2 **Munzur Silsilesi** *Mts* Turk
64D3 **Muomio** Fin
76C1 **Muong Khoua** Laos
76D3 **Muong Man** Viet
76C2 **Muong Nong** Laos
76C1 **Muong Ou Neua** Laos
76C1 **Muong Sai** Laos
76C2 **Muong Sen** Viet
76C1 **Muong Sing** Laos
76C1 **Muong Son** Laos
38J5 **Muonio** Fin
38J5 **Muonio** *R* Sweden/Fin
99E2 **Muqdisho** Somalia
Murabbah = [al Mudawwara]
74D3 **Murakami** Japan
29B5 **Murallón** *Mt* Arg/Chile
61G2 **Murashi** Russian Fed
93D2 **Murat** *R* Turk
53A3 **Muravera** Sardegna
75C1 **Murayama** Japan
90B3 **Murcheh Khvort** Iran
111B2 **Murchison** NZ
106A3 **Murchison** *R* Aust
51B2 **Murcia** Region, Spain
51B2 **Murcia** Spain
54B1 **Mureş** *R* Rom
46E2 **Mureş** *R* Germany
65H6 **Murgab** *R* Turkmenistan
84B2 **Murgha Kibzai** Pak
109D1 **Murgon** Aust
86B2 **Muri** India
35C2 **Muriaé** Brazil
98C3 **Muriege** Angola
64E3 **Murmansk** Russian Fed
61F2 **Murom** Russian Fed
74E2 **Muroran** Japan
50A1 **Muros** Spain
74C4 **Muroto** Japan
75A2 **Muroto-zaki** *C* Japan
20C2 **Murphy** Idaho, USA
22B1 **Murphys** USA
18C2 **Murray** Kentucky, USA
108B2 **Murray** *R* Aust
13C2 **Murray** *R* Can
108A3 **Murray Bridge** Aust
71F4 **Murray,L** PNG
17B1 **Murray,L** USA
106J2 **Murray Seacarp** Pacific O
108B2 **Murrumbidgee** *R* Aust
109C2 **Murrumburrah** Aust
109D2 **Murrurundi** Aust
47B1 **Murten** Switz
108B3 **Murtoa** Aust
110C1 **Murupara** NZ
86A2 **Murwāra** India
109D1 **Murwillimbah** Aust
93D2 **Muş** Turk
54B2 **Musala** *Mt* Bulg
74B2 **Musan** N Korea
91C4 **Musandam** *Pen* Oman
Muscat = Masqat
91C5 **Muscat** Region, Oman
106C3 **Musgrave Range** *Mts* Aust
98B3 **Mushie** Zaire
14A2 **Muskegon** USA
14A2 **Muskegon** *R* USA
18A2 **Muskogee** USA
15C2 **Muskoka,L** Can
95C3 **Musmar** Sudan

99D3 **Musoma** Tanz
8C2 **Musselshell** *R* USA
100A2 **Mussende** Angola
48C2 **Mussidan** France
55C2 **Mustafa-Kemalpasa** Turk
86A1 **Mustang** Nepal
109D2 **Muswellbrook** Aust
95B2 **Mut** Egypt
101C2 **Mutarara** Mozam
101C2 **Mutare** Zim
101C2 **Mutoko** Zim
101D2 **Mutsamudu** Comoros
100B2 **Mutshatsha** Zaire
74E2 **Mutsu** Japan
74E2 **Mutsu wan** *B* Japan
45B2 **Mutton** *I* Irish Rep
72B2 **Mu Us Shamo** *Desert* China
98B3 **Muxima** Angola
63D2 **Muya** Russian Fed
38L6 **Muyezerskiy** Russian Fed
99D3 **Muyinga** Burundi
98C3 **Muyumba** Zaire
82A1 **Muyun Kum** *Desert* Kazakhstan
84C2 **Muzaffarābad** Pak
84C2 **Muzaffargarh** Pak
84D3 **Muzaffarnagar** India
86B1 **Muzaffarpur** India
64H3 **Muzhi** Russian Fed
82C2 **Muztag** *Mt* China
82B2 **Muztagata** *Mt* China
100C2 **Mvuma** Zim
99D3 **Mwanza** Tanz
98C3 **Mwanza** Zaire
98C3 **Mweka** Zaire
98C3 **Mwene Ditu** Zaire
100C3 **Mwenezi** Zim
99C3 **Mwenga** Zaire
99C3 **Mweru** *L* Zambia
100B2 **Mwinilunga** Zambia
83D4 **Myanaung** Burma
Myanma = Burma
86D2 **Myingyan** Burma
76B1 **Myingyao** Burma
76B3 **Myinmoletkat** *Mt* Burma
82D3 **Myitkyina** Burma
76B3 **Myitta** Burma
86C2 **Mymensingh** Bang
69F3 **Myojin** *I* Japan
39F6 **Myrdal** Nor
38B2 **Myrdalsjökur** *Ice Cap* Iceland
17C1 **Myrtle Beach** USA
20B2 **Myrtle Creek** USA
39G7 **Mysen** Nor
56C2 **Myślibórz** Pol
64F3 **Mys Kanin Nos** *C* Russian Fed
59B3 **Myślenice** Pol
69H1 **Mys Lopatka** *C* Russian Fed
87B2 **Mysore** India
60D5 **Mys Sarych** *C* Ukraine
16D2 **Mystic** U3A
61H5 **Mys Tyub-Karagan** *Pt* Kazakhstan
62C2 **Mys Yelizavety** *C* Russian Fed
64H2 **Mys Zhelaniya** *C* Russian Fed
77D3 **My Tho** Viet
20B2 **Mytle Point** USA
101C2 **Mzimba** Malawi
101C2 **Mzuzú** Malawi

N
21C4 **Naalehu** Hawaiian Is
39J6 **Naantali** Fin
45C2 **Naas** Irish Rep
75B2 **Nabari** Japan
61H2 **Naberezhnye Chelny** Russian Fed
12F2 **Nabesna** *R* USA
96D1 **Nabeul** Tunisia
94B2 **Nablus** Israel
101D2 **Nacala** Mozam
20B1 **Naches** USA
101C2 **Nachingwea** Tanz

19B3	**Nacogdoches** USA
76A3	**Nacondam** / Indian O
24B1	**Nacozari** Mexico
85C4	**Nadiäd** India
50B2	**Nador** Mor
90B3	**Nadushan** Iran
59C3	**Nadvornaya** Ukraine
56C1	**Naestved** Den
95B2	**Näfürah** Libya
75A2	**Nagahama** Japan
82D3	**Naga Hills** Burma
75B1	**Nagai** Japan
86C1	**Nägäland** State, India
74D3	**Nagano** Japan
74D3	**Nagaoka** Japan
86C1	**Nagaon** India
87B2	**Nägappattinam** India
85C4	**Nagar Parkar** Pak
74B4	**Nagasaki** Japan
75B2	**Nagashima** Japan
75A2	**Nagato** Japan
85C3	**Nägaur** India
87B3	**Nägercoil** India
85B3	**Nagha Kalat** Pak
84D3	**Nagina** India
74D3	**Nagoya** Japan
85D4	**Nägpur** India
82D2	**Nagqu** China
59B3	**Nagykanizsa** Hung
59B3	**Nagykörös** Hung
69E4	**Naha** Japan
8A2	**Nahanni** Can
84D2	**Nähan** India
4F3	**Nahanni Butte** Can
94B2	**Nahariya** Israel
90A3	**Nahävand** Iran
46D2	**Nahe** R Germany
72D2	**Nahpu** China
72E1	**Naimen Qi** China
7D4	**Nain** Can
90B3	**Nä'in** Iran
84D3	**Naini Tai** India
44C3	**Nairn** Scot
99D3	**Nairobi** Kenya
90B3	**Najafäbäd** Iran
74C2	**Najin** N Korea
75A2	**Nakama** Japan
74E3	**Nakaminato** Japan
75A2	**Nakamura** Japan
75B1	**Nakano** Japan
75A1	**Nakano-shima** / Japan
74C4	**Nakatsu** Japan
75B1	**Nakatsu-gawa** Japan
95C3	**Nak' fa** Eritrea
93E2	**Nakhichevan** Azerbaijan
92B4	**Nakhl** Egypt
74C2	**Nakhodka** Russian Fed
76C3	**Nakhon Pathom** Thai
76C3	**Nakhon Ratchasima** Thai
77C4	**Nakhon Si Thammarat** Thai
12H3	**Nakina** Can
7B4	**Nakina** Ontario, Can
12C3	**Naknek** USA
12C3	**Naknek L** USA
4C4	**Nakrek** USA
39G8	**Nakskov** Den
99D3	**Nakuru** Kenya
13D2	**Nakusp** Can
61F5	**Nal'chik** Russian Fed
87B1	**Nalgonda** India
87B1	**Nallamala Range** Mts India
95A1	**Nälüt** Libya
101H1	**Namaacha** Mozam
65G6	**Namak** L Iran
90C3	**Namakzar-e Shadad** Salt Flat Iran
65J5	**Namangan** Uzbekistan
101C2	**Namapa** Mozam
100A4	**Namaqualand** Region, S Africa
109D1	**Nambour** Aust
109D2	**Nambucca Heads** Aust
77D4	**Nam Can** Viet
82D2	**Nam Co** L China
76D1	**Nam Dinh** Viet
101C2	**Nametil** Mozam
74B4	**Namhae-do** / S Korea
100A2	**Namib Desert** Namibia
100A2	**Namibe** Angola
100A3	**Namibia** Republic, Africa
82D3	**Namjagbarwa Feng** Mt China
71D4	**Namlea** Indon
109C2	**Namoi** R Aust
13D1	**Nampa** Can
20C2	**Nampa** USA
97B3	**Nampala** Mali
76C2	**Nam Phong** Thai
74B3	**Namp'o** N Korea
101C2	**Nampula** Mozam
38G6	**Namsos** Nor
76B1	**Namton** Burma
86D2	**Namtu** Burma
13B2	**Namu** Can
101C2	**Namuno** Mozam
46C1	**Namur** Belg
100A2	**Namutoni** Namibia
74B3	**Namwön** S Korea
13C3	**Nanaimo** Can
74B2	**Nanam** N Korea
109D1	**Nanango** Aust
74D3	**Nanao** Japan
75B1	**Nanatsu-jima** / Japan
73B3	**Nanbu** China
73D4	**Nanchang** China
73B3	**Nanchong** China
49D2	**Nancy** France
87B1	**Nänded** India
109D2	**Nandewar Range** Mts Aust
85C4	**Nandurbar** India
87B1	**Nandyäl** India
98B2	**Nanga Eboko** Cam
84C1	**Nanga Parbat** Mt Pak
78C3	**Nangapinoh** Indon
78C3	**Nangatayap** Indon
74B2	**Nangnim Sanmaek** Mts N Korea
86C1	**Nang Xian** China
67F3	**Nangong** China
87B2	**Nanjangüd** India
72D3	**Nanjing** China
	Nanking = Nanjing
75A2	**Nankoku** Japan
73C4	**Nan Ling** Region, China
76D1	**Nanliu** R China
73B5	**Nanning** China
6F3	**Nanortalik** Greenland
73A5	**Nanpan Jiang** R China
86A1	**Nänpära** India
73D4	**Nanping** China
6A1	**Nansen Sd** Can
99D3	**Nansio** Tanz
48B2	**Nantes** France
13E2	**Nanton** Can
72E3	**Nantong** China
10C2	**Nantucket** / USA
35C1	**Nanuque** Brazil
72C3	**Nanyang** China
72D2	**Nanyang He** L China
99D2	**Nanyuki** Kenya
74D3	**Naoetsu** Japan
85B4	**Naokot** Pak
22A1	**Napa** USA
12B2	**Napaiskak** USA
15C2	**Napanee** Can
65K4	**Napas** Russian Fed
6E3	**Napassoq** Greenland
76D2	**Nape** Laos
110C1	**Napier** NZ
	Naples = Napoli
17B2	**Naples** Florida, USA
19B3	**Naples** Texas, USA
73B5	**Napo** China
32C4	**Napo** R Peru/Ecuador
53B2	**Napoli** Italy
90A2	**Naqadeh** Iran
92C4	**Naqb Ishtar** Jordan
75B2	**Nara** Japan
97B3	**Nara** Mali
107D4	**Naracoorte** Aust
23B1	**Naranjos** Mexico
87C1	**Narasaräopet** India
77C4	**Narathiwat** Thai
86C2	**Narayanganj** Bang
87B1	**Näräyenpet** India
49C3	**Narbonne** France
84D2	**Narendranagar** India
6C2	**Nares Str** Can
58C2	**Narew** R Pol
75C1	**Narita** Japan
85C4	**Narmada** R India
84D3	**Narnaul** India
60E2	**Naro Fominsk** Russian Fed
99D3	**Narok** Kenya
84C2	**Narowal** Pak
107D4	**Narrabri** Aust
109C1	**Narran** L Aust
109C1	**Narran** R Aust
109C2	**Narrandera** Aust
106A4	**Narrogin** Aust
109C2	**Narromine** Aust
85D4	**Narsimhapur** India
87C1	**Narsipatnam** India
6F3	**Narssalik** Greenland
6F3	**Narssaq** Greenland
6F3	**Narssarssuaq** Greenland
75C1	**Narugo** Japan
75A2	**Naruto** Japan
60C2	**Narva** Russian Fed
38H5	**Narvik** Nor
84D3	**Narwäna** India
64G3	**Nar'yan Mar** Russian Fed
108B1	**Narylico** Aust
65J5	**Naryn** Kirghizia
97C4	**Nasarawa** Nig
103D5	**Nasca Ridge** Pacific O
16D1	**Nashua** USA
19B3	**Nashville** Arkansas, USA
11B3	**Nashville** Tennessee, USA
54A1	**Našice** Croatia
85D4	**Näsik** India
99D2	**Nasir** Sudan
13B1	**Nass** R Can
26B1	**Nassau** The Bahamas
16C1	**Nassau** USA
95C2	**Nasser,L** Egypt
39G7	**Nässjö** Sweden
7C4	**Nastapoka Is** Can
100B3	**Nata** Botswana
31D3	**Natal** Brazil
70A3	**Natal** Indon
101H1	**Natal** Province, S Africa
90B3	**Natanz** Iran
7D4	**Natashquan** Can
7D4	**Natashquan** R Can
19B3	**Natchez** USA
19B3	**Natchitoches** USA
108C3	**Nathalia** Aust
6H2	**Nathorsts Land** Region Greenland
13C1	**Nation** R Can
21B3	**National City** USA
75C1	**Natori** Japan
99D3	**Natron** L Tanz
106A4	**Naturaliste,C** Aust
47D1	**Nauders** Austria
56C2	**Nauen** Germany
16C2	**Naugatuck** USA
57C2	**Naumburg** Germany
94B3	**Naur** Jordan
105G4	**Nauru** / Pacific O
63C2	**Naushki** Russian Fed
23B1	**Nautla** Mexico
9C3	**Navajo Res** USA
50A2	**Navalmoral de la Mata** Spain
29B1	**Navarino** / Chile
51B1	**Navarra** Province, Spain
34D3	**Navarro** Arg
19A3	**Navasota** USA
19A3	**Navasota** R USA
50A1	**Navia** R Spain
34A2	**Navidad** Chile
85C4	**Navlakhi** India
60D3	**Navlya** Russian Fed
24B2	**Navojoa** Mexico
55B3	**Návpaktos** Greece
55B3	**Návplion** Greece
85C4	**Navsäri** India
94C2	**Nawá** Syria
86B2	**Nawäda** India
84B2	**Nawah** Afghan
85B3	**Nawrabshah** Pak
73B4	**Naxi** China
55C3	**Náxos** / Greece
23A1	**Nayar** Mexico
90C3	**Nay Band** Iran
91B4	**Näy Band** Iran
74E2	**Nayoro** Japan
94B2	**Nazareth** Israel
32C6	**Nazca** Peru
92A2	**Nazilli** Turk
63B2	**Nazimovo** Russian Fed
13C2	**Nazko** R Can
99D2	**Nazret** Eth
91C5	**Nazwa** Oman
65J4	**Nazyvayevsk** Russian Fed
98B3	**Ndalatando** Angola
98C2	**Ndélé** CAR
98B3	**Ndendé** Gabon
98B1	**Ndjamena** Chad
98B3	**Ndjolé** Gabon
100B2	**Ndola** Zambia
109C1	**Neabul** Aust
108A1	**Neales** R Aust
55B3	**Neápolis** Greece
43C4	**Neath** Wales
109C1	**Nebine** R Aust
65G6	**Nebit Dag** Turkmenistan
8C2	**Nebraska** State, USA
18A1	**Nebraska City** USA
13C2	**Nechako** R Can
19A3	**Neches** R USA
34D3	**Necochea** Arg
86C1	**Nêdong** China
9B3	**Needles** USA
14A2	**Neenah** USA
5J4	**Neepawa** Can
46C1	**Neerpelt** Belg
63C2	**Neftelensk** Russian Fed
99D2	**Negelë** Eth
94B3	**Negev** Desert Israel
60B4	**Negolu** Mt Rom
87B3	**Negombo** Sri Lanka
76A2	**Negrais,C** Burma
32A4	**Negritos** Peru
33E4	**Negro** R Amazonas, Brazil
29C4	**Negro** R Arg
32D2	**Negro** R Urug
79B4	**Negros** / Phil
54C2	**Negru Voda** Rom
90C3	**Nehbändan** Iran
73B4	**Neijiang** China
	Nei Monggol Autonomous Region, China
32B3	**Neiva** Colombia
99D2	**Nejo** Eth
99D2	**Nek'emtë** Eth
60D2	**Nelidovo** Russian Fed
87B2	**Nellore** India
69F2	**Nel'ma** Russian Fed
13D3	**Nelson** Can
110B2	**Nelson** NZ
111B2	**Nelson** NZ
13C3	**Nelson** R Can
108B3	**Nelson,C** Aust
12B2	**Nelson I** USA
97B3	**Néma** Maur
72A1	**Nemagt Uul** Mt Mongolia
58C1	**Neman** R Lithuania
54C1	**Nemira** Mt Rom
74F2	**Nemuro** Japan
63E3	**Nen** R China
41B3	**Nenagh** Irish Rep
12E2	**Nenana** USA
12E2	**Nenana** R USA
43D3	**Nene** R Eng
69C2	**Nenjiang** China
18A2	**Neodesha** USA

Neosho

18B2 Neosho USA
63C2 Nepa Russian Fed
82C3 Nepal Kingdom, Asia
86A1 Nepalganj Nepal
45B1 Nephin Mt Irish Rep
94B3 Neqarot R Israel
34A3 Nequén State, Arg
68D1 Nerchinsk
Russian Fed
52C2 Neretva R Bosnia-
Herzegovina/Croatia
71F2 Nero Deep Pacific O
38C1 Neskaupstaður
Iceland
46B2 Nesle France
7E5 Nesleyville Can
55B2 Néstos R Greece
94B2 Netanya Israel
16B2 Netcong USA
56B2 Netherlands
Kingdom, Europe
3M7 Netherlands Antilles
Is Caribbean S
86C2 Netrakona Bang
6C3 Nettilling L Can
56C2 Neubrandenburg
Germany
47B1 Neuchâtel Switz
46C2 Neufchâteau Belg
48C2 Neufchâtel France
46A2 Neufchâteau-Hay
France
56B2 Neumünster
Germany
52C1 Neunkirchen Austria
46D2 Neunkirchen
Germany
34B3 Neuquén Arg
29B4 Neuquén State, Arg
34B3 Neuquén R Arg
56C2 Neuruppin Germany
46D1 Neuss Germany
46E2 Neustadt Germany
56C2 Neustadt Germany
56C2 Neustrelitz Germany
46D1 Neuwied Germany
8B3 Nevada State, USA
18B2 Nevada USA
34A3 Nevada de Chillán
Mts Arg/Chile
23A2 Nevada de Collima
Mexico
23B2 Nevada de Toluca Mt
Mexico
94B3 Nevatim Israel
60C2 Nevel' Russian Fed
49C2 Nevers France
109C2 Nevertire Aust
27E3 Nevis I Caribbean S
58D2 Nevis R Belorussia/
Lithuania
92B2 Nevşehir Turk
61K2 Nev'yansk
Russian Fed
101C2 Newala Tanz
14A3 New Albany Indiana,
USA
19C3 New Albany
Mississippi, USA
33F2 New Amsterdam
Guyana
109C1 New Angledool Aust
15C3 Newark Delaware,
USA
16B2 Newark New Jersey,
USA
14B2 Newark Ohio, USA
43D3 Newark-upon-Trent
Eng
15D2 New Bedford USA
13B2 New Bella Bella Can
20B1 Newberg USA
11C3 New Bern USA
17B1 Newberry USA
26B2 New Bight
The Bahamas
14B3 New Boston USA
9D4 New Braunfels USA
16C2 New Britain USA
7D5 New Brunswick
Province, Can
16B2 New Brunswick USA
16B2 Newburgh USA
43D4 Newbury Eng

16D1 Newburyport USA
16C2 New Canaan USA
109D2 Newcastle Aust
14A3 New Castle Indiana,
USA
42B2 Newcastle N Ire
14B2 New Castle
Pennsylvania, USA
101G1 Newcastle S Africa
8C2 Newcastle Wyoming,
USA
42D2 Newcastle upon Tyne
Eng
106C2 Newcastle Waters
Aust
45B2 Newcastle West
Irish Rep
84D3 New Delhi India
109D2 New England Range
Mts Aust
12B3 Newenham,C USA
43D4 New Forest,The Eng
7D4 Newfoundland
Province, Can
7E5 Newfoundland I
Can
102F2 Newfoundland Basin
Atlantic O
18B2 New Franklin USA
42B2 New Galloway Scot
101L1 New Georgia I
Solomon Is
7D5 New Glasgow Can
71F4 New Guinea SE Asia
12D3 Newhalen USA
22C3 Newhall USA
10C2 New Hampshire
State, USA
101H1 New Hanover
S Africa
43E4 Newhaven Eng
15D2 New Haven USA
13B1 New Hazelton Can
19B3 New Iberia USA
10C2 New Jersey State,
USA
7C5 New Liskeard Can
16C2 New London USA
106A3 Newman Aust
22B2 Newman USA
43E3 Newmarket Eng
45B2 Newmarket Irish Rep
15C3 New Market USA
9C3 New Mexico State,
USA
16C2 New Milford
Connecticut, USA
17B1 Newnan USA
109C4 New Norfolk Aust
11A3 New Orleans USA
16B2 New Paltz USA
14B2 New Philadelphia
USA
110B1 New Plymouth NZ
18B2 Newport Arkansas,
USA
43D4 Newport Eng
43D4 Newport Kentucky,
USA
20B2 Newport Oregon,
USA
16A2 Newport
Pennsylvania, USA
15D2 Newport Rhode
Island, USA
15D2 Newport Vermont,
USA
43C4 Newport Wales
20C1 Newport
Washington, USA
22D4 Newport Beach USA
11C3 Newport News USA
26B1 New Providence I
Caribbean S
43B4 Newquay Eng
6C3 New Quebec Crater
Can
45C2 New Ross Irish Rep
45C1 Newry N Ire
New Siberian Is =
Novosibirskye
Ostrova
17B2 New Smyrna Beach
USA

107D4 New South Wales
State, Aust
12C3 New Stuyahok USA
18A2 Newton Kansas,
USA
16D1 Newton
Massachusetts, USA
19C3 Newton Mississippi,
USA
16B2 Newton New York,
USA
43C4 Newton Abbot Eng
45C1 Newton Stewart
N Ire
42B2 Newton Stewart
Scot
43C3 Newtown Wales
42B2 Newtownards N Ire
16A2 Newville USA
5F5 New Westminster
Can
10C2 New York State, USA
10C2 New York USA
110 New Zealand
Dominion, SW
Pacific O
105G6 New Zealand Plat
Pacific O
61F2 Neya Russian Fed
91R4 Neyriz Iran
80C2 Neyshābur Iran
60D3 Nezhin Russian Fed
98B3 Ngabé Congo
100B3 Ngami L Botswana
110C1 Ngaruawahia NZ
110C1 Ngaruroro R NZ
110C1 Ngauruhoe,Mt NZ
98B3 Ngo Congo
76D2 Ngoc Linh Mt Viet
98B2 Ngoko R Congo
98B3 Ngoring Hu L China
99D3 Ngorongoro Crater
Tanz
98B3 N'Gounié R Gabon
98B2 Nguigmi Niger
71E3 Ngulu I Pacific O
97D3 Nguru Nig
76D3 Nha Trang Viet
108B3 Nhill Aust
101H1 Nhlangano
Swaziland
76D2 Nhommarath Laos
106C2 Nhulunbuy Aust
97B3 Niafounké Mali
14A1 Niagara USA
15C2 Niagara Falls Can
15C2 Niagara Falls USA
70C3 Niah Malay
97B4 Niakaramandougou
Ivory Coast
97C3 Niamey Niger
99C2 Niangara Zaïre
98C2 Nia Nia Zaïre
70A3 Nias I Indon
25D3 Nicaragua Republic,
Cent America
53C3 Nicastro Italy
49D3 Nice France
26B1 Nicholl's Town
The Bahamas
83D5 Nicobar Is Indian O
92B2 Nicosia Cyprus
25D3 Nicoya,Pen de
Costa Rica
58C2 Nidzica Pol
46D2 Niederbronn France
56B2 Niedersachsen State,
Germany
99C3 Niemba Zaïre
56B2 Nienburg Germany
46D1 Niers R Germany
97B4 Niete,Mt Lib
33F2 Nieuw Amsterdam
Surinam
33F2 Nieuw Nickerie
Surinam
46B1 Nieuwpoort Belg
92B2 Niğde Turk
97C3 Niger Republic,
Africa
97C4 Niger R Nig
97C4 Nigeria Federal
Republic, Africa
55B2 Nigrita Greece

75C1 Nihommatsu Japan
74D3 Niigata Japan
74C4 Niihama Japan
75B2 Nii-jima I Japan
75A2 Niimi Japan
74D3 Niitsu Japan
94B3 Nijil Jordan
56B2 Nijmegen Neth
64E3 Nikel' Russian Fed
97C3 Nikki Benin
74D3 Nikko Japan
60D4 Nikolayev Ukraine
61G4 Nikolayevsk
Russian Fed
63G2 Nikolayevsk-na-
Amure Russian Fed
61G3 Nikol'sk Russian Fed
61G3 Nikol'sk Russian Fed
60D4 Nikopol Ukraine
92C1 Niksar Turk
91D4 Nikshahr Iran
54A2 Nikšić Montenegro,
Yugos
71D4 Nila I Indon
80B3 Nile R N E Africa
14A2 Niles USA
87B2 Nilgiri Hills India
85C4 Nimach India
49C3 Nîmes France
109C3 Nimmitabel Aust
99D2 Nimule Sudan
83B5 Nine Degree Chan
Indian O
104C4 Ninety-East Ridge
Indian O
109C3 Ninety Mile Beach
Aust
73D4 Ningde China
73D4 Ningdu China
68B3 Ningjing Shan Mts
China
76D1 Ningming China
73A4 Ningnan China
72B2 Ningxia Province,
China
72B2 Ning Xian China
73B5 Ninh Binh Vietnam
107D1 Ninigo Is PNG
12D2 Ninilchik USA
8D2 Niobrara R USA
98B3 Nioki Zaïre
97B3 Nioro du Sahel Mali
48B2 Niort France
7B5 Nipawin Can
7B5 Nipigon Can
7B5 Nipigon,L Can
7B5 Nipissing,L Can
14B1 Nipissing Can
87B1 Nirmal India
86B1 Nirmāli India
54B2 Niš Serbia, Yugos
81C4 Nisāb Yemen
75A2 Nishino-shima I
Japan
75A1 Nishino-shima I
Japan
75A2 Nishiwaki Japan
12G2 Nisling R Can
12H2 Nisutlin R Can
7C4 Nitchequon Can
31C6 Niterói Brazil
42C2 Nith R Scot
59B3 Nitra Slovakia
14B3 Nitro USA
78C2 Niut Mt Malay
46C1 Nivelles Belg
49C2 Nivernais Region,
France
38L5 Nivskiy Russian Fed
87B1 Nizāmābād India
94B3 Nizana Hist Site
Israel
61J2 Nizhniye Sergi
Russian Fed
65F4 Nizhniy Novgorod
Russian Fed
61F3 Nizhniy Lomov
Russian Fed
65G4 Nizhniy Tagil
Russian Fed
63B1 Nizhnyaya Tunguska
R Russian Fed
93C2 Nizip Turk
100B2 Njoko R Zambia

99D3 **Njombe** Tanz
98B2 **Nkambé** Cam
101C2 **Nkhata Bay** Malawi
98B2 **Nkongsamba** Cam
97C3 **N'Konni** Niger
86C2 **Noakhali** Bang
12B1 **Noatak** USA
12C1 **Noatak** *R* USA
74C4 **Nobeoka** Japan
47D1 **Noce** *R* Italy
23A1 **Nochistlán** Mexico
23B2 **Nochixtlán** Mexico
19A3 **Nocona** USA
24A1 **Nogales** Sonora, Mexico
9B3 **Nogales** USA
23B2 **Nogales** Veracruz, Mexico
47D2 **Nogara** Italy
75A2 **Nogata** Japan
60E2 **Noginsk** Russian Fed
34D2 **Nogoyá** Arg
34D2 **Nogoyá** *R* Arg
84C3 **Nohar** India
75B2 **Nojima-zaki** *C* Japan
98B2 **Nola** CAR
61G2 **Nolinsk** Russian Fed
16D2 **Nomans Land** *I* USA
12A2 **Nome** USA
46D2 **Nomeny** France
72B1 **Nomgon** Mongolia
5H3 **Nonacho'l** L Can
76C2 **Nong Khai** Thai
101H1 **Nongoma** S Africa
12B1 **Noorvik** USA
13B3 **Nootka Sd** Can
98B3 **Noqui** Angola
7C5 **Noranda** Can
46B1 **Nord** Department, France
64D2 **Nordaustlandet** *I* Barents S
13D2 **Nordegg** Can
38F6 **Nordfjord** *Inlet* Nor
39F8 **Nordfriesische** *Is* Germany
56C2 **Nordhausen** Germany
56B2 **Nordrhein Westfalen** State, Germany
38J4 **Nordkapp** *C* Nor
6E3 **Nordre** Greenland
38H5 **Nord Stronfjället** *Mt* Sweden
1B9 **Nordvik** Russian Fed
45C2 **Nore** *R* Irish Rep
43E3 **Norfolk** County, Eng
8D2 **Norfolk** Nebraska, USA
11C3 **Norfolk** Virginia, USA
107F3 **Norfolk** I Aust
15B1 **Norfolk L** USA
105G5 **Norfolk Ridge** Pacific O
1C10 **Noril'sk** Russian Fed
18C1 **Normal** USA
19A2 **Norman** USA
48B2 **Normandie** Region, France
107D2 **Normanton** Aust
12J1 **Norman Wells** Can
4B3 **Norne** USA
15C2 **Norristown** USA
39H7 **Norrköping** Sweden
39H6 **Norrsundet** Sweden
39H7 **Norrtälje** Sweden
106B4 **Norseman** Aust
63F2 **Norsk** Russian Fed
102J2 **North** *S* N W Europe
42D2 **Northallerton** Eng
106A4 **Northam** Aust
102E3 **North American Basin** Atlantic O
106A3 **Northampton** Aust
43D3 **Northampton** County, Eng
43D3 **Northampton** Eng
15D2 **Northampton** USA
4G3 **North Arm** *B* Can
17B1 **North Augusta** USA
6D1 **North Aulatsivik** *I* Can

13F2 **North Battleford** Can
7C5 **North Bay** Can
20B2 **North Bend** USA
44C3 **North Berwick** Scot
7D5 **North,C** Can
7G4 **North C** NZ
11B3 **North Carolina** State, USA
20B1 **North Cascade Nat Pk** USA
14B1 **North Chan** Can
42B2 **North Chan** Ire/Scot
8C2 **North Dakota** State, USA
43E4 **North Downs** Eng
14C2 **North East** USA
102H2 **North East Atlantic Basin** Atlantic O
4B3 **Northeast C** USA
40B3 **Northern Ireland** UK
27L1 **Northern Range** *Mts* Trinidad
106C2 **Northern Territory** Aust
44C3 **North Esk** *R* Scot
16C1 **Northfield** Massachusetts, USA
12D2 **North Fork** *R* USA
110B1 **North I** NZ
74B3 **North Korea** Republic, S E Asia
North Land = Severnaya Zemlya
19B3 **North Little Rock** USA
1B4 **North Magnetic Pole** Can
17B2 **North Miami** USA
17B2 **North Miami Beach** USA
8C2 **North Platte** USA
8C2 **North Platte** *R* USA
27R3 **North Pt** Barbados
14B1 **North Pt** USA
40B2 **North Rona** *I* Scot
44C2 **North Ronaldsay** *I* Scot
13F2 **North Saskatchewan** *R* Can
40D2 **North Sea** N W Europe
4D3 **North Slope** *Region* USA
109D1 **North Stradbroke** *I* Aust
110B1 **North Taranaki Bight** *B* NZ
9C3 **North Truchas Peak** *Mt* USA
44A3 **North Uist** *I* Scot
42C2 **Northumberland** County, Eng
107E3 **Northumberland Is** Aust
7D5 **Northumberland Str** Can
20B1 **North Vancouver** Can
43E3 **North Walsham** Eng
12F2 **Northway** USA
106A3 **North West C** Aust
84C2 **North West Frontier** Province, Pak
7D4 **North West River** Can
4F3 **North West Territories** Can
42D2 **North York Moors Nat Pk** Eng
12B2 **Norton B** USA
12B2 **Norton Sd** USA
112B1 **Norvegia,C** Ant
16C2 **Norwalk** Connecticut, USA
14B2 **Norwalk** Ohio, USA
39F6 **Norway** Kingdom, Europe
5J4 **Norway House** Can
6A2 **Norwegian B** Can
102H1 **Norwegian Basin** Norwegian S
64A3 **Norwegian S** N W Europe
16C2 **Norwich** Connecticut, USA

43E3 **Norwich** Eng
16D1 **Norwood** Massachusetts, USA
14B3 **Norwood** Ohio, USA
54C2 **Nos Emine** *C* Bulg
74D2 **Noshiro** Japan
54C2 **Nos Kaliakra** *C* Bulg
44E1 **Noss** *I* Scot
91D4 **Nostrābād** Iran
101D2 **Nosy Barren** *I* Madag
101D2 **Nosy Bé** *I* Madag
101E2 **Nosy Boraha** *I* Madag
101D3 **Nosy Varika** Madag
58B2 **Noteć** *R* Pol
5G4 **Notikeuin** Can
53C3 **Noto** Italy
39F7 **Notodden** Nor
75B1 **Noto-hantô** *Pen* Japan
7E5 **Notre Dams B** Can
43D3 **Nottingham** County, Eng
43D3 **Nottingham** Eng
6C3 **Nottingham** *I* Can
6C3 **Nottingham Island** Can
96A2 **Nouadhibou** Maur
97A3 **Nouakchott** Maur
107F3 **Nouméa** Nouvelle Calédonie
97B3 **Nouna** Burkina
107F3 **Nouvelle Calédonie** *I* S W Pacific O
98B3 **Nova Caipemba** Angola
35A2 **Nova Esperança** Brazil
35C2 **Nova Friburgo** Brazil
100A2 **Nova Gaia** Angola
35B2 **Nova Granada** Brazil
35B2 **Nova Horizonte** Brazil
35C1 **Nova Lima** Brazil
Nova Lisboa = Huambo
35A2 **Nova Londrina** Brazil
101C3 **Nova Mambone** Mozam
47C2 **Novara** Italy
7D5 **Nova Scotia** Province, Can
22A1 **Novato** USA
35C1 **Nova Venécia** Brazil
60D4 **Novaya Kakhovka** Ukraine
64G2 **Novaya Zemlya** *I* Barents S
54C2 **Nova Zagora** Bulg
31C2 **Nove Russas** Brazil
54A1 **Nové Zámky** Slovakia
60D2 **Novgorod** Russian Fed
47C2 **Novi Ligure** Italy
54C2 **Novi Pazar** Bulg
54B2 **Novi Pazar** Serbia, Yugos
54A1 **Novi Sad** Serbia, Yugos
61J3 **Novoalekseyevka** Kazakhstan
61F3 **Novoanninskiy** Russian Fed
61E4 **Novocherkassk** Russian Fed
60C3 **Novograd Volynskiy** Ukraine
58D2 **Novogrudok** Russian Fed
30F4 **Novo Hamburgo** Brazil
65H5 **Novokazalinsk** Kazakhstan
65K4 **Novokuznetsk** Russian Fed
112B12 **Novolazarevskaya** *Base* Ant
52C1 **Novo Mesto** Slovenia
60E3 **Novomoskovsk** Russian Fed

60E5 **Novorossiysk** Russian Fed
65K4 **Novosibirsk** Russian Fed
1B8 **Novosibirskiye Ostrova** *I* Russian Fed
61J3 **Novotroitsk** Russian Fed
61G3 **Novo Uzensk** Russian Fed
59C2 **Novovolynsk** Ukraine
61G2 **Novo Vyatsk** Russian Fed
60D3 **Novozybkov** Russian Fed
58C2 **Novy Dwór Mazowiecki** Pol
61K2 **Novyy Lyalya** Russian Fed
61H5 **Novyy Port** Russian Fed
61H5 **Novyy Uzen** Kazakhstan
58B2 **Nowa Sól** Pol
18A2 **Nowata** USA
Nowgong = Nagaon
12D2 **Nowitna** *R* USA
109D2 **Nowra** Aust
90B2 **Now Shahr** Iran
84C2 **Nowshera** Pak
59C3 **Nowy Sącz** Pol
12H3 **Noyes I** USA
46B2 **Noyon** France
97B4 **Nsawam** Ghana
99D1 **Nuba** *Mts* Sudan
81B3 **Nubian Desert** Sudan
34A3 **Nuble** *R* Chile
9D4 **Nueces** *R* USA
5J3 **Nueltin L** Can
26A2 **Nueva Gerona** Cuba
34A3 **Nueva Imperial** Chile
9C4 **Nueva Laredo** Mexico
34D2 **Nueva Palmira** Urug
24B2 **Nueva Rosita** Mexico
26B2 **Nuevitas** Cuba
24B1 **Nuevas Casas Grandes** Mexico
24C2 **Nuevo Laredo** Mexico
6E2 **Nugaal** Region, Somalia
6E2 **Nûgâtsiaq** Greenland
6E2 **Nugssuag** *Pen* Greenland
6E2 **Nûgssuaq** *I* Greenland
108A2 **Nukey Bluff** *Mt* Aust
93D3 **Nukhayb** Iraq
65G5 **Nukus** Uzbekistan
12C2 **Nulato** USA
106B4 **Nullarbor Plain** Aust
97D4 **Numan** Nig
75B1 **Numata** Japan
98C2 **Numatinna** *R* Sudan
74D3 **Numazu** Japan
71E4 **Numfoor** *I* Indon
108C3 **Numurkah** Aust
12B2 **Nunapitchuk** USA
84D2 **Nunkun** *Mt* India
53A2 **Nuoro** Sardegna
91B3 **Nūrābād** Iran
47C2 **Nure** *R* Italy
108A2 **Nuriootpa** Aust
84C1 **Nuristan** *Upland* Afghan
61H3 **Nurlat** Russian Fed
38K6 **Nurmes** Fin
57C2 **Nürnberg** Germany
108C2 **Nurri,Mt** Aust
93D2 **Nusaybin** Turk
12C3 **Nushagak** *R* USA
12C3 **Nushagak B** USA
12C3 **Nushagak Pen** USA
84B3 **Nushki** Pak
7D4 **Nutak** Can
12F2 **Nutzotin Mts** USA
6E2 **Nuuk = Godthåb**
86A1 **Nuwakot** Nepal
87C3 **Nuwara-Eliya** Sri Lanka
6C3 **Nuyukjuak** Can

Nyack

16C2 Nyack USA
99D2 Nyahururu Kenya
108B3 Nyah West Aust
4C3 Nyai USA
68B3 Nyainqentanglha Shan Mts China
99D3 Nyakabindi Tanz
98C1 Nyala Sudan
86B1 Nyalam China
98C2 Nyamlell Sudan
64F3 Nyandoma Russian Fed
100C2 Nyanga Zim
98B3 Nyanga R Gabon
101C2 Nyasa L Malawi/Mozam
76B2 Nyaunglebin Burma
61J2 Nyazepetrovsk Russian Fed
39G7 Nyborg Den
39H7 Nybro Sweden
64J3 Nyda Russian Fed
6D1 Nyeboes Land Region Can
99D3 Nyeri Kenya
101C2 Nyimba Zambia
82D3 Nyingchi China
59C3 Nyiregyháza Hung
99D2 Nyiru,Mt Kenya
38J6 Nykarleby Fin
39F7 Nykøbing Den
39G8 Nykøbing Den
39H7 Nyköping Sweden
100B3 Nylstroom S Africa
109C2 Nymagee Aust
39H7 Nynäshamn Sweden
109C2 Nyngan Aust
47B1 Nyon Switz
98B2 Nyong R Cam
49D3 Nyons France
59B2 Nysa Pol
20C2 Nyssa USA
63D1 Nyurba Russian Fed
99D3 Nzega Tanz
97B4 Nzérékore Guinea
98B3 N'zeto Angola

O

6F3 Oaggsimiut Greenland
8C2 Oahe Res USA
21C4 Oahu I Hawaiian Is
108B2 Oakbank Aust
22B2 Oakdale USA
109D1 Oakey Aust
21A2 Oakland California, USA
20B2 Oakland Oregon, USA
14A3 Oakland City USA
22A2 Oak Lawn USA
22B2 Oakley California, USA
20D2 Oakridge USA
14C2 Oakville Can
111B3 Oamaru NZ
112B7 Oates Land Region, Ant
109C4 Oatlands Aust
23B2 Oaxaca Mexico
23B2 Oaxaca State, Mexico
65J3 Ob' R Russian Fed
75B1 Obama Japan
111A3 Oban NZ
44B3 Oban Scot
75C1 Obanazawa Japan
47D1 Oberammergau Germany
46D1 Oberhausen Germany
47D1 Oberstdorf Germany
71D4 Obi I Indon
33F4 Obidos Brazil
74E2 Obihiro Japan
98C2 Obo CAR
99E1 Obock Djibouti
58B2 Oborniki Pol
60E3 Oboyan Russian Fed
20B2 O'Brien USA
61H3 Obshchiy Syrt Mts Russian Fed
64J3 Obskaya Guba B Russian Fed

97B4 Obuasi Ghana
17B2 Ocala USA
32C2 Ocana Colombia
50B2 Ocaño Spain
12G3 Ocean C USA
15C3 Ocean City Maryland, USA
16B3 Ocean City New Jersey, USA
5F4 Ocean Falls Can
22D4 Oceanside USA
19C3 Ocean Springs USA
61H2 Ocher Russian Fed
44C3 Ochil Hills Scot
17B1 Ochlockonee R USA
27H1 Ocho Rios Jamaica
17B1 Ocmulgee R USA
17B1 Oconee R USA
14A2 Oconto USA
23A1 Ocotlán Jalisco, Mexico
23B2 Ocotlán Oaxaca, Mexico
97B4 Oda Ghana
75A1 Oda Japan
38B2 Ódáðahraun Region, Iceland
74E2 Odate Japan
74D3 Odawara Japan
39F6 Odda Nor
60A2 Odemira Port
55C3 Ödemiş Turk
101G1 Odendaalsrus S Africa
39G7 Odense Den
56C2 Oder R Pol/Germany
9C3 Odessa Texas, USA
60D4 Odessa Ukraine
20C1 Odessa Washington, USA
97B4 Odienné Ivory Coast
59B2 Odra R Pol
31C3 Oeiras Brazil
53C2 Ofanto R Italy
94B3 Ofaqim Israel
45C2 Offaly County, Irish Rep
49D1 Offenbach Germany
49D2 Offenburg Germany
74D3 Oga Japan
99E2 Ogaden Region, Eth
74D3 Ogaki Japan
8C2 Ogallala USA
69G4 Ogasawara Gunto Is Japan
97C4 Ogbomosho Nig
8B2 Ogden Utah, USA
15C2 Ogdensburg USA
17B1 Ogeechee R USA
12G1 Ogilvie Can
4E3 Ogilvie Mts Can
17B1 Oglethorpe,Mt USA
47D2 Oglio R Italy
47B1 Ognon R France
97C4 Ogoja Nig
98A3 Ogooué R Gabon
58C1 Ogre Latvia
96B2 Oguilet Khenachich Well Mali
52C1 Ogulin Croatia
111A3 Ohai NZ
110C1 Ohakune NZ
96C2 Ohanet Alg
111A2 Ohau,L NZ
14A3 Ohio State, USA
14A3 Ohio R USA
100A2 Ohopoho Namibia
57C2 Ohre R Czech Republic
55B2 Ohrid Macedonia
55B2 Ohridsko Jezero L Macedonia/Alb
110B1 Ohura NZ
33G3 Oiapoque French Guiana
68B2 Oijiaojing China
14C2 Oil City USA
21B2 Oildale USA
46B2 Oise Department, France
49C2 Oise R France
74C4 Oita Japan
22C3 Ojai USA
24B2 Ojinaga Mexico

23B2 Ojitlán Mexico
75B1 Ojiya Japan
30C4 Ojos del Salado Mt Arg
23A1 Ojueloz Mexico
60E3 Oka R Russian Fed
100A3 Okahandja Namibia
20C1 Okanagan Falls Can
13D2 Okanagan L Can
20C1 Okanogan USA
20C1 Okanogan R USA
20C1 Okanogan Range Mts Can/USA
84C2 Okara Pak
100A2 Okavango R Angola/Namibia
100B2 Okavango Delta Marsh Botswana
74D3 Okaya Japan
74C4 Okayama Japan
75B2 Okazaki Japan
17B2 Okeechobee USA
17B2 Okeechobee,L USA
17B1 Okefenokee Swamp USA
97C4 Okene Nig
85B4 Okha India
69G1 Okha Russian Fed
86B1 Okhaldunga Nepal
62J3 Okhotsk,S of Russian Fed
69E4 Okinawa I Japan
69E4 Okinawa gunto Arch Japan
74C3 Oki-shoto Is Japan
9D3 Oklahoma State, USA
18A2 Oklahoma City USA
18A2 Okmulgee USA
98B3 Okondja Gabon
98B3 Okoyo Congo
97C4 Okpara R Nig
61J4 Oktyab'sk Kazakhstan
61H3 Oktyabr'skiy Russian Fed
74D2 Okushiri-tö I Japan
38A2 Ólafsvik Iceland
39H7 Öland I Sweden
108B2 Olary Aust
18B2 Olathe USA
29D3 Olavarria Arg
53A2 Olbia Sardegna
14C2 Old Crow Can
56B2 Oldenburg Niedersachsen, Germany
56C2 Oldenburg Schleswig-Holstein, Germany
15C2 Old Forge USA
42C3 Oldham Eng
12D3 Old Harbor USA
41B3 Old Head of Kinsale C Scot
16C2 Old Lyme USA
13E2 Olds Can
72B1 Oldziyt Mongolia
16C2 Olean USA
63F7 Olekma R Russian Fed
63D1 Olekminsk Russian Fed
38L5 Olenegorsk Russian Fed
58D2 Olevsk Ukraine
69F2 Ol'ga Russian Fed
100A3 Olifants R Namibia
55B2 Olimbos Mt Greece
35B2 Olímpia Brazil
23B2 Olinala Mexico
31E3 Olinda Brazil
34C2 Oliva Arg
29C2 Olivares Mt Arg
35C2 Oliveira Brazil
13D3 Oliver Can
30C3 Ollague Chile
30C3 Ollagüe Mt Bol
59A3 Olomouc Czech Republic
68E1 Olochi Russian Fed
39G7 Olofström Sweden
98B3 Olombo Congo

60D1 Olonets Russian Fed
79B3 Olongapa Phil
48B3 Oloron Ste Marie France
68D1 Olovyannaya Russian Fed
46D1 Olpe Germany
58C2 Olsztyn Pol
54B2 Olt R Rom
47B1 Olten Switz
20B1 Olympia USA
20B1 Olympic Nat Pk USA
Olympus = Olimbos
20B1 Olympus,Mt USA
65J4 Om' R Russian Fed
75B1 Omachi Japan
75B2 Omae-zaki C Japan
45C1 Omagh N Ire
18A1 Omaha USA
20C1 Omak USA
91C5 Oman Sultanate, Arabian Pen
91C4 Oman,G of UAE
98A3 Omboué Gabon
99D1 Omdurman Sudan
23B2 Ometepec Mexico
99D1 Om Häjer Eritrea
13B1 Omineca R Can
13B1 Omineca Mts Can
75B1 Omiya Japan
12H3 Ommaney,C USA
4H2 Ommanney B Can
99D2 Omo R Eth
65J4 Omsk Russian Fed
74B4 Omura Japan
74C4 Omuta Japan
61H2 Omutninsk Russian Fed
78D3 Onang Indon
14B1 Onaping L Can
100A2 Oncócua Angola
100A2 Ondangua Namibia
59C3 Ondava R Slovakia
68D2 Öndörhaan Molgolia
83B5 One and Half Degree Chan Indian O
64E3 Onega Russian Fed
64E3 Onega R Russian Fed
15C2 Oneida L USA
8D2 O'Neill USA
16C2 Onekotan I Russian Fed
98C3 Onema Zaire
15D2 Oneonta USA
54C1 Onesti Rom
64E3 Onezhskoye Ozero L Russian Fed
100A2 Ongiva Angola
74B3 Ongjin N Korea
72D1 Ongniud Qi China
87C1 Ongole India
15C2 Onieda L USA
101D3 Onilahy R Madag
97C4 Onitsha Nig
68C2 Onjüül Mongolia
75B1 Ono Japan
75B2 Onohara-jima I Japan
74C4 Onomichi Japan
106A3 Onslow Aust
17C1 Onslow B USA
75B1 Ontake-san Mt Japan
22D3 Ontario California, USA
20C2 Ontario Oregon, USA
7A4 Ontario Province, Can
15C2 Ontario,L Can/USA
51B2 Onteniente Spain
106C3 Oodnadatta Aust
106C4 Ooldea Aust
18A2 Oologah L USA
46B1 Oostende Belg
46B1 Oosterschelde Estuary Neth
100A2 Ootacamund India
13B2 Oosta L Can
69H1 Opala Russian Fed
98C3 Opala Zaire
87C3 Opanake Sri Lanka
61G2 Oparino Russian Fed

59B3 **Opava**
Czech Republic
17A1 **Opelika** USA
19B3 **Opelousas** USA
12C2 **Ophir** USA
58D1 **Opochka**
Russian Fed
59B2 **Opole** Pol
Oporto = Porto
110C1 **Opotiki** NZ
17A1 **Opp** USA
38F6 **Oppdal** Nor
110B1 **Opunake** NZ
54B1 **Oradea** Rom
38B2 **Oraefajökull** Mts
Iceland
85D3 **Orai** India
96B1 **Oran** Alg
30D3 **Orán** Arg
109C2 **Orange** Aust
22D4 **Orange** California,
USA
49C3 **Orange** France
19B3 **Orange** Texas, USA
100A3 **Orange** R S Africa
17B1 **Orangeburg** USA
101G1 **Orange Free State**
Province, S Africa
17B1 **Orange Park** USA
14B2 **Orangeville** Can
56C2 **Oranienburg**
Germany
79C3 **Oras** Phil
54B1 **Orăstie** Rom
54B1 **Oravita** Rom
52B2 **Orbetello** Italy
109C3 **Orbost** Aust
46B1 **Orchies** France
47B2 **Orco** R Italy
106B2 **Ord** R Aust
106B2 **Ord,Mt** Aust
93C1 **Ordu** Turk
39H7 **Örebro** Sweden
8A2 **Oregon** State, USA
14B2 **Oregon** USA
20B1 **Oregon City** USA
39H6 **Oregrund** Sweden
60E2 **Orekhovo Zuyevo**
Russian Fed
60E3 **Orel** Russian Fed
61H3 **Orenburg**
Russian Fed
34D3 **Orense** Arg
50A1 **Orense** Spain
56C1 **Oresund** Str Den/
Sweden
111A3 **Oreti** R NZ
55C3 **Orhaneli** R Turk
68C2 **Orhon Gol** R
Mongolia
23B2 **Oriental** Mexico
108B1 **Orientos** Aust
51B2 **Orihuela** Spain
15C2 **Orillia** Can
33E2 **Orinoco** R Ven
86A2 **Orissa** State, India
53A3 **Oristano** Sardegna
38K6 **Orivesi** L Fin
33F4 **Oriximina** Brazil
23B2 **Orizaba** Mexico
35B1 **Orizona** Brazil
44C2 **Orkney** I Scot
35B2 **Orlândia** Brazil
17B2 **Orlando** USA
48C2 **Orléanais** Region
France
48C2 **Orléans** France
63B2 **Orlik** Russian Fed
82A3 **Ormara** Pak
79B3 **Ormoc** Phil
17B2 **Ormond Beach**
USA
46C2 **Ornain** R France
47B1 **Ornans** France
48B2 **Orne** R France
38H6 **Örnsköldsvik**
Sweden
32C3 **Orocué** Colombia
94B3 **Oron** Israel
Orontes = 'Āṣi
79B4 **Oroquieta** Phil
59C3 **Oroszháza** Hung
21A2 **Oroville** California,
USA

20C1 **Oroville** Washington,
USA
47B1 **Orsières** Switz
65G4 **Orsk** Russian Fed
38F6 **Ørsta** Nor
48B3 **Orthez** France
50A1 **Ortigueira** Spain
47D1 **Ortles** Mts Italy
27L1 **Ortoire** R Trinidad
93E2 **Orūmīyeh** Iran
30C2 **Oruro** Bol
61J2 **Osa** Russian Fed
18B2 **Osage** R USA
75B1 **Osaka** Japan
25D4 **Osa,Pen de** Costa
Rica
18C2 **Osceola** Arkansas,
USA
18B1 **Osceola** Iowa, USA
20C2 **Osgood Mts** USA
15C2 **Oshawa** Can
75B2 **O-shima** I Japan
10B2 **Oshkosh** USA
97C4 **Oshogbo** Nig
7B5 **Oshosh** USA
98B3 **Oshwe** Zaïre
54A1 **Osijek** Croatia
65K5 **Osinniki** Russian Fed
58D2 **Osipovichi**
Belorussia
18B1 **Oskaloosa** USA
60A2 **Oskarshamn** Sweden
39G7 **Oslo** Nor
92C2 **Osmaniye** Turk
56B2 **Osnabrück** Germany
30F4 **Osório** Brazil
29B4 **Osorno** Chile
50B1 **Osorno** Spain
20C1 **Osoyoos** Can
13C1 **Ospika** R Can
107D5 **Ossa,Mt** Aust
16C2 **Ossining** USA
60D2 **Ostashkov**
Russian Fed
Ostend = Oostende
38G6 **Österdalen** V Nor
38G6 **Östersund** Sweden
56B2 **Ostfriesische Inseln**
Is Germany
39H6 **Östhammär** Sweden
53B2 **Ostia** Italy
47D2 **Ostiglia** Italy
59B3 **Ostrava**
Czech Republic
58B2 **Ostróda** Pol
58B2 **Ostroleka** Pol
60C2 **Ostrov** Russian Fed
64J2 **Ostrov Belyy** I
Russian Fed
64H1 **Ostrov Greem Bell** I
Barents S
64F3 **Ostrov Kolguyev** I
Russian Fed
74F2 **Ostrov Kunashir** I
Russian Fed
64F2 **Ostrov**
Mechdusharskiy I
Barents S
90B2 **Ostrov Ogurchinskiy**
I Turkmenistan
64G1 **Ostrov Rudol'fa** I
Barents S
64G2 **Ostrov Vaygach** I
Russian Fed
1B7 **Ostrov Vrangelya** I
Russian Fed
58B2 **Ostrów Wlkp.** Pol
59C2 **Ostrowiec** Pol
58C2 **Ostrów Mazowiecka**
Pol
50A2 **Osuna** Spain
15C2 **Oswego** USA
15C2 **Oswego** USA
43C3 **Oswestry** Eng
59B2 **Oświęcim** Pol
75B1 **Ota** Japan
111B3 **Otago Pen** NZ
110C2 **Otaki** NZ
74E2 **Otaru** Japan
32B3 **Otavalo** Ecuador
100A2 **Otavi** Namibia
75C1 **Otawara** Japan
20C1 **Othello** USA
55B3 **Óthris** Mt Greece

16C1 **Otis** Massachusetts,
USA
16B2 **Otisville** USA
100A3 **Otjiwarongo**
Namibia
72B2 **Otog Qi** China
110C1 **Otorohanga** NZ
55A2 **Otranto** Italy
55A2 **Otranto,Str of** Chan
Italy/Alb
14A2 **Otsego** USA
75B1 **Otsu** Japan
39F6 **Otta** Nor
39F7 **Otta** R Nor
15C1 **Ottawa** Can
18A2 **Ottawa** Kansas, USA
15C1 **Ottawa** R Can
7B4 **Ottawa Is** Can
7B4 **Otter Rapids** Can
6B1 **Otto Fjord** Can
101G1 **Ottosdal** S Africa
18B1 **Ottumwa** USA
46D2 **Ottweiler** Germany
97C4 **Oturkpo** Nig
32B5 **Otusco** Peru
108B3 **Otway,C** Aust
58C2 **Otwock** Pol
47D1 **Ötz** Austria
47D1 **Ötzal** Mts Austria
76C1 **Ou** R Laos
19B3 **Ouachita** R USA
19B3 **Ouachita,L** USA
19B3 **Ouachita Mts** USA
96A2 **Ouadane** Maur
98C2 **Ouadda** CAR
98C1 **Ouaddai** Desert
Region Chad
97B3 **Ouagadougou**
Burkina
97B3 **Ouahigouya** Burkina
98C2 **Ouaka** CAR
97C3 **Oualam** Niger
98C2 **Oualien** Alg
98C2 **Ouanda Djallé** CAR
96A2 **Ouarane** Region,
Maur
96C1 **Ouargla** Alg
98C2 **Ouarra** R CAR
96B1 **Ouarzazate** Mor
51C2 **Ouassel** R Alg
98B2 **Oubangui** R Congo
46B1 **Oudenaarde** Belg
100B4 **Oudtshoorn** S Africa
51B2 **Oued Tlélat** Alg
96B1 **Oued Zem** Mor
98B2 **Ouesso** Congo
96B1 **Ouezzane** Mor
98B2 **Ouham** R Chad
97C4 **Ouidah** Benin
96B1 **Oujda** Mor
38J6 **Oulainen** Fin
38K5 **Oulu** Fin
38K6 **Oulu** R Fin
38K6 **Oulujärvi** L Fin
95B3 **Oum Chalouba** Chad
98B1 **Oum Hadjer** Chad
95B3 **Oum Haouach**
Watercourse Chad
38K5 **Ounas** R Fin
95B3 **Ounianga Kébir**
Chad
46D1 **Our** R Germany
46B2 **Ourcq** R France
Ourense = Orense
31C3 **Ouricuri** Brazil
35B2 **Ourinhos** Brazil
35C2 **Ouro Prêto** Brazil
46C1 **Ourthe** R Belg
42D2 **Ouse** R Eng
43E3 **Ouse** R Eng
40B2 **Outer Hebrides** Is
Scot
22C4 **Outer Santa Barbara**
Chan USA
100A3 **Outjo** Namibia
38K6 **Outokumpu** Fin
108B3 **Ouyen** Aust
47C2 **Ovada** Italy
29B4 **Ovalle** Chile
100A2 **Ovamboland** Region,
Namibia
61H5 **Ova Tyuleni** Is
Kazakhstan
38J5 **Övertorneä** Sweden

50A1 **Oviedo** Spain
60C3 **Ovruch** Ukraine
63E2 **Ovsyanka**
Russian Fed
111A2 **Owaka** NZ
75B2 **Owase** Japan
11B3 **Owensboro** USA
21B2 **Owens L** USA
14B2 **Owen Sound** Can
107D1 **Owen Stanley Range**
Mts PNG
97C4 **Owerri** Nig
97C4 **Owo** Nig
14B2 **Owosso** USA
20C2 **Owyhee** R USA
20C2 **Owyhee Mts** USA
32B6 **Oxapampa** Peru
39H7 **Oxelösund** Sweden
43D4 **Oxford** County, Eng
43D4 **Oxford** Eng
16D1 **Oxford**
Massachusetts, USA
19C3 **Oxford** Mississippi,
USA
45B1 **Ox Mts** Irish Rep
22C3 **Oxnard** USA
74D3 **Oyama** Japan
13E2 **Oyen** Can
98B2 **Oyem** Gabon
44B3 **Oykel** R Scot
39F6 **Øyre** Nor
109C4 **Oyster B** Aust
79B4 **Ozamiz** Phil
17A1 **Ozark** USA
18B2 **Ozark Plat** USA
18B2 **Ozarks,L of the** USA
59C3 **Ozd** Hung
65K5 **Ozero Alakol** L
Kazakhstan/
Russian Fed
65J5 **Ozero Balkhash** L
Kazakhstan
63C2 **Ozero Baykal** L
Kazakhstan
65J4 **Ozero Chany** L
Russian Fed
69F1 **Ozero**
Chukchagirskoye
Russian Fed
69F1 **Ozero Evoron**
Russian Fed
Ozero Chudskoye =
Peipus,L
60D2 **Ozero Il'men** L
Russian Fed
38L5 **Ozero Imandra** L
Russian Fed
82B1 **Ozero Issyk Kul'** L
Kirghizia
69F2 **Ozero Khanka** L
China/Russian Fed
38L5 **Ozero Kovdozero** L
Russian Fed
38L5 **Ozero Kuyto** L
Russian Fed
38L5 **Ozero Pyaozero** L
Russian Fed
65H4 **Ozero Tengiz** L
Kazakhstan
38L5 **Ozero Topozero** L
Russian Fed
65K5 **Ozero Zaysan** L
Kazakhstan
23B1 **Ozuluama** Mexico

P
100A4 **Paarl** S Africa
44A3 **Pabbay** I Scot
58B2 **Pabianice** Pol
86B2 **Pabna** Bang
58D2 **Pabrade** Lithuania
32B5 **Pacasmayo** Peru
23B1 **Pachuca** Mexico
105K6 **Pacific-Antarctic**
Ridge Pacific O
22B2 **Pacific Grove** USA
78C4 **Pacitan** Indon
35C1 **Pacuí** R Brazil
70B4 **Padang** Indon
56B2 **Paderborn** Germany
5J3 **Padlei** Can
86C2 **Padma** R Bang
47D2 **Padova** Italy
9D4 **Padre I** USA

Padstow

43B4 **Padstow** Eng
108B3 **Padthaway** Aust
    Padua = Padova
14A3 **Paducah** Kentucky, USA
11B3 **Paducah** USA
38L5 **Padunskoye More** L Russian Fed
74A3 **Paengnyŏng-do** / S Korea
110C1 **Paeroa** NZ
100C3 **Pafuri** Mozam
52B2 **Pag** / Croatia
79B4 **Pagadian** Phil
70B4 **Pagai Selatan** / Indon
70B4 **Pagai Utara** / Indon
71F2 **Pagan** / Pacific O
78D3 **Pagatan** Indon
55C3 **Pagondhas** Greece
110C2 **Pahiatua** NZ
21C4 **Pahoa** Hawaiian Is
17B2 **Pahokee** USA
39K6 **Pähiska** L Fin
21C4 **Pailola Chan** Hawaiian Is
14B2 **Painesville** USA
9B3 **Painted Desert** USA
42B2 **Paisley** Scot
32A5 **Paita** Peru
38J5 **Pajala** Sweden
00C3 **Pakistan** Republic, Asia
76C2 **Pak Lay** Laos
86D2 **Pakokku** Burma
13E2 **Pakowki L** Can
52C1 **Pakrac** Croatia
54A1 **Paks** Hung
76C2 **Pak Sane** Laos
76D2 **Pakse** Laos
99D2 **Pakwach** Uganda
98B2 **Pala** Chad
52C2 **Palagruža** / Croatia
46B2 **Palaiseau** France
    Palakhat = Palghat
78C3 **Palangkaraya** Indon
87B2 **Palani** India
85C4 **Palanpur** India
100B3 **Palapye** Botswana
17B2 **Palatka** USA
71E3 **Palau Is** Pacific O
76B3 **Palaw** Burma
79A4 **Palawan** / Phil
79A4 **Palawan Pass** Phil
87B3 **Palayankottai** India
39J7 **Paldiski** Estonia
78A3 **Palembang** Indon
50B1 **Palencia** Spain
94A1 **Paleokhorio** Cyprus
53B3 **Palermo** Italy
19A3 **Palestine** USA
86C2 **Paletwa** Burma
87B2 **Pälghät** India
85C3 **Päli** India
85C4 **Pälitäna** India
87B3 **Palk Str** India/ Sri Lanka
61G3 **Pallasovka** Russian Fed
38J5 **Pallastunturi** Mt Fin
111B2 **Palliser B** NZ
111C2 **Palliser,C** NZ
101D2 **Palma** Mozam
51C2 **Palma de Mallorca** Spain
31D3 **Palmares** Brazil
26A5 **Palmar Sur** Costa Rica
97B4 **Palmas,C** Lib
26B2 **Palma Soriano** Cuba
17B2 **Palm Bay** USA
17B2 **Palm Beach** USA
22C3 **Palmdale** USA
31D3 **Palmeira dos Indos** Brazil
12E2 **Palmer** USA
112C3 **Palmer** Base Ant
112C3 **Palmer Arch** Ant
112B3 **Palmer Land** Region Ant
111B3 **Palmerston** NZ
110C2 **Palmerston North** NZ
16B2 **Palmerton** USA
17B2 **Palmetto** USA

53C3 **Palmi** Italy
32B3 **Palmira** Colombia
107D2 **Palm Is** Aust
21B3 **Palm Springs** USA
18B2 **Palmyra** Missouri, USA
16A2 **Palmyra** Pennsylvania, USA
86B2 **Palmyras Pt** India
22A2 **Palo Alto** USA
78B2 **Paloh** Indon
99D1 **Paloich** Sudan
21B3 **Palomar Mt** USA
70D4 **Palopo** Indon
70C4 **Palu** Indon
93C2 **Palu** Turk
84D3 **Palwal** India
97C3 **Pama** Burkina
78C4 **Pamekasan** Indon
78B4 **Pameungpeuk** Indon
48C3 **Pamiers** France
82B2 **Pamir** Mts China
65J6 **Pamir** R Russian Fed
11C3 **Pamlico Sd** USA
9C3 **Pampa** USA
34B2 **Pampa de la Salinas** Salt pan Arg
34B3 **Pampa de la Varita** Plain Arg
32C2 **Pamplona** Colombia
50B1 **Pamplona** Spain
18C2 **Pana** USA
54B2 **Panagyurishte** Bulg
87A1 **Panaji** India
32B2 **Panamá** Panama
32A2 **Panama** Republic, Cent America
26B5 **Panama Canal** Panama
17A1 **Panama City** USA
21B2 **Panamint Range** Mts USA
21B2 **Panamint V** USA
47D2 **Panaro** R Italy
79B3 **Panay** / Phil
54B2 **Pancevo** Serbia, Yugos
79B3 **Pandan** Phil
87B1 **Pandharpur** India
108A1 **Pandie Pandie** Aust
58C1 **Panevežys** Lithuania
65K5 **Panfilov** Kazakhstan
76B1 **Pang** R Burma
99D3 **Pangani** Tanz
99D3 **Pangani** R Tanz
98C3 **Pangi** Zaire
78B4 **Pangkalpinang** Indon
6D3 **Pangnirtung** Can
76B1 **Pangtara** Burma
79B4 **Panguan Group** /s Phil
84D3 **Panipat** India
04D2 **Panjao** Afghan
74B3 **P'anmunjŏm** N Korea
86A2 **Panna** India
35A2 **Panorama** Brazil
53B3 **Pantelleria** / Medit S
23B1 **Pantepec** Mexico
23B1 **Pánuco** Mexico
23B1 **Pánuco** R Mexico
73A4 **Pan Xian** China
53C3 **Paola** Italy
18B2 **Paola** USA
14A3 **Paoli** USA
59B3 **Pápa** Hung
110B1 **Papakura** NZ
23B2 **Papaloapan** R Mexico
23B1 **Papantla** Mexico
44E1 **Papa Stour** / Scot
110B1 **Papatoetoe** NZ
44C2 **Papa Westray** / Scot
107D1 **Papua,G of** PNG
107D1 **Papua New Guinea** Republic, SE Asia
34A2 **Papudo** Chile
76B2 **Papun** Burma
33G4 **Pará** State, Brazil
31B2 **Pará** R Brazil
106A3 **Paraburdoo** Aust
32B6 **Paracas,Pen de** Peru
35B1 **Paracatu** Brazil

35B1 **Paracatu** R Brazil
108A2 **Parachilna** Aust
84C2 **Parachinar** Pak
54B2 **Paracin** Serbia, Yugos
35C1 **Pará de Minas** Brazil
21A2 **Paradise** California, USA
18B2 **Paragould** USA
33E6 **Paragua** R Bol
33E2 **Paragua** R Ven
30E2 **Paraguai** R Brazil
30E4 **Paraguari** Par
30E3 **Paraguay** Republic, S America
30E3 **Paraguay** R Par
31D3 **Paraiba** State, Brazil
35B2 **Paraiba** R Brazil
35C2 **Paraiba do Sul** R Brazil
97C4 **Parakou** Benin
108A2 **Parakylia** Aust
87B3 **Paramakkudi** India
33F2 **Paramaribo** Surinam
69H1 **Paramushir** / Russian Fed
30F3 **Paraná** State, Brazil
34C2 **Parana** Urug
29E2 **Paraná** R Arg
31B4 **Paraná** R Brazil
30A2 **Paraná** R Brazil
30G4 **Paranaguá** Brazil
35A1 **Paranaiba** Brazil
35A1 **Paranaiba** R Brazil
35A2 **Paranapanema** R Brazil
35A2 **Paranavai** Brazil
79B4 **Parang** Phil
35C1 **Paraope** R Brazil
110B2 **Paraparaumu** NZ
87B1 **Parbhani** India
94B2 **Pardes Hanna** Israel
34D3 **Pardo** Arg
35D1 **Pardo** R Bahia, Brazil
35A2 **Pardo** R Mato Grosso do Sul, Brazil
35B1 **Pardo** R Minas Gerais, Brazil
35B2 **Pardo** R Sao Paulo, Brazil
59B2 **Pardubice** Czech Republic
69F4 **Parece Vela** Reef Pacific O
12A2 **Parent** Can
70C4 **Parepare** Indon
34C3 **Parera** Arg
70B4 **Pariaman** Indon
33E1 **Paria,Pen de** Ven
48C2 **Paris** France
19A3 **Paris** Kentucky, USA
19A3 **Paris** Texas, USA
14B3 **Parkersburg** USA
109C2 **Parkes** Aust
16B3 **Parkesburg** USA
14A2 **Park Forest** USA
20B1 **Parksville** Can
87B1 **Parli** India
47D2 **Parma** Italy
14B2 **Parma** USA
31C2 **Parnaíba** Brazil
31C2 **Parnaiba** R Brazil
55B3 **Párnon Óros** Mts Greece
60B2 **Pärnu** Estonia
86B1 **Paro** Bhutan
108B1 **Paroo** R Aust
108B2 **Paroo Channel** R Aust
55C3 **Páros** / Greece
47B2 **Parpaillon** Mts France
34A3 **Parral** Chile
109D2 **Parramatta** Aust
9C4 **Parras** Mexico
6B3 **Parry B** Can
4G2 **Parry Is** Can
7C5 **Parry Sd** Can
14B1 **Parry Sound** Can
57C3 **Parsberg** Germany
5F4 **Parsnip** R Can
18A2 **Parsons** Kansas, USA
14C3 **Parsons** West Virginia, USA

48B2 **Parthenay** France
53B3 **Partinico** Italy
74C2 **Partizansk** Russian Fed
33G4 **Paru** R Brazil
101G1 **Parys** S Africa
19A4 **Pasadena** Texas, USA
22C3 **Pasadena** California, USA
78D3 **Pasangkayu** Indon
76B2 **Pasawing** Burma
19C3 **Pascagoula** USA
54C1 **Paşcani** Rom
20C1 **Pasco** USA
46B1 **Pas-de-Calais** Department, France
39G8 **Pasewalk** Germany
91C4 **Pashū'iyeh** Iran
106B4 **Pasley,C** Aust
29E2 **Paso de los Toros** Urug
29B4 **Paso Limay** Arg
21A2 **Paso Robles** USA
45B3 **Passage West** Irish Rep
16B2 **Passaic** USA
57C3 **Passau** Germany
30E4 **Paso de los Libres** Arg
47D1 **Passo di Stelvio** Mt Italy
30F4 **Passo Fundo** Brazil
35B2 **Passos** Brazil
47B2 **Passy** France
32B4 **Pastaza** R Peru
34C3 **Pasteur** Arg
5H4 **Pas,The** Can
32B3 **Pasto** Colombia
12B2 **Pastol B** USA
47D2 **Pasubio** Mt Italy
78C4 **Pasuruan** Indon
58C1 **Pasvalys** Lithuania
85C4 **Pätan** India
86B1 **Patan** Nepal
108B3 **Patchewollock** Aust
110B1 **Patea** NZ
111B2 **Patea** R NZ
53B3 **Paterno** Italy
16B2 **Paterson** USA
111A3 **Paterson Inlet** B NZ
84D2 **Pathänkot** India
    Pathein = Bassein
84D2 **Patiäla** India
32B6 **Pativilca** Peru
55C3 **Pátmos** / Greece
86B1 **Patna** India
93D2 **Patnos** Turk
63D2 **Patomskoye Nagor'ye** Upland Russian Fed
31D3 **Patos** Brazil
30G1 **Patos de Minas** Brazil
34B2 **Patquia** Arg
55B3 **Pátrai** Greece
35B1 **Patrocinio** Brazil
99E3 **Patta** / Kenya
78D4 **Pattallasang** Indon
77C4 **Pattani** Thai
22B2 **Patterson** California, USA
19B4 **Patterson** Louisiana, USA
12H2 **Patterson,Mt** Can
22C2 **Patterson,Mt** USA
13B1 **Pattullo,Mt** Can
31D3 **Patu** Brazil
86C2 **Patuakhali** Bang
25D3 **Patuca** R Honduras
23A2 **Patzcuaro** Mexico
48B3 **Pau** France
4F3 **Paulatuk** Can
31C3 **Paulistana** Brazil
101H1 **Paulpietersburg** S Africa
31A3 **Pauls Valley** USA
76B2 **Paungde** Burma
84D2 **Pauri** India
38H5 **Pauske** Nor
35C1 **Pavão** Brazil
47C2 **Pavia** Italy
65J4 **Pavlodar** Kazakhstan
61J2 **Pavlovka** Russian Fed

61F2 **Pavlovo** Russian Fed
61F3 **Pavlovsk** Russian Fed
78C3 **Pawan** R Indon
18A2 **Pawhuska** USA
16D2 **Pawtucket** USA
47B1 **Payerne** Switz
20C2 **Payette** USA
7C4 **Payne,L** Can
34D2 **Paysandu** Urug
46A2 **Pays-de-Bray** Region, France
54B2 **Pazardzhik** Bulg
13D1 **Peace** R Can
17B2 **Peace** R USA
13D1 **Peace River** Can
43D3 **Peak District Nat Pk** Eng
108A1 **Peake** R Aust
109C2 **Peak Hill** Aust
71E4 **Peak Mandala** Mt Indon
42D3 **Peak,The** Mt Eng
19B3 **Pearl** R USA
21C4 **Pearl City** Hawaiian Is
21C4 **Pearl Harbor** Hawaiian Is
4H2 **Peary Chan** Can
101C2 **Pebane** Mozam
54B2 **Peć** Serbia, Yugos
35C1 **Peçanha** Brazil
19B4 **Pecan Island** USA
38L5 **Pechenga** Russian Fed
64F3 **Pechora** R Russian Fed
64G3 **Pechorskoye More** S Russian Fed
53C3 **Pecoraro** Mt Italy
9C3 **Pecos** USA
9C3 **Pecos** R USA
59B3 **Pécs** Hung
108A1 **Pedirka** Aust
35C1 **Pedra Azul** Brazil
35B2 **Pedregulho** Brazil
26B3 **Pedro Cays** Is Caribbean S
30C3 **Pedro de Valdivia** Chile
30E3 **Pedro Juan Caballero** Par
34C3 **Pedro Luro** Arg
23B1 **Pedro Mentova** Mexico
87C3 **Pedro,Pt** Sri Lanka
108B2 **Peebinga** Aust
42C2 **Peebles** Scot
17C1 **Pee Dee** R USA
16C2 **Peekskill** USA
42B2 **Peel** Eng
12H1 **Peel** R Can
4J2 **Peel Sd** Can
108A1 **Peera Peera Poolanna** L Aust
13E1 **Peerless L** Can
71E4 **Peg Arfak** Mt Indon
111B2 **Pegasus B** NZ
83D4 **Pegu** Burma
78A3 **Pegunungan Barisan** Mts Indon
78C2 **Pegunungan Iran** Mts Malay/Indon
71E4 **Pegunungan Maoke** Mts Indon
78D3 **Pegunungan Meratus** Mts Indon
78C2 **Pegunungan Muller** Mts Indon
78C3 **Pegunungan Schwanet** Mts Indon
78A3 **Pegunungan Tigapuluh** Mts Indon
76B2 **Pegu Yoma** Mts Burma
34C3 **Pehuajó** Arg
Péipsi Järve = Peipus,L
39K7 **Peipus, Lake** Estonia/Russian Fed
35A2 **Peixe** R Sao Paulo, Brazil
72D3 **Pei Xian** China
78B4 **Pekalongan** Indon

77C5 **Pekan** Malay
78A2 **Pekanbaru** Indon
18C1 **Pekin** USA
Peking = Beijing
77C5 **Pelabohan Kelang** Malay
78D4 **Pelau Pelau Kangean** Is Indon
78C4 **Pelau Pelau Karimunjawa** Arch Indon
78D4 **Pelau Pelau Postilyon** Is Indon
54B1 **Peleaga** Mt Rom
63D2 **Peleduy** Russian Fed
14B2 **Pelee I** Can
71D4 **Peleng** I Indon
12G3 **Pelican** USA
69F1 **Peliny Osipenko** Russian Fed
34C3 **Pellegrini** Arg
38J5 **Pello** Fin
12H2 **Pelly** R Can
6A3 **Pelly Bay** Can
12G2 **Pelly Crossing** Can
12H2 **Pelly Mts** Can
30F5 **Pelotas** Brazil
30F4 **Pelotas** R Brazil
47B2 **Pelvoux** Region, France
78B4 **Pemalang** Indon
78A3 **Pematang** Indon
101D2 **Pemba** Mozam
99D3 **Pemba** I Tanz
13C2 **Pemberton** Can
13D2 **Pembina** R Can
15C1 **Pembroke** Can
17B1 **Pembroke** Can
43B4 **Pembroke** Wales
34A3 **Penco** Chile
78D2 **Penambo Range** Mts Malay
35A2 **Penápolis** Brazil
50A2 **Peñarroya** Spain
51B1 **Penarroya** Mt Spain
50A1 **Peña Trevina** Mt Spain
98B2 **Pende** R Chad
12J3 **Pendelton,Mt** Can
20C1 **Pendleton** USA
20C1 **Pend Oreille** R USA
31D4 **Penedo** Brazil
85D5 **Penganga** R India
73D5 **P'eng-ku Lieh-tao** Is Taiwan
72E2 **Penglai** China
73B4 **Pengshui** China
71E4 **Pegunungan Maoke** Mts Indon
26C4 **Peninsula de la Guajiri** Pen Colombia
27E4 **Peninsula de Paria** Pen Ven
77C5 **Peninsular Malaysia** Malay
10D2 **Peninsule de Gaspé** Pen Can
23A1 **Penjamo** Mexico
87B2 **Penner** R India
42C2 **Pennine Chain** Mts Eng
16B3 **Penns Grove** USA
10C2 **Pennsylvania** State, USA
6D3 **Penny Highlands** Mts Can
108B3 **Penola** Aust
106C4 **Penong** Aust
42C2 **Penrith** Eng
112A **Pensacola** USA
78D1 **Pensiangan** Malay
13D3 **Penticton** Can
44C2 **Pentland Firth** Chan Scot
42C2 **Pentland Hills** Scot
61G3 **Penza** Russian Fed
43B4 **Penzance** Eng
10B2 **Peoria** USA
78A3 **Perabumulih** Indon
77C5 **Perak** R Malay
78A2 **Perawang** Indon
32B3 **Pereira** Colombia

35A2 **Pereira Barreto** Brazil
61F4 **Perelazovskiy** Russian Fed
12D3 **Perenosa B** USA
34C2 **Pergamino** Arg
7C4 **Peribonca** R Can
48C2 **Périgueux** France
25E4 **Perlas Arch de** Is Panama
61J2 **Perm'** Russian Fed
Pernambuco = Recife
31D3 **Pernambuco** State, Brazil
108A2 **Pernatty Lg** Aust
54B2 **Pernik** Bulg
46B2 **Péronne** France
23B2 **Perote** Mexico
49C3 **Perpignan** France
22D4 **Perris** USA
17B1 **Perry** Florida, USA
17B1 **Perry** Georgia, USA
18A2 **Perry** Oklahoma, USA
4H3 **Perry River** Can
14B2 **Perrysburg** USA
12C3 **Perryville** Alaska, USA
18C2 **Perryville** Missouri, USA
106A4 **Perth** Aust
15C2 **Perth** Can
44C3 **Perth** Scot
16B2 **Perth Amboy** USA
32C6 **Peru** Republic, S America
18C1 **Peru** USA
103E5 **Peru-Chile Trench** Pacific O
52B2 **Perugia** Italy
52C2 **Perušic** Croatia
93D2 **Pervari** Turk
61F3 **Pervomaysk** Russian Fed
60D4 **Pervomaysk** Ukraine
61J2 **Pervoural'sk** Russian Fed
52B2 **Pesaro** Italy
22A2 **Pescadero** USA
Pescadores = P'eng-hu Lieh-tao
52B2 **Pescara** Italy
47D2 **Peschiera** Italy
84C2 **Peshawar** Pak
54B2 **Peshkopi** Alb
14A1 **Peshtigo** USA
60E2 **Pestovo** Russian Fed
94B2 **Petah Tiqwa** Israel
21A2 **Petaluma** USA
46C2 **Pétange** Lux
23A2 **Petatlan** Mexico
101C2 **Petauke** Zambia
108A2 **Peterborough** Aust
15C2 **Peterborough** Can
43D3 **Peterborough** Eng
44D3 **Peterhead** Scot
6D1 **Petermann Gletscher** Gl Greenland
106B3 **Petermann Range** Mts Aust
29B3 **Peteroa** Mt Arg/Chile
13F1 **Peter Pond L** Can
12H3 **Petersburg** Alaska, USA
85C4 **Petlad** India
23B2 **Petlalcingo** Mexico
25D2 **Peto** Mexico
63D2 **Petoh Stanovoy Nagor'ye** Upland Russian Fed
34A2 **Petorca** Chile
14B1 **Petoskey** USA
31C3 **Petrolina** Brazil
65H4 **Petropavlovsk** Kazakhstan
35C2 **Petrópolis** Brazil
61G3 **Petrovsk** Russian Fed
68C1 **Petrovsk Zabaykal'skiy** Russian Fed
64E3 **Petrozavodsk** Russian Fed
101G1 **Petrus** S Africa
101G1 **Petrusburg** S Africa

1B7 **Pevek** Russian Fed
46D2 **Pfälzer Wald** Region, Germany
57B3 **Pforzheim** Germany
84D2 **Phagwara** India
85C3 **Phalodi** India
46D2 **Phalsbourg** France
87A1 **Phaltan** India
77B4 **Phangnga** Thai
76C3 **Phanom Dang** Mts Camb
76D3 **Phan Rang** Viet
76D3 **Phan Thiet** Viet
17A1 **Phenix City** USA
76B3 **Phet Buri** Thai
76D3 **Phiafay** Laos
19C3 **Philadelphia** Mississippi, USA
16B2 **Philadelphia** Pennsylvania, USA
Philippeville = Skikda
46C1 **Philippeville** Belg
71D2 **Philippine S** Pacific O
71D2 **Philippines** Republic, S E Asia
104E3 **Philippine Trench** Pacific O
15C2 **Philipsburg** Pennsylvania, USA
12E1 **Philip Smith Mts** USA
79B2 **Phillipine S** Phil
6B1 **Phillips B** Can
16B2 **Phillipsburg** New Jersey, USA
6B2 **Philpots Pen** Can
76C3 **Phnom Penh** Camb
9B3 **Phoenix** Arizona, USA
16B2 **Phoenixville** USA
76C1 **Phong Saly** Laos
Phra Nakhon = Bangkok
76C2 **Phu Bia** Mt Laos
76D3 **Phu Cuong** Viet
77B4 **Phuket** Thai
86A2 **Phulbani** India
76C2 **Phu Miang** Mt Thai
76D2 **Phu Set** Mt Laos
76D1 **Phu Tho** Viet
77D4 **Phu Vinh** Viet
52B2 **Piacenza** Italy
109C2 **Pian** R Aust
52B2 **Pianosa** I Italy
52C2 **Pianosa** I Italy
58C2 **Piaseczno** Pol
54C1 **Piatra-Neamt** Rom
31C3 **Piauí** State, Brazil
47E2 **Piave** R Italy
99D2 **Pibor** R Sudan
99D2 **Pibor Post** Sudan
46B1 **Picardie** Region, France
19C3 **Picayune** USA
47B2 **Pic de Rochebrune** Mt France
34A2 **Pichilemu** Chile
34C3 **Pichi Mahuida** Arg
42D2 **Pickering** Eng
7A4 **Pickle Lake** Can
96A1 **Pico** I Açores
47C1 **Pico Bernina** Mt Switz
51C1 **Pico de Anito** Mt Spain
24B3 **Pico del Infiernillo** Mt Mexico
27C3 **Pico Duarte** Mt Dom Rep
31C3 **Picos** Brazil
50B1 **Picos de Europa** Mt Spain
109D2 **Picton** Can
111B2 **Picton** NZ
95A2 **Pic Toussidé** Mt Chad
35B2 **Piedade** Brazil
22C2 **Piedra** USA
24B2 **Piedras Negras** Mexico
38K6 **Pieksämäki** Fin
38K6 **Pielinen** L Fin
47B2 **Piemonte** Region, Italy

8C2 Pierre USA
59B3 Piešťany Slovakia
101H1 Pietermaritzburg S Africa
100B3 Pietersburg S Africa
101H1 Piet Retief S Africa
60B4 Pietrosu Mt Rom
47E1 Pieve di Cadore Italy
13E2 Pigeon L Can
18B2 Piggott USA
34C3 Pigüé Arg
7A4 Pikangikum L Can
8C3 Pikes Peak USA
100A4 Piketberg S Africa
6F3 Pikintaleq Greenland
82B2 Pik Kommunizma Mt Tajikistan
98B2 Pikounda Congo
82C1 Pik Pobedy Mt China/Kirghizia
34D3 Pila Arg
58B2 Piła Pol
30E4 Pilar Par
30D3 Pilcomayo R Arg/Par
84D3 Pilibhit India
59B2 Pilica R Pol
109C4 Pillar,C Aust
55B3 Pílos Greece
12C3 Pilot Point USA
12B2 Pilot Station USA
19C3 Pilottown USA
33F4 Pimenta Brazil
77C4 Pinang I Malay
26A2 Pinar del Rio Cuba
34B2 Pinas Arg
46C1 Pinche Belg
13E2 Pincher Creek Can
31B2 Pindaré R Brazil
55B3 Pindhos Mts Greece
19B3 Pine Bluff USA
106C2 Pine Creek Aust
22C1 Pinecrest USA
22C2 Pinedale California, USA
22C2 Pine Flat Res USA
64F3 Pinega R Russian Fed
16A2 Pine Grove USA
17B2 Pine Hills USA
17B2 Pine I USA
19B3 Pineland USA
17B2 Pinellas Park USA
5G3 Pine Point Can
26C0 Pinerolo Italy
19B3 Pines,L o'the USA
19B3 Pineville USA
72C3 Pingdingshan China
72B3 Pingguo China
72B2 Pingliang China
72B2 Pingluo China
73D4 Pingtan Dao I China
73E5 P'ing tung Taiwan
72A3 Pingwu China
73D5 Pingxiang Guangxi, China
73C4 Pingxiang Jiangxi, China
31B2 Pinheiro Brazil
70A3 Pini I Indon
55B3 Piniós R Greece
106A4 Pinjarra Aust
13C1 Pink Mountain Can
108B3 Pinnaroo Aust
Pinos,I de, I = Isla de la Juventud
21A2 Pinos,Pt USA
23B2 Pinotepa Nacional Mexico
70C4 Pinrang Indon
60C3 Pinsk Belorussia
32J7 Pinta I Ecuador
61G1 Pinyug Russian Fed
8B3 Pioche USA
52B2 Piombino Italy
6H3 Piórsá Iceland
59B2 Piotrków Trybunalski Pol
44E2 Piper Oilfield N Sea
21B2 Piper Peak Mt USA
10C2 Pipmuacan Res Can
12B2 Piqua USA
35B1 Piracanjuba Brazil
35B2 Piracicaba Brazil

35B2 Piraçununga Brazil
35B2 Piraí do Sul Brazil
55B3 Piraiévs Greece
35B2 Pirajuí Brazil
35A1 Piranhas Brazil
35C1 Pirapora Brazil
35B1 Pirenópolis Brazil
35B1 Pires do Rio Brazil
55B3 Pírgos Greece
Pirineos = Pyrénées
31C2 Piripiri Brazil
46D2 Pirmasens Germany
54B2 Pirot Serbia, Yugos
84C2 Pir Panjal Range Mts Pak
71D4 Piru Indon
22C3 Piru Creek R USA
49E3 Pisa Italy
32B6 Pisco Peru
57C3 Písek Czech Republic
84B2 Pishin Pak
30C4 Pissis Mt Arg
49E3 Pistoia Italy
50B1 Pisuerga R Spain
20B2 Pit R USA
32B3 Pitalito Colombia
105K5 Pitcairn I Pacific O
38H5 Pite R Sweden
38J5 Piteå Sweden
54B2 Pitești Rom
63B2 Pit Gorodok Russian Fed
38L6 Pitkyaranta Russian Fed
44C3 Pitlochry Scot
34A3 Pitrufquén Chile
13B2 Pitt I Can
22B1 Pittsburg California, USA
18B2 Pittsburg Kansas, USA
14C2 Pittsburgh USA
18B2 Pittsfield Illinois, USA
16C1 Pittsfield Massachusetts, USA
109D1 Pittsworth Aust
86A1 Piuthan Nepal
47D1 Pizzo Redorta Mt Italy
32A5 Pjura Peru
7E5 Placentia B Can
22B1 Placerville USA
46B1 Plaine des Flandres Plain Belg/France
96C2 Plaine du Tidikelt Desert Region
9C3 Plainview Texas, USA
22B2 Planada USA
30F2 Planalto de Mato Grosso Plat Brazil
31D3 Planalto do Borborema Plat Brazil
32A1 Planalto do Mato Grosso Mts Brazil
19B3 Plano USA
17B2 Plantation USA
17B2 Plant City USA
50A1 Plasencia Spain
61K3 Plast Russian Fed
69F2 Plastun Russian Fed
96C2 Plateau du Tademait Alg
46D2 Plateau Lorrain Plat France
48C2 Plateaux de Limousin Plat France
51C2 Plateau au Sersou Plat Alg
26C5 Plato Colombia
65G5 Plato Ustyurt Plat Kazakhstan
8C2 Platte R USA
15D2 Plattsburgh USA
18A1 Plattsmouth USA
57C2 Plauen Germany
60B3 Plavsk Russian Fed
23A2 Playa Azul Mexico
32A4 Playas Ecuador
23B2 Playa Vicente Mexico

50A1 Plaza de Moro Almanzor Mt Spain
22B2 Pleasanton California, USA
16B3 Pleasantville USA
14A3 Pleasure Ridge Park USA
76D3 Pleiku Viet
110C1 Plenty,B of NZ
58B2 Pleszew Pol
7C4 Pletipi,L Can
54B2 Pleven Bulg
54A2 Pljevlja Montenegro, Yugos
52C2 Ploče Bosnia-Herzegovina
58B2 Płock Pol
48B2 Plöermel France
54C2 Ploiești Rom
60B3 Płońsk Pol
54B2 Plovdiv Bulg
20C1 Plummer USA
12C2 Plummer,Mt USA
100B3 Plumtree Zim
22B1 Plymouth California, USA
43B4 Plymouth Eng
14A2 Plymouth Indiana, USA
16D2 Plymouth Massachusetts, USA
15C2 Plymouth Pennsylvania, USA
43B4 Plymouth Sd Eng
43C3 Plynlimon Mt Wales
57C3 Plzeň Czech Republic
58B2 Pniewy Pol
38K6 Pnyäselkä L Fin
97B3 Pô Burkina
47E2 Po R Italy
97C4 Pobé Benin
69G2 Pobedino Russian Fed
8B2 Pocatello USA
15C3 Pocomoke City USA
35B2 Poços de Caldas Brazil
54A2 Podgorica Montenegro, Yugos
74B3 Po'hang S Korea
47D2 Po di Volano R Italy
63B1 Podkamennaya R Russian Fed
60E2 Podol'sk Russian Fed
59D3 Podol'skaya Vozvyshennost' Upland Ukraine
60D1 Podporozh'ye Russian Fed
61F1 Podyuga Russian Fed
100A3 Pofadder S Africa
112C9 Poinsett,C Ant
108C2 Point Aust
27E3 Pointe-à-Pitre Guadeloupe
48B2 Pointe de Barfleur Pt France
98B3 Pointe Noire Congo
98A2 Pointe Pongara Pt Gabon
108B3 Point Fairy Aust
27L1 Point Fortin Trinidad
4B3 Point Hope USA
4G3 Point L Can
12B1 Point Lay USA
16B2 Point Pleasant New Jersey, USA
14B3 Point Pleasant W Virginia, USA
47B2 Point St Bernard Mt France
48C2 Poitiers France
48B2 Poitou Region, France
46A2 Poix France
85C3 Pokaran India
109C1 Pokataroo Aust
61G3 Pokrovsk Russian Fed
63E1 Pokrovsk Russian Fed
58B2 Poland Republic, Europe

92B2 Polatli Turk
78D3 Polewali Indon
47A1 Poligny France
55B2 Políyiros Greece
87B2 Pollachi India
79B3 Pololo Is Phil
59D2 Polonnye Ukraine
58D1 Polotsk Russian Fed
60D4 Poltava Russian Fed
52C1 Pölten Austria
64F3 Poluostrov Kanin Pen Russian Fed
61H5 Poluostrov Mangyshlak Pen Kazakhstan
38L5 Poluostrov Rybachiy Pen Russian Fed
64I12 Poluostrov Yamal Pen Russian Fed
38L5 Polyarnyy Murmansk, Russian Fed
1B8 Polyarnyy Yakutskaya, Russian Fed
105H3 Polynesia Region Pacific O
32B5 Pomabamba Peru
35C2 Pomba R Brazil
22D3 Pomona USA
58D1 Pomona Russian Fed
17B2 Pompano Beach USA
16B2 Pompton Lakes USA
18A2 Ponca City USA
27D3 Ponce Puerto Rico
17B2 Ponce de Leon B USA
87B2 Pondicherry India
6C2 Pond Inlet Can
50A1 Ponferrade Spain
98C2 Pongo R Sudan
101H1 Pongola R S Africa
87B2 Ponnani India
86C2 Ponnyadoung Range Mts Burma
13E2 Ponoka Can
64F3 Ponoy Russian Fed
48B2 Pons France
35D1 Ponta da Baleia Pt Brazil
96A1 Ponta Delgada Açores
98B3 Ponta do Padrão Pt Angola
35C2 Ponta dos Búzios Pt Brazil
30F4 Ponta Grossa Brazil
35B2 Pontal Brazil
46D2 Pont-à-Mousson France
30E3 Ponta Pora Brazil
49D2 Pontarlier France
19B3 Pontchartrain,L USA
52B2 Pontedera Italy
52A2 Ponte Leccia Corse
50A1 Pontevedra Spain
18C1 Pontiac Illinois, USA
14B2 Pontiac Michigan, USA
78B3 Pontianak Indon
48B2 Pontivy France
46B2 Pontoise France
108B2 Poopelloe,L Aust
18B2 Poplar Bluff USA
19C3 Poplarville USA
107D1 Popndetta PNG
23B2 Popocatepetl Mt Mexico
98B3 Popokabaka Zaïre
71F4 Popondetta PNG
54C2 Popovo Bulg
85B4 Porbandar India
13A2 Porcher I Can
12F1 Porcupine R Can/USA

52B1	**Poreč** Croatia
35A2	**Porecatu** Brazil
39J6	**Pori** Fin
111B2	**Poririua** NZ
38H5	**Porjus** Sweden
69G2	**Poronaysk** Russian Fed
47B1	**Porrentruy** Switz
38K4	**Porsangen** *Inlet* Nor
39F7	**Porsgrunn** Nor
45C1	**Portadown** N Ire
8D2	**Portage la Prairie** Can
13C3	**Port Alberni** Can
50A2	**Portalegre** Port
9C3	**Portales** USA
100B4	**Port Alfred** S Africa
13B2	**Port Alice** Can
19B3	**Port Allen** USA
20B1	**Port Angeles** USA
26B3	**Port Antonio** Jamaica
45C2	**Portarlington** Irish Rep
19B4	**Port Arthur** USA
108A2	**Port Augusta** Aust
26C3	**Port-au-Prince** Haiti
14B2	**Port Austin** USA
108B3	**Port Campbell** Aust
86B2	**Port Canning** India
7D5	**Port Cartier** Can
111B3	**Port Chalmers** NZ
17B2	**Port Charlotte** USA
16C2	**Port Chester** USA
15C2	**Port Colborne** Can
15C2	**Port Credit** Can
109C4	**Port Davey** Aust
26C3	**Port-de-Paix** Haiti
77C5	**Port Dickson** Malay
100C4	**Port Edward** S Africa
35C1	**Porteirinha** Brazil
14B2	**Port Elgin** Can
100B4	**Port Elizabeth** S Africa
27N2	**Porter Pt** St Vincent and the Grenadines
21B2	**Porterville** USA
107D4	**Port Fairy** Aust
98A3	**Port Gentil** Gabon
19B3	**Port Gibson** USA
12D3	**Port Graham** USA
20B1	**Port Hammond** Can
89E7	**Port Harcourt** Nig
13B2	**Port Hardy** Can
7D5	**Port Hawkesbury** Can
106A3	**Port Hedland** Aust
	Port Heiden = Meshik
43B3	**Porthmadog** Wales
7E4	**Port Hope Simpson** Can
22C3	**Port Hueneme** USA
14B2	**Port Huron** USA
50A2	**Portimão** Port
109D2	**Port Jackson** *B* Aust
16C2	**Port Jefferson** USA
16B2	**Port Jervis** USA
109D2	**Port Kembla** Aust
14B2	**Portland** Indiana, USA
10C2	**Portland** Maine, USA
109C2	**Portland** New South Wales, Aust
20B1	**Portland** Oregon, USA
108B3	**Portland** Victoria, Aust
27H2	**Portland Bight** *B* Jamaica
43C4	**Portland Bill** *Pt* Eng
109C4	**Portland,C** Aust
13A1	**Portland Canal** Can/ USA
110C1	**Portland I** NZ
27H2	**Portland Pt** Jamaica
45C2	**Port Laoise** Irish Rep
108A2	**Port Lincoln** Aust
97A4	**Port Loko** Sierra Leone
101E3	**Port Louis** Mauritius
108B3	**Port MacDonnell** Aust
13B2	**Port McNeill** Can
109D2	**Port Macquarie** Aust
12B3	**Port Moller** USA
107D1	**Port Moresby** PNG
100A3	**Port Nolloth** S Africa
16B3	**Port Norris** USA
89E7	**Port Novo** Benin
50A1	**Porto** Port
30F5	**Pôrto Alegre** Brazil
33F6	**Pôrto Artur** Brazil
30F3	**Pôrto E Cunha** Brazil
52B2	**Portoferraio** Italy
27E4	**Port of Spain** Trinidad
47D2	**Portomaggiore** Italy
97C4	**Porto Novo** Benin
20B1	**Port Orchard** USA
20B2	**Port Orford** USA
96A1	**Porto Santo** *I* Medeira
31D5	**Pôrto Seguro** Brazil
53A2	**Porto Torres** Sardegna
53A2	**Porto Vecchio** Corse
33E5	**Pôrto Velho** Brazil
111A3	**Port Pegasus** *B* NZ
108B3	**Port Phillip** *B* Aust
108A2	**Port Pirie** Aust
44A3	**Portree** Scot
20B1	**Port Renfrew** Can
27J2	**Port Royal** Jamaica
17B1	**Port Royal Sd** USA
45C1	**Portrush** N Ire
92B3	**Port Said** Egypt
17A2	**Port St Joe** USA
100B4	**Port St Johns** S Africa
7E4	**Port Saunders** Can
100C4	**Port Shepstone** S Africa
13A2	**Port Simpson** Can
27Q2	**Portsmouth** Dominica
43D4	**Portsmouth** Eng
14B3	**Portsmouth** Ohio, USA
11C3	**Portsmouth** Virginia, USA
109D2	**Port Stephens** *B* Aust
95C3	**Port Sudan** Sudan
19C3	**Port Sulphur** USA
38K5	**Porttipahdan Tekojärvi** *Res* Fin
50A2	**Portugal** Republic, Europe
14A2	**Port Washington** USA
77C5	**Port Weld** Malay
32D6	**Porvenir** Bol
39K6	**Porvoo** Fin
30E4	**Posadas** Arg
50A2	**Posadas** Spain
47D1	**Poschiavo** Switz
6B2	**Posheim Pen** Can
90C3	**Posht-e Badam** Iran
71D4	**Poso** Indon
58D1	**Postavy** Belorussia
14B2	**Post Clinton** USA
100B3	**Postmasburg** S Africa
52B1	**Postojna** Slovenia
74C2	**Pos'yet** Russian Fed
101G1	**Potchefstroom** S Africa
19B2	**Poteau** USA
53C2	**Potenza** Italy
100B3	**Potgietersrus** S Africa
97D3	**Potiskum** Nig
20C1	**Potlatch** USA
15C3	**Potomac** *R* USA
30C2	**Potosi** Bol
30C4	**Potrerillos** Chile
56C2	**Potsdam** Germany
16B2	**Pottstown** USA
16A2	**Pottsville** USA
16B2	**Poughkeepsie** USA
35B2	**Pouso Alegre** Brazil
110C1	**Poverty B** NZ
61F3	**Povorino** Russian Fed
7C4	**Povungnituk** Can
8C2	**Powder** *R* USA
106C2	**Powell Creek** Aust
9B3	**Powell,L** USA
13C3	**Powell River** Can
8C2	**Power** *R* USA
43C3	**Powys** County, Wales
73D4	**Poyang Hu** *L* China
92B2	**Pozanti** Turk
23B1	**Poza Rica** Mexico
58B2	**Poznan** Pol
30E3	**Pozo Colorado** Par
53B2	**Pozzuoli** Italy
97B4	**Pra** *R* Ghana
76C3	**Prachin Buri** Thai
76B3	**Prachuap Khiri Khan** Thai
59B2	**Pradèd** *Mt* Czech Republic
49C3	**Pradelles** France
35D1	**Prado** *R* Brazil
	Prague = Praha
57C2	**Praha** Czech Republic
97A4	**Praia** Cape Verde
33E5	**Prainha** Brazil
18B2	**Prairie Village** USA
76C3	**Prakhon Chai** Thai
35B1	**Prata** Brazil
35B1	**Prata** *R* Brazil
	Prates = Dongsha Qundao
49E3	**Prato** Italy
16B1	**Prattsville** USA
17A1	**Prattville** USA
48B1	**Prawle Pt** Eng
78D4	**Praya** Indon
47D1	**Predazzo** Italy
63B2	**Predivinsk** Russian Fed
58C2	**Pregolyu** *R* Russian Fed
76D3	**Prek Kak** Camb
56C2	**Prenzlau** Germany
76A3	**Preparis I** Burma
76A2	**Preparis North Chan** Burma
59B3	**Přerov** Czech Republic
23A2	**Presa del Infiernillo** Mexico
9B3	**Prescott** Arizona, USA
19B3	**Prescott** Arkansas, USA
15C2	**Prescott** Can
30D4	**Presidencia Roque Sáenz Peña** Arg
35A2	**Presidente Epitácio** Brazil
112C2	**Presidente Frei** *Base* Ant
23B2	**Presidente Miguel Aleman** *L* Mexico
35A2	**Presidente Prudente** Brazil
35A2	**Presidente Venceslau** Brazil
59C3	**Prešov** Slovakia
58C1	**Preškule** Lithuania
100B3	**Prieska** S Africa
20C1	**Priest L** USA
20C1	**Priest River** USA
55B2	**Prilep** Macedonia, Yugos
60D3	**Priluki** Ukraine
34C2	**Primero** *R* Arg
39K6	**Primorsk** Russian Fed
60E4	**Primorsko-Akhtarsk** Russian Fed
13F2	**Primrose L** Can
5H4	**Prince Albert** Can
4F2	**Prince Albert,C** Can
4G2	**Prince Albert Pen** Can
4G2	**Prince Albert Sd** Can
6C3	**Prince Charles I** Can
112B10	**Prince Charles Mts** Ant
7D5	**Prince Edward I** Can
13C2	**Prince George** Can
4H2	**Prince Gustaf Adolp** *S* Can
5E4	**Prince of Wales I** Can
71F5	**Prince of Wales I** Aust
4H2	**Prince of Wales I** Can
4G2	**Prince of Wales Str** Can
4F2	**Prince Patrick I** Can
6A2	**Prince Regent Inlet** *Str* Can
13A2	**Prince Rupert** Can
107D2	**Princess Charlotte B** Aust
13B2	**Princess Royal I** Can
27L1	**Princes Town** Trinidad
13C3	**Princeton** Can
18C2	**Princeton** Kentucky, USA
18B1	**Princeton** Missouri, USA
16B2	**Princeton** New Jersey, USA
4D3	**Prince William** USA
12E2	**Prince William Sd** USA
97C4	**Principe** *I* W Africa
20B2	**Prineville** USA
12E1	**Pringle,Mt** USA
6F3	**Prins Christian Sund** *Sd* Greenland
112B12	**Prinsesse Astrid Kyst** Region, Ant
112B12	**Prinsesse Ragnhild Kyst** Region, Ant
64B2	**Prins Karls Forland** *I* Barents S
25D3	**Prinzapolca** Nic
58D2	**Pripet** *R* Belorussia
	Pripyat' = Pripet
54B2	**Prizren** Serbia, Yugos
56C2	**Pritzwalk** Germany
61F3	**Privolzhskaya Vozvyshennost'** *Upland* Russian Fed
54B2	**Prizren** Serbia, Yugos
78C4	**Probolinggo** Indon
5G5	**Procatello** USA
87B2	**Proddatur** India
25D2	**Progreso** Mexico
20B2	**Project City** USA
61F5	**Prokhladnyy** Russian Fed
65K4	**Prokop'yevsk** Russian Fed
61F4	**Proletarskaya** Russian Fed
64G2	**Proliv Karskiye Vorota** *Str* Russian Fed
83D4	**Prome** Burma
31D4	**Propriá** Brazil
20B2	**Prospect** Oregon, USA
107D3	**Prosperine** Aust
59B3	**Prostějov** Czech Republic
6D2	**Proven** Greenland
49D3	**Provence** Region, France
16D2	**Providence** USA
15D2	**Provincetown** USA
49C2	**Provins** France
8B2	**Provo** USA

Provost

13E2 **Provost** Can
4D2 **Prudhoe Bay** USA
6D2 **Prudhoe Land**
Greenland
58C2 **Pruszkow** Pol
60C4 **Prut** *R* Romania/
Moldova
60C4 **Prutul** *R* Romania
58C2 **Pruzhany** Belorussia
18A2 **Pryor** USA
59C3 **Przemyś1** Pol
55C3 **Psará** *I* Greece
60C2 **Pskov** Russian Fed
58D2 **Ptich** *R* Belorussia
55B2 **Ptolemais** Greece
32C5 **Pucallpa** Peru
73D4 **Pucheng** China
34A3 **Pucón** Chile
38K5 **Pudasjärvi** Fin
87B2 **Pudukkottai** India
23B2 **Puebla** Mexico
23B2 **Puebla** State, Mexico
50A1 **Puebla de Sanabria**
Spain
50A1 **Puebla de Trives**
Spain
9C2 **Pueblo** USA
34B3 **Puelches** Arg
34B3 **Puelén** Arg
23A2 **Puerta Ixbapa**
Mexico
34D2 **Puente del Inca** Arg
32A5 **Puerta** Peru
30B2 **Puerta Coles** Peru
34B2 **Puerta de los Llanos**
Arg
31D3 **Puerta do Calcanhar**
Pt Brazil
32C1 **Puerta Gallinas**
Colombia
23B2 **Puerta Maldonado** *Pt*
Mexico
32A2 **Puerta Mariato**
Panama
29C5 **Puerta Médanosa** *Pt*
Arg
23A2 **Puerta Mongrove**
Mexico
25E4 **Puerta San Blas** *Pt*
Panama
23A2 **Puerta San Telmo**
Mexico
29B5 **Puerto Aisén** Chile
25D4 **Puerto Armuelles**
Panama
33F6 **Puerto Artur** Brazil
32B3 **Puerto Asis**
Colombia
32D2 **Puerto Ayacucho**
Ven
25D3 **Puerto Barrios**
Guatemala
32C2 **Puerto Berrio**
Colombia
32D1 **Puerto Cabello** Ven
25D3 **Puerto Cabezas** Nic
32D2 **Puerto Carreño**
Colombia
25D4 **Puerto Cortes** Costa
Rica
25D3 **Puerto Cortés**
Honduras
96A2 **Puerto del Rosario**
Canary Is
30F3 **Puerto E Cunha**
Brazil
32C1 **Puerto Fijo** Ven
31B3 **Puerto Franco** Bol
25D2 **Puerto Heath** Bol
25D2 **Puerto Juarez**
Mexico
33E1 **Puerto la Cruz** Ven
50B2 **Puertollano** Spain
27C4 **Puerto Lopez**
Colombia
29D4 **Puerto Madryn** Arg
32D6 **Puerto Maldonado**
Peru
23B2 **Puerto Marquéz**
Mexico
29B4 **Puerto Montt** Chile
30E3 **Puerto Murtinho**
Brazil
29B6 **Puerto Natales** Chile

24A1 **Puerto Peñasco**
Mexico
29D4 **Puerto Pirámides**
Arg
27C3 **Puerto Plata** Dom
Rep
79A4 **Puerto Princesa** Phil
32B3 **Puerto Rico**
Colombia
27D3 **Puerto Rico** *I*
Caribbean S
27D3 **Puerto Rico Trench**
Caribbean S
23A2 **Puerto San Juan de
Lima** Mexico
33G4 **Puerto Santanga**
Brazil
30E2 **Puerto Suárez** Bol
24B2 **Puerto Vallarta**
Mexico
29B4 **Puerto Varas** Chile
30D2 **Puerto Villarroel** Bol
61G3 **Pugachev**
Russian Fed
84C3 **Pugal** India
51C1 **Puigcerdá** Spain
111B2 **Pukaki,L** *L* NZ
74B2 **Pukch'ŏng** N Korea
110B1 **Pukekohe** NZ
111B2 **Puketeraki Range**
Mts NZ
52B2 **Pula** Croatia
15C2 **Pulaski** New York,
USA
71E4 **Pulau Kolepom** *I*
Indon
70A4 **Pulau Pulau Batu** *Is*
Indon
58C2 **Pulawy** Pol
87B2 **Pulicat,L** India
84B1 **Pul-i-Khumri** Afghan
87B3 **Puliyangudi** India
20C1 **Pullman** USA
71E3 **Pulo Anna Merir** *I*
Pacific O
79B2 **Pulog,Mt** Phil
38L5 **Pulozero** Russian Fed
58C2 **Pultusk** Pol
30C4 **Puna de Atacama**
Arg
86B1 **Punakha** Bhutan
84C2 **Punch** Pak
87A1 **Pune** India
23A2 **Punépper** Mexico
98C3 **Punia** Zaire
34A2 **Punitaqui** Chile
84C2 **Punjab** Province, Pak
84D2 **Punjab** State, India
30B2 **Puno** Peru
24A2 **Punta Abreojos** *Pt*
Mexico
53C3 **Punta Alice** *Pt* Italy
34C3 **Punta Alta** *Pt* Arg
29B6 **Punta Arenas** Chile
24A2 **Punta Baja** *Pt*
Mexico
34A2 **Punta Curaumilla** *Pt*
Chile
100A2 **Punta da Marca** *Pt*
Angola
101C3 **Punta de Barra Falsa**
Pt Mozam
29F2 **Punta del Este** Urug
21F2 **Punta Eugenia** *Pt*
Mexico
25D3 **Punta Gorda** Belize
17B2 **Punta Gorda** USA
34A3 **Punta Lavapié** *Pt*
Chile
34A2 **Punta Lengua de
Vaca** *Pt* Chile
53B2 **Punta Licosa** *Pt* Italy
34A1 **Punta Poroto** *Pt*
Chile
9B4 **Punta San Antonia** *Pt*
Mexico
34A2 **Punta Topocalma**
Chile
73C4 **Puqi** China
64J3 **Pur** *R* Russian Fed
19A2 **Purcell** USA
12C1 **Purcell Mt** USA
13D2 **Purcell Mts** Can
34A3 **Purén** Chile

86B2 **Puri** India
87B1 **Pūrna** India
86B1 **Pūrnia** India
76C3 **Pursat** Camb
23A1 **Puruandro** Mexico
33E4 **Purus** *R* Brazil
19C3 **Purvis** USA
78B4 **Purwokerto** Indon
78C4 **Purworejo** Indon
85D5 **Pusad** India
74B3 **Pusan** S Korea
60D2 **Pushkin** Russian Fed
58D1 **Pustoshka**
Russian Fed
82D3 **Puta** Burma
34A2 **Putaendo** Chile
110C1 **Putaruru** NZ
73D4 **Putian** China
16D2 **Putnam** USA
87B3 **Puttalam** Sri Lanka
56C2 **Puttgarden** Germany
32B4 **Putumayo** *R*
Ecuador
78C2 **Putussibau** Indon
38K6 **Puulavesi** *L* Fin
20B1 **Puyallup** USA
49C2 **Puy de Sancy** *Mt*
France
111A3 **Puysegur Pt** NZ
99C3 **Pweto** Zaire
43R3 **Pwllheli** Wales
76B2 **Pyapon** Burma
61F5 **Pyatigorsk**
Russian Fed
Pyê = Prome
74B3 **P'yŏngyang** N Korea
108B3 **Pyramid Hill** Aust
21B1 **Pyramid L** USA
111A2 **Pyramid,Mt** NZ
48B3 **Pyrénées** *Mts* France
58D1 **Pytalovo** Russian Fed
76B2 **Pyu** Burma

Q

94B2 **Qabatiya** Israel
94C3 **Qa'el Hafira** *Mud
Flats* Jordan
94C3 **Qa'el Jinz** *Mud Flats*
Jordan
68B3 **Qaidam Pendi** *Salt
Flat* China
94C2 **Qa Khanna** *Salt
Marsh* Jordan
99D1 **Qala'en Nahl** Sudan
84B2 **Qalat** Afghan
94C1 **Qal'at al Hisn** Syria
81C3 **Qal'at Bishah**
S Arabia
93E3 **Qal'at Sālih** Iraq
68B3 **Qamdo** China
99E1 **Qandala** Somalia
99E2 **Qardho** Somalia
95D2 **Qara** Egypt
90A3 **Qare Shirin** Iran
91A4 **Qaryat al Ulyā**
S Arabia
94C3 **Qasr el Kharana**
Jordan
91D4 **Qasr-e-Qand** Iran
95B2 **Qasr Farafra** Egypt
94C2 **Qatana** Syria
91B4 **Qatar** Emirate,
Arabian Pen
94C3 **Qatrāna** Jordan
95B2 **Qattâra Depression**
Egypt
90C3 **Qāyen** Iran
90A2 **Qazvin** Iran
95C2 **Qena** Egypt
90A2 **Qeydār** Iran
91B4 **Qeys** *I* Iran
90A3 **Qeziot** Israel
73B5 **Qian Jiang** *R* China
72E1 **Qian Shan** *Upland*
China
72E3 **Qidong** China
73B4 **Qijiang** China
84B2 **Qila Saifullah** Pak
72A2 **Qilian** China
68B3 **Qilian Shan** China
72B3 **Qin'an** China
72E2 **Qingdao** China
72A2 **Qinghai** Province,
China

68B3 **Qinghai Hu** *L* China
72D3 **Qingjiang** Jiangsu,
China
73D4 **Qingjiang** Jiangxi,
China
72B3 **Qing Jiang** *R* China
72C2 **Qingshuihe** China
72B2 **Qingshui He** *R* China
72B2 **Qingtongxia** China
72B2 **Qingyang** China
74B2 **Qingyuan** Liaoning,
China
73D4 **Qingyuan** Zhejiang,
China
82C2 **Qing Zang** *Upland*
China
72D2 **Qinhuangdao** China
72B3 **Qin Ling** *Mts* China
73B5 **Qinzhou** China
76E2 **Qionghai** China
73A3 **Qionglai Shan**
Upland China
76D1 **Qiongzhou Haixia** *Str*
China
69E2 **Qiqihar** China
94B2 **Qiryat Ata** Israel
94B3 **Qiryat Gat** Israel
94B2 **Qiryat Shemona**
Israel
94B2 **Qiryat Yam** Israel
94D2 **Qishon** *R* Israel
63A3 **Qitai** China
73C4 **Qiyang** China
72B1 **Qog Qi** China
90B2 **Qolleh-ye Damavand**
Mt Iran
90B3 **Qom** Iran
90B3 **Qomisheh** Iran
**Qomolangma Feng =
Everest,Mt**
94C1 **Qornet es Saouda** *Mt*
Leb
6E3 **Qôrnoq** Greenland
90A2 **Qorveh** Iran
91C4 **Qotābād** Iran
16C1 **Quabbin Res** USA
16B2 **Quakertown** USA
77C3 **Quam Phu Quoc** *I*
Viet
76D2 **Quang Ngai** Viet
76D2 **Quang Tri** Viet
77D4 **Quan Long** Viet
73D5 **Quanzhou** Fujian,
China
73C4 **Quanzhou** Guangxi,
China
5H4 **Qu' Appelle** *R* Can
91C5 **Quarayyāt** Oman
13B2 **Quatsino Sd** Can
90C2 **Quchan** Iran
109C3 **Queanbeyan** Aust
15D1 **Québec** Can
7C4 **Quebec** Province,
Can
35B1 **Quebra-Anzol** *R*
Brazil
34D2 **Quebracho** Urug
30F4 **Quedas do Iguaçu**
Brazil/Arg
16A3 **Queen Anne** USA
13B2 **Queen Bess,Mt** Can
5E4 **Queen Charlotte** *Is*
Can
13B2 **Queen Charlotte Sd**
Can
13B2 **Queen Charlotte Str**
Can
4H1 **Queen Elizabeth Is**
Can
112B9 **Queen Mary Land**
Region, Ant
4H3 **Queen Maud G** Can
112A **Queen Maud Mts** Ant
16C2 **Queens** Borough,
New York, USA
108B3 **Queenscliff** Aust
107D3 **Queensland** State,
Aust
109C4 **Queenstown** Aust
111A3 **Queenstown** NZ
100B4 **Queenstown** S Africa
16A3 **Queenstown** USA
98B3 **Quela** Angola
101C2 **Quelimane** Mozam

34C3 Quemuquemú Arg
13C2 Quensel L Can
34D3 Quequén Arg
34D3 Quequén R Arg
23A1 Querétaro Mexico
23A1 Querétaro State Mexico
13C2 Quesnel Can
84B2 Quetta Pak
25C3 Quezaltenango Guatemala
79B3 Quezon City Phil
100A2 Quibala Angola
98B3 Quibaxe Angola
32B2 Quibdó Colombia
48B2 Quiberon France
98B3 Quicama Nat Pk Angola
73A4 Quijing China
34A2 Quilima Chile
34C2 Quilino Arg
32C6 Quillabamba Peru
30C2 Quillacollo Bol
48C3 Quillan France
5H4 Quill L Can
5H4 Quill Lakes Can
34A2 Quillota Chile
87B3 Quilon India
108B1 Quilpie Aust
34A2 Quilpué Chile
98B3 Quimbele Angola
48B2 Quimper France
48B2 Quimperlé France
21A2 Quincy California, USA
10A3 Quincy Illinois, USA
16D1 Quincy Massachusetts, USA
34B2 Quines Arg
12B3 Quinhagak USA
76D3 Qui Nhon Viet
50B2 Quintanar de la Orden Spain
34A2 Quintero Chile
34C2 Quinto R Arg
34A3 Quirihue Chile
100A2 Quirima Angola
109D2 Quirindi Aust
101D2 Quissanga Mozam
101C3 Quissico Mozam
32B4 Quito Ecuador
31D2 Quixadá Brazil
108A2 Quorn Aust
4G3 Qurlurteuk Can
95C2 Quseir Egypt
6E3 Qutdligssat Greenland
Quthing = Moyeni
73B3 Qu Xian Sichuan, China
73D4 Qu Xian Zhejiang, China
76D2 Quynh Luu Viet
72C2 Quzhou China
86C1 Qüzü China

R

38J6 Raahe Fin
44A3 Raasay I Scot
44A3 Raasay,Sound of Chan Scot
99F1 Raas Caseyr C Somalia
52B2 Rab I Croatia
78D4 Raba Indon
59B3 Rába R Hung
96B1 Rabat Mor
94B3 Rabba Jordan
80B3 Rabigh S Arabia
47B2 Raccorigi Italy
7E5 Race,C Can
48A2 Rachaya Leb
57C3 Rachel Mt Germany
76D3 Rach Gia Viet
14A2 Racine USA
59D3 Rădăuti Rom
58C2 Radom Pol
59B2 Radomsko Pol
58C1 Radviliškis Lithuania
4G3 Rae Can
86A1 Rãe Bareli India
6B3 Rae Isthmus Can

4G3 Rae L Can
110C1 Raetihi NZ
34C2 Rafaela Arg
94B3 Rafah Egypt
98C2 Rafai CAR
93D3 Rafhā Al Jumaymah S Arabia
91C3 Rafsanjān Iran
98C2 Raga Sudan
27R3 Ragged Pt Barbados
53B3 Ragusa Italy
99D1 Rahad R Sudan
84C3 Rahimyar Khan Pak
90B3 Rähjerd Iran
34D2 Raices Arg
87B1 Rāichur India
86A2 Raigarh India
108B3 Rainbow Aust
17A1 Rainbow City USA
20B1 Rainier USA
20B1 Rainier,Mt USA
10A2 Rainy L Can
12D2 Rainy P USA
10A2 Rainy River Can
86A2 Raipur India
87C1 Rājahmundry India
78C2 Rajang R Malay
84C3 Rajanpur Pak
87B3 Rājapālaiyam India
85C3 Rājasthan State, India
84D3 Rājgarh India
85D4 Rājgarh State, India
85C4 Rājkot India
86B2 Rājmahāl Hills India
86A2 Rāj Nāndgaon India
85C4 Rājpipla India
86B2 Rājshahi Bang
85D4 Rājur India
111B2 Rakaia R NZ
78B4 Rakata I Indon
82C3 Raka Zangbo R China
59C3 Rakhov Ukraine
100B3 Rakops Botswana
58D2 Rakov Belorussia
11C3 Raleigh USA
7A5 Ralny L Can
94B2 Rama Israel
94B3 Ramallah Israel
87B3 Rāmanāthapuram India
69G3 Ramapo Deep Pacific O
94B2 Ramat Gan Israel
46A2 Rambouillet France
86B2 Rāmgarh Bihar, India
85C3 Rāmgarh Rajasthan, India
90A3 Rāmhormoz Iran
94B3 Ramla Israel
91C5 Ramlat Al Wahibah Region, Oman
21B3 Ramona USA
84D3 Rāmpur India
84D3 Rāmpura India
90B2 Rāmsar Iran
42B2 Ramsey Eng
16B2 Ramsey I Wales
43E4 Ramsgate Eng
94C2 Ramtha Jordan
71F4 Ramu R PNG
34A2 Rancagua Chile
86A2 Rānchi Plat India
101G1 Randburg S Africa
39G7 Randers Den
101G1 Randfontein S Africa
15D2 Randolph Vermont, USA
111B3 Ranfurly NZ
86C2 Rangamati Bang
111B2 Rangiora NZ
110C1 Rangitaiki R NZ
111B2 Rangitate R NZ
110C1 Rangitikei R NZ
Rangoon = Yangon
86B1 Rangpur India
87B2 Ränibennur India
8A2 Ranier,Mt Mt USA
86B2 Rānīganj India
109C2 Rankins Springs Aust
6A3 Ranklin Inlet Can

85B4 Rann of Kachchh Flood Area India
77B4 Ranong Thai
70A3 Rantauparapat Indon
18C1 Rantoul USA
49D3 Rapallo Italy
34A2 Rapel R Chile
6D3 Raper,C Can
8C2 Rapid City USA
14A1 Rapid River USA
15C3 Rappahannock R USA
47C1 Rapperswil Switz
16B2 Raritan B USA
95C2 Ras Abu Shagara C Sudan
93D2 Ra's al 'Ayn Syria
91C5 Ra's al Hadd C Oman
91C4 Ras al Kaimah UAE
91C4 Ras-al-Kuh C Iran
81D4 Ra's al Madrakah C Oman
91A4 Ra's az Zawr C S Arabia
95C2 Rãs Bãnas C Egypt
94A3 Ras Burün C Egypt
99D1 Ras Dashan Mt Eth
90A3 Ra's-e-Barkan Pt Iran
92A3 Rãs el Kenãyis Pt Egypt
81D4 Ra's Fartak C Yemen
94A3 Ra's Ghãrib Egypt
99D1 Rashad Sudan
94B3 Rashädïya Jordan
92B3 Rashïd Egypt
90A2 Rasht Iran
91C5 Ra's Jibish C Oman
99E1 Ras Khanzira C Somalia
84B3 Ras Koh Mt Pak
95C2 Rãs Muhammad C Egypt
96A2 Ras Nouadhibou C Maur
69H2 Rasshua I Russian Fed
61F3 Rasskazovo Russian Fed
91A4 Ra's Tanãqib C S Arabia
91B4 Ra's Tannürah C S Arabia
57B3 Rastatt Germany
Ras Uarc = Cabo Tres Forcas
99F1 Ras Xaafuun C Somalia
84C3 Ratangarh India
76B3 Rat Buri Thai
85D3 Rath India
56C2 Rathenow Germany
45B2 Rathkeale Irish Rep
45C1 Rathlin I N Ire
45B2 Rath Luirc Irish Rep
85D4 Ratlãm India
87A1 Ratnãgiri India
87C3 Ratnapura Sri Lanka
58C2 Ratno Ukraine
27D1 Rattenberg Austria
39H6 Rättvik Sweden
12H3 Ratz,Mt Can
34D3 Rauch Arg
110C1 Raukumara Range Mts NZ
35C2 Raul Soares Brazil
39J6 Rauma Fin
86A2 Raurkela India
90C3 Rävänsar Iran
59C2 Rava Russkaya Ukraine
16C1 Ravena USA
52B2 Ravenna Italy
57B3 Ravensburg Germany
107D2 Ravenshoe Aust
42E2 Ravenspurn Oilfield N Sea
84C2 Ravi R Pak
84C2 Rawalpindi Pak
93D2 Rawändiz Iran
58B2 Rawicz Pol
106B4 Rawlinna Aust

8C2 Rawlins USA
29C4 Rawson Arg
78C3 Raya Mt Indon
87B2 Rãyadurg India
94C2 Rayak Leb
7E5 Ray,C Can
91C4 Räyen Iran
22C2 Raymond California, USA
20B1 Raymond Washington, USA
109D2 Raymond Terrace Aust
12D1 Ray Mts USA
23B1 Rayon Mexico
90A2 Razan Iran
54C2 Razgrad Bulg
54C2 Razim L Rom
43D4 Reading Eng
16B2 Reading USA
4G3 Read Island Can
16C1 Readsboro USA
34B2 Real de Padre Arg
34C3 Realicó Arg
95B2 Rebiana Well Libya
95B2 Rebiana Sand Sea Libya
38L6 Reboly Russian Fed
106B4 Recherche,Arch of the Is Aust
31E3 Recife Brazil
107F2 Récifs D'Entrecasteaux Nouvelle Calédonie
46D1 Recklinghausen Germany
30E4 Reconquista Arg
19B3 Red R USA
77C4 Redang / Malay
16B2 Red Bank New Jersey, USA
21A1 Red Bluff USA
42D2 Redcar Eng
13E2 Redcliff Can
109D1 Redcliffe Aust
108B2 Red Cliffs Aust
13E2 Red Deer Can
13E2 Red Deer R Can
20B2 Redding USA
10A2 Red L USA
7A4 Red Lake Can
22D3 Redlands USA
16A3 Red Lion USA
20B2 Redmond USA
18A1 Red Oak USA
48B2 Redon France
22C4 Redondo Beach USA
12D2 Redoubt V USA
73B5 Red River Delta Vietnam
80B3 Red Sea Africa/ Arabian Pen
13E2 Redwater Can
22A2 Redwood City USA
14A2 Reed City USA
22C2 Reedley USA
20B2 Reedsport USA
111B2 Reefton NZ
93C2 Refahiye Turk
35D1 Regência Brazil
57C3 Regensburg Germany
96C2 Reggane Alg
53C3 Reggio di Calabria Italy
47D2 Reggio Nell'Emilia Italy
54B1 Reghin Rom
5H4 Regina Can
100A3 Rehoboth Namibia
15C3 Rehoboth Beach USA
94B3 Rehovot Israel
32D1 Reicito Ven
43D4 Reigate Eng
46C2 Reims France
5H4 Reindeer R Can
50B1 Reinosa Spain
16D1 Reisterstown USA
101G1 Reitz S Africa
4H3 Reliance Can
108A2 Remarkable,Mt Aust
78C4 Rembang Indon
91C4 Remeshk Iran

Remscheid

46D1 **Remscheid** Germany
18C2 **Rend,L** USA
56B2 **Rendsburg** Germany
15C1 **Renfrew** Can
78A3 **Rengat** Indon
34A2 **Rengo** Chile
59D3 **Reni** Ukraine
99D1 **Renk** Sudan
6H2 **Renland** *Pen* Greenland
108B2 **Renmark** Aust
107F2 **Rennell** *I* Solomon Is
48B2 **Rennes** France
21B2 **Reno** USA
47D2 **Reno** *R* Italy
15C2 **Renovo** USA
16C1 **Rensselaer** USA
20B1 **Renton** USA
70D4 **Reo** Indon
35B2 **Represa de Furnas** *Dam* Brazil
30E3 **Reprèsa Ilha Grande** *Dam* Brazil
30E3 **Reprèsa Itaipu** *Dam* Brazil
35A2 **Reprèsa Porto Primavera** *Dam* Brazil
35B1 **Reprèsa Três Marias** *Dam* Brazil
20C1 **Republic** USA
41B3 **Republic of Ireland** NW Europe
6B3 **Repulse Bay** Can
15C1 **Réservoir Baskatong** *Res* Can
10C1 **Réservoir de la Grande 2** *Res* Can
10C1 **Réservoir de la Grande 3** *Res* Can
7C4 **Réservoir de la Grande 4** Can
7C5 **Réservoir Cabonga** *Res* Can
7D4 **Réservoir Caniapiscau** *Res* Can
7C5 **Réservoir Gouin** *Res* Can
10D1 **Réservoir Manicouagan** *Res* Can
90B2 **Reshteh-ye Alborz** *Mts* Iran
72A2 **Reshui** China
30E4 **Resistencia** Arg
54B1 **Resita** Rom
6A2 **Resolute** Can
111A3 **Resolution I** NZ
6D3 **Resolution Island** Can
101H1 **Ressano Garcia** Mozam
34B2 **Retamito** Arg
46C2 **Rethel** France
55B3 **Réthímnon** Greece
89K10 **Réunion** *I* Indian O
51C1 **Reus** Spain
47C1 **Reuss** *R* Switz
47D1 **Reutte** Austria
61K3 **Revda** Russian Fed
12D2 **Revelstoke** Can
24A3 **Revillagigedo** *Is* Mexico
12H3 **Revillagigedo I** USA
46C2 **Revin** France
94B3 **Revivim** Israel
86A2 **Rewa** India
84D3 **Rewari** India
8B2 **Rexburg** USA
38A2 **Reykjavík** Iceland
24C2 **Reynosa** Mexico
48B2 **Rezé** France
58D1 **Rezekne** Latvia
61K2 **Rezh** Russian Fed
47C1 **Rhätikon** *Mts* Austria/Switz
94B1 **Rhazir** Republic, Leb
56B2 **Rhein** *R* W Europe
56B2 **Rheine** Germany
47B1 **Rheinfelden** Switz
49D2 **Rheinland Pfalz** Region, Germany
47C1 **Rheinwaldhorn** *Mt* Switz

Rhine = Rhein
16C2 **Rhinebeck** USA
10B2 **Rhinelander** USA
47C2 **Rho** Italy
15D2 **Rhode Island** State, USA
16D2 **Rhode Island Sd** USA
Rhodes = Ródhos
49C3 **Rhône** *R* France
43C3 **Rhyl** Wales
31D4 **Riachão do Jacuipe** Brazil
50A1 **Ria de Arosa** *B* Spain
50A1 **Ria de Betanzos** *B* Spain
50A1 **Ria de Corcubion** *B* Spain
50A1 **Ria de Lage** *B* Spain
50A1 **Ria de Sta Marta** *B* Spain
50A1 **Ria de Vigo** *B* Spain
84C2 **Riäsi** Pak
50A1 **Ribadeo** Spain
35A2 **Ribas do Rio Pardo** Brazil
101C2 **Ribauè** Mozam
42C3 **Ribble** *R* Eng
35B2 **Ribeira** Brazil
35B2 **Ribeirão Prêto** Brazil
32D6 **Riberalta** Bol
15C2 **Rice L** Can
10A2 **Rice Lake** USA
101H1 **Richard's Bay** S Africa
19A3 **Richardson** USA
12G1 **Richardson Mts** Can
8B3 **Richfield** USA
20C1 **Richland** USA
22A2 **Richmond** California, USA
101H1 **Richmond** Natal, S Africa
109D2 **Richmond** New South Wales, Aust
111B2 **Richmond** NZ
107D3 **Richmond** Queensland, Aust
10C3 **Richmond** Virginia, USA
111B2 **Richmond Range** *Mts* NZ
15C2 **Rideau,L** Can
17B1 **Ridgeland** USA
15C2 **Ridgway** USA
27D4 **Riecito** Ven
47D1 **Rienza** *R* Italy
57C2 **Riesa** Germany
29B6 **Riesco** *I* Chile
101F1 **Riet** *R* S Africa
52B2 **Rieti** Italy
50B2 **Rif** *Mts* N Afr
58C1 **Riga** Latvia
60B2 **Riga,G of** Estonia/Latvia
91C4 **Rigan** Iran
20C1 **Riggins** USA
7E4 **Rigolet** Can
39J6 **Riihimaki** Fin
52B1 **Rijeka** Croatia
13E2 **Rimbey** Can
39H7 **Rimbo** Sweden
52B2 **Rimini** Italy
54C1 **Rimnicu Sărat** Rom
54B1 **Rimnicu Vilcea** Rom
10D2 **Rimouski** Can
23A1 **Rincón de Romos** Mexico
39F7 **Ringkøbing** Den
98A2 **Rio Benito** Eq Guinea
32D5 **Rio Branco** Brazil
24B1 **Rio Bravo del Norte** *R* Mexico/USA
32C1 **Riohacha** Colombia
35B2 **Rio Claro** Brazil
27L1 **Rio Claro** Trinidad
34C3 **Rio Colorado** Arg
34C2 **Rio Cuarto** Arg
31D4 **Rio de Jacupe** Brazil
35C2 **Rio de Janeiro** Brazil
35C2 **Rio de Janeiro** State, Brazil
29E3 **Rio de la Plata** *Est* Arg/Urug

29C6 **Rio Gallegos** Arg
29C6 **Rio Grande** Arg
30F5 **Rio Grande** Brazil
26A4 **Rio Grande** Nic
25D3 **Rio Grande** *R* Nic
24B2 **Rio Grande** Mexico/USA
23A1 **Rio Grande de Santiago** Mexico
31D3 **Rio Grande do Norte** State, Brazil
30F4 **Rio Grande do Sul** State, Brazil
103G6 **Rio Grande Rise** Atlantic O
26C4 **Riohacha** Colombia
49C2 **Riom** France
32D4 **Riumbamba** Ecuador
30C2 **Rio Mulatos** Bol
29C3 **Rio Negro** State, Arg
30F4 **Rio Pardo** Brazil
34C2 **Rio Tercero** Arg
33E6 **Rio Theodore Roosevelt** *R* Brazil
29B6 **Rio Turbio** Arg
35A1 **Rio Verde** Brazil
23A1 **Rio Verde** Mexico
14B3 **Ripley** Ohio, USA
14B3 **Ripley** West Virginia, USA
42D2 **Ripon** Eng
22B2 **Ripon** USA
94B3 **Rishon le Zion** Israel
16A3 **Rising Sun** USA
39F7 **Risør** Nor
6E2 **Ritenberk** Greenland
22C2 **Ritter,Mt** USA
20C1 **Ritzville** USA
34B2 **Rivadavia** Arg
34A1 **Rivadavia** Chile
34C3 **Rivadavia Gonzalez Moreno** Arg
47D2 **Riva de Garda** Italy
34B2 **Rivera** Arg
29E2 **Rivera** Urug
22B2 **Riverbank** USA
97B4 **River Cess** Lib
16C2 **Riverhead** USA
108B3 **Riverina** Aust
111A3 **Riversdale** NZ
22D3 **Riverside** USA
13B2 **Rivers Inlet** Can
111A3 **Riverton** NZ
8C2 **Riverton** USA
17B2 **Riviera Beach** USA
7C4 **Rivière aux Feuilles** *R* Can
7D4 **Rivière de la Baleine** *R* Can
7D4 **Rivière du Petit Mècatina** *R* Can
46C2 **Rivigny-sur-Ornain** France
93U1 **Rize** Turk
72D2 **Rizhao** China
Rizhskiy Zaliv = Riga,G of
39F7 **Rjukan** Nor
6B2 **Roanes Pen** Can
49C2 **Roanne** France
17A1 **Roanoke** Alabama, USA
11C3 **Roanoke** Virginia, USA
11C3 **Roanoke** *R* USA
45B3 **Roaringwater B** Irish Rep
38J6 **Robertsforz** Sweden
19B2 **Robert S Kerr Res** USA
97A4 **Robertsport** Lib
7C5 **Roberval** Can
30H6 **Robinson Crusoe** *I* Chile
108B2 **Robinvale** Aust
13D2 **Robson,Mt** Can
24A3 **Roca Partida** *I* Mexico
103G5 **Rocas** *I* Atlantic O
31E2 **Rocas** *I* Brazil
29F2 **Rocha** Urug
42C3 **Rochdale** Eng
48B2 **Rochefort** France
5G3 **Rocher River** Can

108B3 **Rochester** Aust
7C5 **Rochester** Can
43E4 **Rochester** Eng
10A2 **Rochester** Minnesota, USA
15D2 **Rochester** New Hampshire, USA
10C2 **Rochester** New York, USA
10B2 **Rockford** USA
11B3 **Rock Hill** USA
10A2 **Rock Island** USA
108B3 **Rocklands Res** Aust
17B2 **Rockledge** USA
8C2 **Rock Springs** Wyoming, USA
110R2 **Rooks Pt** NZ
109C3 **Rock,The** Aust
16C2 **Rockville** Connecticut, USA
14A3 **Rockville** Indiana, USA
16A3 **Rockville** Maryland, USA
14B1 **Rocky Island L** Can
13E2 **Rocky Mountain House** Can
8B1 **Rocky Mts** Can/USA
12B2 **Rocky Pt** USA
56C2 **Rødbyhavn** Den
34B2 **Rodeo** Arg
49C3 **Rodez** France
55C3 **Ródhos** Greece
55C3 **Ródhos** *I* Greece
52C2 **Rodi Garganico** Italy
54B2 **Rodopi Planina** *Mts* Bulg
106A3 **Roebourne** Aust
46C1 **Roermond** Neth
46B1 **Roeselare** Belg
6B3 **Roes Welcome Sd** Can
18B2 **Rogers** USA
14B1 **Rogers City** USA
20B2 **Rogue** *R* USA
85B3 **Rohn** Pak
84D3 **Rohtak** India
58C1 **Roja** Latvia
35A2 **Rolândia** Brazil
18B2 **Rolla** USA
109C1 **Roma** Aust
52B2 **Roma** Italy
47C2 **Romagnano** Italy
17C1 **Romain,C** USA
54C1 **Roman** Rom
103H5 **Romanche Gap** Atlantic O
71D4 **Romang** *I* Indon
60B4 **Romania** Republic, E Europe
17B2 **Romano,C** USA
49D2 **Romans sur Isère** France
79B3 **Romblon** Phil
Rome = Roma
17A1 **Rome** Georgia, USA
15C2 **Rome** New York, USA
40C2 **Romilly-sur-Seine** France
15C3 **Romney** USA
60D3 **Romny** Ukraine
56B1 **Rømø** *I* Den
47B1 **Romont** Switz
48C2 **Romorantin** France
50A2 **Ronda** Spain
33E6 **Rondônia** Brazil
24F6 **Rondônia** State, Brazil
30F2 **Rondonópolis** Brazil
73B4 **Rong'an** China
73B4 **Rongchang** China
72E2 **Rongcheng** China
73B4 **Rongjiang** China
73B4 **Rong Jiang** *R* China
76A1 **Rongklang Range** *Mts* Burma
39G7 **Rønne** Den
39H7 **Ronneby** Sweden
112B2 **Ronne Ice Shelf** Ant
46B1 **Ronse** Belg
46A1 **Ronthieu** Region, France
9C3 **Roof Butte** *Mt* USA

84D3 Roorkee India
46C1 Roosendaal Neth
112B6 Roosevelt I Ant
106C2 Roper R Aust
33E3 Roraima State, Brazil
33E2 Roraime Mt Ven
38G6 Reros Nor
47C1 Rorschach Switz
38G6 Rørvik Nor
27Q2 Rosalie Dominica
22C3 Rosamond L USA
34C2 Rosario Arg
31C2 Rosário Brazil
34D2 Rosario del Tala Arg
48B2 Roscoff France
45B2 Roscommon County,
  Irish Rep
41B3 Roscommon
  Irish Rep
45C2 Roscrea Irish Rep
27E3 Roseau Dominica
109C4 Rosebery Aust
20B2 Roseburg USA
19A4 Rosenberg USA
57C3 Rosenheim Germany
13F2 Rosetown Can
54B2 Roşiori de Vede Rom
39G7 Roskilde Den
60D3 Roslavl' Russian Fed
61E2 Roslyatino
  Russian Fed
111B2 Ross NZ
12H2 Ross R Can
40B3 Rossan Pt Irish Rep
53C3 Rossano Italy
19C3 Ross Barnet Res USA
15C1 Rosseau L L Can
107E2 Rossel I Solomon Is
112A Ross Ice Shelf Ant
20B1 Ross L USA
13D3 Rossland Can
45C2 Rosslare Irish Rep
111C2 Ross,Mt NZ
97A3 Rosso Maur
43C4 Ross-on-Wye Eng
60E4 Rossosh Russian Fed
4E3 Ross River Can
112B6 Ross S Ant
91B4 Rostāq Iran
56C2 Rostock Germany
  Rostov = Rostov-na-
  Donu
61E4 Rostov-na-Donu
  Russian Fed
17B1 Roswell Georgia,
  USA
9C3 Roswell New
  Mexico, USA
71F2 Rota Pacific O
56B2 Rotenburg
  Niedersachsen,
  Germany
46E1 Rothaar-Geb Region
  Germany
112C3 Rothera Base Ant
42D3 Rotherham Eng
42B2 Rothesay Scot
71D5 Roti I Indon
108C2 Roto Aust
111B2 Rotoiti,L NZ
111B2 Rotoroa,L NZ
110C1 Rotorua NZ
110C1 Rotorua,L NZ
56A2 Rotterdam Neth
46B1 Roubaix France
48C2 Rouen France
42E3 Rough Oilfield N Sea
  Roulers = Roeselare
101E3 Round I Mauritius
109D2 Round Mt Aust
8C2 Roundup USA
44C2 Rousay I Scot
48C3 Roussillon Region,
  France
10C2 Rouyn Can
38K5 Rovaniemi Fin
47D2 Rovereto Italy
47D2 Rovigo Italy
52B1 Rovinj Croatia
59D2 Rovno Ukraine
90A2 Row'ān Iran
109C1 Rowena Aust
6C3 Rowley I Can
106A2 Rowley Shoals Aust

79A3 Roxas Palawan, Phil
79B3 Roxas Panay, Phil
111A3 Roxburgh NZ
45C2 Royal Canal Irish Rep
43D3 Royal Leamington
  Spa Eng
14B2 Royal Oak USA
43E4 Royal Tunbridge
  Wells Eng
48B2 Royan France
48B2 Roye France
43D3 Royston Eng
59C3 Rožňava Slovakia
46B2 Rozoy France
61F3 Rtishchevo
  Russian Fed
99D3 Ruaha Nat Pk Tanz
110C1 Ruahine Range Mts
  NZ
110C1 Ruapehu,Mt NZ
65D3 Rub al Khāli Desert
  S Arabia
44A3 Rubha Hunish Scot
35A2 Rubinéia Brazil
65K4 Rubtsovsk
  Russian Fed
1C2 Ruby USA
91C4 Rudan Iran
90A2 Rūdbār Iran
69F2 Rudnaya Pristan'
  Russian Fed
54B2 Rudoka Planina Mt
  Macedonia
72E3 Rudong China
14B1 Rudyard USA
46A1 Rue France
48C2 Ruffec France
99D3 Rufiji R Tanz
34C2 Rufino Arg
97A3 Rufisque Sen
100B2 Rufunsa Zambia
43D3 Rugby Eng
39G8 Rügen I Germany
56B2 Ruhr R Germany
73D4 Ruijin China
54B2 Rujen Mt Bulg/
  Macedonia
99D3 Rukwa L Tanz
44A3 Rum I Scot
54A1 Ruma Serbia, Yugos
91A4 Rumāh S Arabia
98C2 Rumbek Sudan
26C2 Rum Cay I
  Caribbean S
47A2 Rumilly France
106C2 Rum Jungle Aust
101C2 Rumphi Malawi
111B2 Runanga NZ
110C1 Runaway,C NZ
100C3 Rundi R Zim
100A2 Rundu Namibia
99D3 Rungwa NZ
99D3 Rungwa R Tanz
99D3 Rungwe Mt Tanz
82C2 Ruoqiang China
82C2 Ruo Shui R China
54C1 Rupea Rom
7C4 Rupert R Can
46D1 Rur R Germany
32D6 Rurrenabaque Bol
110C2 Rusape Zim
54C2 Ruse Bulg
18B1 Rushville Illinois,
  USA
108B3 Rushworth Aust
19A3 Rusk USA
17B2 Ruskin USA
110B1 Russell NZ
18B2 Russellville
  Arkansas, USA
18C2 Russellville
  Kentucky, USA
21A2 Russian R USA
62C3 Russian Fed Asia/
  Europe
93E1 Rustavi Georgia
101G1 Rustenburg S Africa
19B3 Ruston USA
99C3 Rutana Burundi
46E1 Rüthen Germany
23B2 Rutla Mexico
15D2 Rutland USA
84D2 Rutog China
  Ruvu = Pangani

101D2 Ruvuma R Tanz/
  Mozam
99D2 Ruwenzori Range
  Mts Uganda/Zaire
101C2 Ruya R Zim
59B3 Ružomberok
  Slovakia
99C3 Rwanda Republic,
  Africa
60E3 Ryazan' Russian Fed
61F3 Ryazhsk Russian Fed
60E2 Rybinsk Russian Fed
60E2 Rybinskoye
  Vodokhranilishche
  Res Russian Fed
13D1 Rycroft Can
43D4 Ryde Eng
43E4 Rye Eng
20C2 Rye Patch Res USA
60D3 Ryl'sk Russian Fed
61G4 Ryn Peski Desert
  Kazakhstan
74D3 Ryōtsu Japan
59D3 Ryskany Moldova
69E4 Ryūkyū Retto Arch
  Japan
59C2 Rzeszów Pol
60D2 Rzhev Russian Fed

S

91B3 Sa'ādatābād Iran
56C2 Saale R Germany
47B1 Saanen Switz
46D2 Saar R Germany
46D2 Saarbrücken
  Germany
46D2 Saarburg Germany
39J7 Saaremaa I Estonia
46D2 Saarland State,
  Germany
46D2 Saarlouis Germany
34C3 Saavedra Arg
54C2 Šabac Serbia, Yugos
51C1 Sabadell Spain
75B1 Sabae Japan
78D1 Sabah State, Malay
26C4 Sabanalarga
  Colombia
70A3 Sabang Indon
87C1 Sabari R India
94B2 Sabastiya Israel
30C2 Sabaya Bol
93C3 Sab'Bi'ār Syria
94C2 Sabhā Jordan
95A2 Sabhā Libya
24B2 Sabinas Mexico
24B2 Sabinas Hidalgo
  Mexico
19A3 Sabine R USA
19B4 Sabine L USA
91B5 Sabkhat Matṭi Salt
  Marsh UAE
94A3 Sabkhet El Bardawil
  Lg Egypt
79B3 Sablayan Phil
7D5 Sable,C Can
17B2 Sable,C USA
7D5 Sable I Can
90C2 Sabzevār Iran
20C1 Sacajawea Peak USA
10A1 Sachigo R Can
57C2 Sachsen State,
  Germany
56C2 Sachsen-Anhalt
  State, Germany
4F2 Sachs Harbour Can
47B1 Säckingen Germany
22B1 Sacramento USA
22B1 Sacramento R USA
21A1 Sacramento V USA
9C3 Sacramento Mts
  USA
81C4 Sa'dah Yemen
54B2 Sadanski Bulg
82D3 Sadiya India
50A2 Sado R Port
74D3 Sado-shima I Japan
85C3 Sādri India
  Safad = Zefat
84A2 Safed Koh Mts
  Afghan
39G7 Saffle Sweden
92C3 Safi Jordan
96B1 Safi Mor

St Francis,C

90D3 Safidabeh Iran
94C1 Şāfītā Syria
93E3 Safwan Iraq
75A2 Saga Japan
76B1 Sagaing Burma
75B2 Sagami-nada B
  Japan
85D4 Sāgar India
16C2 Sag Harbor USA
14B2 Saginaw USA
14B2 Saginaw B USA
26B2 Sagua de Tánamo
  Cuba
26B2 Sagua la Grande
  Cuba
7C5 Saguenay R Can
51B2 Sagunto Spain
94C3 Sahāb Jordan
50A1 Sahagún Spain
96C2 Sahara Desert N
  Africa
84D3 Saharanpur India
84C2 Sahiwal Pak
93D3 Şahrā al Ḥijārah
  Desert Region Iraq
23A1 Sahuayo Mexico
107D1 Saibai I Aust
96C1 Saïda Alg
94B2 Säida Leb
91C4 Sa'idabad Iran
51B2 Saidia Mor
86B1 Saidpur India
84C2 Saidu Pak
75A1 Saigō Japan
  Saigon = Ho Chi Minh
86C2 Saiha India
68D2 Saihan Tal China
75A2 Saijo Japan
74C4 Saiki Japan
75B1 Saitama State, Japan
75A2 Sajama Mt Bol
  Sakai = Sakata
34C3 St Albans Eng
15D2 St Albans Vermont,
  USA
14B3 St Albans West
  Virginia, USA
43C4 St Albans Head C
  Eng
13E2 St Albert Can
46B1 St Amand-les-Eaux
  France
48C2 St Amand-Mont Rond
  France
17A2 St Andrew B USA
44C3 St Andrews Scot
17B1 St Andrew Sd USA
27H1 St Ann's Bay
  Jamaica
7E4 St Anthony Can
108B3 St Arnaud Aust
17B2 St Augustine USA
43B4 St Austell Eng
46D2 St-Avold France
42C2 St Bees Head Pt Eng
47B2 St-Bonnet France
43B4 St Brides B Wales
48B2 St-Brieuc France
15C2 St Catharines Can
27M2 St Catherine,Mt
  Grenada
17B1 St Catherines I USA
43E4 St Catherines Pt Eng
49C2 St Chamond France
18B2 St Charles Missouri,
  USA
14B2 St Clair USA
14B2 St Clair,L Can/USA
14B2 St Clair Shores USA
49D2 St Claud France
10A2 St Cloud USA
27E3 St Croix I
  Caribbean S
43B4 St Davids Head Pt
  Wales
46B2 St Denis France
101E3 St Denis Réunion
46C2 St Dizier France
12F2 St Elias,Mt USA
12G2 St Elias Mts Can
48B2 Saintes France
47B2 St Etienne France
18B2 St Francis R USA
100B4 St Francis,C S Africa

St Gallen

47C1 **St Gallen** Switz
48C3 **St-Gaudens** France
109C1 **St George** Aust
17B1 **St George** South
     Carolina, USA
9B3 **St George** Utah,
     USA
17B2 **St George I** Florida,
     USA
20B2 **St George,Pt** USA
15D1 **St-Georges** Can
27E4 **St George's**
     Grenada
45C3 **St George's Chan**
     Irish Rep/Wales
46A2 **St Germain-en-Laye**
     France
47B2 **St-Gervais** France
47C1 **St Gotthard** P Switz
43B4 **St Govans Head** Pt
     Wales
22A1 **St Helena** USA
103H5 **St Helena** I
     Atlantic O
100A4 **St Helena B** S Africa
17B1 **St Helena Sd** USA
109C4 **St Helens** Aust
42C3 **St Helens** Eng
20B1 **St Helens** USA
20B1 **St Helens,Mt** USA
48B2 **St Helier** Jersey
47B1 **St Hippolyte** France
46C1 **St-Hubert** Belg
7C5 **St-Hyacinthe** Can
14B1 **St Ignace** USA
43B4 **St Ives** Eng
18B2 **St James** Missouri,
     USA
5E4 **St James,C** Can
15D1 **St Jean** Can
48B2 **St Jean-d'Angely**
     France
47B2 **St-Jean-de-**
     Maurienne France
10C2 **St Jean,L** Can
15D1 **St-Jérôme** Can
20C1 **St Joe** R USA
7D5 **Saint John** Can
7E5 **St John's** Can
14B2 **St Johns** Michigan,
     USA
17B2 **St Johns** R USA
15D2 **St Johnsbury** USA
15D1 **St-Joseph** Can
19B3 **St Joseph** Louisiana,
     USA
14A2 **St Joseph** Michigan,
     USA
18B2 **St Joseph** Missouri,
     USA
27L1 **St Joseph** Trinidad
14B2 **St Joseph** R USA
14R1 **St Joseph I** Can
7A4 **St Joseph,L** Can
47B1 **St Julien** France
48C2 **St-Junien** France
46B2 **St-Just-en-Chaussée**
     France
4R? **St Kilda** I Scot
27E3 **St Kitts-Nevis** Is
     Caribbean S
47A1 **St-Laurent** France
7D5 **St Lawrence** R Can
7D5 **Saint Lawrence,G of**
     Can
4A3 **St Lawrence I** USA
15C2 **St Lawrence Seaway**
     Can/USA
48B2 **St Lô** France
97A3 **St Louis** Sen
11A3 **St Louis** USA
27E4 **St Lucia** I
     Caribbean S
101H1 **St Lucia,L** S Africa
44E1 **St Magnus** B Scot
48B2 **St Malo** France
20C1 **St Maries** USA
27E3 **St Martin** I
     Caribbean S
108A2 **St Mary Peak** Mt
     Aust
109C4 **St Marys** Aust
15C2 **St Marys** USA
17B1 **St Marys** R USA

46C2 **Ste-Menehould**
     France
12B2 **St Michael** USA
16A3 **St Michaels** USA
47B2 **St-Michel** France
46C2 **St-Mihiel** France
47C1 **St Moritz** Switz
48B2 **St-Nazaire** France
46C1 **St-Niklaas** Belg
46B1 **St-Omer** France
13E2 **St Paul** Can
10A2 **St Paul** Minnesota,
     USA
97A4 **St Paul** R Lib
17B2 **St Petersburg** USA
7E5 **St Pierre** Can
15D1 **St Pierre,L** Can
4D1 **St Pol Sur Ternoise**
     France
59B3 **St Pölten** Austria
46B2 **St Quentin** France
49D3 **St Raphaël** France
101D2 **St Sébastien** C
     Madag
17B1 **St Simons I** USA
17B1 **St Stephen** USA
14B2 **St Thomas** Can
49D3 **St-Tropez** France
46C1 **St Truiden** Belg
46A1 **St-Valéry-sur-Somme**
     France
27E4 **St Vincent and the**
     Grenadines Is
     Caribbean S
108A2 **St Vincent,G** Aust
46D1 **St-Vith** Germany
46D2 **St Wendel** Germany
71F2 **Saipan** I Pacific O
84B2 **Saiydabad** Afghan
30C2 **Sajama** Mt Bol
74D4 **Sakai** Japan
75A2 **Sakaidi** Japan
75A1 **Sakaiminato** Japan
93D4 **Sakākah** S Arabia
10C1 **Sakami,L** Can
100B2 **Sakania** Zaïre
101D3 **Sakaraha** Madag
60D5 **Sakarya** R Turk
58C1 **Sakasleja** Latvia
74D3 **Sakata** Japan
97C4 **Saketél** Benin
69G1 **Sakhalin** I
     Russian Fed
69E4 **Sakishima gunto** Is
     Japan
97A4 **Sal** I Cape Verde
61F4 **Sal** R Russian Fed
39H7 **Sala** Sweden
34D3 **Saladillo** Arg
34C2 **Saladillo** R Arg
34D3 **Salado** R
     Buenos Aires, Arg
34B3 **Salado** R Mendoza/
     San Luis, Arg
30D4 **Salado** R Sante Fe,
     Arg
97B4 **Salaga** Ghana
76C3 **Sala Hintoun** Camb
98B1 **Salal** Chad
81D4 **Salalah** Oman
34A2 **Salamanca** Chile
23A1 **Salamanca** Mexico
50A1 **Salamanca** Spain
15C2 **Salamanca** USA
98B2 **Salamat** R Chad
71F4 **Salamaua** PNG
15C2 **Salamonica** USA
78D1 **Salang** Indon
38H5 **Salangen** Nor
30C3 **Salar de Arizaro** Arg
30C3 **Salar de Atacama**
     Salt Pan Chile
30C2 **Salar de Coipasa**
     Salt Pan Bol
30C3 **Salar de Uyuni**
     Salt Pan Bol
47C2 **Salasomaggiore**
     Italy
61J3 **Salavat** Russian Fed
70D4 **Salayar** Indon
105L5 **Sala y Gomez** I
     Pacific O
34C3 **Salazar** Arg
48C2 **Salbris** France

12E2 **Salcha** R USA
100A4 **Saldanha** S Africa
94C2 **Saldhad** Syria
34C3 **Saldungaray** Arg
58C1 **Saldus** Latvia
109C3 **Sale** Aust
18C2 **Salem** Illinois, USA
87B2 **Salem** India
16D1 **Salem**
     Massachusetts, USA
16B3 **Salem** New Jersey,
     USA
20B2 **Salem** Oregon, USA
78C4 **Salembu Besar** I
     Indon
39G6 **Salen** Sweden
53B2 **Salerno** Italy
47C3 **Salford** Eng
54A1 **Salgót** Hung
59B3 **Salgótarjan** Hung
31D3 **Salgueiro** Brazil
55C3 **Salihli** Turk
101C2 **Salima** Malawi
39K6 **Salimaa** L Fin
18A2 **Salina** Kansas, USA
53B3 **Salina** I Italy
23B2 **Salina Cruz** Mexico
30C3 **Salina de Arizato**
     Arg
34B3 **Salina Grande**
     Salt pan Arg
34B2 **Salina La Antigua**
     Salt pan Arg
35C1 **Salinas** Ecuador
22B2 **Salinas** USA
22B2 **Salinas** R USA
34B3 **Salinas de Llancaneb**
     Salt Pan Arg
34B2 **Salinas Grandes** Salt
     Pan Arg
19B3 **Saline** R Arkansas,
     USA
27M2 **Salines,Pt** Grenada
31B2 **Salinópolis** Brazil
47A1 **Salins** France
     Salisbury = Harare
43D4 **Salisbury** Eng
15C3 **Salisbury** Maryland,
     USA
6C3 **Salisbury I** Can
43D4 **Salisbury Plain** Eng
38K5 **Salla** Fin
47B2 **Sallanches** France
18B2 **Sallisaw** USA
6C3 **Salluit** Can
86A1 **Sallyana** Nepal
93D2 **Salmas** Iran
38L6 **Salmi** Russian Fed
20C1 **Salmo** Can
8B2 **Salmon** Arg
13D2 **Salmon Arm** Can
8B2 **Salmon River Mts**
     USA
39J6 **Salo** Fin
47D2 **Salò** Italy
49D3 **Salon-de-Provence**
     France
     Salonica =
     Thessaloniki
54D1 **Salonta** Rom
38K8 **Salpausselka** Reginn
     Fin
34B2 **Salsacate** Arg
61F4 **Sal'sk** Russian Fed
94B2 **Salt** Jordan
30C3 **Salta** Arg
30C3 **Salta** State, Arg
24B2 **Saltillo** Mexico
8B2 **Salt Lake City** USA
34C2 **Salto** Arg
34D2 **Salto** Urug
32C3 **Salto Angostura**
     Waterfall Colombia
35D1 **Salto da Divisa** Brazil
33E1 **Salto del Angel**
     Waterfall Ven
30E3 **Salto del Guaira**
     Waterfall Brazil
32C4 **Salto Grande**
     Waterfall Colombia
84C2 **Salt Range** Mts Pak
27H2 **Salt River** Jamaica
17B1 **Saluda** USA
47B2 **Saluzzo** Italy

31D4 **Salvador** Brazil
19B4 **Salvador,L** USA
23A1 **Salvatierra** Mexico
91B5 **Salwah** Qatar
76B1 **Salween** R Burma
93E2 **Sal'yany** Azerbaijan
57C3 **Salzburg** Austria
56C2 **Salzgitter** Germany
56C2 **Salzwedel** Germany
68B1 **Samagaltay**
     Russian Fed
79B4 **Samales Group** Is
     Phil
27D3 **Samaná** Dom Rep
92C2 **Samandaği** Turk
84B1 **Samangan** Afghan
79C3 **Samar** I Phil
65G4 **Samara** Russian Fed
107E2 **Samarai** PNG
78D3 **Samarinda** Indon
80E2 **Samarkand**
     Uzbekistan
93D3 **Sāmarrā'** Iraq
79B3 **Samar S** Phil
86A2 **Sambalpur** India
78B2 **Sambas** Indon
101E2 **Sambava** Madag
84D3 **Sambhal** India
78D3 **Samboja** Indon
59D3 **Sambor** Ukraine
46B1 **Sambre** R France
74B3 **Samch'ŏk** S Korea
99D3 **Same** Tanz
47C1 **Samedan** Switz
46A1 **Samer** France
100B2 **Samfya** Zambia
76B1 **Samka** Burma
76C1 **Sam Neua** Laos
55C3 **Sámos** I Greece
55C2 **Samothráki** I Greece
34C2 **Sampacho** Arg
78D3 **Sampaga** Indon
78C3 **Sampit** Indon
78C3 **Sampit** R Indon
19B3 **Sam Rayburn Res**
     USA
76C3 **Samrong** Camb
56C1 **Samsø** I Den
92C1 **Samsun** Turk
97B3 **San** Mali
76D3 **San** R Camb
81C4 **San'ā'** Yemen
98B2 **Sanaga** R Cam
29C2 **San Agustin** Arg
79C4 **San Agustin,C** Phil
90A2 **Sanandaj** Iran
22B1 **San Andreas** USA
25C3 **San Andrés Tuxtla**
     Mexico
9C3 **San Angelo** USA
53A3 **San Antioco**
     Sardegna
53A3 **San Antioco** I Medlt
     S
34A2 **San Antonio** Chile
9C3 **San Antonio** New
     Mexico, USA
79B2 **San Antonio** USA
9D4 **San Antonio** R
     Texas, USA
51C2 **San Antonio Abad**
     Spain
25D2 **San Antonio,C** Cuba
26A2 **San Antonio de los**
     Banos Cuba
22D3 **San Antonio,Mt** USA
29C4 **San Antonio Oeste**
     Arg
34D3 **San Agustin** Arg
34B2 **San Agustin de**
     Valle Féril Arg
85D4 **Sanawad** India
23A1 **San Bartolo** Mexico
24A3 **San Benedicto** I
     Mexico
22B2 **San Benito** R USA
22B2 **San Benito Mt** USA
22D3 **San Bernardino** USA
34A2 **San Bernardo** Chile
17A2 **San Blas,C** USA
34A3 **San Carlos** Chile
32A1 **San Carlos** Nic
79B2 **San Carlos** Phil

29B4 **San Carlos de Bariloche** Arg
69E4 **San-chung** Taiwan
61G2 **Sanchursk** Russian Fed
34A3 **San Clemente** Chile
22D4 **San Clemente** USA
21B3 **San Clemente I** USA
34C2 **San Cristóbal** Arg
25C3 **San Cristóbal** Mexico
32C2 **San Cristóbal** Ven
32J7 **San Cristóbal I** Ecuador
107F2 **San Cristobal I** Solomon Is
25E2 **Sancti Spiritus** Cuba
78C3 **Sandai** Indon
70C3 **Sandakan** Malay
44C2 **Sanday** I Scot
9C3 **Sanderson** USA
13F1 **Sandfly L** Can
21B3 **San Diego** USA
92B2 **Sandikli** Turk
86A1 **Sandila** India
39F7 **Sandnes** Nor
38G5 **Sandnessjøen** Nor
98C3 **Sandoa** Zaire
59C2 **Sandomierz** Pol
38D3 **Sandoy** Føroyar
20C1 **Sandpoint** USA
49D2 **Sandrio** Italy
18A2 **Sand Springs** USA
106A3 **Sandstone** Aust
73C4 **Sandu** China
14B2 **Sandusky** USA
39H6 **Sandviken** Sweden
7A4 **Sandy L** Can
34C2 **San Felipe** Baja Cal, Mexico
34A2 **San Felipe** Chile
23A1 **San Felipe** Guanajuato, Mexico
27D4 **San Felipe** Ven
51C1 **San Feliu de Guixols** Spain
28A5 **San Felix** I Pacific O
34A2 **San Fernando** Chile
79B2 **San Fernando** Phil
79B2 **San Fernando** Phil
50A2 **San Fernando** Spain
27E4 **San Fernando** Trinidad
22C3 **San Fernando** USA
32D2 **San Fernando** Ven
17B2 **Sanford** Florida, USA
12F2 **Sanford,Mt** USA
34C2 **San Francisco** Arg
27C3 **San Francisco** Dom Rep
22A2 **San Francisco** USA
22A2 **San Francisco B** USA
24B2 **San Francisco del Oro** Mexico
23A1 **San Francisco del Rincon** Mexico
22D3 **San Gabriel Mts** USA
85C5 **Sangamner** India
18C2 **Sangamon** R USA
71F2 **Sangan** I Pacific O
87B1 **Sangareddi** India
78D4 **Sangeang** I Indon
22C2 **Sanger** USA
72C2 **Sanggan He** R China
78C2 **Sanggau** Indon
98B2 **Sangha** R Congo
85B3 **Sanghar** Pak
76B2 **Sangkhla Buri** Thai
78D2 **Sangkulirang** Indon
87A1 **Sängli** India
98B2 **Sangmélima** Cam
9B3 **San Gorgonio Mt** USA
9C3 **Sangre de Cristo** Mts USA
34C2 **San Gregorio** Arg
22A2 **San Gregorio** USA
84D2 **Sangrür** India
30E4 **San Ignacio** Arg
79B3 **San Isidro** Phil
32B2 **San Jacinto** Colombia
21B3 **San Jacinto Peak** Mt USA

34A3 **San Javier** Chile
34D2 **San Javier** Santa Fe, Arg
74D3 **Sanjö** I Japan
31C6 **São João del Rei** Brazil
22B2 **San Joaquin** R USA
22B2 **San Joaquin Valley** USA
32A1 **San José** Costa Rica
25C3 **San José** Guatemala
79B2 **San Jose** Luzon, Phil
79B3 **San Jose** Mindoro, Phil
22B2 **San Jose** USA
9B4 **San Jose** I Mexico
30D2 **San José de Chiquitos** Bol
34D2 **San José de Feliciano** Arg
34B2 **San José de Jachal** Arg
34C2 **San José de la Dormida** Arg
31B6 **São Jose do Rio Prêto** Brazil
24B2 **San José del Cabo** Mexico
34B2 **San Juan** Arg
27D3 **San Juan** Puerto Rico
34B2 **San Juan** State, Arg
27L1 **San Juan** Trinidad
32D2 **San Juan** Ven
26B2 **San Juan** Mt Cuba
8C3 **San Juan** Mts USA
34B2 **San Juan** R Arg
23B2 **San Juan** R Mexico
25D3 **San Juan** R Nic/ Costa Rica
23B2 **San Juan Bautista** Mexico
30E4 **San Juan Bautista** Par
22B2 **San Juan Bautista** USA
25D3 **San Juan del Norte** Nic
27D4 **San Juan de los Cayos** Ven
23A1 **San Juan de la Lagoz** Mexico
23A1 **San Juan del Rio** Mexico
25D3 **San Juan del Sur** Nic
20B1 **San Juan Is** USA
23B2 **San Juan Tepozcolula** Mexico
29C5 **San Julián** Arg
34C2 **San Justo** Arg
60D2 **Sankt-Peterburg** Russian Fed
98C3 **Sankuru** R Zaire
22A2 **San Leandro** USA
93C2 **Şanlıurfa** Turk
32B3 **San Lorenzo** Ecuador
34C2 **San Lorenzo** Arg
22B2 **San Lucas** USA
34B2 **San Luis** Arg
34B2 **San Luis** State, Arg
23A1 **San Luis de la Paz** Mexico
21A2 **San Luis Obispo** USA
23A1 **San Luis Potosi** Mexico
22B2 **San Luis Res** USA
53A3 **Sanluri** Sardegna
33D2 **San Maigualida** Mts Ven
34A2 **San Manuel** Arg
34A2 **San Marcos** Chile
23B2 **San Marcos** Mexico
52B2 **San Marino** Republic, Europe
34B2 **San Martin** Mendoza, Arg
112C3 **San Martin** Base Ant
47D1 **San Martino di Castroza** Italy
23B2 **San Martin Tuxmelacan** Mexico
30E2 **San Matias** Bol
72C3 **Sanmenxia** China

25D3 **San Miguel** El Salvador
22B3 **San Miguel I** USA
23A1 **San Miguel del Allende** Mexico
34D3 **San Miguel del Monte** Arg
30C4 **San Miguel de Tucumán** Arg
73D4 **Sanming** China
9B3 **San Nicolas I** USA
34C2 **San Nicolás de los Arroyos** Arg
101G1 **Sannieshof** S Africa
97B4 **Sanniquellie** Lib
59C3 **Sanok** Pol
26B5 **San Onofre** Colombia
22D4 **San Onofre** USA
79B3 **San Pablo** Phil
22A1 **San Pablo B** USA
34D2 **San Pedro** Buenos Aires, Arg
97B4 **San Pédro** Ivory Coast
30D3 **San Pedro** Jujuy, Arg
30E3 **San Pedro** Par
22C4 **San Pedro Chan** USA
9C4 **San Pedro de los Colonias** Mexico
25D3 **San Pedro Sula** Honduras
53A3 **San Pietro** I Medit S
24A1 **San Quintin** Mexico
34B2 **San Rafael** Arg
22A2 **San Rafael** USA
22C3 **San Rafael Mts** USA
49D3 **San Remo** Italy
34C2 **San Salvador** Arg
26C2 **San Salvador** I Caribbean S
32J7 **San Salvador** I Ecuador
30C3 **San Salvador de Jujuy** Arg
51B1 **San Sebastian** Spain
53C2 **San Severo** Italy
30C2 **Santa Ana** Bol
25C3 **Santa Ana** Guatemala
22D4 **Santa Ana** USA
22D4 **Santa Ana Mts** USA
34A3 **Santa Bárbara** Chile
24B2 **Santa Barbara** Mexico
22C3 **Santa Barbara** USA
22C4 **Santa Barbara** I USA
22B3 **Santa Barbara Chan** USA
22C4 **Santa Barbara Res** USA
22C4 **Santa Catalina** I USA
22C4 **Santa Catalina,G of** USA
30F4 **Santa Catarina** State, Brazil
26B2 **Santa Clara** Cuba
22B2 **Santa Clara** USA
22C3 **Santa Clara** R USA
29C6 **Santa Cruz** Arg
30D2 **Santa Cruz** Bol
34A2 **Santa Cruz** Chile
79B3 **Santa Cruz** Phil
29B5 **Santa Cruz** State, Arg
22A2 **Santa Cruz** USA
22C4 **Santa Cruz** I USA
35D1 **Santa Cruz Cabralia** Brazil
22C3 **Santa Cruz Chan** USA
96A2 **Santa Cruz de la Palma** Canary Is
26B2 **Santa Cruz del Sur** Cuba
96A2 **Santa Cruz de Tenerife** Canary Is
100B2 **Santa Cruz do Cuando** Angola
35B2 **Santa Cruz do Rio Pardo** Brazil
22A2 **Santa Cruz Mts** USA
34D2 **Santa Elena** Arg

Santo Domingo

33E8 **Santa Elena** Ven
34C2 **Santa Fe** Arg
34C2 **Santa Fe** State, Arg
9C3 **Santa Fe** USA
35A1 **Santa Helena de Goiás** Brazil
73B3 **Santai** China
29B6 **Santa Inés** I Chile
34B3 **Santa Isabel** La Pampa, Arg
34C2 **Santa Isabel** Sante Fe, Arg
107E1 **Santa Isabel I** Solomon Is
21A2 **Santa Lucia** Ra USA
21A2 **Santa Lucia Range** Mts USA
97A4 **Santa Luzia** I Cape Verde
9B4 **Santa Margarita** I Mexico
22D4 **Santa Margarita** R USA
30F4 **Santa Maria** Brazil
26C4 **Santa Maria** Colombia
21A3 **Santa Maria** USA
96A1 **Santa Maria** I Açores
23B1 **Santa Maria** R Queretaro, Mexico
23A1 **Santa Maria del Rio** Mexico
32C1 **Santa Marta** Colombia
22C3 **Santa Monica** USA
22C4 **Santa Monica B** USA
29E2 **Santana do Livramento** Brazil
32B3 **Santander** Colombia
50B1 **Santander** Spain
51C2 **Santañy** Spain
22C3 **Santa Paula** USA
31C2 **Santa Quitéria** Brazil
33G4 **Santarem** Brazil
50A2 **Santarém** Port
22A1 **Santa Rosa** California, USA
25D3 **Santa Rosa** Honduras
34C3 **Santa Rosa** La Pampa, Arg
34B2 **Santa Rosa** Mendoza, Arg
34B2 **Santa Rosa** San Luis, Arg
22B3 **Santa Rosa** I USA
24A2 **Santa Rosalia** Mexico
20C2 **Santa Rosa Range** Mts USA
31D3 **Santa Talhada** Brazil
35C1 **Santa Teresa** Brazil
53A2 **Santa Teresa di Gallura** Sardegna
22B3 **Santa Ynez** R USA
22B3 **Santa Ynez Mts** USA
17C1 **Santee** R USA
47C2 **Santhia** Italy
34A2 **Santiago** Chile
27C3 **Santiago** Dom Rep
32A2 **Santiago** Panama
79B2 **Santiago** Phil
32B4 **Santiago** R Peru
50A1 **Santiago de Compostela** Spain
26B2 **Santiago de Cuba** Cuba
30D4 **Santiago del Estero** Arg
30D4 **Santiago del Estero** State, Arg
22D4 **Santiago Peak** Mt USA
31C5 **Santo** State, Brazil
35A2 **Santo Anastácio** Brazil
30F4 **Santo Angelo** Brazil
97A4 **Santo Antão** I Cape Verde
35A2 **Santo Antonio da Platina** Brazil
27D3 **Santo Domingo** Dom Rep

Santos

35B2 **Santos** Brazil
35C2 **Santos Dumont** Brazil
30E4 **Santo Tomé** Arg
29B5 **San Valentín** *Mt* Chile
34A2 **San Vicente** Chile
98B3 **Sanza Pomba** Angola
30E4 **São Borja** Brazil
35B2 **São Carlos** Brazil
33G5 **São Félix** Mato Grosso, Brazil
35C2 **São Fidélis** Brazil
35C1 **São Francisco** Brazil
31D3 **São Francisco** *R* Brazil
30G4 **São Francisco do Sul** Brazil
35B1 **São Gotardo** Brazil
99D3 **Sao Hill** Tanz
35C2 **São João da Barra** Brazil
35B2 **São João da Boa Vista** Brazil
35C1 **São João da Ponte** Brazil
35C2 **São João del Rei** Brazil
35B2 **São Joaquim da Barra** Brazil
96A1 **São Jorge** *I* Açores
35B2 **São José do Rio Prêto** Brazil
35B2 **São Jose dos Campos** Brazil
31C2 **São Luis** Brazil
35B1 **São Marcos** *R* Brazil
35C1 **São Maria do Suaçui** Brazil
35D1 **São Mateus** Brazil
35C1 **São Mateus** *R* Brazil
96A1 **São Miguel** *I* Açores
49C2 **Saône** *R* France
97A4 **São Nicolau** *I* Cape Verde
35B2 **São Paulo** Brazil
35A2 **São Paulo** State, Brazil
31C3 **São Raimundo Nonato** Brazil
35B1 **São Romão** Brazil
35B2 **São Sebastia do Paraiso** Brazil
35A1 **São Simão** Goias, Brazil
35B2 **São Simão** Sao Paulo, Brazil
97A4 **São Tiago** *I* Cape Verde
97C4 **São Tomé** *I* W Africa
97C4 **São Tomé and Príncipe** Republic. W Africa
96B2 **Saoura** *Watercourse* Alg
35B2 **São Vicente** Brazil
97A4 **São Vincente** *I* Cape Verde
55C2 **Sápai** Greece
78U4 **Sape** Indon
97C4 **Sapele** Nig
74E2 **Sapporo** Japan
53C2 **Sapri** Italy
18A2 **Sapulpa** USA
90A2 **Saqqez** Iran
10C2 **Saquenay** *R* Can
90A2 **Sarāb** Iran
54A2 **Sarajevo** Bosnia-Herzegovina
90D2 **Sarakhs** Iran
61J3 **Saraktash** Russian Fed
63A2 **Sarala** Russian Fed
15D2 **Saranac L** USA
15D2 **Saranac Lake** USA
55B3 **Sarandë** Alb
79C4 **Sarangani Is** Phil
61G3 **Saransk** Russian Fed
61H2 **Sarapul** Russian Fed
17B2 **Sarasota** USA
54C1 **Sarata** Ukraine
15D2 **Saratoga Springs** USA

78C2 **Saratok** Malay
61G3 **Saratov** Russian Fed
61G3 **Saratovskoye Vodokhranilishche** *Res* Russian Fed
67F4 **Sarawak** State, Malay
92A2 **Saraykoy** Turk
90C3 **Sarbisheh** Iran
47D1 **Sarca** *R* Italy
95A2 **Sardalas** Libya
90A2 **Sar Dasht** Iran
52A2 **Sardegna** *I* Medit S
Sardinia = Sardegna
38H5 **Sarektjåkkå** *Mt* Sweden
84C2 **Sargodha** Pak
98B2 **Sarh** Chad
90B2 **Sāri** Iran
94B2 **Sarida** *R* Isreal
93D1 **Sarikamiş** Turk
31D3 **Sarina** Aust
47B1 **Sarine** *R* Switz
90A2 **Sarir Tibesti** *Desert* Libya
74B3 **Sariwŏn** N Korea
48B2 **Sark** *I* UK
92C2 **Sarkišla** Turk
11E4 **Sarmi** Indon
29C5 **Sarmiento** Arg
39G6 **Särna** Sweden
47C1 **Sarnen** Switz
14B2 **Sarnia** Can
58D2 **Sarny** Ukraine
6E2 **Saroaq** Greenland
84B2 **Sarobi** Afghan
78A3 **Sarolangun** Indon
55B3 **Saronikós Kólpos** *G* Greece
47C2 **Saronno** Italy
55C2 **Saros Körfezi** *B* Turk
39G7 **Sarpsborg** Nor
46D2 **Sarralbe** France
46D2 **Sarrebourg** France
46D2 **Sarreguemines** France
46D2 **Sarre-Union** France
51B1 **Sarrion** Spain
85B3 **Sartanahu** Pak
53A2 **Sartène** Corse
48B2 **Sarthe** *R* France
61H4 **Sarykamys** Kazakhstan
65H5 **Sarysu** *R* Kazakhstan
86A2 **Sasarām** India
74B4 **Sasebo** Japan
5H4 **Saskatchewan** Province, Can
5H4 **Saskatchewan** *R* Can
5H4 **Saskatoon** Can
13F2 **Saskatoon** Can
101G1 **Sasolburg** S Africa
61F3 **Sasovo** Russian Fed
97B4 **Sassandra** Ivory Coast
97B4 **Sassandra** *R* Ivory Coast
53A2 **Sassari** Sardegna
56C2 **Sassnitz** Germany
47D2 **Sassuolo** Italy
34C2 **Sastre** Arg
87A1 **Sātāra** India
4G2 **Satellite B** Can
78D4 **Satengar** *Is* Indon
39H6 **Säter** Sweden
17B1 **Satilla** *R* USA
61J2 **Satka** Russian Fed
86A2 **Satna** India
85C4 **Sätpura Range** *Mts* India
54B1 **Satu Mare** Rom
34D2 **Sauce** Arg
39F7 **Sauda** Nor
80C3 **Saudi Arabia** Kingdom, Arabian Pen
46D2 **Sauer** *R* Germany/Lux
46D1 **Sauerland** Region, Germany
38B1 **Sauðárkrókur** Iceland

14A2 **Saugatuck** USA
16C1 **Saugerties** USA
13B2 **Saugstad,Mt** Can
7B5 **Sault Sainte Marie** Can
14B1 **Sault Ste Marie** Can
14B1 **Sault Ste Marie** USA
71E4 **Saumlaki** Indon
48B2 **Saumur** France
98C3 **Saurimo** Angola
27M2 **Sauteurs** Grenada
54A2 **Sava** *R* Serbia, Yugos
97C4 **Savalou** Benin
17B1 **Savannah** Georgia, USA
17B1 **Savannah** *R* USA
76C2 **Savannakhet** Laos
26B3 **Savanna la Mar** Jamaica
7A4 **Savant Lake** Can
76D2 **Savarane** Laos
97C4 **Savé** Benin
101C3 **Save** *R* Mozam
90B3 **Sāveh** Iran
46D2 **Saverne** France
47B2 **Savigliano** Italy
46D2 **Savigny** France
49D2 **Savoie** *Region* France
49D3 **Savona** Italy
38K6 **Savonlinna** Fin
4A3 **Savoonga** USA
38K5 **Savukoski** Fin
71D4 **Savu S** Indon
76A1 **Saw** Burma
85D3 **Sawai Mādhopur** India
78A2 **Sawang** Indon
76B2 **Sawankhalok** Thai
75C1 **Sawara** Japan
12E1 **Sawtooth Mt** USA
106B2 **Sawu** *I* Indon
97C3 **Say** Niger
84B1 **Sayghan** Afghan
81C3 **Sayhūt** Yemen
61G4 **Saykhin** Kazakhstan
68D2 **Saynshand** Mongolia
61H5 **Say-Utes** Kazakhstan
16C2 **Sayville** USA
13B2 **Sayward** Can
57C3 **Sázava** *R* Czech Republic
51C2 **Sbisseb** *R* Alg
42C2 **Scafell Pike** *Mt* Eng
44E1 **Scalloway** Scot
44C2 **Scapa Flow** *Sd* Scot
15C2 **Scarborough** Can
42D2 **Scarborough** Eng
27E4 **Scarborough** Tobago
44A2 **Scarp** *I* Scot
46B2 **Scarrff** Irish Rep
52A1 **Schaffhausen** Switz
57C3 **Scharding** Austria
46D1 **Scharteberg** *Mt* Germany
7D4 **Schefferville** Can
46B1 **Schelde** *R* Belg
10C2 **Schenectady** USA
47D2 **Cchio** Italy
46D1 **Schleiden** Germany
56B2 **Schleswig** Germany
56B2 **Schleswig Holstein** State, Germany
16B1 **Schoharie** USA
71F4 **Schouten Is** PNG
7B5 **Schreiber** Can
21B2 **Schurz** USA
16A2 **Schuykill Haven** USA
16B2 **Schuylkill** *R* USA
57B3 **Schwabische Alb** *Upland* Germany
57B3 **Schwarzwald** *Upland* Germany
12C1 **Schwatka Mts** USA
47D1 **Schwaz** Austria
57C2 **Schweinfurt** Germany
101G1 **Schweizer Reneke** S Africa
56C2 **Schwerin** Germany
47C1 **Schwyz** Switz
53B3 **Sciacca** Italy

14B3 **Scioto** *R* USA
109D2 **Scone** Aust
6H2 **Scoresby Sd** Greenland
103F7 **Scotia Ridge** Atlantic O
103F7 **Scotia S** Atlantic O
44B3 **Scotland** Country, UK
112B7 **Scott Base** Ant
13B2 **Scott,C** Can
9C2 **Scott City** USA
112C6 **Scott I** Ant
6C2 **Scott Inlet** *B* Can
20B2 **Scott,Mt** USA
106B2 **Scott Reef** Timor S
8C2 **Scottsbluff** USA
17A1 **Scottsboro** USA
109C4 **Scottsdale** Aust
10C2 **Scranton** USA
47D1 **Scuol** Switz
Scutari = Shkodër
5J4 **Seal** *R* Can
108B3 **Sea Lake** Aust
18B2 **Searcy** USA
22B2 **Seaside** California, USA
20B1 **Seaside** Oregon, USA
16B3 **Ceaside Park** U3A
20B1 **Seattle** USA
22A1 **Sebastopol** USA
58D1 **Sebez** Russian Fed
17B2 **Sebring** USA
111A3 **Secretary I** NZ
18B2 **Sedalia** USA
46C2 **Sedan** France
111B2 **Seddonville** NZ
94B3 **Sede Boqer** Israel
94B3 **Sederot** Israel
97A3 **Sédhiou** Sen
94B3 **Sedom** Israel
100A3 **Seeheim** Namibia
71E4 **Sefton,Mt** NZ
77C5 **Segamat** Malay
51B2 **Segorbe** Spain
97B3 **Ségou** Mali
Segovia = Coco
50B1 **Segovia** Spain
51C1 **Segre** *R* Spain
97B4 **Séguéla** Ivory Coast
96A2 **Seguia el Hamra** *Watercourse* Mor
34C2 **Segundo** *R* Arg
78D2 **Seguntur** Indon
50B2 **Segura** *R* Spain
85B3 **Sehwan** Pak
46D2 **Seille** *R* France
38J6 **Seinäjoki** Fin
48C2 **Seine** *R* France
46B2 **Seine-et-Marne** Department, France
99D3 **Sékenke** Tanz
99D1 **Sek'ot'a** Eth
20B1 **Selah** USA
71E4 **Selaru** *I* Indon
78B3 **Selat Bangka** *Str* Indon
78A3 **Selat Berhala** *B* Indon
71E4 **Selat Dampier** *Str* Indon
78B3 **Selat Gaspar** *Str* Indon
78D4 **Selat Lombok** *Str* Indon
78B4 **Selat Sape** *Str* Indon
78B4 **Selat Sunda** *Str* Indon
71D4 **Selat Wetar** *Chan* Indon
12B1 **Selawik** USA
12C1 **Selawik** *R* USA
12B1 **Selawik L** USA
42D3 **Selby** Eng
55C3 **Selcuk** Turk
12D3 **Seldovia** USA
100B3 **Selebi Pikwe** Botswana
6H3 **Selfoss** Iceland
95B2 **Selima Oasis** Sudan
5J4 **Selkirk** Can
42C2 **Selkirk** Scot

Shimabara

13D2 Selkirk Mts Can
22C2 Selma California, USA
50B2 Selouane Mor
12H2 Selous,Mt Can
78B3 Selta Karimata *Str* Indon
32C5 Selvas Region, Brazil
107D3 Selwyn Aust
4E3 Selwyn Mts Can
78C4 Semarang Indon
61E2 Semenov Russian Fed
12C3 Semidi *Is* USA
60E3 Semiluki Russian Fed
19A2 Seminole Oklahoma, USA
17B1 Seminole,L USA
65K4 Semipalatinsk Kazakhstan
79B3 Semirara *Is* Phil
90B3 Semirom Iran
78C2 Semitau Indon
90B2 Semnan Iran
46C2 Semois *R* Belg
23B2 Sempoala Hist Site, Mexico
32D5 Sena Madureira Brazil
100B2 Senanga Zambia
19C3 Senatobia USA
74E3 Sendai Honshū, Japan
74C4 Sendai Kyūshū, Japan
85D4 Sendwha India
15C2 Seneca Falls USA
97A3 Senegal Republic, Africa
97A3 Sénégal *R* Maur Sen
101G1 Senekal S Africa
31D4 Senhor do Bonfim Brazil
52B2 Senigallia Italy
52C2 Senj Croatia
69E4 Senkaku Gunto *Is* Japan
46B2 Senlis France
99D1 Sennar Sudan
7C5 Senneterre Can
49C2 Sens France
54A1 Senta Serbia, Yugos
98C3 Sentery Zaïre
13C2 Sentinel Peak *Mt* Can
85D4 Seoni India
Seoul = Soul
110B2 Separation Pt NZ
76D2 Sepone Laos
24 Sept-Iles Can
95A2 Séquédine Niger
21B2 Sequoia Nat Pk, USA
71D4 Seram *I* Indon
78B4 Serang Indon
78B2 Serasan *I* Indon
54A2 Serbia Republic, Yugos
61F3 Serdobsk Russian Fed
77C5 Seremban Malay
99D3 Serengeti Nat Pk Tanz
100C2 Serenje Zambia
59D3 Seret *R* Ukraine
61G2 Sergach Russian Fed
65H3 Sergino Russian Fed
31D4 Sergipe State, Brazil
60E2 Segiyev Posad
78C2 Seria Brunei
78C2 Serian Malay
55B3 Sérifos *I* Greece
47C2 Serio *R* Italy
95B2 Serir Calanscio *Desert* Libya
46C2 Sermaize-les-Bains France
71D4 Sermata *I* Indon
61H3 Sernovodsk Russian Fed
65H4 Serov Russian Fed
100B3 Serowe Botswana
50A2 Serpa Port

60E3 Serpukhov Russian Fed
35B2 Serra da Canastra *Mts* Brazil
50A1 Serra da Estrela *Mts* Port
35B2 Serra da Mantiqueira *Mts* Brazil
35A1 Serra da Mombuca Brazil
35C1 Serra do Cabral *Mt* Brazil
33F5 Serra do Cachimbo *Mts* Brazil
35A1 Serra do Caiapó *Mts* Brazil
35A2 Serra do Cantu *Mts* Brazil
35C2 Serra do Caparaó *Mts* Brazil
31C5 Serra do Chifre Brazil
35C1 Serra do Espinhaço *Mts* Brazil
35B2 Serra do Mar *Mts* Brazil
35A2 Serra do Mirante *Mts* Brazil
33G3 Serra do Navio Brazil
35B2 Serra do Paranapiacaba *Mts* Brazil
33F6 Serra dos Caiabis *Mts* Brazil
35A2 Serra dos Dourados *Mts* Brazil
33E6 Serra dos Parecis *Mts* Brazil
35B1 Serra dos Pilões *Mts* Brazil
35A1 Serra Dourada *Mts* Brazil
33F6 Serra Formosa Brazil
55B2 Sérrai Greece
25D3 Serrana Bank *Is* Caribbean S
51B1 Serrana de Cuenca *Mts* Spain
35A1 Serranópolis Brazil
33E3 Serra Pacaraima *Mts* Brazil/Ven
33E3 Serra Parima *Mts* Brazil
33G3 Serra Tumucumaque Brazil
46B2 Serre *R* France
34B2 Serrezuela Arg
31D4 Serrinha Brazil
6G3 Serrmilik Greenland
35C1 Serro Brazil
35A2 Sertanópolis Brazil
72A3 Sêrtar China
78C3 Seruyan *R* Indon
100A2 Sesfontein Namibia
100B2 Sesheke Zambia
47B2 Sestriere Italy
74D2 Setana Japan
49C3 Sète France
35C1 Sete Lagoas Brazil
96C1 Sétif Alg
75B1 Seto Japan
75A2 Seto Naikai *S* Japan
96B1 Settat Mor
42C2 Settle Eng
5G4 Settler Can
50A2 Sétubal Port
93E1 Sevan,Oz *L* Armenia
60D5 Sevastopol' Ukraine
7B4 Severn *R* Can
43C3 Severn *R* Eng
1B9 Severnaya Zemlya *I* Russian Fed
63C2 Severo-Baykalskoye Nagorye *Mts* Russian Fed
60E4 Severo Donets Ukraine
64E3 Severodvinsk Russian Fed
64H3 Severo Sos'va *R* Russian Fed
8B3 Sevier *R* USA
8B3 Sevier *L* USA
50A2 Sevilla Spain

Seville = Sevilla
54C2 Sevlievo Bulg
97A4 Sewa *R* Sierra Leone
12E2 Seward Alaska, USA
18A1 Seward Nebraska, USA
12A1 Seward Pen USA
13D1 Sexsmith Can
89K8 Seychelles *Is* Indian O
38C1 Seyðisfjörður Iceland
92C2 Seyhan Turk
60E3 Seym *R* Russian Fed
108C3 Seymour Aust
16C2 Seymour Connecticut, USA
14A3 Seymour Indiana, USA
46B2 Sézanne France
96D1 Sfax Tunisia
54C1 Sfinto Gheorghe Rom
56A2 's-Gravenhage Neth
72B3 Shaanxi Province, China
98C3 Shabunda Zaïre
82B2 Shache China
112C9 Shackleton Ice Shelf Ant
85B3 Shadadkot Pak
91B3 Shādhām *R* Iran
43C4 Shaftesbury Eng
29G8 Shag Rocks *Is* South Georgia
90A3 Shāhābād Iran
94C2 Shahbā Syria
91C3 Shahdap Iran
86A2 Shahdol India
90A2 Shāhīn Dezh Iran
90C3 Shāh Kūh Iran
91C3 Shahr-e Bābak Iran
Shahresa = Qomisheh
90B3 Shahr Kord Iran
87B1 Shājābād India
84D3 Shājahānpur India
85D4 Shājapur India
61F4 Shakhty Russian Fed
61G2 Shakhun'ya Russian Fed
97C4 Shaki Nig
12B2 Shaktoolik USA
61J2 Shamary Russian Fed
99D2 Shambe Sudan
16B1 Shamokin USA
72D2 Shandong Province, China
73C5 Shangchuan Dao *I* China
72C1 Shangdu China
73E3 Shanghai China
72C3 Shangnan China
100B2 Shangombo Zambia
73D4 Shangra China
73B5 Shangsi China
72C3 Shang Xian China
41B3 Shannon *R* Irish Rep
72D3 Shanqiu China
72B3 Shansonggang China
63F2 Shantarskiye Ostrova *I* Russian Fed
73D5 Shantou China
72C2 Shanxi Province, China
72D3 Shan Xian China
73C5 Shaoguan China
73E4 Shaoxing China
73C4 Shaoyang China
44C2 Shapinsay *I* Scot
90C2 Shaqqā Syria
72A1 Sharhulsan Mongolia
90C2 Sharīfābād Iran
91C4 Sharjah UAE
106A3 Shark B Aust
90C2 Sharlauk Turkmenistan
94B2 Sharon,Plain of Israel
61G2 Sharya Russian Fed
99D2 Shashemanē Eth
73C3 Shashi China

20B2 Shasta *L* USA
20B2 Shasta,Mt USA
93E3 Shaṭṭ al Gharrat *R* Iraq
94B3 Shaubak Jordan
13F3 Shaunavon Can
22C2 Shave *L* USA
16B2 Shawangunk Mt USA
15D1 Shawinigan Can
19A2 Shawnee Oklahoma, USA
73D4 Sha Xian China
106B3 Shay Gap Aust
94C2 Shaykh Miskin Syria
99E1 Shaykh 'Uthmān Yemen
60E3 Shchekino Russian Fed
60E3 Shchigry Russian Fed
60D3 Shchors Ukraine
65J4 Shchuchinsk Kazakhstan
99E2 Shebele *R* Eth
14A2 Sheboygan USA
98B2 Shebshi *Mts* Nig
12F1 Sheenjek *R* USA
45C1 Sheep Haven *Estuary* Irish Rep
43E4 Sheerness Eng
94B2 Shefar'am Israel
42D3 Sheffield Eng
84C2 Sheikhupura Pak
13B1 Shelagyote Peak *Mt* Can
16C1 Shelburne Falls USA
14A2 Shelby Michigan, USA
8B2 Shelby Montana, USA
14A3 Shelbyville Indiana, USA
12H2 Sheldon,Mt Can
12D3 Shelikof Str USA
109D2 Shellharbour Aust
111A3 Shelter Pt NZ
20B1 Shelton USA
93E1 Shemakha Azerbaijan
18A1 Shenandoah USA
15C3 Shenandoah *R* USA
15C3 Shenandoah Nat Pk USA
97C4 Shendam Nig
95C2 Shendi Sudan
72C2 Shenmu China
72E1 Shenyang China
73C5 Shenzhen China
85D3 Sheopur India
59D2 Shepetovka Ukraine
108C3 Shepparton Aust
6B2 Sherard,C Can
43C4 Sherborne Eng
97A4 Sherbro *I* Sierra Leone
15D1 Sherbrooke Can
85C3 Shergarh India
19B3 Sheridan Arkansas, USA
8C2 Sheridan Wyoming, USA
19A3 Sherman USA
56B2 s-Hertogenbosh Neth
12H3 Sheslay Can
40C1 Shetland *Is* Scot
52C2 Shevchenko = Aktau
91B4 Sheyk Sho'eyb *I* Iran
69H2 Shiashkotan *I* Russian Fed
84B1 Shibarghan Afghan
74D3 Shibata Japan
95C1 Shibin el Kom Egypt
75B1 Shibukawa Japan
72C2 Shijiazhuang China
84B3 Shikarpur Pak
67G3 Shikoku *I* Japan
74C4 Shikoku-sanchi *Mts* Japan
86B1 Shiliguri India
68D1 Shilka Russian Fed
68D1 Shilka *R* Russian Fed
16B2 Shillington USA
86C1 Shillong India
61F3 Shilovo Russian Fed
75A2 Shimabara Japan

75B2 **Shimada** Japan
69E1 **Shimanovsk**
    Russian Fed
74D3 **Shimizu** Japan
84D2 **Shimla** India
75B2 **Shimoda** Japan
87B2 **Shimoga** India
74C4 **Shimonoseki** Japan
75B1 **Shinano** *R* Japan
91C5 **Shinās** Oman
74D4 **Shingū** Japan
75C1 **Shinjo** Japan
74D3 **Shinminato** Japan
94C1 **Shinshār** Syria
93D2 **Shinyanga** Tanz
74E3 **Shiogama** Japan
75B2 **Shiono-misaki** *C*
    Japan
73A5 **Shiping** China
16A2 **Shippensburg** USA
72B3 **Shiquan** China
75C1 **Shirakawa** Japan
75B1 **Shirane-san** *Mt*
    Japan
75B1 **Shirane-san** *Mt*
    Japan
91B4 **Shiraz** Iran
90B3 **Shir Kūh** Iran
75B1 **Shirotori** Japan
90C2 **Shirvān** Iran
12A1 **Shishmaref** USA
12A1 **Shishmaref Inlet**
    USA
4B3 **Shishmaret** China
72B2 **Shitanjing** China
14A3 **Shively** USA
85D3 **Shivpuri** India
94B3 **Shivta** *Hist Site*
    Israel
101C2 **Shiwa Ngandu**
    Zambia
72C3 **Shiyan** China
72B2 **Shizuishan** China
75B1 **Shizuoka** Japan
54A2 **Shkodër** Alb
109D2 **Shoalhaven** *R* Aust
75A2 **Shobara** Japan
87B2 **Shoranūr** India
87B1 **Shorāpur** India
21B2 **Shoshone Mts** USA
60D3 **Shostka** Ukraine
19B3 **Shreveport** USA
43C3 **Shrewsbury** Eng
43C3 **Shropshire** County,
    Eng
72E1 **Shuanglia** China
69F2 **Shuangyashan**
    China
61J4 **Shubar-Kuduk**
    Kazakhstan
72D2 **Shu He** *R* China
73A4 **Shuicheng** China
84C3 **Shujaabad** Pak
85D4 **Shujālpur** India
08B2 **Shule He** China
54C2 **Shumen** Bulg
61G2 **Shumerlya**
    Russian Fed
73D4 **Shuncheng** China
12C1 **Shungnak** USA
72C2 **Shuo Xian** China
01C4 **Shūr Gaz** Iran
100B2 **Shurugwi** Zim
15D2 **Shuswap L** Can
61F2 **Shuya** Russian Fed
12D3 **Shuyak I** USA
82D3 **Shwebo** Burma
76B2 **Shwegyin** Burma
84A2 **Siah Koh** *Mts*
    Afghan
84C2 **Sialkot** Pak
    Sian = Xi'an
79C4 **Siarao** *I* Phil
82A1 **Siaton** Phil
58C1 **Siauliai** Lithuania
65G4 **Sibay** Russian Fed
101H1 **Sibayi L** S Africa
52C2 **Šibenik** Croatia
70A4 **Siberut** *I* Indon
84B3 **Sibi** Pak
68C1 **Sibirskoye**
    Russian Fed
98B3 **Sibiti** Congo
99D3 **Sibiti** *R* Tanz

54B1 **Sibiu** Rom
70A3 **Sibolga** Indon
86C1 **Sibsāgar** India
78C2 **Sibu** Malay
79B4 **Sibuguay B** Phil
98B2 **Sibut** CAR
79B3 **Sibuyan** *I* Phil
79B3 **Sibuyan S** Phil
73A3 **Sichuan** Province,
    China
53B3 **Sicilia** / Medit S
53B3 **Sicilian** *Chan* Italy/
    Tunisia
    Sicily = Sicilia
32C6 **Sicuani** Peru
85C4 **Siddhapur** India
87B1 **Siddipet** India
86A2 **Sidhi** India
95B1 **Sidi Barrani** Egypt
96B1 **Sidi Bel Abbès** Alg
96B1 **Sidi Kacem** Mor
44C3 **Sidlaw Hills** Scot
112B5 **Sidley,Mt** Ant
20B1 **Sidney** Can
8C2 **Sidney** Nebraska,
    USA
15C2 **Sidney** New York,
    USA
14B2 **Sidney** Ohio, USA
17B1 **Sidney Lanier,L**
    USA
    Sidon = Säida
58C2 **Siedlce** Pol
46D1 **Sieg** *R* Germany
46D1 **Siegburg** Germany
46D1 **Siegen** Germany
76C3 **Siem Reap** Camb
52B2 **Siena** Italy
58B2 **Sierpc** Pol
23B2 **Sierra Andrés Tuxtla**
    Mexico
34B3 **Sierra Auca Mahuida**
    Mts Arg
9C3 **Sierra Blanca** USA
51B1 **Sierra de Albarracin**
    Mts Spain
50B2 **Sierra de Alcaraz** *Mts*
    Spain
34B2 **Sierra de Cordoba**
    Mts Arg
50A1 **Sierra de Gredos** *Mts*
    Spain
50A2 **Sierra de Guadalupe**
    Mts Spain
50B1 **Sierra de**
    Guadarrama *Mts*
    Spain
51B1 **Sierra de Guara** *Mts*
    Spain
51B1 **Sierra de Gudar** *Mts*
    Spain
23B2 **Sierra de Juárez**
    Mexico
34C3 **Sierra de la Ventana**
    Mts Arg
51C1 **Sierra del Codi** *Mts*
    Spain
34B2 **Sierra del Morro** *Mt*
    Arg
34B3 **Sierra del Nevádo**
    Mts Arg
24B2 **Sierra de los**
    Alamitos *Mts*
    Mexico
50B2 **Sierra de los Filabres**
    Spain
23A1 **Sierra de los**
    Huicholes Mexico
23B2 **Sierra de Miahuatlán**
    Mexico
23A1 **Sierra de Morones**
    Mts Mexico
50A2 **Sierra de Ronda** *Mts*
    Spain
34B2 **Sierra de San Luis**
    Mts Arg
50B2 **Sierra de Segura** *Mts*
    Spain
50B1 **Sierra de Urbion** *Mts*
    Spain
34B2 **Sierra de Uspallata**
    Mts Arg
34B2 **Sierra de Valle Fértil**
    Mts Arg

23B2 **Sierra de Zongolica**
    Mexico
34C2 **Sierra Grande** *Mts*
    Arg
97A4 **Sierra Leone**
    Republic, Africa
97A4 **Sierra Leone,C** Sierra
    Leone
79B2 **Sierra Madre** *Mts*
    Phil
23A2 **Sierra Madre del Sur**
    Mts Mexico
24B2 **Sierra Madre**
    Occidental *Mts*
    Mexico
24C2 **Sierra Madre Oriental**
    Mts Mexico
34D2 **Sierra Malanzan** *Mts*
    Arg
9C4 **Sierra Mojada**
    Mexico
50A2 **Sierra Morena** *Mts*
    Spain
50B2 **Sierra Nevada** *Mts*
    Spain
21A2 **Sierra Nevada** *Mts*
    USA
32C1 **Sierra Nevada de**
    Santa Marta *Mts*
    Colombia
34B2 **Sierra Pié de Palu**
    Mts Arg
47B1 **Sierre** Switz
55B3 **Sifnos** *I* Greece
59C3 **Sighetu Marmaţiei**
    Rom
54B1 **Sighişoara** Rom
38B1 **Siglufjördur** Iceland
50B1 **Sigüenza** Spain
97B3 **Siguiri** Guinea
    Sihanoukville =
    Kompong Som
85E4 **Sihora** India
93D2 **Siirt** Turk
68B3 **Sikai Hu** *L* China
85D3 **Sikar** India
84B2 **Sikaram** *Mt* Afghan
97B3 **Sikasso** Mali
18C2 **Sikeston** USA
55C3 **Sikinos** *I* Greece
55B3 **Sikionia** Greece
86B1 **Sikkim** State, India
50A1 **Sil** *R* Spain
47D1 **Silandro** Italy
23A1 **Silao** Mexico
79B3 **Silay** Phil
86C2 **Silchar** India
96C2 **Silet** Alg
86A1 **Silgarhi** Nepal
92B2 **Silifke** Turk
92D2 **Siling Co** *L* China
54C2 **Silistra** Bulg
39F7 **Silkeborg** Den
4/E1 **Sillian** Austria
18B2 **Siloam Springs** USA
19B3 **Silsbee** USA
95A3 **Siltou** *Well* Chad
58C1 **Šilute** Lithuania
93D2 **Silvan** Turk
35B1 **Silvania** Brazil
85C4 **Silvassa** India
2182 **Silver City** Nevada,
    USA
9C3 **Silver City** New
    Mexico, USA
20B2 **Silver Lake** USA
16A3 **Silver Spring** USA
13B2 **Silverthrone Mt** Can
108B2 **Silverton** Aust
47C1 **Silvretta** *Mts*
    Austria/Switz
78C2 **Simanggang** Malay
76C1 **Simao** China
90A3 **Simareh** *R* Iran
55C3 **Simav** Turk
55C3 **Simav** *R* Turk
61G3 **Simbirsk**
    Russian Fed
15C2 **Simcoe,L** Can
70A3 **Simeulue** *I* Indon
60D5 **Simferopol'** Ukraine
55B3 **Sími** *I* Greece
56D3 **Simmern** Germany
13B2 **Simoon Sound** Can

49D2 **Simplon** *Mt* Switz
47C1 **Simplon** *P* Switz
4C2 **Simpson,C** USA
106C3 **Simpson Desert** Aust
6B3 **Simpson Pen** Can
39G7 **Simrishamn** Sweden
69H2 **Simushir** *I*
    Russian Fed
99E2 **Sina Dhaqa** Somalia
92B4 **Sinai** *Pen* Egypt
32B2 **Sincelejo** Colombia
17B1 **Sinclair,L** USA
85D3 **Sind** *R* India
85B3 **Sindh** Region, Pak
55C3 **Sindirği** Turk
86B2 **Sindri** India
50A2 **Sines** Port
99D1 **Singa** Sudan
77C5 **Singapore** Republic,
    S E Asia
77C5 **Singapore,Str of**
    S E Asia
78D4 **Singaraja** Indon
99D3 **Singida** Tanz
78B2 **Singkawang** Indon
109D2 **Singleton** Aust
78A3 **Singtep** *I* Indon
76B1 **Singu** Burma
53A2 **Siniscola** Sardgena
93D2 **Sinjar** Iraq
84B2 **Sinkai Hills** *Mts*
    Afghan
95C3 **Sinkat** Sudan
82C1 **Sinkiang**
    Autonomous Region,
    China
33G2 **Sinnamary** French
    Guiana
92C1 **Sinop** Turk
54B1 **Sintana** Rom
78C2 **Sintang** Indon
50A2 **Sintra** Port
32B2 **Sinú** *R* Colombia
74A2 **Sinŭiju** N Korea
59B3 **Siofok** Hung
47B1 **Sion** Switz
8D2 **Sioux City** USA
8D2 **Sioux Falls** USA
10A2 **Sioux Lookout** Can
79B4 **Sipalay** Phil
27L1 **Siparia** Trinidad
69E2 **Siping** China
112B3 **Siple** *Base* Ant
112B5 **Siple I** Ant
79B3 **Sipocot** Phil
70A4 **Sipora** Indon
79B4 **Siquijor** *I* Phil
87B2 **Sira** India
53C3 **Siracusa** Italy
86B2 **Sirajganj** Bang
13C2 **Sir Alexander,Mt** Can
91B5 **Sir Bani Yās** *I* UAE
106C2 **Sir Edward Pellew**
    Group *Is* Aust
54C1 **Siret** *R* Rom
12J2 **Sir James**
    McBrien,Mt Can
87B2 **Sir Kālahasti** India
13D2 **Sir Laurier,Mt** Can
93D1 **Şirnak** Turk
85C4 **Sirohi** India
87B1 **Sironcha** India
85D4 **Sironj** India
55B3 **Siros** *I* Greece
9184 **Sirri** *I* Iran
84D3 **Sirsa** India
13D2 **Sir Sandford,Mt** Can
87A2 **Sirsi** India
95A1 **Sirte Desert** Libya
95A1 **Sirte,G of** Libya
52C1 **Sisak** Croatia
76C2 **Sisaket** Thai
76C3 **Sisophon** Camb
46C2 **Sissonne** France
90D3 **Sistan** Region, Iran/
    Afghan
49D3 **Sisteron** France
63B2 **Sistig Khem**
    Russian Fed
86A1 **Sītāpur** India
55C3 **Sitia** Greece
4E4 **Sitka** USA
12D3 **Sitkalidak I** USA
12D3 **Sitkinak** *I* USA

76B2 Sittang *R* Burma
46C1 Sittard Neth
86C2 Sittwe Burma
78C4 Situbondo Indon
92C2 Sivas Turk
93C2 Siverek Turk
92B2 Sivrihisar Turk
95B2 Siwa Egypt
84D2 Siwalik Range *Mts* India
86A1 Siwalik Range *Mts* Nepal
72D3 Siyang China
56C1 Sjaelland *I* Den
39G7 Skagen Den
39F7 Skagerrak *Str* Nor/ Den
20B1 Skagit *R* USA
20B1 Skagit Mt Can
4E4 Skagway USA
39G7 Skara Sweden
59C2 Skarzysko-Kamlenna Pol
5F4 Skeena *R* Can
13B1 Skeena Mts Can
4D3 Skeenjek *R* USA
42E3 Skegness Eng
38H5 Skellefte *R* Sweden
38J6 Skelleftea Sweden
55B3 Skiathos *I* Greece
13B3 Skibbereen Irish Rep
5E4 Skidegate Can
58C2 Skiemiewice Pol
39F7 Skien Nor
96C1 Skikda Alg
74C4 Skikoku */* Japan
42D3 Skipton Eng
55B3 Skiros */* Greece
39F7 Skive Den
56B1 Skjern Den
6F3 Skjoldungen Greenland
14A2 Skokie USA
55B3 Skópelos */* Greece
54B2 Skopje Macedonia
39G7 Skövde Sweden
63E2 Skovorodino Russian Fed
4C3 Skwentna USA
58B2 Skwierzyna Pol
40B2 Skye */* Scot
39G7 Slagelse Den
45C2 Slaney *R* Irish Rep
54B2 Slatina Rom
78C4 Slaung Indon
5G3 Slave *R* Can
13E1 Slave Lake Can
65J4 Slavgorod Russian Fed
59D2 Slavuta Ukraine
60E4 Slavyansk Ukraine
44B3 Sleat,Sound of *Chan* Scot
12C2 Sleetmute USA
45C2 Sleeve Bloom *Mts* Irish Rep
19C3 Slidell USA
16B2 Slide Mt USA
45B1 Sligo County, Irish Rep
41B3 Sligo Irish Rep
41B3 Sligo *B* Irish Rep
54C2 Sliven Bulg
54C2 Slobozia Rom
13D3 Slocan Can
58D2 Slonim Belorussia
43D4 Slough Eng
22B2 Slough *R* USA
59B3 Slovakia Republic, Europe
52B1 Slovenia Republic, Europe
56C2 Slubice Pol
59D2 Sluch' *R* Ukraine
58B2 Slupsk Pol
58B2 Slutsk Belorussia
58D2 Slutsk *R* Belorussia
41A3 Slyne Head *Pt*
63C2 Slyudyanka Russian Fed
7D4 Smallwood Res Can
54B2 Smederevo Serbia, Yugos

54B2 Smederevska Palanka Serbia, Yugos
60D4 Smela Ukraine
15C2 Smethport USA
13E1 Smith Can
4F3 Smith Arm *B* Can
13B2 Smithers Can
7C3 Smith I Can
13B2 Smith Sd Can
15C2 Smiths Falls Can
109C4 Smithton Aust
13D1 Smoky *R* Can
109D2 Smoky C Aust
13E2 Smoky Lake Can
38F6 Smøla */* Nor
60D3 Smolensk Russian Fed
55B2 Smólikas *Mt* Greece
54B2 Smolyan Bulg
58D2 Smorgon' Belorussia
16B3 Smyrna Delaware, USA
17B1 Smyrna Georgia, USA
42B2 Snaefell *Mt* Eng
38B2 Snæfell *Mt* Iceland
8B2 Snake *R* USA
8B2 Snake River Canyon USA
56B2 Sneek Neth
45B3 Sneem Irish Rep
22B2 Snelling USA
59B2 Snežka *Mt* Pol/ Czech Republic
38F6 Snohetta *Mt* Nor
20B1 Snohomish USA
20B1 Snoqualmie P USA
76D3 Snoul Camb
43B3 Snowdon *Mt* Wales
43B3 Snowdonia Nat Pk Wales
4G3 Snowdrift Can
5H4 Snow Lake Can
108A2 Snowtown Aust
9C3 Snowy Mts Aust
9C3 Snyder USA
78B4 Soan-kundo */ S Korea
99D2 Sobat *R* Sudan
31C2 Sobral Brazil
58C2 Sochaczew Pol
61E5 Sochi Russian Fed
9C3 Socorro USA
24A3 Socorro */ Mexico
34A2 Socos Chile
81D4 Socotra */ Yemen
38K5 Sodankylä Fin
39H6 Söderhamn Sweden
39H7 Södertälje Sweden
99C1 Sodiri Sudan
99D2 Sodo Eth
46E1 Soest Germany
101C2 Sofala Mozam
Sofia = Sofiya
54B2 Sofiya Bulg
69G4 Sofu Gan */ Japan
32C2 Sogamoso Colombia
39F6 Sognefjorden *Inlet* Nor
82D2 Sog Xian China
95C2 Sohag Egypt
84D3 Sohipat India
46B1 Soignies Belg
46B2 Soissons France
85C3 Sojat India
74A3 Sojoson-man *B* N Korea
92A2 Söke Turk
97C4 Sokodé Togo
61E2 Sokol Russian Fed
58C2 Sokolka Pol
97B3 Sokolo Mali
6H3 Søkongens Øy */ Greenland
99D1 Sokota Eth
97C3 Sokoto Nig
97C3 Sokoto *R* Nig
111A3 Solander I NZ
79B2 Solano Phil
87B1 Solapur India
47D1 Soldhall Hall Austria
47D1 Sölden Austria
12D2 Soldotna USA
26C4 Soledad Colombia

43D4 Solent *Sd* Eng
46B1 Solesmes France
58D2 Soligorsk Belorussia
61J2 Solikamsk Russian Fed
32C4 Solimões *R* Peru
46D1 Solingen Germany
38H6 Sollefteå Sweden
61H3 Sol'lletsk Russian Fed
70B4 Solok Indon
105G4 Solomon */s* Pacific O
47B1 Solothurn Switz
39F8 Soltau Germany
22B3 Solvang USA
42C2 Solway Firth *Estuary* Eng/Scot
100B2 Solwezi Zambia
75C1 Sõma Japan
55C3 Soma Turk
81C5 Somalia Republic, E Africa
54A1 Sombor Serbia, Yugos
107D2 Somerset Aust
43C4 Somerset County, Eng
7D2 Somerset Massachusetts, USA
15C2 Somerset Pennsylvania, USA
100B4 Somerset East S Africa
6A2 Somerset I Can
16B3 Somers Point USA
16B2 Somerville USA
19A3 Somerville Res USA
54B1 Somes *R* Rom
46B2 Somme Department, France
46B2 Somme *R* France
46C2 Sommesous France
86A2 Son *R* India
39F8 Sonch'ŏn N Korea
39F8 Sønderborg Den
6E3 Søndre Strømfjord Greenland
47C1 Sondrio Italy
76D3 Song Ba *R* Viet
76D3 Song Cau Viet
101C2 Songea Tanz
73E3 Songjiang China
77C4 Songkhla Thai
74B3 Songnim N Korea
77C5 Sông Pahang *R* Malay
72A3 Songpan China
72C1 Sonid Youqi China
76C1 Son La Viet
85B3 Sonmiani Pak
85B3 Sonmiani Bay Pak
22A1 Sonoma USA
22B2 Sonora California, USA
24A2 Sonora */ Mexico
9B3 Sonoran Desert USA
22C1 Sonora P USA
25D3 Sonsonate El Salvador
71E3 Sonsorol */ Pacific O
10B2 Soo Canals Can/USA
13C3 Sooke Can
58B2 Sopot Pol
59B3 Sopron Hung
22B2 Soquel USA
53B2 Sora Italy
94B3 Sored *R* Israel
15D1 Sorel Can
109C4 Sorell Aust
92C2 Sorgun Turk
50B1 Soria Spain
38J5 Sørkjosen Nor
64C2 Sørksop */ Barents S
61H4 Sor Mertvyy Kultuk Plain Kazakhstan
35B2 Sorocaba Brazil
61H3 Sorochinsk Russian Fed
71F3 Soroi */ Pacific O
60C4 Soroki Moldova
71E4 Sorong Indon
71E4 Sorong Province, Indon
99D2 Soroti Uganda

38J4 Sørøya */ Nor
53B2 Sorrento Italy
38K5 Sorsatunturi *Mt* Fin
38H5 Sorsele Sweden
79B3 Sorsogon Phil
38L6 Sortavala Russian Fed
74B3 Sõsan S Korea
59B2 Sosnowiec Pol
65H4 Sos'va Russian Fed
98B2 Souanké Congo
97B4 Soubré Ivory Coast
16B2 Souderton USA
27P2 Soufrière St Lucia
27N2 Soufrière *Mt* St Vincent and the Grenadines
48C3 Souillac France
96C1 Souk Ahras Alg
74B3 Soul S Korea
51C2 Soummam *R* Alg
Sour = Tyr
101G1 Sources,Mt aux Lesotho
31D3 Sousa Brazil
96D1 Sousse Tunisia
100B4 South Africa Republic, Africa
15C2 South Amboy USA
14B2 Southampton Can
43D4 Southampton Eng
16C2 Southampton USA
6B3 Southampton I Can
28F6 South Atlantic O
7D4 South Aulatsivik I Can
106B3 South Australia State, Aust
104E3 South Australian Basin Indian O
19C3 Southaven USA
17B2 South Bay USA
14B1 South Baymouth Can
14A2 South Bend Indiana, USA
20B1 South Bend Washington, USA
16D1 Southbridge USA
South Cape = Ka Lae
11B3 South Carolina State, USA
70C2 South China S
8C2 South Dakota State, USA
16C1 South Deerfield USA
43D4 South Downs Eng
109C4 South East C Aust
111A2 Southen Alps *Mts* NZ
5H4 Southend Can
43E4 Southend-on-Sea Eng
111A2 Southern Alps *Mts* NZ
106A4 Southern Cross Aust
5J4 Southern Indian L Can
27H2 Southfield Jamaica
105G5 South Fiji Basin Pacific O
12D2 South Fork *R* Alaska, USA
22B1 South Fork *R* California, USA
28F8 South Georgia */ S Atlantic O
43C4 South Glamorgan County, Wales
14A2 South Haven USA
5J3 South Henik L Can
104F3 South Honshu Ridge Pacific O
111A2 South I NZ
16C2 Southington USA
74B3 South Korea Republic, S E Asia
21A2 South Lake Tahoe USA
112C6 South Magnetic Pole Ant
19C4 South Miami USA
16A3 South Mt USA

South Nahanni

4F3 **South Nahanni** *R* Can
26G1 **South Negril Pt** Jamaica
103F8 **South Orkney** *Is* Atlantic O
8C2 **South Platte** *R* USA
80E **South Pole** Ant
42C3 **Southport** Eng
27R3 **South Pt** Barbados
16B2 **South River** USA
44C2 **South Ronaldsay** *I* Scot
103G7 **South Sandwich Trench** Atlantic O
22A2 **South San Francisco** USA
5H4 **South Saskatchewan** *R* Can
42D2 **South Shields** Eng
110B1 **South Taranaki Bight** *B* NZ
44A3 **South Uist** *I* Scot
South West Africa = Namibia
107D5 **South West C** Aust
105J5 **South West Pacific Basin** Pacific O
103D5 **South West Peru Ridge** Pacific O
43D3 **South Yorkshire** *(unclear)* Eng
58C1 **Sovetsk** Russian Fed
61G2 **Sovetsk** Russian Fed
101G1 **Soveto** S Africa
98B3 **Soyo** Congo Angola
60D3 **Sozh** *R* Belorussia
46C1 **Spa** Belg
50A1 **Spain** Kingdom
Spalato = Split
43D3 **Spalding** Eng
14B1 **Spanish** *R* Can
26B3 **Spanish Town** Jamaica
21B2 **Sparks** USA
11B3 **Spartanburg** USA
55B3 **Sparti** Greece
69F2 **Spassk Dal'niy** Russian Fed
27R3 **Speightstown** Barbados
12E2 **Spenard** USA
14A3 **Spencer** Indiana, USA
8D2 **Spencer** Iowa, USA
6A3 **Spencer Bay** Can
108A3 **Spencer,C** Aust
108A2 **Spencer G** Aust
6C3 **Spencer I** Can
111B2 **Spenser Mts** NZ
45C1 **Sperrin** *Mts* N Ire
44C3 **Spey** *R* Scot
57B3 **Speyer** Germany
27K1 **Speyside** Tobago
47B1 **Spiez** Switz
12F1 **Spike Mt** USA
20C1 **Spirit Lake** USA
5G4 **Spirit River** Can
Spitsbergen = Svalbard
64C2 **Spitsbergen** *I* Barents S
57C3 **Spittal** Austria
38F6 **Spjelkavik** Nor
52C2 **Split** Croatia
47C1 **Splügen** Switz
20C1 **Spokane** USA
55C3 **Sporádhes** *Is* Greece
20C2 **Spray** USA
56C2 **Spree** *R* Germany
100A3 **Springbok** S Africa
18B2 **Springdale** USA
10B3 **Springfield** Illinois, USA
10C2 **Springfield** Massachusetts, USA
18B2 **Springfield** Missouri, USA
14B3 **Springfield** Ohio, USA
20B2 **Springfield** Oregon, USA
15D2 **Springfield** Vermont, USA

100B4 **Springfontein** S Africa
101G1 **Springs** S Africa
41D3 **Spurn Head** *Pt* Eng
13C3 **Squamish** Can
60E3 **Sredne-Russkaya Vozvyshennost** *Upland* Russian Fed
63B1 **Sredne Sibirskoye Ploskogorye** *Tableland* Russian Fed
61J2 **Sredniy Ural** *Mts* Russian Fed
76D3 **Srepok** *R* Camb
68D1 **Sretensk** Russian Fed
70C3 **Sre Umbell** Camb
83C5 **Sri Lanka** Republic, S Asia
84C2 **Srinagar** Pak
87A1 **Srivardhan** India
58B2 **Sroda Wlk.** Pol
30H6 **Sta Clara** *I* Chile
32J7 **Sta Cruz** *I* Ecuador
56B2 **Stade** Germany
44A3 **Staffa** *I* Scot
43C3 **Stafford** County, Eng
43C3 **Stafford** Eng
16C2 **Stafford Springs** USA
Stalingrad = Volgograd
6A1 **Stallworthy,C** Can
59C2 **Stalowa Wola** Pol
32J7 **Sta Maria** *I* Ecuador
16C2 **Stamford** Connecticut, USA
16B1 **Stamford** New York, USA
100A3 **Stampriet** Namibia
101G1 **Standerton** S Africa
14B2 **Standish** USA
101H1 **Stanger** S Africa
22B2 **Stanislaus** *R* USA
54B2 **Stanke Dimitrov** Bulg
109C4 **Stanley** Aust
29E6 **Stanley** Falkland Is
87B2 **Stanley Res** India
Stanleyville = Kisangani
25D3 **Stann Creek** Belize
63E2 **Stanovoy Khrebet** *Mts* Russian Fed
47C1 **Stans** Switz
109D1 **Stanthorpe** Aust
54B2 **Stara Planina** *Mts* Bulg
60D2 **Staraya Russa** Russian Fed
54C2 **Stara Zagora** Bulg
58B2 **Stargard Szczecinski** Pol
19C3 **Starkville** USA
57C3 **Starnberg** Germany
58B2 **Starogard Gdanski** Pol
59D3 **Starokonstantinov** Ukraine
43C4 **Start Pt** Eng
60E3 **Staryy Oskol** Russian Fed
15C2 **State College** USA
16B2 **Staten I** USA
17B1 **Statesboro** USA
15C3 **Staunton** USA
39F7 **Stavanger** Nor
46C1 **Stavelot** Belg
61F4 **Stavropol'** Russian Fed
108B3 **Stawell** Aust
58B2 **Stawno** Pol
20B2 **Stayton** USA
12B2 **Stebbins** USA
12F2 **Steele,Mt** Can
16A2 **Steelton** USA
20C2 **Steens Mt** USA
6E2 **Steenstrups Gletscher** *Gl* Greenland
4H2 **Stefansson I** Can
101H1 **Stegi** Swaziland

47D1 **Steinach** Austria
8D2 **Steinbach** Can
38G6 **Steinkjer** Nor
13C2 **Stein Mt** Can
23B2 **Stemaco** Mexico
46C2 **Stenay** France
56C2 **Stendal** Germany
110B2 **Stephens,C** NZ
108B2 **Stephens Creek** Aust
14A1 **Stephenson** USA
12H3 **Stephens Pass** USA
7E5 **Stephenville** Can
100B4 **Sterkstroom** S Africa
8C2 **Sterling** Colorado, USA
14B2 **Sterling Heights** USA
61J3 **Sterlitamak** Russian Fed
13E2 **Stettler** Can
14B2 **Steubenville** USA
4D3 **Stevens Village** USA
13B1 **Stewart** Can
21B2 **Stewart** USA
12G2 **Stewart** *R* Can
12G2 **Stewart Crossing** Can
111A3 **Stewart I** NZ
107F1 **Stewart Is** Solomon Is
4E3 **Stewart River** Can
(unclear) **Steyerm** *(unclear)* Russian Fed
101G1 **Steyn** S Africa
57C3 **Steyr** Austria
12G3 **Stika** USA
12H3 **Stikine** *R* Can
12H3 **Stikine Ranges** *Mts* Can
18A2 **Stillwater** Oklahoma, USA
21B2 **Stillwater Range** *Mts* USA
108A2 **Stirling** Aust
44C3 **Stirling** Scot
16C1 **Stockbridge** USA
59B3 **Stockerau** Austria
39H7 **Stockholm** Sweden
42C3 **Stockport** Eng
22B2 **Stockton** California, USA
42D2 **Stockton** Eng
18B2 **Stockton L** USA
43C3 **Stoke-on-Trent** Eng
38A2 **Stokkseyri** Iceland
38G5 **Stokmarknes** Nor
39K8 **Stolbtsy** Belorussia
58D2 **Stolin** Belorussia
16B3 **Stone Harbor** USA
44C3 **Stonehaven** Scot
19A3 **Stonewall** USA
12D2 **Stony** *R* USA
38H5 **Storavan** *L* Sweden
38G6 **Støren** Nor
109C4 **Storm B** Aust
44A2 **Stornoway** Scot
59D3 **Storozhinets** Ukraine
16C2 **Storrs** USA
38G6 **Stors168jon** *L* Sweden
38H5 **Storuman** Sweden
16D1 **Stoughton** USA
45C3 **Strabane** N Ire
109C4 **Strahan** Aust
56C2 **Stralsund** Germany
38F6 **Stranda** Nor
39H7 **Strängnäs** Sweden
42B2 **Stranraer** Scot
49D2 **Strasbourg** France
15C3 **Strasburg** USA
14B2 **Stratford** Can
15C2 **Stratford** Connecticut, USA
110B1 **Stratford** NZ
43D3 **Stratford-on-Avon** Eng
108A3 **Strathalbyn** Aust
42B2 **Strathclyde** Region, Scot
13E2 **Strathmore** USA
18C1 **Streator** USA
47C2 **Stresa** Italy
53C3 **Stretto di Messina** *Str* Italy/Sicily
38D3 **Streymoy** Føroyar

53C3 **Stroboli** *I* Italy
6E3 **Strømfjord** Greenland
44C2 **Stromness** Scot
18A1 **Stromsburg** USA
38H6 **Stromsund** Sweden
38G6 **Ströms Vattudal** *L* Sweden
21J **Stronsay** *I* Scot
43C4 **Stroud** Eng
16B2 **Stroudsburg** USA
54B2 **Struma** *R* Bulg
43B3 **Strumble Head** *Pt* Wales
55B2 **Strumica** Macedonia
59C3 **Stryy** Ukraine
59C3 **Stryy** *R* Ukraine
108B1 **Strzelecki Creek** *R* Aust
17B2 **Stuart** Florida, USA
18C3 **Stuart** *R* Can
12B2 **Stuart I** USA
13C2 **Stuart L** Can
47D1 **Stubaier Alpen** *Mts* Austria
76D3 **Stung Sen** Camb
76D3 **Stung Treng** Camb
112C7 **Sturge I** Ant
110A1 **Sturgeon Bay** USA
14C1 **Sturgeon Falls** Can
18C2 **Sturgis** Kentucky, USA
14A2 **Sturgis** Michigan, USA
106B2 **Sturt Creek** *R* Aust
108B1 **Sturt Desert** Aust
100B4 **Stutterheim** S Africa
19B3 **Stuttgart** USA
57B3 **Stuttgart** Germany
38A1 **Stykkisholmur** Iceland
59D2 **Styr'** *R* Ukraine
35C1 **Suaqui Grande** *R* Brazil
81B4 **Suakin** Sudan
73E5 **Su-ao** Taiwan
34C2 **Suardi** Arg
78B2 **Subi I** Indon
54A1 **Subotica** Serbia, Yugos
60C4 **Suceava** Rom
64B1 **Suck** *R* Irish Rep
30C2 **Sucre** Bol
35A1 **Sucuriú** *R* Brazil
98C1 **Sudan** Republic, Africa
14B1 **Sudbury** Can
43E3 **Sudbury** Eng
99C2 **Sudd** *Swamp* Sudan
33F2 **Suddie** Guyana
08C2 **Sue** *R* Sudan
4H2 **Suerdrup Is** Can
92B4 **Suez** Egypt
92B3 **Suez Canal** Egypt
92C4 **Suez G** Egypt
16B2 **Suffern** USA
43E3 **Suffolk** County, Eng
109D2 **Sugarloaf Pt** Aust
91C6 **Suhar** Oman
68C1 **Sühbaatar** Mongolia
84B3 **Sui** Pak
72C2 **Suide** China
69E2 **Suihua** China
73B3 **Suining** China
46C2 **Suippes** France
41B3 **Suir** *R* Irish Rep
73C3 **Sui Xian** China
72E1 **Suizhong** China
85C3 **Sujängarth** India
78B4 **Sukabumi** Indon
78B4 **Sukadana** Borneo, Indon
78B4 **Sukadana** Sumatra, Indon
74E3 **Sukagawa** Japan
78C3 **Sukaraya** Indon
60E3 **Sukhinichi** Russian Fed
61F2 **Sukhona** *R* Russian Fed
61F5 **Sukhumi** Georgia
6E3 **Sukkertoppen** Greenland

6E3 Sukkertoppen L Greenland
38L6 Sukkozero Russian Fed
85B3 Sukkur Pak
87C1 Sukma India
95A2 Süknah Libya
100A3 Sukses Namibia
75A2 Sukumo Japan
13C1 Sukunka R Can
60E3 Sula R Russian Fed
84B3 Sulaiman Range Mts Pak
70C4 Sulawesi I Indon
54C1 Sulina Rom
38H5 Sulitjelma Nor
32A4 Sullana Peru
18B2 Sullivan USA
13B2 Sullivan Bay Can
13E2 Sullivan L Can
52B2 Sulmona Italy
19B3 Sulphur Louisiana, USA
19A3 Sulphur Oklahoma, USA
19A3 Sulphur Springs USA
86A1 Sultānpur India
79B4 Sulu Arch Phil
70C3 Sulu S Philip
30D4 Sumampa Arg
70B4 Sumatera I Indon
70C4 Sumba I Indon
78D4 Sumbawa I Indon
78D4 Sumbawa Besar Indon
99D3 Sumbawanga Tanz
100A2 Sumbe Angola
44E2 Sumburgh Head Pt Scot
78C4 Sumenep Indon
69G3 Sumisu I Japan
13D3 Summerland Can
5F4 Summit Lake Can
21B2 Summit Mt USA
111B2 Sumner,L NZ
75A2 Sumoto Japan
17B1 Sumter USA
60D3 Sumy Ukraine
16A2 Sunbury USA
34C2 Sunchales Arg
74B3 Sunch'ŏn N Korea
74B4 Sunch'ŏn S Korea
86A2 Sundargarh India
86B2 Sunderbans Swamp India
42D2 Sunderland Eng
13E2 Sundre Can
15C1 Sundridge Can
38H6 Sundsvall Sweden
38D3 Suduroy Føroyar
78D3 Sungaianyar Indon
78A3 Sungaipenuh Indon
20C1 Sunnyside USA
21A2 Sunnyvale USA
63D1 Suntar Russian Fed
97B4 Sunyani Ghana
75A2 Suŏ-nada B Japan
38K6 Suonejoki Fin
86B1 Supaul India
18A1 Superior Nebraska, USA
10A2 Superior Wisconsin, USA
10B2 Superior,L Can/USA
76C3 Süphan Buri Thai
93D2 Süphan Dağ Turk
71E4 Supiori I Indon
93E3 Suq ash Suyukh Iraq
72D3 Suqian China
91C5 Sür Oman
61G3 Sura R Russian Fed
78C4 Surabaya Indon
75B2 Suraga-wan B Japan
78C4 Surakarta Indon
109C1 Surat Aust
85C4 Sūrat India
84C3 Süratgarh India
77B4 Surat Thani Thai
85C4 Surendranagar India
16B3 Surf City USA
64J3 Surgut Russian Fed
87B1 Suriapet India
49D2 Sürich Switz

79C4 Surigao Phil
76C3 Surin Thai
33F3 Surinam Republic, S America
43D4 Surrey County, Eng
47C1 Sursee Switz
95A1 Surt Libya
38A2 Surtsey I Iceland
78A3 Surulangan Indon
47B2 Susa Italy
75A2 Susa Japan
75A2 Susaki Japan
21A1 Susanville USA
47D1 Süsch Switz
12E2 Susitna R USA
16A3 Susquehanna R USA
16B2 Sussex USA
43D4 Sussex West Eng
13B1 Sustut Peak Mt Can
100B4 Sutherland S Africa
84C2 Sutlej R Pak
21A2 Sutter Creek USA
14B3 Sutton USA
12C3 Sutwik I USA
74D3 Suwa Japan
58C2 Suwałki Pol
17B2 Suwannee R USA
94B2 Suweilih Jordan
74B3 Suwŏn S Korea
72D3 Su Xian China
75B1 Suzaka Japan
73E3 Suzhou China
74D3 Suzu Japan
75B2 Suzuka Japan
75B1 Suzu-misaki C Japan
64C2 Svalbard Is Barents S
59C3 Svalyava Ukraine
38G5 Svartisen Mt Nor
78D3 Svay Rieng Camb
38G6 Sveg Sweden
39G7 Svendborg Den
       Sverdlovsk = Yekaterinburg
6A1 Sverdrup Chan Can
69F2 Svetlaya Russian Fed
58C2 Svetlogorsk Russian Fed
39K6 Svetogorsk Russian Fed
54B2 Svetozarevo Serbia, Yugos
54C2 Svilengrad Bulg
58D2 Svir' Belorussia
59B3 Svitavy Czech Republic
69E1 Svobodnyy Russian Fed
38G5 Svolvaer Nor
107E3 Swain Reefs Aust
17B1 Swainsboro USA
100A3 Swakopmund Namibia
42D2 Swale R Eng
70C3 Swallow Reef I S E Asia
87B2 Swämimalli India
25D3 Swan I Honduras
43D4 Swanage Eng
108B3 Swan Hill Aust
13D2 Swan Hills Can
13D2 Swan Hills Mts Can
26A3 Swan I Caribbean S
5H4 Swan River Can
43C4 Swansea Wales
43C4 Swansea B Wales
101G1 Swartruggens S Africa
       Swatow = Shantou
101H1 Swaziland Kingdom, S Africa
39G7 Sweden Kingdom, N Europe
20B2 Sweet Home USA
9C3 Sweetwater USA
100B4 Swellendam S Africa
59B2 Świdnica Pol
58B2 Świdwin Pol
58B2 Świebodzin Pol
58B2 Świecie Pol
5H4 Swift Current Can
43D4 Swindon Eng
45B2 Swinford Irish Rep

56C2 Świnoujście Pol
49D2 Switzerland Federal Republic, Europe
45C2 Swords Irish Rep
109D2 Sydney Aust
7D5 Sydney Can
64G3 Syktyvkar Russian Fed
17A1 Sylacauga USA
38G6 Sylarna Mt Sweden
86C2 Sylhet Bang
56B1 Sylt I Germany
14B2 Sylvania USA
112C11 Syowa Base Ant
       Syracuse = Siracusa
15C2 Syracuse USA
65H5 Syr Darya R Kazakhstan
93C2 Syria Republic, S W Asia
61J2 Sysert' Russian Fed
61G3 Syzran' Russian Fed
56C2 Szczecin Pol
58C2 Szczecinek Pol
58C2 Szczytno Pol
59C3 Szeged Hung
59B3 Székesfehérvár Hung
59B3 Szekszard Hung
59B3 Szolnok Hung
59B3 Szombathely Hung
58B2 Szprotawa Pol

T

90C3 Tabas Iran
23A1 Tabasco Mexico
32D4 Tabatinga Brazil
76C3 Tabeng Camb
79B3 Tablas I Phil
100A4 Table Mt S Africa
12F1 Table Mt USA
18B2 Table Rock Res USA
78B3 Taboali Indon
57C3 Tábor Czech Republic
99D3 Tabora Tanz
97B4 Tabou Ivory Coast
90A2 Tabriz Iran
92C4 Tabūk S Arabia
23A2 Tacámbaro Mexico
82C1 Tacheng China
79C3 Tacloban Phil
30B2 Tacna Peru
8A2 Tacoma USA
99E1 Tadjoura Djibouti
87B2 Tädpatri India
74B3 Taebaek Sanmaek Mts S Korea
74B3 Taegu S Korea
74B4 Taehŭksan I S Korea
74B3 Taejŏn S Korea
51B1 Tafalla Spain
96C2 Tafasaset Watercourse Alg
43C4 Taff R Wales
94B3 Tafila Jordan
60E4 Taganrog Ukraine
97A3 Tagant Region, Maur
79B4 Tagbilaran Phil
96B2 Taguenout Hagguerete Well Maur
107E2 Tagula I Solomon Is
79C4 Tagum Phil
       Tagus = Tejo
96C2 Tahat Mt Alg
105J4 Tahiti I Pacific O
21A2 Tahoe City USA
21A2 Tahoe,L USA
97C3 Tahoua Niger
72D2 Tai'an China
72B3 Taibai Shan Mt China
72D1 Taibus Qi China
73E5 T'ai-chung Taiwan
111B3 Taieri R NZ
72C2 Taihang Shan China
110C1 Taihape NZ
72E3 Tai Hu L China
108A3 Tailem Bend Aust
44B3 Tain Scot

73E5 T'ai-nan Taiwan
35C1 Taiobeiras Brazil
73E5 T'ai pei Taiwan
77C5 Taiping Malay
75C1 Taira Japan
78A3 Tais Indon
75A1 Taisha Japan
29B5 Taitao,Pen de Chile
73E5 T'ai-tung Taiwan
38K5 Taivelkoski Fin
69E4 Taiwan Republic, China
       Taiwan Haixia = Formosa Str
72C2 Taiyuan China
72D3 Taizhou China
81C4 Ta'izz Yemen
82A2 Tajikistan Republic, Asia
50B1 Tajo R Spain
76B2 Tak Thai
74D3 Takada Japan
75A2 Takahashi Japan
110B2 Takaka NZ
74C4 Takamatsu Japan
74D3 Takaoka Japan
110B1 Takapuna NZ
74D3 Takasaki Japan
75B1 Takayama Japan
74D3 Takefu Japan
70A3 Takengon Indon
76C3 Takeo Camb
75A2 Takeo Japan
       Take-shima = Tok-do
90A2 Takestan Iran
75A2 Taketa Japan
4G3 Takjvak L Can
99D1 Takkaze R Eritrea/Eth
13B1 Takla L Can
13B1 Takla Landing Can
12B2 Taksleslek L USA
1J2 Taku Arm R Can
23A1 Tala Mexico
59B3 Talabanya Hung
84C2 Talagang Pak
34A2 Talagante Chile
87B3 Talaimannar Sri Lanka
97C3 Talak Desert Region, Niger
78A3 Talangbetutu Indon
32A4 Talara Peru
50B2 Talavera de la Reina Spain
34A3 Talca Chile
34A3 Talcahuano Chile
86B2 Tälcher India
82B1 Taldy Kurgan Kazakhstan
71D4 Taliabu Indon
84B1 Taligan Afghan
99D2 Tali Post Sudan
78D4 Taliwang Indon
12D2 Talkeetna USA
12E2 Talkeetna Mts USA
17A1 Talladega USA
93D2 Tall 'Afar Iraq
17B1 Tallahassee USA
94B1 Tall Bisah Syria
60B2 Tallinn Estonia
92C3 Tall Kalakh Syria
19B3 Tallulah USA
60D4 Tal'noye Ukraine
58C2 Talpaki Russian Fed
30B4 Taltal Chile
109C1 Talwood Aust
78D1 Tamabo Range Mts Malay
97B4 Tamale Ghana
96C2 Tamanrasset Alg
96C2 Tamanrasset Watercourse Alg
16B2 Tamaqua USA
       Tamatave = Toamasina
23A2 Tamazula Jalisco, Mexico
23B2 Tamazulapán Mexico
23B1 Tamazunchale Mexico
97A3 Tambacounda Sen
61F3 Tambov Russian Fed
50A1 Tambre R Spain
98C2 Tambura Sudan

Tamchaket

97A3 **Tamchaket** Maur
50A1 **Tamega** *R* Port
23B1 **Tamiahua** Mexico
87B2 **Tamil Nadu** State, India
76D2 **Tam Ky** Viet
17B2 **Tampa** USA
17B2 **Tampa B** USA
39J6 **Tampere** Fin
23B1 **Tampico** Mexico
68D2 **Tamsagbulag** Mongolia
86C2 **Tamu** Burma
23B1 **Tamuis** Mexico
109D2 **Tamworth** Aust
43D3 **Tamworth** Eng
38K4 **Tana** Nor
99D1 **Tana** *R* Eth
99E3 **Tana** *R* Kenya
38K5 **Tana** *R* Nor/Fin
75B2 **Tanabe** Japan
38K4 **Tanafjord** *Inlet* Nor
78D3 **Tanahgrogot** Indon
71E4 **Tanahmerah** Indon
12D1 **Tanana** USA
12E2 **Tanana** *R* USA
  **Tananarive =
  Antananarivo**
47C2 **Tanaro** *R* Italy
74B2 **Tanch'ŏn** N Korea
34D3 **Tandil** Arg
78B2 **Tandjong Datu** *Pt* Indon
71E4 **Tandjung d'Urville** *C* Indon
78D3 **Tandjung Layar** *C* Indon
78D2 **Tandjung Lumut** *C* Indon
78D2 **Tandjung Mangkalihet** *C* Indon
78C3 **Tandjung Sambar** *C* Indon
78C2 **Tandjung Sirik** *C* Malay
71E4 **Tandjung Vals** *C* Indon
85B3 **Tando Adam** Pak
85B3 **Tando Muhammad Khan** Pak
108B2 **Tandou L** Aust
87B1 **Tanduti** Indon
110C1 **Taneatua** NZ
76B2 **Tanen Range** *Mts* Burma/Thai
96B2 **Tanezrouft** *Desert Region* Alg
91C4 **Tang** Iran
99D3 **Tanga** Tanz
60E4 **Tanganrog** Russian Fed
99C3 **Tanganyika,L** Tanz/Zaïre
90D1 **Tanger** Mor
82C2 **Tanggula Shan** *Mts* China
  Tangier = Tanger
78A2 **Tanjungpinang** Indon
82C2 **Tangra Yumco** *L* China
72D2 **Tangshan** China
79B4 **Tangub** Phil
63C2 **Tanguy** Russian Fed
78C3 **Tanintharyi = Tenasserim**
79B4 **Tanjay** Phil
101D3 **Tanjona Ankaboa** *C* Madag
101D2 **Tanjona Babaomby** *C* Madag
101D2 **Tanjona Vilanandro** *C* Madag
101D3 **Tanjona Vohimena** *C* Madag
78C4 **Tanjong Bugel** *C* Indon
78B4 **Tanjong Cangkuang** *C* Indon
78C3 **Tanjong Puting** *C* Indon
78C3 **Tanjong Selatan** *C* Indon
78D3 **Tanjung** Indon

70A3 **Tanjungbalai** Indon
78A3 **Tanjung Jabung** *Pt* Indon
78B3 **Tanjungpandan** Indon
78B4 **Tanjung Priok** Indon
78D2 **Tanjungredeb** Indon
78D2 **Tanjungselor** Indon
84C2 **Tank** Pak
68B1 **Tannu Ola** *Mts* Russian Fed
97B4 **Tano** *R* Ghana
97C3 **Tanout** Niger
23B1 **Tanquián** Mexico
73E4 **Tan-shui** Taiwan
86A1 **Tansing** Nepal
95C1 **Tanta** Egypt
96A2 **Tan-Tan** Mor
4B3 **Tanunak** USA
99D3 **Tanzania** Republic, Africa
72A3 **Tao He** *R* China
72B2 **Taole** China
78B1 **Taourirt** Mor
60C2 **Tapa** Estonia
25C3 **Tapachula** Mexico
33F4 **Tapajós** *R* Brazil
34C3 **Tapalquén** Arg
70B4 **Tapan** Indon
111A3 **Tapanui** NZ
32D5 **Tapaua** *R* Brazil
85D4 **Tapi** *R* India
86B1 **Taplejung** Nepal
35B2 **Tapuaenuku** *Mt* NZ
79B4 **Tapuaritinga** Brazil
33E4 **Tapurucuara** Brazil
109D1 **Tara** Aust
65J4 **Tara** Russian Fed
65J4 **Tara** *R* Russian Fed
54A2 **Tara** *R* Bosnia-Herzegovina/Montenegro, Yugos
97D4 **Taraba** *R* Nig
30D2 **Tarabuco** Bol
  Tarābulus = Tripoli
50B1 **Taracón** Spain
110C1 **Taradale** Nz
78D2 **Tarakan** Indon
44A3 **Taransay** *I* Scot
53C2 **Taranto** Italy
32B5 **Tarapoto** Peru
49C2 **Tarare** France
110C2 **Tararua Range** *Mts* NZ
96C2 **Tarat** Alg
110C1 **Tarawera** NZ
51B1 **Tarazona** Spain
44C3 **Tarbat Ness** *Pen* Scot
84C2 **Tarbela Res** Pak
42B2 **Tarbert** Strathclyde, Scot
44A3 **Tarbert** Western Isles, Scot
48C3 **Tarbes** France
106C4 **Tarcoola** Aust
109C2 **Tarcoon** Aust
109D2 **Taree** Aust
96A2 **Tarfaya** Mor
95A1 **Tarhūnah** Libya
91B5 **Tarif** UAE
30D3 **Tarija** Bol
87B2 **Tarikere** India
81C4 **Tarim** Yemen
99D3 **Tarime** Tanz
82C1 **Tarim He** *R* China
82C2 **Tarim Pendi** *Basin* China
84B2 **Tarin Kut** Afghan
18A1 **Tarkio** USA
79B2 **Tarlac** Phil
32B6 **Tarma** Peru
49C3 **Tarn** *R* France
59C2 **Tarnobrzeg** Pol
59C3 **Tarnów** Pol
107D3 **Taroom** Aust
51C1 **Tarragona** Spain
114A3 **Tarraleah** Aust
51C1 **Tarrasa** Spain
16C2 **Tarrytown** USA
92B2 **Tarsus** Turk
44D2 **Tartan** *Oilfield* N Sea

47D2 **Tartaro** *R* Italy
60C2 **Tartu** Estonia
92C3 **Tartūs** Syria
35C1 **Tarumirim** Brazil
70A3 **Tarutung** Indon
52B1 **Tarvisio** Italy
80D1 **Tashauz** Turkmenistan
86C1 **Tashigang** Bhutan
82A1 **Tashkent** Uzbekistan
65K4 **Tashtagol** Russian Fed
63A2 **Tashtyp** Russian Fed
78B4 **Tasikmalaya** Indon
94B2 **Tasil** Syria
6E2 **Tasiussaq** Greenland
95A3 **Tasker** *Well* Niger
110B2 **Tasman B** NZ
107D5 **Tasmania** *I* Aust
111B2 **Tasman Mts** NZ
109C4 **Tasman Pen** Aust
107E4 **Tasman S** NZ Aust
92C1 **Taşova** Turk
96C2 **Tassili du Hoggar** Alg
96C2 **Tassili N'jjer** *Desert Region, Alg*
96B2 **Tata** Mor
96D1 **Tataouine** Tunisia
65J4 **Tatarsk** Russian Fed
60G2 **Tatarskiy Proliv** *Str* Russian Fed
61G2 **Tatarstan** Russian Fed
75B1 **Tateyama** Japan
5G3 **Tathlina L** Can
12E2 **Tatitlek** USA
13C2 **Tatla Lake** Can
59B3 **Tatry** *Mts* Pol/Slovakia
75A2 **Tatsuno** Japan
85B4 **Tatta** Pak
31D4 **Tatuí** Brazil
93D2 **Tatvan** Turk
31C3 **Tauá** Brazil
35B2 **Taubaté** Brazil
110C1 **Taumarunui** NZ
101F1 **Taung** S Africa
76B2 **Taungdwingyi** Burma
76B1 **Taung-gyi** Burma
76A2 **Taungup** Burma
84C2 **Taunsa** Pak
43C4 **Taunton** Eng
16D2 **Taunton** USA
46E1 **Taunus** Region, Germany
110C1 **Taupo** NZ
110C1 **Taupo,L** NZ
58C1 **Taurage** Lithuania
110C1 **Tauranga** NZ
110C1 **Tauranga Harbour** *B* NZ
110B1 **Tauroa Pt** NZ
7A3 **Tavani** Can
65H4 **Tavda** *R* Russian Fed
43B4 **Tavistock** Eng
76B3 **Tavoy** Burma
76B3 **Tavoy Pt** Burma
92A2 **Tavşanli** Turk
111B2 **Tawa** NZ
19A3 **Tawakoni,L** USA
18C2 **Taylorville** USA
70C3 **Tawau** Malay
98C1 **Taweisha** Sudan
79B4 **Tawitawi** *I* Phil
79B4 **Tawitawi Group** *Is* Phil
23B2 **Taxco** Mexico
23B2 **Taxcoco** Mexico
44C3 **Tay** *R* Scot
78C3 **Tayan** Indon
12B1 **Taylor** Alaska, USA
13C1 **Taylor** Can
14B2 **Taylor** Michigan, USA
19A3 **Taylor** Texas, USA
18C2 **Taylorville** USA
80B3 **Tayma'** S Arabia
63B1 **Taymura** *R* Russian Fed
76D3 **Tay Ninh** Viet
63B2 **Tayshet** Russian Fed

68B2 **Tayshir** Mongolia
44C3 **Tayside** Region, Scot
79A3 **Taytay** Phil
90D3 **Tayyebāt** Iran
96B1 **Taza** Mor
95B2 **Tazirbu** Libya
12E2 **Tazlina L** USA
64J3 **Tazovskiy** Russian Fed
65F5 **Tbilisi** Georgia
98B3 **Tchibanga** Gabon
95A2 **Tchigaï,Plat du** Niger
97C3 **Tchin Tabaradene** Niger
98B2 **Tcholliré** Cam
58B2 **Tczew** Pol
111A3 **Te Anau** NZ
111A3 **Te Anau,L** NZ
110C1 **Te Aroha** NZ
110C1 **Te Awamutu** NZ
96C1 **Tébessa** Alg
23A2 **Teboman** Mexico
23A2 **Tecaltlán** Mexico
21B3 **Tecate** Mexico
61K2 **Techa** *R* Russian Fed
23A2 **Tecolotlán** Mexico
23A2 **Tecpan** Mexico
54C1 **Tecuci** Rom
18A1 **Tecumseh** USA
  **Tedzhen =
  Turkmenistan**
65H6 **Tedzhen** *R* Turkmenistan
42D2 **Tees** *R* Eng
33E4 **Tefé** Brazil
78B4 **Tegal** Indon
78B4 **Tegineneng** Indon
25D3 **Tegucigalpa** Honduras
21B3 **Tehachapi Mts** USA
21B2 **Tehachapi P** USA
4J3 **Tehek L** Can
90B2 **Tehrān** Iran
23B2 **Tehuacán** Mexico
23B2 **Tehuantepec** Mexico
23B2 **Tehuitzingo** Mexico
43B3 **Teifi** *R* Wales
50A2 **Tejo** *R* Port
23A2 **Tejupilco** Mexico
111B2 **Tekapo,L** NZ
82B1 **Tekeli** Kazakhstan
92A1 **Tekirdağ** Turk
55C2 **Tekir Dağlari** *Mts* Turk
86C2 **Teknaf** Bang
110C1 **Te Kuiti** NZ
25D3 **Tela** Honduras
94B2 **Tel Aviv Yafo** Israel
34B3 **Telén** Arg
21E2 **Telescope Peak** *Mt* USA
33F5 **Teles Pires** *R* Brazil
47D1 **Telfs** Austria
63A2 **Teli** Russian Fed
94B3 **Tell el Meise** *Mt* Jordan
12A1 **Teller** USA
87B2 **Tellichorry** India
77C5 **Telok Anson** Malay
78D2 **Telok Darvel** Malay
71E4 **Télok Flamingo** *B* Indon
78C3 **Télok Kumai** *B* Indon
78B4 **Télok Pelabuanratu** *B* Indon
78D4 **Télok Saleh** *B* Indon
78C3 **Télok Sampit** *B* Indon
78B3 **Télok Sukadona** *B* Indon
64G3 **Tel'pos-iz** *Mt* Russian Fed
58C1 **Telšiai** Lithuania
78C3 **Telukbatang** Indon
71E4 **Teluk Berau** *B* Indon
78B4 **Telukbetung** Indon
70D4 **Teluk Bone** *B* Indon
71E4 **Teluk Cendrawasih** *B* Indon
78D3 **Teluk Mandar** *B* Indon
71D4 **Teluk Tolo** *B* Indon

70D3 **Teluk Tomini** *B* Indon
71D3 **Teluk Weda** *B* Indon
14B1 **Temagami,L** Can
23B2 **Temascal** Mexico
78A3 **Tembesi** *R* Indon
78A3 **Tembilahan** Indon
27E5 **Temblador** Ven
77C5 **Temerloh** Malay
65G5 **Temir** Kazakhstan
65J4 **Temirtau** Kazakhstan
15C1 **Temiscaming** Can
109C2 **Temora** Aust
9B3 **Tempe** USA
19A3 **Temple** USA
45C2 **Templemore**
    Irish Rep
23B1 **Tempoal** Mexico
34A3 **Temuco** Chile
111B2 **Temuka** NZ
32B4 **Tena** Ecuador
87C1 **Tenāli** India
23B2 **Tenancingo** Mexico
76B3 **Tenasserim** Burma
43B4 **Tenby** Wales
99E1 **Tendaho** Eth
83D5 **Ten Degree Chan**
    Indian O
98B1 **Ténéré** *Desert*
    Region Niger
96A2 **Tenerife** *I* Canary Is
76B1 **Teng** *R* Burma
78D3 **Tenggarong** Indon
72A2 **Tengger Shamo**
    Desert China
112C2 **Teniente Jubany**
    Base Ant
112C2 **Teniente Rodolfo**
    Marsh Martin *Base*
    Ant
87B3 **Tenkäsi** India
100B2 **Tenke** Zaïre
97B3 **Tenkodogo** Burkina
106C2 **Tennant Creek** Aust
11B3 **Tennessee** *State*,
    USA
18C2 **Tennessee** *R* USA
34A2 **Teno** Chile
78D1 **Tenom** Malay
25C3 **Tenosique** Mexico
109D1 **Tenterfield** Aust
17B2 **Ten Thousand Is**
    USA
23A1 **Teocaltiche** Mexico
35C1 **Teófilo Otóni** Brazil
23B2 **Teotihiucan** Hist Site,
    Mexico
23B2 **Teotitlan** Mexico
24B2 **Tepehuanes** Mexico
23A2 **Tepeji** Mexico
23A1 **Tepic** Mexico
57C2 **Teplice**
    Czech Republic
110C1 **Te Puke** NZ
23A1 **Tequila** Mexico
23B2 **Tequistepec** Mexico
51C1 **Ter** *R* Spain
97C3 **Téra** Niger
75B1 **Teradomari** Japan
52B2 **Teramo** Italy
96A1 **Terceira** *I* Açores
59D3 **Terebovlya** Ukraine
31C3 **Teresina** Brazil
35C2 **Teresópolis** Brazil
92C1 **Terme** Turk
80E2 **Termez** Uzbekistan
52B2 **Termoli** Italy
71D3 **Ternate** Indon
52B2 **Terni** Italy
59D3 **Ternopol** Ukraine
13B2 **Terrace** Can
53B2 **Terracina** Italy
100B3 **Terrafirma** S Africa
112C8 **Terre Adélie** *Region*,
    Ant
19B4 **Terre Bonne B** USA
14A3 **Terre Haute** USA
19A3 **Terrell** USA
56B2 **Terschelling** *I* Neth
51B1 **Teruel** Spain
4C2 **Teshekpuk** USA
4C2 **Teshekpuk L** USA
74E2 **Teshio** *R* Japan

68B2 **Tesiyn Gol** *Mts*
    Mongolia
12H2 **Teslin** Can
12H3 **Teslin** *R* Can
12H2 **Teslin L** Can
63B3 **Teslyn Gol** *R*
    Mongolia
96C2 **Tessalit** Mali
97C3 **Tessaoua** Niger
101C2 **Tete** Mozam
23A2 **Tetela** Mexico
96B1 **Tetouan** Mor
61G2 **Tetyushi**
    Russian Fed
30D3 **Teuco** *R* Arg
23A1 **Teúl de Gonzalez**
    Ortega Mexico
71D4 **Teun** *I* Indon
52B2 **Tevere** *R* Italy
42C2 **Teviot** *R* Scot
65J4 **Tevriz** Russian Fed
111A3 **Te Waewae B** NZ
78C3 **Tewah** Indon
109D1 **Tewantin** Aust
72A3 **Têwo** China
19B3 **Texarkana** USA
19B3 **Texarkana,L** USA
109D1 **Texas** Aust
9C3 **Texas** *State*, USA
19B4 **Texas City** USA
56A2 **Texel** *I* Neth
19A3 **Texoma,L** USA
101G1 **Teyateyaneng**
    Lesotho
23B2 **Teziutlán** Mexico
86C1 **Tezpur** India
76C1 **Tha** Laos
101G1 **Thabana Ntlenyana**
    Mt Lesotho
101G1 **Thaba Putsoa** *Mt*
    Lesotho
76B3 **Thagyettaw** Burma
76D1 **Thai Binh** Viet
76C2 **Thailand** *Kingdom*,
    S E Asia
76C3 **Thailand,G of** Thai
76D1 **Thai Nguyen** Viet
76C2 **Thakhek** Laos
84C2 **Thal** Pak
77C4 **Thale Luang** *L* Thai
109D1 **Thallon** Aust
110C1 **Thames** NZ
43E4 **Thames** *R* Eng
76D2 **Thanh Hoah** Viet
87B2 **Thanjavur** India
        Thanlwin = Salween
85C3 **Thar Desert** India
108B1 **Thargomindah** Aust
55B2 **Thásos** *I* Greece
76B2 **Thaton** Burma
76B2 **Thayetmyo** Burma
5F5 **The Dalles** USA
91B4 **The Gulf** S W Asia
4H3 **Thelon** *R* Can
107E3 **Theodore** Aust
9B3 **Theodore Roosevelt L**
    USA
55B2 **Thermaïkós Kólpos**
    G Greece
8C2 **Thermopolis** USA
4F2 **Thesiger B** Can
14B1 **Thessalon** Can
55B2 **Thessaloníki** Greece
43E3 **Thetford** Eng
15D1 **Thetford Mines** Can
101G1 **Theunissen** S Africa
19B4 **Thibodaux** USA
5J4 **Thicket Portage** Can
8D2 **Thief River Falls** USA
20B2 **Thielsen,Mt** USA
49C2 **Thiers** France
97A3 **Thiès** Sen
99D3 **Thika** Kenya
86B1 **Thimphu** Bhutan
49D2 **Thionville** France
55C3 **Thíra** *I* Greece
42D2 **Thirsk** Eng
        Thiruvananthapuram
        = Trivandrum
39F7 **Thisted** Den
55B3 **Thívai** Greece
48C2 **Thiviers** France
17B1 **Thomaston** Georgia,
    USA

45C2 **Thomastown**
    Irish Rep
17B1 **Thomasville** Georgia,
    USA
6A2 **Thom Bay** Can
5J4 **Thompson** Can
18B1 **Thompson** *R* USA
4G3 **Thompson Landing**
    Can
13C2 **Thompson R** Can
16C2 **Thompsonville** USA
17B1 **Thomson** USA
107D3 **Thomson** *R* Aust
76C3 **Thon Buri** Thai
76B2 **Thongwa** Burma
47B1 **Thonon-les-Bains**
    France
42C2 **Thornhill** Scot
48B2 **Thouars** France
15C2 **Thousand Is** Can/
    USA
13E2 **Three Hills** Can
7G4 **Three Kings Is** NZ
76B2 **Three Pagodas P**
    Thai
14A2 **Three Rivers**
    Michigan, USA
20B2 **Three Sisters** *Mt* USA
        Thríssur = Trichūr
6D2 **Thule** Greenland
47B1 **Thun** Switz
10B2 **Thunder Bay** Can
47B1 **Thuner See** *L* Switz
77B4 **Thung Song** Thai
47C1 **Thur** *R* Switz
57C2 **Thüringen** *State*,
    Germany
57C2 **Thüringer Wald**
    Upland Germany
45C2 **Thurles** Irish Rep
71F5 **Thursday I** Aust
44C2 **Thurso** Scot
11284 **Thurston I** Ant
47C1 **Thusis** Switz
108B1 **Thylungra** Aust
73B5 **Tiandong** China
73B5 **Tian'e** China
72D2 **Tianjin** China
73B5 **Tianlin** China
82C1 **Tiān Shan** *Mts* C
    Asia
72B3 **Tianshui** China
72A2 **Tianzhu** China
96C1 **Tiaret** Alg
35A2 **Tibagi** *R* Brazil
94B2 **Tiberias** Israel
94B2 **Tiberias,L** Israel
        Tiber,R = Tevere,R
95A2 **Tibesti** *Mountain*
    Region Chad
82C2 **Tibet** *Autonomous*
    Region, China
108B1 **Tibooburra** Aust
86A1 **Tibrikot** Nepal
24A2 **Tiburón** *I* Mexico
97B3 **Tichitt** Maur
96A2 **Tichla** Mor
47C2 **Ticino** *R* Italy/Switz
15D2 **Ticonderoga** USA
25D2 **Ticul** Mexico
97A3 **Tidjikja** Maur
47C1 **Tiefencastel** Switz
74A2 **Tieling** China
46B1 **Tielt** Belg
46C1 **Tienen** Belg
65J5 **Tien Shan** *Mts*
    China/Kirghizia
72D2 **Tientsin** China
39H6 **Tierp** Sweden
23B2 **Tierra Blanca** Mexico
23B2 **Tierra Colorada**
    Mexico
29C6 **Tierra del Fuego**
    Territory, Arg
28C8 **Tierra del Fuego** *I*
    Arg/Chile
35B2 **Tietê** Brazil
35A2 **Tiete** *R* Brazil
17B1 **Tifton** USA
32B4 **Tigre** *R* Peru
33E2 **Tigre** *R* Ven
93E3 **Tigris** *R* Iraq
23B1 **Tihuatlán** Mexico

21B3 **Tijuana** Mexico
85D4 **Tikamgarh** India
60D2 **Tikhin** Russian Fed
61F4 **Tikhoretsk**
    Russian Fed
93D3 **Tikrit** Iraq
1B8 **Tiksi** Russian Fed
46C1 **Tilburg** Neth
43E4 **Tilbury** Eng
30C3 **Tilcara** Arg
108B1 **Tilcha** Aust
76A1 **Tilin** Burma
97C3 **Tillabéri** Niger
20B1 **Tillamook** USA
97C3 **Tillia** Niger
55C3 **Tílos** *I* Greece
108B2 **Tilpa** Aust
32B3 **Tiluá** Colombia
64G3 **Timanskiy Kryazh**
    Mts Russian Fed
111B2 **Timaru** NZ
60E4 **Timashevsk**
    Russian Fed
55B3 **Timbákion** Greece
19B4 **Timbalier B** USA
97B3 **Timbédra** Maur
        Timbuktu =
        Tombouctou
97B3 **Timétrine Monts** *Mts*
    Mali
97C3 **Timia** Niger
96C2 **Timis** *R* Rom
54B1 **Timişoara** Rom
10B2 **Timmins** Can
106B1 **Timor** *I* Indon
106B2 **Timor S** Aust/Indon
34C3 **Timote** Arg
79C4 **Tinaca Pt** Phil
27D5 **Tinaco** Ven
87B2 **Tindivanam** India
96B2 **Tindouf** Alg
96B2 **Tinfouchy** Alg
96C2 **Tin Fouye** Alg
6F3 **Tingmiarmuit**
    Greenland
32B5 **Tingo Maria** Peru
97B3 **Tingrela** Ivory Coast
86B1 **Tingri** China
71F2 **Tinian** Pacific O
30C4 **Tinogasta** Arg
55C3 **Tinos** *I* Greece
43B4 **Tintagel Head** *Pt*
    Eng
96C2 **Tin Tarabine**
    Watercourse Alg
108B3 **Tintinara** Aust
96C2 **Tin Zaouaten** Alg
22C2 **Tioga P** USA
77C5 **Tioman** *I* Malay
47D1 **Tione** Italy
45C2 **Tipperary** County,
    Irish Rep
41B3 **Tipperary** Irish Rep
18B2 **Tipton** Missouri,
    USA
87B2 **Tiptūr** India
23A2 **Tiquicheo** Mexico
55A2 **Tiranë** Alb
47D1 **Tirano** Italy
60C4 **Tiraspol** Moldova
87B2 **Tirchchirāppalli** India
55A3 **Tira** Turk
93C1 **Tirebolu** Turk
44A3 **Tiree** *I* Scot
54C2 **Tîrgovişte** Rom
54B1 **Tîrgu Jiu** Rom
54B1 **Tîrgu Mureş** Rom
84C1 **Tirich Mir** *Mt* Pak
96A2 **Tiris** Region, Mor
61J3 **Tirlyanskiy**
    Russian Fed
54B1 **Tîrnăveni** Rom
55B3 **Tírnavos** Greece
85D4 **Tirodi** India
47D1 **Tirol** Province,
    Austria
53A2 **Tirso** *R* Sardegna
87B3 **Tiruchchendūr** India
87B3 **Tirunelveli** India
87B2 **Tirupati** India
87B2 **Tiruppattūr** India
87B2 **Tiruppur** India
87B2 **Tiruvannāmalai** India
19A3 **Tishomingo** USA

Tisīyah

94C2 **Tisīyah** Syria
59C3 **Tisza** *R* Hung
86A2 **Titlagarh** India
54B2 **Titov Veles**
Macedonia
98C2 **Titule** Zaire
17B2 **Titusville** USA
43C4 **Tiverton** Eng
52B2 **Tivoli** Italy
23B2 **Tixtla** Mexico
99E2 **Tiyeglow** Somalia
23B2 **Tizayuca** Mexico
25D2 **Tizimin** Mexico
96C1 **Tizi Ouzou** Alg
96B2 **Tiznit** Mor
23A1 **Tizpan el Alto**
Mexico
23B2 **Tlacolula** Mexico
23B2 **Tlacotalpan** Mexico
23A2 **Tlalchana** Mexico
23B2 **Tlalnepantla** Mexico
23B2 **Tlalpan** Mexico
23A1 **Tlaltenango** Mexico
23B2 **Tlancualpicán**
Mexico
23B2 **Tlapa** Mexico
23B2 **Tlapacoyan** Mexico
23A1 **Tlaquepaque** Mexico
23B2 **Tlaxcala** Mexico
23B2 **Tlaxcala** State,
Mexico
23B2 **Tlaxiaco** Mexico
96B1 **Tlemcen** Alg
101D2 **Toamasina** Madag
34C3 **Toay** Arg
75B2 **Toba** Japan
84B2 **Toba and Kakar**
Ranges *Mts* Pak
27E4 **Tobago** *I*
Caribbean S
13C2 **Toba Inlet** *Sd* Can
71D3 **Tobelo** Indon
14B1 **Tobermory** Can
44A3 **Tobermory** Scot
71E3 **Tobi** *I* Pacific O
21B2 **Tobin,Mt** USA
65H4 **Tobol** *R* Kazakhstan
70D4 **Toboli** Indon
65H4 **Tobol'sk** Russian Fed
Tobruk = Tubruq
31B2 **Tocantins** *R* Brazil
31B3 **Tocantins** State,
Brazil
17B1 **Toccoa** USA
47C1 **Toce** *R* Italy
30B3 **Tocopilla** Chile
30C3 **Tocorpuri** *Mt* Chile
32D1 **Tocuyo** *R* Ven
85D3 **Toda** India
47C1 **Tödi** *Mt* Switz
75A1 **Todong** S Korea
9B4 **Todos Santos**
Mexico
13E2 **Tofield** Can
13B3 **Tofino** Can
12B3 **Togiak** USA
12B3 **Togiak B** USA
97C4 **Togo** Republic, Africa
72C1 **Togtoh** China
12F2 **Tok** USA
74E2 **Tokachi** *R* Japan
75B1 **Tokamachi** Japan
95C3 **Tokar** Sudan
69E4 **Tokara Retto** *Arch*
Japan
92C1 **Tokat** Turk
74B3 **Tökchök-kundo** *Arch*
S Korea
75A1 **Tok-do** *I* S Korea
82B1 **Tokmak** Kirghizia
110C1 **Tokomaru Bay** NZ
12H3 **Toku** *R* Can/USA
78C3 **Tokung** Indon
69E4 **Tokuno** *I* Japan
74C4 **Tokushima** Japan
75A2 **Tokuyama** Japan
74D3 **Tökyö** Japan
110C1 **Tolaga Bay** NZ
101D3 **Tôlañaro** Madag
30F3 **Toledo** Brazil
50B2 **Toledo** Spain
14B2 **Toledo** USA
19B3 **Toledo Bend Res**
USA

101D3 **Toliara** Madag
23B1 **Toliman** Mexico
32B3 **Tolima** *Mt* Colombia
51B1 **Tolosa** Spain
29B3 **Toltén** Chile
23B2 **Toluca** Mexico
61G3 **Tol'yatti** Russian Fed
74E2 **Tomakomai** Japan
78D1 **Tomani** Malay
58C2 **Tomaszów**
Mazowiecka Pol
11B3 **Tombigbee** *R* USA
98B3 **Tomboco** Angola
35C2 **Tombos** Brazil
97B3 **Tombouctou** Mali
100A2 **Tombua** Angola
34A3 **Tomé** Chile
50B2 **Tomelloso** Spain
50A2 **Tomer** Port
106B3 **Tomkinson Range**
Mts Aust
63E2 **Tommot**
Russian Fed
55B2 **Tomorrit** *Mt* Alb
65K4 **Tomsk** Russian Fed
16B3 **Toms River** USA
25C3 **Tonalá** Mexico
20C1 **Tonasket** USA
15C2 **Tonawanda** USA
105H4 **Tonga** *Is* Pacific O
101H1 **Tongaat** S Africa
73U3 **Longcheng** China
72B2 **Tongchuan** China
72A2 **Tongde** China
46C1 **Tongeren** Belg
76E2 **Tonggu Jiao** *I* China
73A5 **Tonghai** China
74B3 **Tonghua** China
74B3 **Tongjosón-man**
N Korea
76D1 **Tongkin,G of** China/
Viet
72E1 **Tonglia** China
73D3 **Tongling** China
108B2 **Tongo** Aust
34A2 **Tongoy** Chile
73B4 **Tongren** Guizhou,
China
72A2 **Tongren** Qinghai,
China
86C1 **Tongsa** Bhutan
76B1 **Tongta** Burma
68B3 **Tongtian He** *R* China
44B2 **Tongue** Scot
72D2 **Tong Xian** China
72B2 **Tongxin** China
73B4 **Tongzi** China
9C4 **Tonich** Mexico
99C2 **Tonj** Sudan
85D3 **Tonk** India
18A2 **Tonkawa** USA
76C3 **Tonle Sap** *L* Camb
21B2 **Tonopah** USA
12E2 **Tonsina** USA
8B2 **Tooele** USA
109D1 **Toogoolawah** Aust
108B1 **Toompine** Aust
109D1 **Toowoomba** Aust
22C1 **Topaz L** USA
18A2 **Topeka** USA
23B2 **Topolobampo**
Mexico
20B1 **Toppenish** USA
99D2 **Tor** Eth
55C3 **Torbalï** Turk
90C2 **Torbat-e-Heydariyeh**
Iran
90D2 **Torbat-e Jäm** Iran
12D2 **Torbert,Mt** USA
50A1 **Tordesillas** Spain
56C2 **Torgau** Germany
46B1 **Torhout** Belg
69G3 **Tori** *I* Japan
47B2 **Torino** Italy
99D2 **Torit** Sudan
35A1 **Torixoreu** Brazil
50A1 **Tormes** *R* Spain
13E2 **Tornado Mt** Can
38J5 **Torne** *L* Sweden
38H5 **Torneträsk** Sweden
7D4 **Torngat** *Mts* Can
38J5 **Tornio** Fin
34C3 **Tornquist** Arg
15C2 **Toronto** Can

60D2 **Toropets**
Russian Fed
99D2 **Tororo** Uganda
92B2 **Toros Daǧlari** *Mts*
Turk
43C4 **Torquay** Eng
22C4 **Torrance** USA
50A2 **Torrão** Port
51C1 **Torreblanca** Spain
53B2 **Torre del Greco** Italy
50B1 **Torrelavega** Spain
50B2 **Torremolinos** Spain
108A2 **Torrens,L** Aust
24B2 **Torreón** Mexico
47B2 **Torre Pellice** Italy
107D2 **Torres Str** Aust
50A2 **Torres Vedras** Port
16C2 **Torrington**
Connecticut, USA
8C2 **Torrington**
Wyoming, USA
9C4 **Torrón** Mexico
38D3 **Tórshavn** Føroyar
47C2 **Tortona** Italy
51C1 **Tortosa** Spain
90C2 **Torüd** Iran
58B2 **Toruń** Poland
40B2 **Tory** *I* Irish Rep
60D2 **Torzhok** Russian Fed
75A2 **Tosa** Japan
74C4 **Tosa-shimizu** Japan
74C4 **Tosa-wan** *B* Japan
74C4 **Tosashimizu** Japan
Toshkent = Tashkent
60D2 **Tosno** Russian Fed
75A2 **Tosu** Japan
92B1 **Tosya** Turk
61F1 **Tot'ma** Russian Fed
43C4 **Totnes** Eng
33F2 **Totness** Surinam
23B2 **Totolapan** Mexico
51B2 **Totona** Spain
109C2 **Tottenham** Aust
74C3 **Tottori** Japan
97B4 **Touba** Ivory Coast
97A3 **Touba** Sen
96B1 **Toubkal** *Mt* Mor
97B3 **Tougan** Burkina
96C1 **Touggourt** Alg
97A3 **Tougué** Guinea
46C2 **Toul** France
49D3 **Toulon** France
49D3 **Toulouse** France
48C3 **Toumodi** Ivory Coast
76B2 **Toungoo** Burma
46B1 **Tourcoing** France
96A2 **Tourine** Maur
46B1 **Tournai** Belg
48C2 **Tours** France
74E2 **Towada** Japan
74E2 **Towada-ko** *L* Japan
15C2 **Towanda** USA
107D2 **Townsville** Aust
16A3 **Towson** USA
43C4 **Towy** *R* Wales
74D3 **Toyama** Japan
75B1 **Toyama-wan** *B*
Japan
75B2 **Toyohashi** Japan
75B2 **Toyonaka** Japan
75A1 **Toyooka** Japan
74D3 **Toyota** Japan
96C1 **Tozeur** Tunisia
93C1 **Trabzon** Turk
22B2 **Tracy** California, USA
34A3 **Traiguén** Chile
13D3 **Trail** Can
41B3 **Tralee** Irish Rep
45B2 **Tralee B** Irish Rep
45C2 **Tramore** Irish Rep
39G7 **Tranås** Sweden
77B4 **Trang** Thai
71E4 **Trangan** *I* Indon
109C2 **Trangie** Aust
12E2 **Transalaskan Pipeline**
USA
100B3 **Transvaal** Province,
S Africa
Transylvanian Alps =
Munţii Carpaţii
Meridionali
53B3 **Trapani** Italy

109C3 **Traralgon** Aust
97A3 **Trarza** Region, Maur
76C3 **Trat** Thai
108B2 **Traveller's** *L* Aust
56C2 **Travemünde**
Germany
14A2 **Traverse City** USA
12C1 **Traverse Peak** *Mt*
USA
111B2 **Travers,Mt** NZ
47C2 **Trebbia** *R* Italy
59B3 **Třebíč**
Czech Republic
54A2 **Trebinje** Bosnia-
Herzegovina
57C3 **Trebon**
Czech Republic
29F2 **Treinta y Tres** Urug
29C4 **Trelew** Arg
39G7 **Trelleborg** Sweden
43B3 **Tremadog B** Wales
15D1 **Tremblant,Mt** Can
13C2 **Trembleur L** Can
14A2 **Tremont** USA
59B3 **Trenčín** Slovakia
34C3 **Trenque Lauquén**
Arg
43D3 **Trent** *R* Eng
47D1 **Trentino** Region,
Italy
47D1 **Trento** Italy
15C2 **Trenton** Can
18B1 **Trenton** Missouri,
USA
16B2 **Trenton** New Jersey,
USA
7E5 **Trepassey** Can
34C3 **Tres Arroyos** Arg
35B2 **Tres Corações** Brazil
30F3 **Três Lagoas** Brazil
34C3 **Tres Lomas** Arg
35C2 **Três Rios** Brazil
47C2 **Treviglio** Italy
47E2 **Treviso** Italy
47C2 **Trezzo** Italy
87B2 **Trichūr** India
108C2 **Trida** Aust
46D2 **Trier** Germany
52B1 **Trieste** Italy
45C2 **Trim** Irish Rep
87C3 **Trincomalee**
Sri Lanka
33E6 **Trinidad** Bol
25D2 **Trinidad** Urug
9C3 **Trinidad** USA
34C3 **Trinidad** *I*
27E4 **Trinidad** *I*
Caribbean S
103G6 **Trindade** *I* Atlantic O
27E4 **Trinidad & Tobago**
Republic Caribbean S
19A3 **Trinity** USA
9D3 **Trinity** *R* USA
7E5 **Trinity B** Can
12D3 **Trinity Is** USA
17A1 **Trion** USA
94B1 **Tripoli** Leb
95A1 **Tripoli** Libya
55B3 **Trípolis** Greece
86C2 **Tripura** State, India
103H6 **Tristan da Cunha** *Is*
Atlantic O
87B3 **Trivandrum** India
59B3 **Trnava** Slovakia
107E1 **Trobriand Is** PNG
15D1 **Trois-Rivières** Can
65H4 **Troitsk** Russian Fed
39G7 **Trollhättan** Sweden
38F6 **Trollheimen** *Mt* Nor
89K9 **Tromelin** *I* Indian O
38H5 **Tromsø** Nor
38G6 **Trondheim** Nor
38G6 **Trondheimfjord** *Inlet*
Nor
42B2 **Troon** Scot
102J3 **Tropic of Cancer**
102J6 **Tropic of Capricorn**
96B2 **Troudenni** Mali
7A4 **Trout L** Ontario, Can
17A1 **Troy** Alabama, USA
16C1 **Troy** New York, USA
14B2 **Troy** Ohio, USA
54B2 **Troyan** Bulg

49C2 **Troyes** France
91B5 **Trucial Coast** Region, UAE
21A2 **Truckee** *R* USA
25D3 **Trujillo** Honduras
32B5 **Trujillo** Peru
50A2 **Trujillo** Spain
32C2 **Trujillo** Ven
109C2 **Trundle** Aust
7D5 **Truro** Can
43B4 **Truro** Eng
68B2 **Tsagaan Nuur** *L* Mongolia
68B1 **Tsagan-Tologoy** Russian Fed
101D2 **Tsaratanana** Madag
100B3 **Tsau** Botswana
99D3 **Tsavo** Kenya
99D3 **Tsavo Nat Pk** Kenya
65J4 **Tselinograd** Kazakhstan
100A3 **Tses** Namibia
68C2 **Tsetserleg** Mongolia
97C4 **Tsévié** Togo
100B3 **Tshabong** Botswana
100B3 **Tshane** Botswana
98B3 **Tshela** Zaire
98C3 **Tshibala** Zaire
98C3 **Tshikapa** Zaire
98C3 **Tshuapa** *R* Zaire
101D3 **Tsihombe** Madag
61F4 **Tsimlyanskoye Vodokhranilishche** *Res* Russian Fed
Tsinan = Jinan
Tsingtao = Qingdao
101D2 **Tsiroanomandidy** Madag
13B2 **Tsitsutl Peak** *Mt* Can
58D2 **Tsna** *R* Belorussia
72B1 **Tsogt Ovoo** Mongolia
68C2 **Tsomog** Mongolia
75B2 **Tsu** Japan
75B1 **Tsubata** Japan
74E3 **Tsuchiura** Japan
74E2 **Tsugaru-kaikyō** *Str* Japan
100A2 **Tsumeb** Namibia
100A3 **Tsumis** Namibia
75B1 **Tsunugi** Japan
74D3 **Tsuruga** Japan
74D3 **Tsuruoka** Japan
75B1 **Tsushima** Japan
74B4 **Tsushima** *I* Japan
74C3 **Tsuyama** Japan
50A1 **Tua** *R* Port
45B2 **Tuam** Irish Rep
60E5 **Tuapse** Russian Fed
111A3 **Tuatapere** NZ
30G4 **Tubarão** Brazil
94B2 **Tubas** Israel
79A4 **Tubbataha Reefs** *Is* Phil
57B3 **Tübingen** Germany
95B1 **Tubruq** Libya
16B3 **Tuckerton** USA
9B3 **Tucson** USA
30C4 **Tucumán** State, Arg
34B2 **Tucunuco** Arg
33E2 **Tucupita** Ven
51B1 **Tudela** Spain
93C3 **Tudmur** Syria
101H1 **Tugela** *R* S Africa
109D2 **Tuggerah** *L* Aust
12D3 **Tugidak** *I* USA
79B2 **Tuguegarao** Phil
72D2 **Tuhai He** *R* China
4E3 **Tuktoyaktuk** Can
58C1 **Tukums** Latvia
99D3 **Tukuyu** Tanz
84B1 **Tukzar** Afghan
60E3 **Tula** Russian Fed
23B1 **Tulancingo** Mexico
78A3 **Tulangbawang** *R* Indon
32B3 **Tulcán** Colombia
60C5 **Tulcea** Rom
100B3 **Tuli** USA
94B2 **Tulkarm** Israel
18B2 **Tulle** France
19B3 **Tullos** USA
45C2 **Tullow** Irish Rep

18A2 **Tulsa** USA
93C3 **Tulūl ash Shāmiyah** *Desert Region* Syria/ S Arabia
63C2 **Tulun** Russian Fed
78C4 **Tulungagung** Indon
32B3 **Tumaco** Colombia
109C3 **Tumbarumba** Aust
32A4 **Tumbes** Ecuador
108A2 **Tumby Bay** Aust
74B2 **Tumen** China
87B2 **Tumkūr** India
75C4 **Tumpat** Malay
85B1 **Tumsar** India
97B3 **Tumu** Ghana
109C3 **Tumut** Aust
109C3 **Tumut** *R* Aust
27L1 **Tunapuna** Trinidad
93C2 **Tunceli** Turk
99D3 **Tunduma** Zambia
101C2 **Tunduru** Tanz
54C2 **Tundzha** *R* Bulg
87B1 **Tungabhadra** *R* India
68D4 **Tung-Chiang** Taiwan
38B2 **Tungnafellsjökull** *Mts* Iceland
12J2 **Tungsten** Can
63B1 **Tunguska** *R* Russian Fed
87C1 **Tuni** India
96D1 **Tunis** Tunisia
88E4 **Tunisia** Republic, N Africa
32C2 **Tunja** Colombia
12B2 **Tuntutuliak** USA
12B2 **Tununak** USA
34B2 **Tunuyán** Arg
34B2 **Tunuyán** *R* Arg
22C2 **Tuolumne Meadows** USA
35A2 **Tupã** Brazil
35B1 **Tupaciguara** Brazil
19C3 **Tupelo** USA
30C3 **Tupiza** Bol
15D2 **Tupper Lake** USA
34B2 **Tupungato** Arg
29C2 **Tupungato** *Mt* Arg
86C1 **Tura** India
63C1 **Tura** Russian Fed
62A2 **Tura** *R* Russian Fed
90C2 **Turan** Iran
63B2 **Turan** Russian Fed
93C3 **Turayf** S Arabia
80E3 **Turbat** Pak
32B2 **Turbo** Colombia
54B1 **Turda** Rom
63A3 **Turfan Depression** China
65H4 **Turgay** Kazakhstan
63B3 **Turgen Uul** *Mt* Mongolia
54C2 **Turgovishte** Bulg
92A2 **Turgutlu** Turk
92C1 **Turhal** Turk
39K7 **Türi** Estonia
51B2 **Turia** *R* Spain
Turin = Torino
61K2 **Turinsk** Russian Fed
69F2 **Turiy Rog** Russian Fed
99D2 **Turkana,L** Kenya/Eth
80E1 **Turkestan** Region, C Asia
82A1 **Turkestan** Kazakhstan
92C2 **Turkey** Republic, W Asia
80D1 **Turkmenistan** Republic, Asia
90B2 **Turkmenskiy Zaliv** *B* Turkmenistan
27C2 **Turks Is** Caribbean S
39J6 **Turku** Fin
99D2 **Turkwel** *R* Kenya
22B2 **Turlock** USA
22B2 **Turlock L** USA
110C2 **Turnagain,C** NZ
25D3 **Turneffe** *I* Belize
16C1 **Turners Falls** USA
46C1 **Turnhout** Belg
13F1 **Turnor L** Can
54B2 **Turnu Măgurele** Rom
63A3 **Turpan** China
26B2 **Turquino** *Mt* Cuba
80E1 **Turtkul'** Uzbekistan

18A2 **Turtle Creek Res** USA
13F2 **Turtle L** Can
63A1 **Turukhansk** Russian Fed
68C1 **Turuntayevo** Russian Fed
35A1 **Turvo** *R* Goias, Brazil
35B2 **Turvo** *R* São Paulo, Brazil
58C2 **Tur'ya** *R* Ukraine
19C3 **Tuscaloosa** USA
18C2 **Tuscola** USA
90C3 **Tusharik** Iran
Tutera = Tudela
87B3 **Tuticorin** India
54C2 **Tutrakan** Bulg
57B3 **Tuttlingen** Germany
68C2 **Tuul Gol** *R* Mongolia
105G4 **Tuvalu** *Is* Pacific O
63B2 **Tuvinskaya Respublika,** Russian Fed
23A2 **Tuxpan** Jalisco, Mexico
24B2 **Tuxpan** Nayarit, Mexico
23B1 **Tuxpan** Veracruz, Mexico
23B2 **Tuxtepec** Mexico
25C3 **Tuxtla Gutiérrez** Mexico
50A1 **Túy** Spain
76D3 **Tuy Hoa** Viet
92B2 **Tuz Gölü** *Salt L* Turk
93D3 **Tuz Khurmātū** Iraq
54A2 **Tuzla** Bosnia- Herzegovina
60E2 **Tver'** Russian Fed
42C2 **Tweed** *R* Eng/Scot
109D1 **Tweed Heads** Aust
42C2 **Tweedsmuir Hills** Scot
7E5 **Twillingate** Can
21B2 **Twin Falls** USA
111B2 **Twins,The** *Mt* NZ
14A2 **Two Rivers** USA
63E2 **Tygda** Russian Fed
19A3 **Tyler** USA
65K3 **Tym** *R* Russian Fed
69G1 **Tymovskoye** Russian Fed
42D2 **Tyne** *R* Eng
42D2 **Tyne and Wear** Metropolitan County, Eng
42D2 **Tynemouth** Eng
38G6 **Tynset** Nor
12D3 **Tyonek** USA
94B2 **Tyr** Leb
45C1 **Tyrone** County, N Ire
108B3 **Tyrrell,L** Aust
53B2 **Tyrrhenian S** Italy
65H4 **Tyumen'** Russian Fed
43B3 **Tywyn** Wales
55B3 **Tzoumérka** *Mt* Greece

U

99E2 **Uarsciek** Somalia
35C2 **Ubá** Brazil
35C1 **Ubaí** Brazil
98B2 **Ubangi** *R* CAR
47B2 **Ubaye** *R* France
75A2 **Ube** Japan
50B2 **Ubeda** Spain
6E2 **Ubekendt Ejland** *I* Greenland
35B1 **Uberaba** Brazil
35B1 **Uberlândia** Brazil
76C2 **Ubon Ratchathani** Thai
58D2 **Ubort** *R* Belorussia
98C3 **Ubundi** Zaire
32C5 **Ucayali** *R* Peru
84C3 **Uch** Pak
63F2 **Uchar** *R* Russian Fed
74E2 **Uchiura-wan** *B* Japan
82B2 **Uda** *R* Russian Fed
85C4 **Udaipur** India
86B1 **Udaipur Garhi** Nepal

34D3 **Udaquoila** Arg
39G7 **Uddevalla** Sweden
38H5 **Uddjaur** *L* Sweden
87B1 **Udgir** India
84D2 **Udhampur** India
61H2 **Udmurtskaya Respublika,** Russian Fed
76C2 **Udon Thani** Thai
63F2 **Udskaya Guba** *B* Russian Fed
87A2 **Udupi** India
75B1 **Ueda** Japan
99C2 **Uele** *R* Zaire
56C2 **Uelzen** Germany
98C2 **Uere** *R* Zaire
61J3 **Ufa** Russian Fed
61J2 **Ufa** *R* Russian Fed
100A3 **Ugab** *R* Namibia
99D3 **Ugalla** *R* Tanz
12D3 **Ugak B** USA
99D2 **Uganda** Republic, Africa
12C3 **Ugashik B** USA
12C3 **Ugashik L** USA
47B2 **Ugine** France
69G2 **Uglegorsk** Russian Fed
60E2 **Uglich** Russian Fed
60E3 **Ugra** *R* Russian Fed
44A3 **Uig** Scot
98B3 **Uige** Angola
61H4 **Uil** Kazakhstan
8B2 **Uinta Mts** USA
100B4 **Uitenhage** S Africa
59C3 **Ujfehértó** Hung
75B2 **Uji** Japan
99C3 **Ujiji** Tanz
30C3 **Ujina** Chile
85D4 **Ujjain** India
70C4 **Ujung Pandang** Indon
99D3 **Ukerewe** *I* Tanz
86C1 **Ukhrul** India
21A2 **Ukiah** California, USA
20C1 **Ukiah** Oregon, USA
58C1 **Ukmerge** Lithuania
60C4 **Ukraine** Republic, Europe
68C2 **Ulaanbaatar** Mongolia
72C1 **Ulaan Uul** Mongolia
82C1 **Ulangar Hu** *L* China
68C1 **Ulan Ude** Russian Fed
72A3 **Ulan Ul Hu** *L* China
34B2 **Ulapes** Arg
74B3 **Ulchin** S Korea
54D2 **Ulcinj** Montenegro, Yugos
68D2 **Uldz** Mongolia
68B2 **Uliastay** Mongolia
58D1 **Ulla** Lithuania
109D3 **Ulladulla** Aust
44B3 **Ullapool** Scot
38H5 **Ullsfjorden** *Inlet* Nor
74C3 **Ullŭng-do** *I* S Korea
57C3 **Ulm** Germany
108A1 **Uloowaranie,L** Aust
74B3 **Ulsan** S Korea
45C1 **Ulster** Region, N Ire
65K5 **Ulungur He** *R* China
65K5 **Ulungur Hu** *L* China
44A3 **Ulva** *I* Scot
42C2 **Ulverston** Eng
109C4 **Ulverstone** Aust
63G2 **Ulya** *R* Russian Fed
60D4 **Uman** Ukraine
6E2 **Umanak** Greenland
86A2 **Umaria** India
85B3 **Umarkot** Pak
108A1 **Umaroona,L** Aust
20C1 **Umatilla** USA
38L5 **Umba** Russian Fed
99D3 **Umba** *R* Tanz
38H6 **Ume** *R* Sweden
38J6 **Umea** Sweden
101H1 **Umfolozi** *R* S Africa
4C3 **Umiat** USA
91C4 **Umm al Qaiwain** UAE

Umm as Samīm

91C5 **Umm as Samīm** *Salt Marsh* Oman
99C1 **Umm Bell** Sudan
98C1 **Umm Keddada** Sudan
99D1 **Umm Ruwaba** Sudan
91B5 **Umm Sa'id** Qatar
20B2 **Umpqua** *R* USA
85D4 **Umred** India
100B4 **Umtata** S Africa
35A2 **Umuarama** Brazil
52C1 **Una** *R* Bosnia-Herzegovina/Croatia
35B1 **Unai** Brazil
12B2 **Unalakleet** USA
80C3 **Unayzah** S Arabia
16C2 **Uncasville** USA
101G1 **Underberg** S Africa
60D3 **Uneeha** Russian Fed
94B3 **Uneisa** Jordan
7D4 **Ungava B** Can
30F4 **União de Vitória** Brazil
34B3 **Unión** Arg
18B2 **Union** Missouri, USA
17B1 **Union** S Carolina, USA
14C2 **Union City** Pennsylvania, USA
17A1 **Union Springs** USA
15C3 **Uniontown** USA
91B5 **United Arab Emirates** Arabian Pen
36C3 **United Kingdom** Kingdom, W Europe
2H4 **United States of America**
6B1 **United States Range** *Mts* Can
13F2 **Unity** Can
20C2 **Unity** USA
46D1 **Unna** Germany
86A1 **Unnao** India
44E1 **Unst** *I* Scot
13A1 **Unuk** *R* USA
92C1 **Unye** Turk
61F2 **Unzha** *R* Russian Fed
33E2 **Upata** Ven
98C3 **Upemba Nat Pk** Zaïre
6E2 **Upernavik** Greenland
22D3 **Upland** USA
100B3 **Uplington** S Africa
14B2 **Upper Arlington** USA
13D2 **Upper Arrow L** Can
111C2 **Upper Hutt** NZ
20B2 **Upper Klamath L** USA
20B2 **Upper L** USA
45C1 **Upper Lough Erne** *L* N Ire
27L1 **Upper Manzanilla** Trinidad
39H7 **Uppsala** Sweden
72B1 **Urad Qianqi** China
74A3 **Uraïrah** S Arabia
61H3 **Ural** *R* Kazakhstan
109D2 **Uralla** Aust
61H3 **Ural'sk** Kazakhstan
65G4 **Uralskiy Khrebet** *Mts* Russian Fed
5H4 **Uranium City** Can
75B1 **Urawa** Japan
18C1 **Urbana** Illinois, USA
14B2 **Urbana** Ohio, USA
52B2 **Urbino** Italy
42C2 **Ure** *R* Eng
61G2 **Uren'** Russian Fed
80E1 **Urgench** Uzbekistan
84B2 **Urgun** Afghan
55C3 **Urla** Turk
54B2 **Uroševac** Serbia, Yugos
31B4 **Uruaçu** Brazil
23A2 **Uruapan** Mexico
35B1 **Urucuia** *R* Brazil
30E4 **Uruguaiana** Brazil
29E2 **Uruguay** Republic, S America
29E2 **Uruguay** *R* Urug
82C1 **Ürümqi** China
69H2 **Urup** *I* Russian Fed
84B2 **Uruzgan** Afghan

61F3 **Uryupinsk** Russian Fed
61H2 **Urzhum** Russian Fed
54C2 **Urziceni** Rom
82C1 **Usa** China
75A2 **Usa** Japan
64G3 **Usa** *R* Russian Fed
92A2 **Uşak** Turk
100A3 **Usakos** Namibia
99D3 **Ushashi** Tanz
65J5 **Ush Tobe** Kazakhstan
29C6 **Ushuaia** Arg
63E2 **Ushumun** Russian Fed
43C4 **Usk** *R* Wales
92A1 **Usküdar** Turk
63C2 **Usolye Sibirskoye** Russian Fed
34B2 **Uspallata** Arg
69F2 **Ussuriysk** Russian Fed
47C1 **Uster** Switz
53B3 **Ustica** *I* Italy
57C2 **Ustí nad Labem** Czech Republic
65J4 **Ust'Ishim** Kazakhstan
58B2 **Ustka** Pol
65K5 **Ust'-Kamenogorsk** Kazakhstan
63B2 **Ust Karabula** Russian Fed
61J2 **Ust'Katav** Russian Fed
63C2 **Ust'-Kut** Russian Fed
61E4 **Ust Labinsk** Russian Fed
63F1 **Ust'Maya** Russian Fed
1C8 **Ust'Nera** Russian Fed
63E2 **Ust'Nyukzha** Russian Fed
63C2 **Ust'Ordynskiy** Russian Fed
64G3 **Ust'Tsil'ma** Russian Fed
63F2 **Ust'Umal'ta** Russian Fed
75A2 **Usuki** Japan
25C3 **Usumacinta** *R* Guatemala/Mexico
101H1 **Usutu** *R* Swaziland
8B3 **Utah** State, USA
8B2 **Utah L** USA
58D1 **Utena** Russian Fed
85B3 **Uthal** Pak
10C2 **Utica** USA
51B2 **Utiel** Spain
13D1 **Utikuma L** Can
56B2 **Utrecht** Neth
101H1 **Utrecht** S Africa
50A2 **Utrera** Spain
38K5 **Utsjoki** Fin
74D3 **Utsunomiya** Japan
76C2 **Uttaradit** Thai
86A1 **Uttar Pradesh** State, India
65H4 **Uval** Russian Fed
107E3 **Uvéa** *I* Nouvelle Calédonie
99D3 **Uvinza** Tanz
99C3 **Uvira** Zaïre
6E2 **Uvkusigssat**
39J6 **Uvsikaupunki** Fin
68B1 **Uvs Nuur** *L* China
74C4 **Uwajima** Japan
72B2 **Uxin Qi** China
63B2 **Uyar** Russian Fed
30C3 **Uyuni** Bol
80E1 **Uzbekistan** Republic, Asia
48C2 **Uzerche** France
59C3 **Uzhgorod** Ukraine
54A2 **Užice** Serbia, Yugos
60E3 **Uzlovaya** Russian Fed
92A1 **Uzunköprü** Turk

V
101F1 **Vaal** *R* S Africa
101G1 **Vaal Dam** *Res* S Africa

100B3 **Vaalwater** S Africa
38J6 **Vaasa** Fin
59B3 **Vác** Hung
30F4 **Vacaria** Brazil
35C1 **Vacaria** *R* Minas Gerais, Brazil
21A2 **Vacaville** USA
85C4 **Vadodara** India
38K4 **Vadsø** Nor
47C1 **Vaduz** Leichtenstein
38D3 **Vágar** Føroyar
29E3 **Va Gesell** Arg
59B3 **Váh** *R* Slovakia
87B2 **Vaigai** *R* India
65K3 **Vakh** *R* Russian Fed
60B4 **Vâlcea** Rom
29C4 **Valcheta** Arg
47D2 **Valdagno** Italy
60D2 **Valday** Russian Fed
60D2 **Valdayskaya Vozvyshennost'** *Upland* Russian Fed
32D2 **Val de la Pascua** Ven
36D2 **Valdepeñas** Spain
12E2 **Valdez** USA
29B3 **Valdivia** Chile
46B2 **Val d'Oise** *Department* France
17B1 **Valdosta** USA
20C2 **Vale** USA
13D2 **Valemount** Can
31D4 **Valença** Bahia, Brazil
35C2 **Valença** Rio de Janeiro, Brazil
49C3 **Valence** France
51B2 **Valencia** Region, Spain
51B2 **Valencia** Spain
32D1 **Valencia** Ven
45A3 **Valencia** *I* Irish Rep
50A2 **Valencia de Alcantara** Spain
46B1 **Valenciennes** France
47C2 **Valenza** Italy
32C2 **Valera** Ven
39K7 **Valga** Estonia
54A2 **Valjevo** Serbia, Yugos
Valka = Valga
39J6 **Valkeakoski** Fin
25D2 **Valladolid** Mexico
50B1 **Valladolid** Spain
47B2 **Valle d'Aosta** Region, Italy
27D5 **Valle de la Pascua** Ven
23A1 **Valle de Santiago** Mexico
47B2 **Valle d'Isére** France
32C1 **Valledupar** Colombia
97C3 **Vallée de l'Azaouak** *V* Niger
97C3 **Vallée Tilemsi** *V* Mali
30D2 **Valle Grande** Bol
22A1 **Vallejo** USA
30B4 **Vallenar** Chile
53B3 **Valletta** Malta
8D2 **Valley City** USA
28D2 **Valley Falls** USA
15D1 **Valleyfield** Can
13D1 **Valleyview** Can
47E2 **Valli di Comacchio** *Lg* Italy
51C1 **Valls** Spain
58D1 **Valmiera** Latvia
35A2 **Valparaíso** Brazil
34A2 **Valparaíso** Chile
23A1 **Valparaiso** Mexico
17A1 **Valparaiso** USA
101G1 **Vals** *R* S Africa
85C4 **Valsad** India
60E3 **Valuyki** Russian Fed
50A2 **Valverde del Camino** Spain
38J6 **Vammala** Fin
93D2 **Van** Turk
63C1 **Vanavara** Russian Fed
18B2 **Van Buren** Arkansas, USA
13C3 **Vancouver** Can
20B1 **Vancouver** USA
5F5 **Vancouver I** Can
12G2 **Vancouver,Mt** Can

18C2 **Vandalia** Illinois, USA
14B3 **Vandalia** Ohio, USA
13C2 **Vanderhoof** Can
106C2 **Van Diemen G** *Gulf* Aust
39G7 **Vänern** *L* Sweden
39G7 **Vänersborg** Sweden
101D3 **Vangaindrano** Madag
93D2 **Van Gölü** *Salt L* Turk
76C2 **Vang Vieng** Laos
9C3 **Van Horn** USA
15C1 **Vanier** Can
1C6 **Vankarem** Russian Fed
38H6 **Vännäs** Sweden
48B2 **Vannes** France
47B2 **Vanoise** *Mts* France
100A4 **Vanrhynsdorp** S Africa
6B3 **Vansittart I** Can
105G4 **Vanuatu** *Is* Pacific O
14B2 **Van Wert** USA
47C2 **Varallo** Italy
90B2 **Varämin** Iran
86A1 **Väränasi** India
38K4 **Varangerfjord** *Inlet* Nor
38A5 **Varangerhalvøya** *Pen* Nor
52C1 **Varazdin** Croatia
39G7 **Varberg** Sweden
39F7 **Varde** Den
38L4 **Vardø** Nor
58C2 **Varéna** Lithuania
47C2 **Varenna** Italy
47C2 **Varese** Italy
35B2 **Varginha** Brazil
38K6 **Varkaus** Fin
54C2 **Varna** Bulg
39G7 **Värnamo** Sweden
17B1 **Varnville** USA
35C1 **Várzea da Palma** Brazil
47C2 **Varzi** Italy
50B1 **Vascongadas** Region, Spain
60D3 **Vasil'kov** Ukraine
14B2 **Vassar** USA
39H7 **Västerås** Sweden
39H7 **Västervik** Sweden
52B2 **Vasto** Italy
65J4 **Vasyugan** *R* Russian Fed
38B2 **Vatnajökull** *Mts* Iceland
38A1 **Vatneyri** Iceland
54C1 **Vatra Dornei** Rom
39G7 **Vättern** *L* Sweden
9C3 **Vaughn** USA
32C3 **Vaupés** *R* Colombia
13E2 **Vauxhall** Can
87C3 **Vavuniya** Sri Lanka
39G7 **Växjö** Sweden
64G2 **Vaygach, Ostrov** *I* Russian Fed
34C2 **Vedia** Arg
38G5 **Vega** *I* Nor
13E2 **Vegreville** Can
39F7 **Vejle** Den
52C2 **Velebit** *Mts* Croatia
52C1 **Velenje** Slovenia
35C1 **Velhas** *R* Brazil
39K7 **Velikaya** *R* Russian Fed
60D2 **Velikiye Luki** Russian Fed
61G1 **Velikiy Ustyug** Russian Fed
54C2 **Veliko Türnovo** Bulg
97A3 **Vélingara** Sen
87B2 **Vellore** India
61F1 **Vel'sk** Russian Fed
87B3 **Vembanad L** India
34C2 **Venado Tuerto** Arg
35B2 **Vençeslau Braz** Brazil
49C2 **Vendôme** France
12E1 **Venetie** USA
47D2 **Veneto** Region, Italy
47E2 **Venezia** Italy

32D2 Venezuela Republic, S America
87A1 Vengurla India
12C3 Veniaminof V USA
87B2 Venkatagiri India
56B2 Venlo Neth
58C1 Venta R Latvia
101G1 Ventersburg S Africa
58C1 Ventspils Latvia
32D3 Ventuari R Ven
22C3 Ventura USA
60D1 Vepsovskaya Vozvyshennost' Upland Russian Fed
30D4 Vera Arg
51B2 Vera Spain
23B2 Veracruz Mexico
23B1 Veracruz State, Mexico
85C4 Veräval India
47C2 Verbania Italy
47C2 Vercelli Italy
35A1 Verde R Goias, Brazil
23A1 Verde R Jalisco, Mexico
35A1 Verde R Mato Grosso do Sul, Brazil
23B2 Verde R Oaxaca, Mexico
Verde,C = Cap Vert
35C1 Verde Grande R Brazil
34C3 Verde,Pen Arg
49D3 Verdon R France
46C2 Verdun France
101G1 Vereeniging S Africa
61H2 Vereshchagino Russian Fed
97A3 Verga,C Guinea
34D3 Vergara Arg
50A1 Verín Spain
63D2 Verkh Angara R Russian Fed
61J3 Verkhneural'sk Russian Fed
63E1 Verkhnevilyuysk Russian Fed
1C8 Verkhoyansk Russian Fed
35A1 Vermelho R Brazil
13E2 Vermilion Can
10C2 Vermont State, USA
22B2 Vernalis USA
13D2 Vernon Can
46A2 Vernon France
9D3 Vernon USA
17B2 Vero Beach USA
54B2 Veroia Greece
47D2 Verolanuova Italy
47D2 Verona Italy
46A2 Versailles France
101H1 Verulam S Africa
46C1 Verviers Belg
46B2 Vervins France
46C2 Vesle R France
49D2 Vesoul France
38G5 Vesterälen Is Nor
38G5 Vestfjorden Inlet Nor
38A2 Vestmannaeyjar Iceland
53B2 Vesuvio Mt Italy
59B3 Veszprém Hung
39H7 Vetlanda Sweden
61F2 Vetluga R Russian Fed
46B1 Veurne Belg
47B1 Vevey Switz
46A1 Vexin Region, France
47A2 Veynes France
50A1 Viana do Castelo Port
Vientiane = Viangchan
49E3 Viareggio Italy
39F7 Viborg Den
53C3 Vibo Valentia Italy
Vic = Vich
112C2 Viceconodoro Marambio Base Ant
52B1 Vicenza Italy
51C1 Vich Spain
32D3 Vichada R Colombia
61F2 Vichuga Russian Fed

49C2 Vichy France
19B3 Vicksburg USA
35C2 Vicosa Brazil
106C4 Victor Harbour Aust
34C2 Victoria Arg
13C3 Victoria Can
34A3 Victoria Chile
78D1 Victoria Malay
108B3 Victoria State, Aust
9D4 Victoria USA
106C2 Victoria R Aust
26B2 Victoria de las Tunas Cuba
100B2 Victoria Falls Zambia/Zim
4G2 Victoria,L Can
108B2 Victoria,L Aust
99D3 Victoria,L C Africa
112B7 Victoria Land Region, Ant
86C2 Victoria,Mt Burma
99D2 Victoria Nile R Uganda
111B2 Victoria Range Mts NZ
106C2 Victoria River Downs Aust
4H3 Victoria Str Can
15D1 Victoriaville Can
100B4 Victoria West S Africa
34B3 Victorica Arg
21B3 Victorville USA
34A2 Vicuña Chile
34C2 Vicuña Mackenna Arg
17B1 Vidalia USA
54C2 Vídele Rom
54B2 Vidin Bulg
85D4 Vidisha India
58D1 Vidzy Belorussia
29D4 Viedma Arg
26A4 Viejo Costa Rica
Vielha = Viella
51C1 Viella Spain
Vienna = Wien
18C2 Vienna Illinois, USA
14B3 Vienna W Virginia, USA
49C2 Vienne France
48C2 Vienne R France
76C2 Vientiane Laos
47C1 Vierwaldstätter See L Switz
48C2 Vierzon France
53C2 Vieste Italy
70B2 Vietnam Republic, S E Asia
76D1 Vietri Viet
27P2 Vieux Fort St Lucia
79B2 Vigan Phil
47C2 Vigevano Italy
48B3 Vignemale Mt France
50A1 Vigo Spain
87C1 Vijayawāda India
55A2 Vijosë R Alb
38B2 Vik Iceland
54B2 Vikhren Mt Bulg
13E2 Viking Can
38G6 Vikna I Nor
101C2 Vila da Maganja Mozam
101C1 Vila Machado Mozam
101C3 Vilanculos Mozam
Vilanova i la Geltrú = Villanueva-y-Geltrú
50A1 Vila Real Port
101C2 Vila Vasco da Gama Mozam
35C2 Vila Velha Brazil
58D2 Vileyka Belorussia
38H6 Vilhelmina Sweden
33E6 Vilhena Brazil
60C2 Viljandi Estonia
101G1 Viljoenskroon S Africa
9C3 Villa Ahumada Mexico
34B2 Villa Atuel Arg
50A1 Villaba Spain
23A2 Villa Carranza Mexico

52B1 Villach Austria
34B2 Villa Colon Arg
34C2 Villa Constitución Arg
34C1 Villa de María Arg
23A1 Villa de Reyes Mexico
34B2 Villa Dolores Arg
47D2 Villafranca di Verona Italy
34C2 Villa General Mitre Arg
34B2 Villa General Roca Arg
34D2 Villaguay Arg
25C3 Villahermosa Mexico
23A1 Villa Hidalgo Mexico
34C2 Villa Huidobro Arg
34C3 Villa Iris Arg
34C2 Villa María Arg
30D3 Villa Montes Bol
23A1 Vilianeuva Mexico
50A1 Villa Nova de Gaia Port
50A2 Villanueva de la Serena Spain
51C1 Villanueva-y-Geltrú Spain
34B3 Villa Regina Arg
51B2 Villarreal Spain
29B3 Villarrica Chile
30E4 Villarrica Par
50B2 Villarrobledo Spain
34D2 Villa San José Arg
34C2 Villa Valeria Arg
32C3 Villavicencio Colombia
49C2 Villefranche France
7C5 Ville-Marie Can
51B2 Villena Spain
46B2 Villeneuve-St-Georges France
48C3 Villeneuve-sur-Lot France
19B3 Ville Platte USA
46B2 Villers-Cotterêts France
49C2 Villeurbanne France
101G1 Villiers S Africa
87B2 Villupuram India
58D2 Vilnius Lithuania
63D1 Vilyuy R Russian Fed
63E1 Vilyuysk Russian Fed
34A2 Viña del Mar Chile
51C1 Vinaroz Spain
14A3 Vincennes USA
38H5 Vindel R Sweden
85D4 Vindhya Range Mts India
16B3 Vineland USA
16D2 Vineyard Haven USA
76D2 Vinh Viet
76D3 Vinh Cam Ranh B Viet
77D4 Vinh Loi Viet
77D3 Vinh Long Viet
38J2 Vinita USA
54A1 Vinkovci Croatia
60C4 Vinnitsa Ukraine
112B3 Vinson Massif Upland Ant
100A3 Vioolsdrift S Africa
47D1 Vipiteno Italy
79B3 Virac Phil
87B2 Virddhächalam India
100A2 Virei Angola
35C1 Virgem da Lapa Brazil
101G1 Virginia S Africa
10C3 Virginia State, USA
10A2 Virginia USA
21B2 Virginia City USA
27E3 Virgin Is Caribbean S
52C1 Virovitica Croatia
46C2 Virton Belg
87B2 Virudunagar India
52C2 Vis I Croatia
21B2 Visalia USA
79B3 Visayan S Phil
39H7 Visby Sweden
4H2 Viscount Melville Sd Can

54A2 Višegrad Bosnia-Herzegovina
50A1 Viseu Port
83C4 Vishākhapatnam India
47B1 Visp Switz
49C1 Vissingen Neth
21B3 Vista USA
Vistula = Wisla
57C3 Vitavia R Czech Republic
87A1 Vite India
60D2 Vitebsk Belorussia
52B2 Viterbo Italy
50A1 Vitigudino Spain
63D2 Vitim R Russian Fed
50B1 Vitora Spain
31C6 Vitória Brazil
31C4 Vitória da Conquista Brazil
48B2 Vitré France
46C2 Vitry-le-Francois France
41J2 Vittangi Sweden
53B3 Vittoria Italy
47E2 Vittorio Veneto Italy
69H2 Vityaz Depth Pacific O
50A1 Vivero Spain
63B1 Vivi R Russian Fed
34D3 Vivorata Arg
63C2 Vizhne-Angarsk Russian Fed
83C4 Vizianagaram India
54B1 Vlădeasa Mt Rom
61F5 Vladikavkaz Russian Fed
65F4 Vladimir Russian Fed
59C2 Vladimir Volynskiy Ukraine
74C2 Vladivostok Russian Fed
56A2 Vlieland I Neth
46B1 Vlissingen Neth
55A2 Vlorë Alb
57C3 Vöcklabruck Austria
76D3 Voeune Sai Camb
47C2 Voghera Italy
101D2 Vohibinany Madag
101E2 Vohimarina Madag
99D3 Voi Kenya
97B4 Voinjama Lib
49D2 Voiron France
54A1 Vojvodina Aut Republic Serbia, Yugos
26A5 Volcán Baru Mt Panama
23B2 Volcán Citlaltepetl Mt Mexico
30C3 Volcán Lullaillaco Mt Chile
34A3 Volcáno Copahue Mt Chile
34A3 Volcáno Domuyo Mt Arg
Volcano Is = Kazan Retto
29B3 Volcáno Lanín Mt Arg
30C3 Volcán Ollagüe Mt Chile
34A3 Volcáno Llaima Mt Chile
34B2 Volcáno Maipo Mt Arg
34A3 Volcáno Peteroa Mt Chile
34B3 Volcáno Tromen V Arg
23A2 Volcán Paracutin Mt Mexico
32B3 Volcán Puracé Mt Colombia
34A2 Volcán Tinguiririca Mt Arg/Chile
61J2 Volchansk Russian Fed
61G4 Volga R Russian Fed
61F4 Volgodonsk Russian Fed

Volgograd

61F4 **Volgograd**
   Russian Fed
61G3 **Volgogradskoye**
   Vodokhranilishche
   Res Russian Fed
60D2 **Volkhov** Russian Fed
60D2 **Volkhov** *R*
   Russian Fed
58C2 **Volkovysk** Belorussia
101G1 **Volksrust** S Africa
61F2 **Vologda** Russian Fed
48B2 **Volognes** France
55B3 **Vólos** Greece
61G3 **Vol'sk** Russian Fed
22B2 **Volta** USA
97B3 **Volta Blanche** *R*
   Burkina
97B4 **Volta,L** Ghana
97B3 **Volta Noire** *R*
   Burkina
35C2 **Volta Redonda** Brazil
97B3 **Volta Rouge** *R*
   Burkina
61F4 **Volzhskiy**
   Russian Fed
12D2 **Von Frank Mt** USA
6J3 **Vopnafjörður** Iceland
47C1 **Voralberg** Province,
   Austria
47C1 **Vorder Rhein** *R*
   Switz
56C1 **Vordingborg** Den
04I3 **Vorkutá** Russian Fed
39G6 **Vorma** *R* Nor
60E3 **Voronezh**
   Russian Fed
38M5 **Voron'ya** *R*
   Russian Fed
39K7 **Võru** Estonia
49D2 **Vosges** *Mt* France
39F6 **Voss** Nor
63B2 **Vostochnyy Sayan**
   Mts Russian Fed
112B9 **Vostok** *Base* Ant
61H2 **Votkinsk**
   Russian Fed
46C2 **Vouziers** France
60D4 **Voznesensk** Ukraine
54B2 **Vranje** Serbia, Yugos
54B2 **Vratsa** Bulg
54A1 **Vrbas** Serbia, Yugos
52C2 **Vrbas** *R* Serbia,
   Yugos
52B1 **Vrbovsko** Bosnia-
   Herzegovina
101G1 **Vrede** S Africa
33F2 **Vreed en Hoop**
   Guyana
54B1 **Vršac** Serbia, Yugos
52C2 **Vrtoče** Bosnia-
   Herzegovina
100B3 **Vryburg** S Africa
101H1 **Vryheid** S Africa
54A1 **Vukovar** Croatia
13F2 **Vulcan** Can
53B3 **Vulcano** *I* Italy
77D3 **Vung Tau** Viet
38J5 **Vuollerim** Sweden
38L6 **Vyartsilya**
   Russian Fed
61H2 **Vyatka** *R*
   Russian Fed
69F2 **Vyazemskiy**
   Russian Fed
60D2 **Vyaz'ma** Russian Fed
61F2 **Vyazniki** Russian Fed
60C1 **Vyborg** Russian Fed
64G3 **Vym'** *R* Russian Fed
43C3 **Vyrnwy** *R* Wales
60D2 **Vyshiy Volochek**
   Russian Fed
59B3 **Vyškov**
   Czech Republic
60E1 **Vytegra** Russian Fed

W

97B3 **Wa** Ghana
13E1 **Wabasca** Can
5G4 **Wabasca** *R* Can
13E1 **Wabasca L** Can
14A2 **Wabash** USA
14A3 **Wabash** *R* USA
5J4 **Wabowden** Can
7D4 **Wabush** Can

17B2 **Waccasassa B** USA
16D1 **Wachusett Res** USA
19A3 **Waco** USA
85B3 **Wad** Pak
95A2 **Waddán** Libya
5F4 **Waddington,Mt** Can
93E4 **Wadi al Bāţin**
   Watercourse Iraq
93D3 **Wadi al Ghudāf**
   Watercourse Iraq
94C2 **Wadi al Harir** *V* Syria
93D3 **Wadi al Mirah**
   Watercourse Iraq/
   S Arabia
93D3 **Wadi al Ubayyid**
   Watercourse Iraq
93D3 **Wadi Ar'ar**
   Watercourse
   S Arabia
91A5 **Wadi as Hsabá'**
   Watercourse
   S Arabia
92C3 **Wadi as Sirhân** *V*
   Jordan/S Arabia
94C2 **Wadi az Zaydi** *V*
   Syria
94C3 **Wadi edh Dhab'i** *V*
   Jordan
94A3 **Wadi el 'Arish** *V*
   Egypt
94C3 **Wadi el Ghadaf** *V*
   Jordan
94B3 **Wadi el Hasa** *V*
   Jordan
94C3 **Wadi el Janab** *V*
   Jordan
94B3 **Wadi el Jeib** *V* Israel/
   Jordan
95B3 **Wadi el Milk**
   Watercourse Sudan
92A3 **Wadi el Natrun**
   Watercourse Egypt
94B3 **Wadi es Sir** Jordan
94B3 **Wadi Fidan** *V* Jordan
94B3 **Wadi Hareidin** *V*
   Egypt
93D3 **Wadi Hawrān** *R* Iraq
95B3 **Wadi Howa**
   Watercourse Sudan
98C1 **Wadi Ibra**
   Watercourse Sudan
94C2 **Wadi Luhfi**
   Watercourse Jordan
94B3 **Wadi Mujib** *V*
   Jordan
94B3 **Wadi Qitaiya** *V*
   Egypt
80B3 **Wadi Sha'it**
   Watercourse Egypt
99D1 **Wad Medani** Sudan
93E4 **Wafra** Kuwait
6B3 **Wager B** Can
6A3 **Wager Bay** Can
54A1 **Wagga Wagga** Aust
108A4 **Wagin** Aust
95A2 **Wāha** Libya
21C4 **Wahiawa** Hawaiian Is
18A1 **Wahoo** USA
8D2 **Wahpeton** USA
87A1 **Wai** India
111B2 **Waiau** NZ
111A0 **Waiau** *R* NZ
111B2 **Waiau** *R* NZ
71E3 **Waigeo** *I* Indon
110C1 **Waihi** NZ
110C1 **Waikaremoana,L** NZ
110C1 **Waikato** *R* NZ
108A2 **Waikerie** Aust
111B3 **Waikouaiti** NZ
21C4 **Wailuku** Hawaiian Is
111B2 **Waimakariri** *R* NZ
111B2 **Waimate** NZ
21C4 **Waimea** Hawaiian Is
106B1 **Waingapu** Indon
13E2 **Wainwright** Can
4B2 **Wainwright** USA
111B2 **Waipara** NZ
110C2 **Waipukurau** NZ
111C2 **Wairarapa,L** NZ
111B2 **Wairau** *R* NZ
110C1 **Wairoa** NZ
110C1 **Wairoa** *R* NZ
111B2 **Waitaki** *R* NZ
110B1 **Waitara** NZ

110C1 **Waitomo** NZ
110B1 **Waiuku** NZ
75B1 **Wajima** Japan
99E2 **Wajir** Kenya
75B1 **Wakasa-wan** *B*
   Japan
111A3 **Wakatipu,L** NZ
74D4 **Wakayama** Japan
42D3 **Wakefield** Eng
27H1 **Wakefield** Jamaica
16D2 **Wakefield** Rhode
   Island, USA
76B2 **Wakema** Burma
69G2 **Wakkanai** Japan
108B3 **Wakool** *R* Aust
59B2 **Wałbrzych** Pol
109D2 **Walcha** Aust
58B2 **Walcz** Pol
46D1 **Waldbröl** Germany
16B2 **Walden** USA
43C3 **Wales** Country, UK
12A1 **Wales** USA
6B3 **Wales I** Can
109C2 **Walgett** Aust
112B4 **Walgreen Coast**
   Region, Ant
99C3 **Walikale** Zaire
21B2 **Walker L** USA
14B2 **Walkerton** Can
8B2 **Wallace** USA
108A2 **Wallaroo** Aust
109C3 **Walla Walla** Aust
20C1 **Walla Walla** USA
16C2 **Wallingford** USA
105H4 **Wallis and Futuna** *Is*
   Pacific O
20C1 **Wallowa** USA
20C1 **Wallowa Mts** *Mts*
   USA
109C1 **Wallumbilla** Aust
18A2 **Walnut Ridge** USA
110C1 **Walouru** NZ
43D3 **Walsall** Eng
9C3 **Walsenburg** USA
9C3 **Walsenburgh** USA
17A1 **Walterboro** USA
17A1 **Walter F George Res**
   USA
16D1 **Waltham** USA
100A3 **Walvis Bay** Namibia
103J6 **Walvis Ridge**
   Atlantic O
97C4 **Wamba** Nig
98B3 **Wamba** *R* Zaire
18A2 **Wamego** USA
84B2 **Wana** Pak
108B1 **Wanaaring** Aust
111A2 **Wanaka** NZ
111A2 **Wanaka,L** NZ
14B1 **Wanapitei L** Can
109C1 **Wandoan** Aust
108B3 **Wanganella** Aust
110C1 **Wanganui** NZ
110C1 **Wanganui** *R* NZ
109C3 **Wangaratta** Aust
99E2 **Wanle Weyne**
   Somalia
76E2 **Wanning** China
87B1 **Wanparti** India
73B3 **Wanxian** China
73B3 **Wanyuan** China
13D2 **Wapiti** *R* Can
18B2 **Wappapello,L** USA
16C1 **Wappingers Falls**
   USA
87B1 **Warangal** India
109C4 **Waratah** Aust
108C3 **Waratah B** Aust
108A1 **Warburton** *R* Aust
109C1 **Ward** *R* Aust
101G1 **Warden** S Africa
99E2 **Warder** Eth
85D4 **Wardha** India
111A3 **Ward,Mt** NZ
5F4 **Ware** Can
16C1 **Ware** USA
16D2 **Wareham** USA
109C1 **Warialda** Aust
76C2 **Warin Chamrap**
   Thai
100B3 **Warmbad** S Africa
16B2 **Warminster** USA
21B2 **Warm Springs** USA

56C2 **Warnemünde**
   Germany
20B2 **Warner Mts** USA
17B1 **Warner Robins** USA
108B3 **Warracknabeal** Aust
108A1 **Warrandirinna,L** Aust
107D3 **Warrego** *R* Aust
19B3 **Warren** Arkansas,
   USA
109C2 **Warren** Aust
16D2 **Warren**
   Massachusetts, USA
14B2 **Warren** Ohio, USA
15C2 **Warren**
   Pennsylvania, USA
45C1 **Warrenpoint** N Ire
18B2 **Warrensburg** USA
101F1 **Warrenton** S Africa
15C3 **Warrenton** USA
97C4 **Warri** Nig
108A1 **Warrina** Aust
42C3 **Warrington** Eng
108B3 **Warrnambool** Aust
58C2 **Warszawa = Warsaw**
58C2 **Warszawa** Pol
59B2 **Warta** *R* Pol
109D1 **Warwick** Aust
43D3 **Warwick** County,
   Eng
43D3 **Warwick** Eng
16B2 **Warwick** New York,
   USA
16D2 **Warwick** Rhode
   Island, USA
8B3 **Wasatch Range** *Mts*
   USA
101H1 **Wasbank** S Africa
21B2 **Wasco** USA
4H2 **Washburn L** Can
85D4 **Wāshim** India
10C3 **Washington** District
   of Columbia, USA
17B1 **Washington** Georgia,
   USA
14A3 **Washington** Indiana,
   USA
18B2 **Washington**
   Missouri, USA
16B2 **Washington** New
   Jersey, USA
14B2 **Washington**
   Pennsylvania, USA
8A2 **Washington** State,
   USA
14B3 **Washington Court**
   House USA
6D1 **Washington Land**
   Can
15D2 **Washington,Mt** USA
43E3 **Wash,The** Eng
85A3 **Washuk** Pak
12E2 **Wasilla** USA
7C4 **Waskaganish** Can
26A4 **Waspán** Nic
70D4 **Watampone** Indon
16C2 **Waterbury** USA
45C2 **Waterford** County,
   Irish Rep
41B3 **Waterford** Irish Rep
45C2 **Waterford Harbour**
   Irish Rep
46C1 **Waterloo** Belg
10A2 **Waterloo** Can
15C2 **Watertown** New
   York, USA
101H1 **Waterval-Boven**
   S Africa
10D2 **Waterville** Maine,
   USA
16C1 **Watervliet** USA
5G4 **Waterways** Can
43D4 **Watford** Eng
15C2 **Watkins Glen** USA
8C1 **Watrous** Can
99C2 **Watsa** Zaire
12J2 **Watson Lake** Can
22B2 **Watsonville** USA
71F4 **Wau** PNG
99C2 **Wau** Sudan
7B5 **Wawa** Can
109D2 **Wauchope** Aust
17B2 **Wauchula** USA
14A2 **Waukegan** USA
10B2 **Wausau** USA

14A2 **Wauwatosa** USA
106C2 **Wave Hill** Aust
43E3 **Waveney** R Eng
14B3 **Waverly** Ohio, USA
46C1 **Wavre** Belg
10B2 **Wawa** Can
95A2 **Wāw Al Kabīr** Libya
95A2 **Wāw an Nāmūs** Well Libya
22C2 **Wawona** USA
19A3 **Waxahachie** USA
106C2 **Waycross** USA
17B1 **Waynesboro** Georgia, USA
19C3 **Waynesboro** Mississippi, USA
16A3 **Waynesboro** Pennsylvania, USA
15C3 **Waynesboro** Virginia, USA
18B2 **Waynesville** Missouri, USA
84B2 **Wazi Khwa** Afghan
43E4 **Weald,The** Upland Eng
42C2 **Wear** R Eng
19A3 **Weatherford** Texas, USA
20B2 **Weaverville** USA
14B1 **Webbwood** Can
16D1 **Webster** USA
18B2 **Webster Groves** USA
29D6 **Weddell I** Falkland Is
112C2 **Weddell S** Ant
13C2 **Wedge Mt** Can
20B2 **Weed** USA
101H1 **Weenen** S Africa
109C2 **Wee Waa** Aust
72D1 **Weichang** China
57C3 **Weiden** Germany
72D2 **Weifang** China
72E2 **Weihai** China
72C3 **Wei He** R Henan, China
72C2 **Wei He** R Shaanxi, China
109C1 **Weilmoringle** Aust
73A4 **Weining** China
107D2 **Weipa** Aust
14B2 **Weirton** USA
20C2 **Weiser** USA
72D3 **Weishan Hu** L China
57C2 **Weissenfels** Germany
17A1 **Weiss L** USA
99D1 **Weldiya** Eth
101G1 **Welkom** S Africa
15C2 **Welland** Can
43D3 **Welland** R Eng
106C2 **Wellesley Is** Aust
12G2 **Wellesley L** Can
43D3 **Wellingborough** Eng
109C2 **Wellington** Kansas, USA
18A2 **Wellington** Kansas, USA
111B2 **Wellington** NZ
6A2 **Wellington Chan** Can
13C2 **Wells** Can
43C4 **Wells** Eng
110B1 **Wellsford** NZ
106B3 **Wells,L** Aust
57C3 **Wels** Austria
43C3 **Welshpool** Wales
13D1 **Wembley** Can
7C4 **Wemindji** Can
20B1 **Wenatchee** USA
20C1 **Wenatchee** R USA
97B4 **Wenchi** Ghana
72E2 **Wenden** China
73E4 **Wenling** China
32J7 **Wenman** I Ecuador
73A5 **Wenshan** China
107D4 **Wenthaggi** Aust
108B2 **Wentworth** Aust
72A3 **Wen Xian** China
73E4 **Wenzhou** China
73C4 **Wenzhu** China
101G1 **Wepener** S Africa
12G1 **Wernecke Mts** Can
57C2 **Werra** R Germany
109D2 **Werris Creek** Aust
56B2 **Wesel** Germany
56B2 **Weser** R Germany
106C2 **Wessel Is** Aust

14A2 **West Allis** USA
104C4 **West Australian Basin** Indian O
104C5 **West Australian Ridge** Indian O
19C3 **West B** USA
86B2 **West Bengal** State, India
43D3 **West Bromwich** Eng
16B3 **West Chester** USA
46D1 **Westerburg** Germany
56B2 **Westerland** Germany
16D2 **Westerly** USA
106A3 **Western Australia** State, Aust
87A1 **Western Ghats** Mts India
44A3 **Western Isles** Scot
96A2 **Western Sahara** Region, Mor
105H4 **Western Samoa** Is Pacific O
46B1 **Westerschelde** Estuary Neth
46D1 **Westerwald** Region, Germany
49D1 **Westfalen** Region, Germany
29D6 **West Falkland** I Falkland Is
16C1 **Westfield** Massachusetts, USA
15C2 **Westfield** New York, USA
18C2 **West Frankfort** USA
109C1 **Westgate** Aust
43C4 **West Glamorgan** County, Wales
102E3 **West Indies** Is Caribbean S
13E2 **Westlock** Can
14B2 **West Lorne** Can
45C2 **Westmeath** County, Irish Rep
18A1 **West Memphis** USA
43D3 **West Midlands** County, Eng
43D4 **Westminster** Eng
16A3 **Westminster** Maryland, USA
17B1 **Westminster** S Carolina, USA
100B3 **West Nicholson** Zim
78D1 **Weston** Malay
14B3 **Weston** USA
43C4 **Weston-super-Mare** Eng
17B2 **West Palm Beach** USA
18B2 **West Plains** USA
22B1 **West Point** California, USA
19C3 **West Point** Mississippi, USA
16C2 **West Point** USA
12F2 **West Point** Mt USA
45B2 **Westport** Irish Rep
111B2 **Westport** NZ
40C2 **Westray** I Scot
13C2 **West Road** R Can
45C2 **West Sole** Oilfield N Sea
11B3 **West Virginia** State, USA
22C1 **West Walker** R USA
109C2 **West Wyalong** Aust
42D3 **West Yorkshire** County, Eng
71D4 **Wetar** I Indon
13E2 **Wetaskiwin** Can
99D3 **Wete** Tanz
46E1 **Wetzlar** Germany
Wevok = Cape Lisburne
71F4 **Wewak** PNG
19A2 **Wewoka** USA
45C2 **Wexford** County, Irish Rep
45C2 **Wexford** Irish Rep
5H5 **Weybridge** Can
43C4 **Weymouth** Eng
16D1 **Weymouth** USA

110C1 **Whakatane** NZ
110C1 **Whakatane** R NZ
44E1 **Whalsay** I Scot
110B1 **Whangarei** NZ
42D3 **Wharfe** R Eng
19A4 **Wharton** USA
111B2 **Whataroa** NZ
16A3 **Wheaton** Maryland, USA
8B3 **Wheeler Peak** Mt Nevada, USA
9C3 **Wheeler Peak** Mt New Mexico, USA
14B2 **Wheeling** USA
13C3 **Whistler** Can
15C2 **Whitby** Can
42D2 **Whitby** Eng
18B2 **White** R Arkansas, USA
12F2 **White** R Can
14A3 **White** R Indiana, USA
8C2 **White** R S Dakota, USA
7E4 **White B** Can
108B2 **White Cliffs** Aust
40C2 **White Coomb** Mt Scot
13D2 **Whitecourt** Can
14A1 **Whitefish Pt** USA
7D4 **Whitegull L** Can
15D2 **Whitehall** New York, USA
16B2 **Whitehall** Pennsylvania, USA
42C2 **Whitehaven** Eng
12G2 **Whitehorse** Can
110C1 **White I** NZ
19B4 **White L** USA
109C4 **Whitemark** Aust
21B2 **White Mountain Peak** Mt USA
12E1 **White Mts** Alaska, USA
15D2 **White Mts** New Hampshire, USA
99D1 **White Nile** R Sudan
16C2 **White Plains** USA
7B5 **White River** Can
15D2 **White River Junction** USA
White S = Beloye More
13B2 **Whitesail L** Can
20B1 **White Salmon** USA
17C1 **Whiteville** USA
97B4 **White Volta** R Ghana
42B2 **Whithorn** Scot
17B1 **Whitmire** USA
21B2 **Whitney,Mt** USA
12E2 **Whittier** Alaska, USA
22C4 **Whittier** California, USA
5H3 **Wholdia L** Can
108A2 **Whyalla** Aust
18A2 **Wiarton** Can
9D3 **Wichita Falls** USA
44C2 **Wick** Scot
45C2 **Wicklow** County, Irish Rep
45C2 **Wicklow** Irish Rep
45C2 **Wicklow** Mts Irish Rep
109C1 **Widgeegoara** R Aust
46D1 **Wied** R Germany
59B2 **Wielun** Pol
59B3 **Wien** Austria
59B3 **Wiener Neustadt** Austria
58C2 **Wieprz** R Pol
46E1 **Wiesbaden** Germany
42C3 **Wigan** Eng
19C3 **Wiggins** USA
42B2 **Wigtown** Scot
42B2 **Wigtown B** Scot
20C1 **Wil** Switz
20C1 **Wilbur** USA
108B2 **Wilcannia** Aust
21B2 **Wildcat Peak** Mt USA
47B1 **Wildhorn** Mt Switz

13E2 **Wild Horse** Can
47D1 **Wildspitze** Mt Austria
17B2 **Wildwood** Florida, USA
16B3 **Wildwood** New Jersey, USA
101G1 **Wilge** R S Africa
56B2 **Wilhelmshaven** Germany
15C2 **Wilkes-Barre** USA
112B8 **Wilkes Land** Ant
13F2 **Wilkie** Can
20B2 **Willamette** R USA
108B2 **Willandra** R Aust
20B1 **Willapa B** USA
9C3 **Willcox** USA
27D4 **Willemstad** Curaçao
108A1 **William Creek** Aust
108B3 **William,Mt** Aust
21A2 **Williams** California, USA
13C2 **Williams Lake** Can
15C2 **Williamsport** USA
16C1 **Williamstown** Massachusetts, USA
14B3 **Williamstown** W Virginia, USA
16C2 **Willimantic** USA
16B2 **Willingboro** USA
13D2 **Willingdon,Mt** Can
107E2 **Willis Group** Is Aust
17B2 **Williston** Florida, USA
100B4 **Williston** S Africa
13C1 **Williston L** Can
8D2 **Willmar** USA
108A3 **Willoughby,C** Aust
13C2 **Willow** R Can
20B2 **Willow Ranch** USA
21A2 **Willows** USA
18B2 **Willow Springs** USA
108A2 **Wilmington** Aust
16B3 **Wilmington** Delaware, USA
17C1 **Wilmington** N Carolina, USA
7A5 **Wilnona** USA
13D1 **Wilson** USA
108B1 **Wilson** R Aust
6B3 **Wilson,C** Can
22C3 **Wilson,Mt** California, USA
20B1 **Wilson,Mt** Oregon, USA
109C3 **Wilsons Promontory** Pen Aust
43D4 **Wiltshire** County, Eng
46C2 **Wiltz** Lux
106B3 **Wiluna** Aust
14A2 **Winamac** USA
101G1 **Winburg** S Africa
16C1 **Winchendon** USA
15C1 **Winchester** USA
43D4 **Winchester** Eng
16C1 **Winchester** New Hampshire, USA
15C3 **Winchester** Virginia, USA
42C2 **Windermere** Eng
100A3 **Windhoek** Namibia
107D3 **Windorah** Aust
8C2 **Wind River Range** Mts USA
109D2 **Windsor** Aust
16C2 **Windsor** Connecticut, USA
43D4 **Windsor** Eng
7D5 **Windsor** Nova Scotia, Can
14B2 **Windsor** Ontario, Can
15D1 **Windsor** Quebec, Can
17B1 **Windsor Forest** USA
16C2 **Windsor Locks** USA
27E4 **Windward Is** Caribbean S
26C3 **Windward Pass** Caribbean S
13E1 **Winefred L** Can
18A2 **Winfield** Kansas, USA
109D2 **Wingham** Aust

Winifreda

34C3 Winifreda Arg
7B4 Winisk R Can
7B4 Winisk L Can
76B2 Winkana Burma
20B1 Winlock USA
97B4 Winneba Ghana
14A2 Winnebago,L USA
20C2 Winnemucca USA
19B3 Winnfield USA
5J4 Winnipeg Can
5J4 Winnipeg,L Can
5J4 Winnipegosis Can
4J4 Winnipegosis,L Can
15D2 Winnipesaukee,L USA
10A2 Winona Minnesota, USA
19C3 Winona Mississippi, USA
15D2 Winooski USA
9B3 Winslow USA
16C2 Winsted USA
11B3 Winston-Salem USA
46E1 Winterberg Germany
17B2 Winter Garden USA
17B2 Winter Park USA
22B1 Winters USA
47C1 Winterthur Switz
107D3 Winton Aust
111A3 Winton NZ
43±3 Wisbech Eng
10B2 Wisconsin State, USA
7B5 Wisconsin Rapids USA
12D1 Wiseman USA
58B2 Wisla R Pol
56C2 Wismar Germany
33F2 Witagron Surinam
101G1 Witbank S Africa
9D3 Witchita Falls USA
43D3 Witham R Eng
42E3 Withernsea Eng
43D4 Witney Eng
46D1 Witten Germany
56C2 Wittenberg Germany
106A3 Wittenoom Aust
46D1 Wittlich Germany
58B2 Wladyslawowo Pol
58B2 Wloclawek Pol
58C2 Wlodawa Pol
109C3 Wodonga Aust
47C1 Wohlen Switz
71E4 Wokam Indon
43D4 Woking Eng
71F3 Woleai / Pacific O
20B2 Wolf Creek USA
8C2 Wolf Point USA
57C3 Wolfsberg Austria
56C2 Wolfsburg Germany
5H4 Wollaston L Can
5H4 Wollaston Lake Can
4C3 Wollaston Pen Con
109C3 Wollongong Aust
101G1 Wolmaransstad S Africa
59B2 Wolow Pol
108B3 Wolseley Aust
43C3 Wolverhampton Lng
16A2 Womelsdorf USA
109D1 Wondai Aust
74B3 Wonju S Korea
108B2 Wonominta R Aust
13C1 Wonowon Can
74B3 Wŏnsan N Korea
108C3 Wonthaggi Aust
108A2 Woocalla Aust
16B3 Woodbine USA
15C3 Woodbridge USA
5G4 Wood Buffalo Nat Pk Can
109D1 Woodburn Aust
20B1 Woodburn USA
16B3 Woodbury USA
12F1 Woodchopper USA
21A2 Woodland California, USA
20B1 Woodland Washington, USA
107E1 Woodlark / PNG
106C4 Woodmera Aust
106C3 Woodroffe,Mt Aust
14B2 Woodstock Ontario, Can

16B3 Woodstown USA
110C2 Woodville NZ
19B3 Woodville USA
108A2 Woomera Aust
15D2 Woonsocket USA
14B2 Wooster USA
43C3 Worcester Eng
100A4 Worcester S Africa
16D1 Worcester USA
47E1 Wörgl Austria
42C2 Workington Eng
8C2 Worland USA
46E2 Worms Germany
43B4 Worms Head Pt Wales
43D4 Worthing Eng
8D2 Worthington USA
71D4 Wowoni / Indon
12H3 Wrangell USA
12H3 Wrangell I USA
12F2 Wrangell Mts USA
40B2 Wrath,C Scot
43C3 Wrexham Wales
17B1 Wrightsville USA
22D3 Wrightwood USA
4F3 Wrigley Can
59B2 Wroclaw Pol
58B2 Września Pol
69E2 Wuchang China
76E1 Wuchuan China
72E2 Wuda China
72C2 Wuding He R China
72A3 Wudu China
73C4 Wugang China
72B2 Wuhai China
73C3 Wuhan China
73D3 Wuhu China
73D5 Wuhua China
72D2 Wüjang China
72B1 Wujia He R China
73B4 Wu Jiang R China
97C4 Wukari Nig
73B4 Wuling Shan Mts China
97D4 Wum Cam
73A4 Wumeng Shan Upland China
46D1 Wuppertal Germany
72B2 Wuqi China
72D2 Wuqing China
57B3 Würzburg Germany
57C2 Wurzen Germany
72C2 Wutai Shan Mt China
71F4 Wuvulu / Pacific O
72A2 Wuwei China
73E3 Wuxi China
73E3 Wuxing China
72C2 Wuyang China
73D4 Wuyi Shan Mts China
72B1 Wuyuan China
76D2 Wuzhi Shan Mts China
72B2 Wuzhong China
73C5 Wuzhou China
14B2 Wyandotte USA
109C1 Wyandra Aust
43C4 Wye R Eng
43C4 Wylye R Eng
43E3 Wymondham Eng
106B2 Wyndham Aust
18B2 Wynne USA
4G2 Wynniatt B Can
109C4 Wynyard Aust
8C2 Wyoming State, USA
14A2 Wyoming USA
109D2 Wyong Aust

X
84D1 Xaidulla China
72D1 Xai Moron He R China
101C3 Xai Xai Mozam
23B2 Xachinguis Mexico
100A2 Xangongo Angola
46D1 Xanten Germany
55B2 Xánthi Greece
100B3 Xau,L Botswana
14B3 Xenia USA
72A2 Xiahe China
73D5 Xiamen China
72B3 Xi'an China

73B4 Xianfeng China
73C3 Xiangfan China
73C4 Xiang Jiang R China
73C4 Xiangtan Province, China
73C4 Xianning China
72B3 Xianyang China
73C4 Xiao Shui R China
73D4 Xiapu China
73A4 Xichang China
23B1 Xicotepec Mexico
76C2 Xieng Khouang Laos
73B4 Xifeng China
86B1 Xigazê China
72A1 Xi He R China
72B2 Xiji China
73C5 Xi Jiang R China
72E1 Xiliao He R China
73B5 Xilin China
23B1 Xilitla Mexico
73B4 Xinfeng China
72C1 Xinghe China
73D5 Xingning China
73B4 Xingren China
72C2 Xingtai China
33C4 Xingu R Brazil
68B2 Xingxingxia China
73A4 Xingyi China
72A2 Xining China
72E2 Xinjin Liaoning, China
73A3 Xinjin Sichuan, China
72D2 Xinwen China
72C2 Xin Xian China
72C2 Xinxiang China
73C3 Xinyang China
73C5 Xinyi Guangdong, China
72D3 Xinyi Jiangsu, China
72D1 Xi Ujimqin Qi China
74A2 Xiuyan China
23B2 Xochimilco Mexico
73D3 Xuancheng China
73B3 Xuanhan China
72D1 Xuanhua China
73A4 Xuanwei China
72C3 Xuchang China
99E2 Xuddur Somalia
72A2 Xunhua China
73C5 Xun Jiang R China
69E2 Xunke China
73C5 Xunwu China
73C4 Xupu China
76E1 Xuwen China
73A4 Xuyong China
72D3 Xuzhou China

Y
73A4 Ya'an China
108B3 Yaapeet Aust
98B2 Yabassi Cam
68C1 Yablonovyy Khrebet Mts Russian Fed
94C2 Yabrüd Syria
20B2 Yachats USA
30D3 Yacuiba Bol
87B1 Yādgir India
95A1 Yafran Libya
23A1 Yahualica Mexico
98C3 Yahuma Zaire
75B1 Yaita Japan
75B2 Yaizu Japan
73A4 Yajiang China
20B1 Yakima USA
20B1 Yakima R USA
97B3 Yako Burkina
98C2 Yakoma Zaire
74E2 Yakumo Japan
12G3 Yakutat B USA
63E1 Yakutsk Russian Fed
77C4 Yala Thai
23B2 Yalalag Mexico
98C3 Yaloun R China
68B3 Yalong R China
73A4 Yalong Jiang R China
54C2 Yalova Turk
60D5 Yalta Ukraine
73B2 Yalu Jiang R China
74D3 Yamagata Japan
74C4 Yamaguchi Japan

68D1 Yamarovka Russian Fed
109D1 Yamba New S Wales, Aust
108B2 Yamba S Australia, Aust
99C2 Yambio Sudan
54C2 Yambol Bulg
71E4 Yamdena / Indon
Yam Kinneret = Tiberias,L
108B1 Yamma Yamma,L Aust
97B4 Yamoussoukro Ivory Coast
85D3 Yamuna R India
86C1 Yamzho Yumco L China
63F1 Yana R Russian Fed
108B3 Yanac Aust
75A2 Yanagawa Japan
87C1 Yanam India
72B2 Yan'an China
80B3 Yanbu'al Bahr S Arabia
108B2 Yancannia Aust
72E3 Yancheng China
72B2 Yanchi China
108B1 Yandama R Aust
98C2 Yangambi Zaire
72C1 Yang He R China
73C5 Yangjiang China
76B2 Yangon Burma
72C2 Yangquan China
73C5 Yangshan China
73C3 Yangtze Gorges China
72E3 Yangtze,Mouths of the China
72D3 Yangzhou China
73B4 Yanhe China
74B2 Yanji China
108C3 Yanko R Aust
8D2 Yankton USA
68A2 Yanqqi China
72D1 Yan Shan Hills China
108B1 Yantabulla Aust
72E2 Yantai China
72D2 Yanzhou China
98B2 Yaoundé Cam
71E4 Yapen / Indon
71E3 Yap Is Pacific O
24B2 Yaqui R Mexico
61G2 Yaransk Russian Fed
32C3 Yari R Colombia
74D3 Yariga-dake Mt Japan
82B2 Yarkant He R China
86C1 Yarlung Zangbo Jiang R China
7D5 Yarmouth Can
94B2 Yarmūk R Syria/Jordan
61E2 Yaroslavl' Russian Fed
94B2 Yarqon R Israel
109C3 Yarram Aust
109D1 Yarraman Aust
109C3 Yarrawonga Aust
60D2 Yartsevo Russian Fed
63B1 Yartsevo Russian Fed
74C4 Yarumal Colombia
97C3 Yashi Nig
97C4 Yashikera Nig
61F4 Yashkul' Russian Fed
84C1 Yasin Pak
59C3 Yasinya Ukraine
109C2 Yass Aust
109C2 Yass R Aust
75A1 Yasugi Japan
18A2 Yates Center USA
98C2 Yatolema Zaire
74C4 Yatsushiro Japan
94B3 Yatta Israel
32C4 Yavari Peru
85D4 Yavatmäl India
74C4 Yawatahama Japan
76D2 Ya Xian China
90B3 Yazd Iran
90B3 Yazd-e Khvāst Iran
19B3 Yazoo R USA

The ᐧᐧᐧ es

TRAVELER'S
POCKET ATLAS

T I M E S   B O O K S

R A N D O M   H O U S E